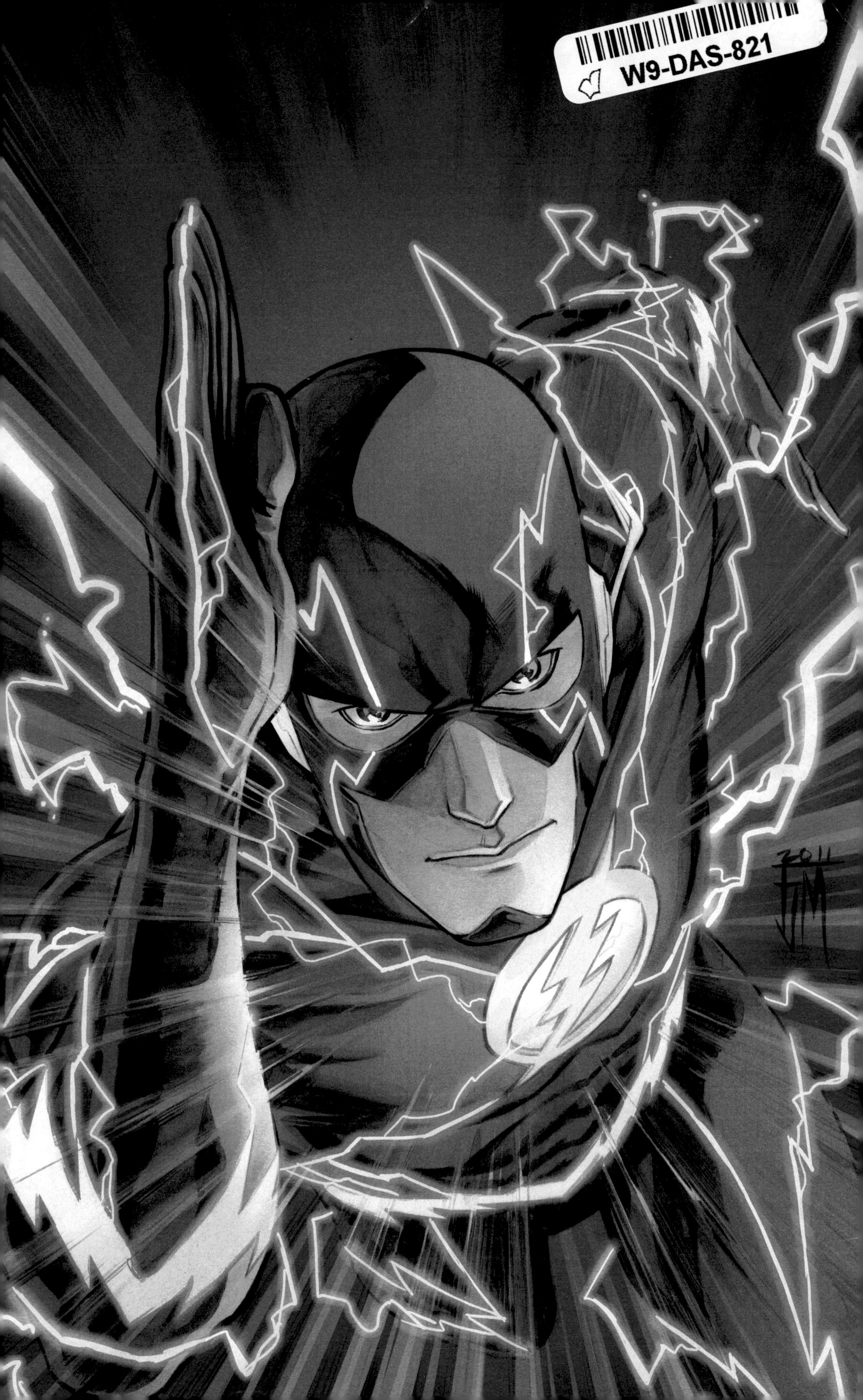

FRANCIS MANAPUL and BRIAN BUCCELLATO
cover art

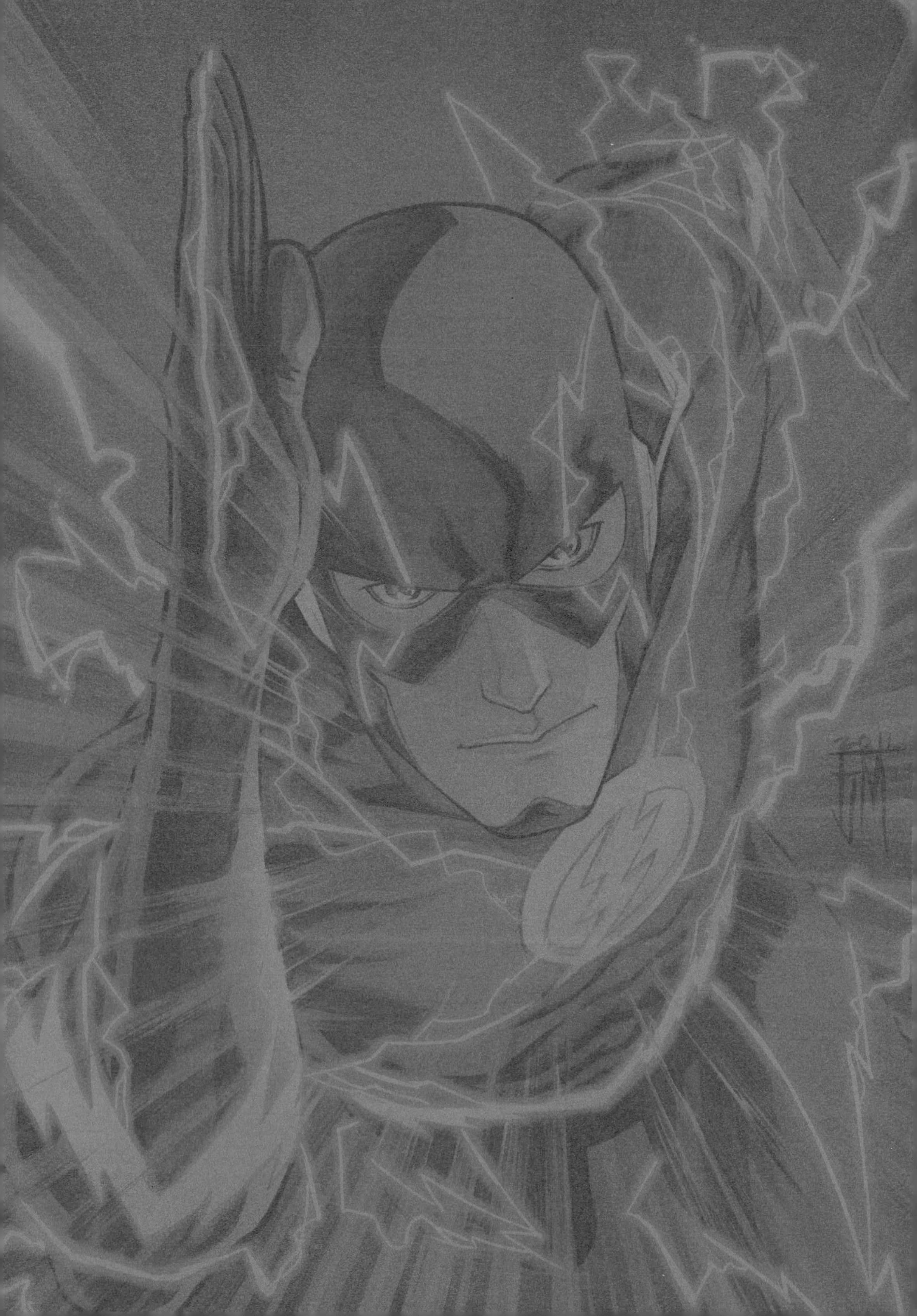

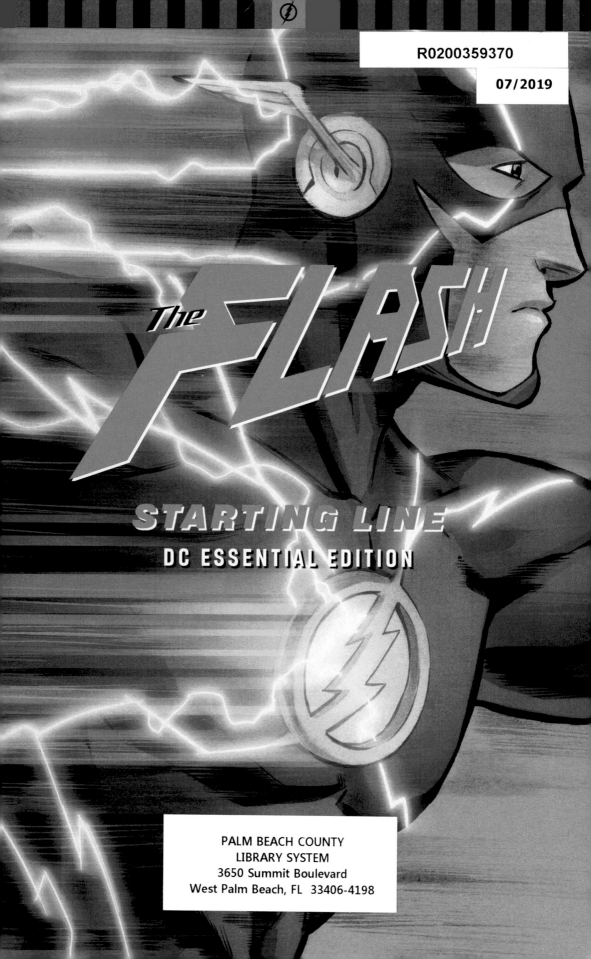

R0200359370

07/2019

PALM BEACH COUNTY
LIBRARY SYSTEM
3650 Summit Boulevard
West Palm Beach, FL 33406-4198

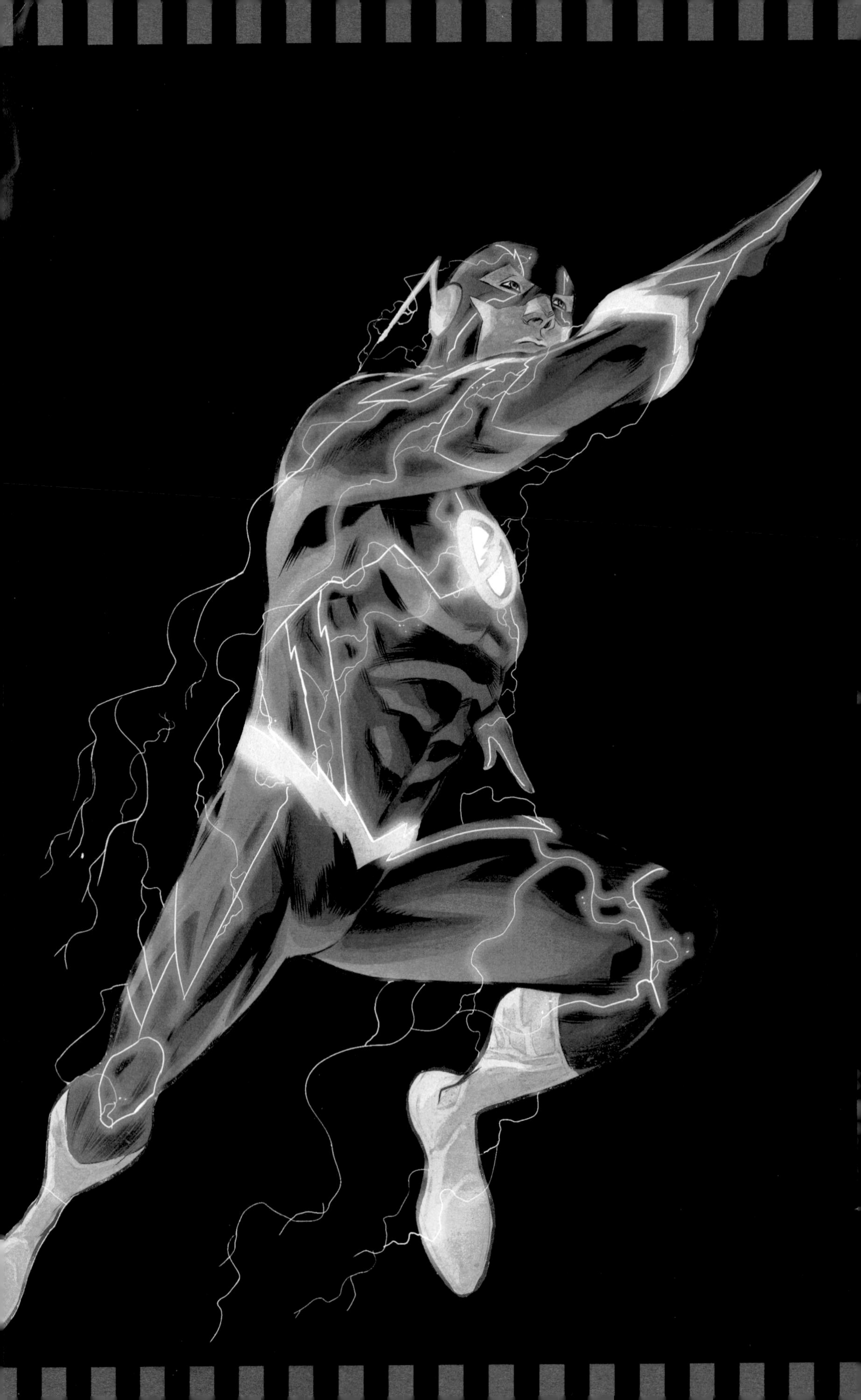

The FLASH

STARTING LINE

DC ESSENTIAL EDITION

FRANCIS MANAPUL and **BRIAN BUCCELLATO**
story

FRANCIS MANAPUL
MARCUS TO • SCOTT KOLINS • DIOGENES NEVES
WES CRAIG • MARCIO TAKARA
art

RAY McCARTHY • OCLAIR ALBERT
inks

BRIAN BUCCELLATO
IAN HERRING • MIKE ATIYEH • HI-FI
colors

SAL CIPRIANO
CARLOS M. MANGUAL • WES ABBOTT
DEZI SIENTY • PAT BROSSEAU
letters

BRIAN CUNNINGHAM, MATT IDELSON, WIL MOSS, JOEY CAVALIERI Editors – Original Series
CHRIS CONROY, HARVEY RICHARDS Associate Editors – Original Series
DARREN SHAN, KYLE ANDRUKIEWICZ Assistant Editors – Original Series
JEB WOODARD Group Editor – Collected Editions
ERIC SEARLEMAN Editor – Collected Edition
STEVE COOK Design Director – Books
MEGEN BELLERSEN Publication Design

BOB HARRAS Senior VP – Editor-in-Chief, DC Comics
PAT McCALLUM Executive Editor, DC Comics

DAN DiDIO Publisher
JIM LEE Publisher & Chief Creative Officer
AMIT DESAI Executive VP – Business & Marketing Strategy, Direct to Consumer & Global Franchise Management
BOBBIE CHASE VP & Executive Editor, Young Reader & Talent Development
MARK CHIARELLO Senior VP – Art, Design & Collected Editions
JOHN CUNNINGHAM Senior VP – Sales & Trade Marketing
BRIAR DARDEN VP – Business Affairs
ANNE DePIES Senior VP – Business Strategy, Finance & Administration
DON FALLETTI VP – Manufacturing Operations
LAWRENCE GANEM VP – Editorial Administration & Talent Relations
ALISON GILL Senior VP – Manufacturing & Operations
JASON GREENBERG VP – Business Strategy & Finance
HANK KANALZ Senior VP – Editorial Strategy & Administration
JAY KOGAN Senior VP – Legal Affairs
NICK J. NAPOLITANO VP – Manufacturing Administration
LISETTE OSTERLOH VP – Digital Marketing & Events
EDDIE SCANNELL VP – Consumer Marketing
COURTNEY SIMMONS Senior VP – Publicity & Communications
JIM (SKI) SOKOLOWSKI VP – Comic Book Specialty Sales & Trade Marketing
NANCY SPEARS VP – Mass, Book, Digital Sales & Trade Marketing
MICHELE R. WELLS VP – Content Strategy

THE FLASH: STARTING LINE DC ESSENTIAL EDITION

Published by DC Comics. Compilation, cover and all new material Copyright © 2018 DC Comics. All Rights Reserved. Originally published in single magazine form in THE FLASH 0-12 and THE FLASH ANNUAL 1. Copyright © 2011, 2012 DC Comics. All Rights Reserved. All characters, their distinctive likenesses and related elements featured in this publication are trademarks of DC Comics. The stories, characters and incidents featured in this publication are entirely fictional. DC Comics does not read or accept unsolicited submissions of ideas, stories or artwork.

DC Comics, 2900 West Alameda Ave., Burbank, CA 91505
Printed by LSC Communications, Kendallville, IN, USA. 9/21/18. First Printing.
ISBN: 978-1-4012-8476-3

Library of Congress Cataloging-in-Publication Data is available.

PEFC Certified
Printed on paper from
sustainably managed
forests and controlled
sources
PEFC/29-31-337
www.pefc.org

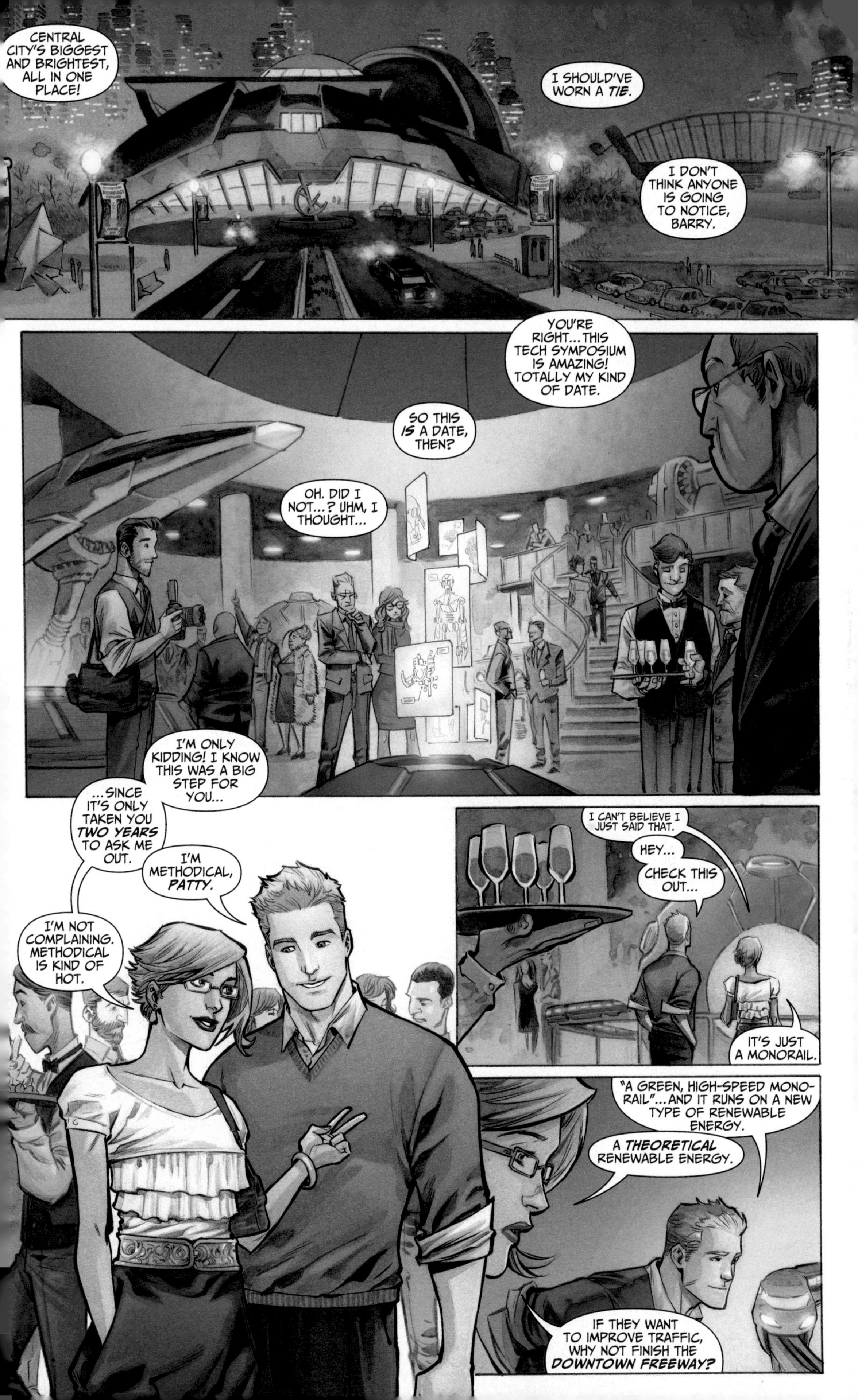
CENTRAL CITY'S BIGGEST AND BRIGHTEST, ALL IN ONE PLACE!
I SHOULD'VE WORN A *TIE*.
I DON'T THINK ANYONE IS GOING TO NOTICE, BARRY.
YOU'RE RIGHT... THIS TECH SYMPOSIUM IS AMAZING! TOTALLY MY KIND OF DATE.
SO THIS *IS* A DATE, THEN?
OH. DID I NOT...? UHM, I THOUGHT...
I'M ONLY KIDDING! I KNOW THIS WAS A BIG STEP FOR YOU...
...SINCE IT'S ONLY TAKEN YOU ***TWO YEARS*** TO ASK ME OUT.
I'M METHODICAL, *PATTY*.
I'M NOT COMPLAINING. METHODICAL IS KIND OF HOT.
I CAN'T BELIEVE I JUST SAID THAT.
HEY...
CHECK THIS OUT...
IT'S JUST A MONORAIL.
"A GREEN, HIGH-SPEED MONO-RAIL"... AND IT RUNS ON A NEW TYPE OF RENEWABLE ENERGY.
A ***THEORETICAL*** RENEWABLE ENERGY.
IF THEY WANT TO IMPROVE TRAFFIC, WHY NOT FINISH THE ***DOWNTOWN FREEWAY?***

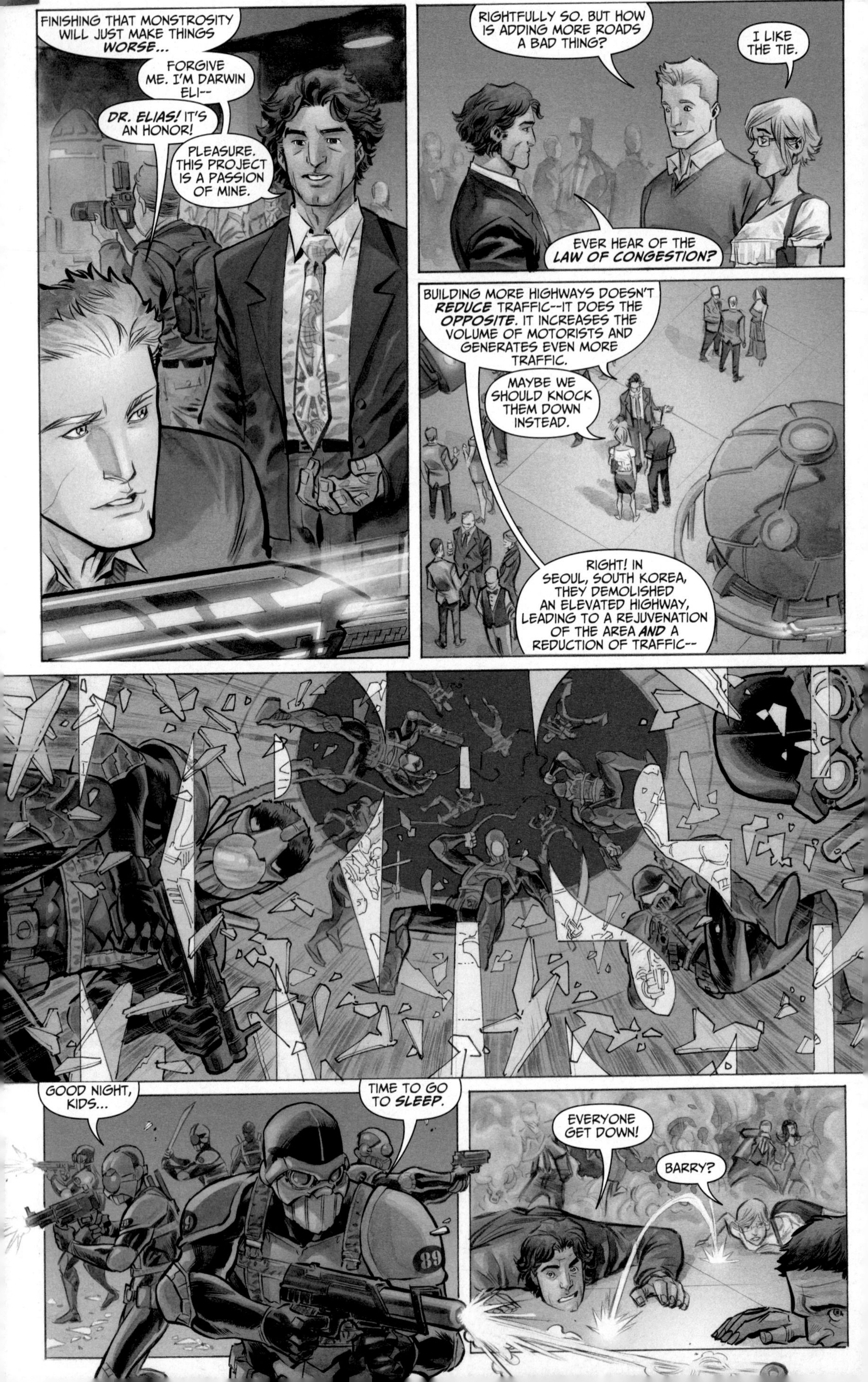
FINISHING THAT MONSTROSITY WILL JUST MAKE THINGS WORSE...
FORGIVE ME. I'M DARWIN ELI--
DR. ELIAS! IT'S AN HONOR!
PLEASURE. THIS PROJECT IS A PASSION OF MINE.
RIGHTFULLY SO. BUT HOW IS ADDING MORE ROADS A BAD THING?
I LIKE THE TIE.
EVER HEAR OF THE LAW OF CONGESTION?
BUILDING MORE HIGHWAYS DOESN'T REDUCE TRAFFIC--IT DOES THE OPPOSITE. IT INCREASES THE VOLUME OF MOTORISTS AND GENERATES EVEN MORE TRAFFIC.
MAYBE WE SHOULD KNOCK THEM DOWN INSTEAD.
RIGHT! IN SEOUL, SOUTH KOREA, THEY DEMOLISHED AN ELEVATED HIGHWAY, LEADING TO A REJUVENATION OF THE AREA AND A REDUCTION OF TRAFFIC--
GOOD NIGHT, KIDS...
TIME TO GO TO SLEEP.
EVERYONE GET DOWN!
BARRY?

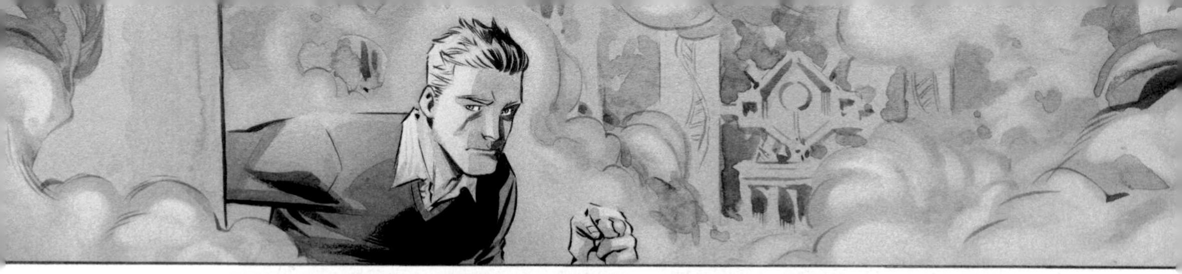

STORY BY FRANCIS MANAPUL & BRIAN BUCCELLATO

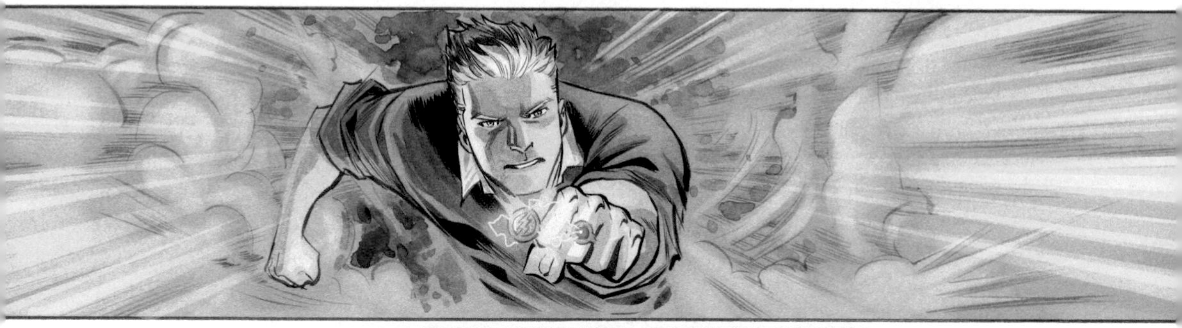

ART BY FRANCIS MANAPUL

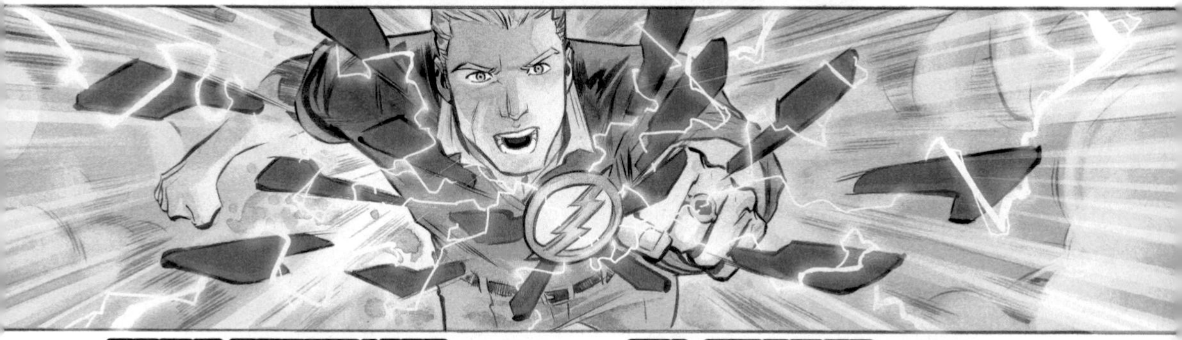

BRIAN BUCCELLATO COLORS SAL CIPRIANO LETTERS

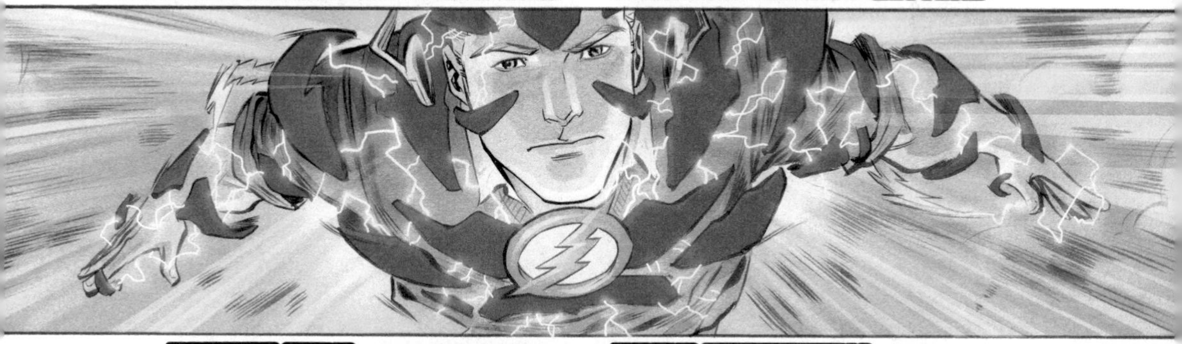

DARREN SHAN ASSISTANT EDITOR BRIAN CUNNINGHAM EDITOR

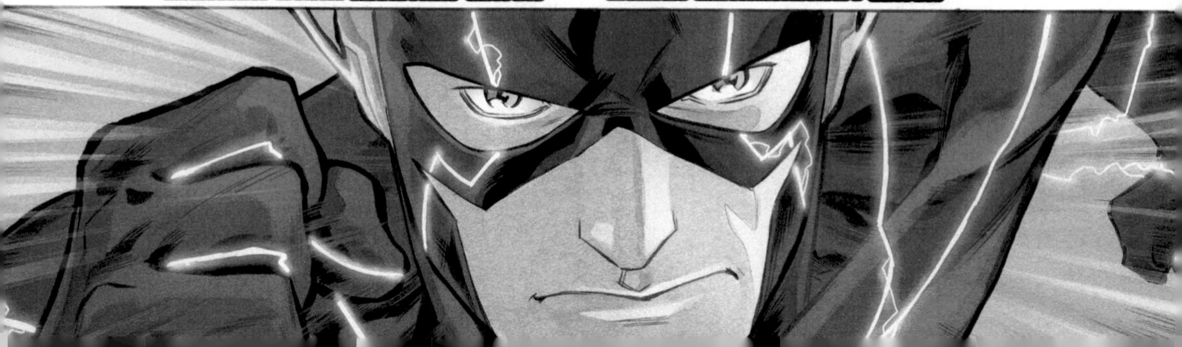

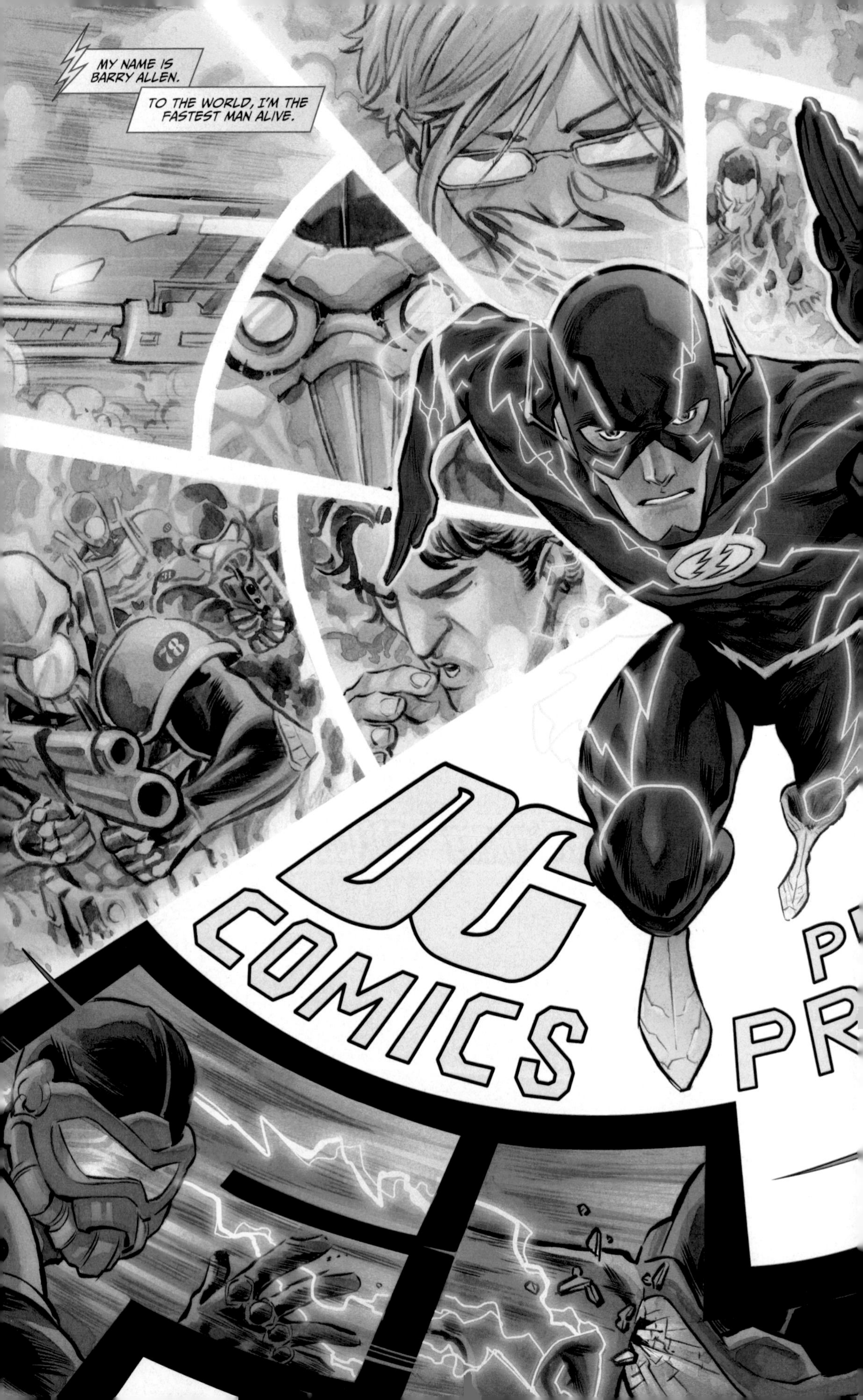
MY NAME IS BARRY ALLEN.
TO THE WORLD, I'M THE FASTEST MAN ALIVE.
DC COMICS

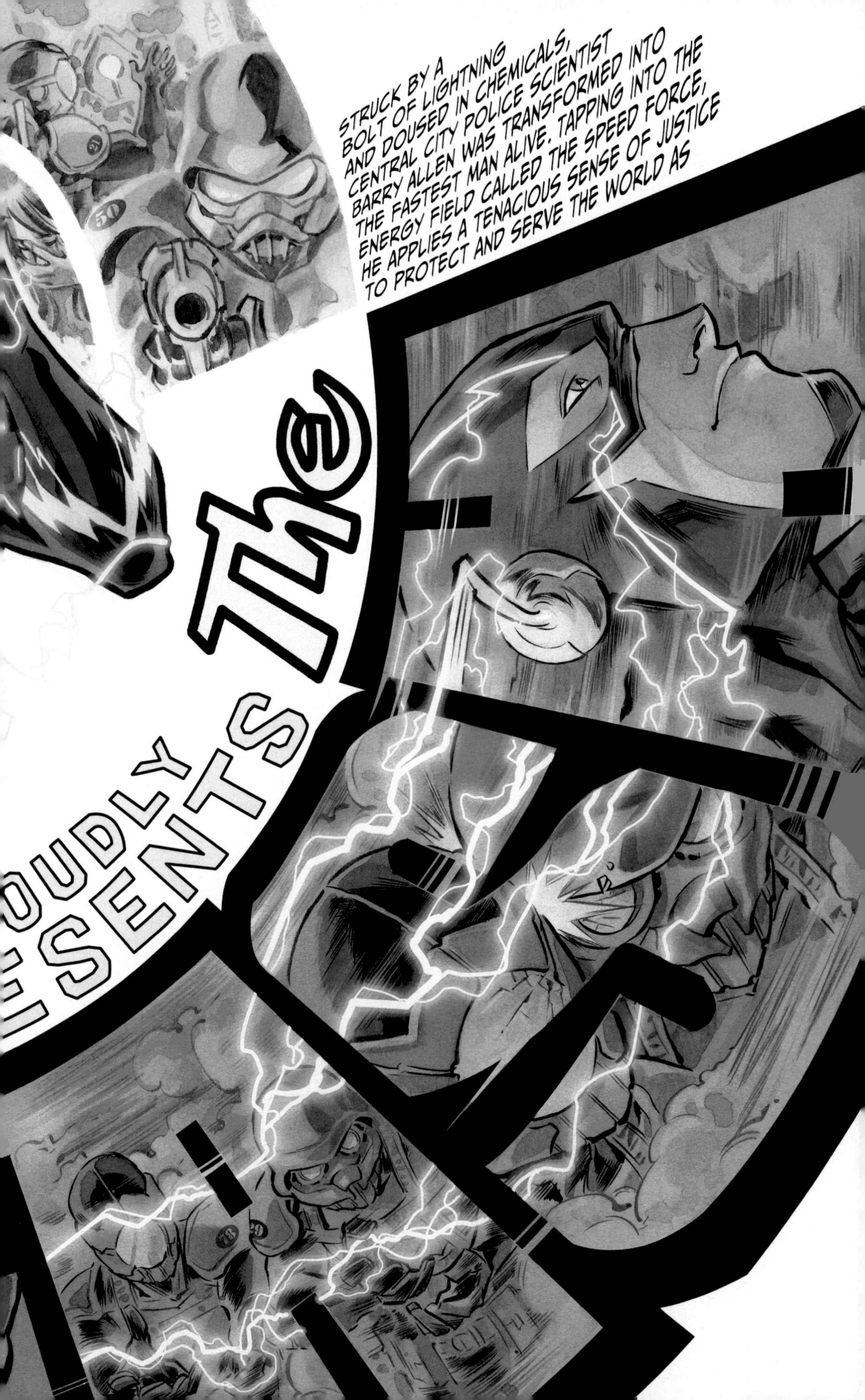
STRUCK BY A BOLT OF LIGHTNING AND DOUSED IN CHEMICALS, CENTRAL CITY POLICE SCIENTIST BARRY ALLEN WAS TRANSFORMED INTO THE FASTEST MAN ALIVE. TAPPING INTO THE ENERGY FIELD CALLED THE SPEED FORCE, HE APPLIES A TENACIOUS SENSE OF JUSTICE TO PROTECT AND SERVE THE WORLD AS
OUDLY
ESENTS The

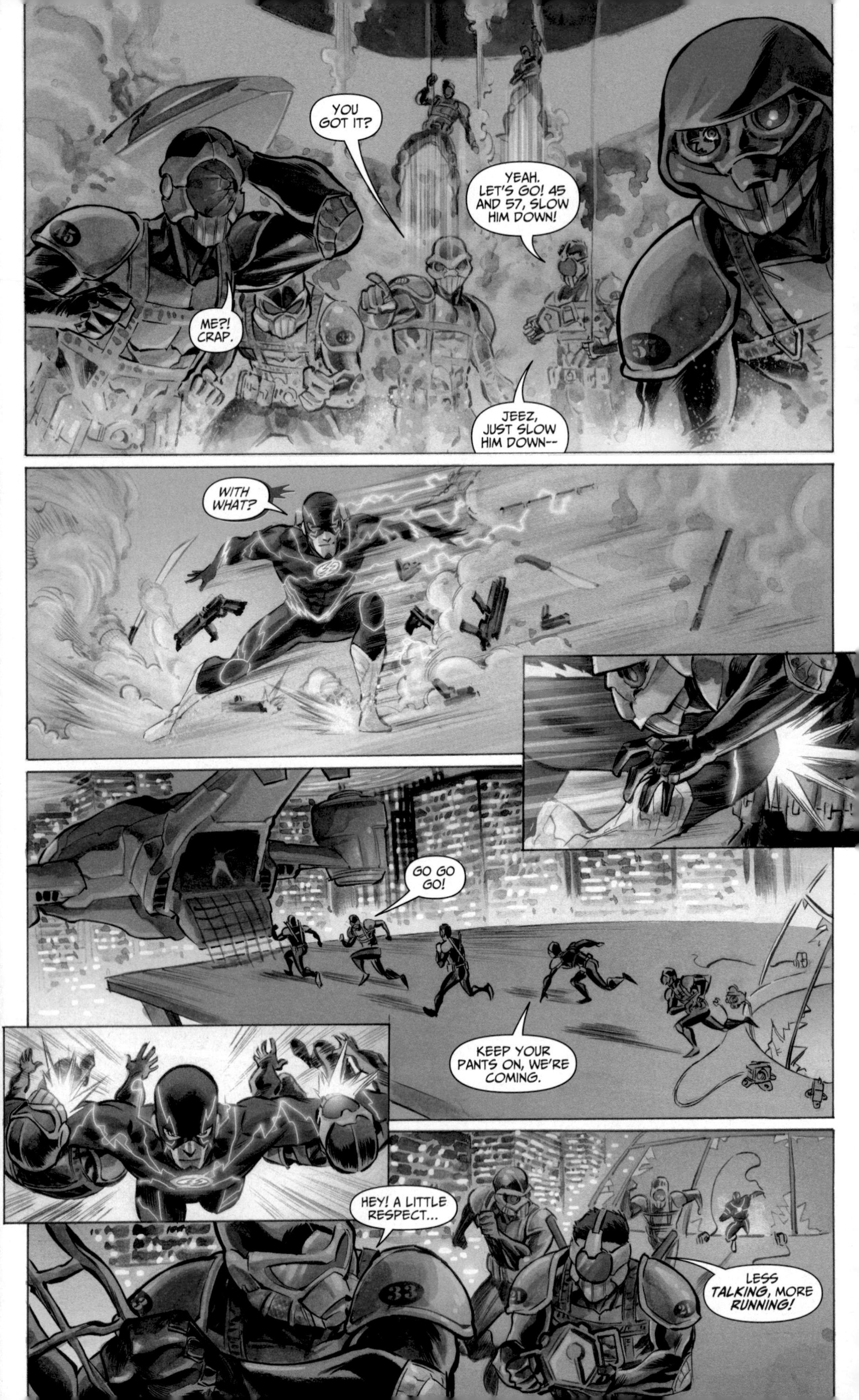
YOU GOT IT?
YEAH. LET'S GO! 45 AND 57, SLOW HIM DOWN!
ME?! CRAP.
JEEZ, JUST SLOW HIM DOWN--
WITH WHAT?
GO GO GO!
KEEP YOUR PANTS ON, WE'RE COMING.
HEY! A LITTLE RESPECT...
LESS TALKING, MORE RUNNING!

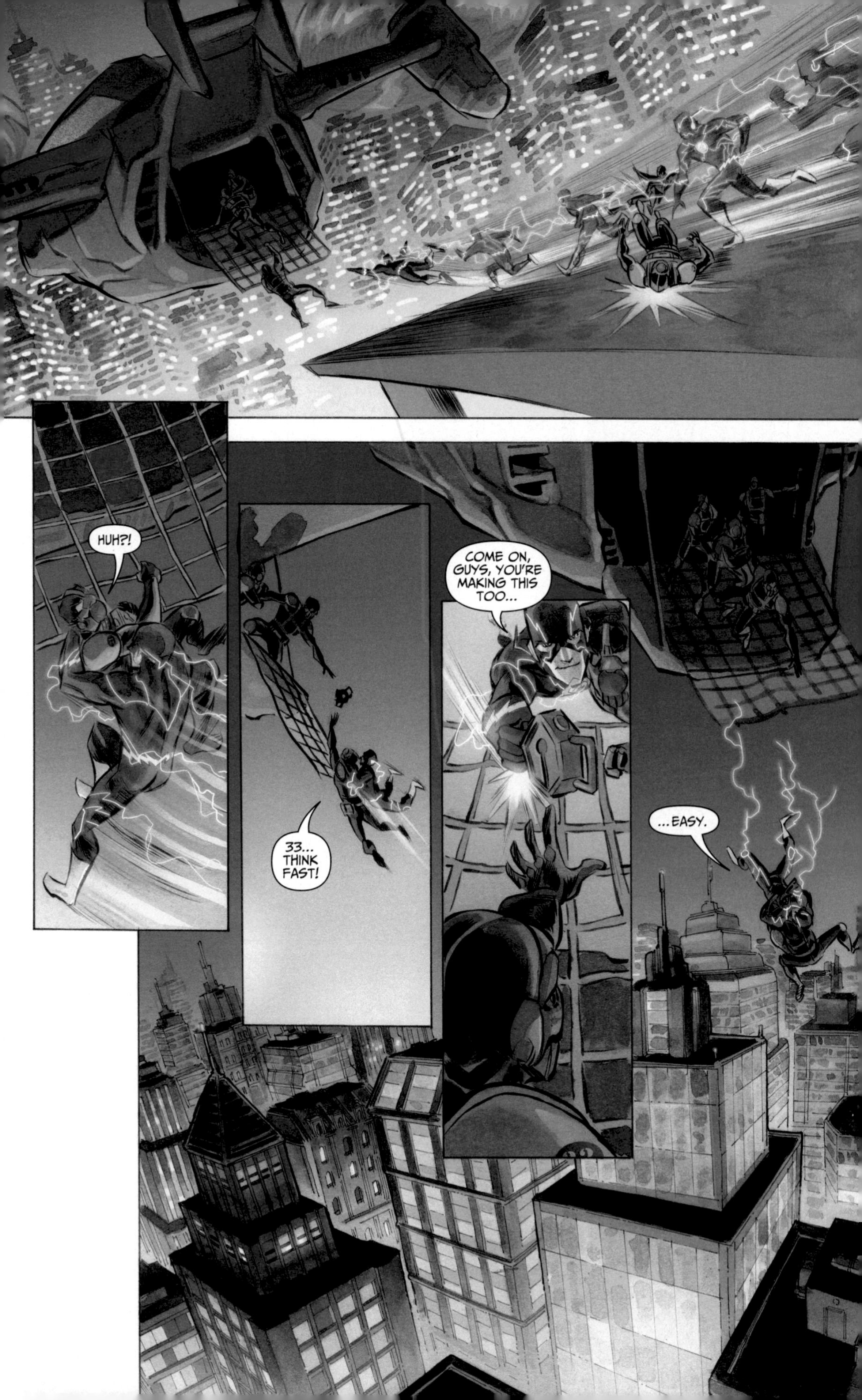
HUH?!
33... THINK FAST!
COME ON, GUYS, YOU'RE MAKING THIS TOO...
...EASY.

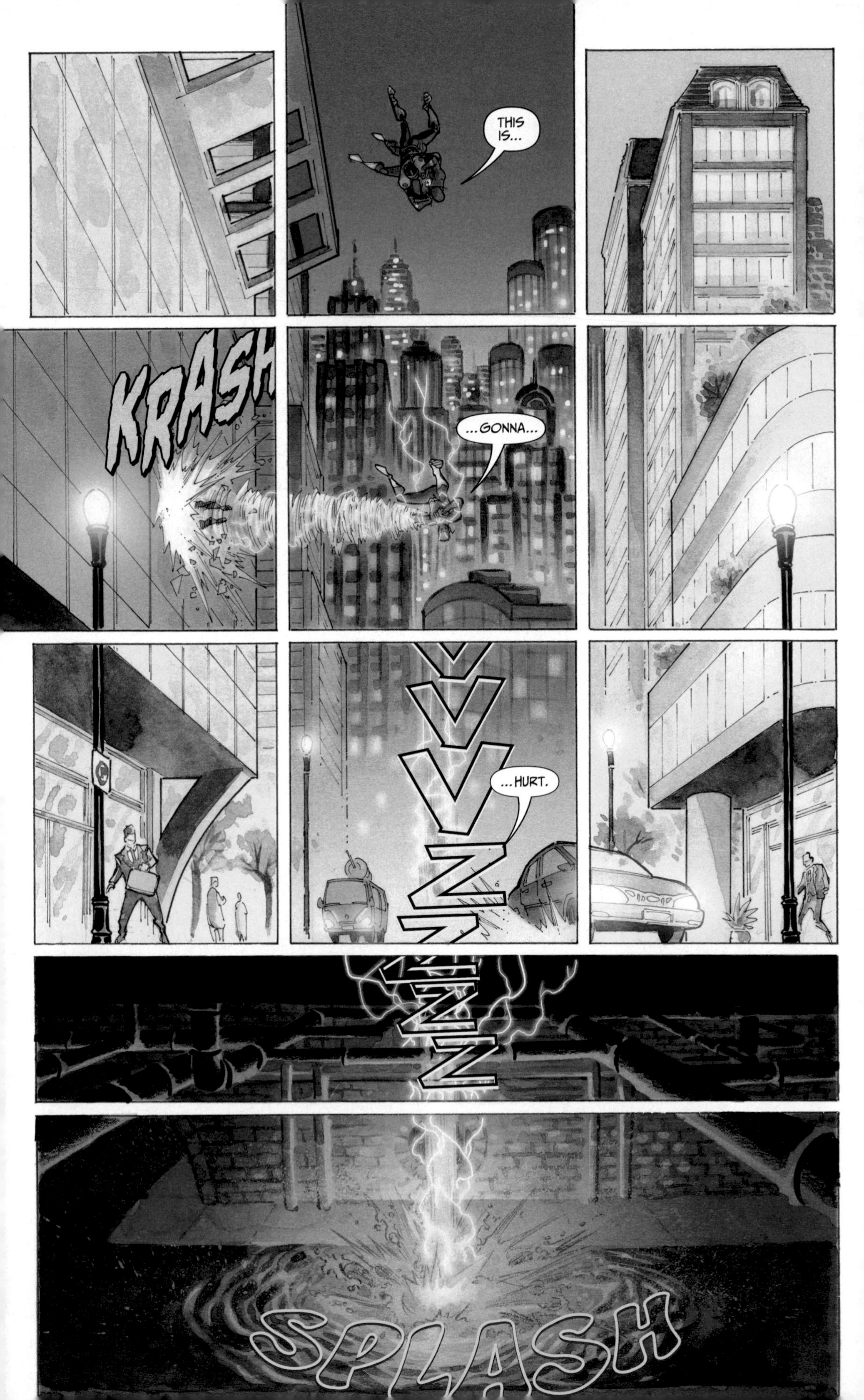
THIS IS...
KRASH
...GONNA...
...HURT.
VVVVZZZZZ
SPLASH

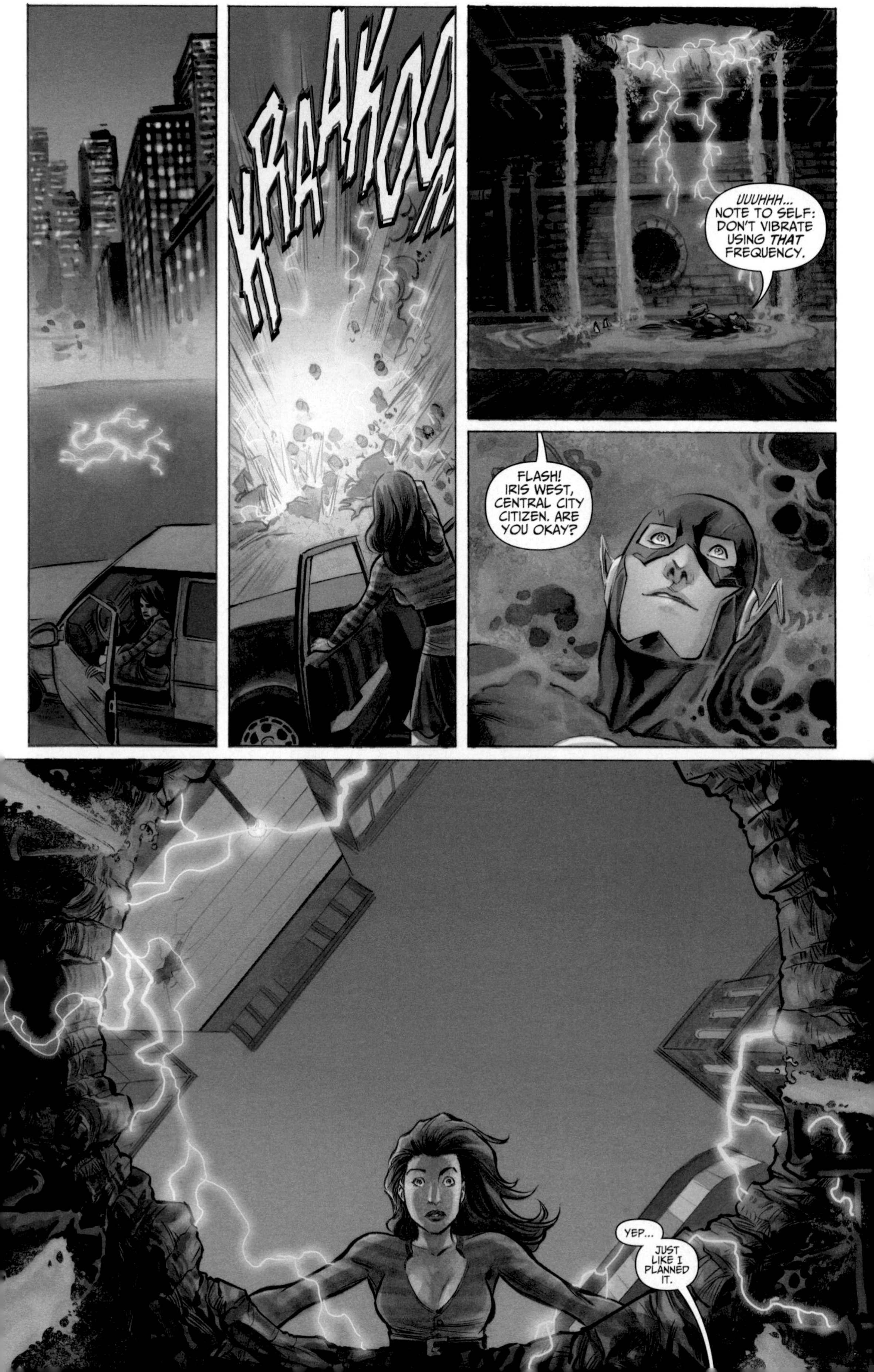
KRAKOO
UUUHHH... NOTE TO SELF: DON'T VIBRATE USING THAT FREQUENCY.
FLASH! IRIS WEST, CENTRAL CITY CITIZEN. ARE YOU OKAY?
YEP...
JUST LIKE I PLANNED IT.

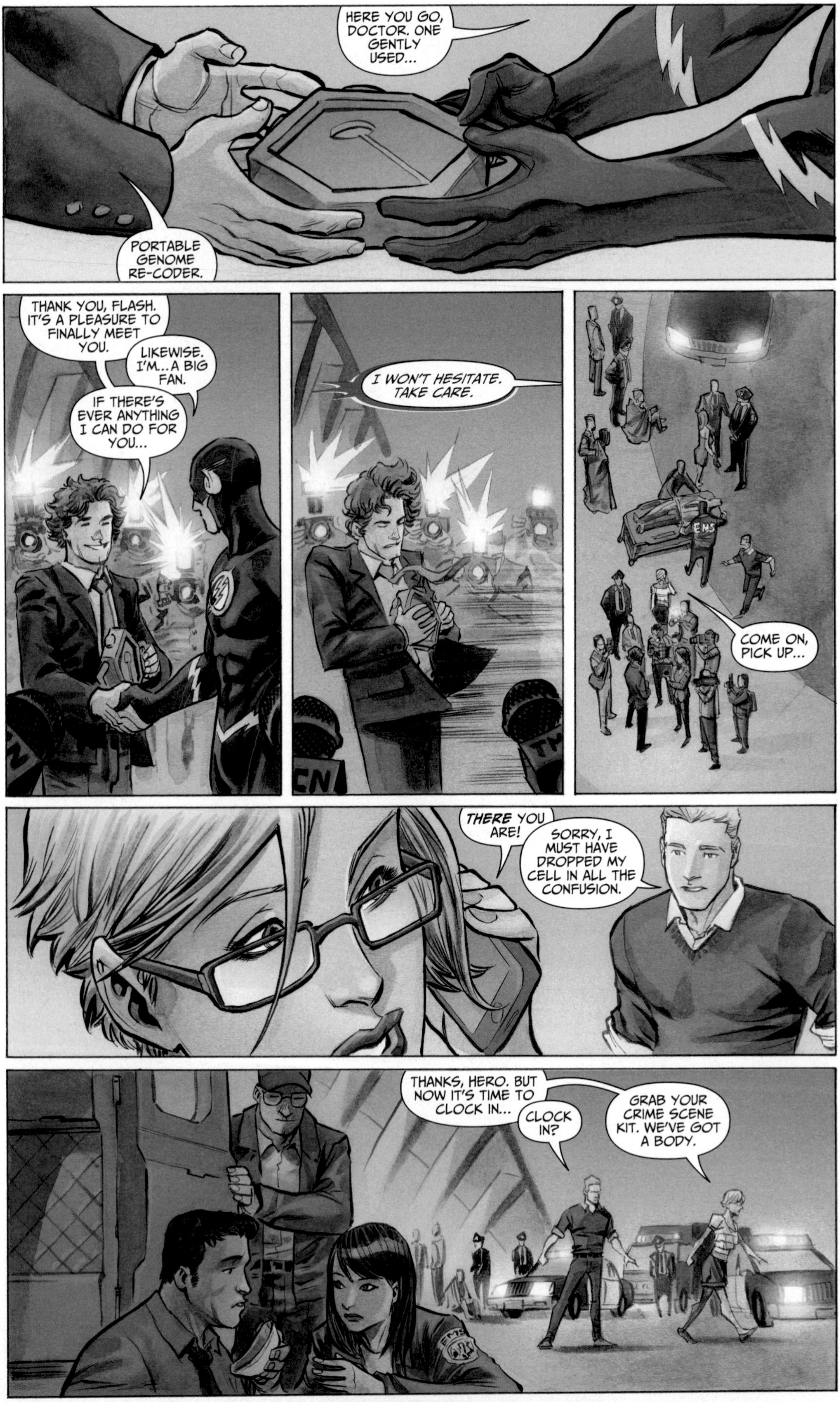
HERE YOU GO, DOCTOR. ONE GENTLY USED...
PORTABLE GENOME RE-CODER.
THANK YOU, FLASH. IT'S A PLEASURE TO FINALLY MEET YOU.
LIKEWISE. I'M...A BIG FAN.
IF THERE'S EVER ANYTHING I CAN DO FOR YOU...
I WON'T HESITATE. TAKE CARE.
COME ON, PICK UP...
THERE YOU ARE!
SORRY, I MUST HAVE DROPPED MY CELL IN ALL THE CONFUSION.
THANKS, HERO. BUT NOW IT'S TIME TO CLOCK IN...
CLOCK IN?
GRAB YOUR CRIME SCENE KIT. WE'VE GOT A BODY.

LOOK AT THIS... LITTLE PATTY SPIVOT! OUT OF THE LAB COAT AND GETTING HER HANDS DIRTY, FOR A CHANGE.

NICE TO SEE YOU, TOO, TONY. WHAT HAPPENED?

THE FLASH HAPPENED. PUT HIM THROUGH A PLATE GLASS WINDOW.

KILLED ON IMPACT?

WE'LL FIND OUT...

MANUEL?!

HUH? YOU MEAN--

"--YOU KNOW THIS GUY?"

I TOLDJA IT WAS A BAD IDEA.

NO WAY, BARRY. SHE WAS TOTALLY WORTH IT.

WORTH GETTING A BEAT DOWN FROM THE WHOLE RUGBY TEAM, MANUEL?

AT LEAST YOU'RE OUT OF THE DORM FOR ONCE, GETTING FRESH AIR.

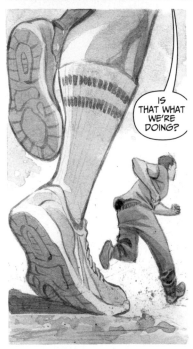

IS THAT WHAT WE'RE DOING?

I THOUGHT WE WERE FLEEING FROM ANOTHER ANGRY MOB...

...INSTEAD OF PREPPING FOR YOUR *HUGE* INTERVIEW TOMORROW.

WHATEVER. YOU KNOW WHAT YOUR PROBLEM IS?

YOU HAVEN'T FOUND SOMEONE WORTH TAKING A BEATING FOR.

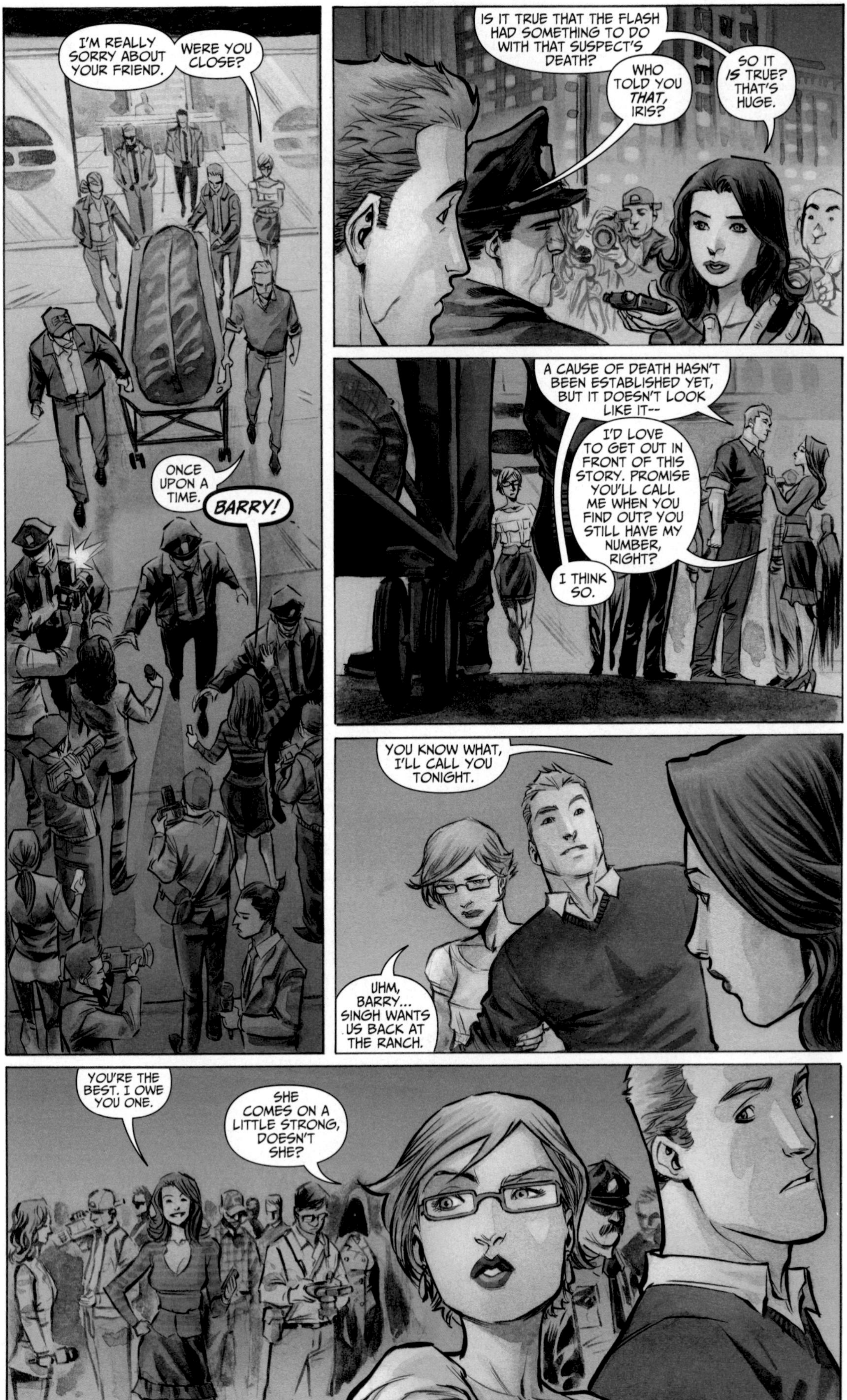
I'M REALLY SORRY ABOUT YOUR FRIEND.
WERE YOU CLOSE?
ONCE UPON A TIME.
BARRY!
IS IT TRUE THAT THE FLASH HAD SOMETHING TO DO WITH THAT SUSPECT'S DEATH?
WHO TOLD YOU THAT, IRIS?
SO IT IS TRUE? THAT'S HUGE.
A CAUSE OF DEATH HASN'T BEEN ESTABLISHED YET, BUT IT DOESN'T LOOK LIKE IT--
I'D LOVE TO GET OUT IN FRONT OF THIS STORY. PROMISE YOU'LL CALL ME WHEN YOU FIND OUT? YOU STILL HAVE MY NUMBER, RIGHT?
I THINK SO.
YOU KNOW WHAT, I'LL CALL YOU TONIGHT.
UHM, BARRY... SINGH WANTS US BACK AT THE RANCH.
YOU'RE THE BEST. I OWE YOU ONE.
SHE COMES ON A LITTLE STRONG, DOESN'T SHE?

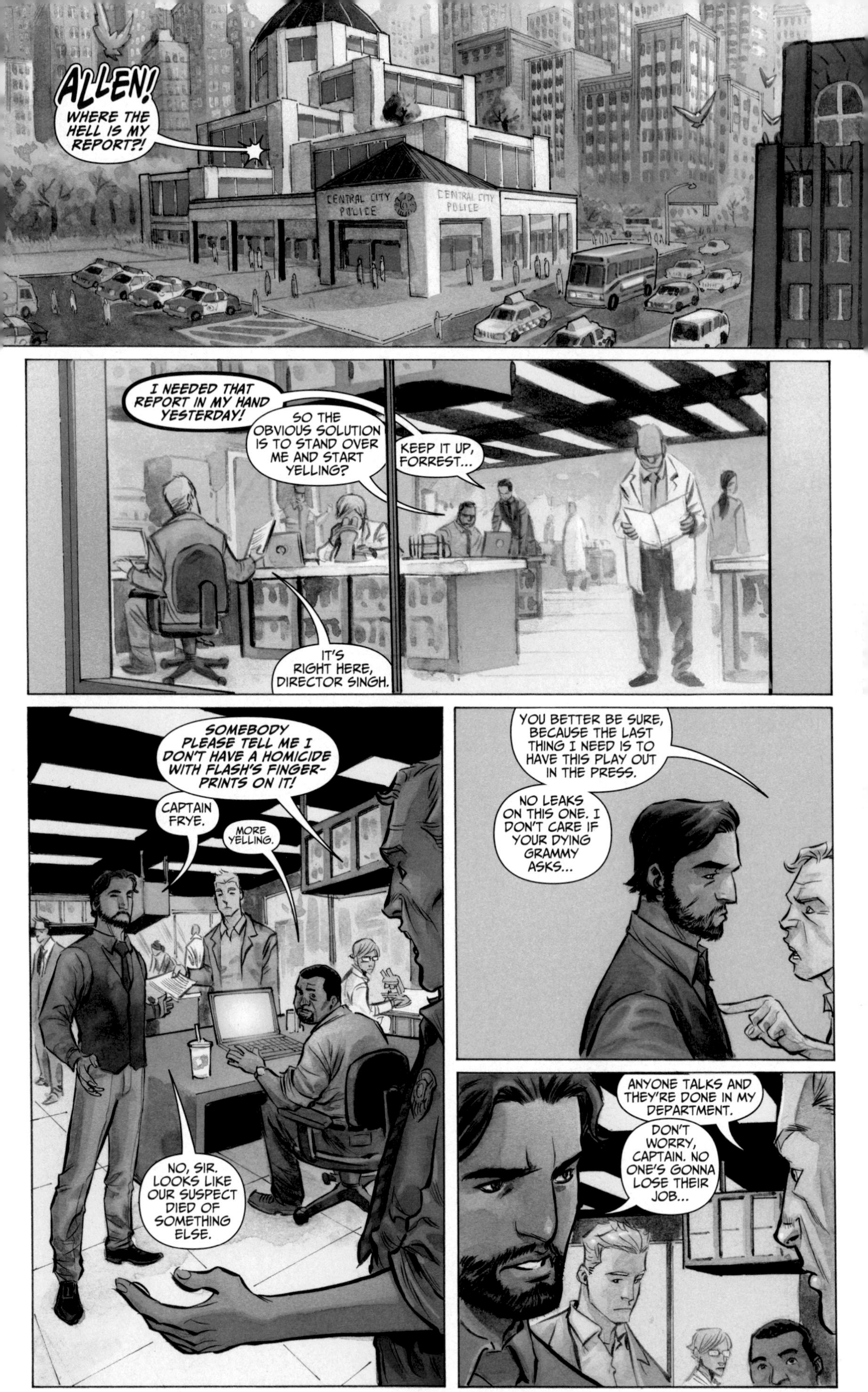
ALLEN!
WHERE THE HELL IS MY REPORT?!
CENTRAL CITY POLICE
CENTRAL CITY POLICE
I NEEDED THAT REPORT IN MY HAND YESTERDAY!
SO THE OBVIOUS SOLUTION IS TO STAND OVER ME AND START YELLING?
KEEP IT UP, FORREST...
IT'S RIGHT HERE, DIRECTOR SINGH.
SOMEBODY PLEASE TELL ME I DON'T HAVE A HOMICIDE WITH FLASH'S FINGER-PRINTS ON IT!
CAPTAIN FRYE.
MORE YELLING.
NO, SIR. LOOKS LIKE OUR SUSPECT DIED OF SOMETHING ELSE.
YOU BETTER BE SURE, BECAUSE THE LAST THING I NEED IS TO HAVE THIS PLAY OUT IN THE PRESS.
NO LEAKS ON THIS ONE. I DON'T CARE IF YOUR DYING GRAMMY ASKS...
ANYONE TALKS AND THEY'RE DONE IN MY DEPARTMENT.
DON'T WORRY, CAPTAIN. NO ONE'S GONNA LOSE THEIR JOB...

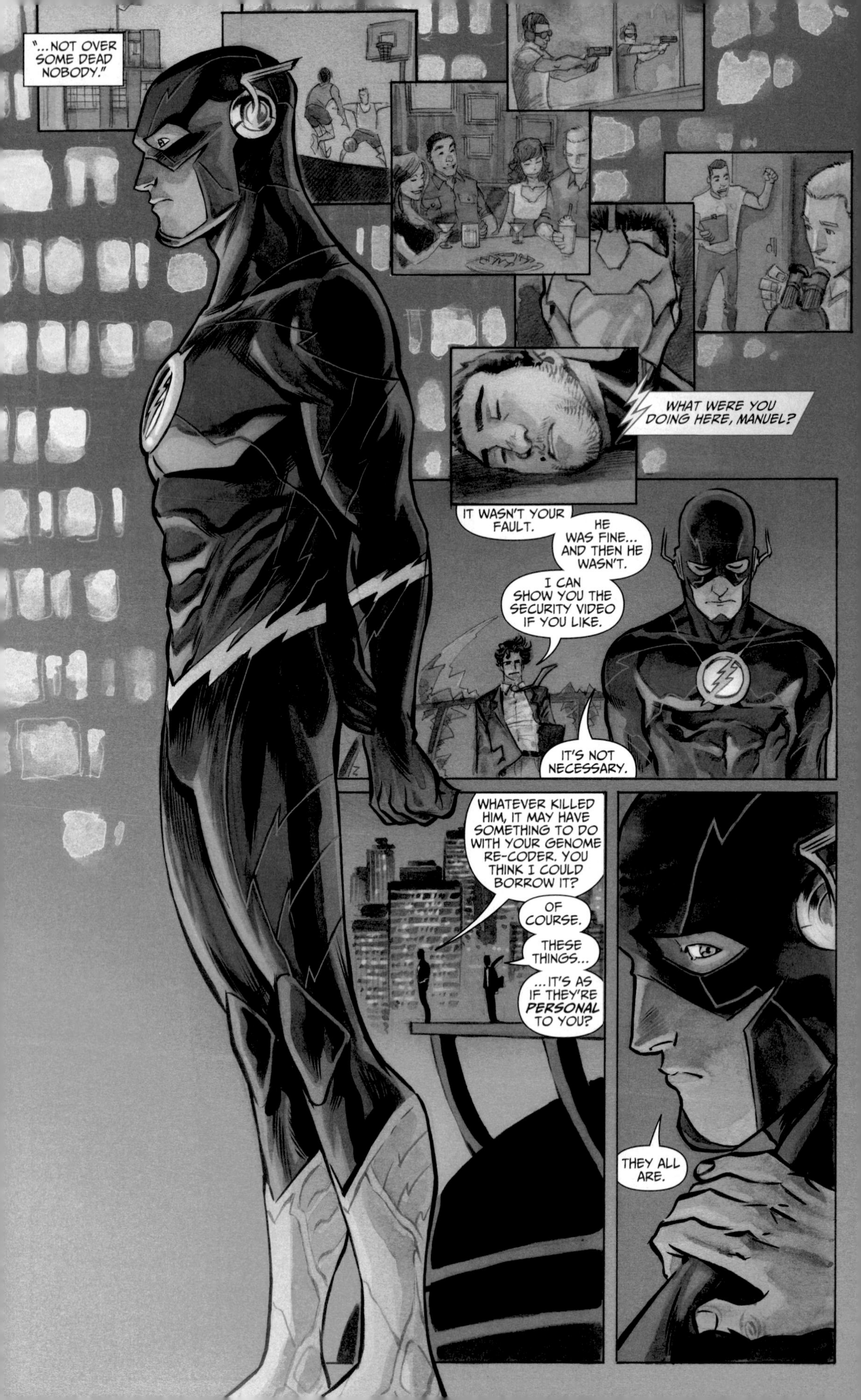
"...NOT OVER SOME DEAD NOBODY."
WHAT WERE YOU DOING HERE, MANUEL?
IT WASN'T YOUR FAULT.
HE WAS FINE... AND THEN HE WASN'T.
I CAN SHOW YOU THE SECURITY VIDEO IF YOU LIKE.
IT'S NOT NECESSARY.
WHATEVER KILLED HIM, IT MAY HAVE SOMETHING TO DO WITH YOUR GENOME RE-CODER. YOU THINK I COULD BORROW IT?
OF COURSE.
THESE THINGS...
...IT'S AS IF THEY'RE PERSONAL TO YOU?
THEY ALL ARE.

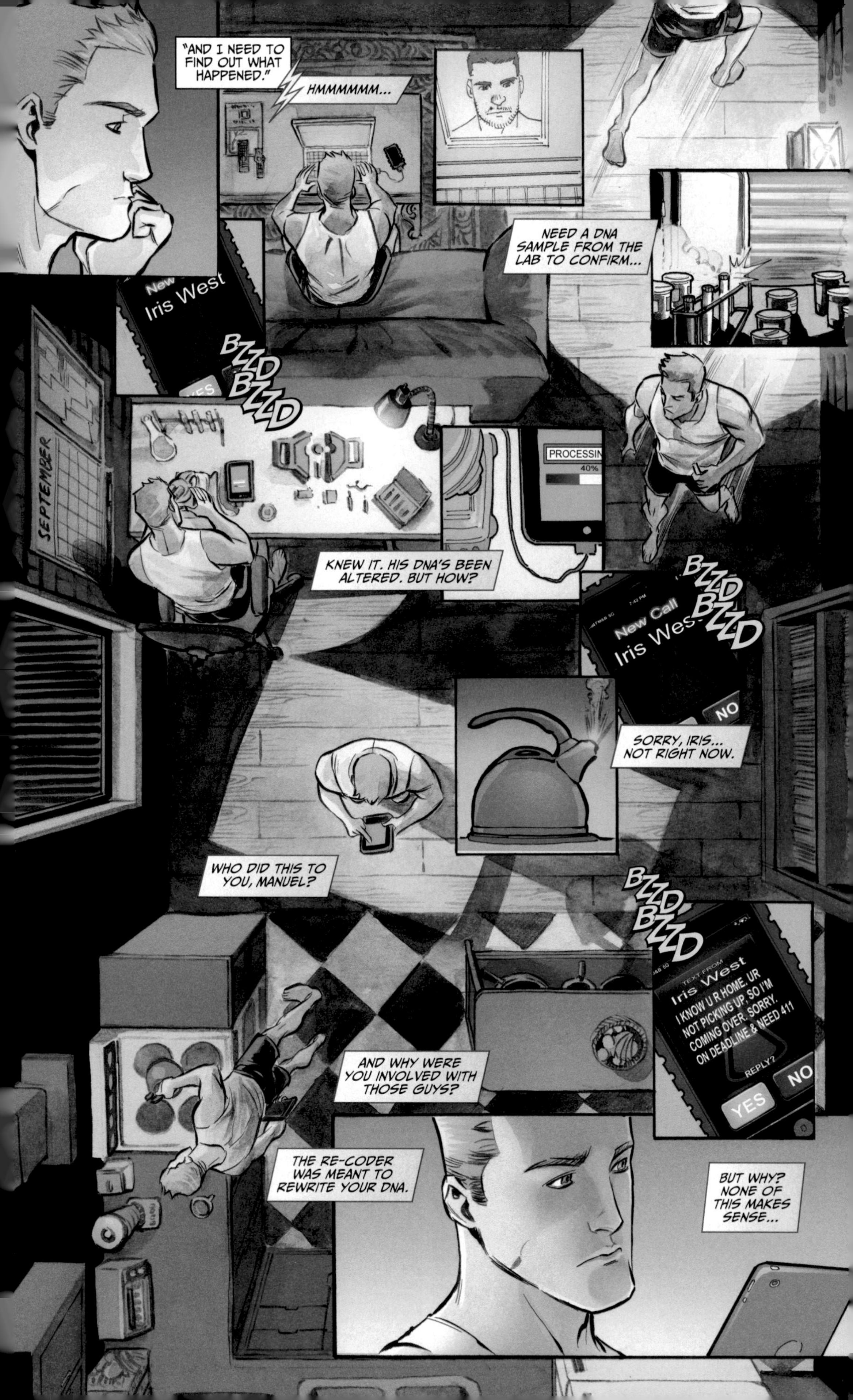
"AND I NEED TO FIND OUT WHAT HAPPENED."
HMMMMMM...
NEED A DNA SAMPLE FROM THE LAB TO CONFIRM...
Iris West
BZZD BZZD
SEPTEMBER
PROCESSIN
40%
KNEW IT. HIS DNA'S BEEN ALTERED. BUT HOW?
New Call
Iris Wes
BZZD BZZD
NO
SORRY, IRIS... NOT RIGHT NOW.
WHO DID THIS TO YOU, MANUEL?
BZZD BZZD
TEXT FROM
Iris West
I KNOW U R HOME. UR NOT PICKING UP, SO I'M COMING OVER. SORRY. ON DEADLINE & NEED 411
REPLY?
YES
NO
AND WHY WERE YOU INVOLVED WITH THOSE GUYS?
THE RE-CODER WAS MEANT TO REWRITE YOUR DNA.
BUT WHY? NONE OF THIS MAKES SENSE...

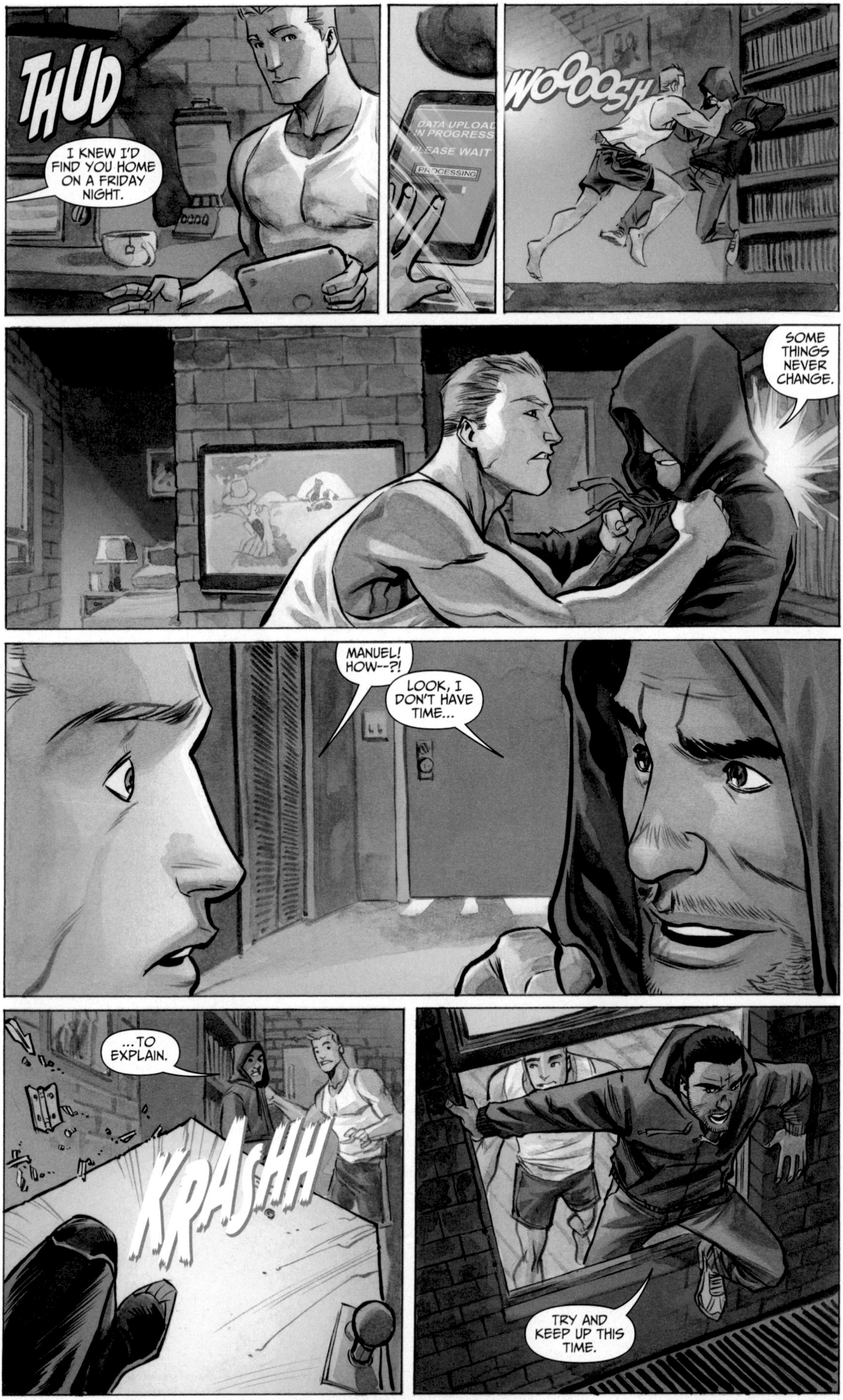
THUD
I KNEW I'D FIND YOU HOME ON A FRIDAY NIGHT.
DATA UPLOAD IN PROGRESS
PLEASE WAIT
PROCESSING
WOOOOSH
SOME THINGS NEVER CHANGE.
MANUEL! HOW--?!
LOOK, I DON'T HAVE TIME...
...TO EXPLAIN.
KRASHH
TRY AND KEEP UP THIS TIME.

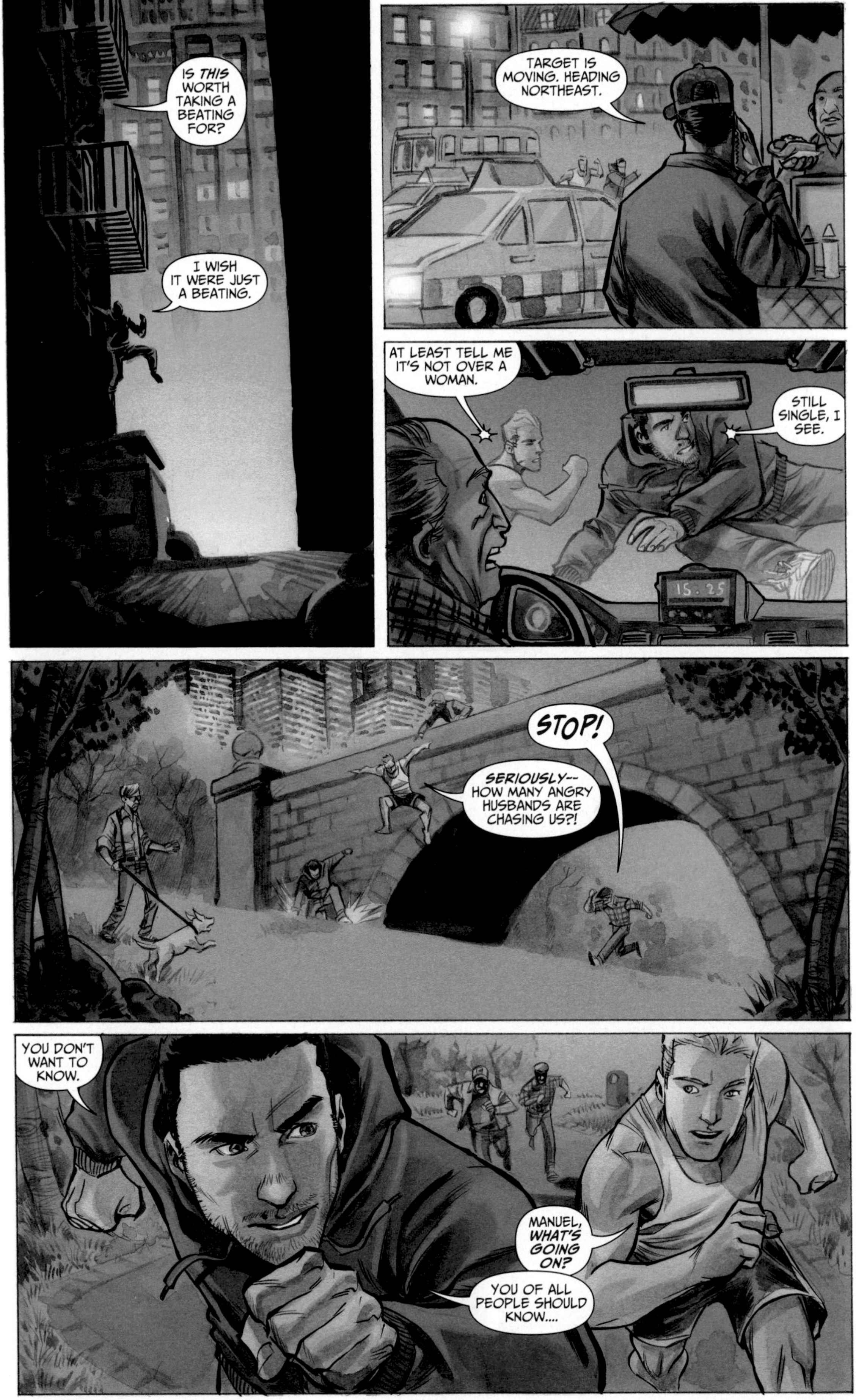
IS *THIS* WORTH TAKING A BEATING FOR?
I WISH IT WERE JUST A BEATING.
TARGET IS MOVING. HEADING NORTHEAST.
AT LEAST TELL ME IT'S NOT OVER A WOMAN.
STILL SINGLE, I SEE.
15.25
STOP!
SERIOUSLY-- HOW MANY ANGRY HUSBANDS ARE CHASING US?!
YOU DON'T WANT TO KNOW.
MANUEL, *WHAT'S GOING ON?*
YOU OF ALL PEOPLE SHOULD KNOW....

...WE'RE ALWAYS RUNNING FROM SOMETHING.

HE'S HALF RIGHT.

MY MOM ONCE TOLD ME THAT "LIFE IS LOCOMOTION..."

"IF YOU'RE NOT MOVING, YOU'RE NOT LIVING.

"BUT THERE COMES A TIME WHEN YOU'VE GOT TO STOP RUNNING *AWAY* FROM THINGS...

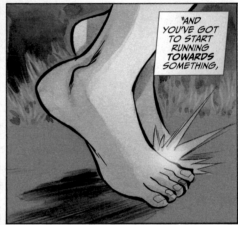

"AND YOU'VE GOT TO START RUNNING *TOWARDS* SOMETHING,

"YOU'VE GOT TO FORGE AHEAD.

BARRY?!

"KEEP MOVING."

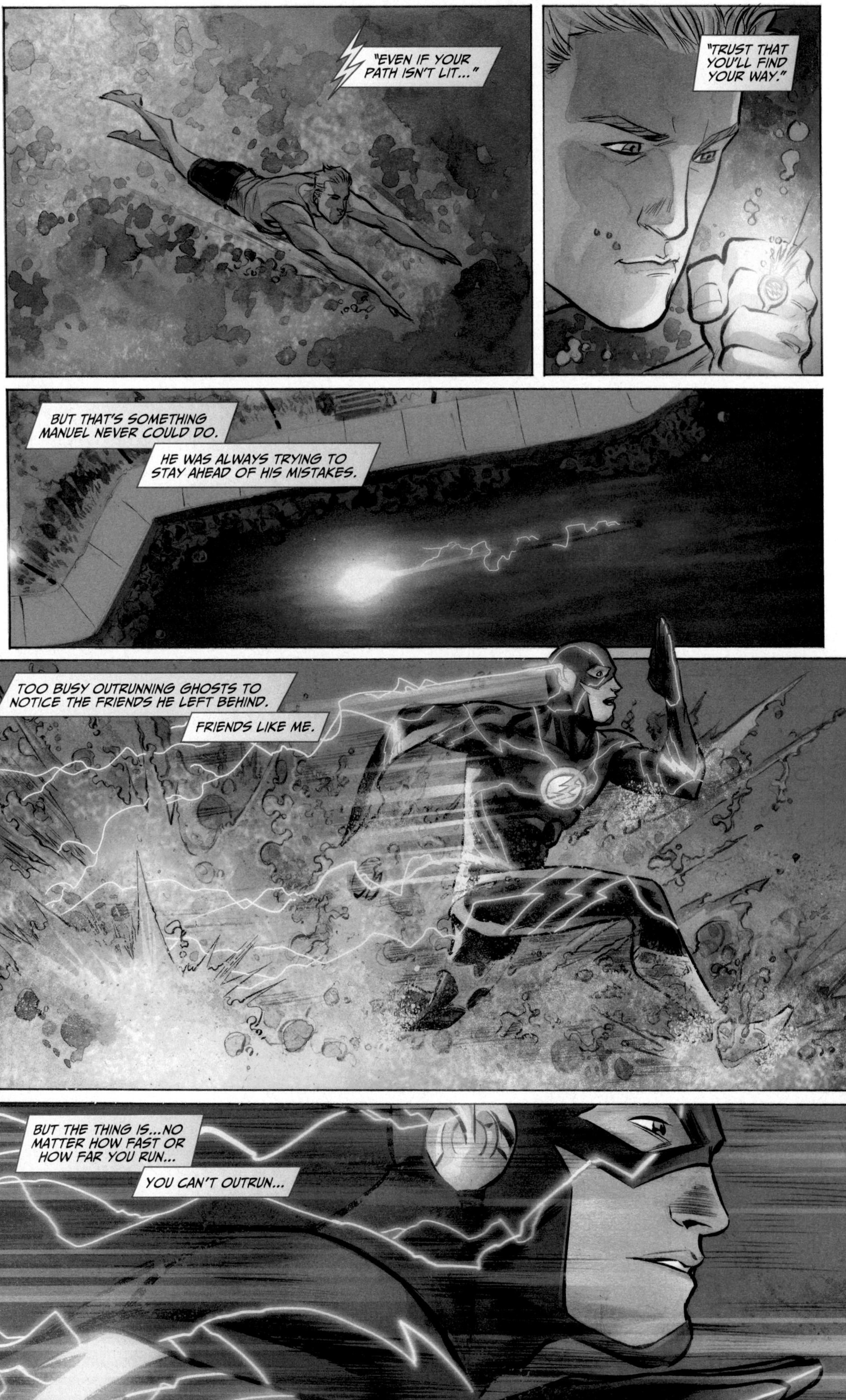
"EVEN IF YOUR PATH ISN'T LIT..."
"TRUST THAT YOU'LL FIND YOUR WAY."
BUT THAT'S SOMETHING MANUEL NEVER COULD DO.
HE WAS ALWAYS TRYING TO STAY AHEAD OF HIS MISTAKES.
TOO BUSY OUTRUNNING GHOSTS TO NOTICE THE FRIENDS HE LEFT BEHIND.
FRIENDS LIKE ME.
BUT THE THING IS...NO MATTER HOW FAST OR HOW FAR YOU RUN...
YOU CAN'T OUTRUN...

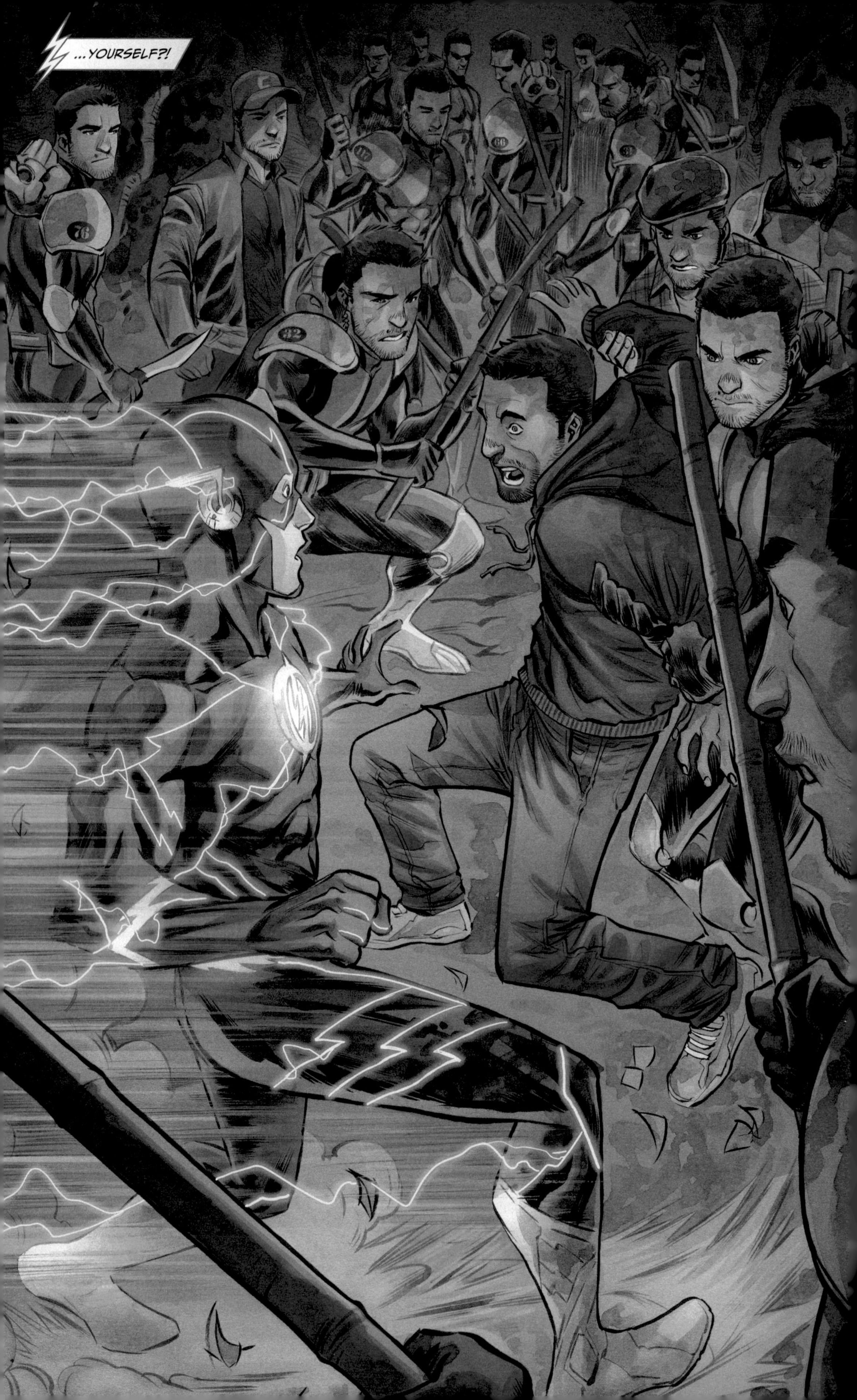
...YOURSELF?!

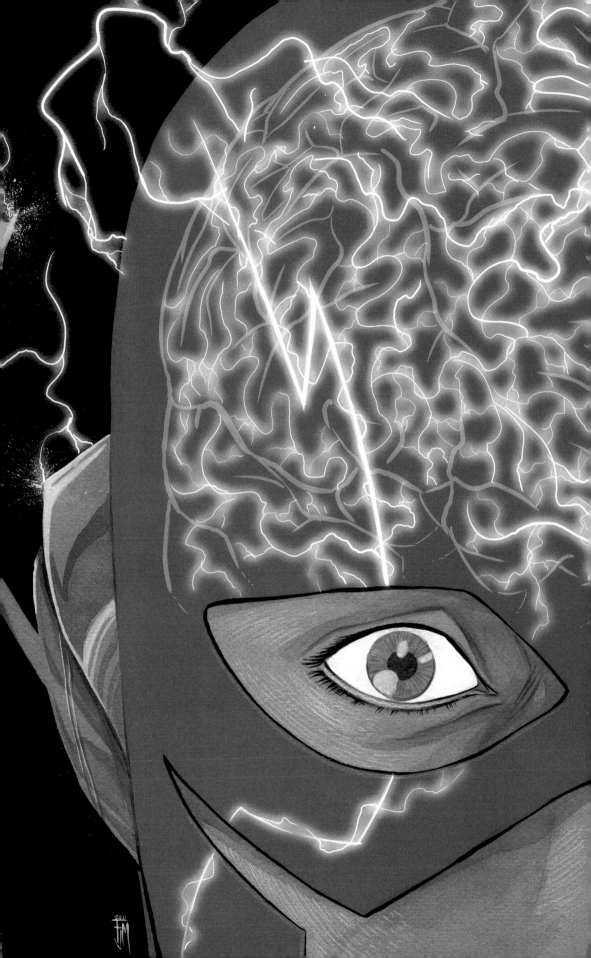

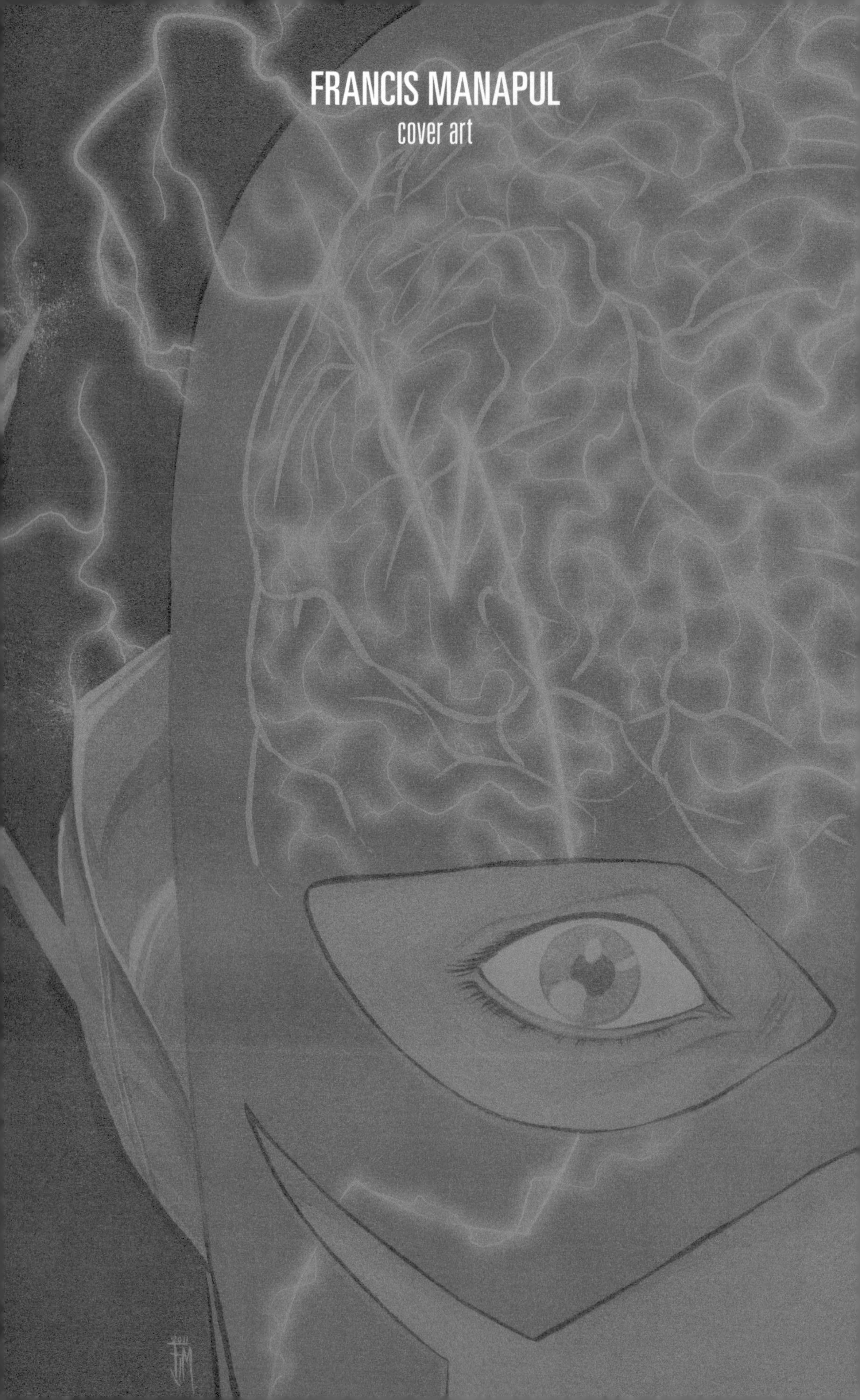

FRANCIS MANAPUL
cover art

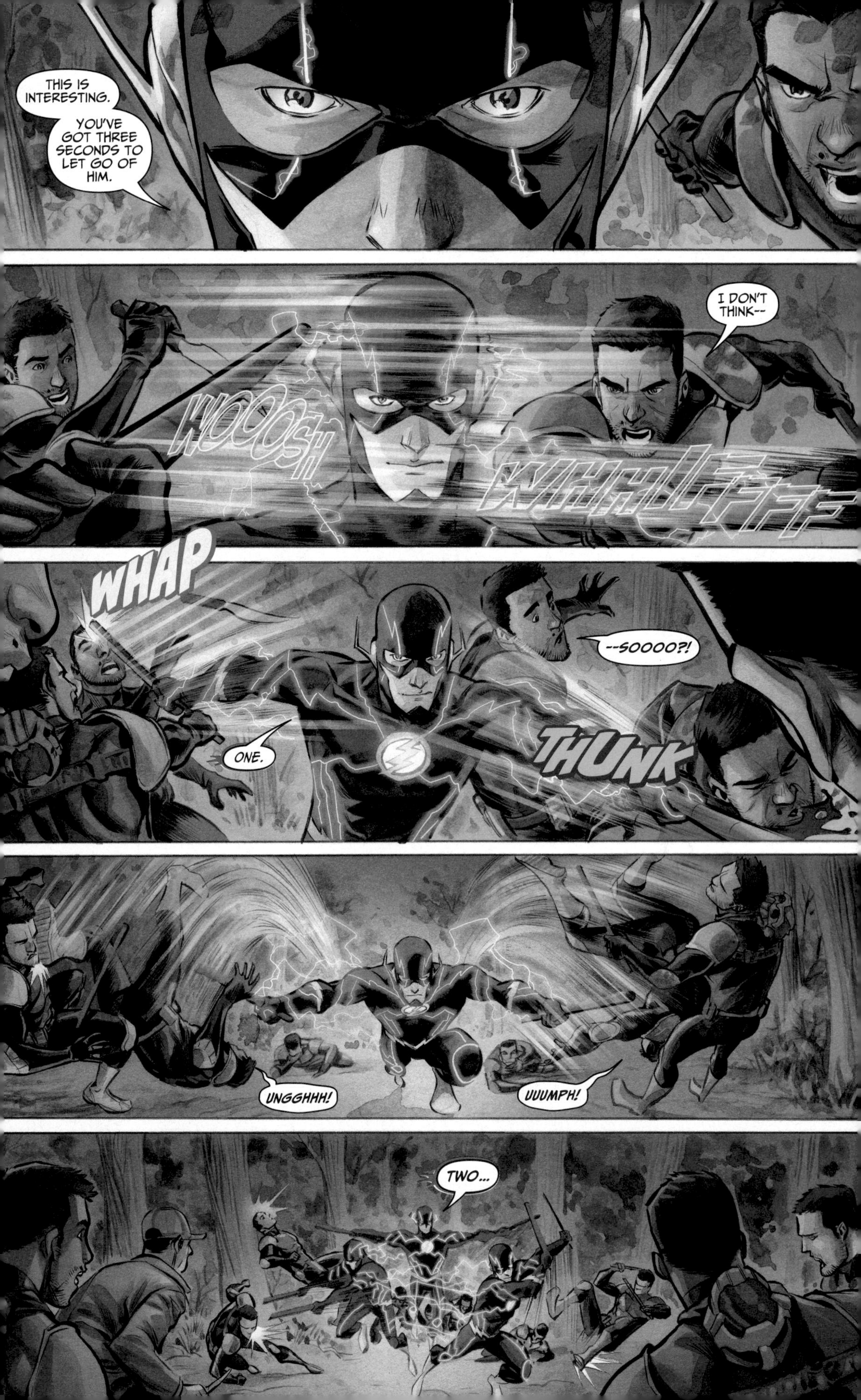
THIS IS INTERESTING.
YOU'VE GOT THREE SECONDS TO LET GO OF HIM.
I DON'T THINK--
WOOOSH
WHHUFFFF
WHAP
--SOOOO?!
ONE.
THUNK
UNGGHHH!
UUUMPH!
TWO...

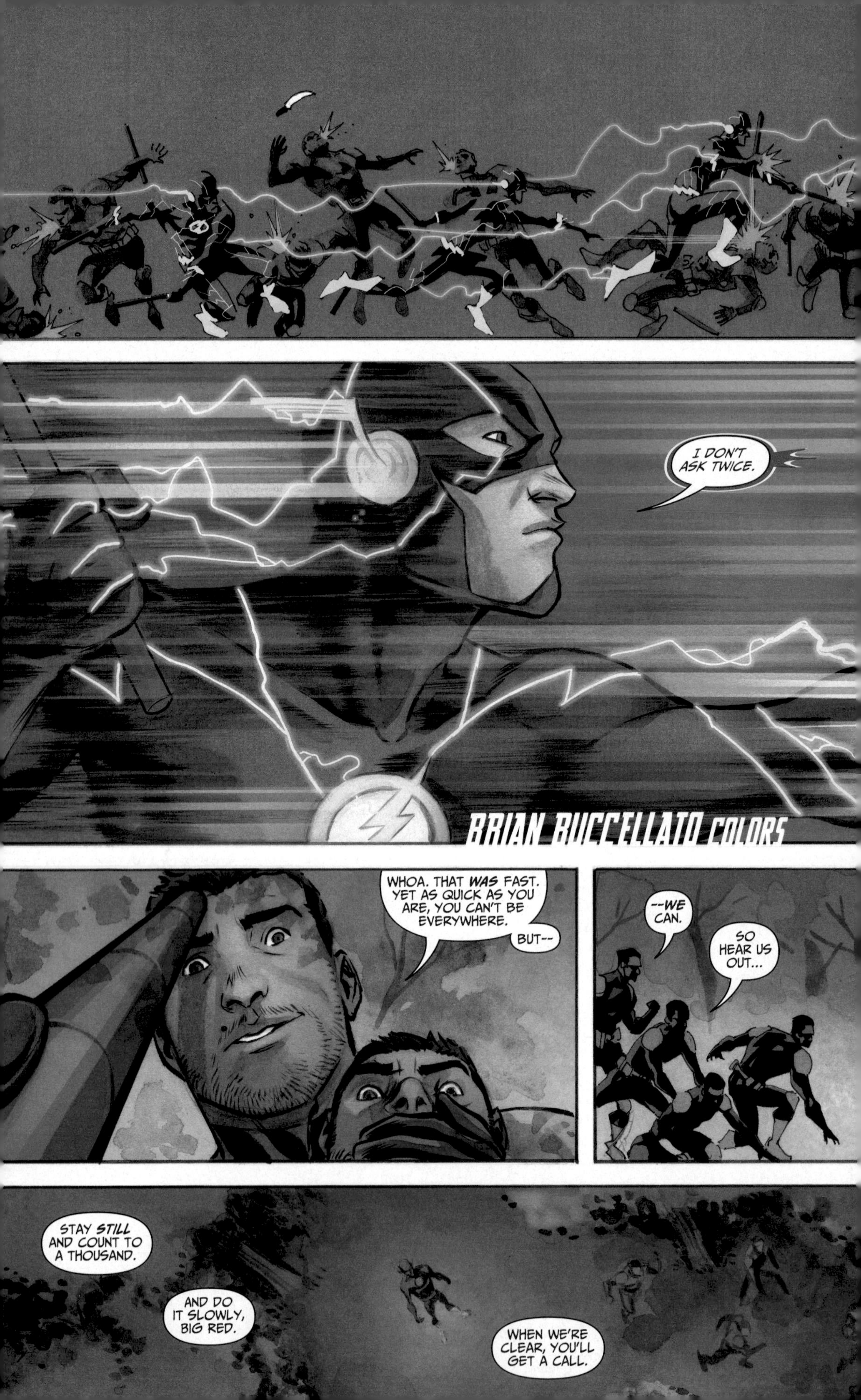
I DON'T ASK TWICE.
BRIAN BUCCELLATO COLORS
WHOA. THAT WAS FAST. YET AS QUICK AS YOU ARE, YOU CAN'T BE EVERYWHERE.
BUT--
--WE CAN.
SO HEAR US OUT...
STAY STILL AND COUNT TO A THOUSAND.
AND DO IT SLOWLY, BIG RED.
WHEN WE'RE CLEAR, YOU'LL GET A CALL.

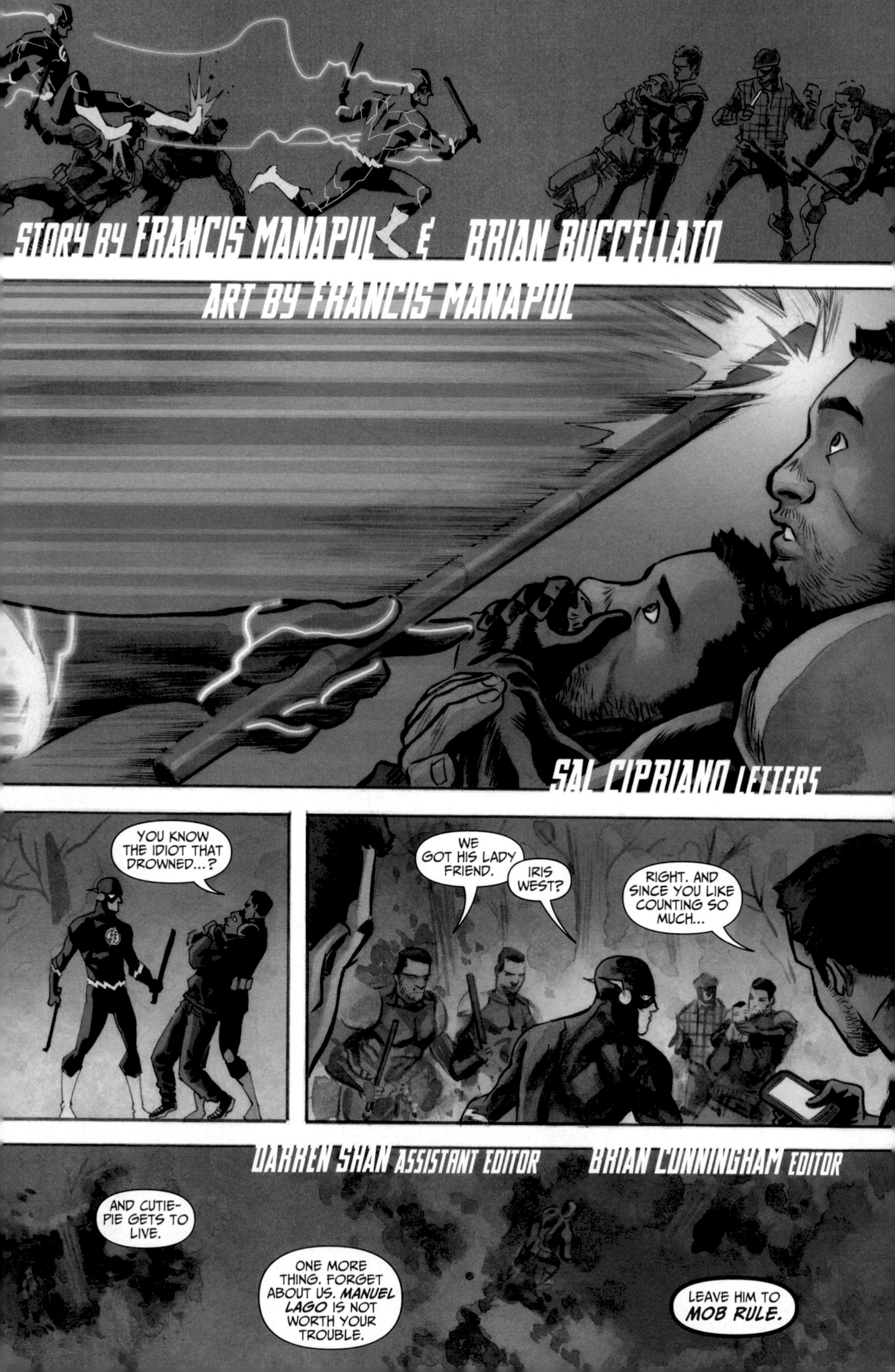
STORY BY FRANCIS MANAPUL & BRIAN BUCCELLATO
ART BY FRANCIS MANAPUL
SAL CIPRIANO LETTERS
YOU KNOW THE IDIOT THAT DROWNED...?
WE GOT HIS LADY FRIEND.
IRIS WEST?
RIGHT. AND SINCE YOU LIKE COUNTING SO MUCH...
DARREN SHAN ASSISTANT EDITOR
BRIAN CUNNINGHAM EDITOR
AND CUTIE-PIE GETS TO LIVE.
ONE MORE THING. FORGET ABOUT US. MANUEL LAGO IS NOT WORTH YOUR TROUBLE.
LEAVE HIM TO MOB RULE.

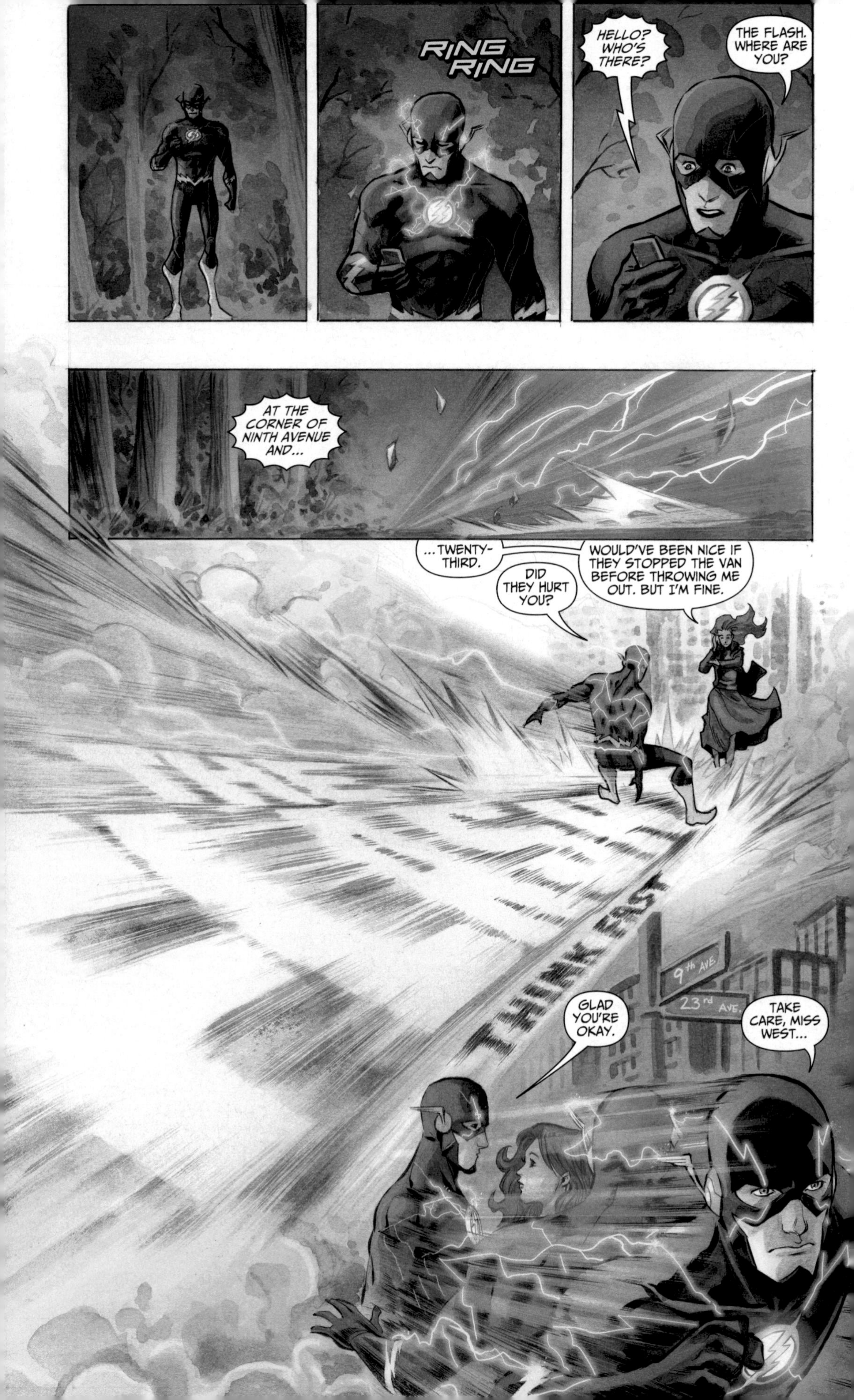
RING RING
HELLO? WHO'S THERE?
THE FLASH. WHERE ARE YOU?
AT THE CORNER OF NINTH AVENUE AND...
...TWENTY-THIRD.
DID THEY HURT YOU?
WOULD'VE BEEN NICE IF THEY STOPPED THE VAN BEFORE THROWING ME OUT. BUT I'M FINE.
THINK FAST
9th AVE.
23rd AVE.
GLAD YOU'RE OKAY.
TAKE CARE, MISS WEST...

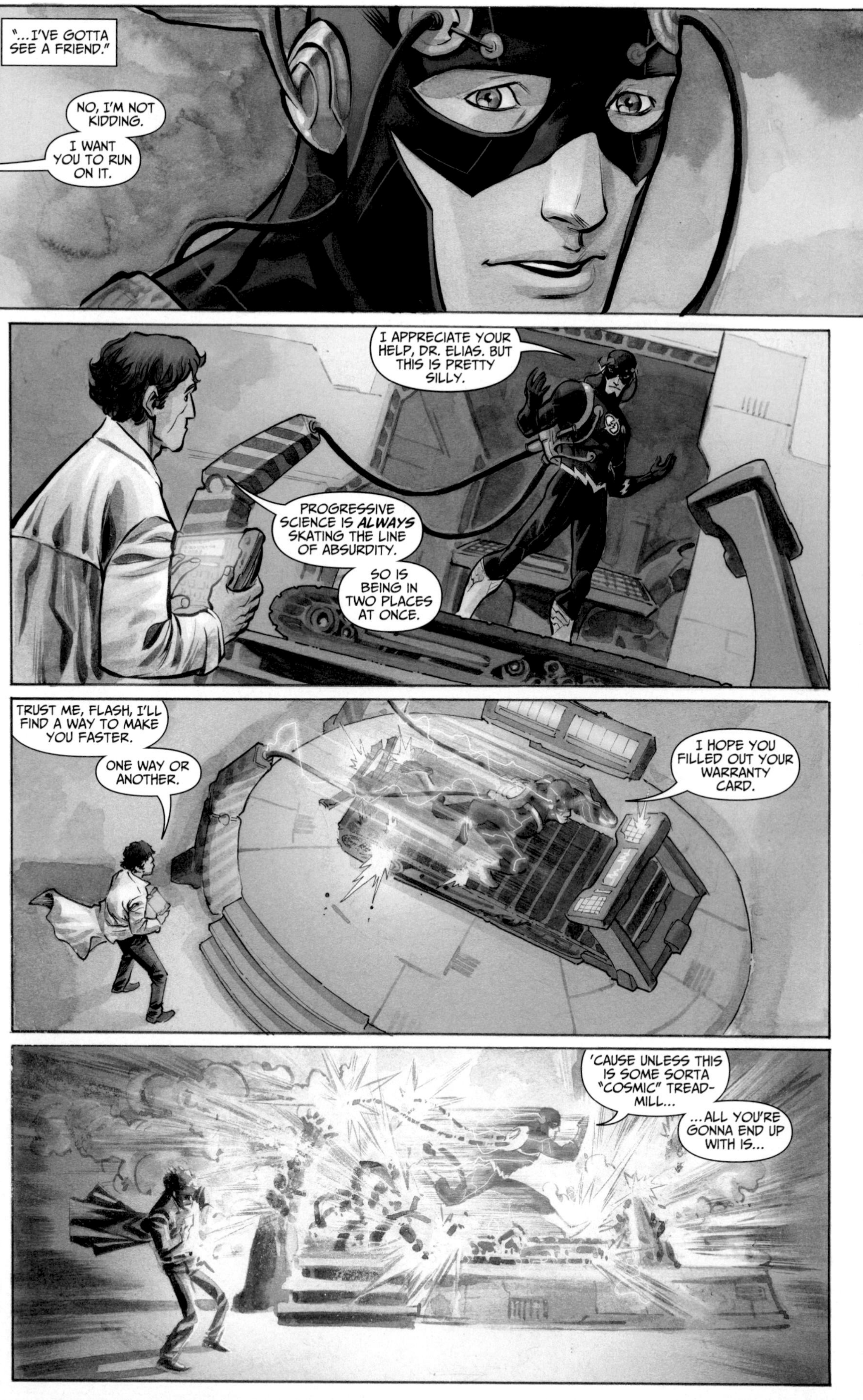
"...I'VE GOTTA SEE A FRIEND."
NO, I'M NOT KIDDING.
I WANT YOU TO RUN ON IT.
I APPRECIATE YOUR HELP, DR. ELIAS. BUT THIS IS PRETTY SILLY.
PROGRESSIVE SCIENCE IS ALWAYS SKATING THE LINE OF ABSURDITY.
SO IS BEING IN TWO PLACES AT ONCE.
TRUST ME, FLASH, I'LL FIND A WAY TO MAKE YOU FASTER.
ONE WAY OR ANOTHER.
I HOPE YOU FILLED OUT YOUR WARRANTY CARD.
'CAUSE UNLESS THIS IS SOME SORTA "COSMIC" TREAD-MILL...
...ALL YOU'RE GONNA END UP WITH IS...

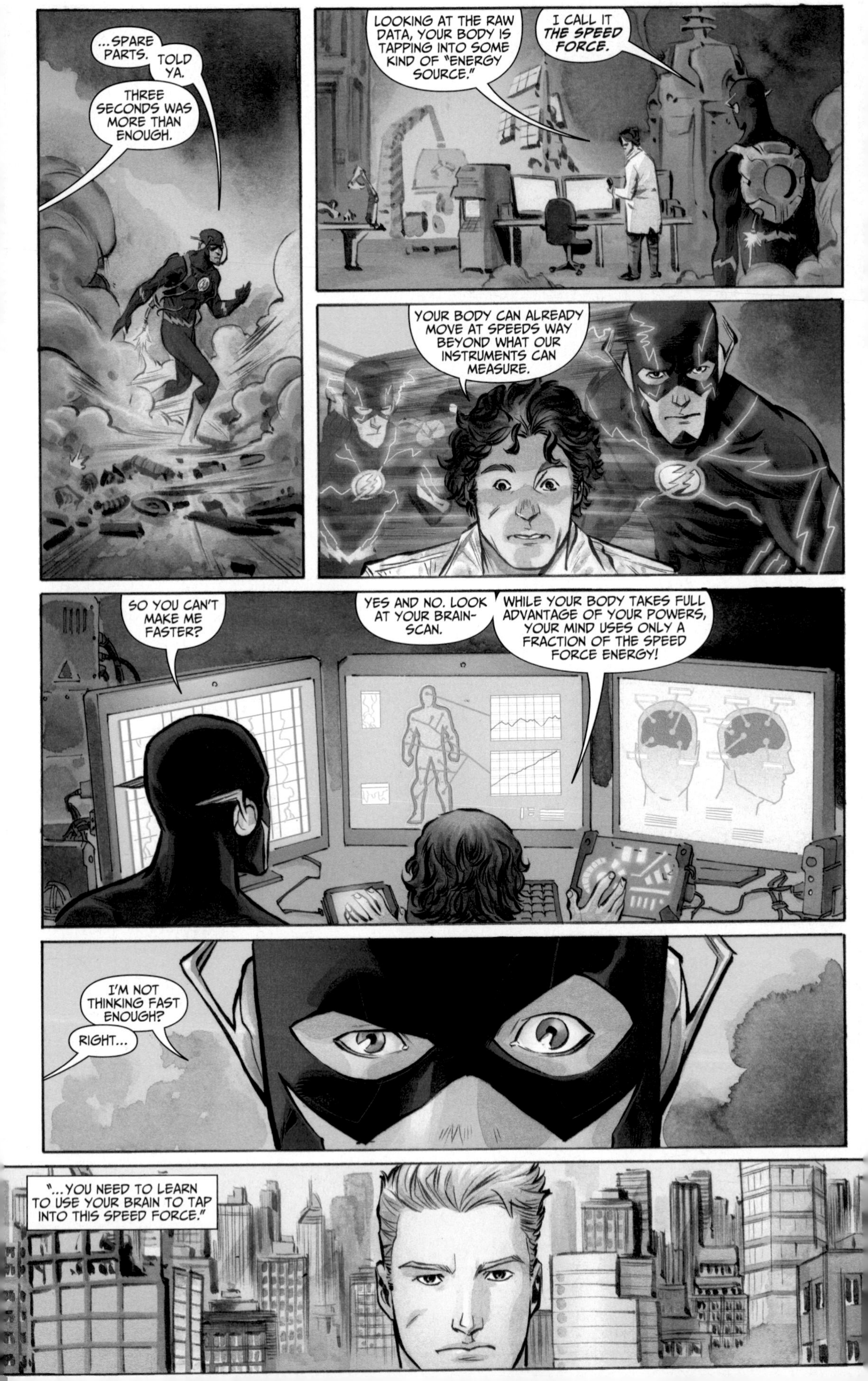
...SPARE PARTS.
TOLD YA.
THREE SECONDS WAS MORE THAN ENOUGH.
LOOKING AT THE RAW DATA, YOUR BODY IS TAPPING INTO SOME KIND OF "ENERGY SOURCE."
I CALL IT THE SPEED FORCE.
YOUR BODY CAN ALREADY MOVE AT SPEEDS WAY BEYOND WHAT OUR INSTRUMENTS CAN MEASURE.
SO YOU CAN'T MAKE ME FASTER?
YES AND NO. LOOK AT YOUR BRAIN-SCAN.
WHILE YOUR BODY TAKES FULL ADVANTAGE OF YOUR POWERS, YOUR MIND USES ONLY A FRACTION OF THE SPEED FORCE ENERGY!
I'M NOT THINKING FAST ENOUGH?
RIGHT...
"...YOU NEED TO LEARN TO USE YOUR BRAIN TO TAP INTO THIS SPEED FORCE."

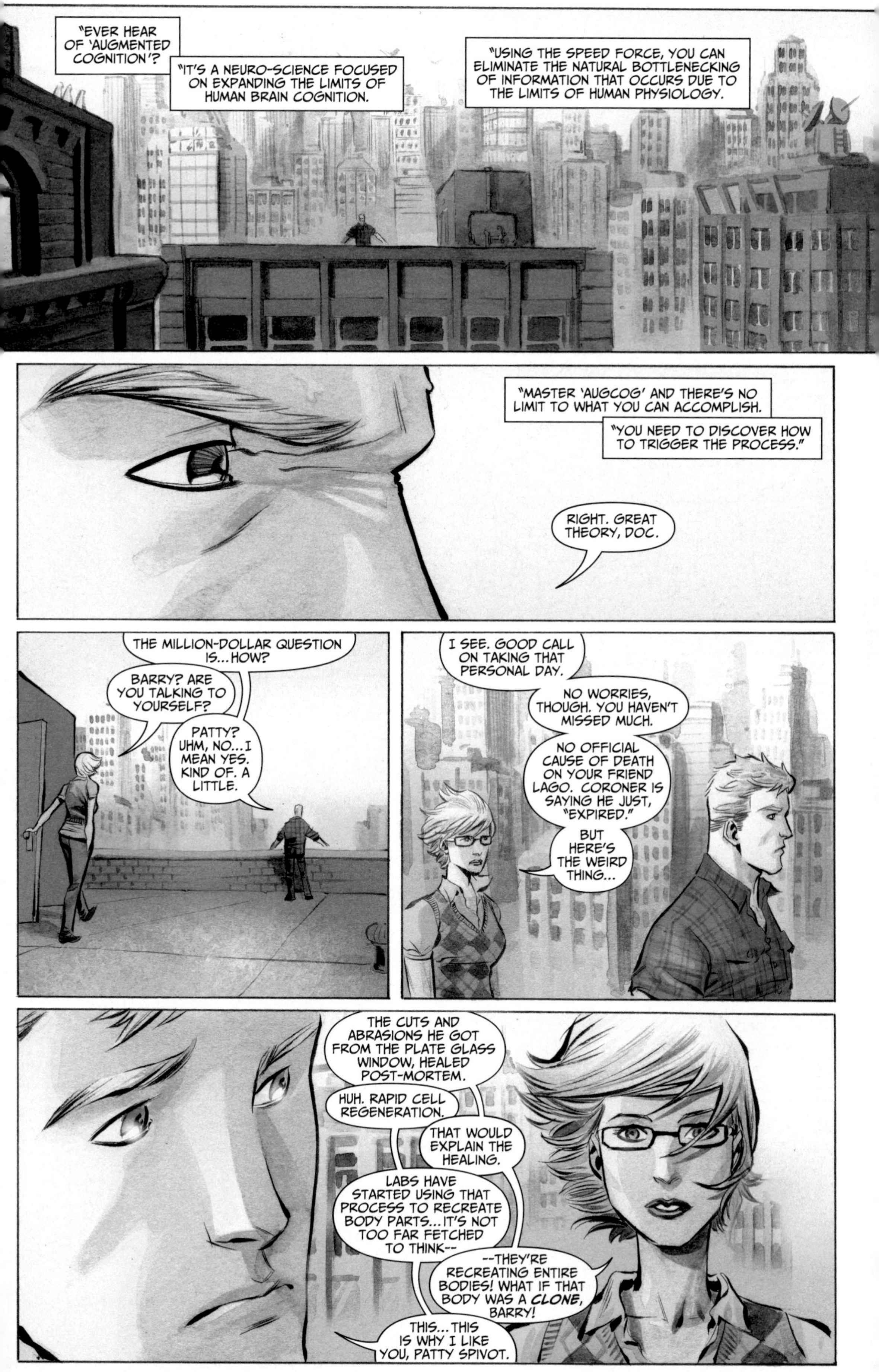
"EVER HEAR OF 'AUGMENTED COGNITION'?
"IT'S A NEURO-SCIENCE FOCUSED ON EXPANDING THE LIMITS OF HUMAN BRAIN COGNITION.
"USING THE SPEED FORCE, YOU CAN ELIMINATE THE NATURAL BOTTLENECKING OF INFORMATION THAT OCCURS DUE TO THE LIMITS OF HUMAN PHYSIOLOGY.
"MASTER 'AUGCOG' AND THERE'S NO LIMIT TO WHAT YOU CAN ACCOMPLISH.
"YOU NEED TO DISCOVER HOW TO TRIGGER THE PROCESS."
RIGHT. GREAT THEORY, DOC.
THE MILLION-DOLLAR QUESTION IS...HOW?
BARRY? ARE YOU TALKING TO YOURSELF?
PATTY? UHM, NO...I MEAN YES. KIND OF. A LITTLE.
I SEE. GOOD CALL ON TAKING THAT PERSONAL DAY.
NO WORRIES, THOUGH. YOU HAVEN'T MISSED MUCH.
NO OFFICIAL CAUSE OF DEATH ON YOUR FRIEND LAGO. CORONER IS SAYING HE JUST, "EXPIRED."
BUT HERE'S THE WEIRD THING...
THE CUTS AND ABRASIONS HE GOT FROM THE PLATE GLASS WINDOW, HEALED POST-MORTEM.
HUH. RAPID CELL REGENERATION.
THAT WOULD EXPLAIN THE HEALING.
LABS HAVE STARTED USING THAT PROCESS TO RECREATE BODY PARTS...IT'S NOT TOO FAR FETCHED TO THINK--
--THEY'RE RECREATING ENTIRE BODIES! WHAT IF THAT BODY WAS A *CLONE*, BARRY!
THIS...THIS IS WHY I LIKE YOU, PATTY SPIVOT.

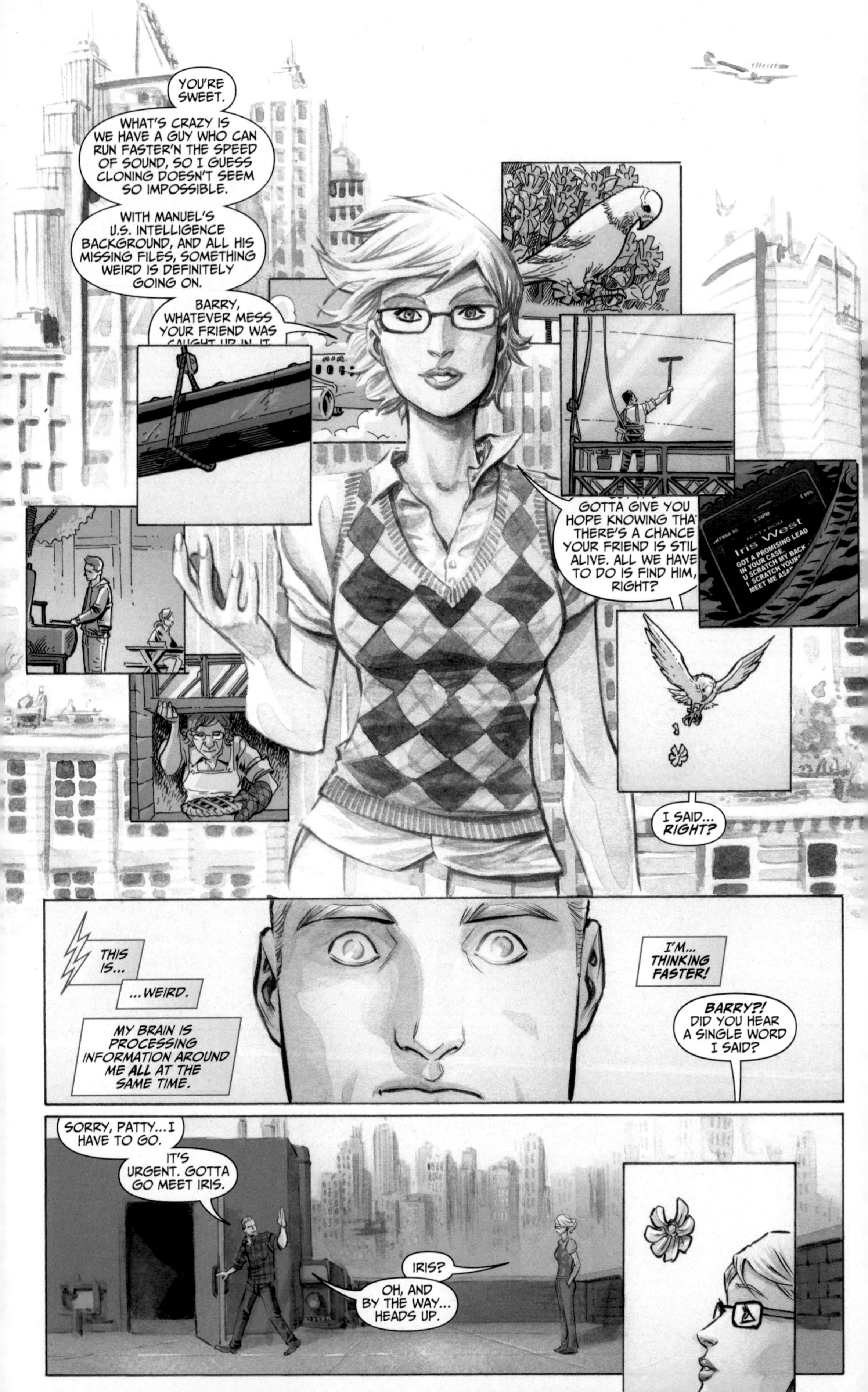
YOU'RE SWEET.
WHAT'S CRAZY IS WE HAVE A GUY WHO CAN RUN FASTER'N THE SPEED OF SOUND, SO I GUESS CLONING DOESN'T SEEM SO IMPOSSIBLE.
WITH MANUEL'S U.S. INTELLIGENCE BACKGROUND, AND ALL HIS MISSING FILES, SOMETHING WEIRD IS DEFINITELY GOING ON.
BARRY, WHATEVER MESS YOUR FRIEND WAS
GOTTA GIVE YOU HOPE KNOWING THA THERE'S A CHANCE YOUR FRIEND IS STIL ALIVE. ALL WE HAVE TO DO IS FIND HIM, RIGHT?
3:24PM
TEXT FROM
Iris West
GOT A PROMISING LEAD IN YOUR CASE. U SCRATCH MY BACK... I SCRATCH YOUR
I SAID... RIGHT?
THIS IS...
...WEIRD.
MY BRAIN IS PROCESSING INFORMATION AROUND ME ALL AT THE SAME TIME.
I'M... THINKING FASTER!
BARRY?! DID YOU HEAR A SINGLE WORD I SAID?
SORRY, PATTY...I HAVE TO GO.
IT'S URGENT. GOTTA GO MEET IRIS.
IRIS?
OH, AND BY THE WAY... HEADS UP.

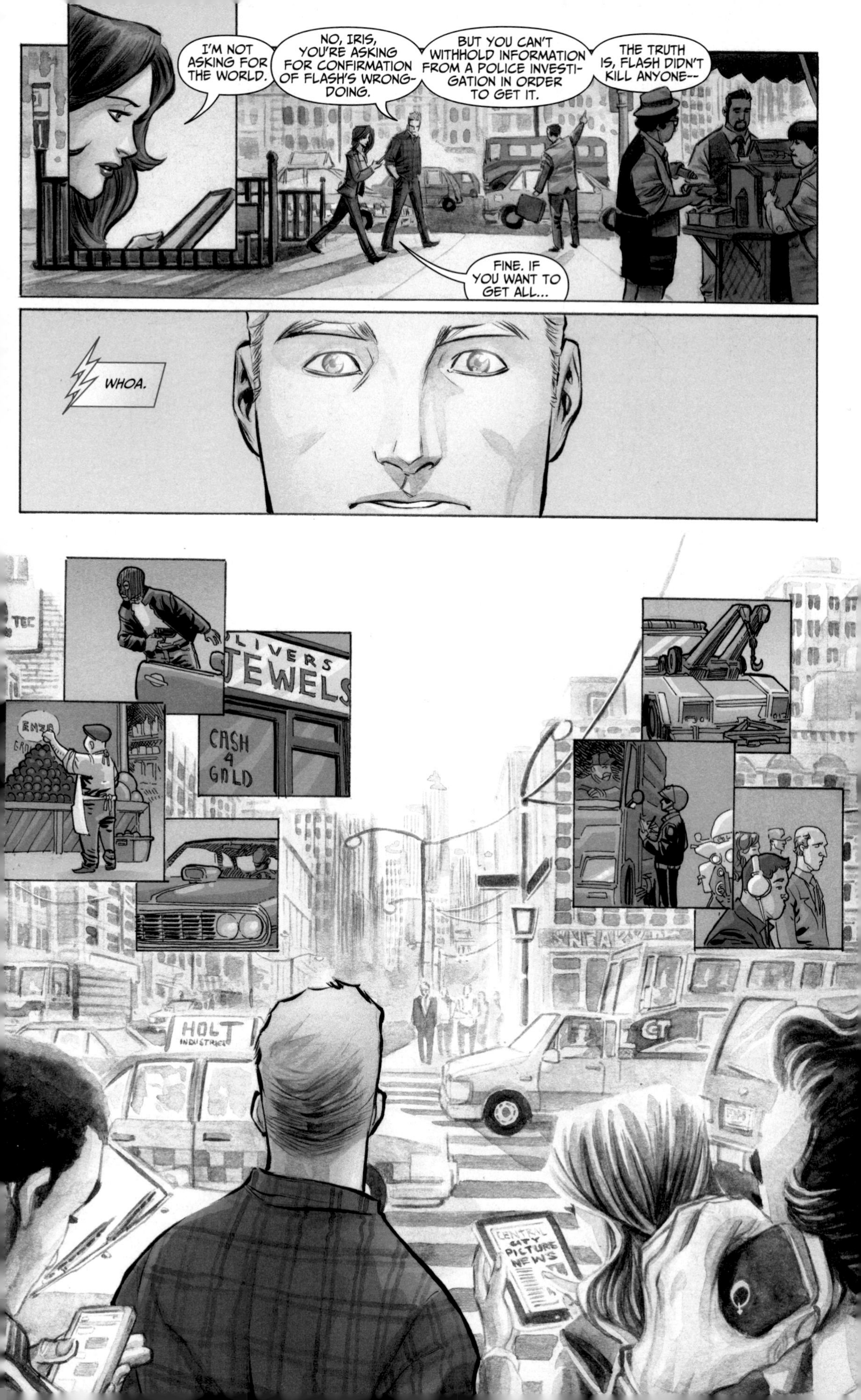

I'M NOT ASKING FOR THE WORLD.
NO, IRIS, YOU'RE ASKING FOR CONFIRMATION OF FLASH'S WRONG-DOING.
BUT YOU CAN'T WITHHOLD INFORMATION FROM A POLICE INVESTI-GATION IN ORDER TO GET IT.
THE TRUTH IS, FLASH DIDN'T KILL ANYONE--
FINE. IF YOU WANT TO GET ALL...
WHOA.
OLIVERS JEWELS
CASH 4 GOLD
ENZO
HOLT INDUSTRIES
CENTRAL CITY PICTURE NEWS

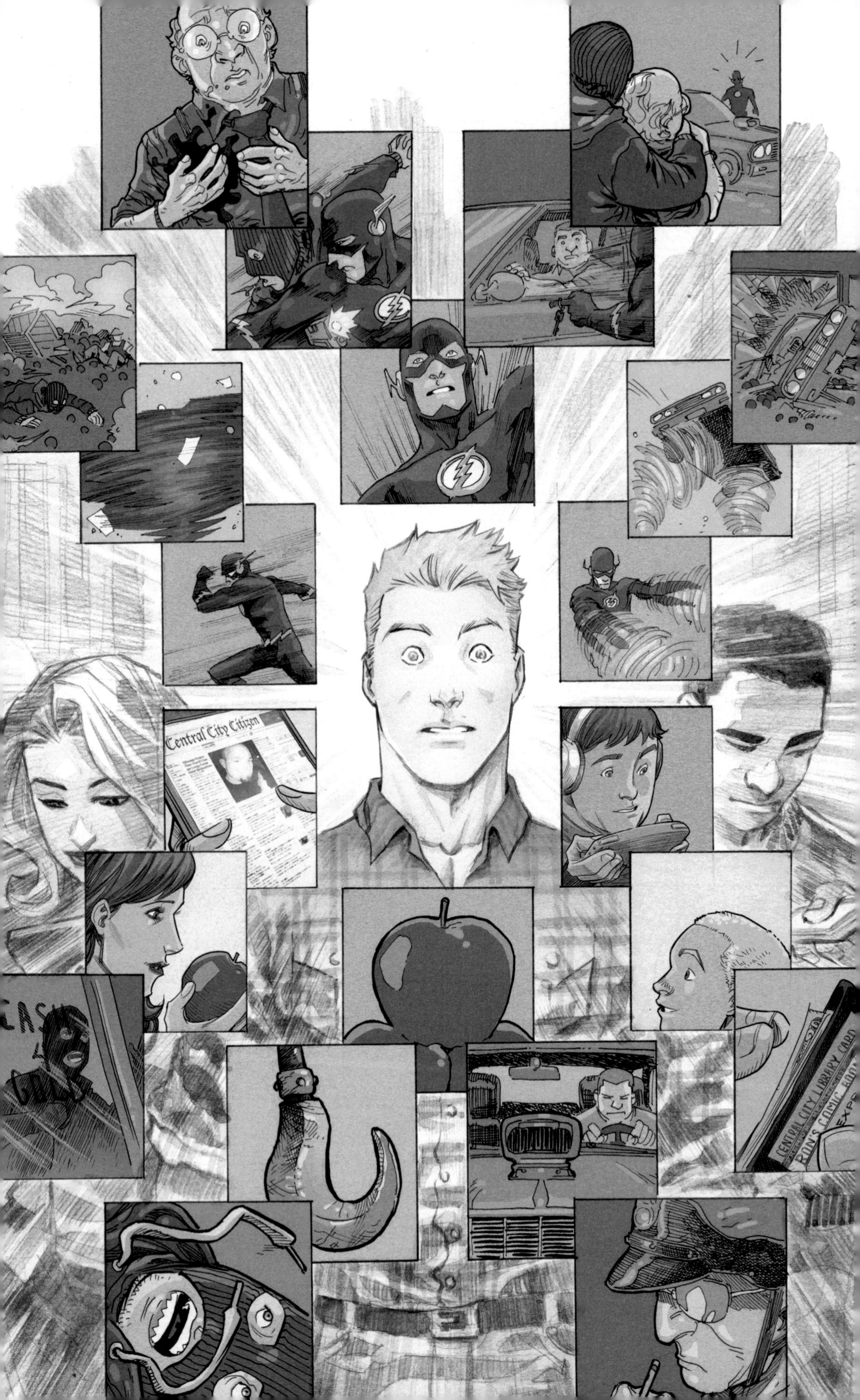
Central City Citizen
CENTRAL CITY LIBRARY CARD

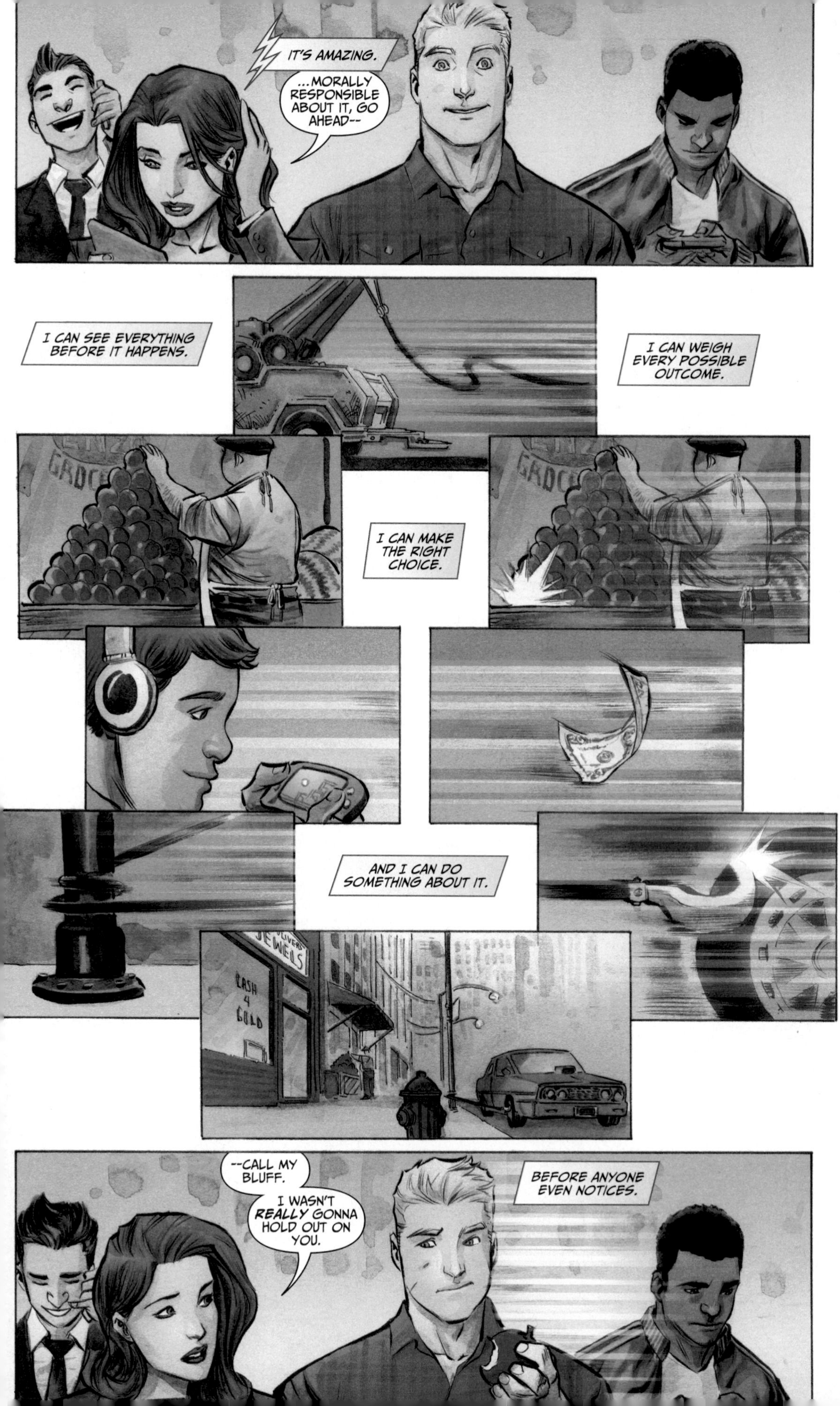
IT'S AMAZING.
...MORALLY RESPONSIBLE ABOUT IT, GO AHEAD--
I CAN SEE EVERYTHING BEFORE IT HAPPENS.
I CAN WEIGH EVERY POSSIBLE OUTCOME.
I CAN MAKE THE RIGHT CHOICE.
AND I CAN DO SOMETHING ABOUT IT.
JEWELS
CASH 4 GOLD
--CALL MY BLUFF.
I WASN'T *REALLY* GONNA HOLD OUT ON YOU.
BEFORE ANYONE EVEN NOTICES.

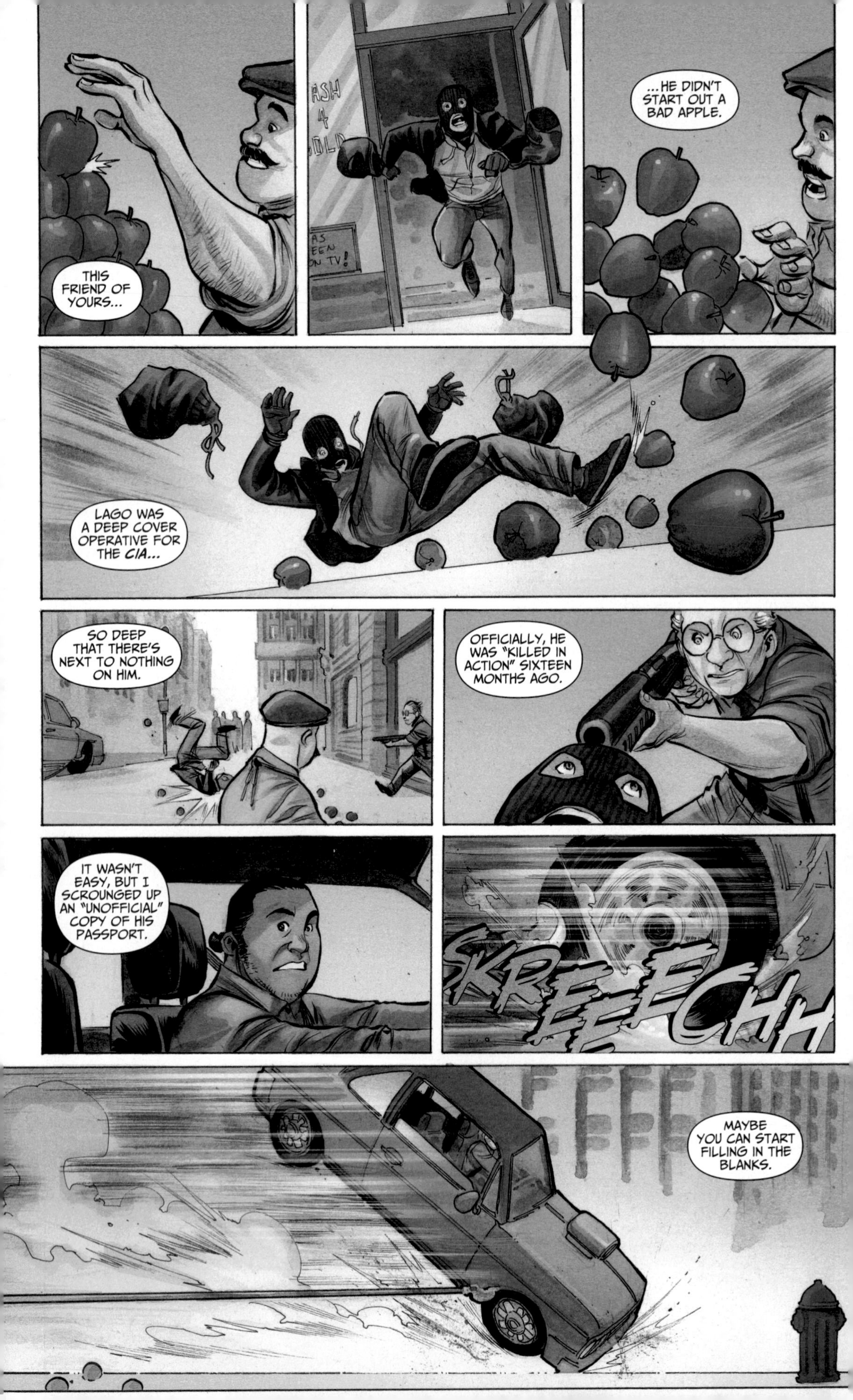
THIS FRIEND OF YOURS...
CASH 4 GOLD
AS SEEN ON TV!
...HE DIDN'T START OUT A BAD APPLE.
LAGO WAS A DEEP COVER OPERATIVE FOR THE CIA...
SO DEEP THAT THERE'S NEXT TO NOTHING ON HIM.
OFFICIALLY, HE WAS "KILLED IN ACTION" SIXTEEN MONTHS AGO.
IT WASN'T EASY, BUT I SCROUNGED UP AN "UNOFFICIAL" COPY OF HIS PASSPORT.
SKREEEECHH
MAYBE YOU CAN START FILLING IN THE BLANKS.

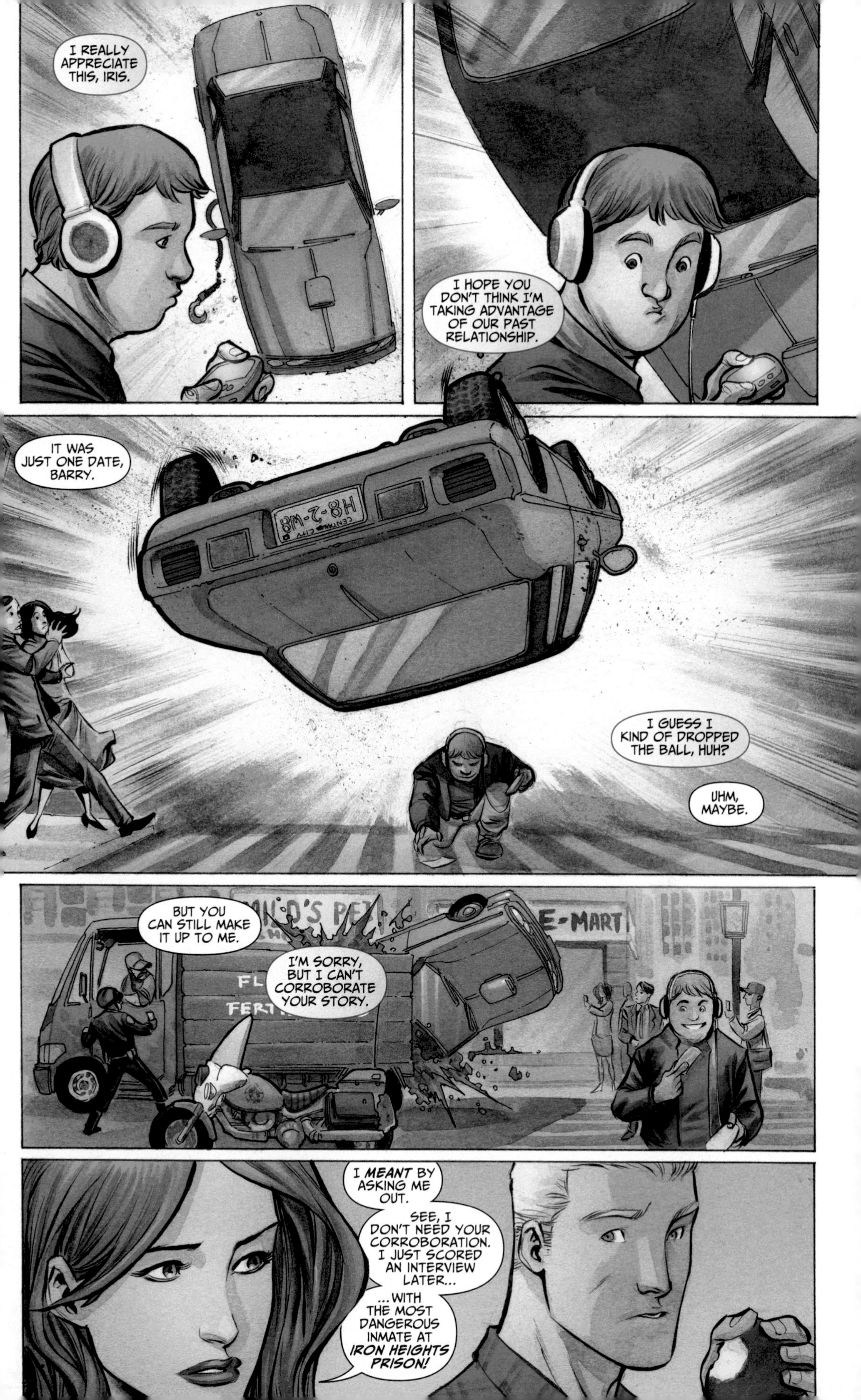
I REALLY APPRECIATE THIS, IRIS.
I HOPE YOU DON'T THINK I'M TAKING ADVANTAGE OF OUR PAST RELATIONSHIP.
IT WAS JUST ONE DATE, BARRY.
I GUESS I KIND OF DROPPED THE BALL, HUH?
UHM, MAYBE.
BUT YOU CAN STILL MAKE IT UP TO ME.
I'M SORRY, BUT I CAN'T CORROBORATE YOUR STORY.
E-MART
I *MEANT* BY ASKING ME OUT.
SEE, I DON'T NEED YOUR CORROBORATION. I JUST SCORED AN INTERVIEW LATER...
...WITH THE MOST DANGEROUS INMATE AT *IRON HEIGHTS PRISON!*

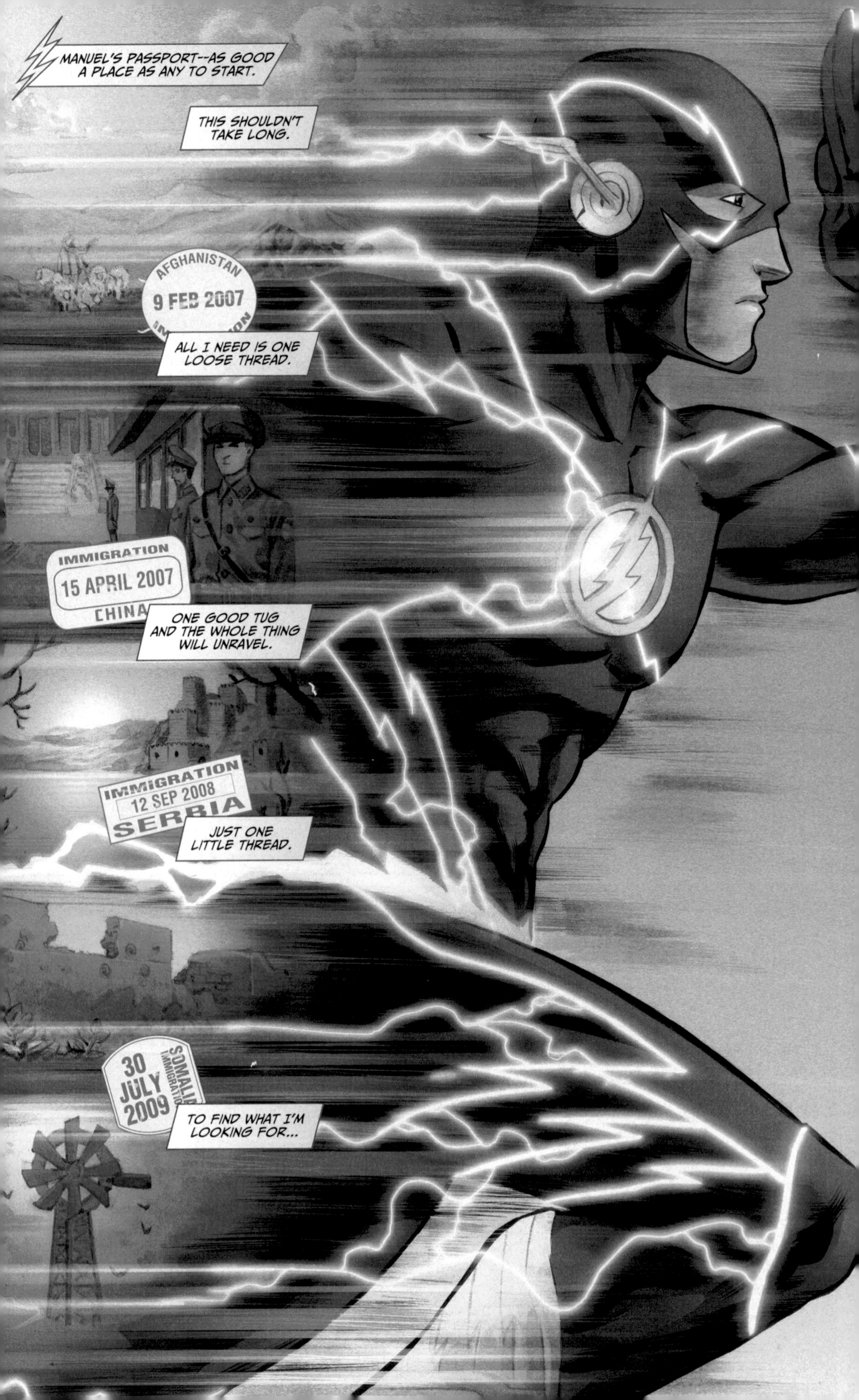
MANUEL'S PASSPORT--AS GOOD A PLACE AS ANY TO START.
THIS SHOULDN'T TAKE LONG.
AFGHANISTAN
9 FEB 2007
ALL I NEED IS ONE LOOSE THREAD.
IMMIGRATION
15 APRIL 2007
CHINA
ONE GOOD TUG AND THE WHOLE THING WILL UNRAVEL.
IMMIGRATION
12 SEP 2008
SERBIA
JUST ONE LITTLE THREAD.
30 JULY 2009
TO FIND WHAT I'M LOOKING FOR...

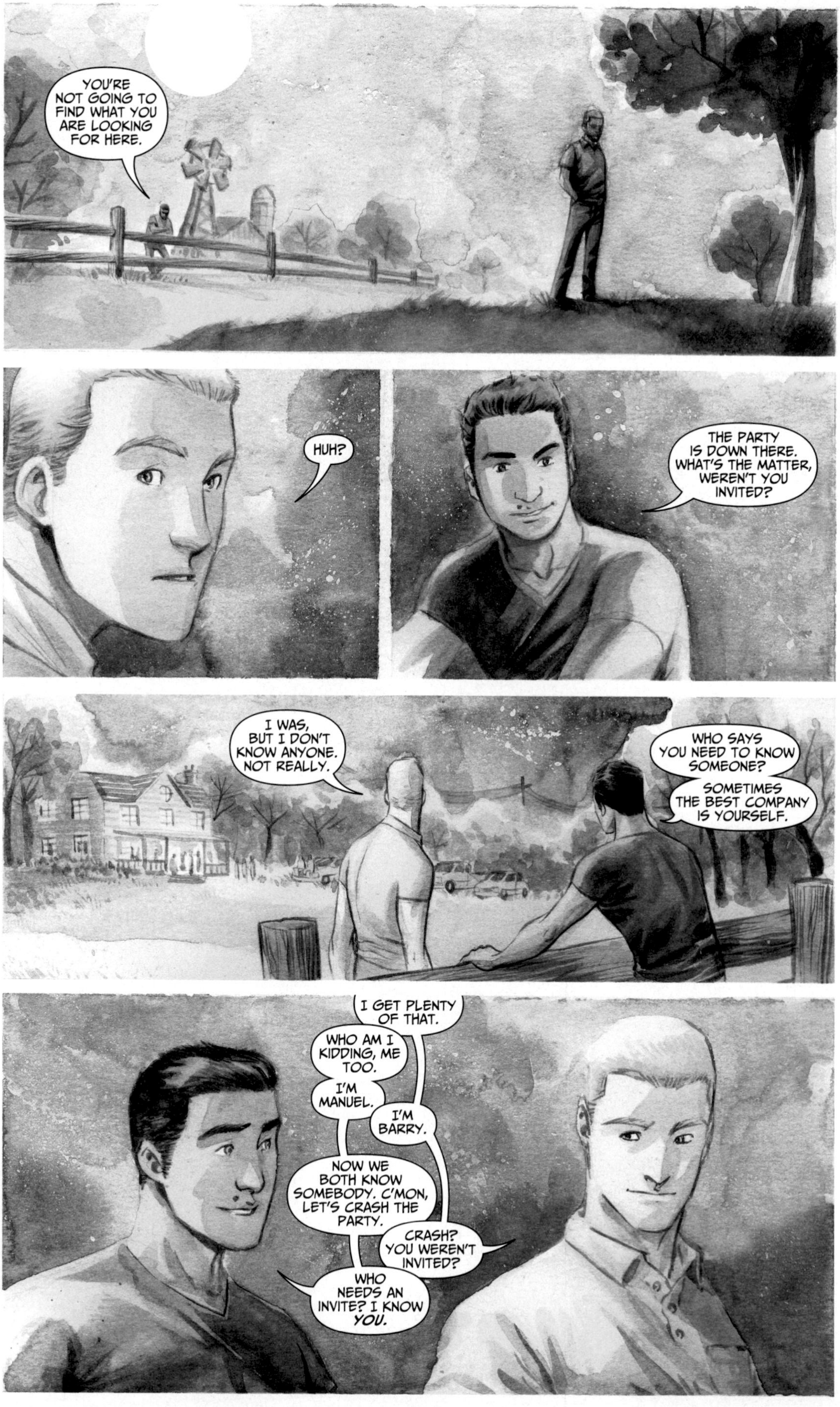
YOU'RE NOT GOING TO FIND WHAT YOU ARE LOOKING FOR HERE.
HUH?
THE PARTY IS DOWN THERE. WHAT'S THE MATTER, WEREN'T YOU INVITED?
I WAS, BUT I DON'T KNOW ANYONE. NOT REALLY.
WHO SAYS YOU NEED TO KNOW SOMEONE?
SOMETIMES THE BEST COMPANY IS YOURSELF.
I GET PLENTY OF THAT.
WHO AM I KIDDING, ME TOO.
I'M MANUEL.
I'M BARRY.
NOW WE BOTH KNOW SOMEBODY. C'MON, LET'S CRASH THE PARTY.
CRASH? YOU WEREN'T INVITED?
WHO NEEDS AN INVITE? I KNOW *YOU*.

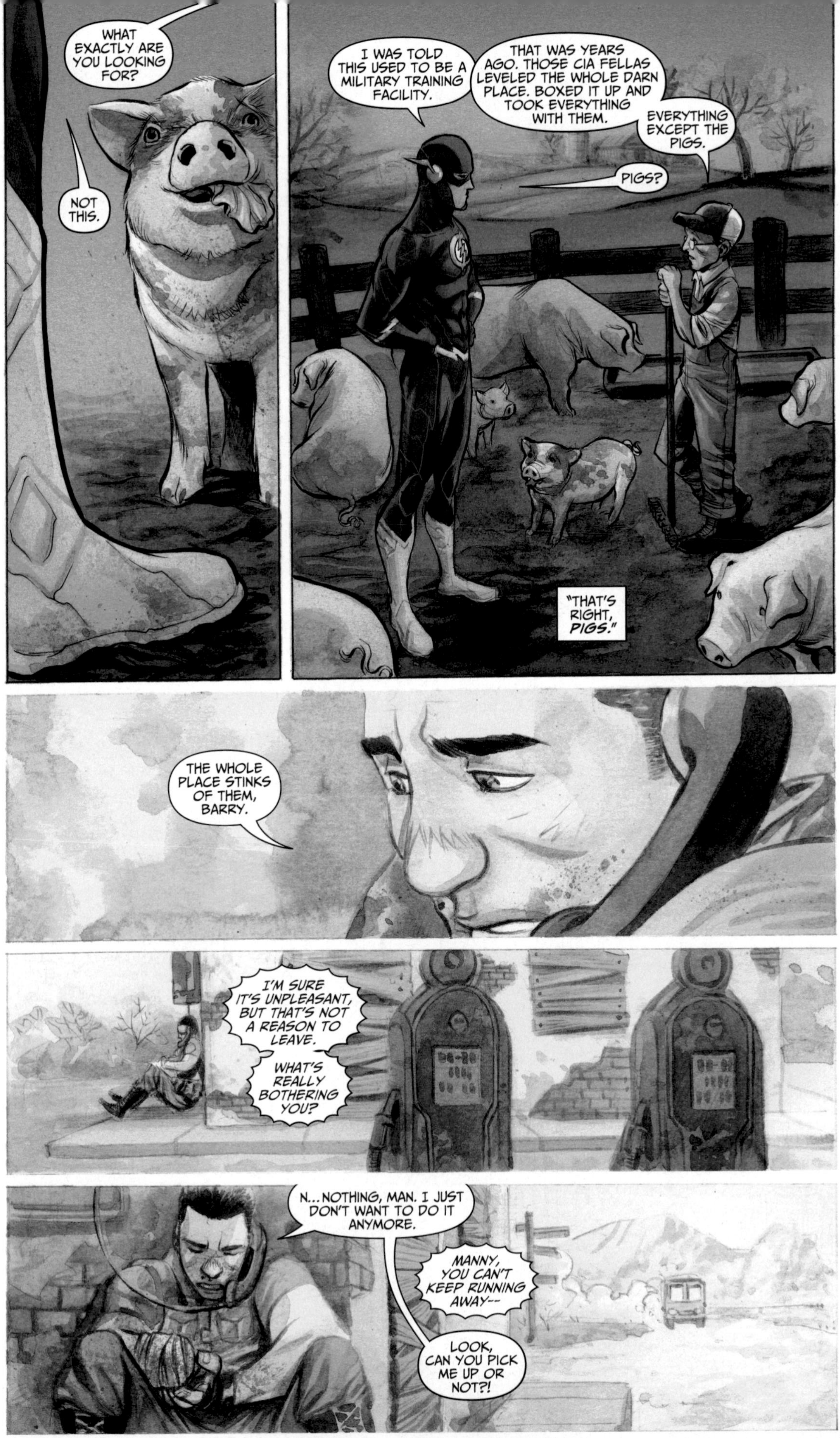
WHAT EXACTLY ARE YOU LOOKING FOR?
NOT THIS.
I WAS TOLD THIS USED TO BE A MILITARY TRAINING FACILITY.
THAT WAS YEARS AGO. THOSE CIA FELLAS LEVELED THE WHOLE DARN PLACE. BOXED IT UP AND TOOK EVERYTHING WITH THEM.
EVERYTHING EXCEPT THE PIGS.
PIGS?
"THAT'S RIGHT, PIGS."
THE WHOLE PLACE STINKS OF THEM, BARRY.
I'M SURE IT'S UNPLEASANT, BUT THAT'S NOT A REASON TO LEAVE.
WHAT'S REALLY BOTHERING YOU?
N...NOTHING, MAN. I JUST DON'T WANT TO DO IT ANYMORE.
MANNY, YOU CAN'T KEEP RUNNING AWAY--
LOOK, CAN YOU PICK ME UP OR NOT?!

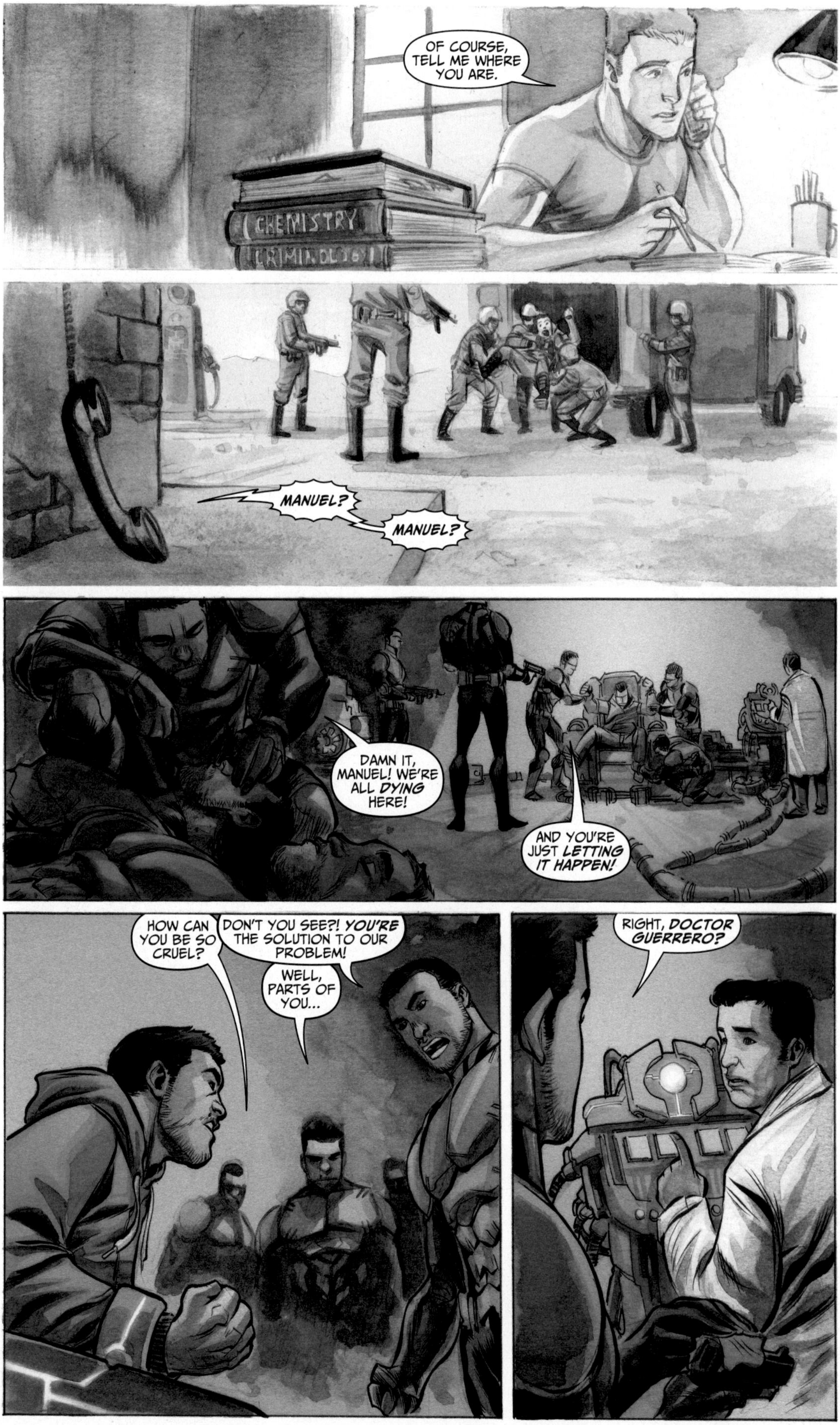
OF COURSE, TELL ME WHERE YOU ARE.
CHEMISTRY
MANUEL?
MANUEL?
DAMN IT, MANUEL! WE'RE ALL DYING HERE!
AND YOU'RE JUST LETTING IT HAPPEN!
HOW CAN YOU BE SO CRUEL?
DON'T YOU SEE?! YOU'RE THE SOLUTION TO OUR PROBLEM!
WELL, PARTS OF YOU...
RIGHT, DOCTOR GUERRERO?

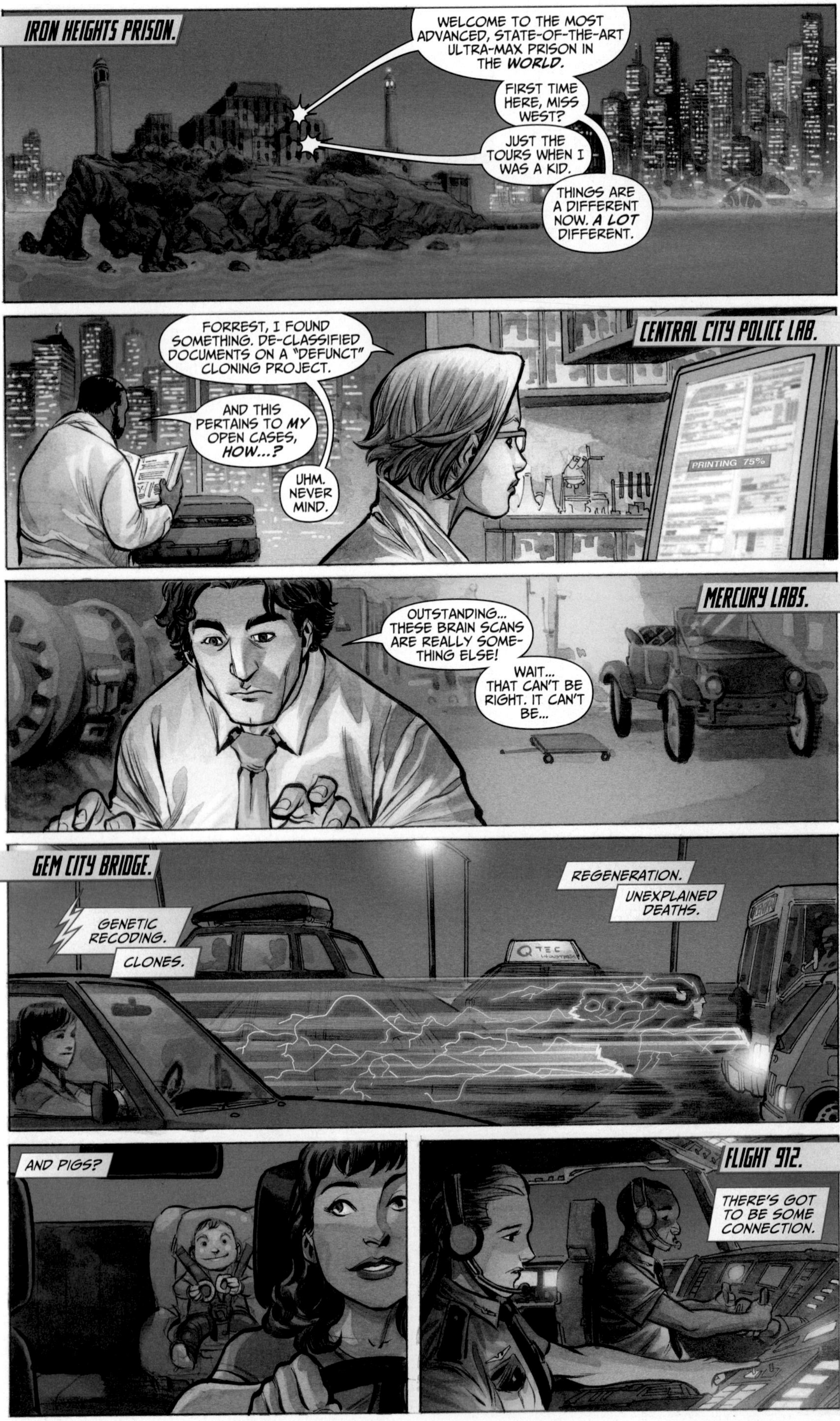
IRON HEIGHTS PRISON.
WELCOME TO THE MOST ADVANCED, STATE-OF-THE-ART ULTRA-MAX PRISON IN THE WORLD.
FIRST TIME HERE, MISS WEST?
JUST THE TOURS WHEN I WAS A KID.
THINGS ARE A DIFFERENT NOW. A LOT DIFFERENT.
CENTRAL CITY POLICE LAB.
FORREST, I FOUND SOMETHING. DE-CLASSIFIED DOCUMENTS ON A "DEFUNCT" CLONING PROJECT.
AND THIS PERTAINS TO MY OPEN CASES, HOW...?
UHM. NEVER MIND.
PRINTING 75%
MERCURY LABS.
OUTSTANDING... THESE BRAIN SCANS ARE REALLY SOME-THING ELSE!
WAIT... THAT CAN'T BE RIGHT. IT CAN'T BE...
GEM CITY BRIDGE.
GENETIC RECODING.
CLONES.
REGENERATION.
UNEXPLAINED DEATHS.
AND PIGS?
FLIGHT 912.
THERE'S GOT TO BE SOME CONNECTION.

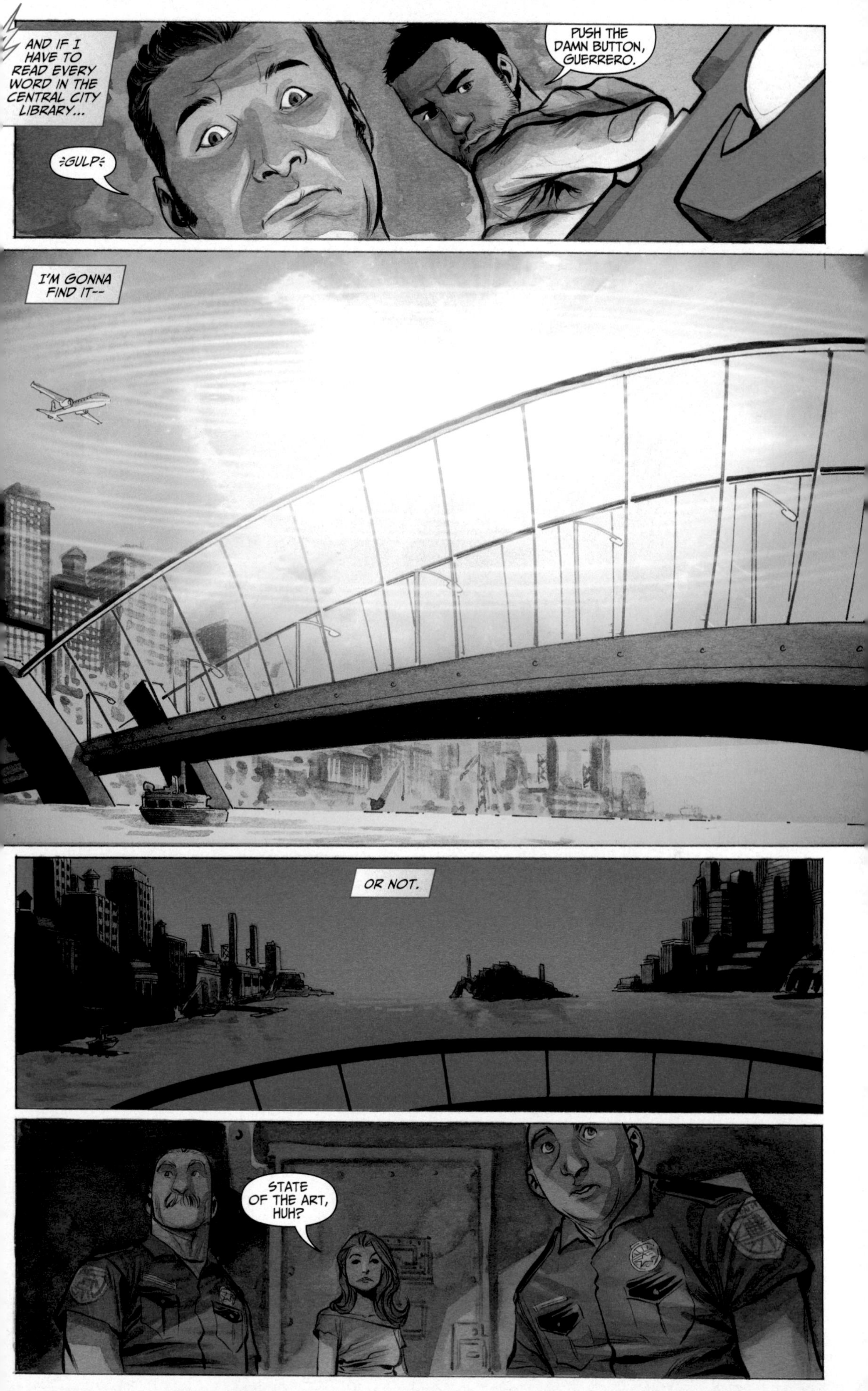
AND IF I HAVE TO READ EVERY WORD IN THE CENTRAL CITY LIBRARY...
PUSH THE DAMN BUTTON, GUERRERO.
GULP
I'M GONNA FIND IT--
OR NOT.
STATE OF THE ART, HUH?

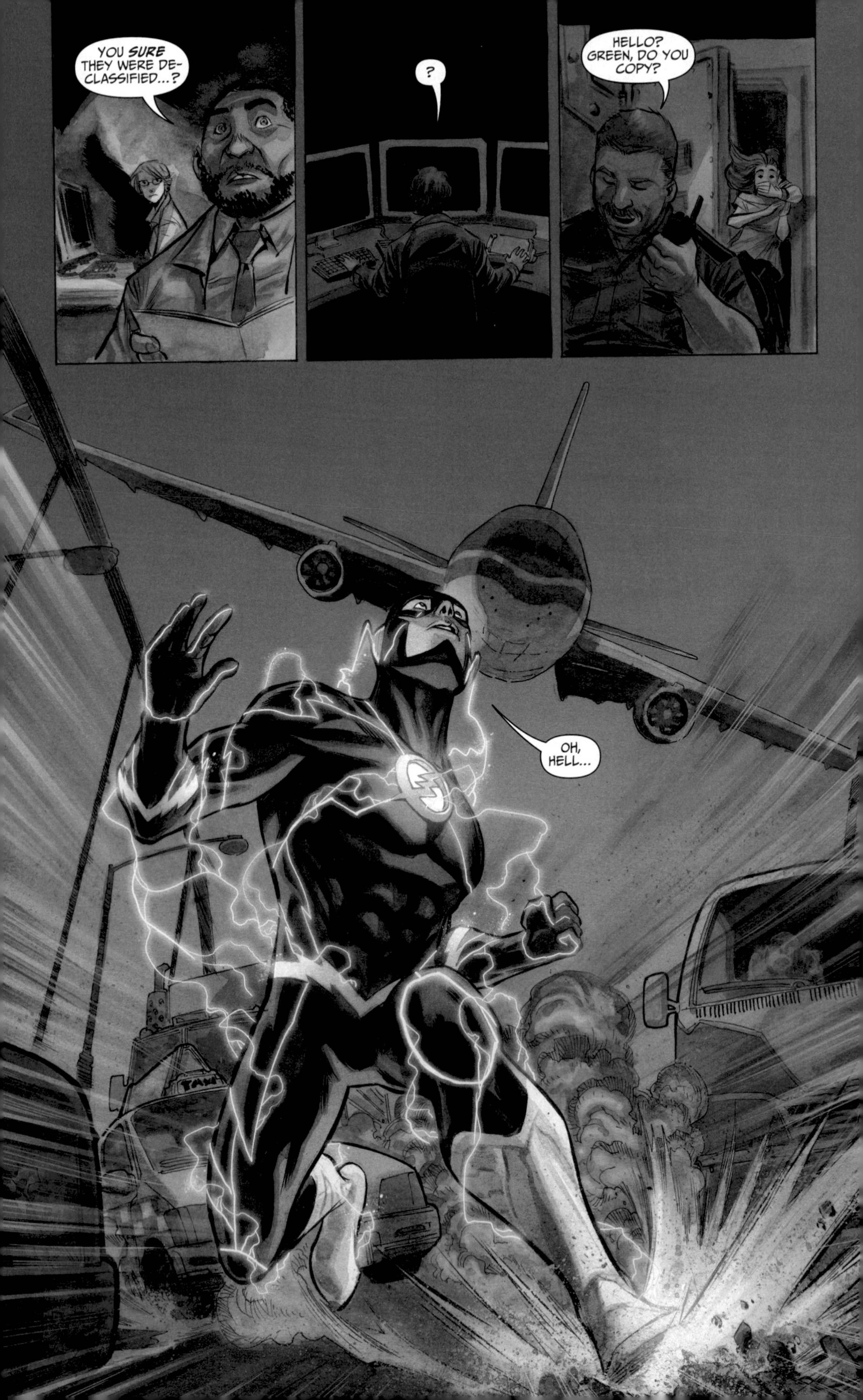
YOU SURE THEY WERE DE-CLASSIFIED...?
?
HELLO? GREEN, DO YOU COPY?
OH, HELL...

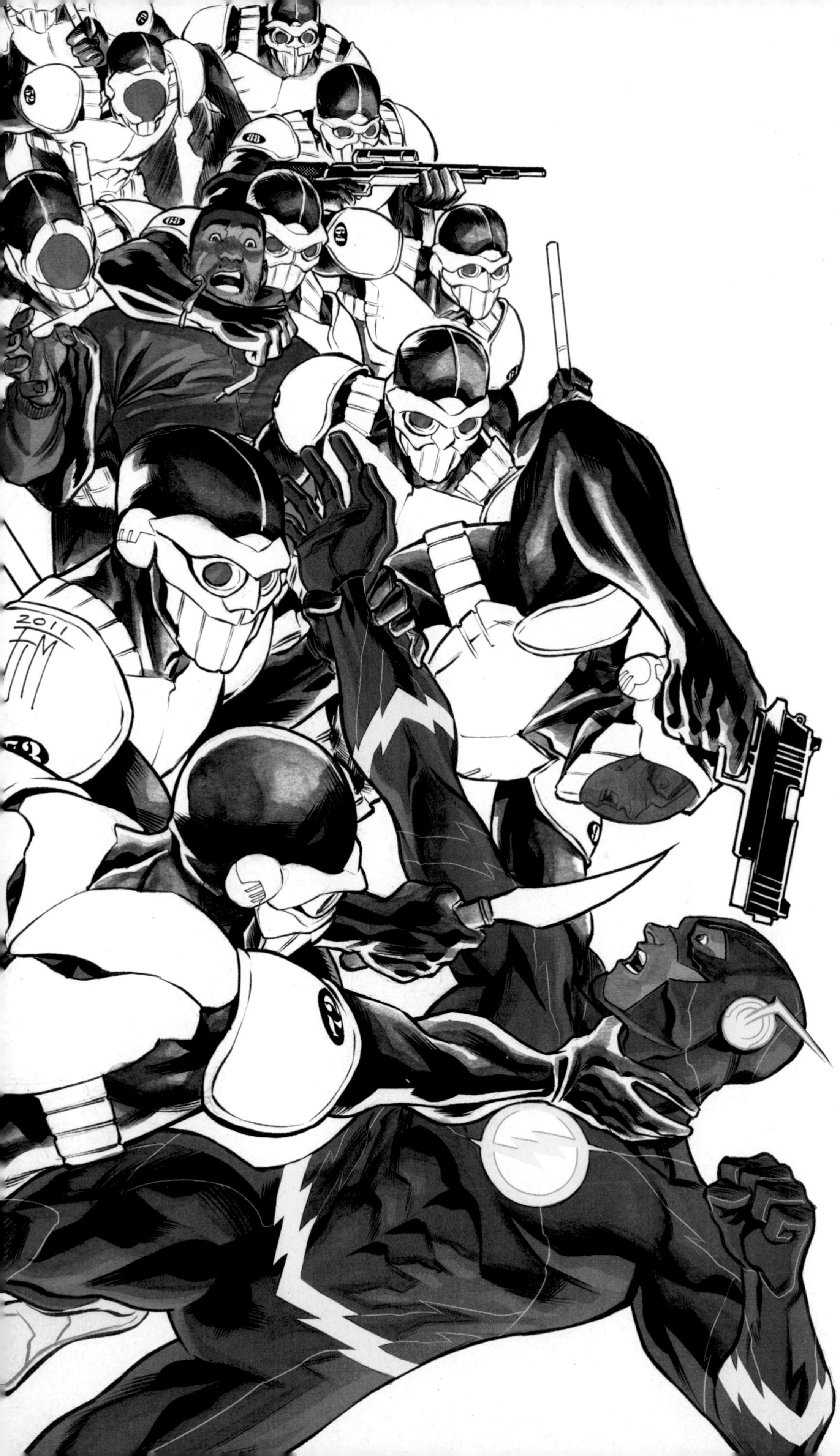
2011

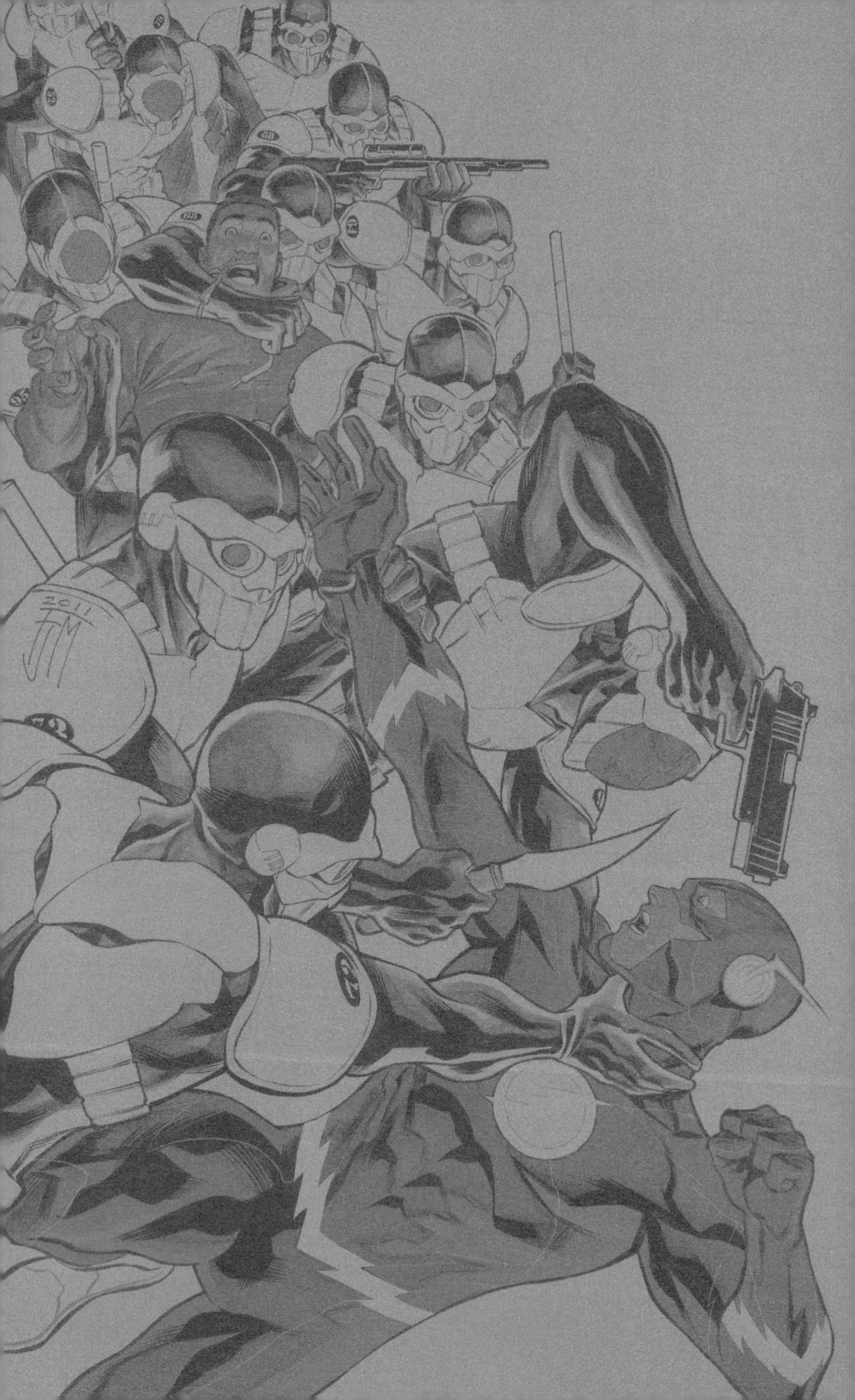
2011

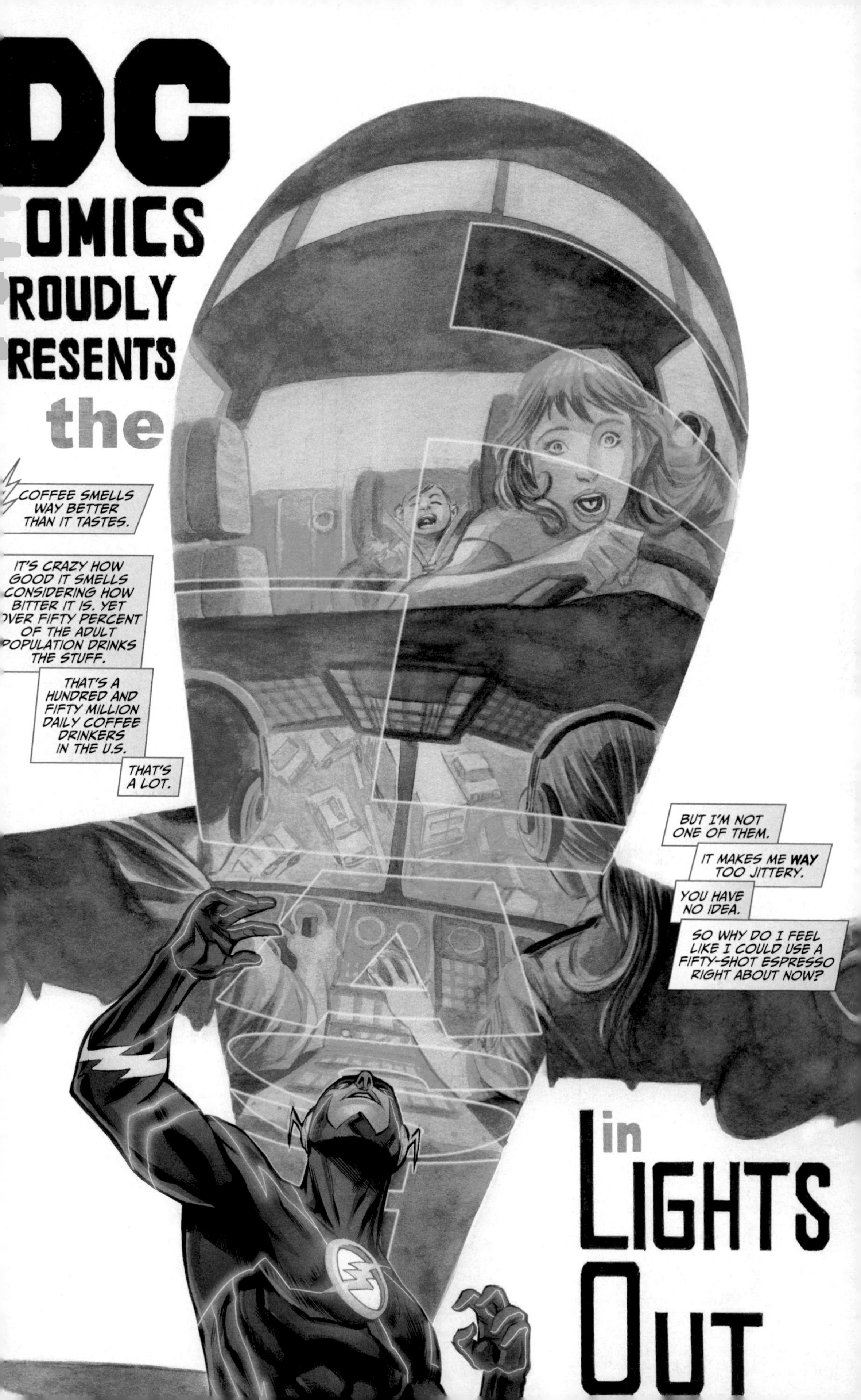
DC
OMICS
ROUDLY
RESENTS
the
COFFEE SMELLS WAY BETTER THAN IT TASTES.
IT'S CRAZY HOW GOOD IT SMELLS CONSIDERING HOW BITTER IT IS. YET OVER FIFTY PERCENT OF THE ADULT POPULATION DRINKS THE STUFF.
THAT'S A HUNDRED AND FIFTY MILLION DAILY COFFEE DRINKERS IN THE U.S.
THAT'S A LOT.
BUT I'M NOT ONE OF THEM.
IT MAKES ME **WAY** TOO JITTERY.
YOU HAVE NO IDEA.
SO WHY DO I FEEL LIKE I COULD USE A FIFTY-SHOT ESPRESSO RIGHT ABOUT NOW?
in
LIGHTS
OUT

story by
francis manapul
& brian buccellato

I DON'T KNOW WHY I'M THINKING ABOUT COFFEE.

GUESS I'M A LITTLE A.D.D. SINCE I LEARNED THAT MY BRAIN CAN TAP INTO THE SPEED FORCE.

KREESH SKREEEE

CREATING VORTEXES.

THESE AREN'T THINGS I WAS TAUGHT.

WOOOSH

I DIDN'T GET A MANUAL WITH MY POWERS.

MOST OF THEM I STUMBLED ACROSS AS I FUMBLED MY WAY THROUGH THE EARLY DAYS.

LIKE MY ABILITY TO VIBRATE THROUGH SOLID OBJECTS.

HOW'D I LEARN TO DO THAT? TOTAL ACCIDENT.

A QUADRUPLE SHOT OF ESPRESSO OVER ICE, WHILE PULLING AN ALL-NIGHTER IN THE LAB.

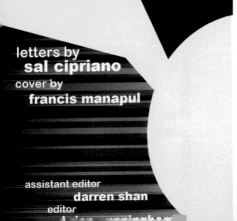

letters by
sal cipriano
cover by
francis manapul

assistant editor
darren shan
editor

THAT WAS MY FIRST AND LAST COFFEE EXPERIENCE.

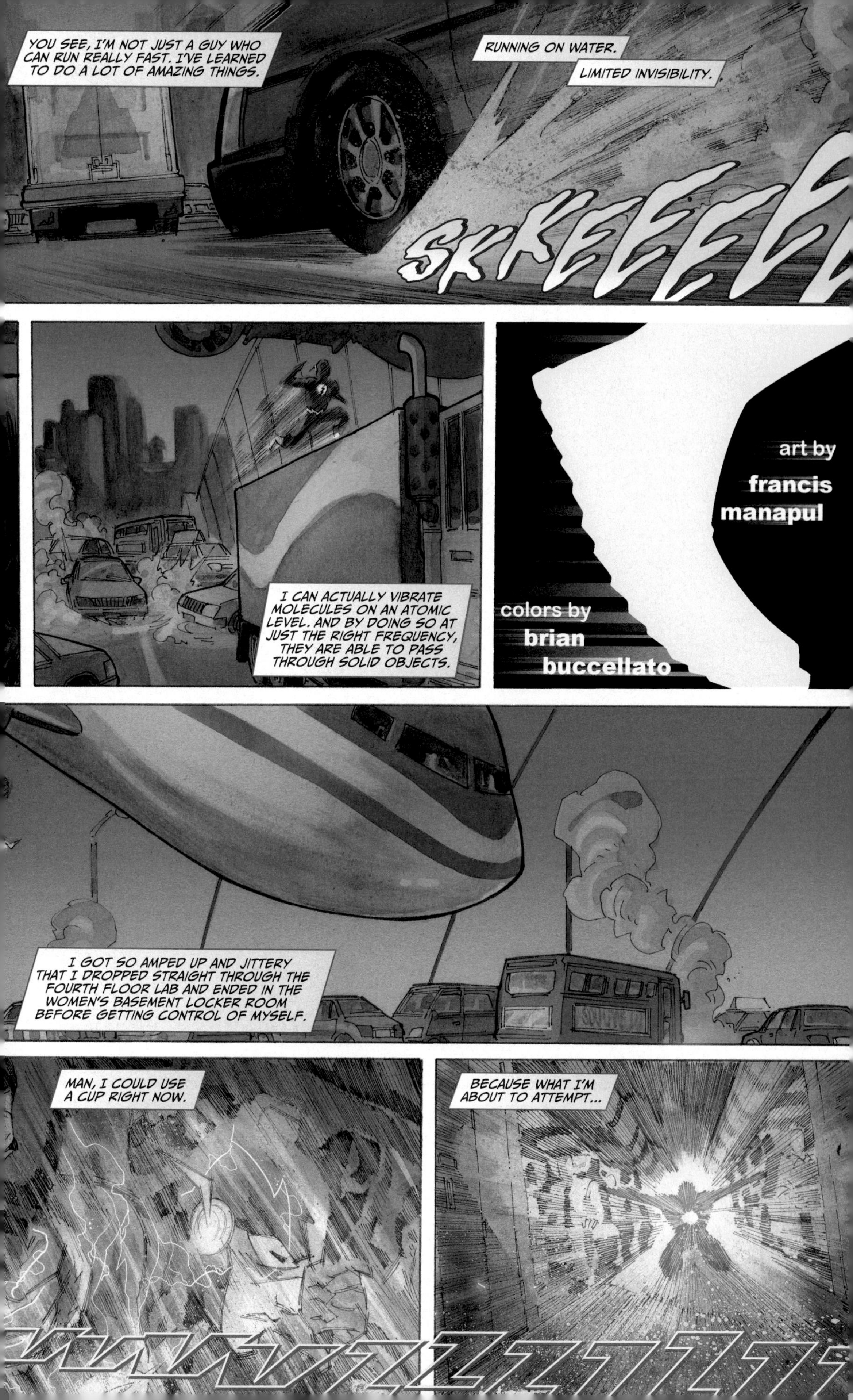
YOU SEE, I'M NOT JUST A GUY WHO CAN RUN REALLY FAST. I'VE LEARNED TO DO A LOT OF AMAZING THINGS.
RUNNING ON WATER.
LIMITED INVISIBILITY.
SKREEEEE
I CAN ACTUALLY VIBRATE MOLECULES ON AN ATOMIC LEVEL. AND BY DOING SO AT JUST THE RIGHT FREQUENCY, THEY ARE ABLE TO PASS THROUGH SOLID OBJECTS.
art by
francis
manapul
colors by
brian
buccellato
I GOT SO AMPED UP AND JITTERY THAT I DROPPED STRAIGHT THROUGH THE FOURTH FLOOR LAB AND ENDED IN THE WOMEN'S BASEMENT LOCKER ROOM BEFORE GETTING CONTROL OF MYSELF.
MAN, I COULD USE A CUP RIGHT NOW.
BECAUSE WHAT I'M ABOUT TO ATTEMPT...

...IS A MIRACLE.

COME ON, BARRY...

KEEP...IT... TOGETHER...

JUST...A LITTLE...

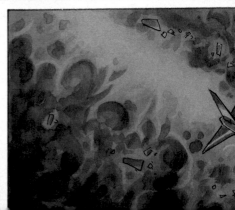

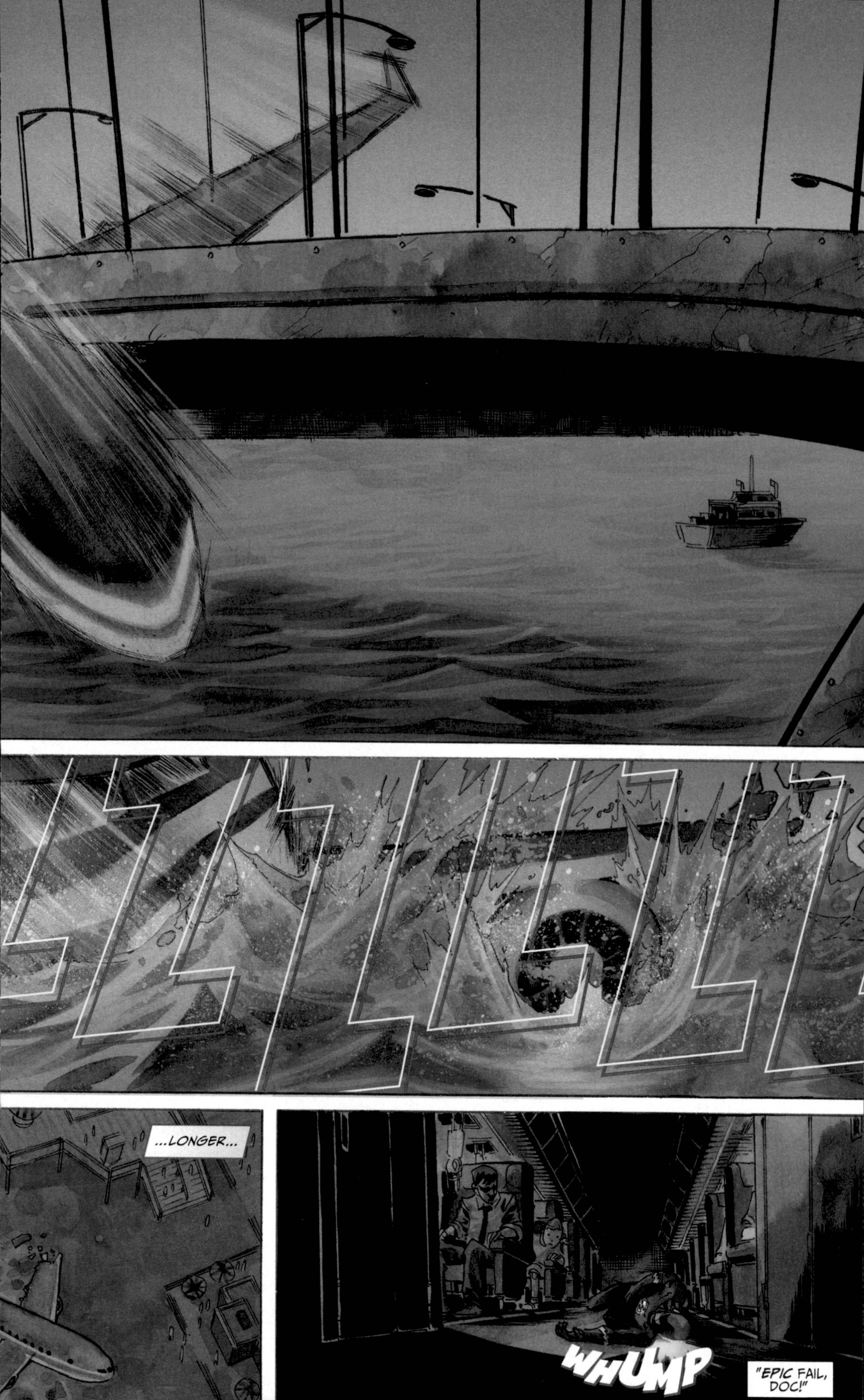
...LONGER...
WHUMP
"EPIC FAIL, DOC!"

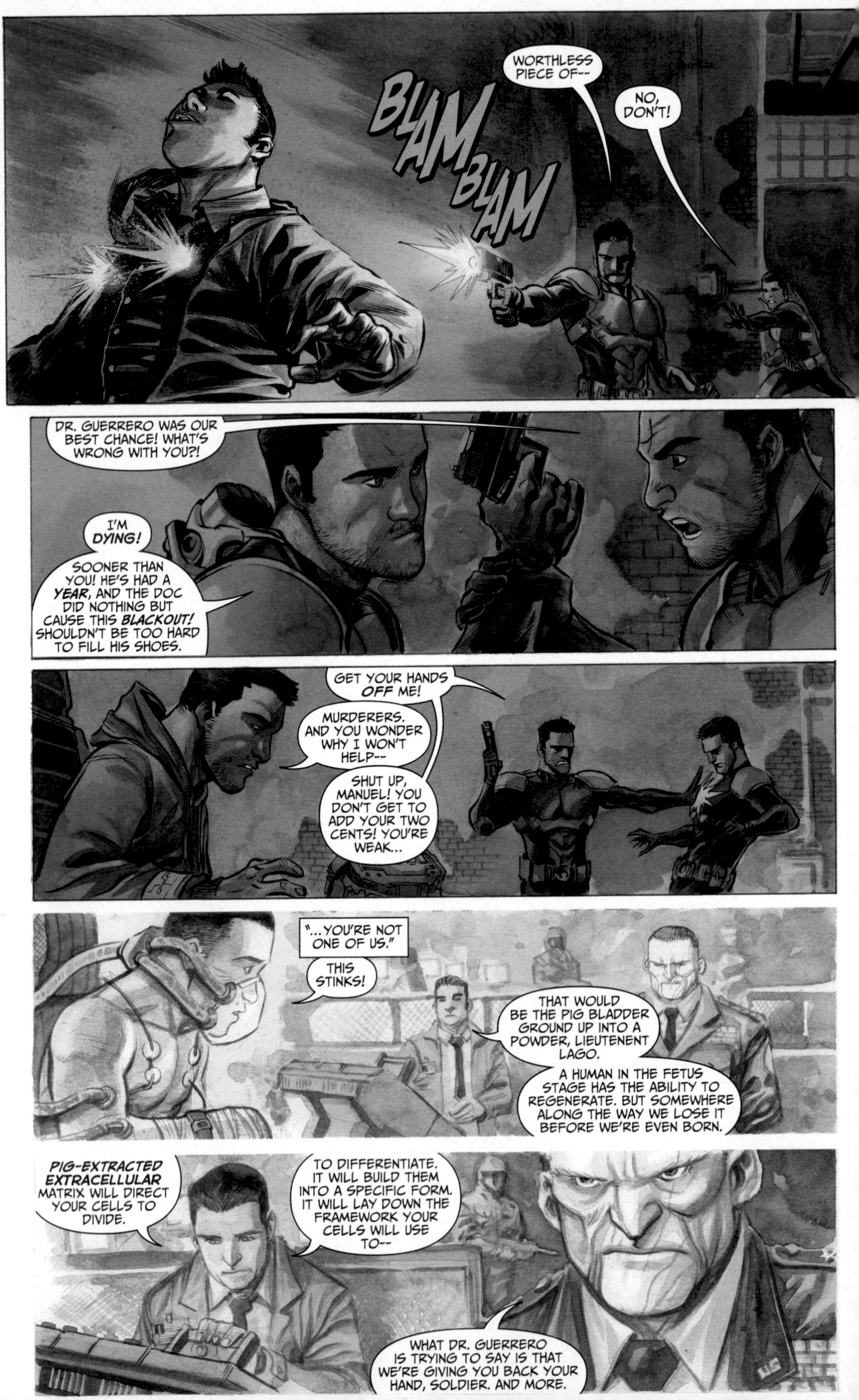
BLAM
BLAM
WORTHLESS PIECE OF--
NO, DON'T!
DR. GUERRERO WAS OUR BEST CHANCE! WHAT'S WRONG WITH YOU?!
I'M *DYING!*
SOONER THAN YOU! HE'S HAD A *YEAR*, AND THE DOC DID NOTHING BUT CAUSE THIS *BLACKOUT!* SHOULDN'T BE TOO HARD TO FILL HIS SHOES.
GET YOUR HANDS *OFF* ME!
MURDERERS. AND YOU WONDER WHY I WON'T HELP--
SHUT UP, MANUEL! YOU DON'T GET TO ADD YOUR TWO CENTS! YOU'RE WEAK...
"...YOU'RE NOT ONE OF US."
THIS STINKS!
THAT WOULD BE THE PIG BLADDER GROUND UP INTO A POWDER, LIEUTENENT LAGO.
A HUMAN IN THE FETUS STAGE HAS THE ABILITY TO REGENERATE. BUT SOMEWHERE ALONG THE WAY WE LOSE IT BEFORE WE'RE EVEN BORN.
PIG-EXTRACTED EXTRACELLULAR MATRIX WILL DIRECT YOUR CELLS TO DIVIDE.
TO DIFFERENTIATE. IT WILL BUILD THEM INTO A SPECIFIC FORM. IT WILL LAY DOWN THE FRAMEWORK YOUR CELLS WILL USE TO--
WHAT DR. GUERRERO IS TRYING TO SAY IS THAT WE'RE GIVING YOU BACK YOUR HAND, SOLDIER. AND MORE.

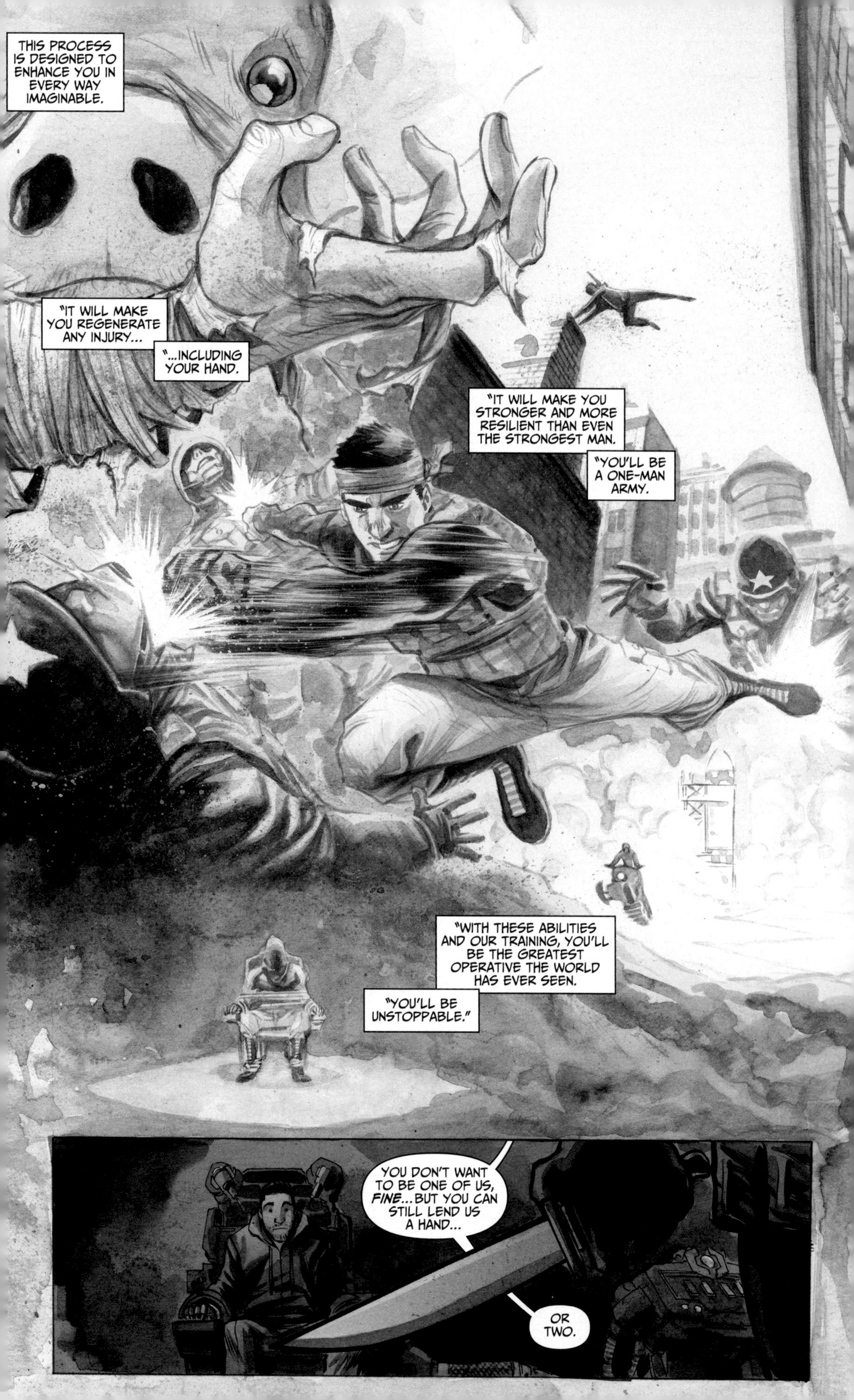
THIS PROCESS IS DESIGNED TO ENHANCE YOU IN EVERY WAY IMAGINABLE.
"IT WILL MAKE YOU REGENERATE ANY INJURY...
"...INCLUDING YOUR HAND.
"IT WILL MAKE YOU STRONGER AND MORE RESILIENT THAN EVEN THE STRONGEST MAN.
"YOU'LL BE A ONE-MAN ARMY.
"WITH THESE ABILITIES AND OUR TRAINING, YOU'LL BE THE GREATEST OPERATIVE THE WORLD HAS EVER SEEN.
"YOU'LL BE UNSTOPPABLE."
YOU DON'T WANT TO BE ONE OF US, *FINE*...BUT YOU CAN STILL LEND US A HAND...
OR TWO.

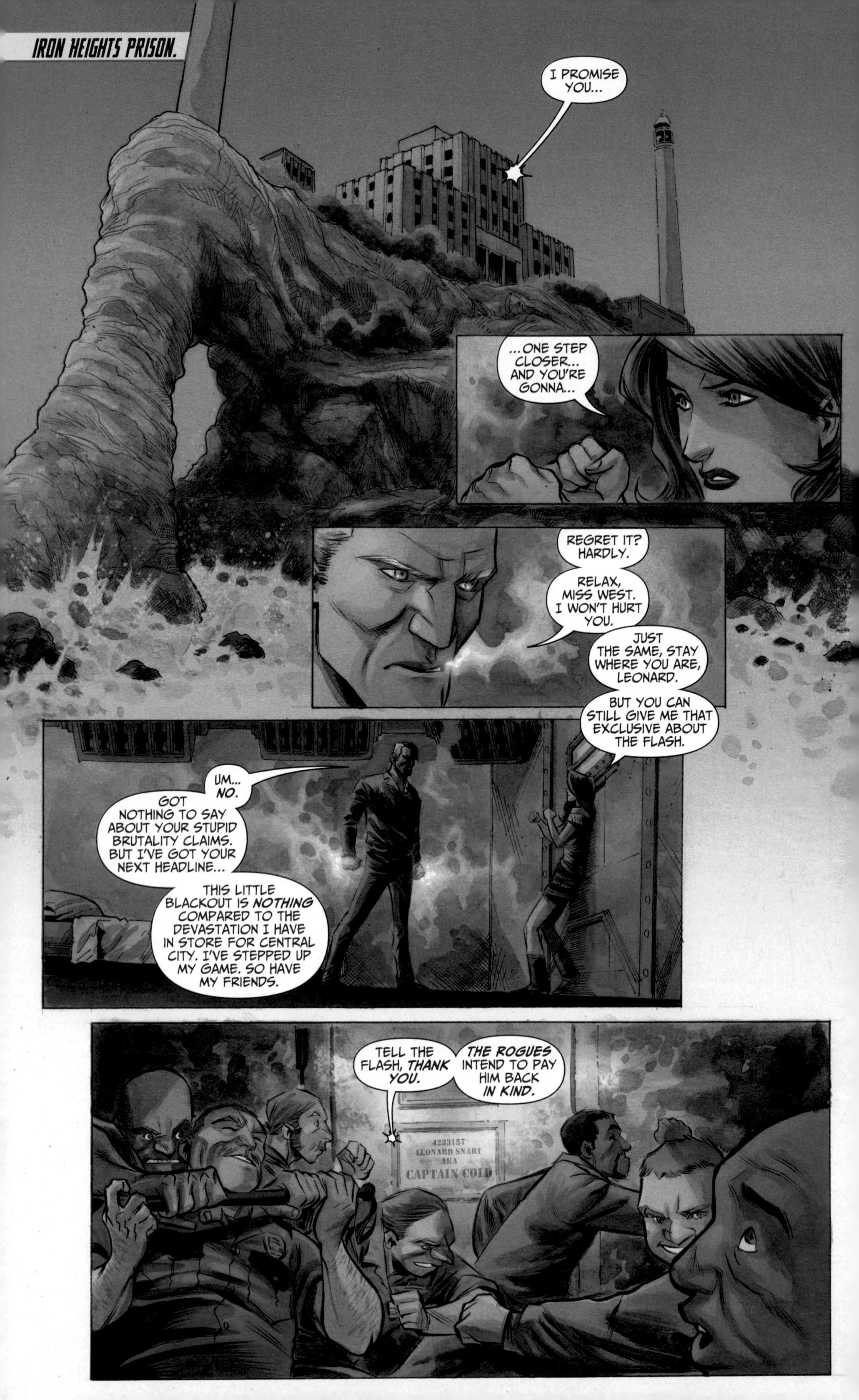
IRON HEIGHTS PRISON.
I PROMISE YOU...
...ONE STEP CLOSER... AND YOU'RE GONNA...
REGRET IT? HARDLY.
RELAX, MISS WEST. I WON'T HURT YOU.
JUST THE SAME, STAY WHERE YOU ARE, LEONARD.
BUT YOU CAN STILL GIVE ME THAT EXCLUSIVE ABOUT THE FLASH.
UM... NO.
GOT NOTHING TO SAY ABOUT YOUR STUPID BRUTALITY CLAIMS. BUT I'VE GOT YOUR NEXT HEADLINE...
THIS LITTLE BLACKOUT IS NOTHING COMPARED TO THE DEVASTATION I HAVE IN STORE FOR CENTRAL CITY. I'VE STEPPED UP MY GAME. SO HAVE MY FRIENDS.
TELL THE FLASH, THANK YOU.
THE ROGUES INTEND TO PAY HIM BACK IN KIND.
4283157
LEONARD SNART
AKA
CAPTAIN COLD

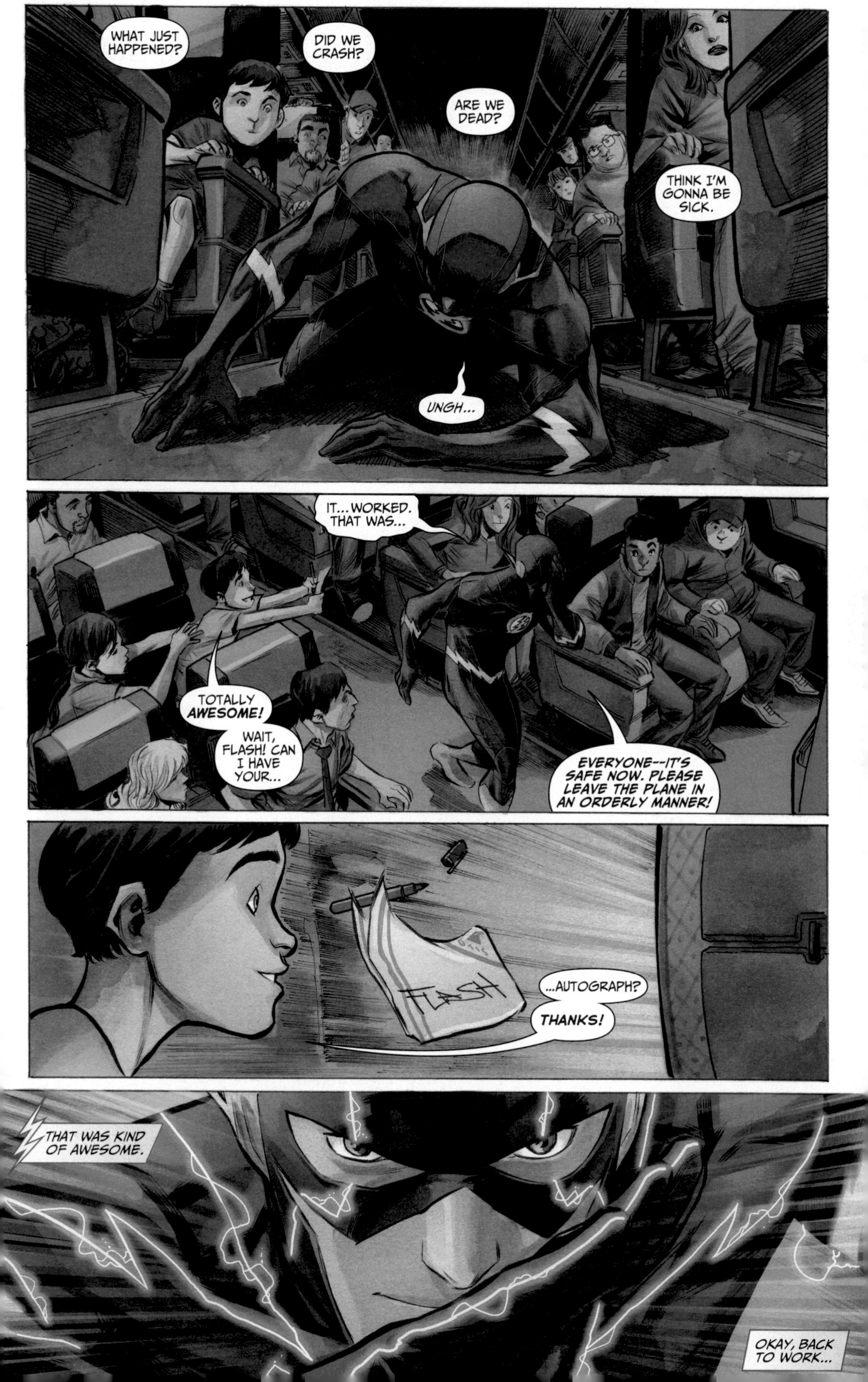
WHAT JUST HAPPENED?
DID WE CRASH?
ARE WE DEAD?
THINK I'M GONNA BE SICK.
UNGH...
IT... WORKED. THAT WAS...
TOTALLY AWESOME!
WAIT, FLASH! CAN I HAVE YOUR...
EVERYONE--IT'S SAFE NOW. PLEASE LEAVE THE PLANE IN AN ORDERLY MANNER!
FLASH
...AUTOGRAPH?
THANKS!
THAT WAS KIND OF AWESOME.
OKAY, BACK TO WORK...

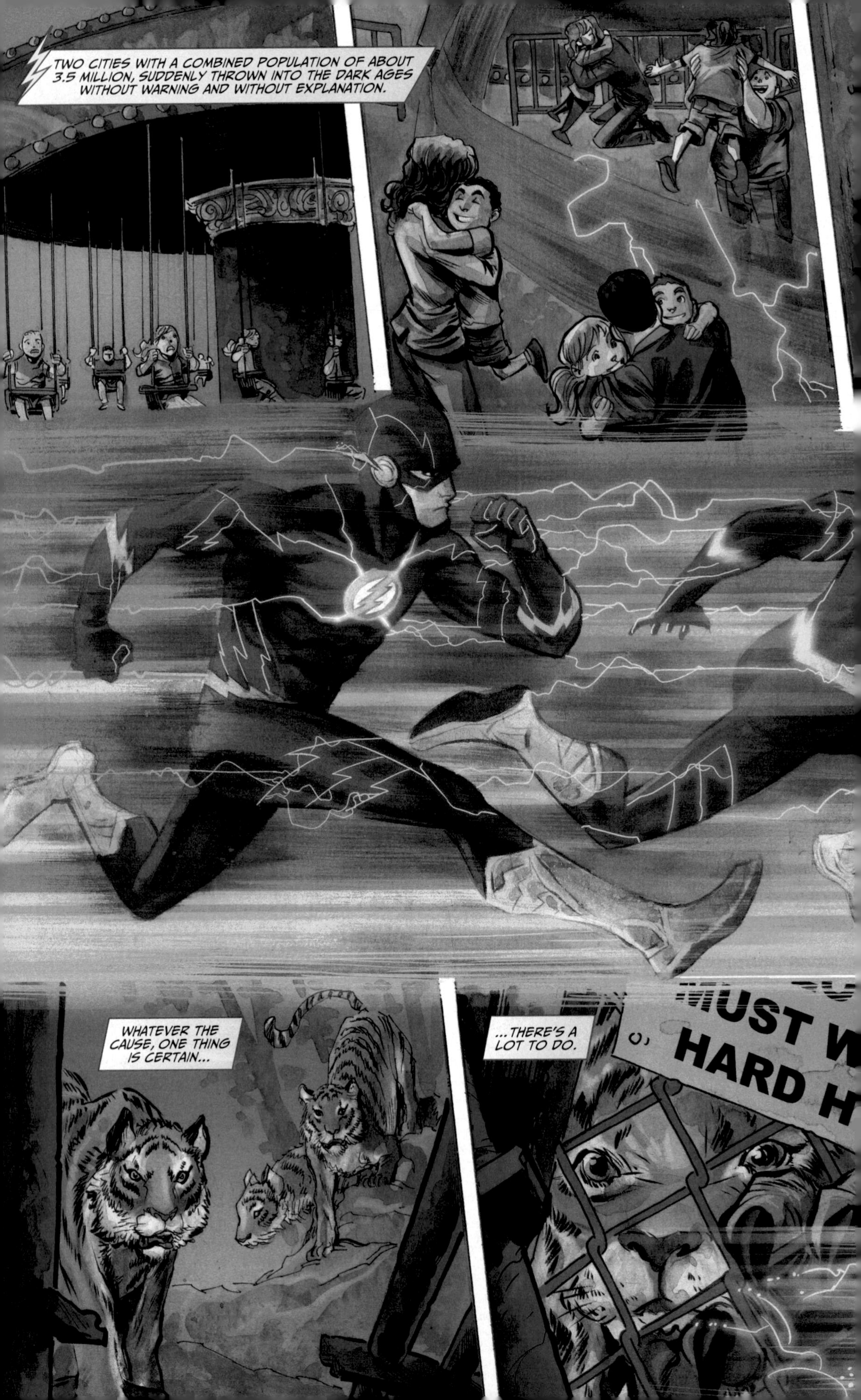
TWO CITIES WITH A COMBINED POPULATION OF ABOUT 3.5 MILLION, SUDDENLY THROWN INTO THE DARK AGES WITHOUT WARNING AND WITHOUT EXPLANATION.
WHATEVER THE CAUSE, ONE THING IS CERTAIN...
...THERE'S A LOT TO DO.
MUST W
HARD H

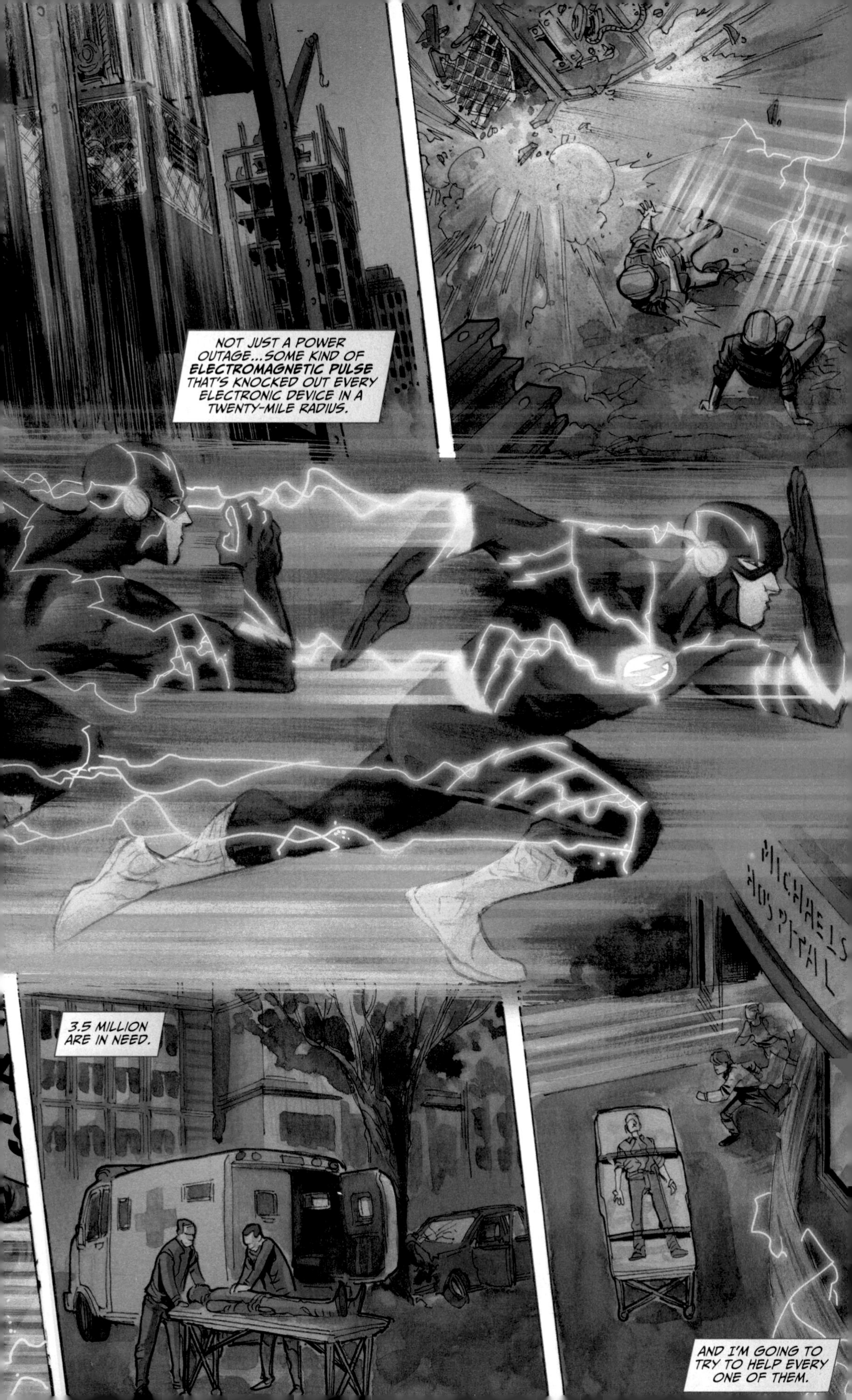
NOT JUST A POWER OUTAGE...SOME KIND OF **ELECTROMAGNETIC PULSE** THAT'S KNOCKED OUT EVERY ELECTRONIC DEVICE IN A TWENTY-MILE RADIUS.
3.5 MILLION ARE IN NEED.
AND I'M GOING TO TRY TO HELP EVERY ONE OF THEM.

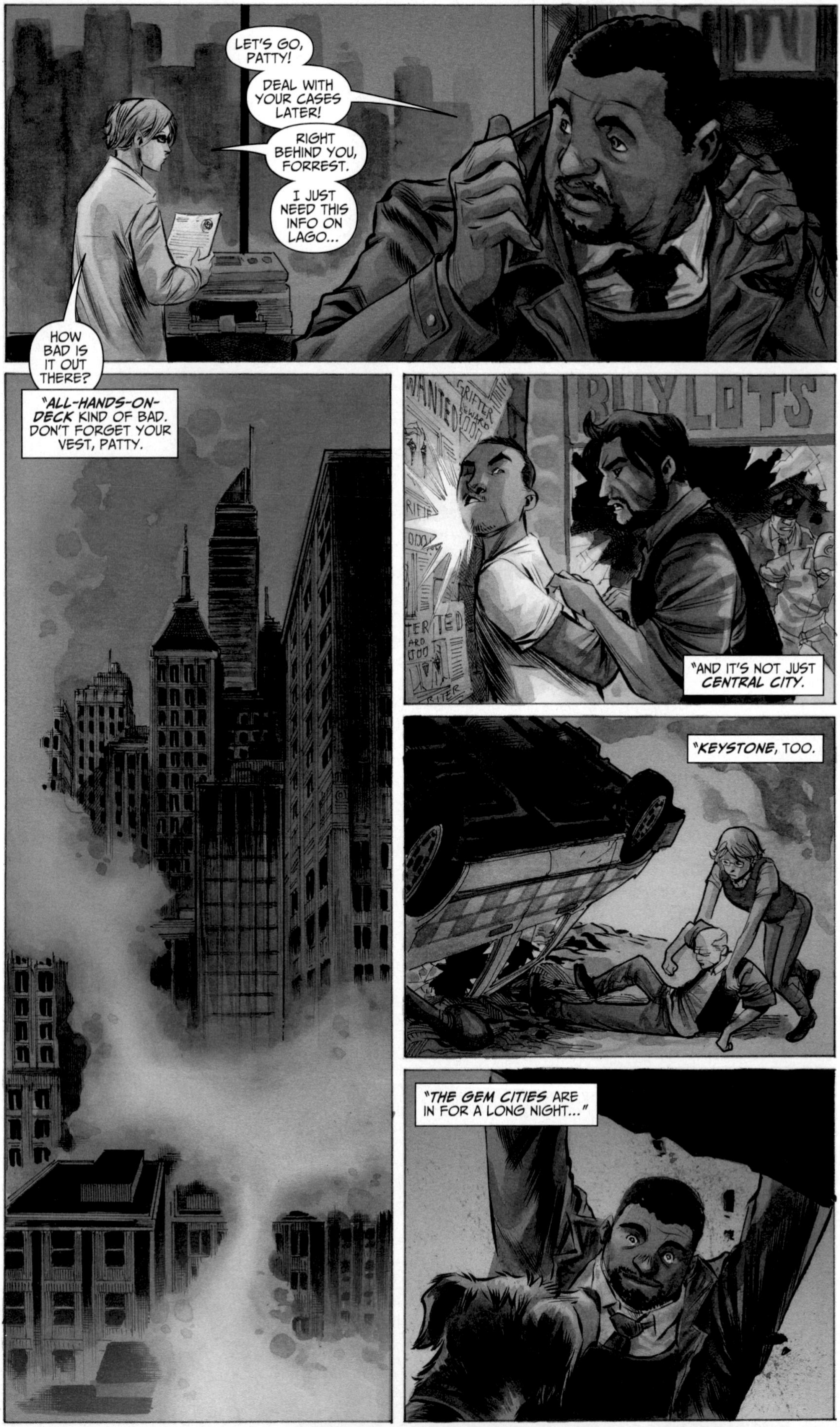
LET'S GO, PATTY!
DEAL WITH YOUR CASES LATER!
RIGHT BEHIND YOU, FORREST.
I JUST NEED THIS INFO ON LAGO...
HOW BAD IS IT OUT THERE?
"ALL-HANDS-ON-DECK KIND OF BAD. DON'T FORGET YOUR VEST, PATTY.
BUYLOTS
"AND IT'S NOT JUST CENTRAL CITY.
"KEYSTONE, TOO.
"THE GEM CITIES ARE IN FOR A LONG NIGHT..."

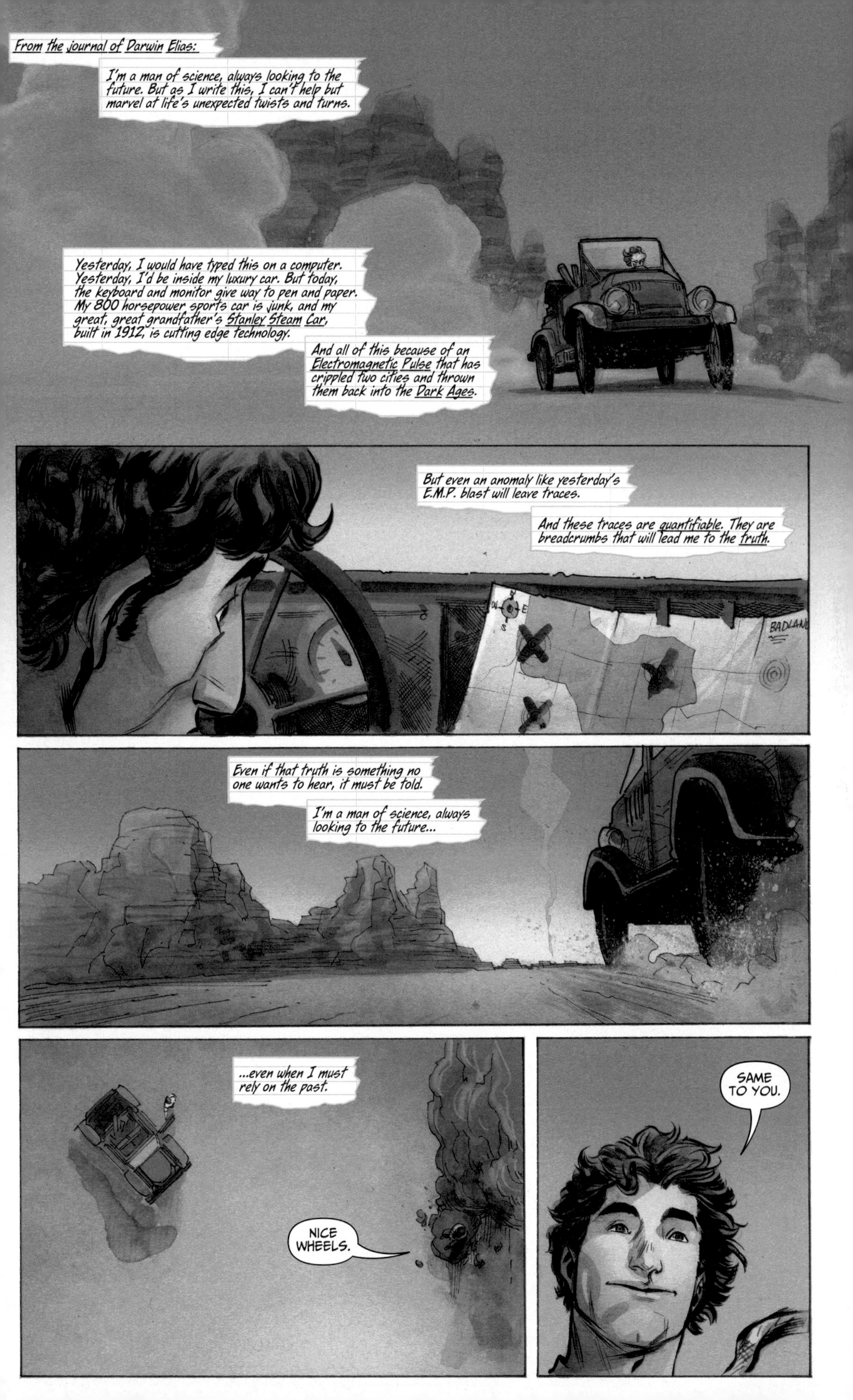
From the journal of Darwin Elias:
I'm a man of science, always looking to the future. But as I write this, I can't help but marvel at life's unexpected twists and turns.
Yesterday, I would have typed this on a computer. Yesterday, I'd be inside my luxury car. But today, the keyboard and monitor give way to pen and paper. My 800 horsepower sports car is junk, and my great, great grandfather's Stanley Steam Car, built in 1912, is cutting edge technology.
And all of this because of an Electromagnetic Pulse that has crippled two cities and thrown them back into the Dark Ages.
But even an anomaly like yesterday's E.M.P. blast will leave traces.
And these traces are quantifiable. They are breadcrumbs that will lead me to the truth.
Even if that truth is something no one wants to hear, it must be told.
I'm a man of science, always looking to the future...
...even when I must rely on the past.
NICE WHEELS.
SAME TO YOU.

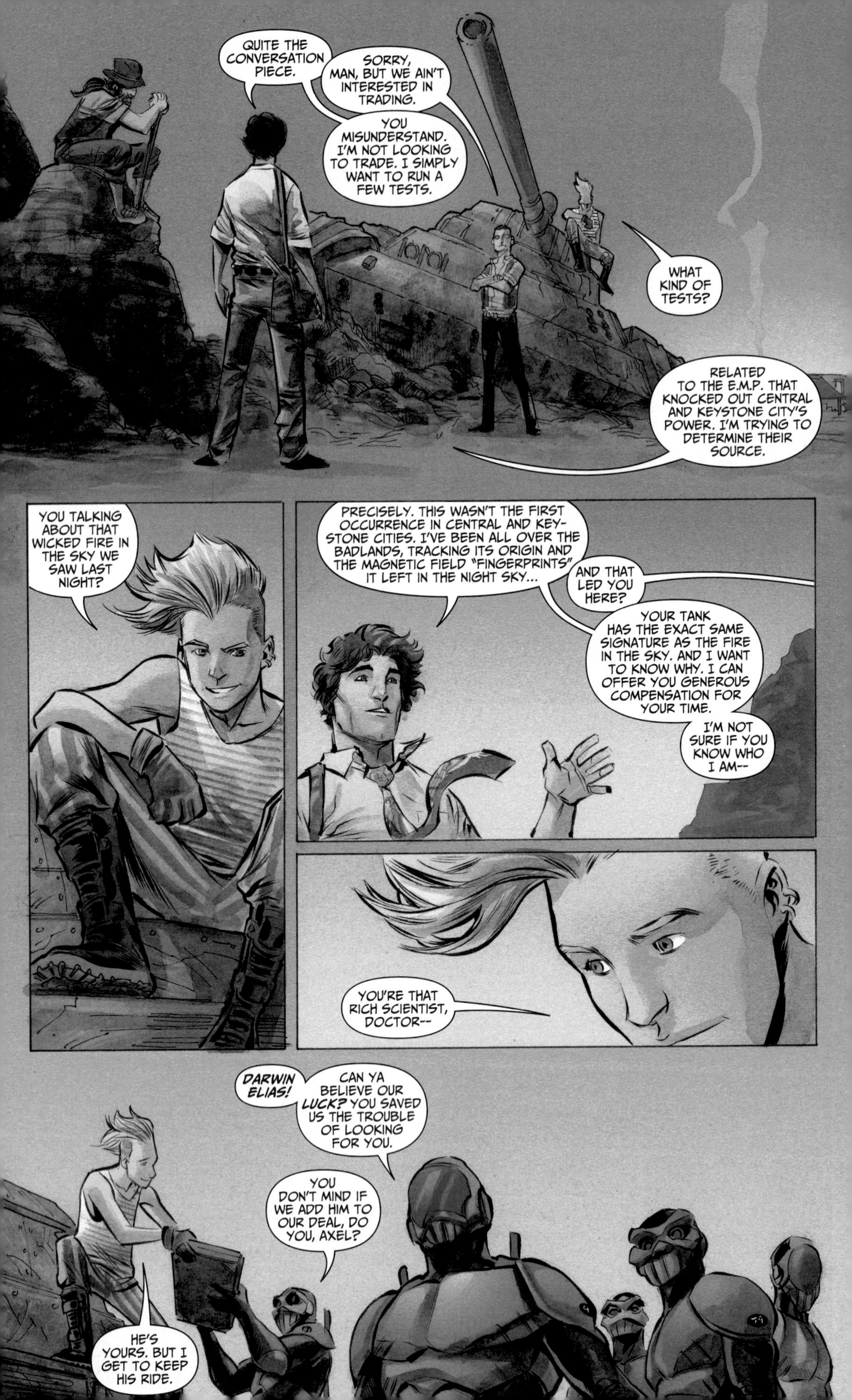
QUITE THE CONVERSATION PIECE.
SORRY, MAN, BUT WE AIN'T INTERESTED IN TRADING.
YOU MISUNDERSTAND. I'M NOT LOOKING TO TRADE. I SIMPLY WANT TO RUN A FEW TESTS.
WHAT KIND OF TESTS?
RELATED TO THE E.M.P. THAT KNOCKED OUT CENTRAL AND KEYSTONE CITY'S POWER. I'M TRYING TO DETERMINE THEIR SOURCE.
YOU TALKING ABOUT THAT WICKED FIRE IN THE SKY WE SAW LAST NIGHT?
PRECISELY. THIS WASN'T THE FIRST OCCURRENCE IN CENTRAL AND KEY-STONE CITIES. I'VE BEEN ALL OVER THE BADLANDS, TRACKING ITS ORIGIN AND THE MAGNETIC FIELD "FINGERPRINTS" IT LEFT IN THE NIGHT SKY...
AND THAT LED YOU HERE?
YOUR TANK HAS THE EXACT SAME SIGNATURE AS THE FIRE IN THE SKY. AND I WANT TO KNOW WHY. I CAN OFFER YOU GENEROUS COMPENSATION FOR YOUR TIME.
I'M NOT SURE IF YOU KNOW WHO I AM--
YOU'RE THAT RICH SCIENTIST, DOCTOR--
DARWIN ELIAS!
CAN YA BELIEVE OUR LUCK? YOU SAVED US THE TROUBLE OF LOOKING FOR YOU.
YOU DON'T MIND IF WE ADD HIM TO OUR DEAL, DO YOU, AXEL?
HE'S YOURS. BUT I GET TO KEEP HIS RIDE.

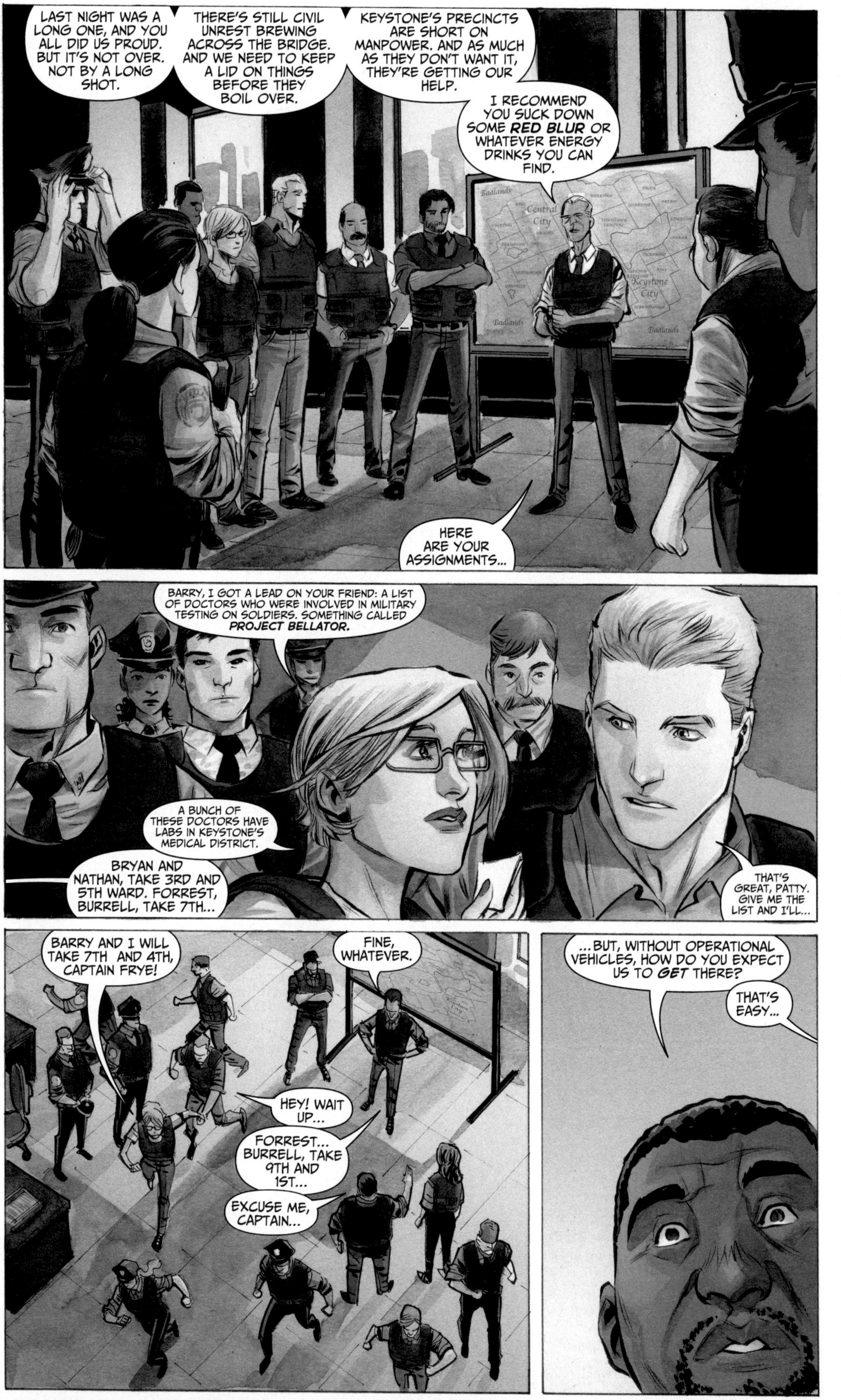
LAST NIGHT WAS A LONG ONE, AND YOU ALL DID US PROUD. BUT IT'S NOT OVER. NOT BY A LONG SHOT.
THERE'S STILL CIVIL UNREST BREWING ACROSS THE BRIDGE. AND WE NEED TO KEEP A LID ON THINGS BEFORE THEY BOIL OVER.
KEYSTONE'S PRECINCTS ARE SHORT ON MANPOWER. AND AS MUCH AS THEY DON'T WANT IT, THEY'RE GETTING OUR HELP.
I RECOMMEND YOU SUCK DOWN SOME **RED BLUR** OR WHATEVER ENERGY DRINKS YOU CAN FIND.
Badlands
Central City
Keystone City
Badlands
Badlands
HERE ARE YOUR ASSIGNMENTS...
BARRY, I GOT A LEAD ON YOUR FRIEND: A LIST OF DOCTORS WHO WERE INVOLVED IN MILITARY TESTING ON SOLDIERS. SOMETHING CALLED ***PROJECT BELLATOR.***
A BUNCH OF THESE DOCTORS HAVE LABS IN KEYSTONE'S MEDICAL DISTRICT.
BRYAN AND NATHAN, TAKE 3RD AND 5TH WARD. FORREST, BURRELL, TAKE 7TH...
THAT'S GREAT, PATTY. GIVE ME THE LIST AND I'LL...
BARRY AND I WILL TAKE 7TH AND 4TH, CAPTAIN FRYE!
FINE, WHATEVER.
HEY! WAIT UP...
FORREST... BURRELL, TAKE 9TH AND 1ST...
EXCUSE ME, CAPTAIN...
...BUT, WITHOUT OPERATIONAL VEHICLES, HOW DO YOU EXPECT US TO *GET* THERE?
THAT'S EASY...

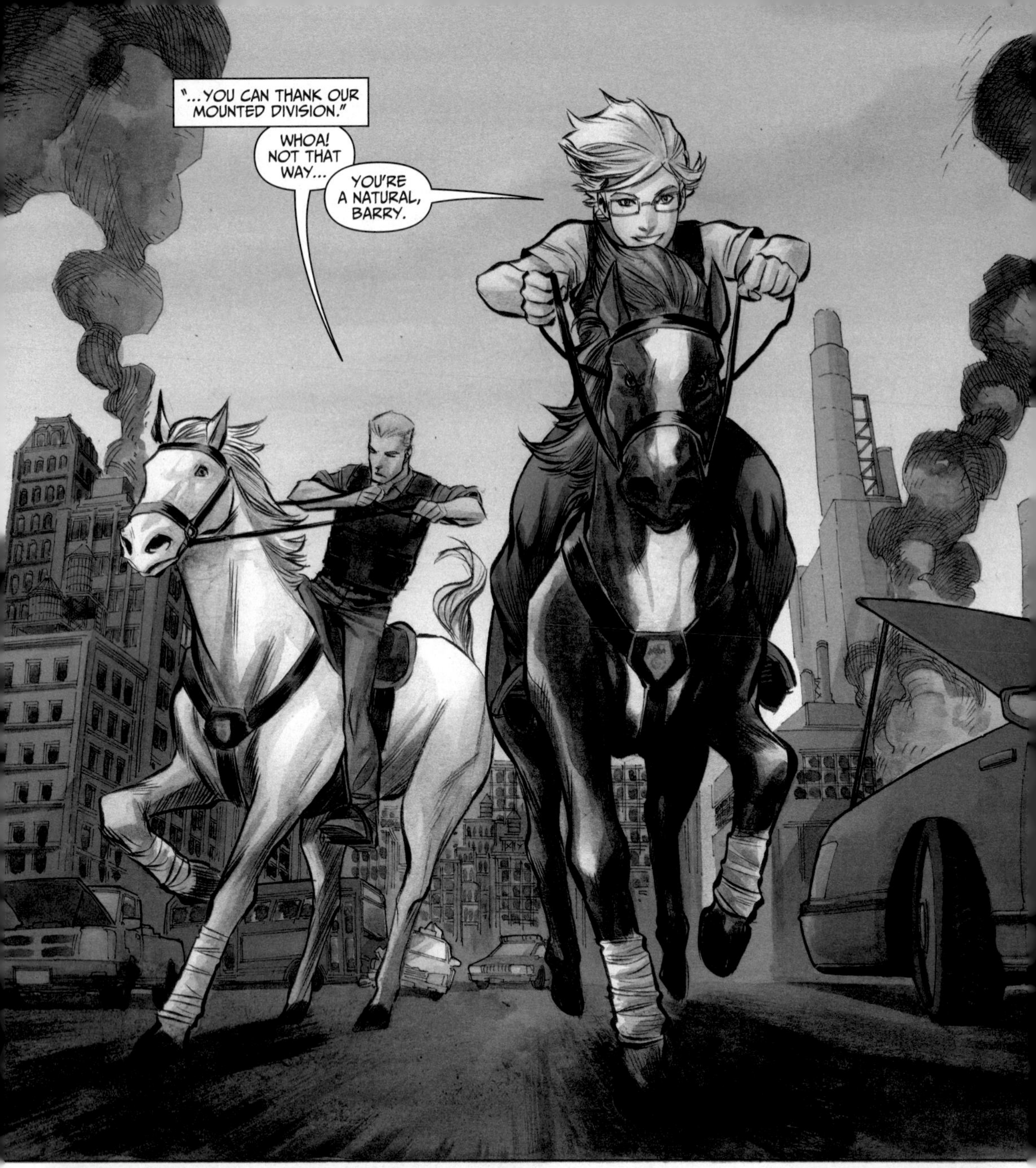
"...YOU CAN THANK OUR MOUNTED DIVISION."
WHOA! NOT THAT WAY...
YOU'RE A NATURAL, BARRY.

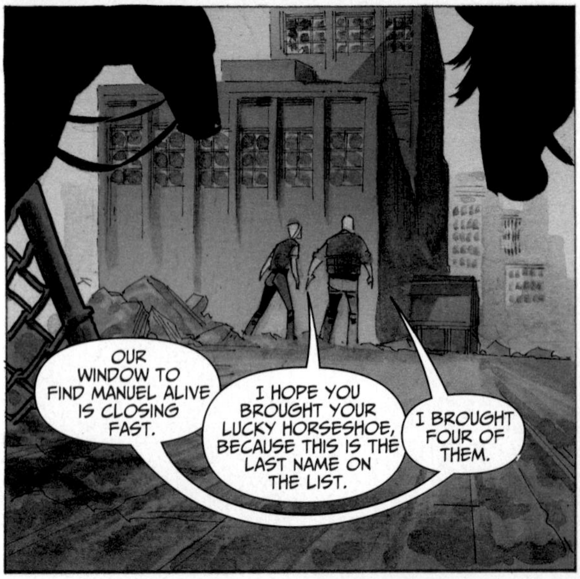
OUR WINDOW TO FIND MANUEL ALIVE IS CLOSING FAST.
I HOPE YOU BROUGHT YOUR LUCKY HORSESHOE, BECAUSE THIS IS THE LAST NAME ON THE LIST.
I BROUGHT FOUR OF THEM.

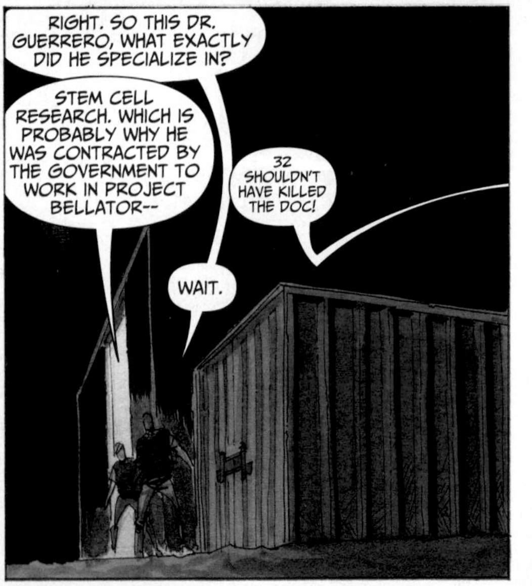
RIGHT. SO THIS DR. GUERRERO, WHAT EXACTLY DID HE SPECIALIZE IN?
STEM CELL RESEARCH. WHICH IS PROBABLY WHY HE WAS CONTRACTED BY THE GOVERNMENT TO WORK IN PROJECT BELLATOR--
32 SHOULDN'T HAVE KILLED THE DOC!
WAIT.

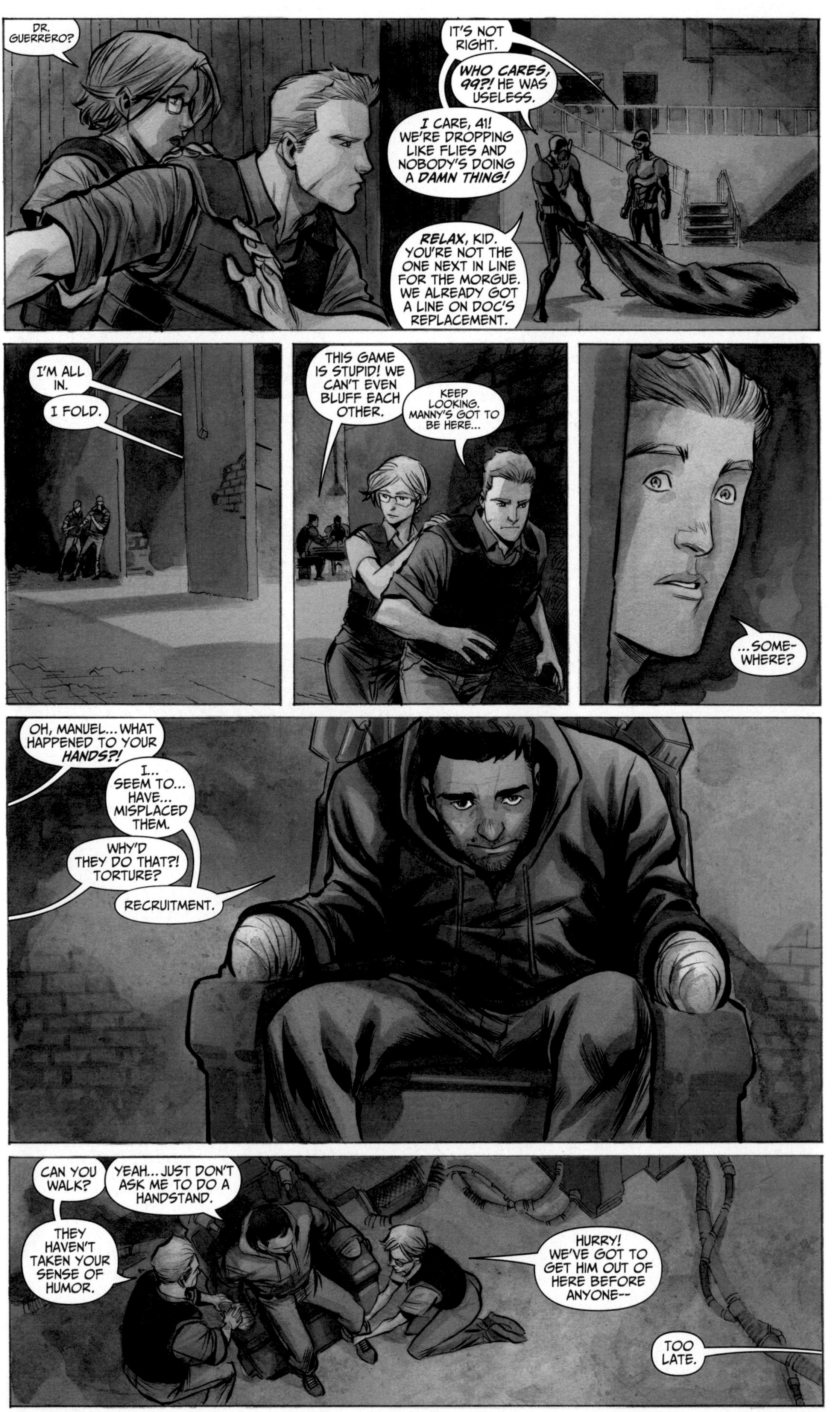
DR. GUERRERO?
IT'S NOT RIGHT.
WHO CARES, 99?! HE WAS USELESS.
I CARE, 41! WE'RE DROPPING LIKE FLIES AND NOBODY'S DOING A DAMN THING!
RELAX, KID. YOU'RE NOT THE ONE NEXT IN LINE FOR THE MORGUE. WE ALREADY GOT A LINE ON DOC'S REPLACEMENT.
I'M ALL IN.
I FOLD.
THIS GAME IS STUPID! WE CAN'T EVEN BLUFF EACH OTHER.
KEEP LOOKING. MANNY'S GOT TO BE HERE...
...SOME-WHERE?
OH, MANUEL... WHAT HAPPENED TO YOUR HANDS?!
I... SEEM TO... HAVE... MISPLACED THEM.
WHY'D THEY DO THAT?! TORTURE?
RECRUITMENT.
CAN YOU WALK?
YEAH... JUST DON'T ASK ME TO DO A HANDSTAND.
THEY HAVEN'T TAKEN YOUR SENSE OF HUMOR.
HURRY! WE'VE GOT TO GET HIM OUT OF HERE BEFORE ANYONE--
TOO LATE.

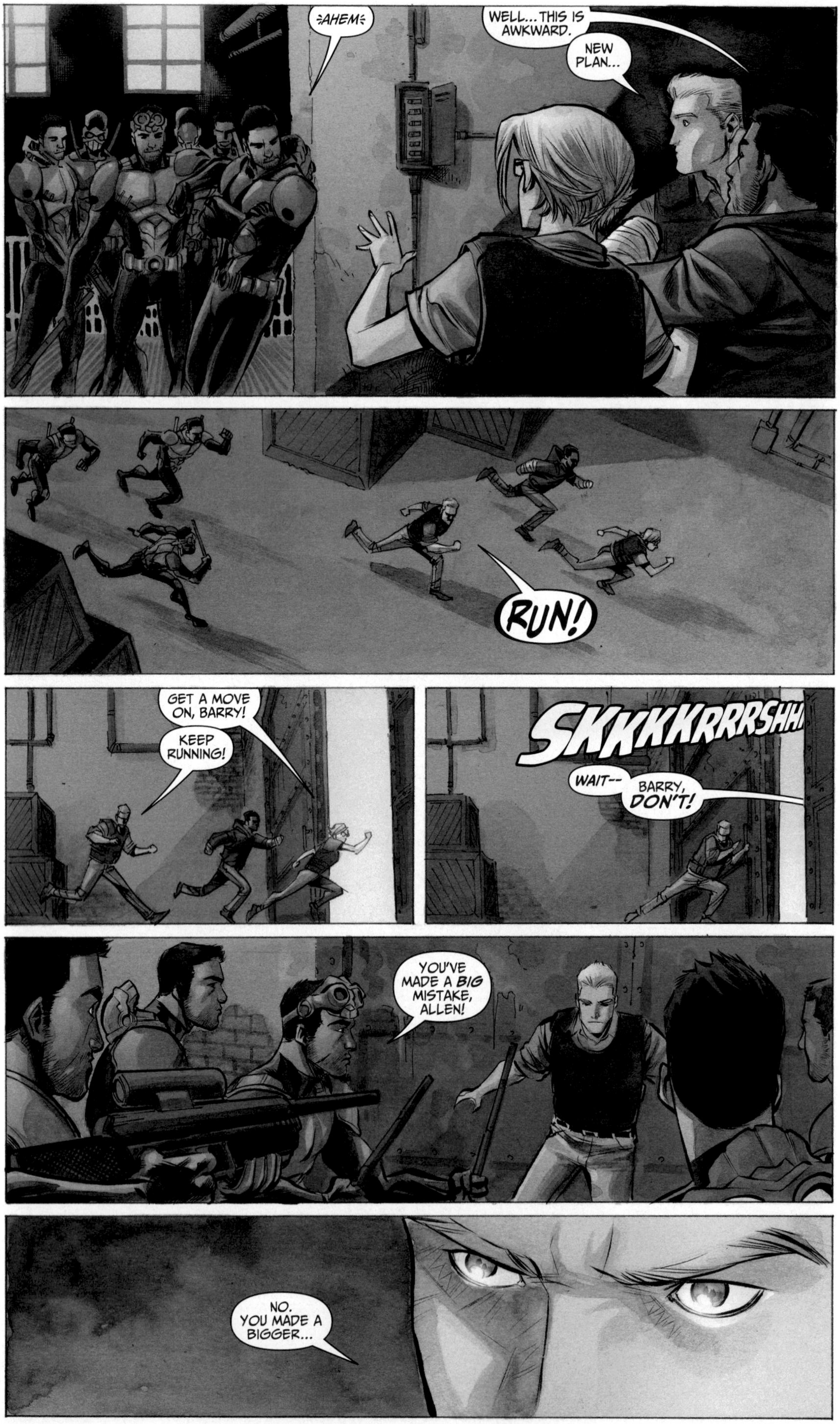
AHEM
WELL... THIS IS AWKWARD.
NEW PLAN...
RUN!
GET A MOVE ON, BARRY!
KEEP RUNNING!
SKKKKRRRSHH
WAIT--
BARRY, DON'T!
YOU'VE MADE A BIG MISTAKE, ALLEN!
NO. YOU MADE A BIGGER...

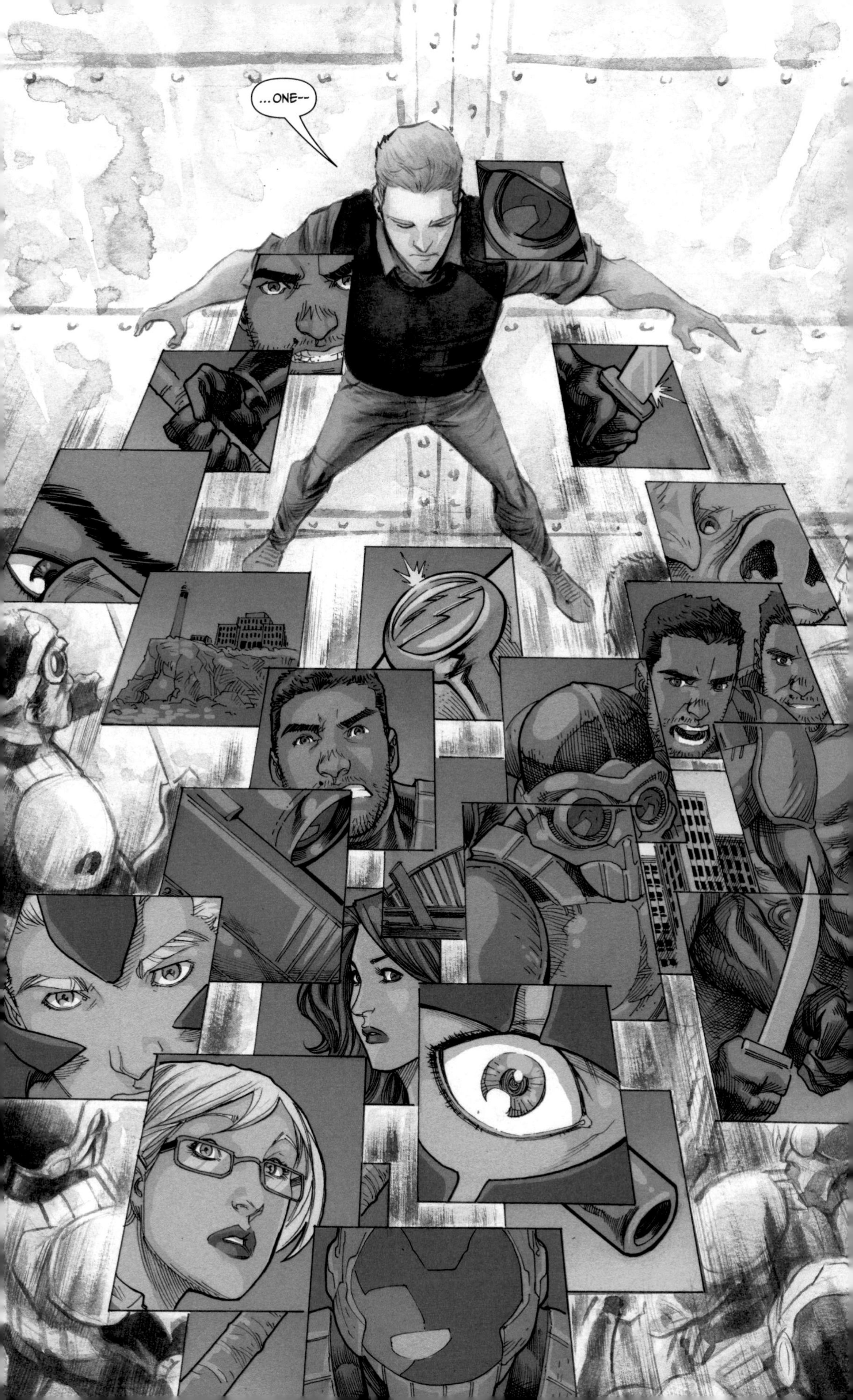
...ONE--

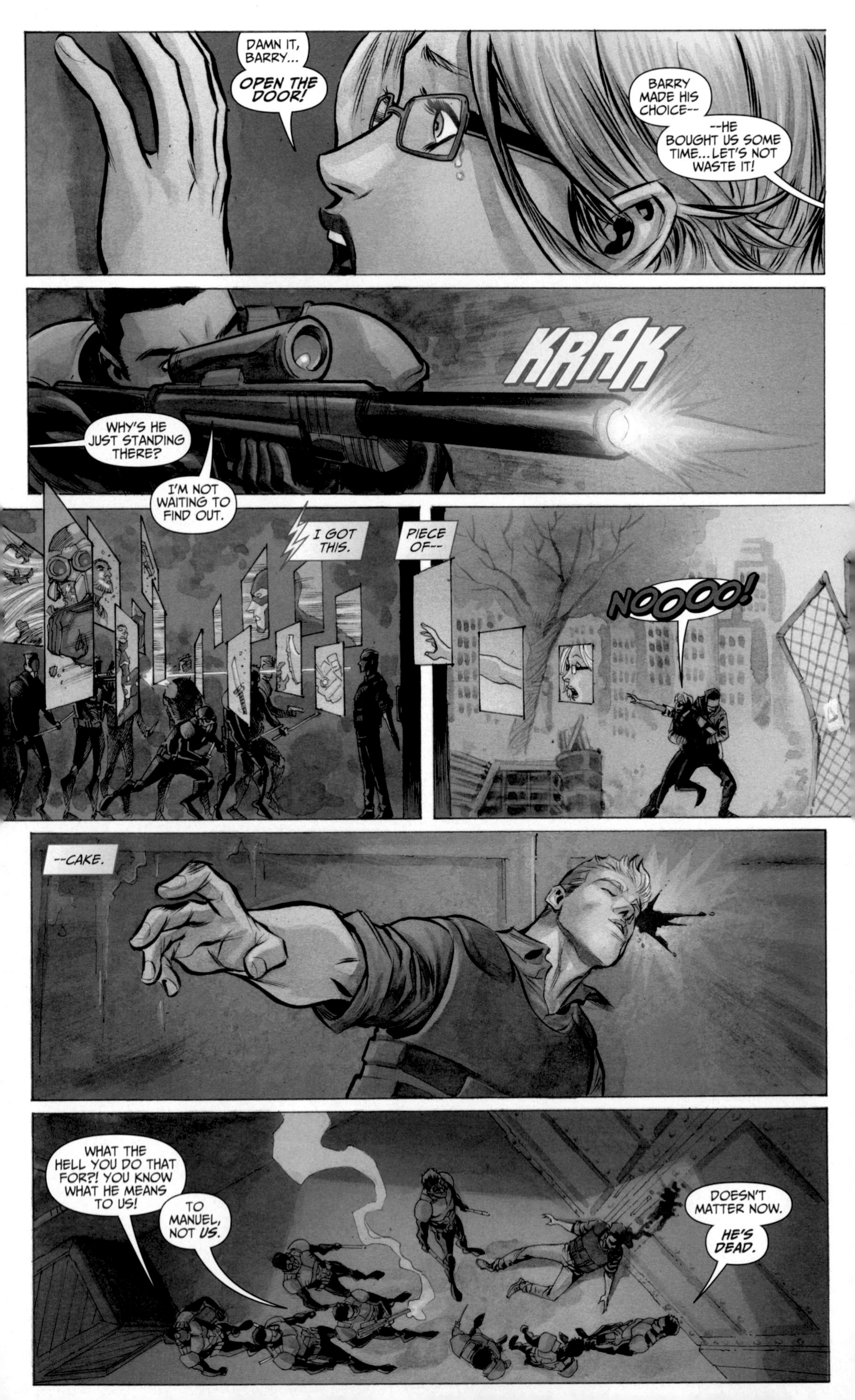
DAMN IT, BARRY... OPEN THE DOOR!
BARRY MADE HIS CHOICE--
--HE BOUGHT US SOME TIME... LET'S NOT WASTE IT!
KRAK
WHY'S HE JUST STANDING THERE?
I'M NOT WAITING TO FIND OUT.
I GOT THIS.
PIECE OF--
NOOOOO!
--CAKE.
WHAT THE HELL YOU DO THAT FOR?! YOU KNOW WHAT HE MEANS TO US!
TO MANUEL, NOT US.
DOESN'T MATTER NOW.
HE'S DEAD.

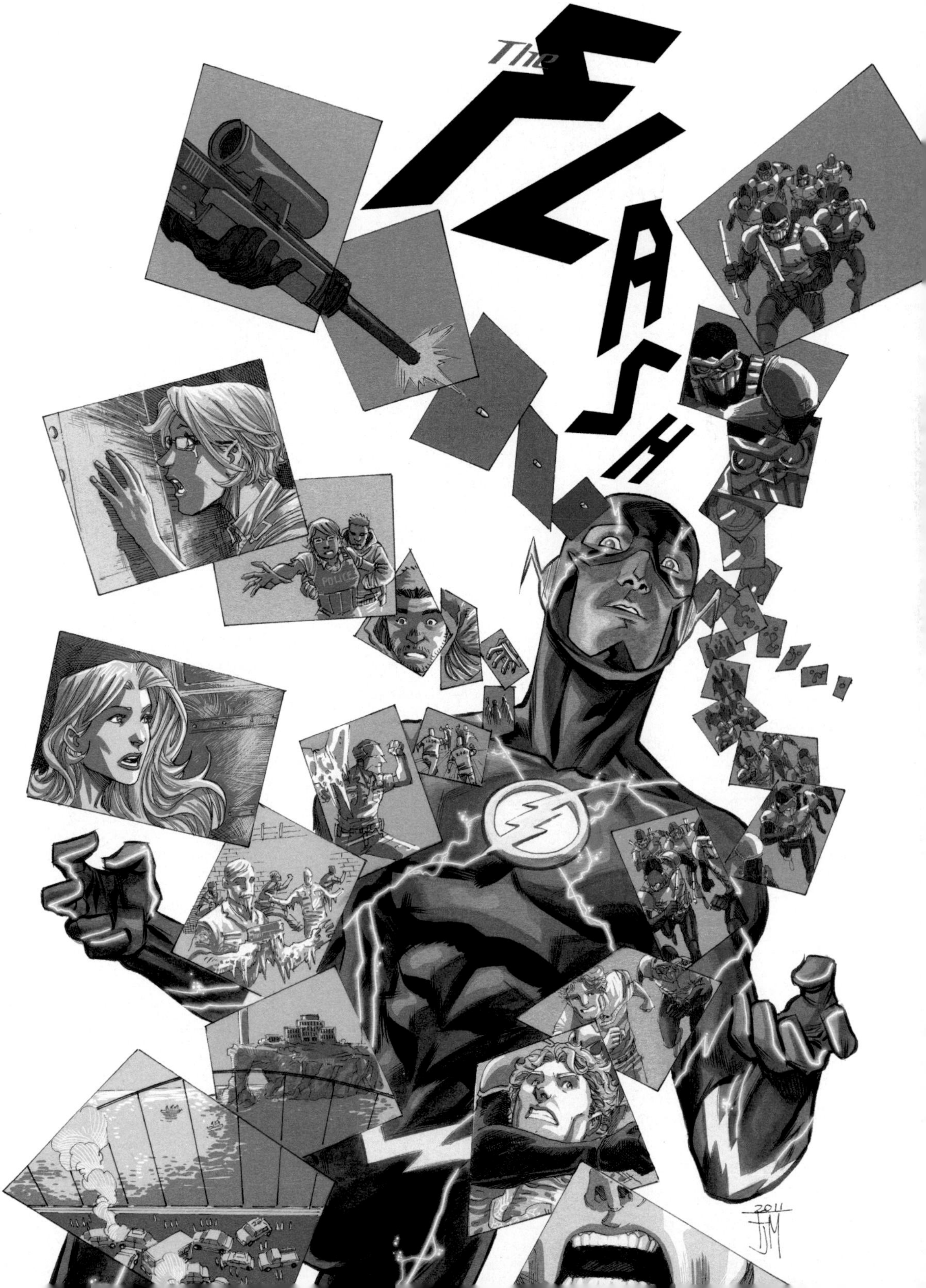
The FLASH
2011

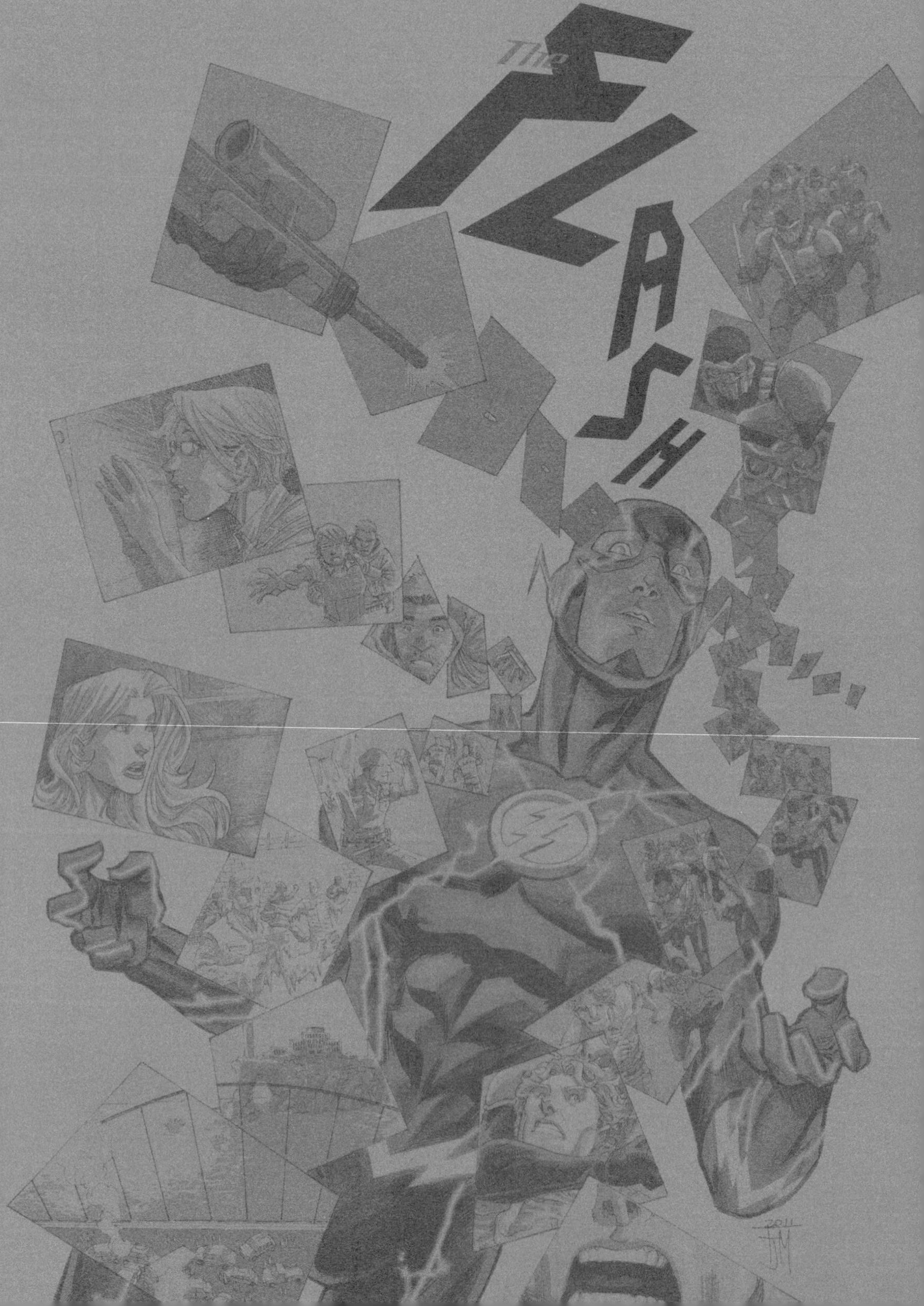
The
FLASH

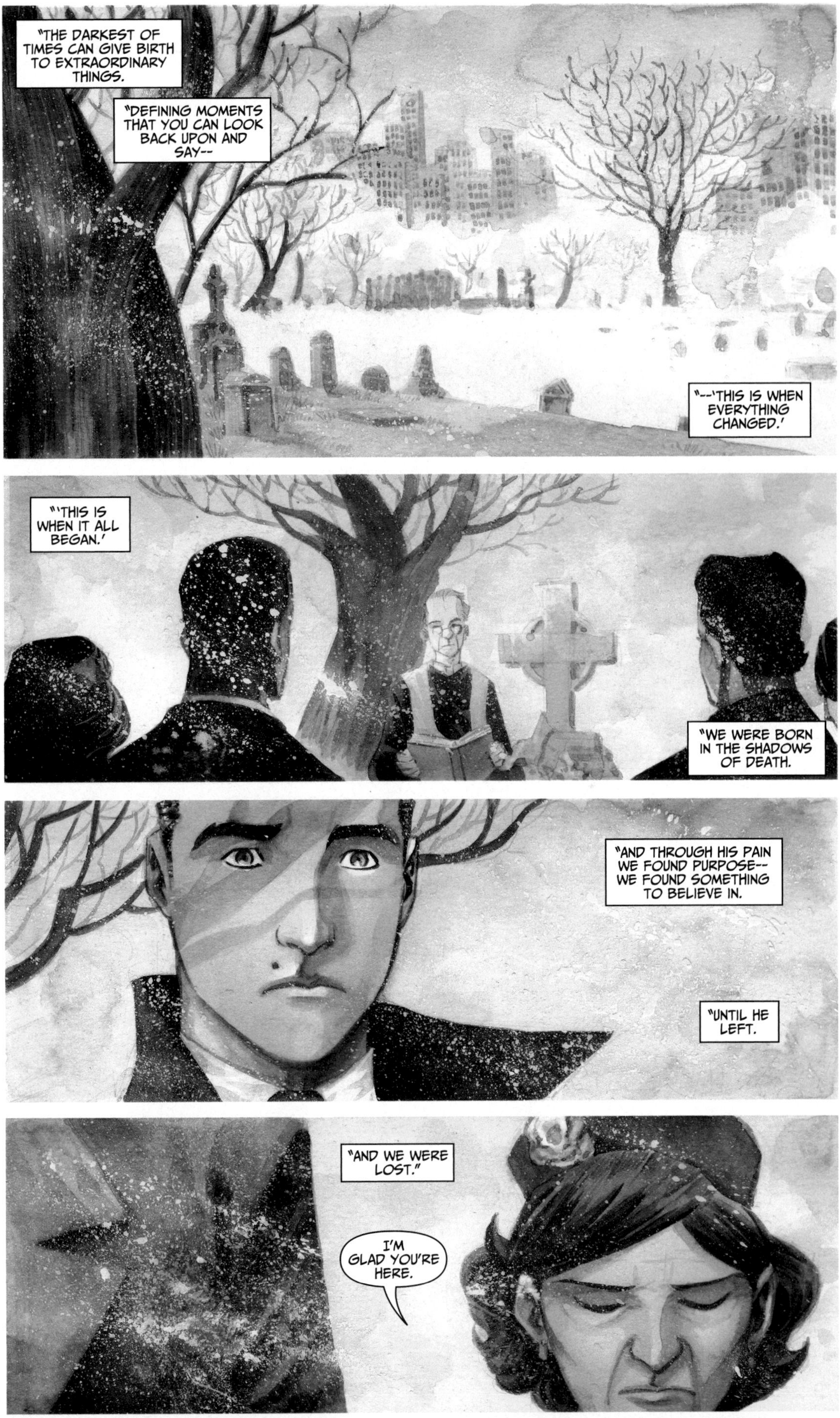
"THE DARKEST OF TIMES CAN GIVE BIRTH TO EXTRAORDINARY THINGS.
"DEFINING MOMENTS THAT YOU CAN LOOK BACK UPON AND SAY--
"--'THIS IS WHEN EVERYTHING CHANGED.'
"'THIS IS WHEN IT ALL BEGAN.'
"WE WERE BORN IN THE SHADOWS OF DEATH.
"AND THROUGH HIS PAIN WE FOUND PURPOSE-- WE FOUND SOMETHING TO BELIEVE IN.
"UNTIL HE LEFT.
"AND WE WERE LOST."
I'M GLAD YOU'RE HERE.

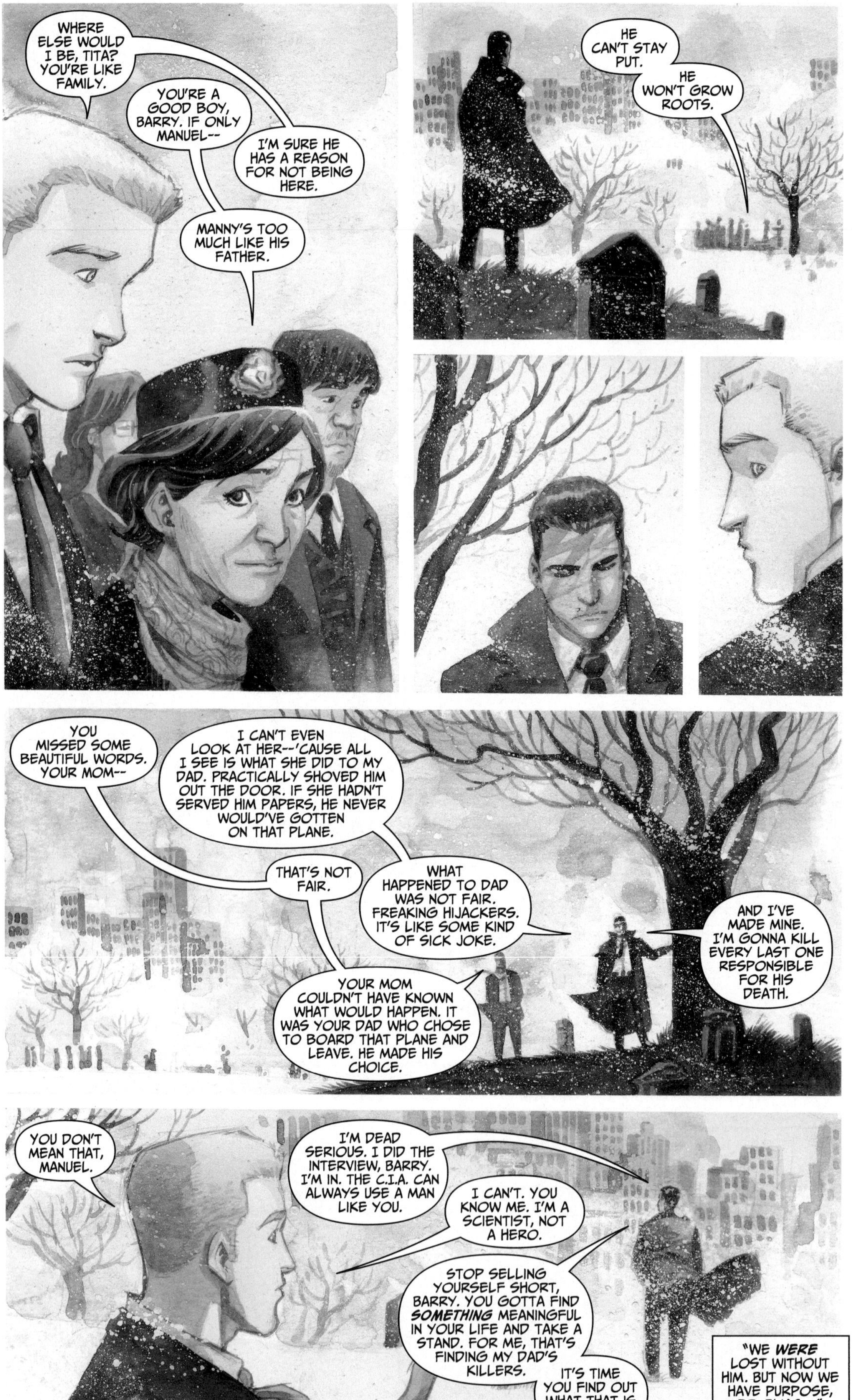

WHERE ELSE WOULD I BE, TITA? YOU'RE LIKE FAMILY.
YOU'RE A GOOD BOY, BARRY. IF ONLY MANUEL--
I'M SURE HE HAS A REASON FOR NOT BEING HERE.
MANNY'S TOO MUCH LIKE HIS FATHER.
HE CAN'T STAY PUT.
HE WON'T GROW ROOTS.
YOU MISSED SOME BEAUTIFUL WORDS. YOUR MOM--
I CAN'T EVEN LOOK AT HER--'CAUSE ALL I SEE IS WHAT SHE DID TO MY DAD. PRACTICALLY SHOVED HIM OUT THE DOOR. IF SHE HADN'T SERVED HIM PAPERS, HE NEVER WOULD'VE GOTTEN ON THAT PLANE.
THAT'S NOT FAIR.
WHAT HAPPENED TO DAD WAS NOT FAIR. FREAKING HIJACKERS. IT'S LIKE SOME KIND OF SICK JOKE.
YOUR MOM COULDN'T HAVE KNOWN WHAT WOULD HAPPEN. IT WAS YOUR DAD WHO CHOSE TO BOARD THAT PLANE AND LEAVE. HE MADE HIS CHOICE.
AND I'VE MADE MINE. I'M GONNA KILL EVERY LAST ONE RESPONSIBLE FOR HIS DEATH.
YOU DON'T MEAN THAT, MANUEL.
I'M DEAD SERIOUS. I DID THE INTERVIEW, BARRY. I'M IN. THE C.I.A. CAN ALWAYS USE A MAN LIKE YOU.
I CAN'T. YOU KNOW ME. I'M A SCIENTIST, NOT A HERO.
STOP SELLING YOURSELF SHORT, BARRY. YOU GOTTA FIND *SOMETHING* MEANINGFUL IN YOUR LIFE AND TAKE A STAND. FOR ME, THAT'S FINDING MY DAD'S KILLERS.
IT'S TIME YOU FIND OUT WHAT THAT IS FOR YOU.
"WE *WERE* LOST WITHOUT HIM. BUT NOW WE HAVE PURPOSE, DR. ELIAS--"

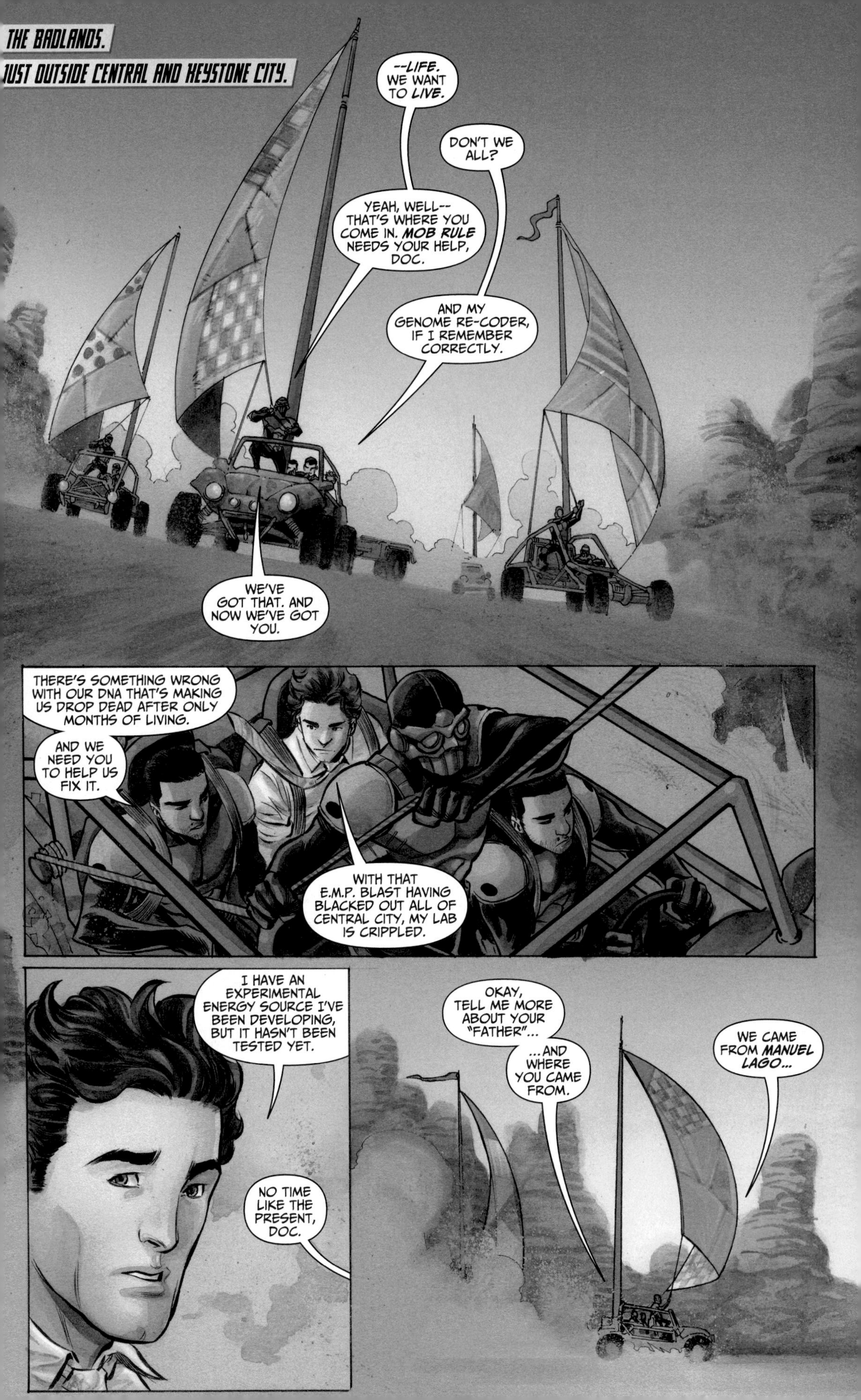
THE BADLANDS.
JUST OUTSIDE CENTRAL AND KEYSTONE CITY.
--LIFE. WE WANT TO LIVE.
DON'T WE ALL?
YEAH, WELL-- THAT'S WHERE YOU COME IN. MOB RULE NEEDS YOUR HELP, DOC.
AND MY GENOME RE-CODER, IF I REMEMBER CORRECTLY.
WE'VE GOT THAT. AND NOW WE'VE GOT YOU.
THERE'S SOMETHING WRONG WITH OUR DNA THAT'S MAKING US DROP DEAD AFTER ONLY MONTHS OF LIVING.
AND WE NEED YOU TO HELP US FIX IT.
WITH THAT E.M.P. BLAST HAVING BLACKED OUT ALL OF CENTRAL CITY, MY LAB IS CRIPPLED.
I HAVE AN EXPERIMENTAL ENERGY SOURCE I'VE BEEN DEVELOPING, BUT IT HASN'T BEEN TESTED YET.
NO TIME LIKE THE PRESENT, DOC.
OKAY, TELL ME MORE ABOUT YOUR "FATHER"...
...AND WHERE YOU CAME FROM.
WE CAME FROM MANUEL LAGO...

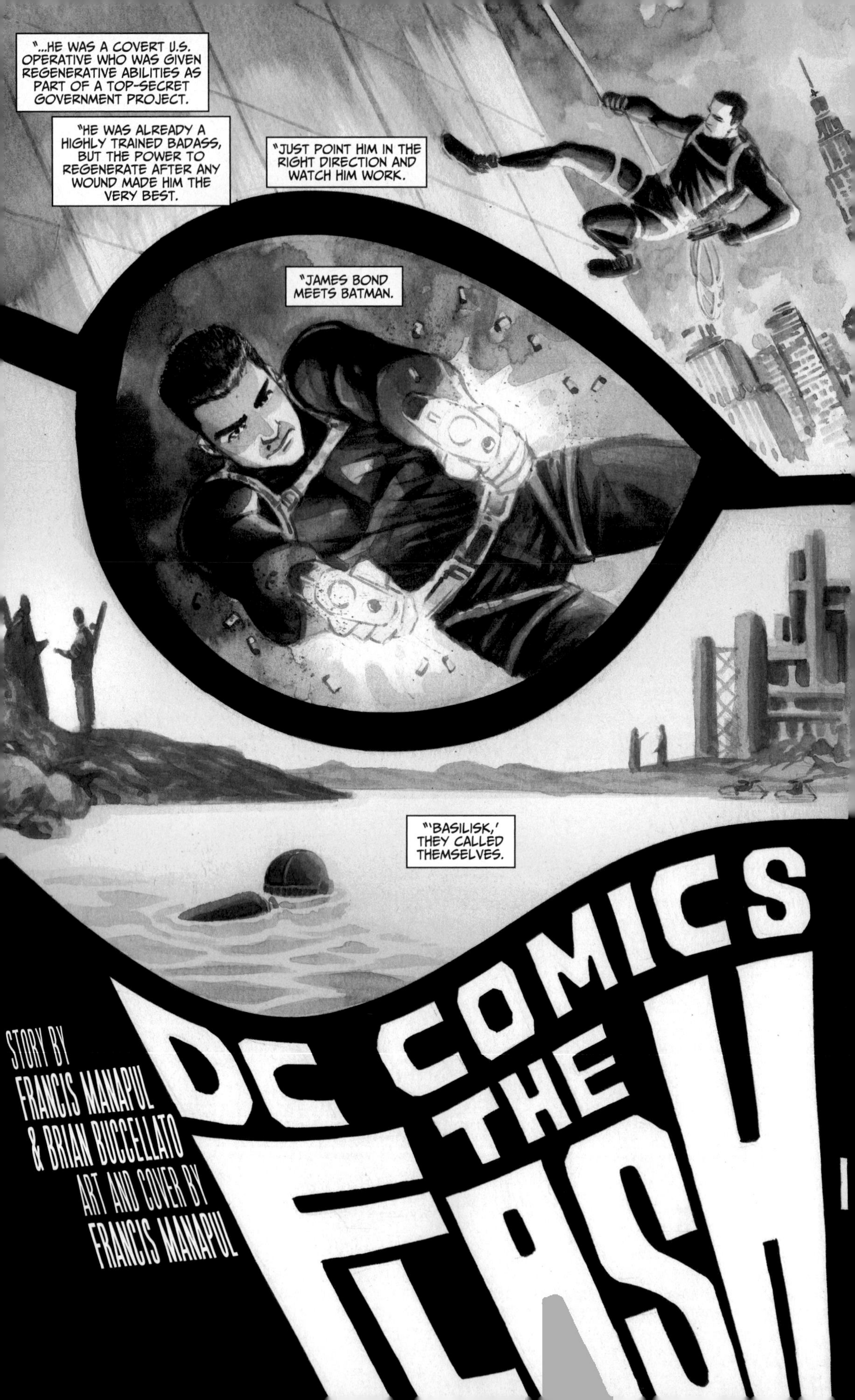
"...HE WAS A COVERT U.S. OPERATIVE WHO WAS GIVEN REGENERATIVE ABILITIES AS PART OF A TOP-SECRET GOVERNMENT PROJECT.
"HE WAS ALREADY A HIGHLY TRAINED BADASS, BUT THE POWER TO REGENERATE AFTER ANY WOUND MADE HIM THE VERY BEST.
"JUST POINT HIM IN THE RIGHT DIRECTION AND WATCH HIM WORK.
"JAMES BOND MEETS BATMAN.
"'BASILISK,' THEY CALLED THEMSELVES.
DC COMICS
THE FLASH
STORY BY FRANCIS MANAPUL & BRIAN BUCCELLATO
ART AND COVER BY FRANCIS MANAPUL

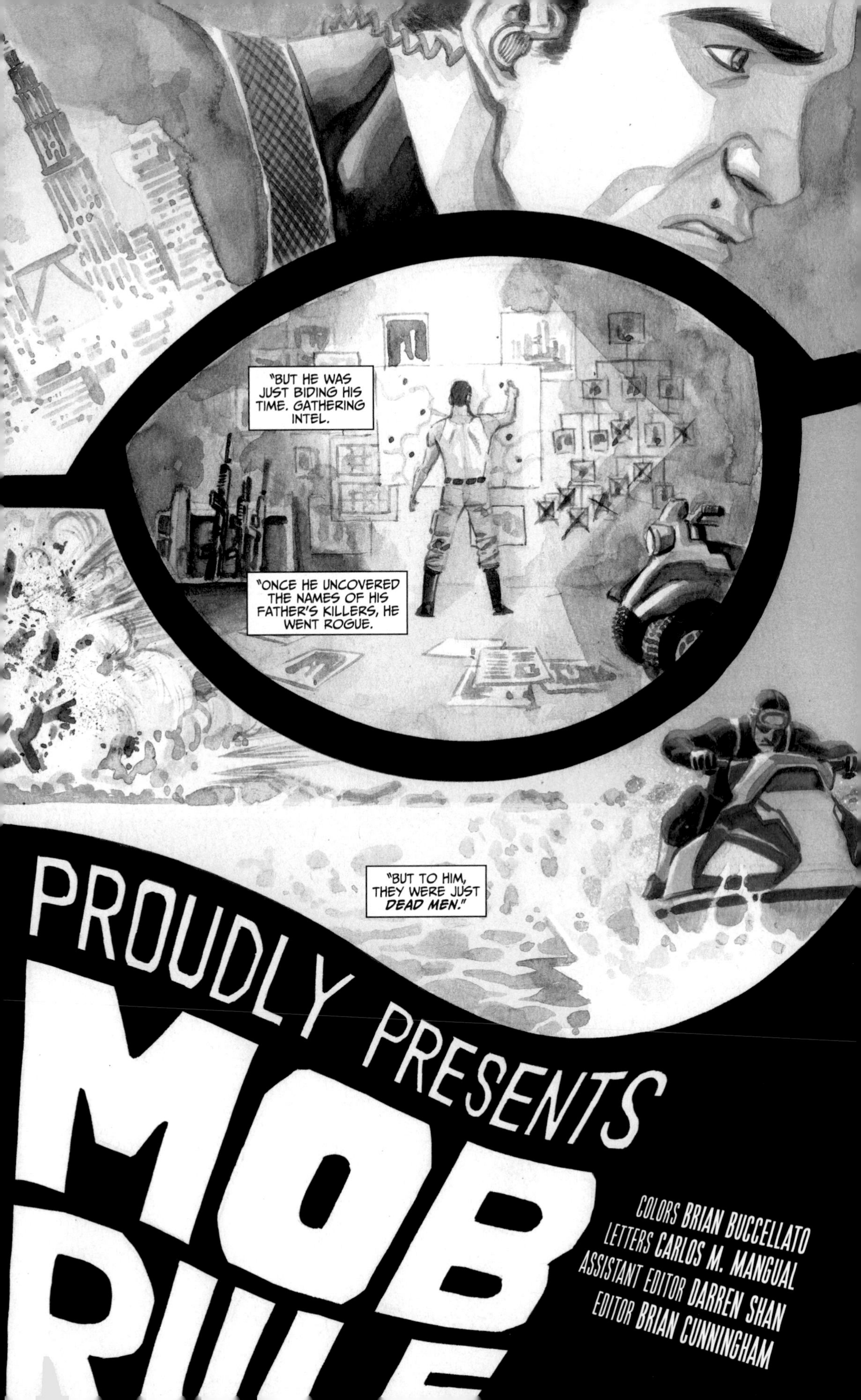
"BUT HE WAS JUST BIDING HIS TIME. GATHERING INTEL.
"ONCE HE UNCOVERED THE NAMES OF HIS FATHER'S KILLERS, HE WENT ROGUE.
"BUT TO HIM, THEY WERE JUST DEAD MEN."
PROUDLY PRESENTS
MOB RULE
COLORS BRIAN BUCCELLATO
LETTERS CARLOS M. MANGUAL
ASSISTANT EDITOR DARREN SHAN
EDITOR BRIAN CUNNINGHAM

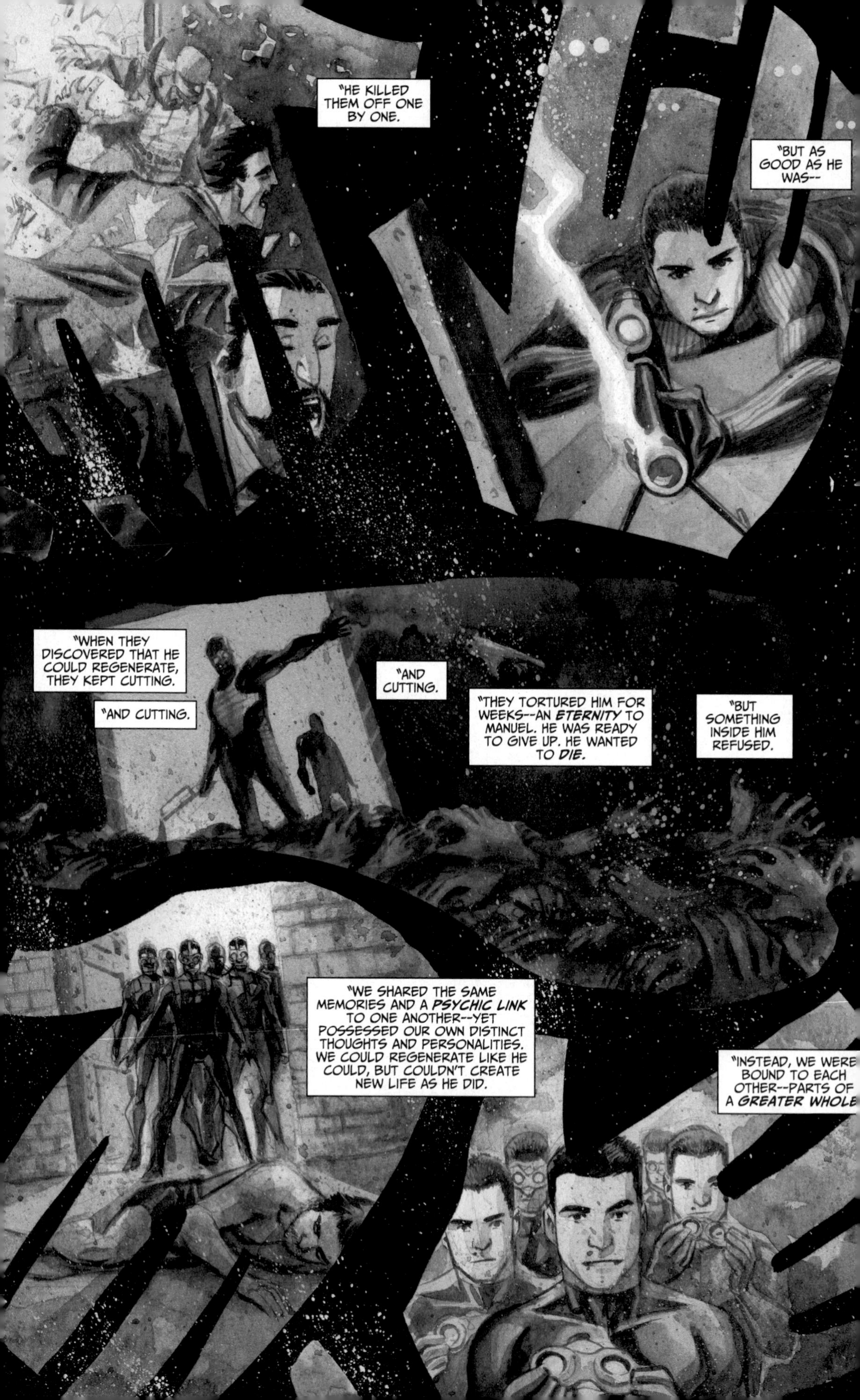
"HE KILLED THEM OFF ONE BY ONE.
"BUT AS GOOD AS HE WAS--
"WHEN THEY DISCOVERED THAT HE COULD REGENERATE, THEY KEPT CUTTING.
"AND CUTTING.
"AND CUTTING.
"THEY TORTURED HIM FOR WEEKS--AN *ETERNITY* TO MANUEL. HE WAS READY TO GIVE UP. HE WANTED TO *DIE.*
"BUT SOMETHING INSIDE HIM REFUSED.
"WE SHARED THE SAME MEMORIES AND A *PSYCHIC LINK* TO ONE ANOTHER--YET POSSESSED OUR OWN DISTINCT THOUGHTS AND PERSONALITIES. WE COULD REGENERATE LIKE HE COULD, BUT COULDN'T CREATE NEW LIFE AS HE DID.
"INSTEAD, WE WERE BOUND TO EACH OTHER--PARTS OF A *GREATER WHOLE*

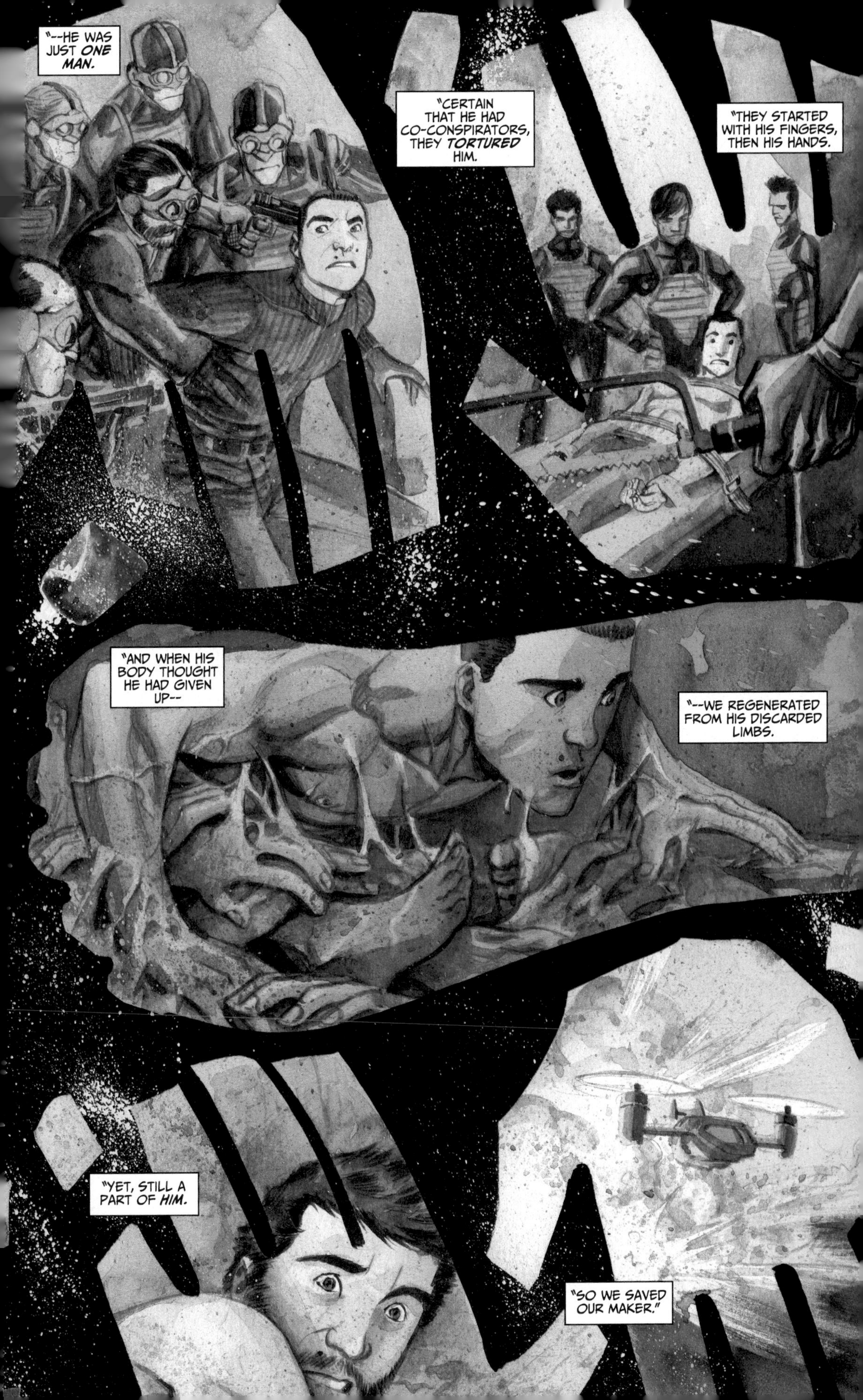
"--HE WAS JUST ONE MAN.
"CERTAIN THAT HE HAD CO-CONSPIRATORS, THEY TORTURED HIM.
"THEY STARTED WITH HIS FINGERS, THEN HIS HANDS.
"AND WHEN HIS BODY THOUGHT HE HAD GIVEN UP--
"--WE REGENERATED FROM HIS DISCARDED LIMBS.
"YET, STILL A PART OF HIM.
"SO WE SAVED OUR MAKER."

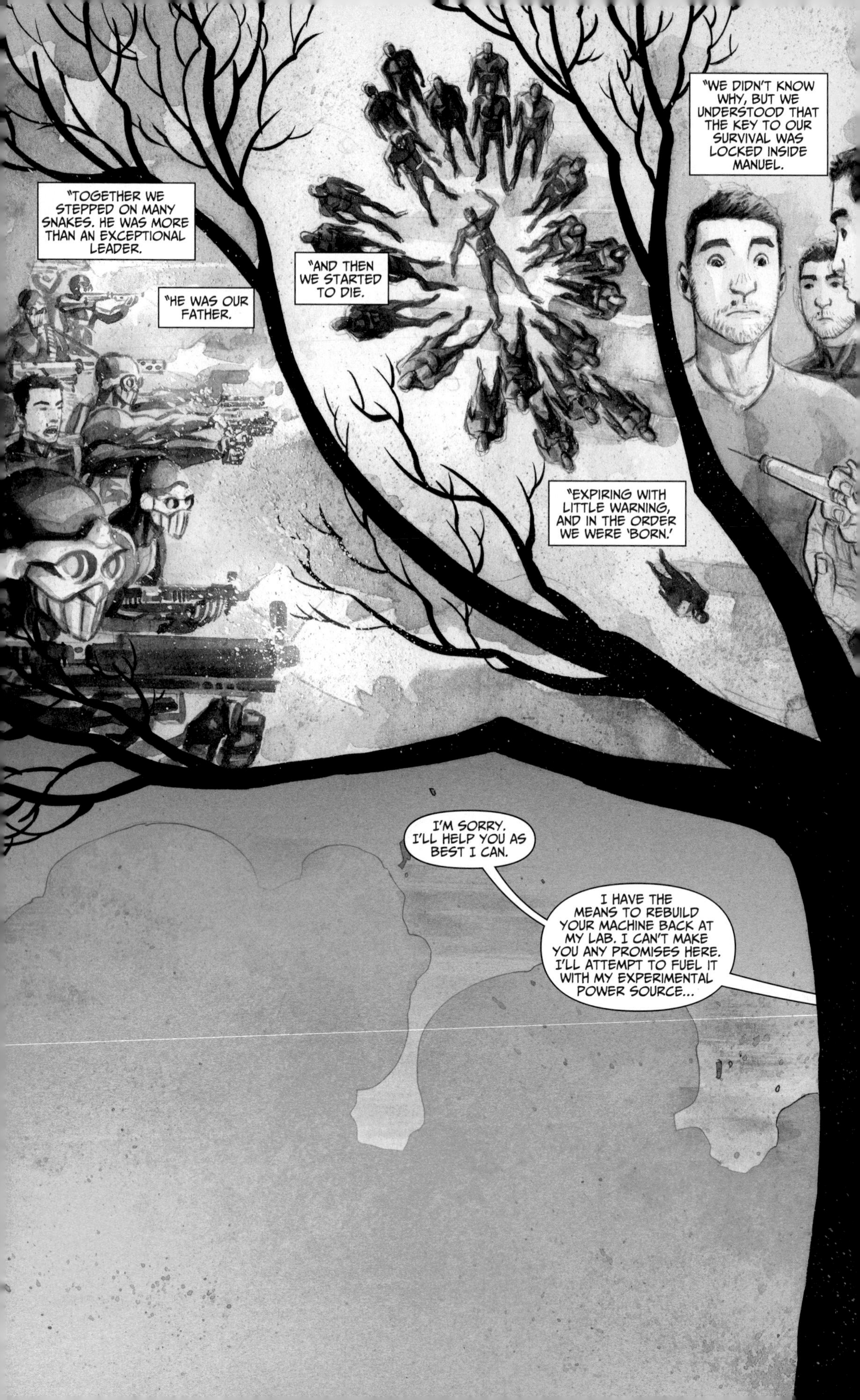
"TOGETHER WE STEPPED ON MANY SNAKES. HE WAS MORE THAN AN EXCEPTIONAL LEADER.
"HE WAS OUR FATHER.
"AND THEN WE STARTED TO DIE.
"EXPIRING WITH LITTLE WARNING, AND IN THE ORDER WE WERE 'BORN.'
"WE DIDN'T KNOW WHY, BUT WE UNDERSTOOD THAT THE KEY TO OUR SURVIVAL WAS LOCKED INSIDE MANUEL.
I'M SORRY. I'LL HELP YOU AS BEST I CAN.
I HAVE THE MEANS TO REBUILD YOUR MACHINE BACK AT MY LAB. I CAN'T MAKE YOU ANY PROMISES HERE. I'LL ATTEMPT TO FUEL IT WITH MY EXPERIMENTAL POWER SOURCE...

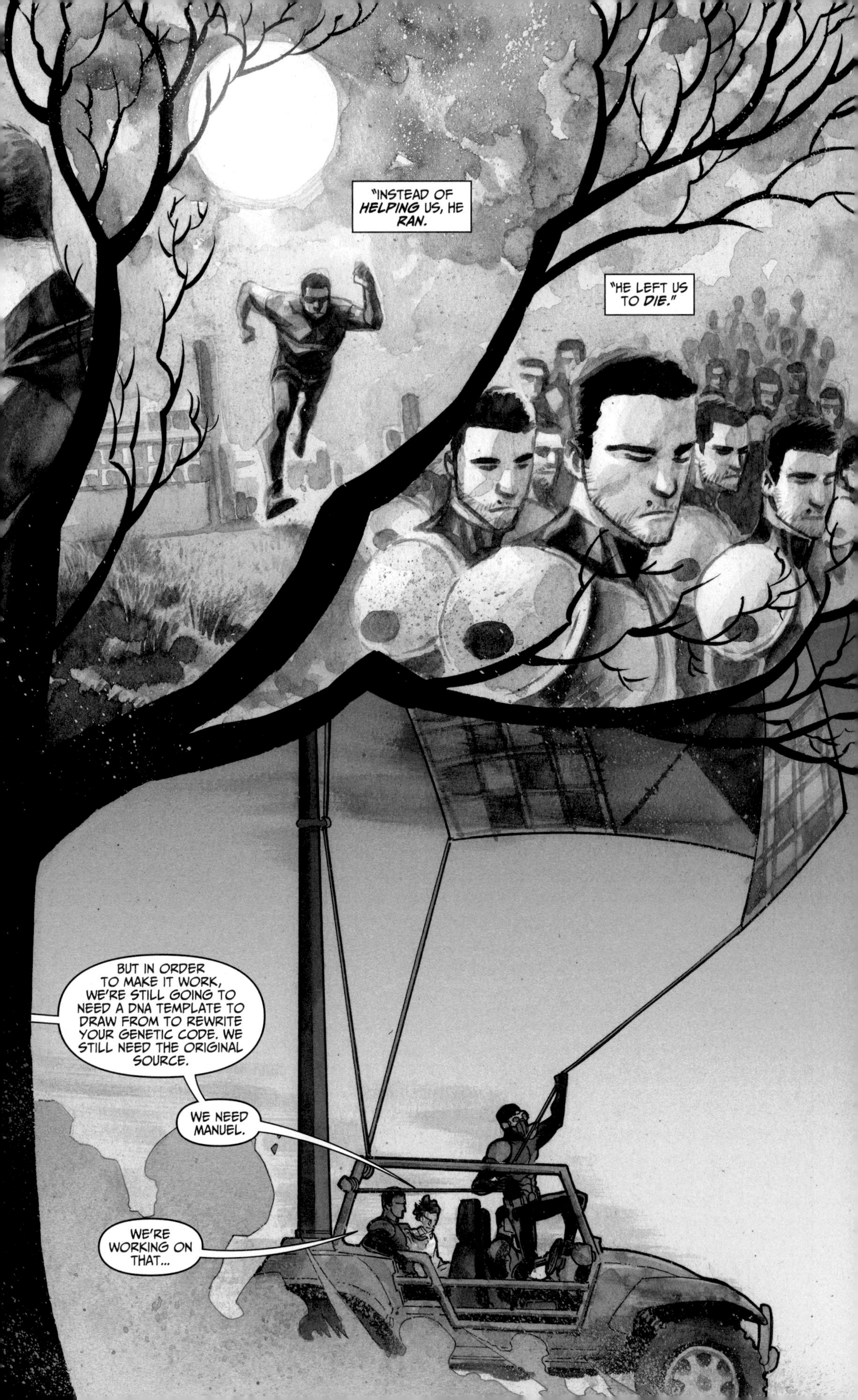
"INSTEAD OF HELPING US, HE RAN.
"HE LEFT US TO DIE."
BUT IN ORDER TO MAKE IT WORK, WE'RE STILL GOING TO NEED A DNA TEMPLATE TO DRAW FROM TO REWRITE YOUR GENETIC CODE. WE STILL NEED THE ORIGINAL SOURCE.
WE NEED MANUEL.
WE'RE WORKING ON THAT...

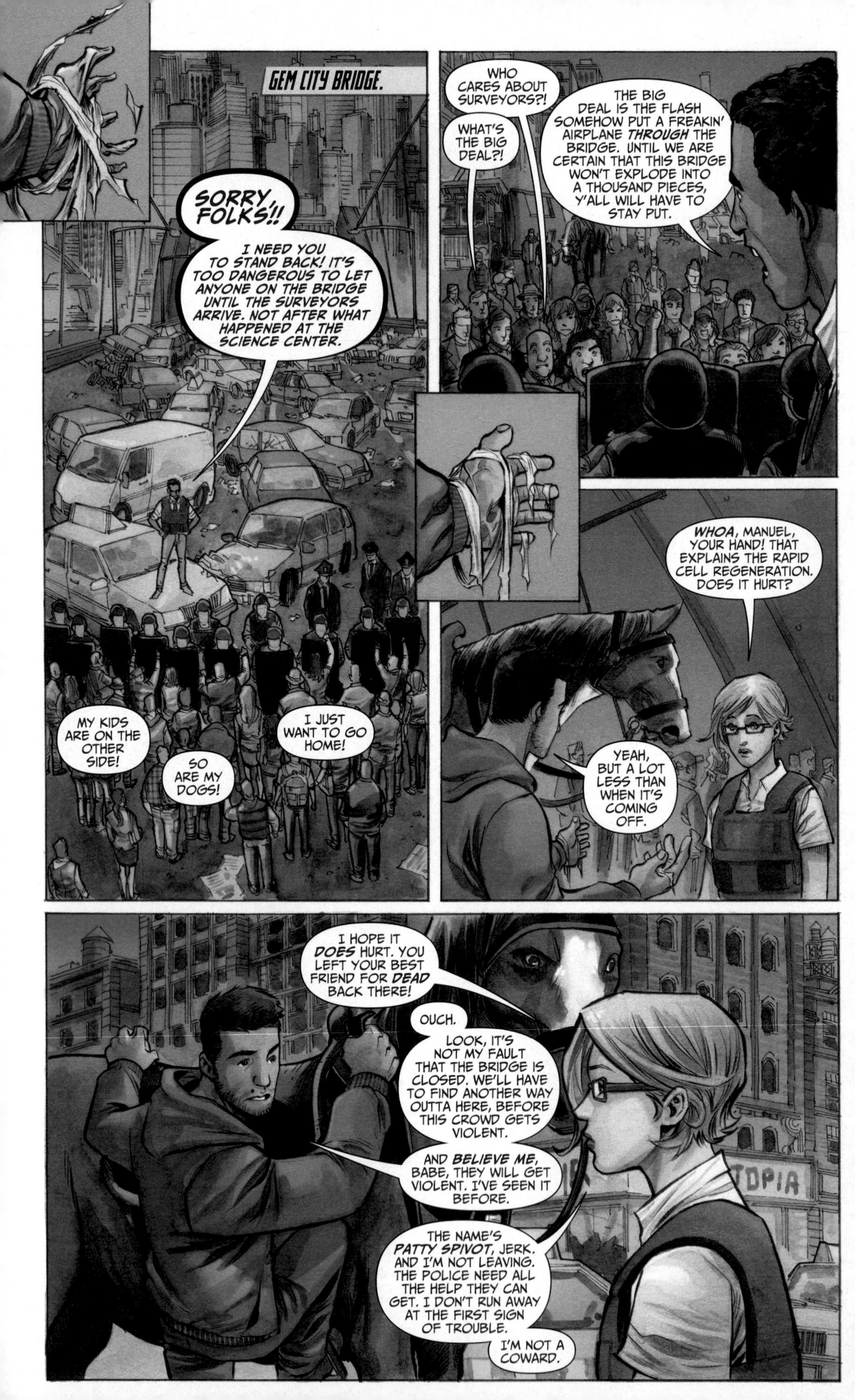
GEM CITY BRIDGE.
SORRY, FOLKS!!
I NEED YOU TO STAND BACK! IT'S TOO DANGEROUS TO LET ANYONE ON THE BRIDGE UNTIL THE SURVEYORS ARRIVE. NOT AFTER WHAT HAPPENED AT THE SCIENCE CENTER.
MY KIDS ARE ON THE OTHER SIDE!
SO ARE MY DOGS!
I JUST WANT TO GO HOME!
WHO CARES ABOUT SURVEYORS?!
WHAT'S THE BIG DEAL?!
THE BIG DEAL IS THE FLASH SOMEHOW PUT A FREAKIN' AIRPLANE THROUGH THE BRIDGE. UNTIL WE ARE CERTAIN THAT THIS BRIDGE WON'T EXPLODE INTO A THOUSAND PIECES, Y'ALL WILL HAVE TO STAY PUT.
WHOA, MANUEL, YOUR HAND! THAT EXPLAINS THE RAPID CELL REGENERATION. DOES IT HURT?
YEAH, BUT A LOT LESS THAN WHEN IT'S COMING OFF.
I HOPE IT DOES HURT. YOU LEFT YOUR BEST FRIEND FOR DEAD BACK THERE!
OUCH.
LOOK, IT'S NOT MY FAULT THAT THE BRIDGE IS CLOSED. WE'LL HAVE TO FIND ANOTHER WAY OUTTA HERE, BEFORE THIS CROWD GETS VIOLENT.
AND BELIEVE ME, BABE, THEY WILL GET VIOLENT. I'VE SEEN IT BEFORE.
THE NAME'S PATTY SPIVOT, JERK. AND I'M NOT LEAVING. THE POLICE NEED ALL THE HELP THEY CAN GET. I DON'T RUN AWAY AT THE FIRST SIGN OF TROUBLE.
I'M NOT A COWARD.

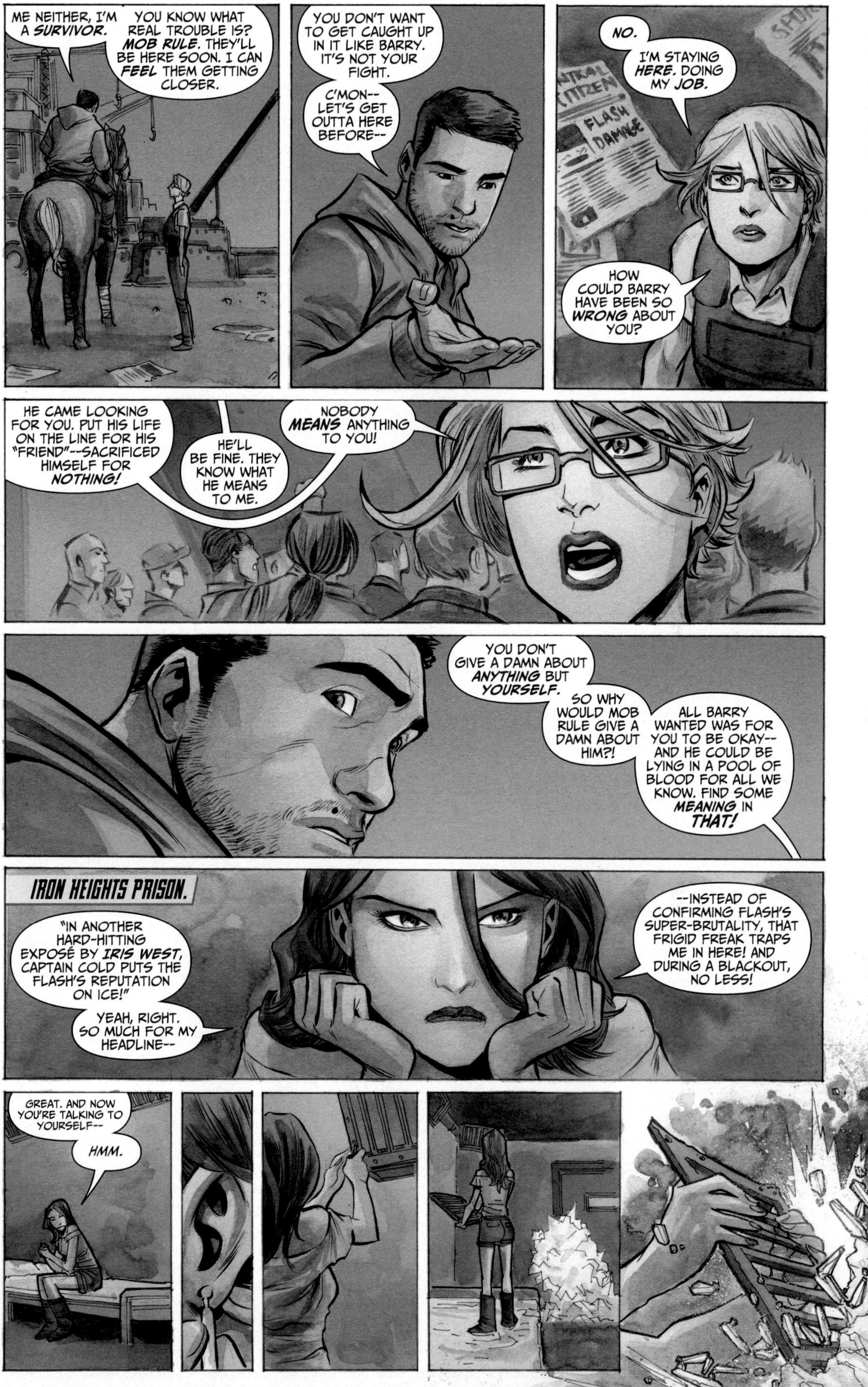
ME NEITHER, I'M A SURVIVOR.
YOU KNOW WHAT REAL TROUBLE IS? MOB RULE. THEY'LL BE HERE SOON. I CAN FEEL THEM GETTING CLOSER.
YOU DON'T WANT TO GET CAUGHT UP IN IT LIKE BARRY. IT'S NOT YOUR FIGHT.
C'MON-- LET'S GET OUTTA HERE BEFORE--
NO.
I'M STAYING HERE. DOING MY JOB.
FLASH DAMAGE
HOW COULD BARRY HAVE BEEN SO WRONG ABOUT YOU?
HE CAME LOOKING FOR YOU. PUT HIS LIFE ON THE LINE FOR HIS "FRIEND"--SACRIFICED HIMSELF FOR NOTHING!
HE'LL BE FINE. THEY KNOW WHAT HE MEANS TO ME.
NOBODY MEANS ANYTHING TO YOU!
YOU DON'T GIVE A DAMN ABOUT ANYTHING BUT YOURSELF.
SO WHY WOULD MOB RULE GIVE A DAMN ABOUT HIM?!
ALL BARRY WANTED WAS FOR YOU TO BE OKAY-- AND HE COULD BE LYING IN A POOL OF BLOOD FOR ALL WE KNOW. FIND SOME MEANING IN THAT!
IRON HEIGHTS PRISON.
"IN ANOTHER HARD-HITTING EXPOSÉ BY IRIS WEST, CAPTAIN COLD PUTS THE FLASH'S REPUTATION ON ICE!"
YEAH, RIGHT. SO MUCH FOR MY HEADLINE--
--INSTEAD OF CONFIRMING FLASH'S SUPER-BRUTALITY, THAT FRIGID FREAK TRAPS ME IN HERE! AND DURING A BLACKOUT, NO LESS!
GREAT. AND NOW YOU'RE TALKING TO YOURSELF--
HMM.

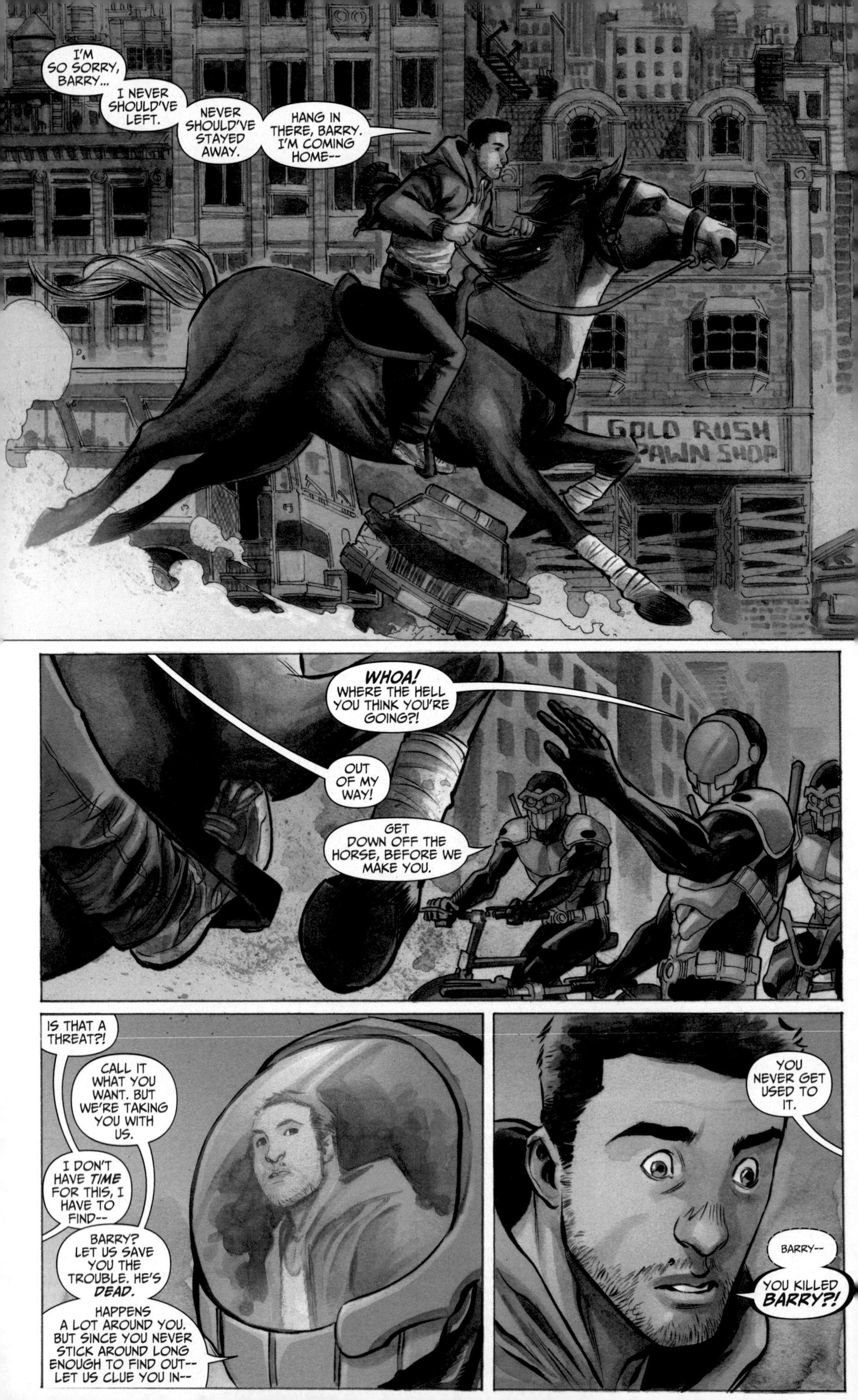
I'M SO SORRY, BARRY...
I NEVER SHOULD'VE LEFT.
NEVER SHOULD'VE STAYED AWAY.
HANG IN THERE, BARRY. I'M COMING HOME--
GOLD RUSH PAWN SHOP
WHOA! WHERE THE HELL YOU THINK YOU'RE GOING?!
OUT OF MY WAY!
GET DOWN OFF THE HORSE, BEFORE WE MAKE YOU.
IS THAT A THREAT?!
CALL IT WHAT YOU WANT. BUT WE'RE TAKING YOU WITH US.
I DON'T HAVE *TIME* FOR THIS, I HAVE TO FIND--
BARRY? LET US SAVE YOU THE TROUBLE. HE'S *DEAD*.
HAPPENS A LOT AROUND YOU. BUT SINCE YOU NEVER STICK AROUND LONG ENOUGH TO FIND OUT-- LET US CLUE YOU IN--
YOU NEVER GET USED TO IT.
BARRY--
YOU KILLED *BARRY?!*

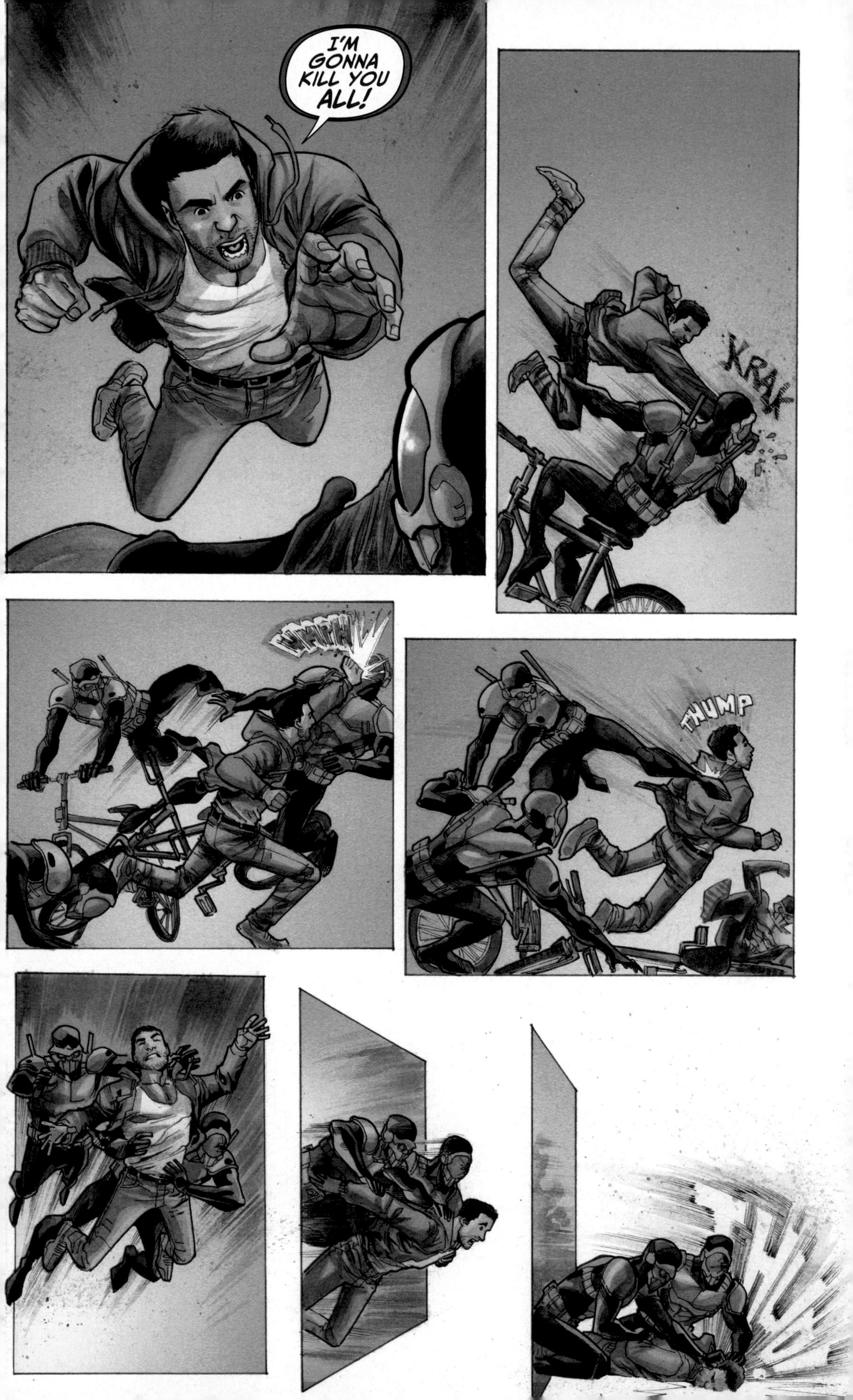
I'M GONNA KILL YOU ALL!
KRAK
THUMP

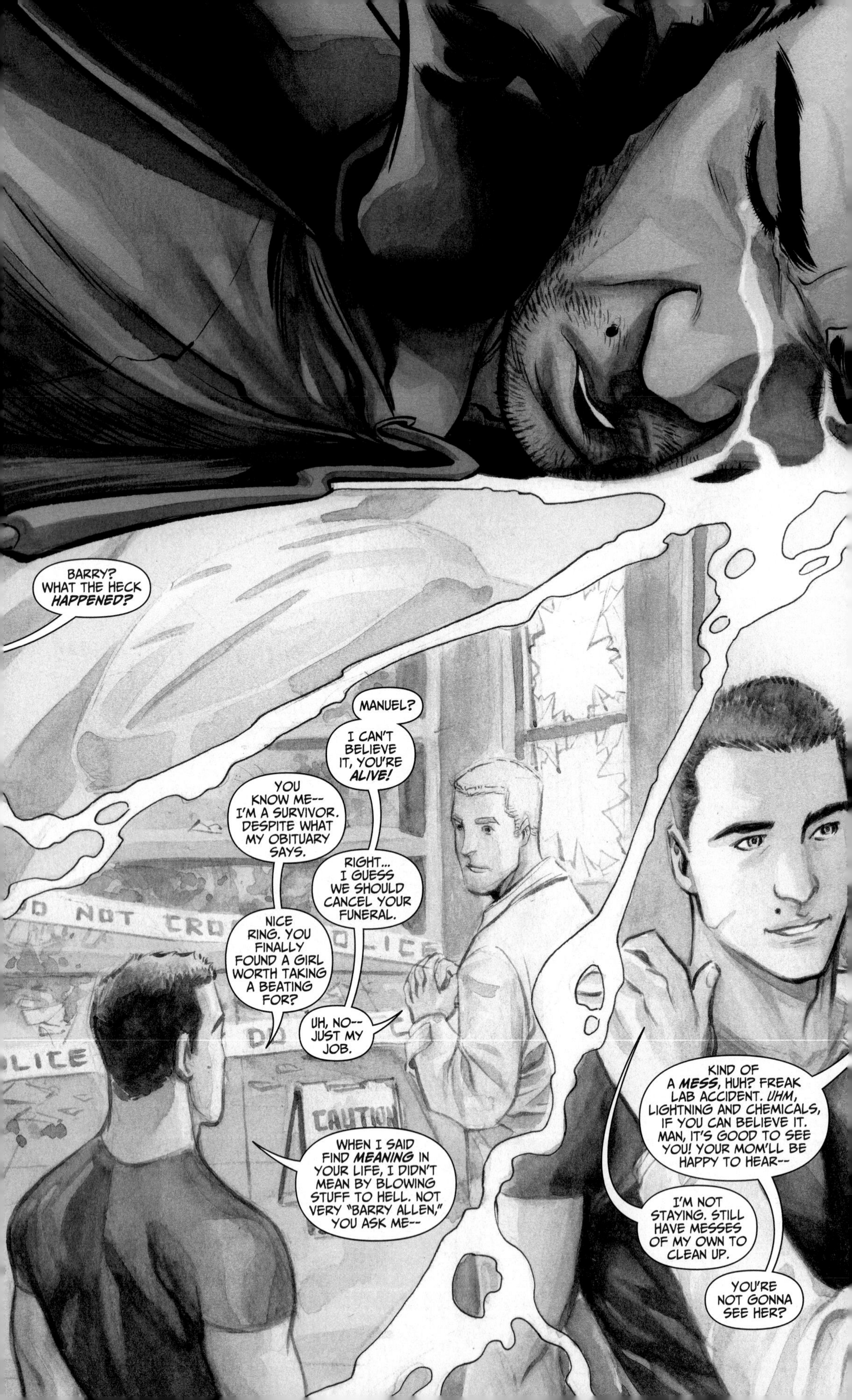
BARRY? WHAT THE HECK *HAPPENED?*
MANUEL?
I CAN'T BELIEVE IT, YOU'RE *ALIVE!*
YOU KNOW ME-- I'M A SURVIVOR. DESPITE WHAT MY OBITUARY SAYS.
RIGHT... I GUESS WE SHOULD CANCEL YOUR FUNERAL.
NICE RING. YOU FINALLY FOUND A GIRL WORTH TAKING A BEATING FOR?
UH, NO-- JUST MY JOB.
DO NOT CRO
POLICE
DO
POLICE
CAUTION
WHEN I SAID FIND *MEANING* IN YOUR LIFE, I DIDN'T MEAN BY BLOWING STUFF TO HELL. NOT VERY "BARRY ALLEN," YOU ASK ME--
KIND OF A *MESS*, HUH? FREAK LAB ACCIDENT. *UHM*, LIGHTNING AND CHEMICALS, IF YOU CAN BELIEVE IT. MAN, IT'S GOOD TO SEE YOU! YOUR MOM'LL BE HAPPY TO HEAR--
I'M NOT STAYING. STILL HAVE MESSES OF MY OWN TO CLEAN UP.
YOU'RE NOT GONNA SEE HER?

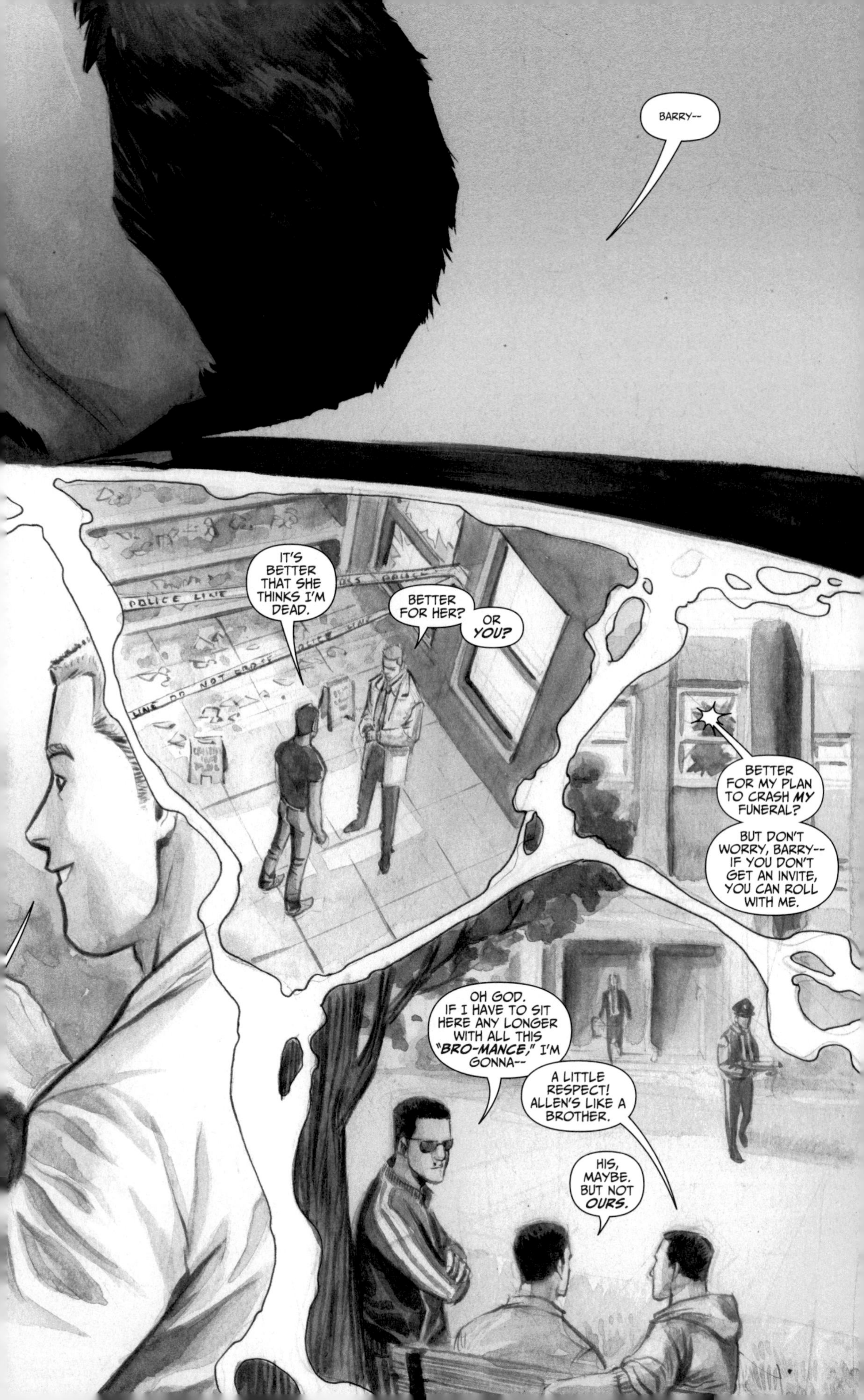
BARRY--
IT'S BETTER THAT SHE THINKS I'M DEAD.
BETTER FOR HER?
OR YOU?
BETTER FOR MY PLAN TO CRASH MY FUNERAL?
BUT DON'T WORRY, BARRY-- IF YOU DON'T GET AN INVITE, YOU CAN ROLL WITH ME.
OH GOD. IF I HAVE TO SIT HERE ANY LONGER WITH ALL THIS "BRO-MANCE," I'M GONNA--
A LITTLE RESPECT! ALLEN'S LIKE A BROTHER.
HIS, MAYBE. BUT NOT OURS.

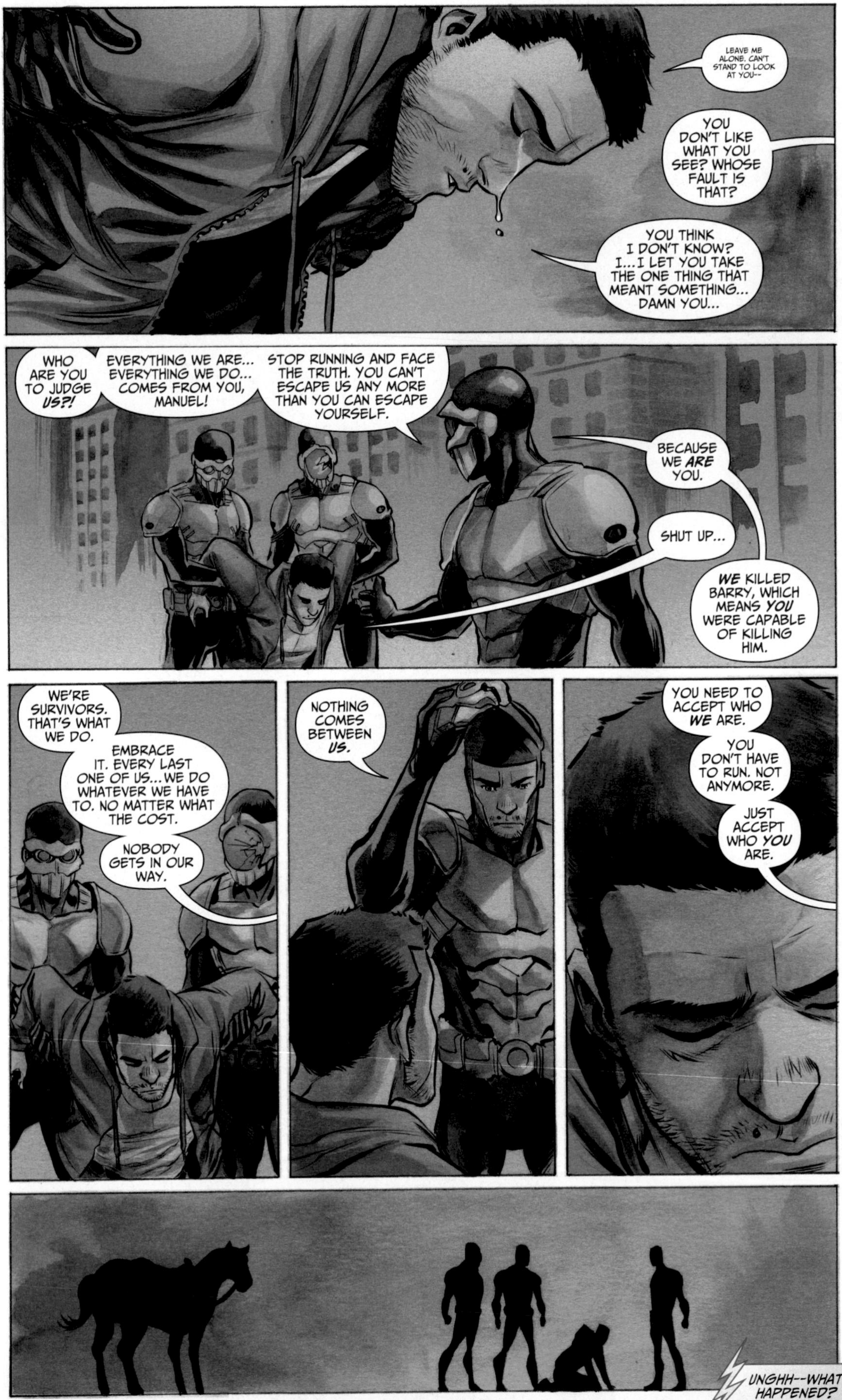
LEAVE ME ALONE. CAN'T STAND TO LOOK AT YOU--
YOU DON'T LIKE WHAT YOU SEE? WHOSE FAULT IS THAT?
YOU THINK I DON'T KNOW? I...I LET YOU TAKE THE ONE THING THAT MEANT SOMETHING... DAMN YOU...
WHO ARE YOU TO JUDGE US?!
EVERYTHING WE ARE... EVERYTHING WE DO... COMES FROM YOU, MANUEL!
STOP RUNNING AND FACE THE TRUTH. YOU CAN'T ESCAPE US ANY MORE THAN YOU CAN ESCAPE YOURSELF.
BECAUSE WE ARE YOU.
SHUT UP...
WE KILLED BARRY, WHICH MEANS YOU WERE CAPABLE OF KILLING HIM.
WE'RE SURVIVORS. THAT'S WHAT WE DO.
EMBRACE IT. EVERY LAST ONE OF US...WE DO WHATEVER WE HAVE TO. NO MATTER WHAT THE COST.
NOBODY GETS IN OUR WAY.
NOTHING COMES BETWEEN US.
YOU NEED TO ACCEPT WHO WE ARE.
YOU DON'T HAVE TO RUN. NOT ANYMORE.
JUST ACCEPT WHO YOU ARE.
UNGHH--WHAT HAPPENED?

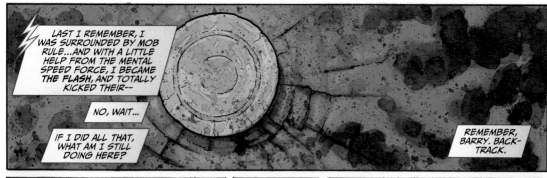

LAST I REMEMBER, I WAS SURROUNDED BY MOB RULE...AND WITH A LITTLE HELP FROM THE MENTAL SPEED FORCE, I BECAME THE FLASH, AND TOTALLY KICKED THEIR--

NO, WAIT...

IF I DID ALL THAT, WHAT AM I STILL DOING HERE?

REMEMBER, BARRY. BACK-TRACK.

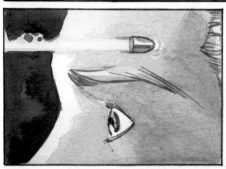

I REMEMBER... I ALMOST ATE A BULLET, THEN MY INSTINCTS KICKED IN.

LUCKILY, **SENSORY NEURONS** ARE AMAZING. THEY TAKE EXTERNAL STIMULI AND SEND SIGNALS TO MY CENTRAL NERVOUS SYSTEM.

THE SUPER-SPEED HELPS TOO. MY BODY SENDS PAIN MESSAGES TO MY BRAIN AT SUCH VELOCITY THAT THE **FEMTOSECOND** I FEEL SOMETHING, I WILL REACT.

I CAN FEEL THE SLIGHTEST CHANGES IN THE AIR PRESSURE AROUND ME... WHICH PRETTY MUCH MAKES ME **UNTOUCHABLE.**

HONESTLY, IT ALMOST NEVER COMES TO THAT BECAUSE EVEN A SPEEDING BULLET ISN'T FAST ENOUGH TO CATCH ME OFF GUARD.

THAT DOESN'T CHANGE THE FACT THAT I DON'T HAVE A HANDLE ON MY MENTAL ABILITIES...AND BECAUSE OF THAT I ALMOST **DIED.**

I GOT LOST IN MY THOUGHTS. I GOT LOST IN **PROBABILITIES.** I COULDN'T TELL THE DIFFERENCE BETWEEN WHAT I'D **DONE** AND WHAT I WAS **ABOUT TO DO.**

I FROZE.

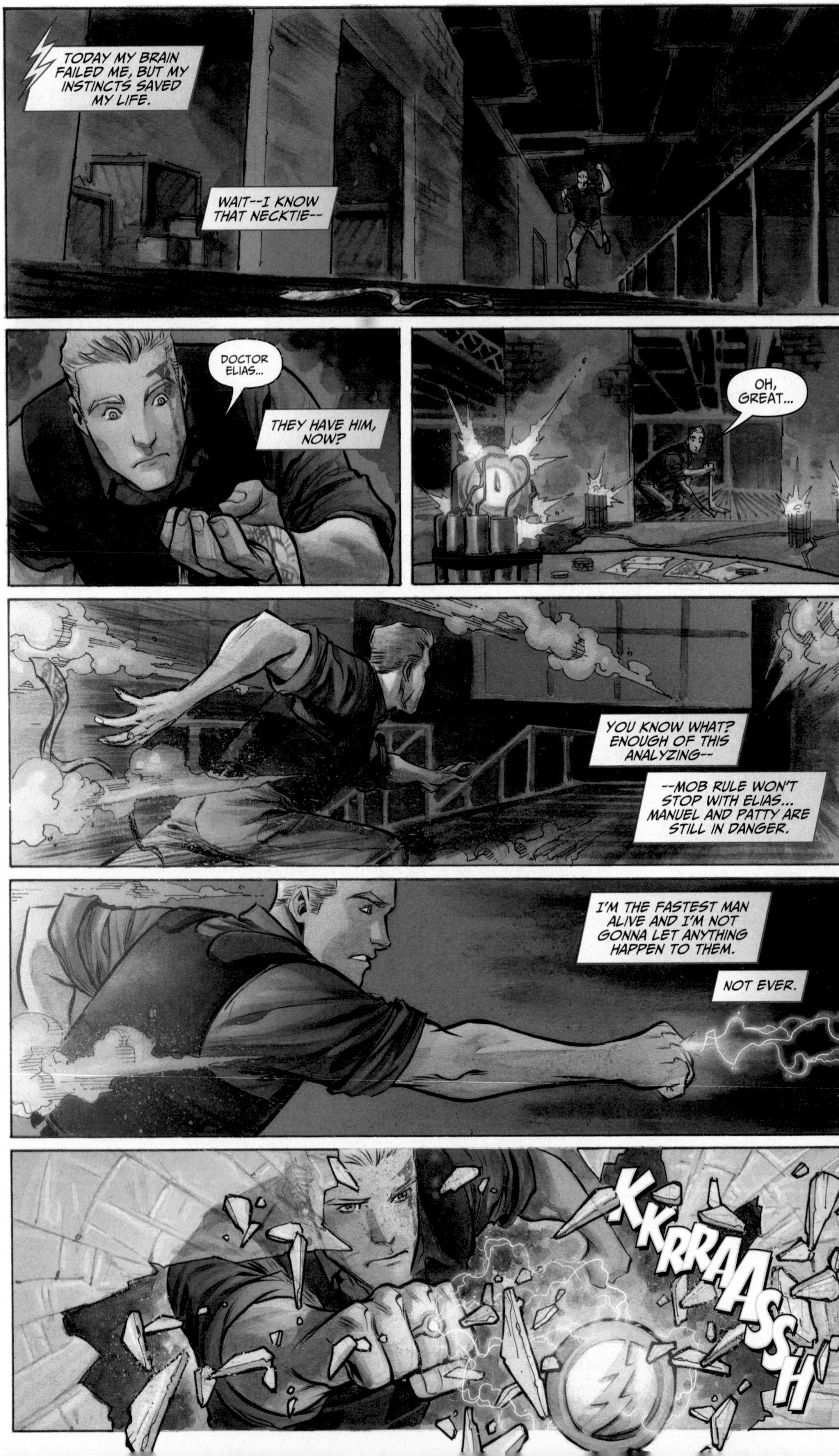
TODAY MY BRAIN FAILED ME, BUT MY INSTINCTS SAVED MY LIFE.
WAIT--I KNOW THAT NECKTIE--
DOCTOR ELIAS...
THEY HAVE HIM, NOW?
OH, GREAT...
YOU KNOW WHAT? ENOUGH OF THIS ANALYZING--
--MOB RULE WON'T STOP WITH ELIAS... MANUEL AND PATTY ARE STILL IN DANGER.
I'M THE FASTEST MAN ALIVE AND I'M NOT GONNA LET ANYTHING HAPPEN TO THEM.
NOT EVER.
KKRRAASSH

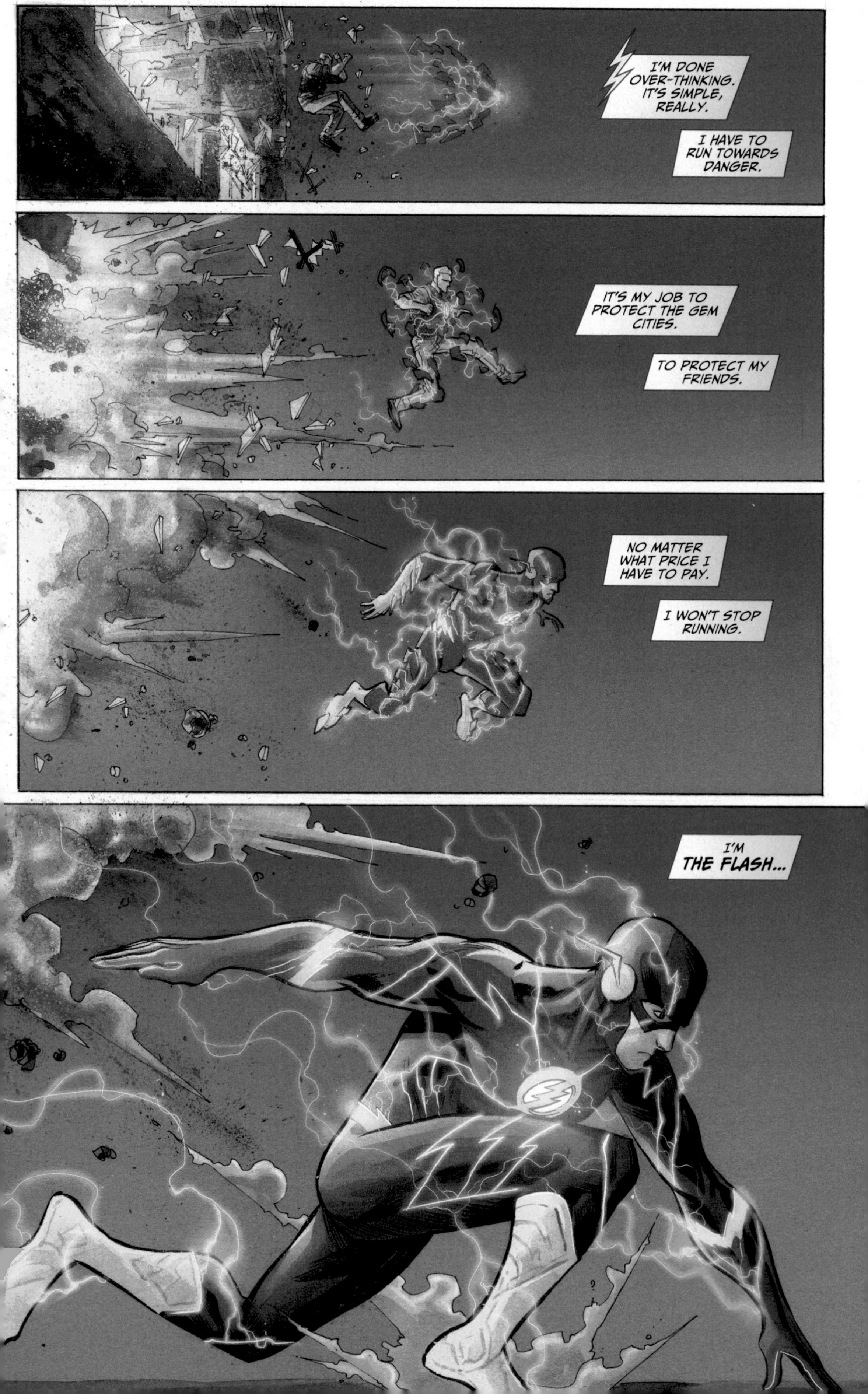
I'M DONE OVER-THINKING. IT'S SIMPLE, REALLY.
I HAVE TO RUN TOWARDS DANGER.
IT'S MY JOB TO PROTECT THE GEM CITIES.
TO PROTECT MY FRIENDS.
NO MATTER WHAT PRICE I HAVE TO PAY.
I WON'T STOP RUNNING.
I'M THE FLASH...

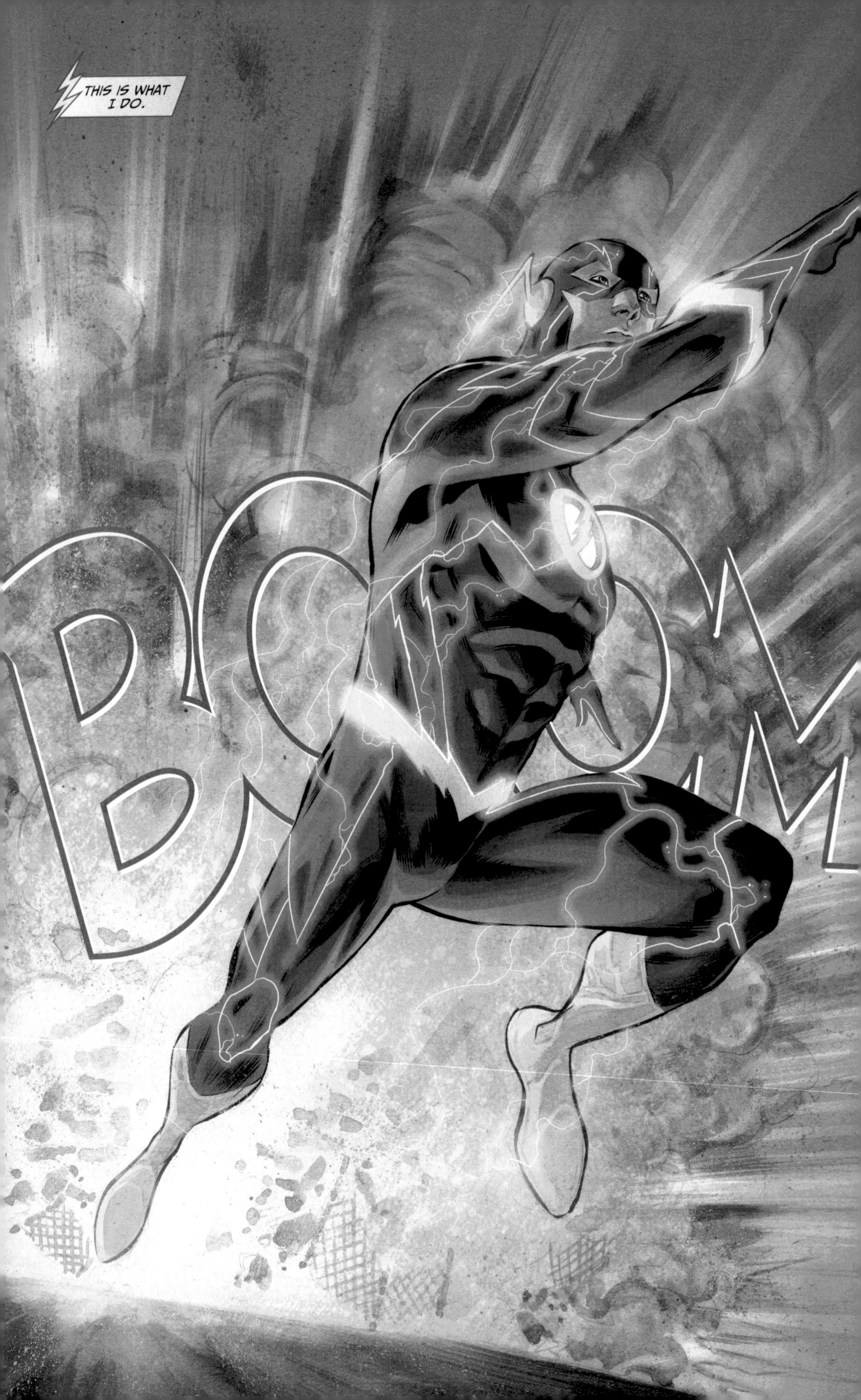
THIS IS WHAT I DO.
BOOM

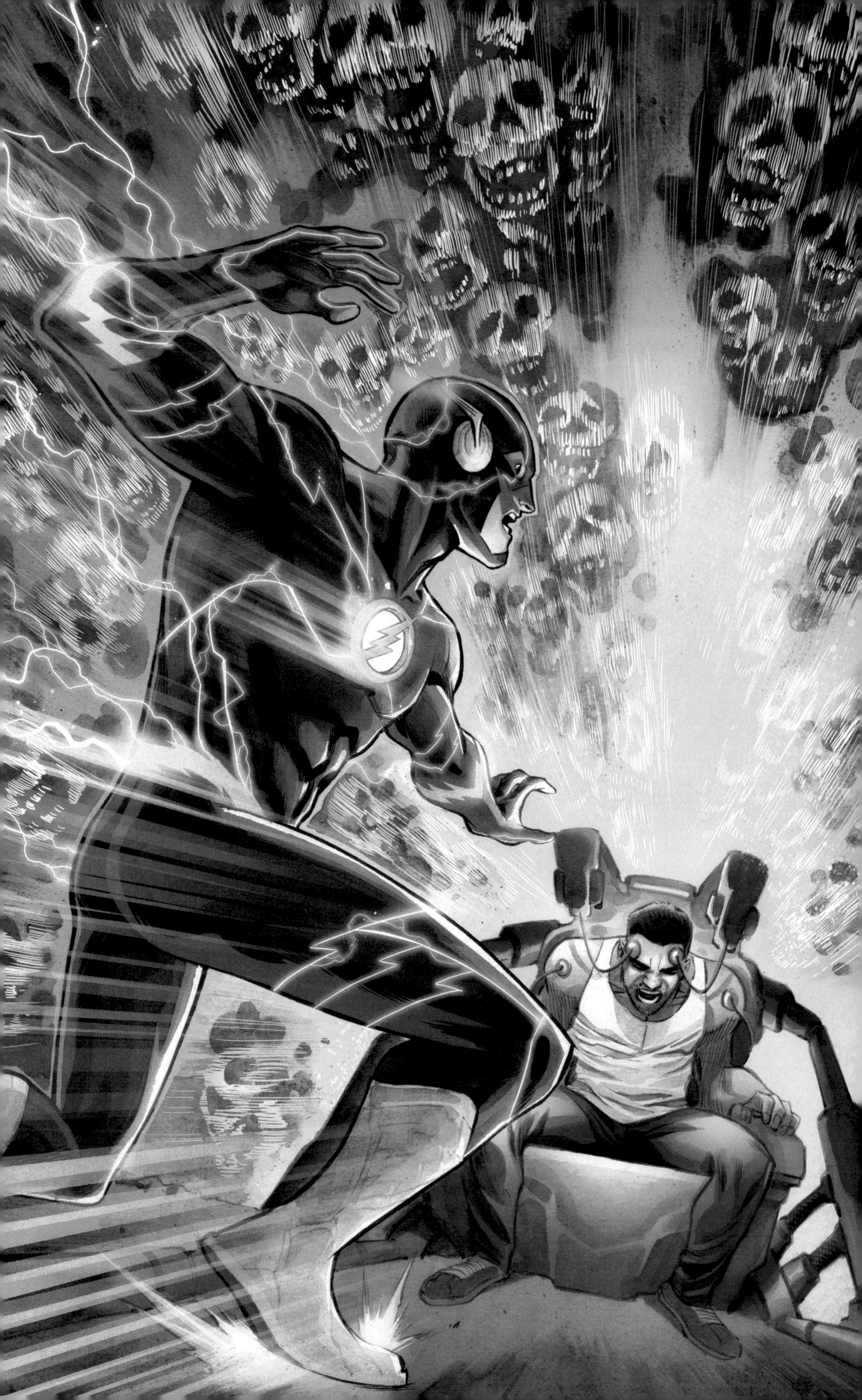

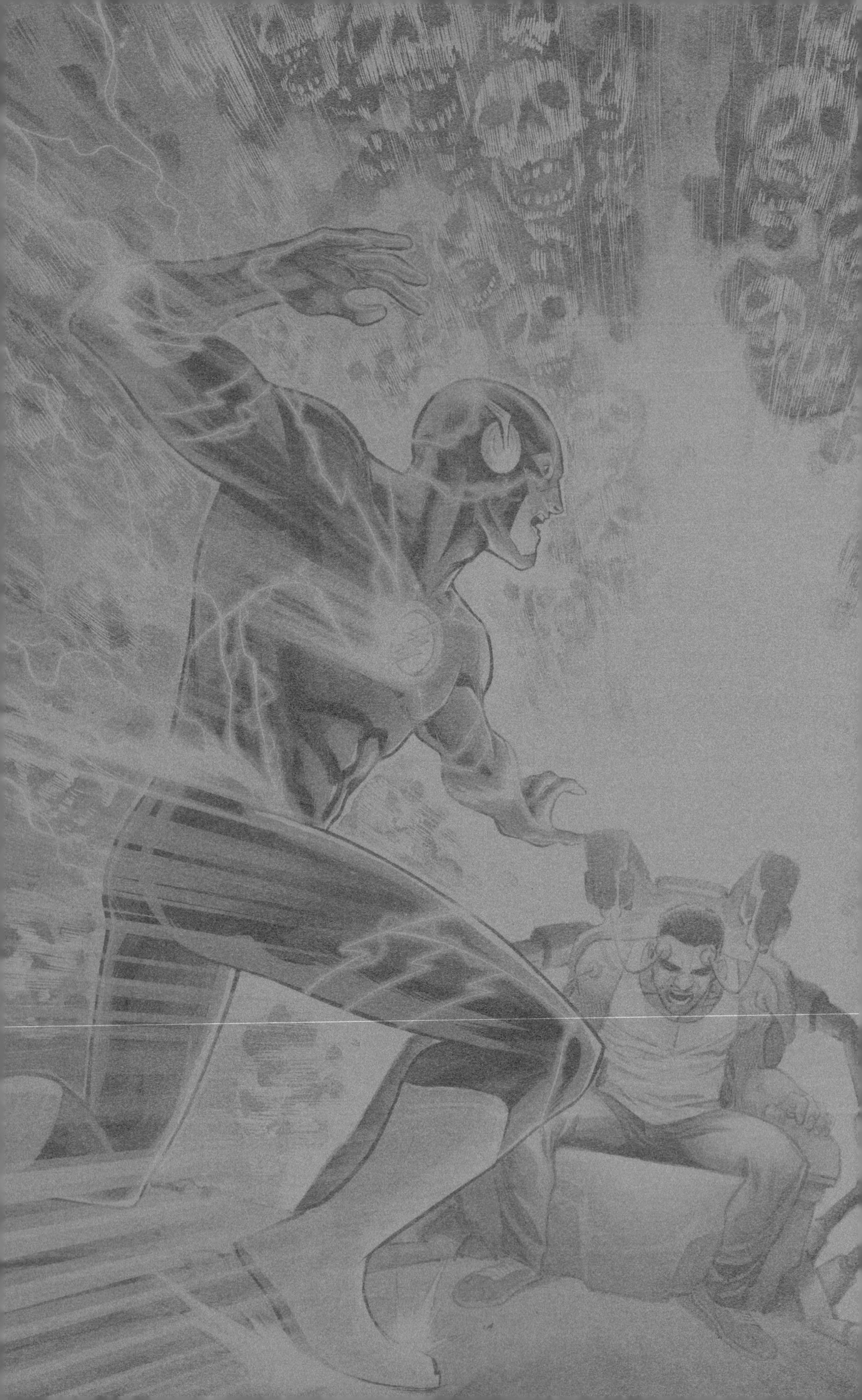

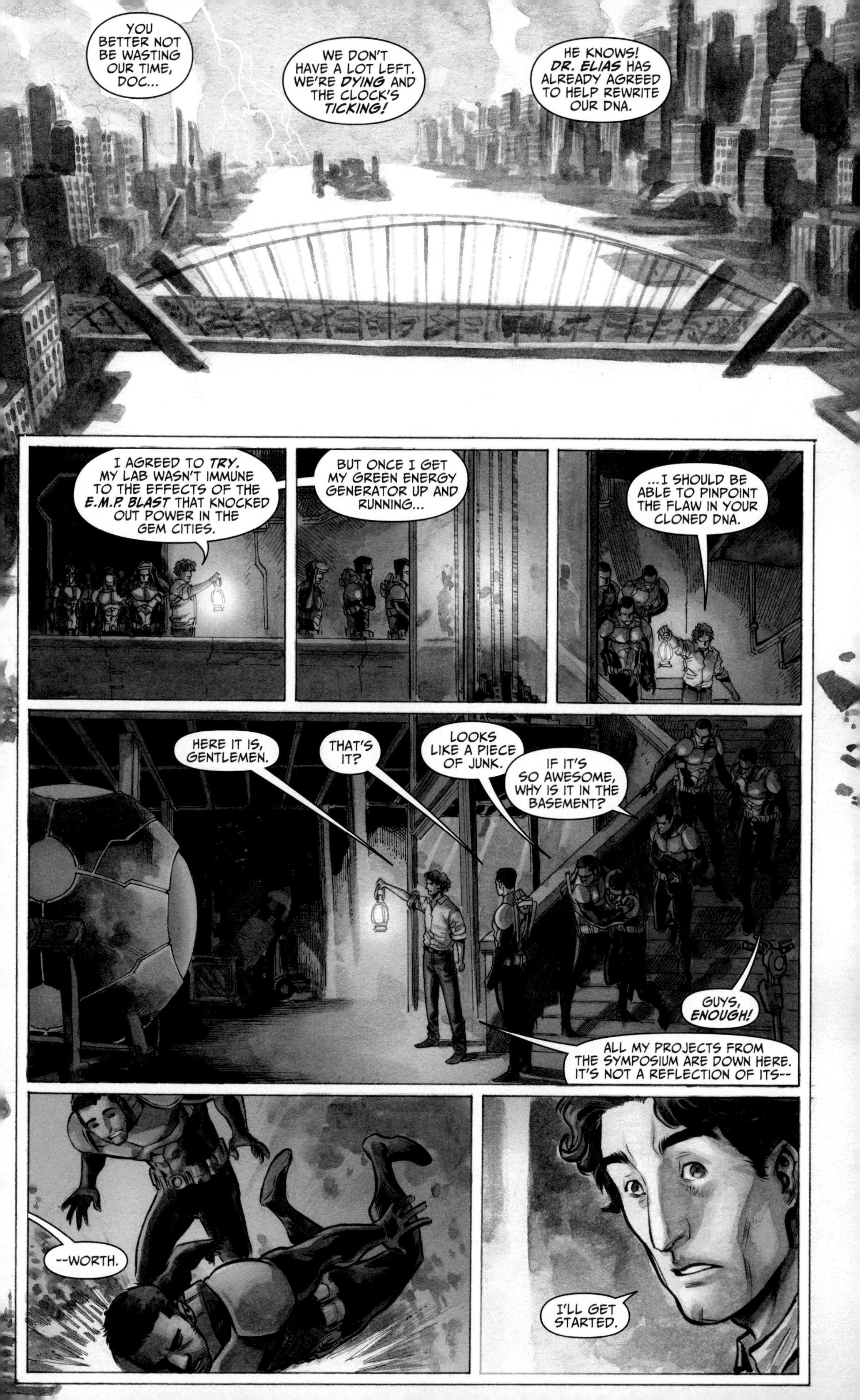
YOU BETTER NOT BE WASTING OUR TIME, DOC...
WE DON'T HAVE A LOT LEFT. WE'RE DYING AND THE CLOCK'S TICKING!
HE KNOWS! DR. ELIAS HAS ALREADY AGREED TO HELP REWRITE OUR DNA.
I AGREED TO TRY. MY LAB WASN'T IMMUNE TO THE EFFECTS OF THE E.M.P. BLAST THAT KNOCKED OUT POWER IN THE GEM CITIES.
BUT ONCE I GET MY GREEN ENERGY GENERATOR UP AND RUNNING...
...I SHOULD BE ABLE TO PINPOINT THE FLAW IN YOUR CLONED DNA.
HERE IT IS, GENTLEMEN.
THAT'S IT?
LOOKS LIKE A PIECE OF JUNK.
IF IT'S SO AWESOME, WHY IS IT IN THE BASEMENT?
GUYS, ENOUGH!
ALL MY PROJECTS FROM THE SYMPOSIUM ARE DOWN HERE. IT'S NOT A REFLECTION OF ITS--
--WORTH.
I'LL GET STARTED.

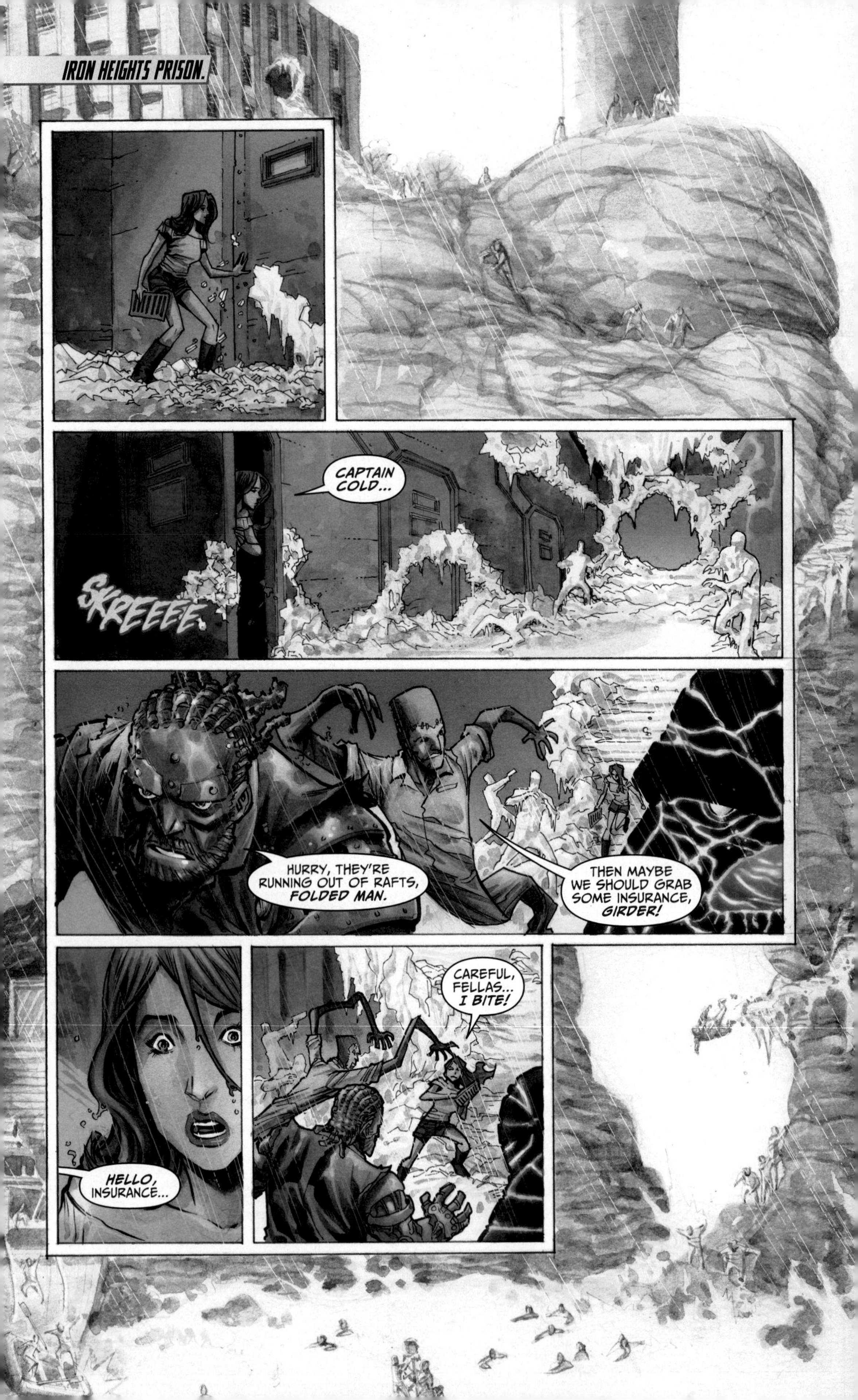
IRON HEIGHTS PRISON.
CAPTAIN COLD...
SKREEEEE
HURRY, THEY'RE RUNNING OUT OF RAFTS, FOLDED MAN.
THEN MAYBE WE SHOULD GRAB SOME INSURANCE, GIRDER!
HELLO, INSURANCE...
CAREFUL, FELLAS... I BITE!

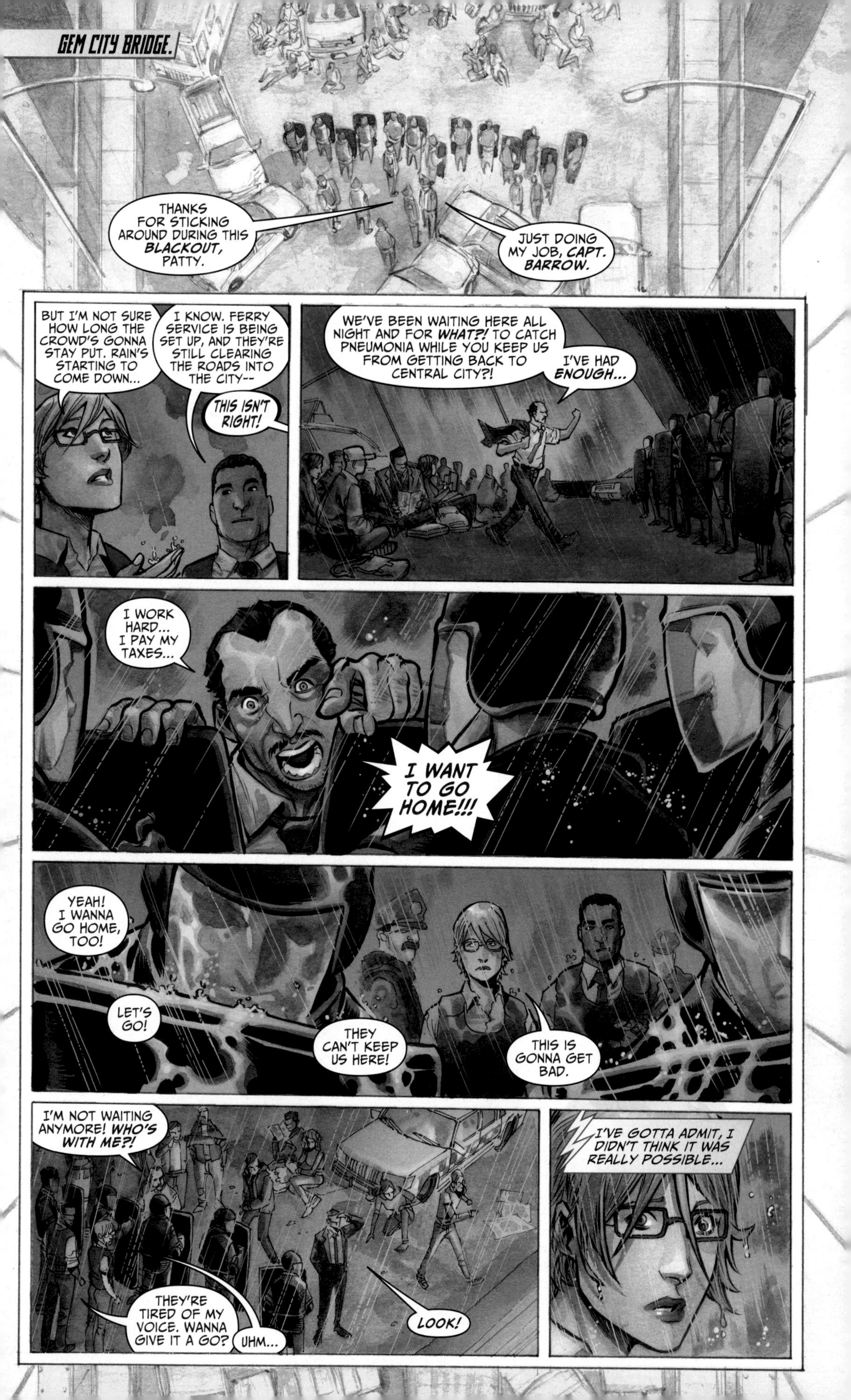
GEM CITY BRIDGE.
THANKS FOR STICKING AROUND DURING THIS BLACKOUT, PATTY.
JUST DOING MY JOB, CAPT. BARROW.
BUT I'M NOT SURE HOW LONG THE CROWD'S GONNA STAY PUT. RAIN'S STARTING TO COME DOWN...
I KNOW. FERRY SERVICE IS BEING SET UP, AND THEY'RE STILL CLEARING THE ROADS INTO THE CITY--
THIS ISN'T RIGHT!
WE'VE BEEN WAITING HERE ALL NIGHT AND FOR WHAT?! TO CATCH PNEUMONIA WHILE YOU KEEP US FROM GETTING BACK TO CENTRAL CITY?!
I'VE HAD ENOUGH...
I WORK HARD... I PAY MY TAXES...
I WANT TO GO HOME!!!
YEAH! I WANNA GO HOME, TOO!
LET'S GO!
THEY CAN'T KEEP US HERE!
THIS IS GONNA GET BAD.
I'M NOT WAITING ANYMORE! WHO'S WITH ME?!
THEY'RE TIRED OF MY VOICE. WANNA GIVE IT A GO?
UHM...
LOOK!
I'VE GOTTA ADMIT, I DIDN'T THINK IT WAS REALLY POSSIBLE...

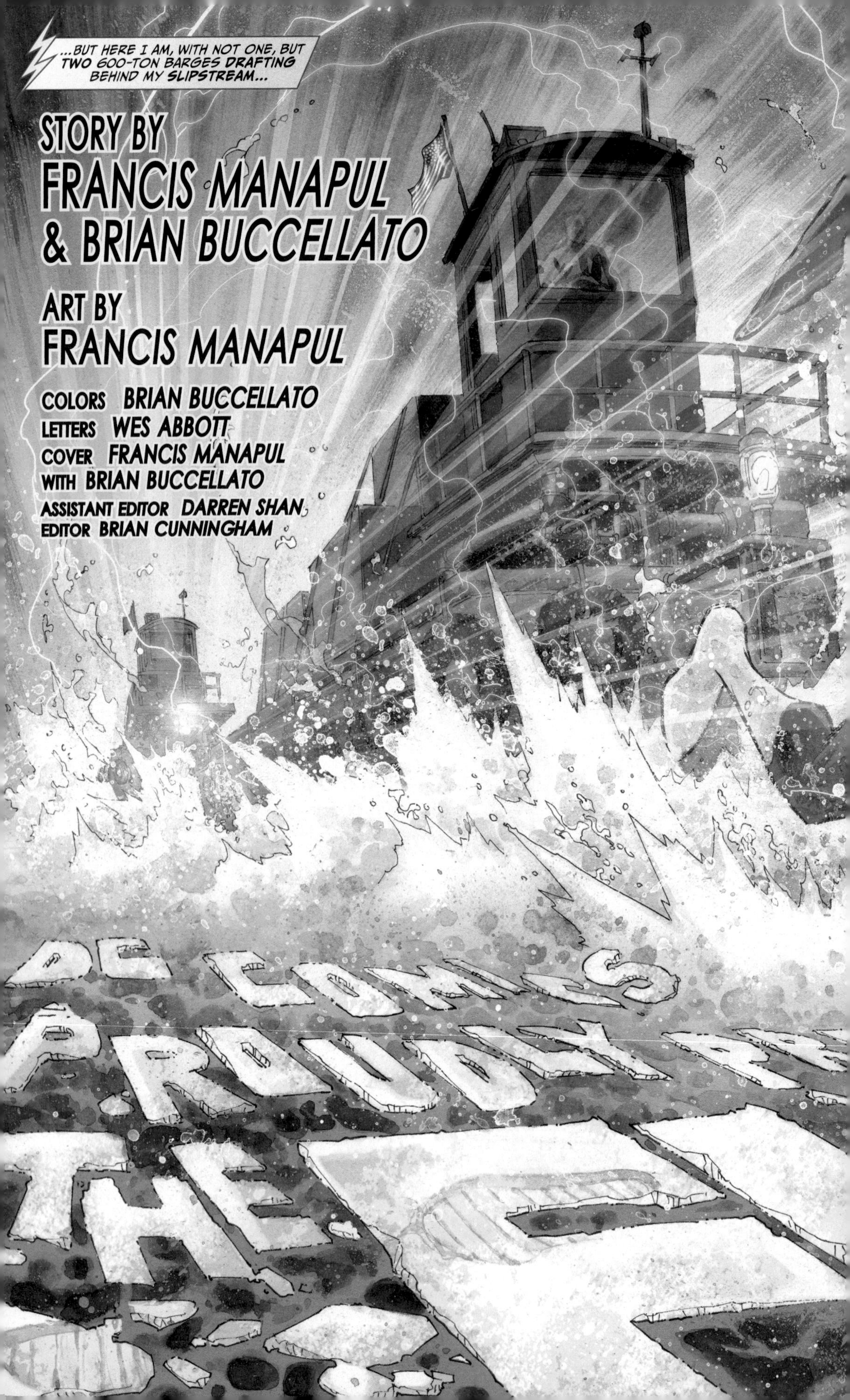
...BUT HERE I AM, WITH NOT ONE, BUT TWO 600-TON BARGES DRAFTING BEHIND MY SLIPSTREAM...
STORY BY FRANCIS MANAPUL & BRIAN BUCCELLATO
ART BY FRANCIS MANAPUL
COLORS BRIAN BUCCELLATO
LETTERS WES ABBOTT
COVER FRANCIS MANAPUL WITH BRIAN BUCCELLATO
ASSISTANT EDITOR DARREN SHAN
EDITOR BRIAN CUNNINGHAM
DC COMICS
PROUDLY
THE

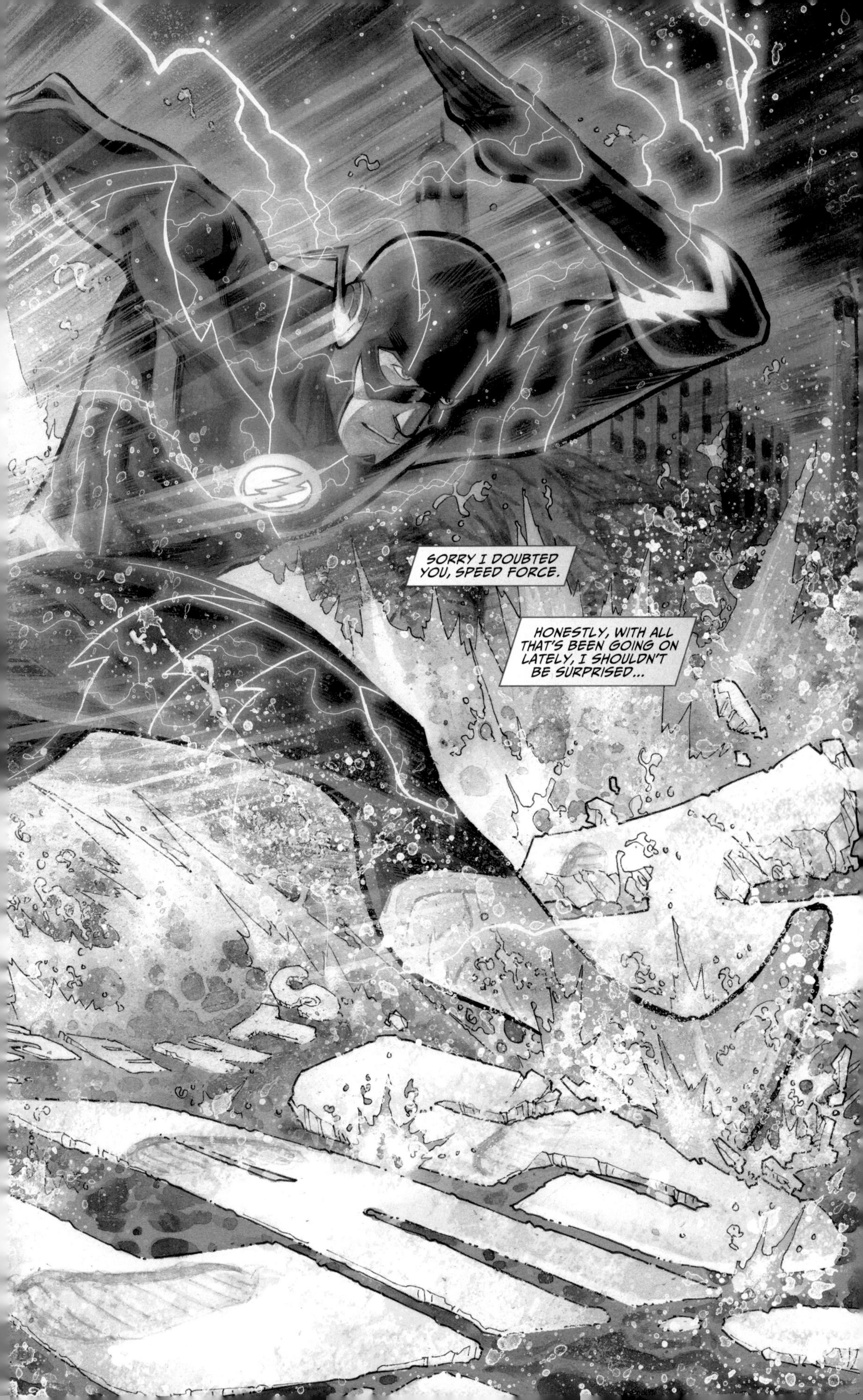
SORRY I DOUBTED YOU, SPEED FORCE.
HONESTLY, WITH ALL THAT'S BEEN GOING ON LATELY, I SHOULDN'T BE SURPRISED...

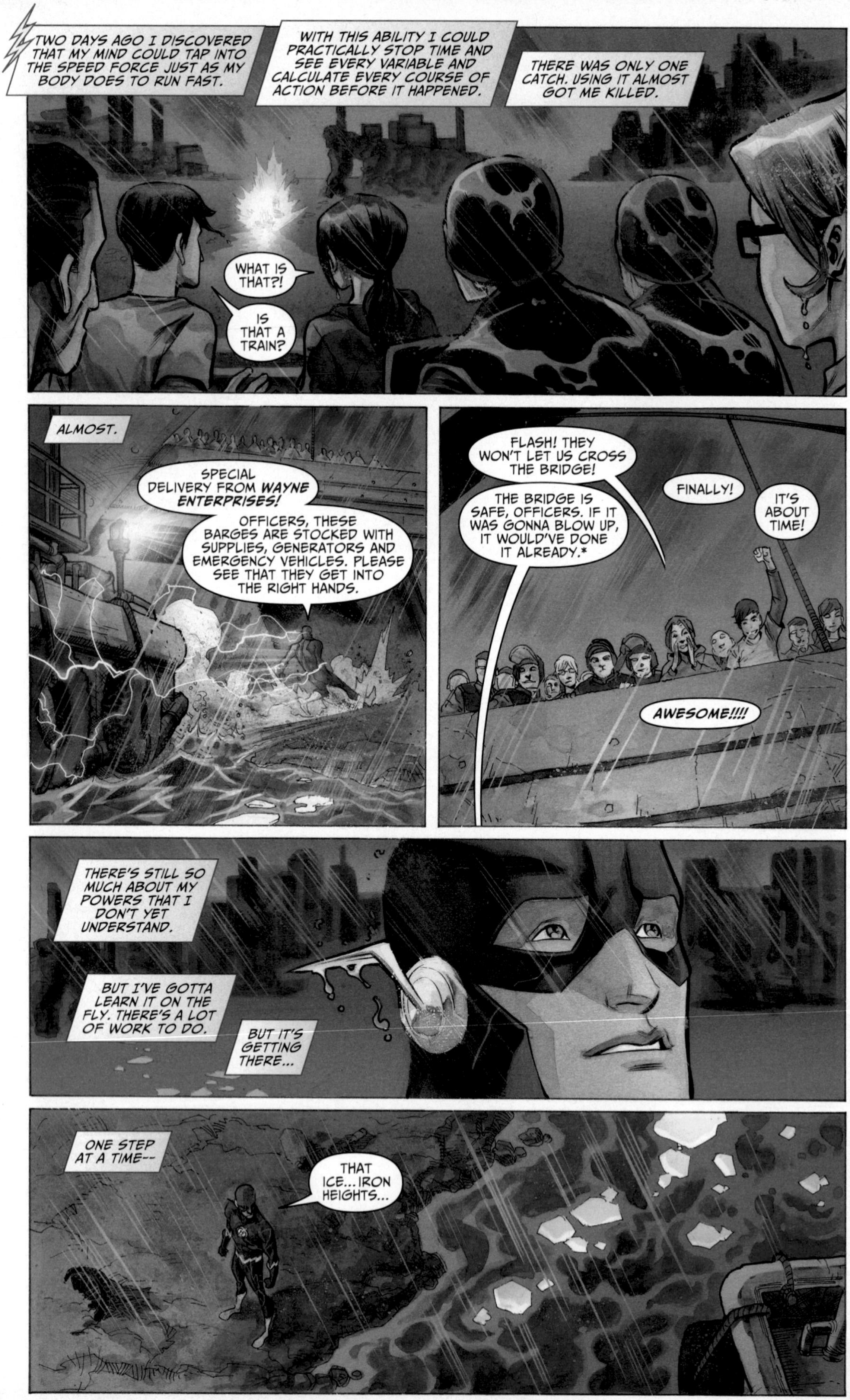
TWO DAYS AGO I DISCOVERED THAT MY MIND COULD TAP INTO THE SPEED FORCE JUST AS MY BODY DOES TO RUN FAST.
WITH THIS ABILITY I COULD PRACTICALLY STOP TIME AND SEE EVERY VARIABLE AND CALCULATE EVERY COURSE OF ACTION BEFORE IT HAPPENED.
THERE WAS ONLY ONE CATCH. USING IT ALMOST GOT ME KILLED.
WHAT IS THAT?!
IS THAT A TRAIN?
ALMOST.
SPECIAL DELIVERY FROM WAYNE ENTERPRISES!
OFFICERS, THESE BARGES ARE STOCKED WITH SUPPLIES, GENERATORS AND EMERGENCY VEHICLES. PLEASE SEE THAT THEY GET INTO THE RIGHT HANDS.
FLASH! THEY WON'T LET US CROSS THE BRIDGE!
THE BRIDGE IS SAFE, OFFICERS. IF IT WAS GONNA BLOW UP, IT WOULD'VE DONE IT ALREADY.*
FINALLY!
IT'S ABOUT TIME!
AWESOME!!!!
THERE'S STILL SO MUCH ABOUT MY POWERS THAT I DON'T YET UNDERSTAND.
BUT I'VE GOTTA LEARN IT ON THE FLY. THERE'S A LOT OF WORK TO DO.
BUT IT'S GETTING THERE...
ONE STEP AT A TIME--
THAT ICE... IRON HEIGHTS...

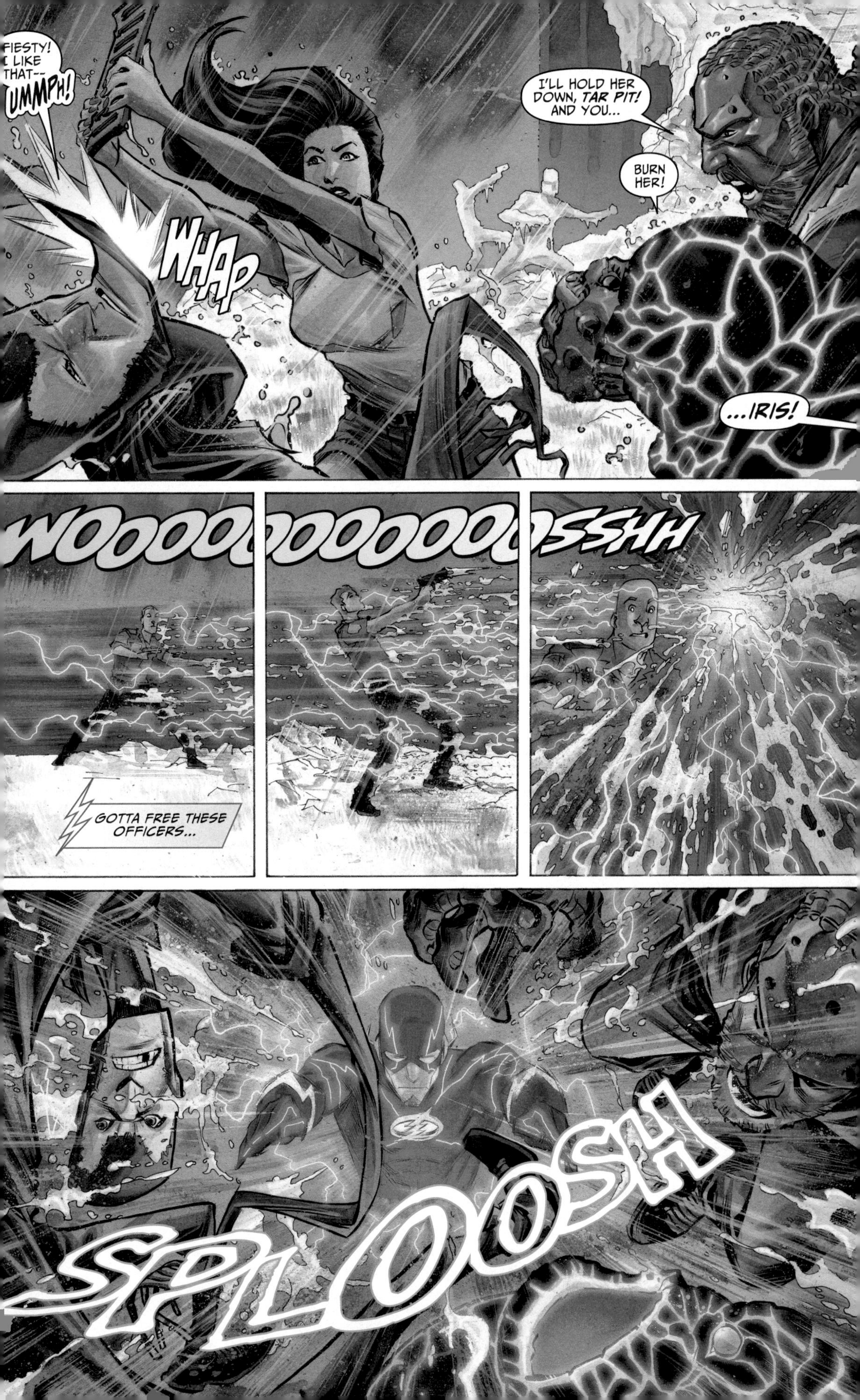
FIESTY! I LIKE THAT--
UMMPH!
WHAP
I'LL HOLD HER DOWN, TAR PIT! AND YOU...
BURN HER!
...IRIS!
WOOOOOOOOOOOOSSHH
GOTTA FREE THESE OFFICERS...
SPLOOSH

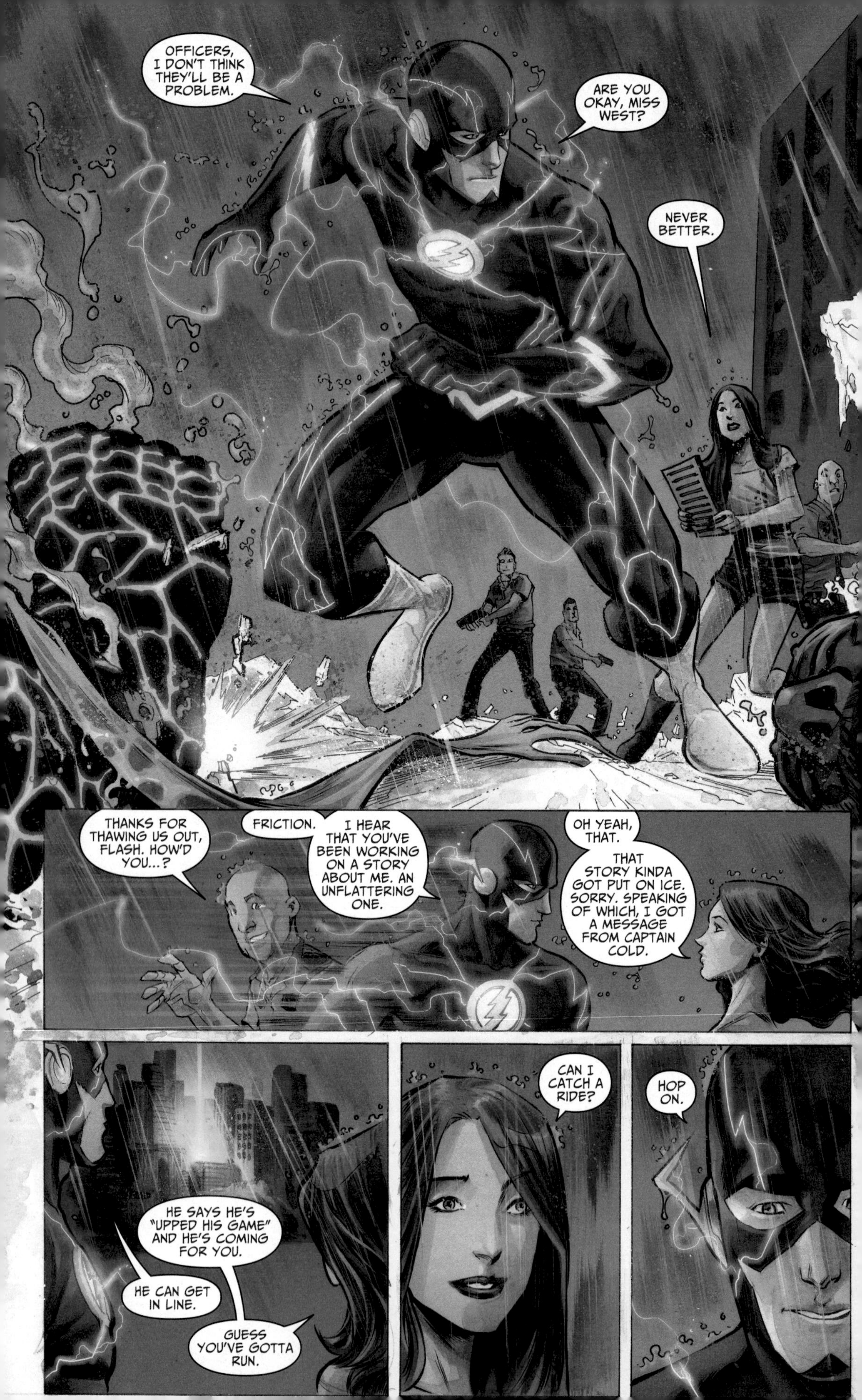

OFFICERS, I DON'T THINK THEY'LL BE A PROBLEM.
ARE YOU OKAY, MISS WEST?
NEVER BETTER.
THANKS FOR THAWING US OUT, FLASH. HOW'D YOU...?
FRICTION.
I HEAR THAT YOU'VE BEEN WORKING ON A STORY ABOUT ME. AN UNFLATTERING ONE.
OH YEAH, THAT.
THAT STORY KINDA GOT PUT ON ICE. SORRY. SPEAKING OF WHICH, I GOT A MESSAGE FROM CAPTAIN COLD.
HE SAYS HE'S "UPPED HIS GAME" AND HE'S COMING FOR YOU.
HE CAN GET IN LINE.
GUESS YOU'VE GOTTA RUN.
CAN I CATCH A RIDE?
HOP ON.

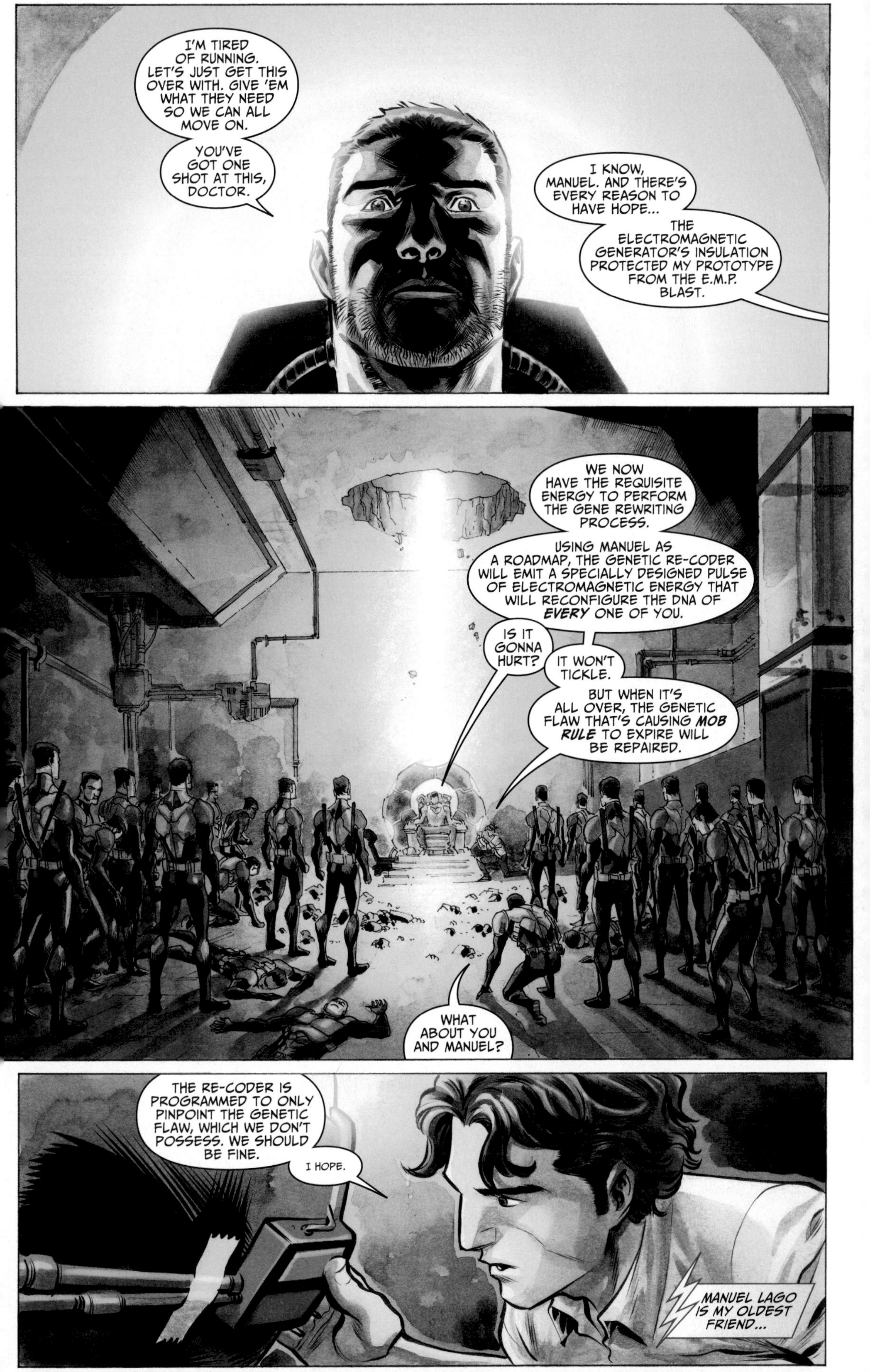
I'M TIRED OF RUNNING. LET'S JUST GET THIS OVER WITH. GIVE 'EM WHAT THEY NEED SO WE CAN ALL MOVE ON.
YOU'VE GOT ONE SHOT AT THIS, DOCTOR.
I KNOW, MANUEL. AND THERE'S EVERY REASON TO HAVE HOPE...
THE ELECTROMAGNETIC GENERATOR'S INSULATION PROTECTED MY PROTOTYPE FROM THE E.M.P. BLAST.
WE NOW HAVE THE REQUISITE ENERGY TO PERFORM THE GENE REWRITING PROCESS.
USING MANUEL AS A ROADMAP, THE GENETIC RE-CODER WILL EMIT A SPECIALLY DESIGNED PULSE OF ELECTROMAGNETIC ENERGY THAT WILL RECONFIGURE THE DNA OF *EVERY* ONE OF YOU.
IS IT GONNA HURT?
IT WON'T TICKLE.
BUT WHEN IT'S ALL OVER, THE GENETIC FLAW THAT'S CAUSING *MOB RULE* TO EXPIRE WILL BE REPAIRED.
WHAT ABOUT YOU AND MANUEL?
THE RE-CODER IS PROGRAMMED TO ONLY PINPOINT THE GENETIC FLAW, WHICH WE DON'T POSSESS. WE SHOULD BE FINE.
I HOPE.
MANUEL LAGO IS MY OLDEST FRIEND...

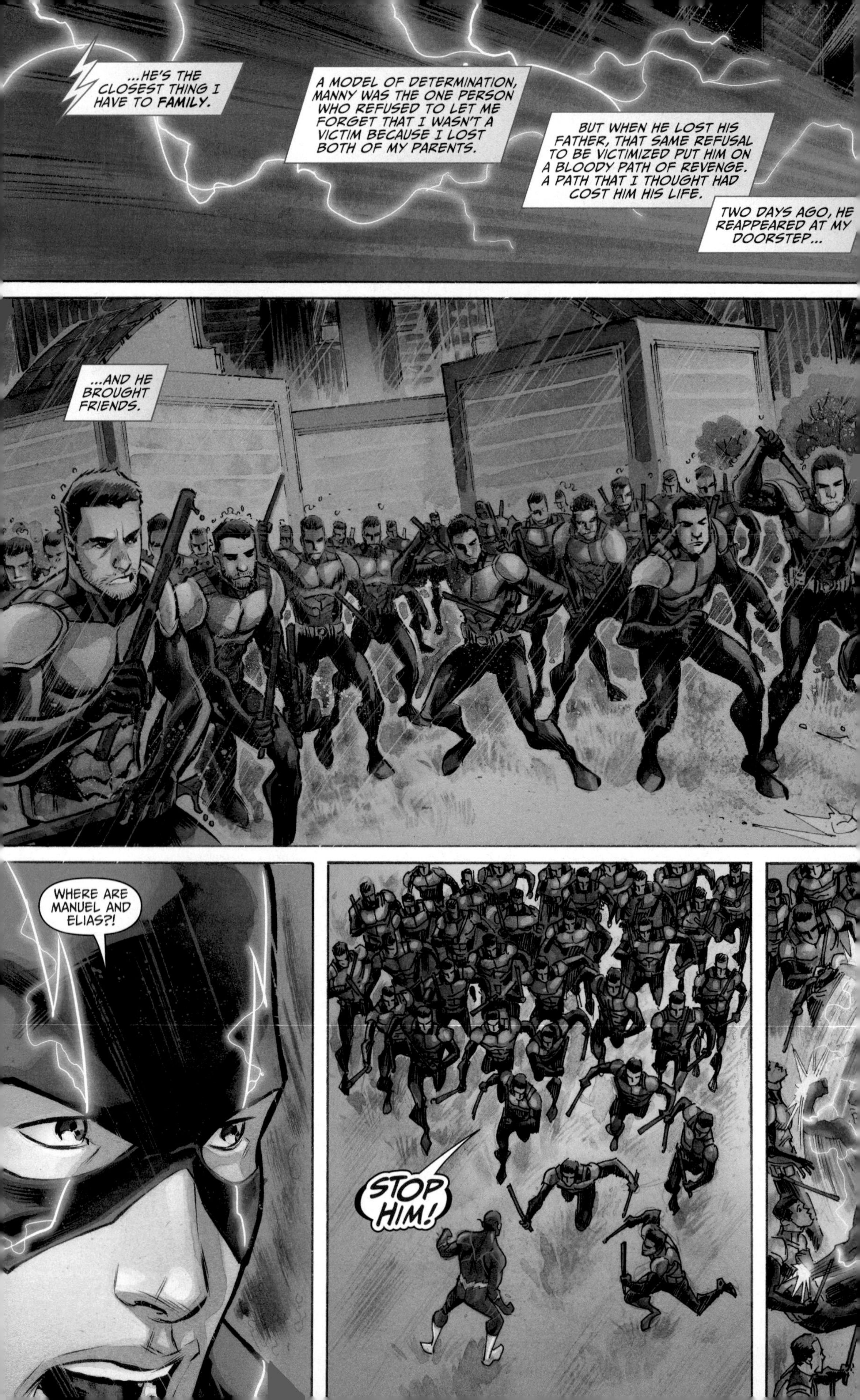
...HE'S THE CLOSEST THING I HAVE TO FAMILY.
A MODEL OF DETERMINATION, MANNY WAS THE ONE PERSON WHO REFUSED TO LET ME FORGET THAT I WASN'T A VICTIM BECAUSE I LOST BOTH OF MY PARENTS.
BUT WHEN HE LOST HIS FATHER, THAT SAME REFUSAL TO BE VICTIMIZED PUT HIM ON A BLOODY PATH OF REVENGE. A PATH THAT I THOUGHT HAD COST HIM HIS LIFE.
TWO DAYS AGO, HE REAPPEARED AT MY DOORSTEP...
...AND HE BROUGHT FRIENDS.
WHERE ARE MANUEL AND ELIAS?!
STOP HIM!

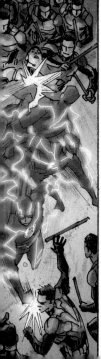

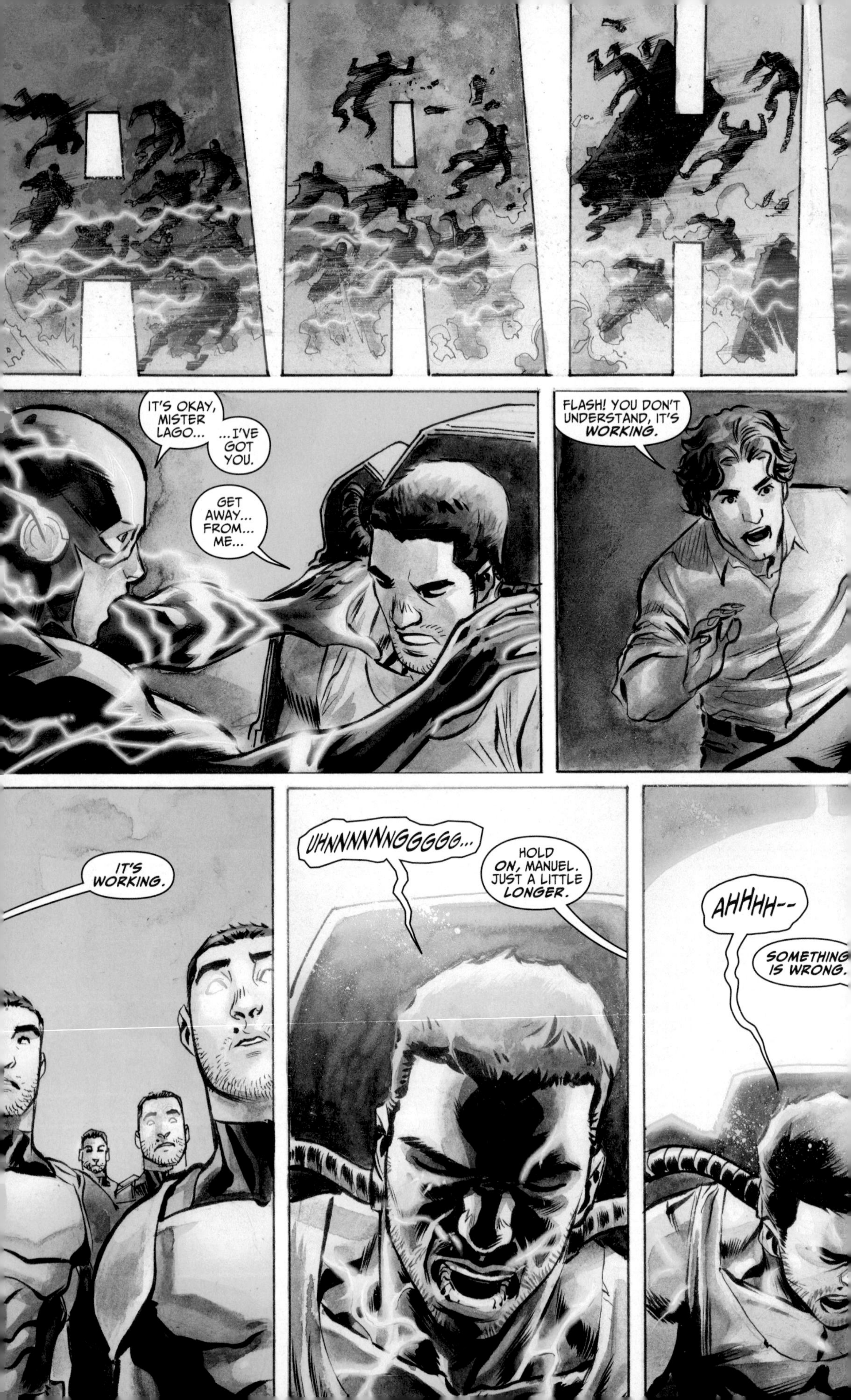
IT'S OKAY, MISTER LAGO...
...I'VE GOT YOU.
GET AWAY... FROM... ME...
FLASH! YOU DON'T UNDERSTAND, IT'S WORKING.
IT'S WORKING.
UHNNNNNNGGGGG...
HOLD ON, MANUEL. JUST A LITTLE LONGER.
AHHHH--
SOMETHING IS WRONG.

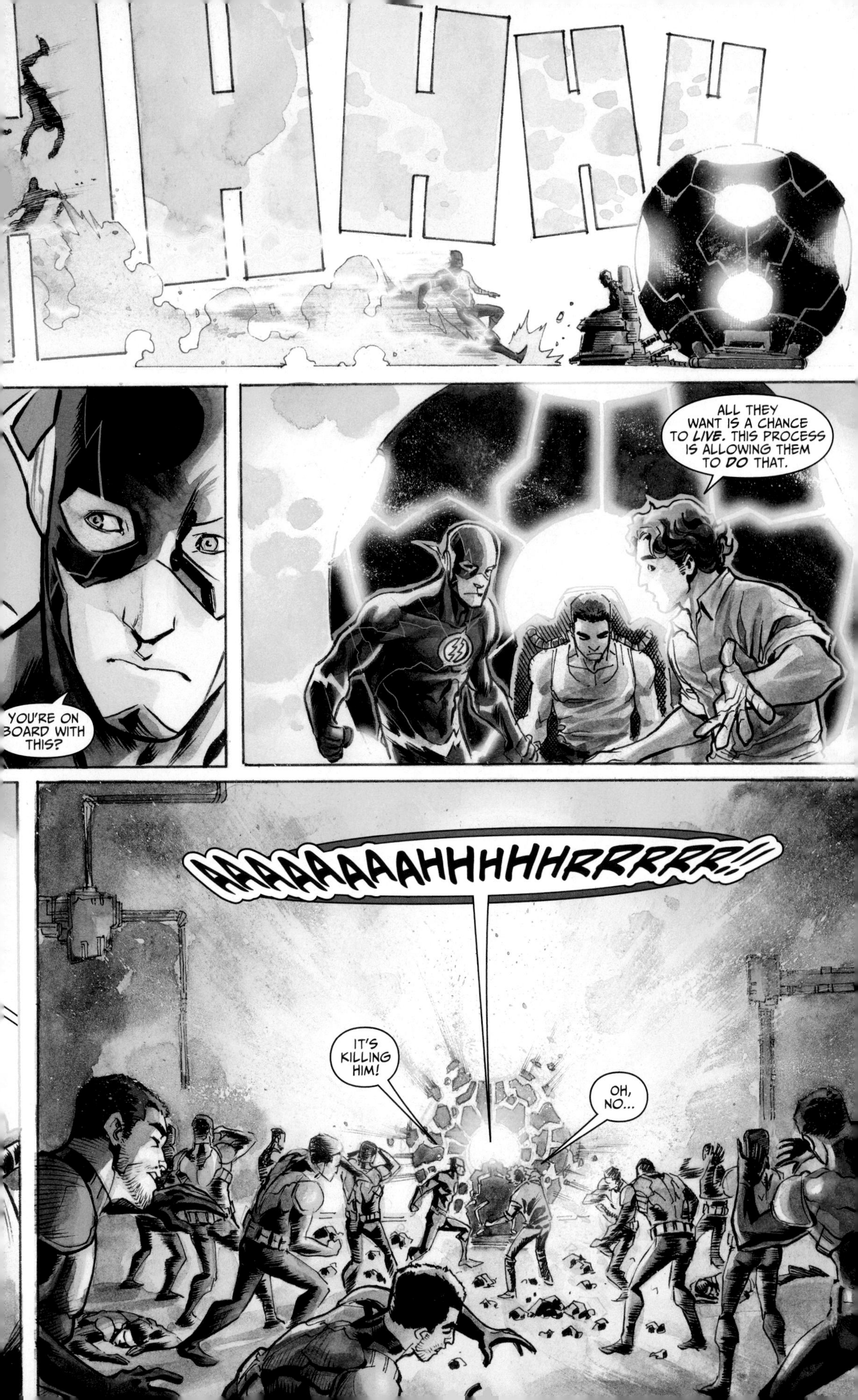
YOU'RE ON BOARD WITH THIS?
ALL THEY WANT IS A CHANCE TO LIVE. THIS PROCESS IS ALLOWING THEM TO DO THAT.
AAAAAAAAAHHHHHRRRRRR!!
IT'S KILLING HIM!
OH, NO...

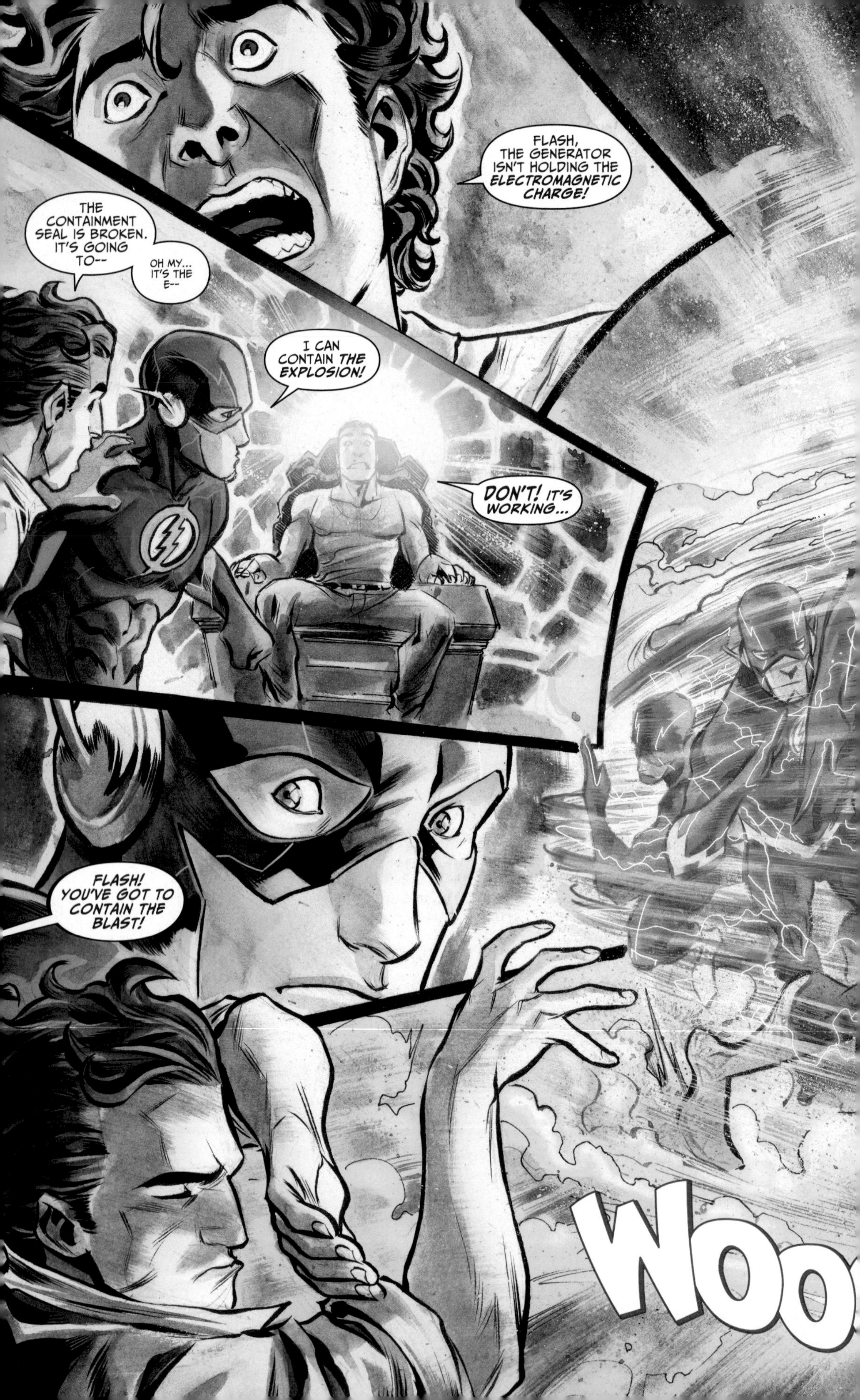
FLASH, THE GENERATOR ISN'T HOLDING THE ELECTROMAGNETIC CHARGE!
THE CONTAINMENT SEAL IS BROKEN. IT'S GOING TO--
OH MY... IT'S THE E--
I CAN CONTAIN THE EXPLOSION!
DON'T! IT'S WORKING...
FLASH! YOU'VE GOT TO CONTAIN THE BLAST!
WOO

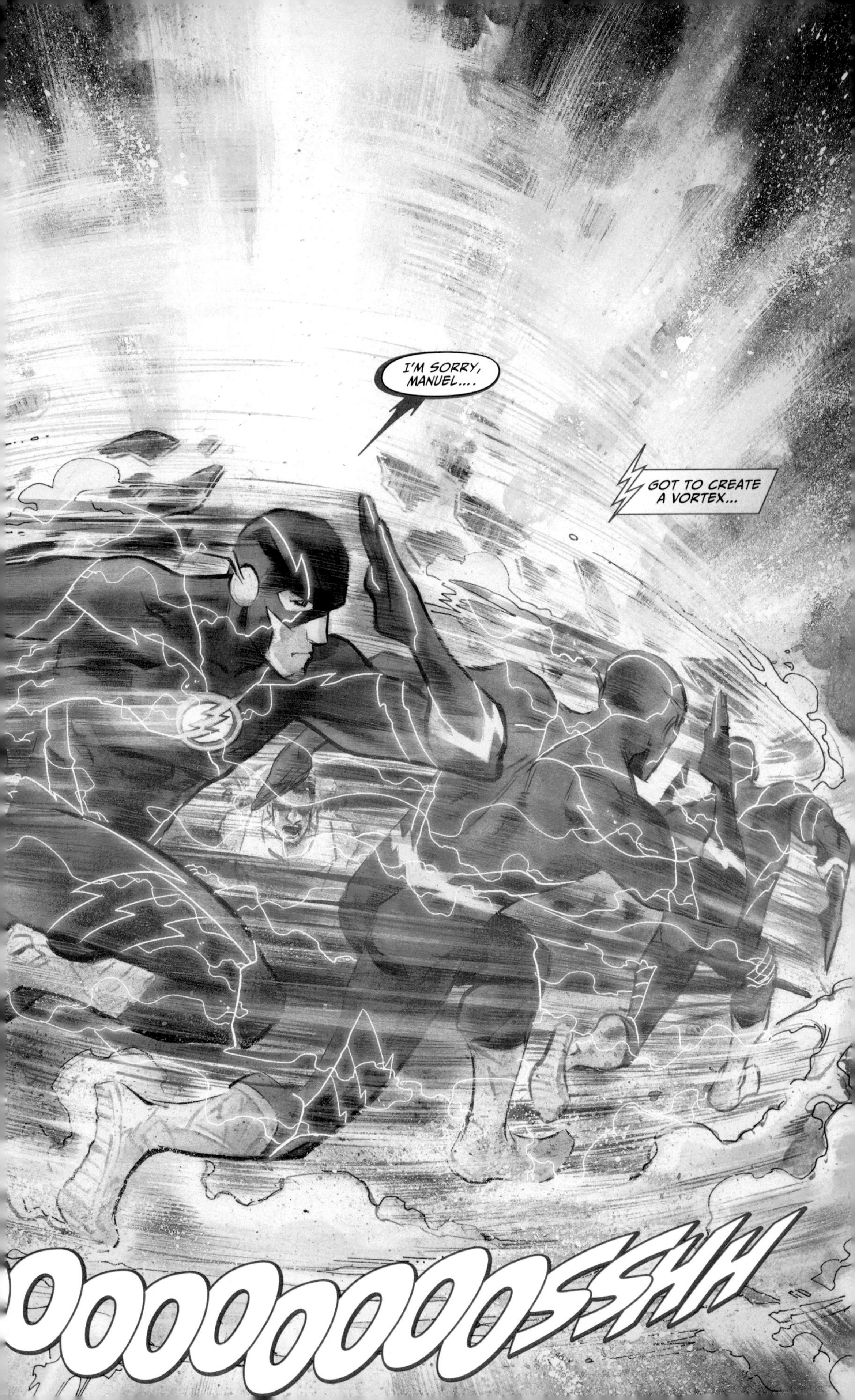
I'M SORRY, MANUEL....
GOT TO CREATE A VORTEX...
OOOOOOOOOSSHH

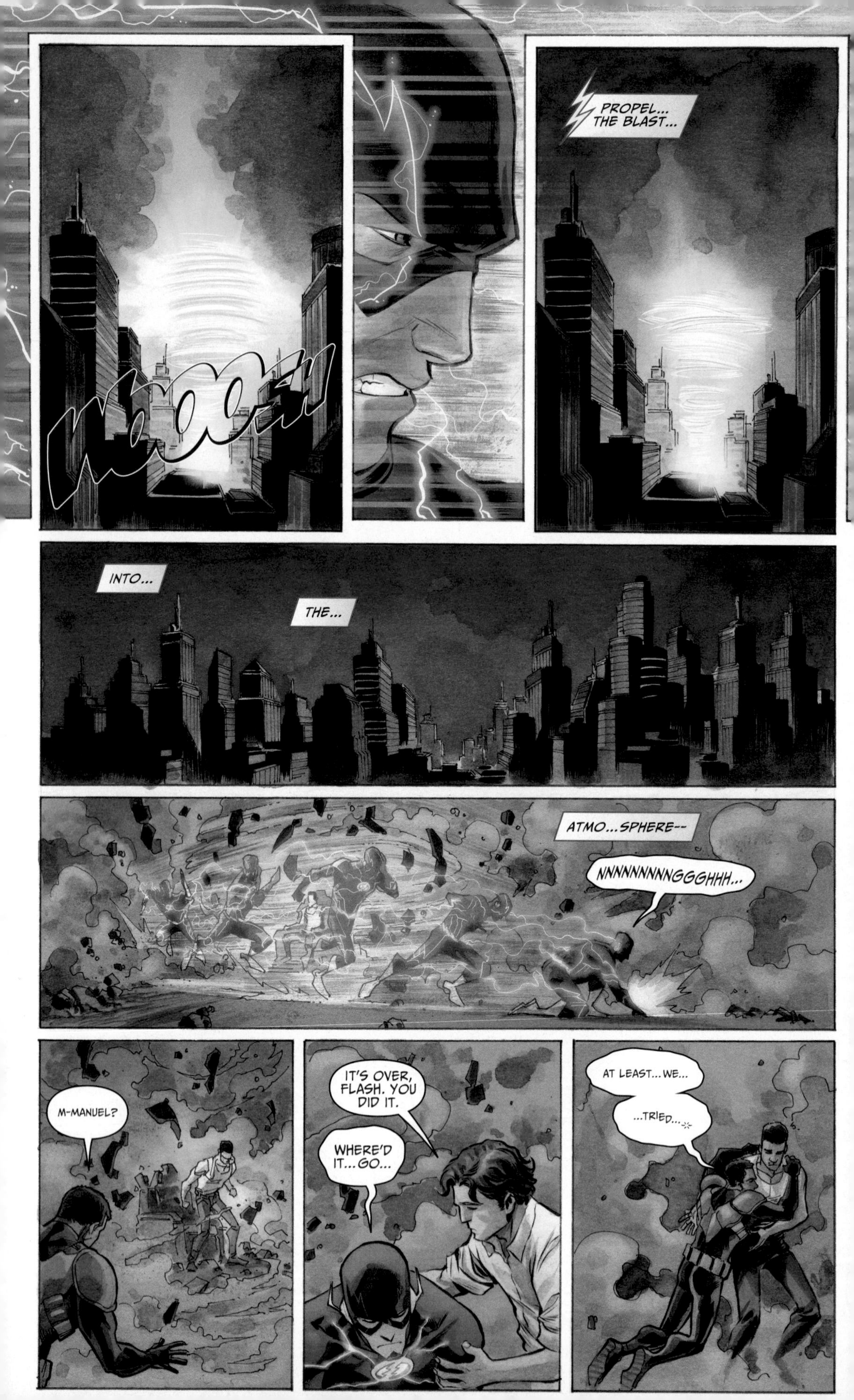
WHOOSH
PROPEL... THE BLAST...
INTO...
THE...
ATMO...SPHERE--
NNNNNNNNNGGGHHH...
M-MANUEL?
IT'S OVER, FLASH. YOU DID IT.
WHERE'D IT...GO...
AT LEAST...WE...
...TRIED...

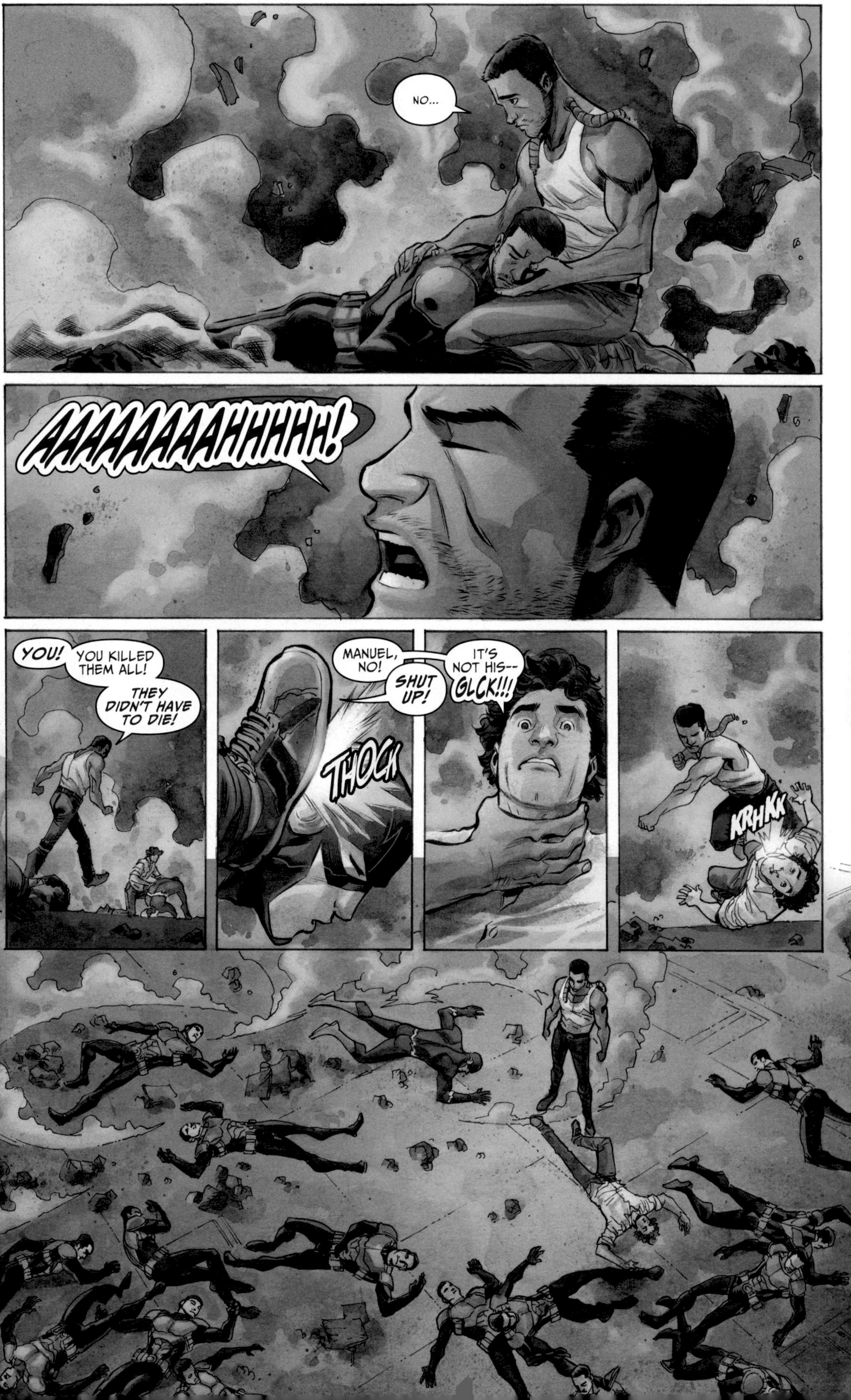
NO...
AAAAAAAAAHHHHH!
YOU!
YOU KILLED THEM ALL!
THEY DIDN'T HAVE TO DIE!
THOCK
MANUEL, NO!
SHUT UP!
IT'S NOT HIS--
GLCK!!!
KRHKK

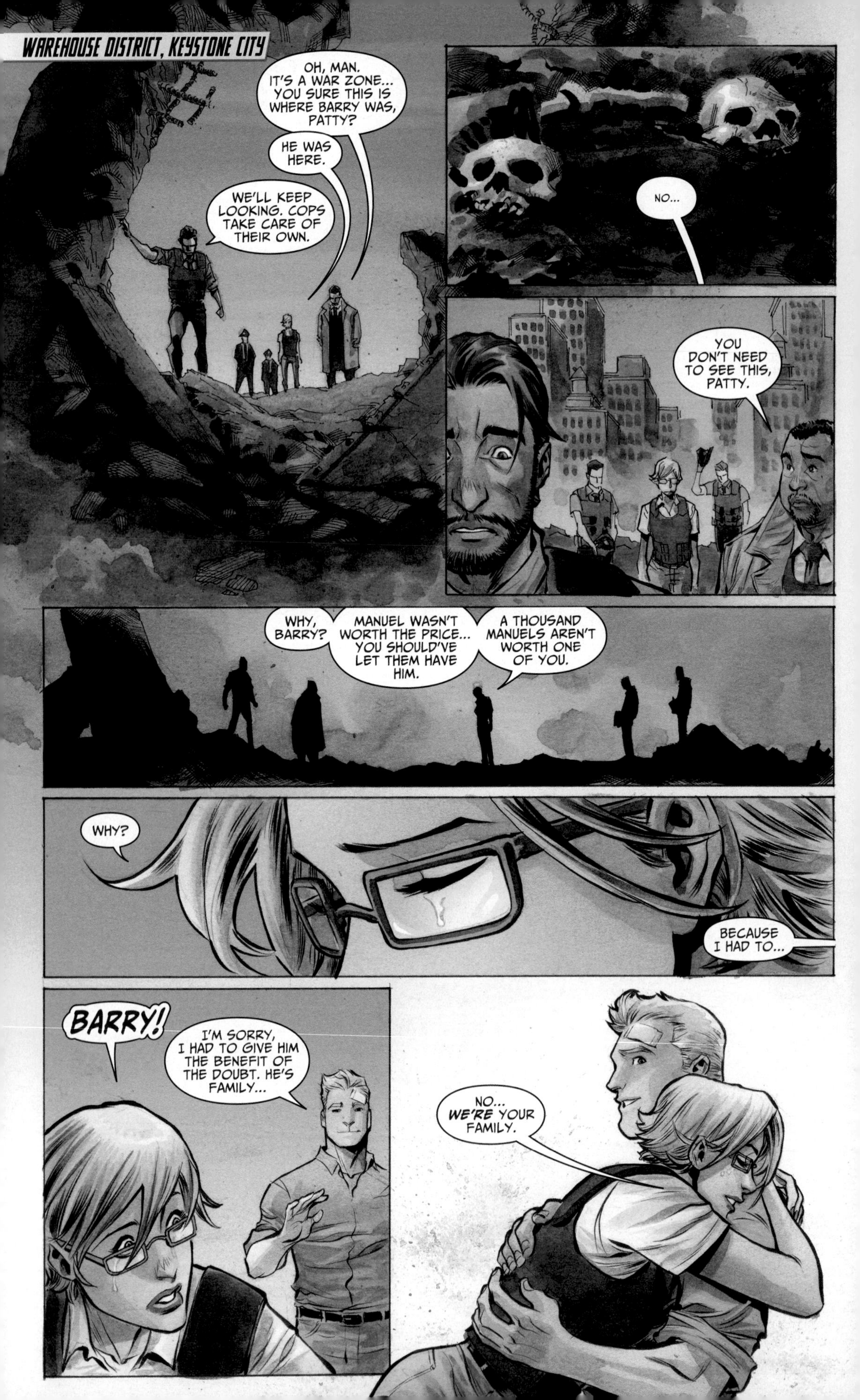
WAREHOUSE DISTRICT, KEYSTONE CITY
OH, MAN. IT'S A WAR ZONE... YOU SURE THIS IS WHERE BARRY WAS, PATTY?
HE WAS HERE.
WE'LL KEEP LOOKING. COPS TAKE CARE OF THEIR OWN.
NO...
YOU DON'T NEED TO SEE THIS, PATTY.
WHY, BARRY?
MANUEL WASN'T WORTH THE PRICE... YOU SHOULD'VE LET THEM HAVE HIM.
A THOUSAND MANUELS AREN'T WORTH ONE OF YOU.
WHY?
BECAUSE I HAD TO...
BARRY!
I'M SORRY, I HAD TO GIVE HIM THE BENEFIT OF THE DOUBT. HE'S FAMILY...
NO... WE'RE YOUR FAMILY.

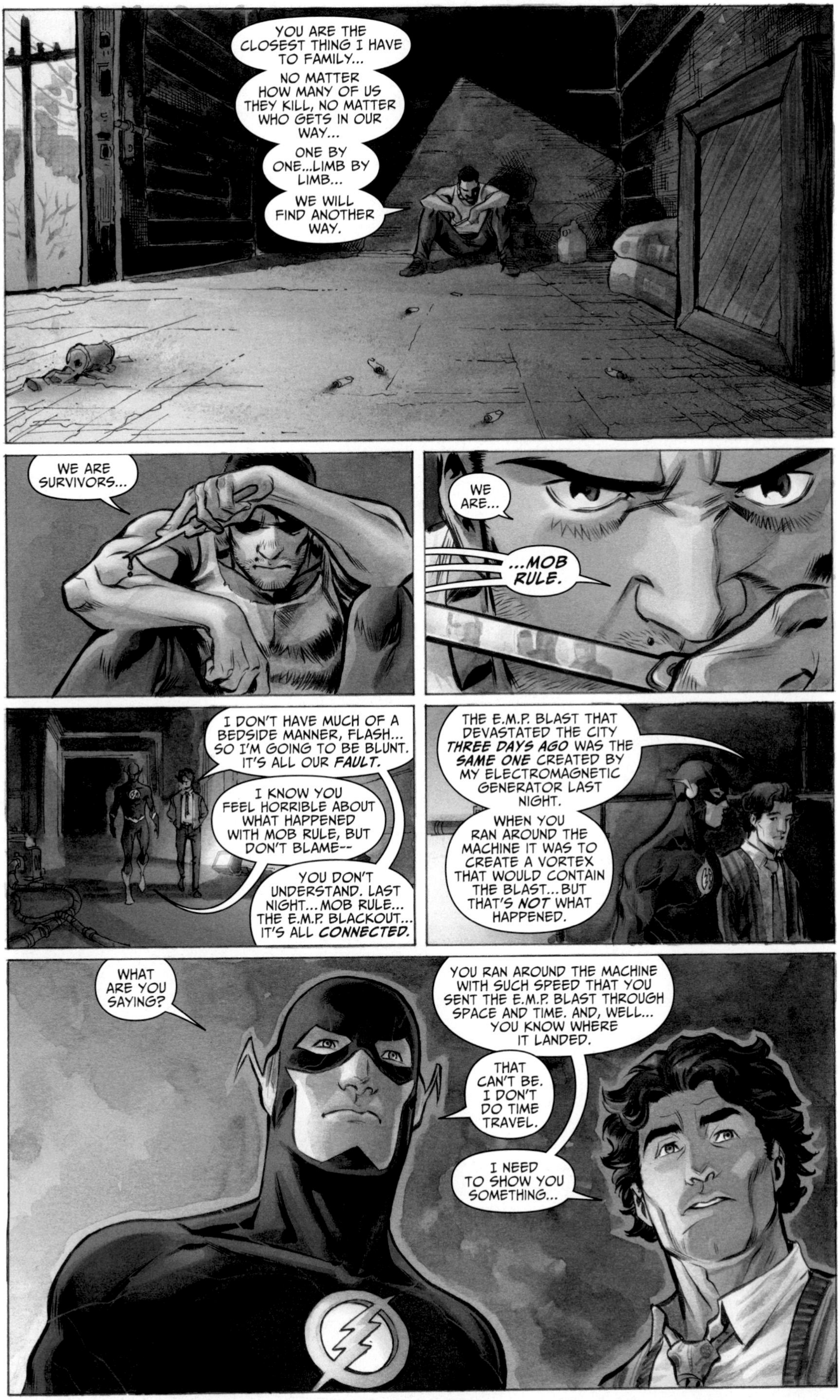
YOU ARE THE CLOSEST THING I HAVE TO FAMILY...
NO MATTER HOW MANY OF US THEY KILL, NO MATTER WHO GETS IN OUR WAY...
ONE BY ONE...LIMB BY LIMB...
WE WILL FIND ANOTHER WAY.
WE ARE SURVIVORS...
WE ARE...
...MOB RULE.
I DON'T HAVE MUCH OF A BEDSIDE MANNER, FLASH... SO I'M GOING TO BE BLUNT. IT'S ALL OUR FAULT.
I KNOW YOU FEEL HORRIBLE ABOUT WHAT HAPPENED WITH MOB RULE, BUT DON'T BLAME--
YOU DON'T UNDERSTAND. LAST NIGHT...MOB RULE... THE E.M.P. BLACKOUT... IT'S ALL CONNECTED.
THE E.M.P. BLAST THAT DEVASTATED THE CITY THREE DAYS AGO WAS THE SAME ONE CREATED BY MY ELECTROMAGNETIC GENERATOR LAST NIGHT.
WHEN YOU RAN AROUND THE MACHINE IT WAS TO CREATE A VORTEX THAT WOULD CONTAIN THE BLAST...BUT THAT'S NOT WHAT HAPPENED.
WHAT ARE YOU SAYING?
YOU RAN AROUND THE MACHINE WITH SUCH SPEED THAT YOU SENT THE E.M.P. BLAST THROUGH SPACE AND TIME. AND, WELL... YOU KNOW WHERE IT LANDED.
THAT CAN'T BE. I DON'T DO TIME TRAVEL.
I NEED TO SHOW YOU SOMETHING...

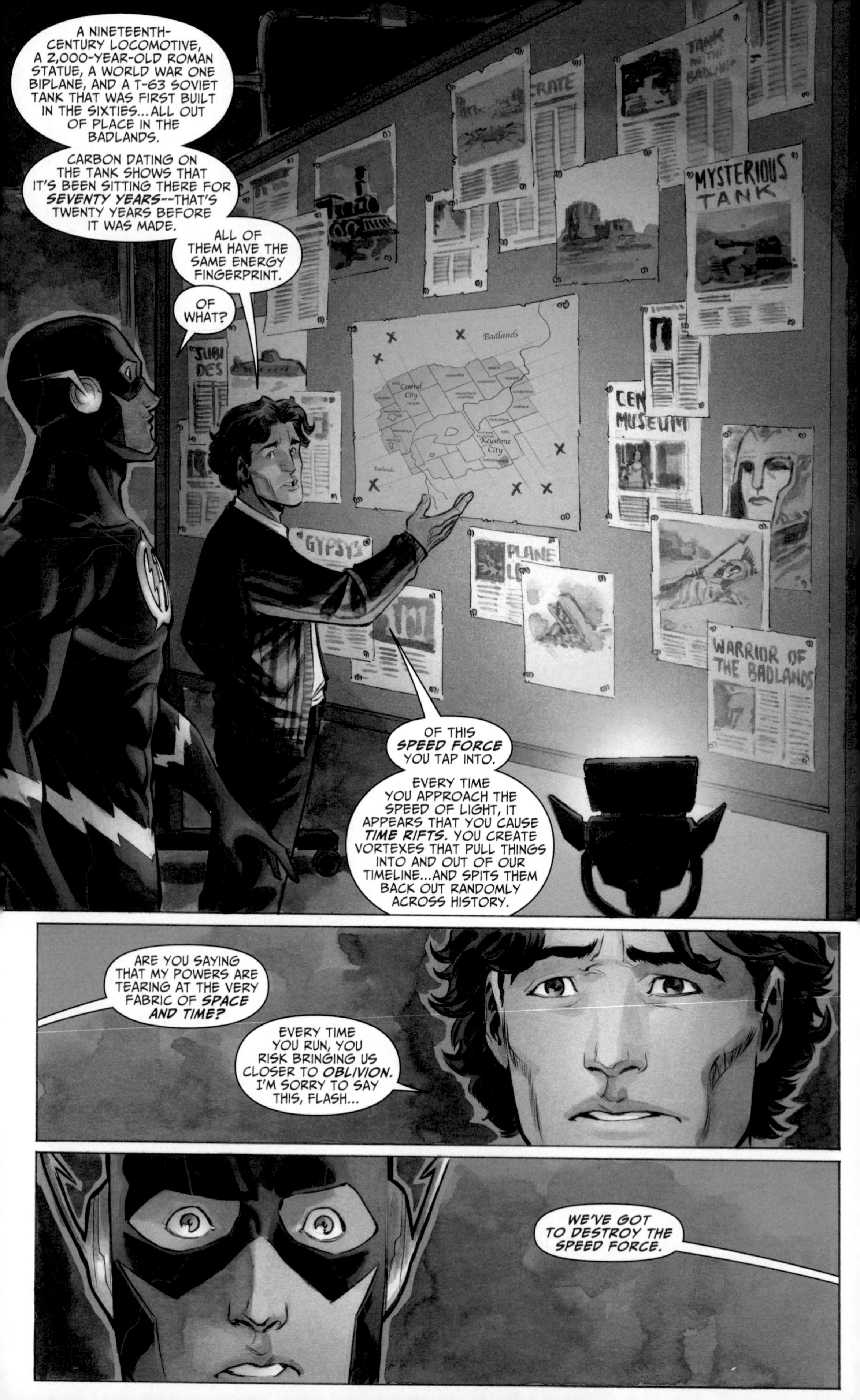
A NINETEENTH-CENTURY LOCOMOTIVE, A 2,000-YEAR-OLD ROMAN STATUE, A WORLD WAR ONE BIPLANE, AND A T-63 SOVIET TANK THAT WAS FIRST BUILT IN THE SIXTIES...ALL OUT OF PLACE IN THE BADLANDS.
CARBON DATING ON THE TANK SHOWS THAT IT'S BEEN SITTING THERE FOR *SEVENTY YEARS*--THAT'S TWENTY YEARS BEFORE IT WAS MADE.
ALL OF THEM HAVE THE SAME ENERGY FINGERPRINT.
OF WHAT?
MYSTERIOUS TANK
Badlands
Central City
Keystone City
Badlands
CEN MUSEUM
GYPSYS
PLANE
WARRIOR OF THE BADLANDS
OF THIS *SPEED FORCE* YOU TAP INTO.
EVERY TIME YOU APPROACH THE SPEED OF LIGHT, IT APPEARS THAT YOU CAUSE *TIME RIFTS.* YOU CREATE VORTEXES THAT PULL THINGS INTO AND OUT OF OUR TIMELINE...AND SPITS THEM BACK OUT RANDOMLY ACROSS HISTORY.
ARE YOU SAYING THAT MY POWERS ARE TEARING AT THE VERY FABRIC OF *SPACE AND TIME?*
EVERY TIME YOU RUN, YOU RISK BRINGING US CLOSER TO *OBLIVION.* I'M SORRY TO SAY THIS, FLASH...
WE'VE GOT TO DESTROY THE SPEED FORCE.

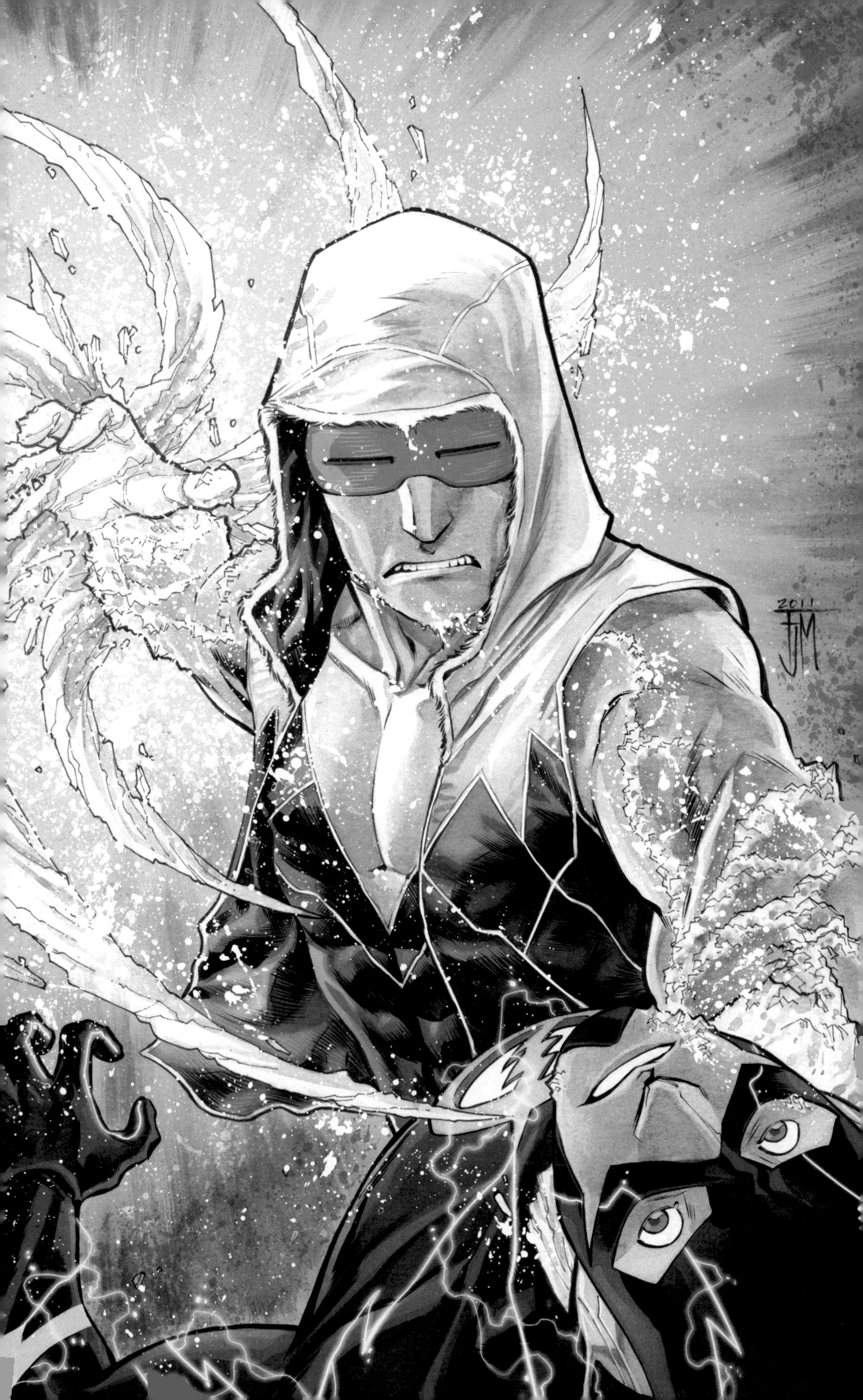
2011

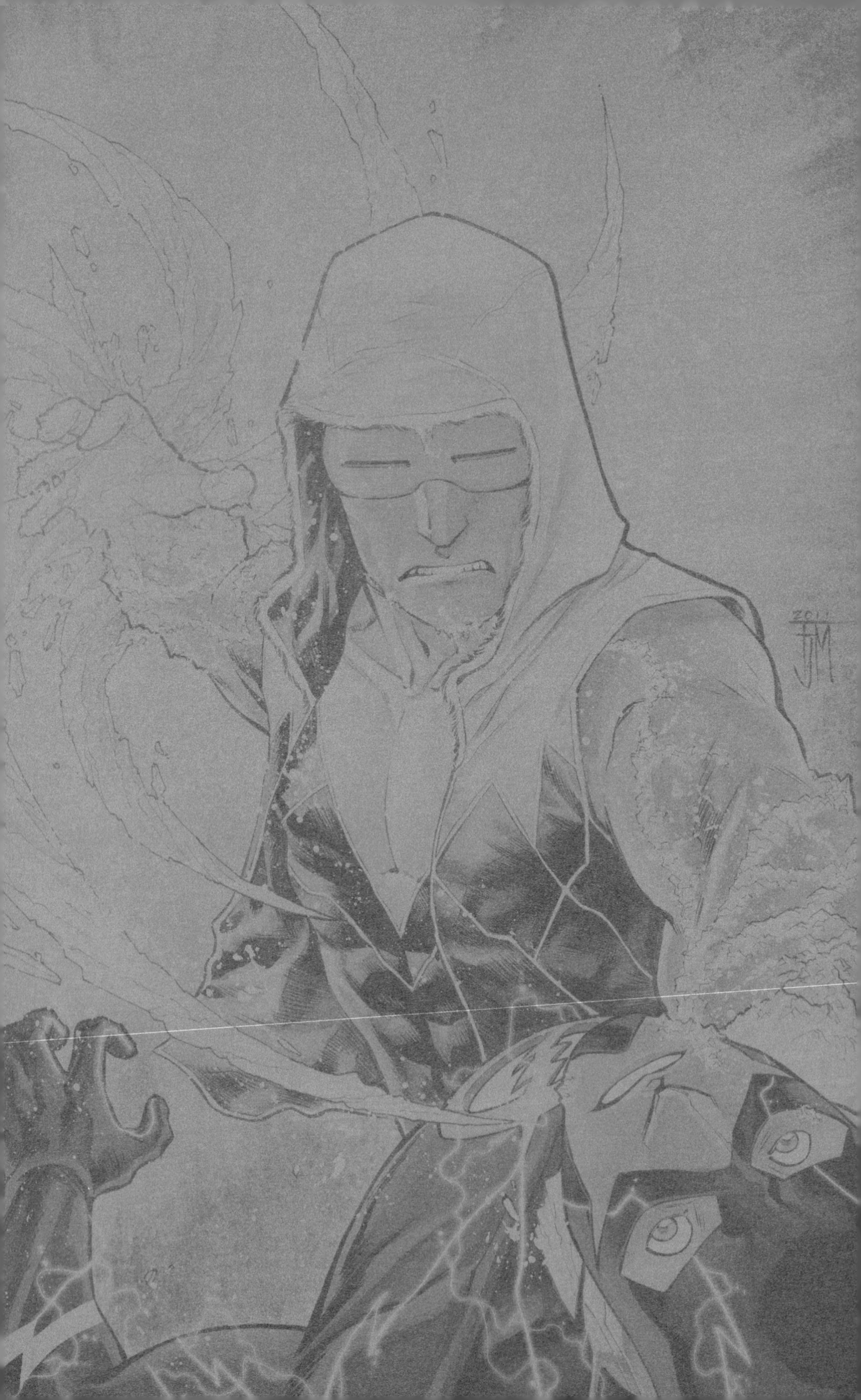

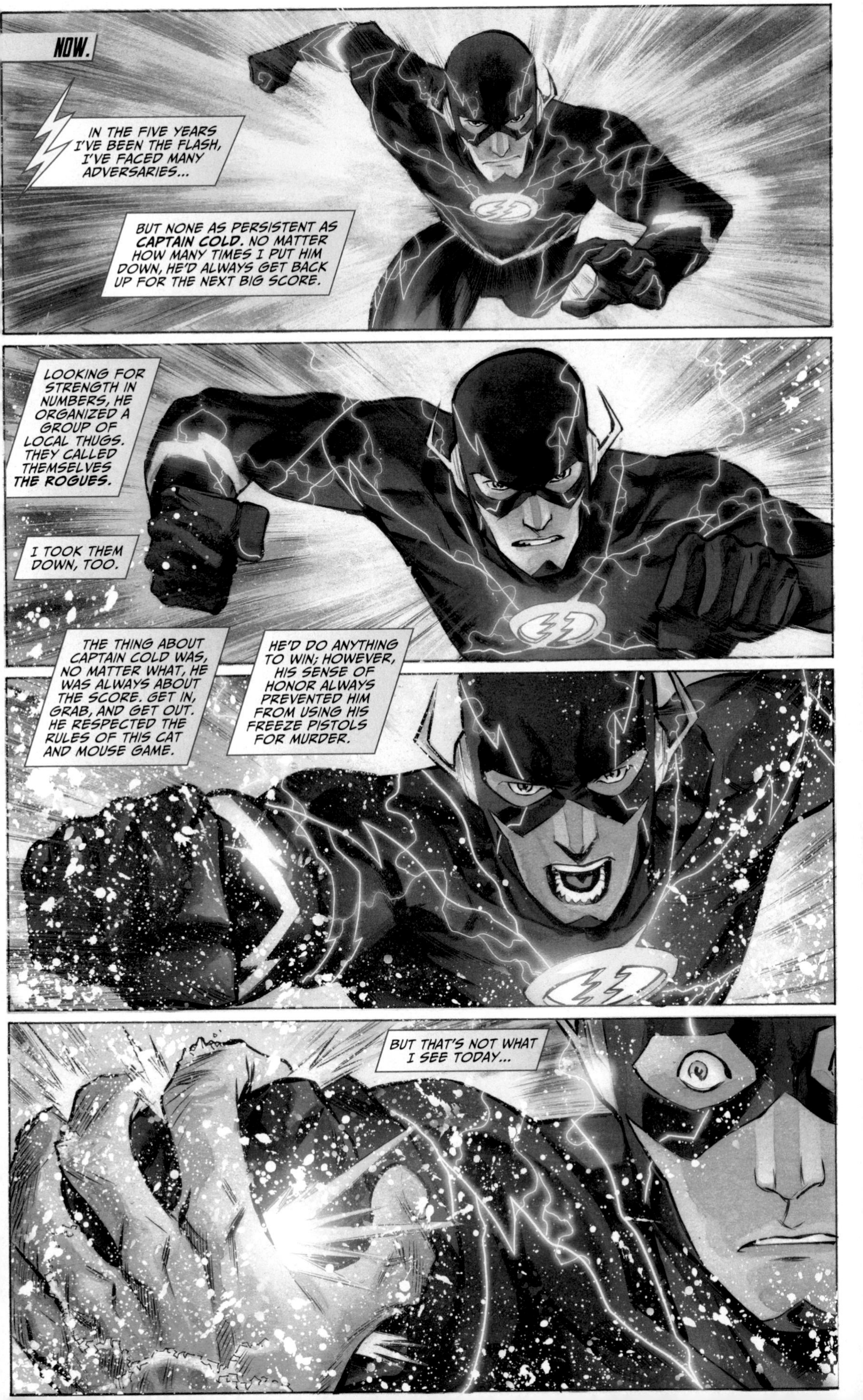
NOW.
IN THE FIVE YEARS I'VE BEEN THE FLASH, I'VE FACED MANY ADVERSARIES...
BUT NONE AS PERSISTENT AS **CAPTAIN COLD.** NO MATTER HOW MANY TIMES I PUT HIM DOWN, HE'D ALWAYS GET BACK UP FOR THE NEXT BIG SCORE.
LOOKING FOR STRENGTH IN NUMBERS, HE ORGANIZED A GROUP OF LOCAL THUGS. THEY CALLED THEMSELVES **THE ROGUES.**
I TOOK THEM DOWN, TOO.
THE THING ABOUT CAPTAIN COLD WAS, NO MATTER WHAT, HE WAS ALWAYS ABOUT THE SCORE. GET IN, GRAB, AND GET OUT. HE RESPECTED THE RULES OF THIS CAT AND MOUSE GAME.
HE'D DO ANYTHING TO WIN; HOWEVER, HIS SENSE OF HONOR ALWAYS PREVENTED HIM FROM USING HIS FREEZE PISTOLS FOR MURDER.
BUT THAT'S NOT WHAT I SEE TODAY...

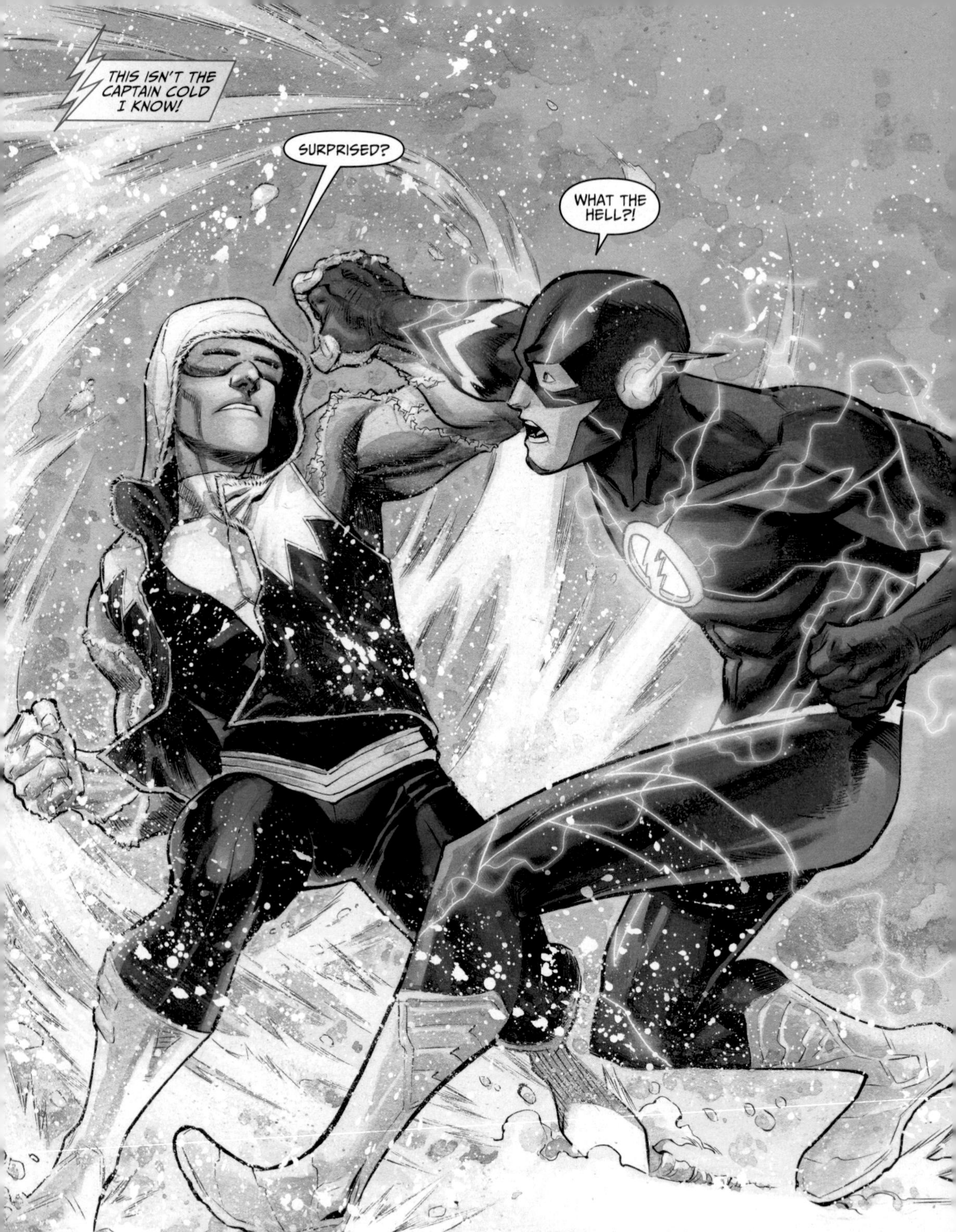
THIS ISN'T THE CAPTAIN COLD I KNOW!
SURPRISED?
WHAT THE HELL?!
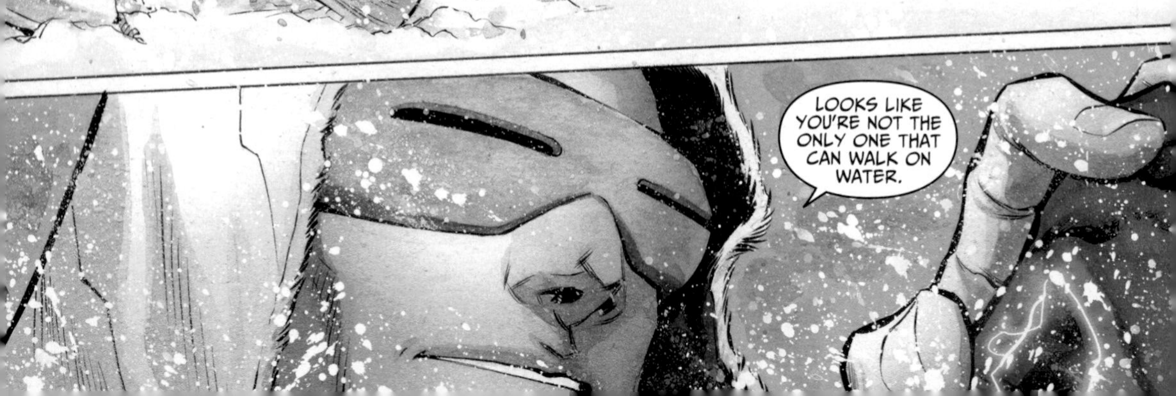
LOOKS LIKE YOU'RE NOT THE ONLY ONE THAT CAN WALK ON WATER.

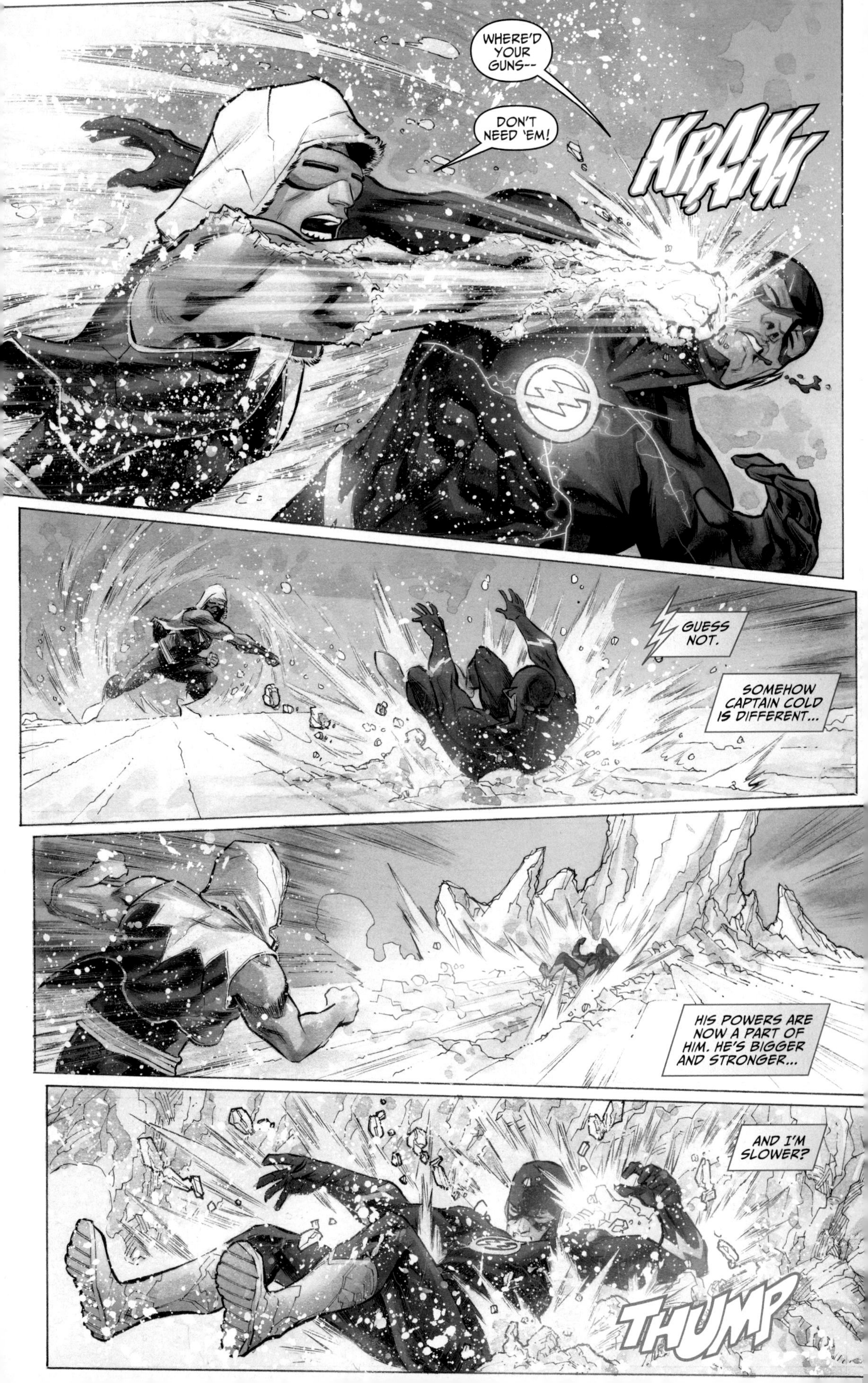
WHERE'D YOUR GUNS--
DON'T NEED 'EM!
KRAKK
GUESS NOT.
SOMEHOW CAPTAIN COLD IS DIFFERENT...
HIS POWERS ARE NOW A PART OF HIM. HE'S BIGGER AND STRONGER...
AND I'M SLOWER?
THUMP

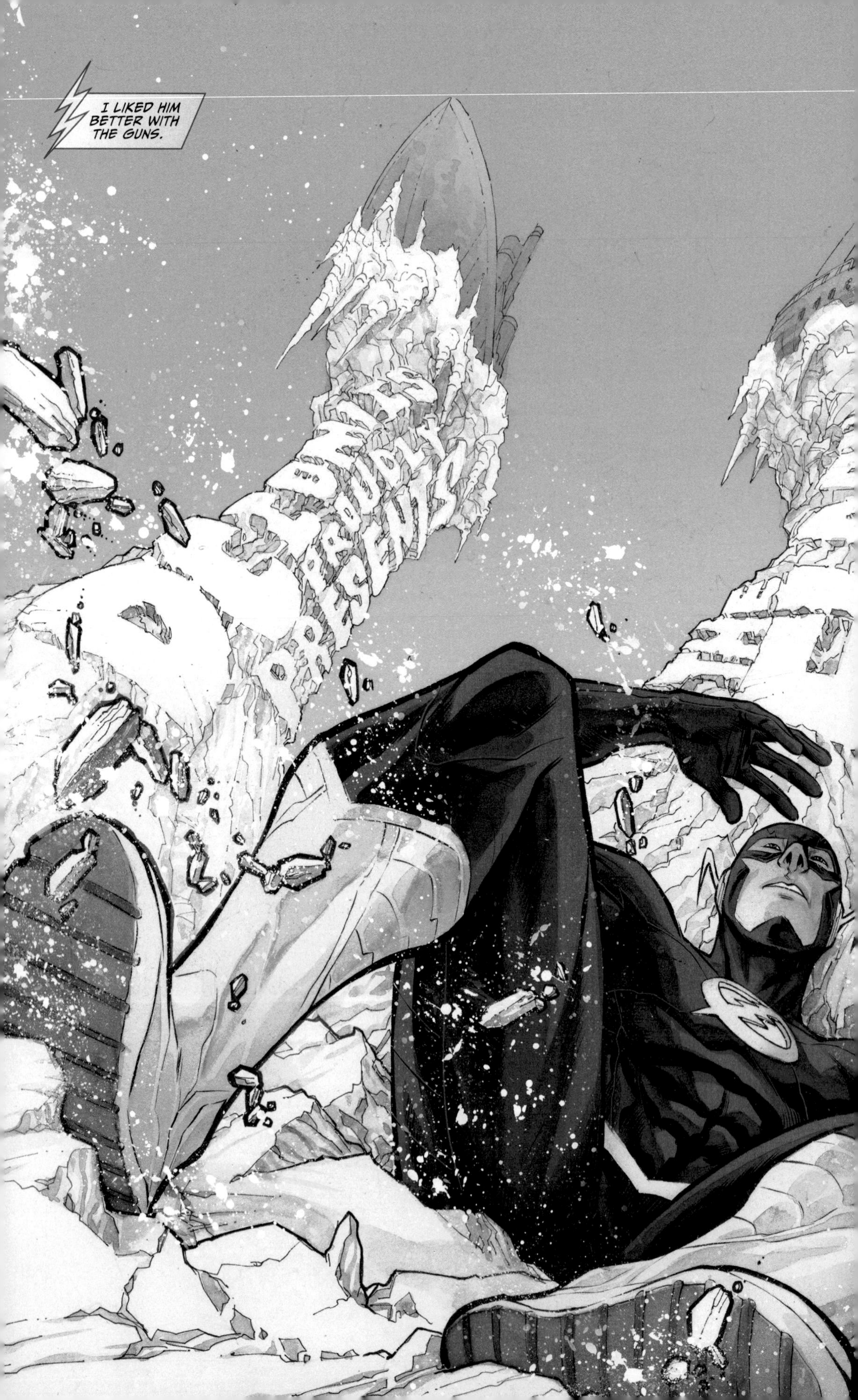
I LIKED HIM BETTER WITH THE GUNS.

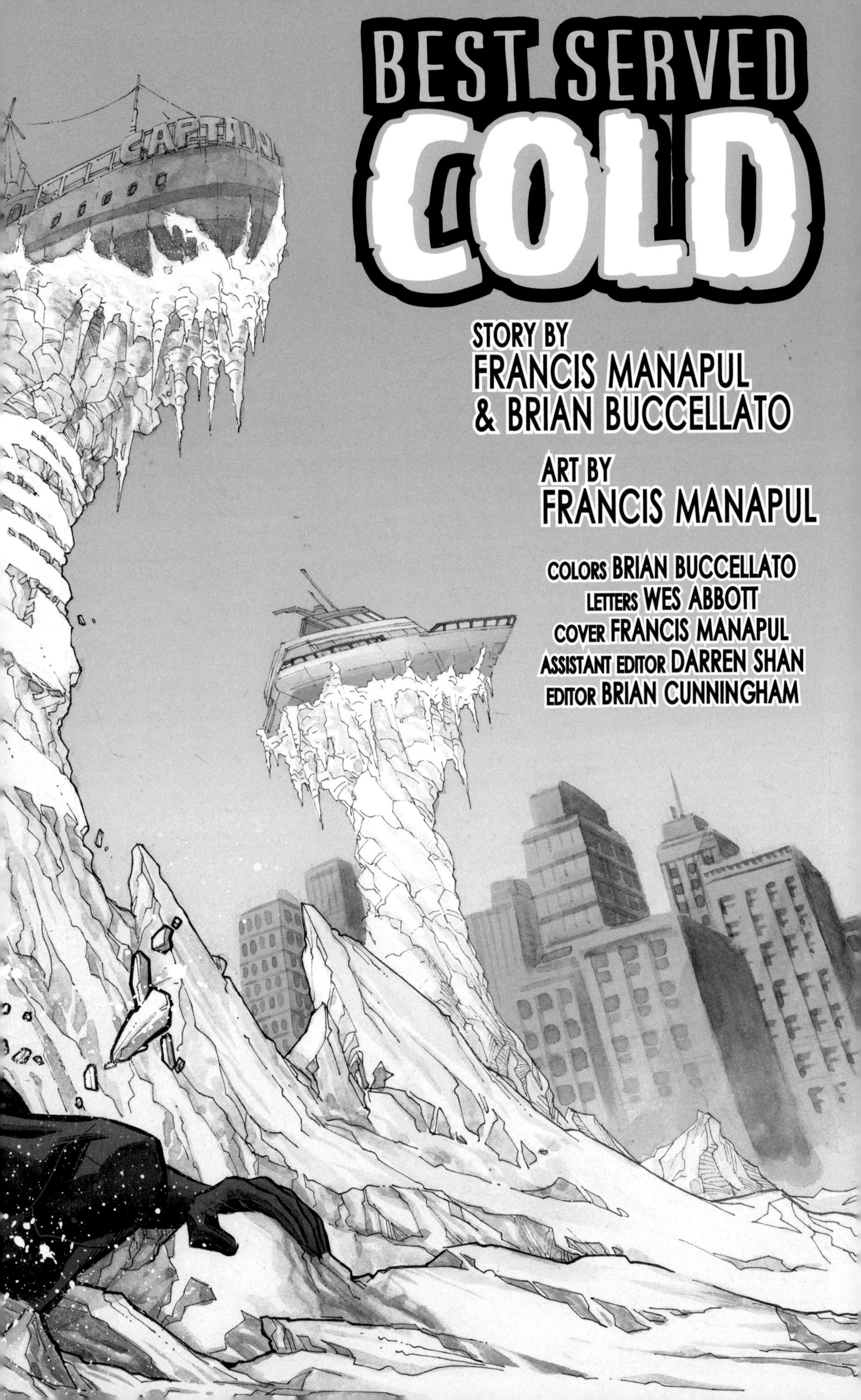
BEST SERVED
COLD
STORY BY
FRANCIS MANAPUL
& BRIAN BUCCELLATO
ART BY
FRANCIS MANAPUL
COLORS BRIAN BUCCELLATO
LETTERS WES ABBOTT
COVER FRANCIS MANAPUL
ASSISTANT EDITOR DARREN SHAN
EDITOR BRIAN CUNNINGHAM

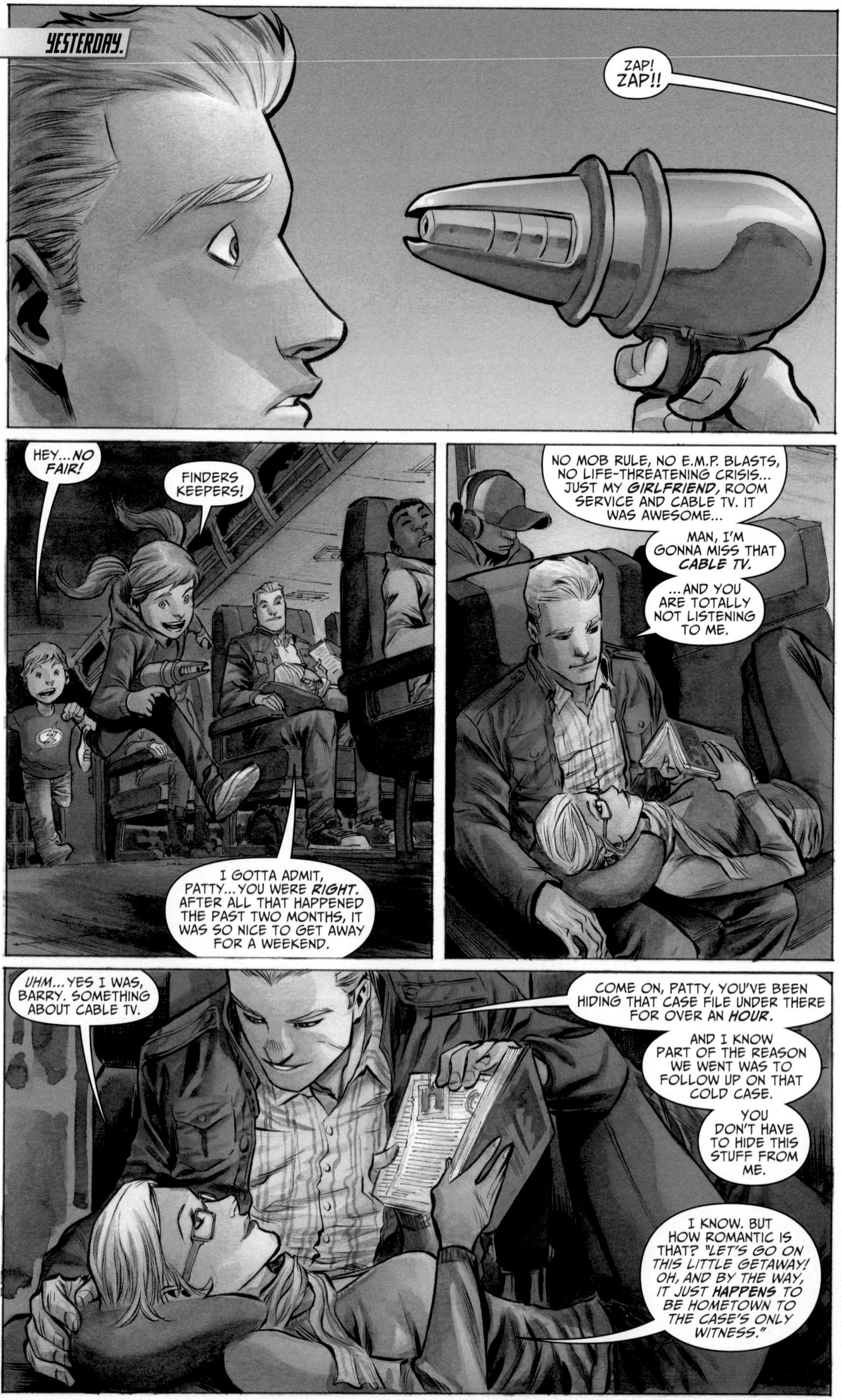

YESTERDAY.
ZAP! ZAP!!
HEY...NO FAIR!
FINDERS KEEPERS!
I GOTTA ADMIT, PATTY...YOU WERE RIGHT. AFTER ALL THAT HAPPENED THE PAST TWO MONTHS, IT WAS SO NICE TO GET AWAY FOR A WEEKEND.
NO MOB RULE, NO E.M.P. BLASTS, NO LIFE-THREATENING CRISIS... JUST MY GIRLFRIEND, ROOM SERVICE AND CABLE TV. IT WAS AWESOME...
MAN, I'M GONNA MISS THAT CABLE TV.
...AND YOU ARE TOTALLY NOT LISTENING TO ME.
UHM...YES I WAS, BARRY. SOMETHING ABOUT CABLE TV.
COME ON, PATTY, YOU'VE BEEN HIDING THAT CASE FILE UNDER THERE FOR OVER AN HOUR.
AND I KNOW PART OF THE REASON WE WENT WAS TO FOLLOW UP ON THAT COLD CASE.
YOU DON'T HAVE TO HIDE THIS STUFF FROM ME.
I KNOW. BUT HOW ROMANTIC IS THAT? "LET'S GO ON THIS LITTLE GETAWAY! OH, AND BY THE WAY, IT JUST HAPPENS TO BE HOMETOWN TO THE CASE'S ONLY WITNESS."

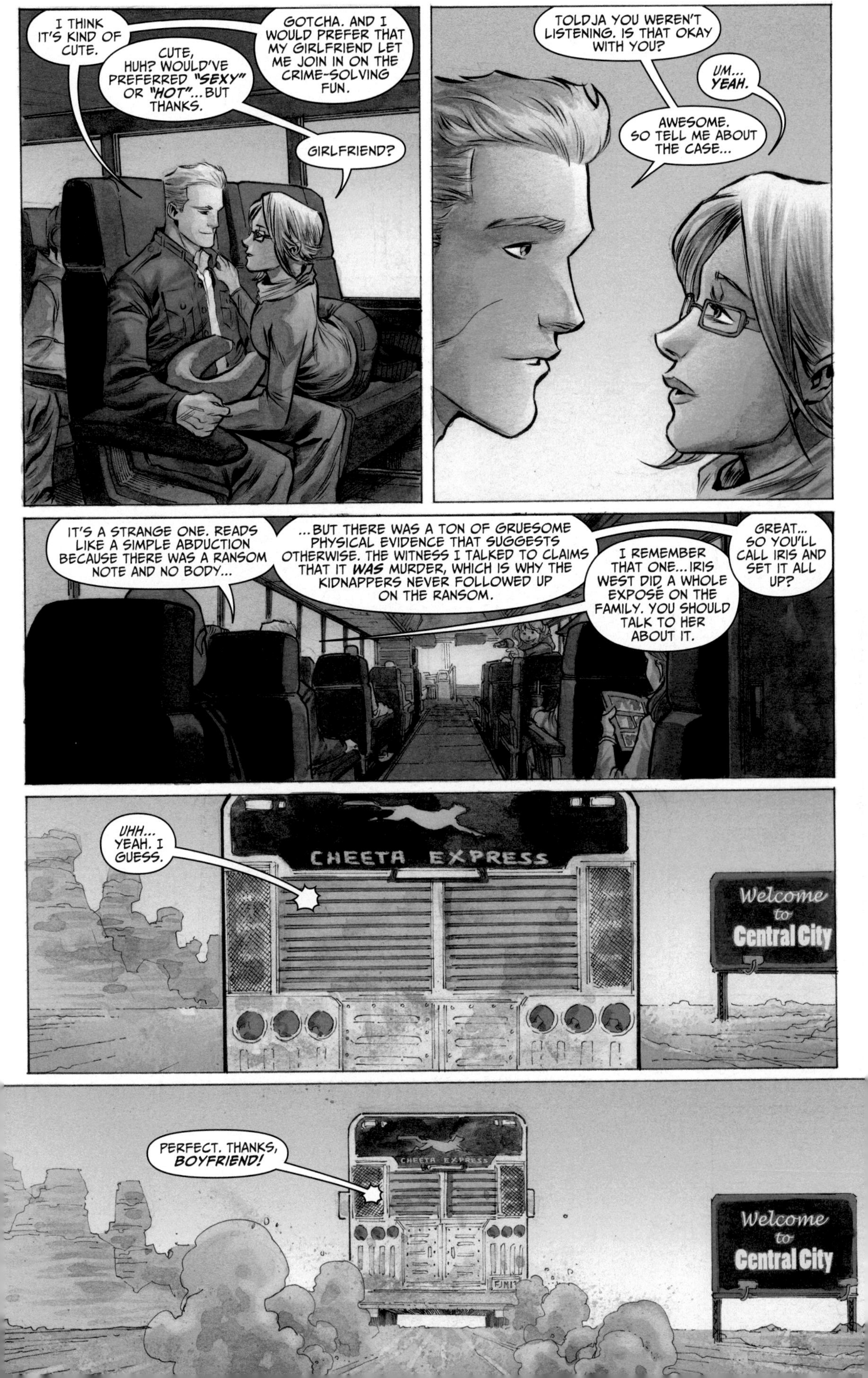
I THINK IT'S KIND OF CUTE.
CUTE, HUH? WOULD'VE PREFERRED "SEXY" OR "HOT"... BUT THANKS.
GOTCHA. AND I WOULD PREFER THAT MY GIRLFRIEND LET ME JOIN IN ON THE CRIME-SOLVING FUN.
GIRLFRIEND?
TOLDJA YOU WEREN'T LISTENING. IS THAT OKAY WITH YOU?
UM... YEAH.
AWESOME. SO TELL ME ABOUT THE CASE...
IT'S A STRANGE ONE. READS LIKE A SIMPLE ABDUCTION BECAUSE THERE WAS A RANSOM NOTE AND NO BODY...
...BUT THERE WAS A TON OF GRUESOME PHYSICAL EVIDENCE THAT SUGGESTS OTHERWISE. THE WITNESS I TALKED TO CLAIMS THAT IT WAS MURDER, WHICH IS WHY THE KIDNAPPERS NEVER FOLLOWED UP ON THE RANSOM.
I REMEMBER THAT ONE... IRIS WEST DID A WHOLE EXPOSÉ ON THE FAMILY. YOU SHOULD TALK TO HER ABOUT IT.
GREAT... SO YOU'LL CALL IRIS AND SET IT ALL UP?
UHH... YEAH. I GUESS.
CHEETA EXPRESS
Welcome to Central City
PERFECT. THANKS, BOYFRIEND!
CHEETA EXPRESS
Welcome to Central City

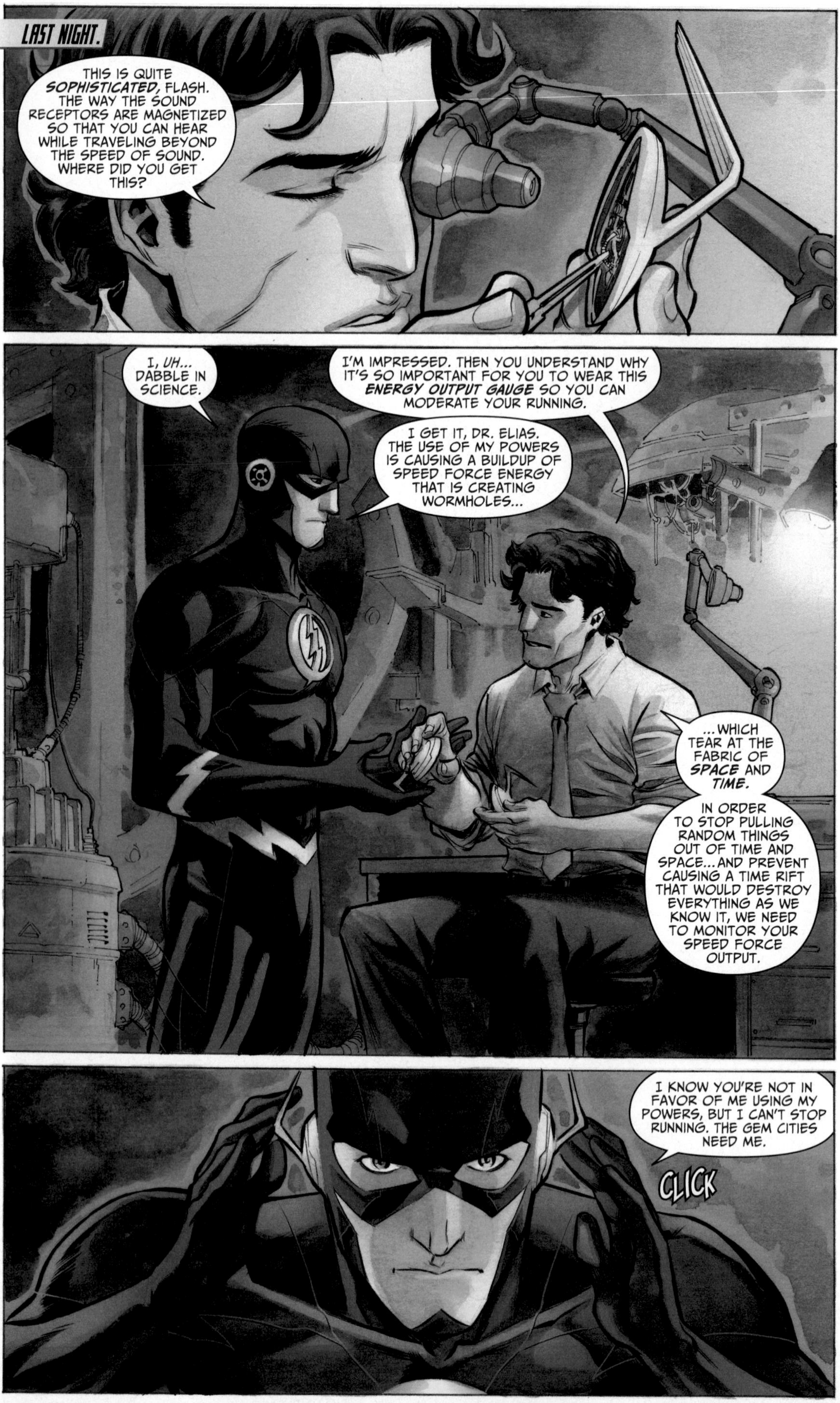
LAST NIGHT.
THIS IS QUITE SOPHISTICATED, FLASH. THE WAY THE SOUND RECEPTORS ARE MAGNETIZED SO THAT YOU CAN HEAR WHILE TRAVELING BEYOND THE SPEED OF SOUND. WHERE DID YOU GET THIS?
I, UH... DABBLE IN SCIENCE.
I'M IMPRESSED. THEN YOU UNDERSTAND WHY IT'S SO IMPORTANT FOR YOU TO WEAR THIS ENERGY OUTPUT GAUGE SO YOU CAN MODERATE YOUR RUNNING.
I GET IT, DR. ELIAS. THE USE OF MY POWERS IS CAUSING A BUILDUP OF SPEED FORCE ENERGY THAT IS CREATING WORMHOLES...
...WHICH TEAR AT THE FABRIC OF SPACE AND TIME.
IN ORDER TO STOP PULLING RANDOM THINGS OUT OF TIME AND SPACE...AND PREVENT CAUSING A TIME RIFT THAT WOULD DESTROY EVERYTHING AS WE KNOW IT, WE NEED TO MONITOR YOUR SPEED FORCE OUTPUT.
I KNOW YOU'RE NOT IN FAVOR OF ME USING MY POWERS, BUT I CAN'T STOP RUNNING. THE GEM CITIES NEED ME.
CLICK

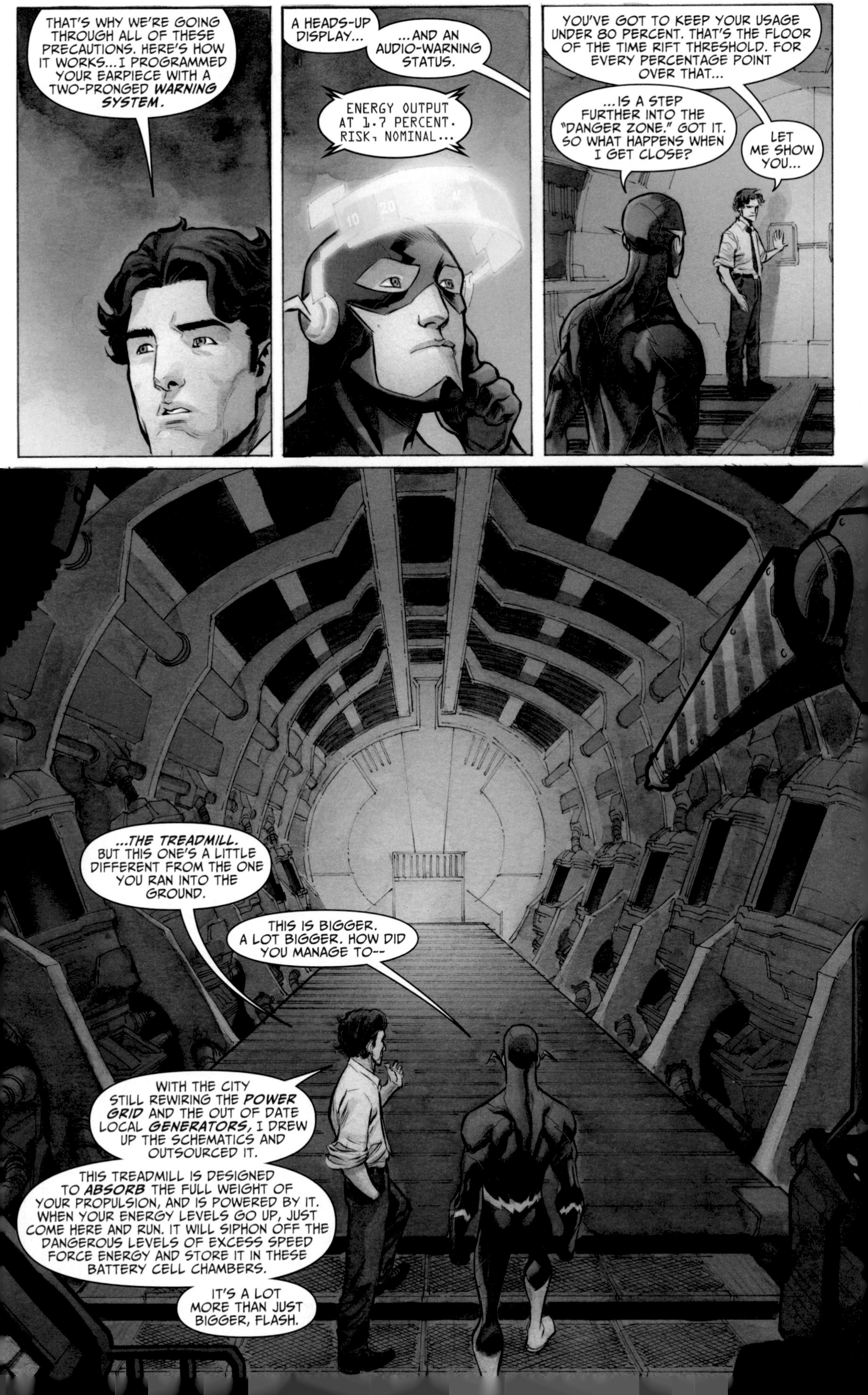
THAT'S WHY WE'RE GOING THROUGH ALL OF THESE PRECAUTIONS. HERE'S HOW IT WORKS...I PROGRAMMED YOUR EARPIECE WITH A TWO-PRONGED WARNING SYSTEM.
A HEADS-UP DISPLAY...
...AND AN AUDIO-WARNING STATUS.
ENERGY OUTPUT AT 1.7 PERCENT. RISK, NOMINAL...
10
20
YOU'VE GOT TO KEEP YOUR USAGE UNDER 80 PERCENT. THAT'S THE FLOOR OF THE TIME RIFT THRESHOLD. FOR EVERY PERCENTAGE POINT OVER THAT...
...IS A STEP FURTHER INTO THE "DANGER ZONE." GOT IT. SO WHAT HAPPENS WHEN I GET CLOSE?
LET ME SHOW YOU...
...THE TREADMILL. BUT THIS ONE'S A LITTLE DIFFERENT FROM THE ONE YOU RAN INTO THE GROUND.
THIS IS BIGGER. A LOT BIGGER. HOW DID YOU MANAGE TO--
WITH THE CITY STILL REWIRING THE POWER GRID AND THE OUT OF DATE LOCAL GENERATORS, I DREW UP THE SCHEMATICS AND OUTSOURCED IT.
THIS TREADMILL IS DESIGNED TO ABSORB THE FULL WEIGHT OF YOUR PROPULSION, AND IS POWERED BY IT. WHEN YOUR ENERGY LEVELS GO UP, JUST COME HERE AND RUN. IT WILL SIPHON OFF THE DANGEROUS LEVELS OF EXCESS SPEED FORCE ENERGY AND STORE IT IN THESE BATTERY CELL CHAMBERS.
IT'S A LOT MORE THAN JUST BIGGER, FLASH.

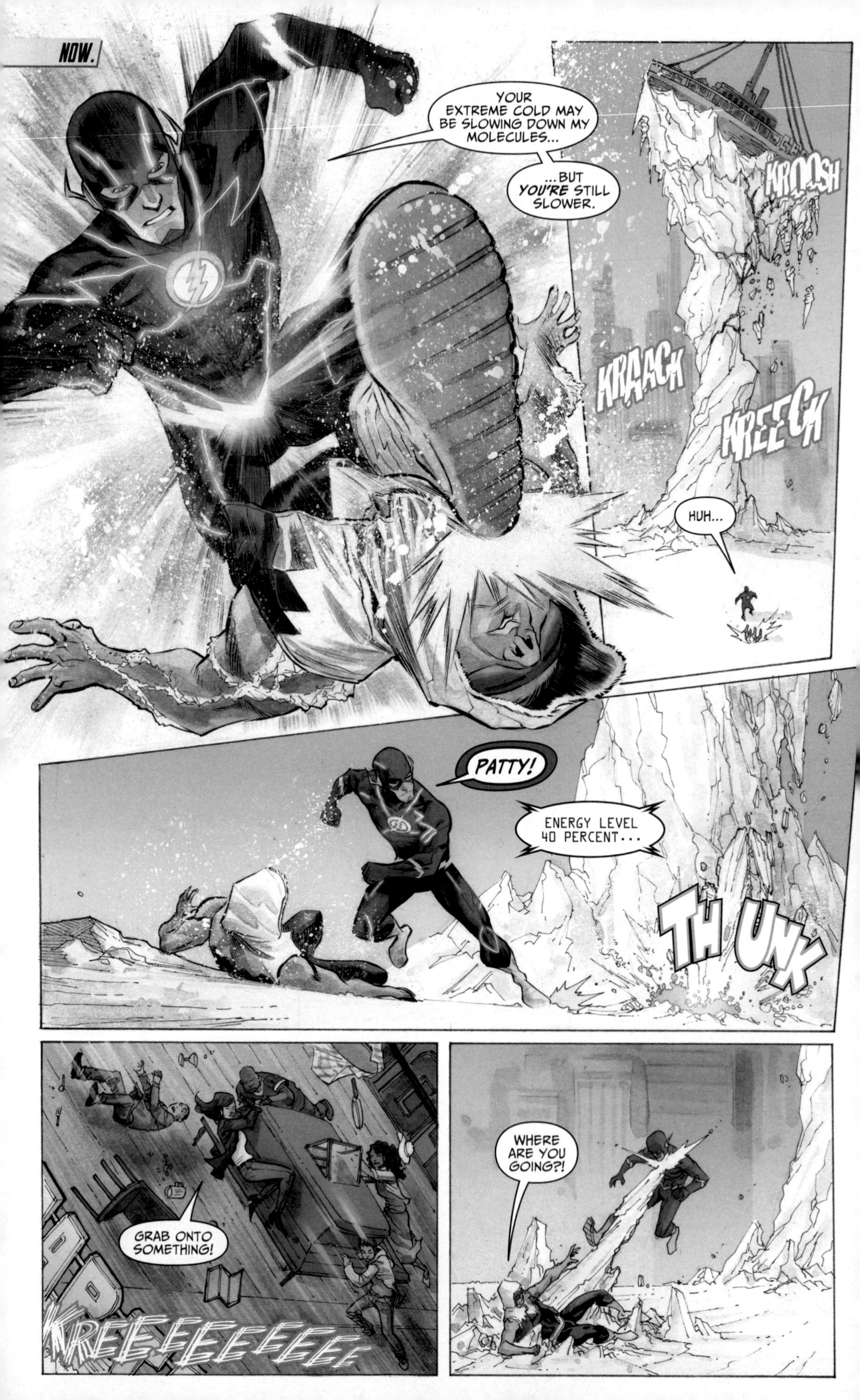
NOW.
YOUR EXTREME COLD MAY BE SLOWING DOWN MY MOLECULES...
...BUT YOU'RE STILL SLOWER.
KROOSH
KRAACK
KREECH
HUH...
PATTY!
ENERGY LEVEL 40 PERCENT...
THUNK
GRAB ONTO SOMETHING!
KREEEEEEEEEE
WHERE ARE YOU GOING?!

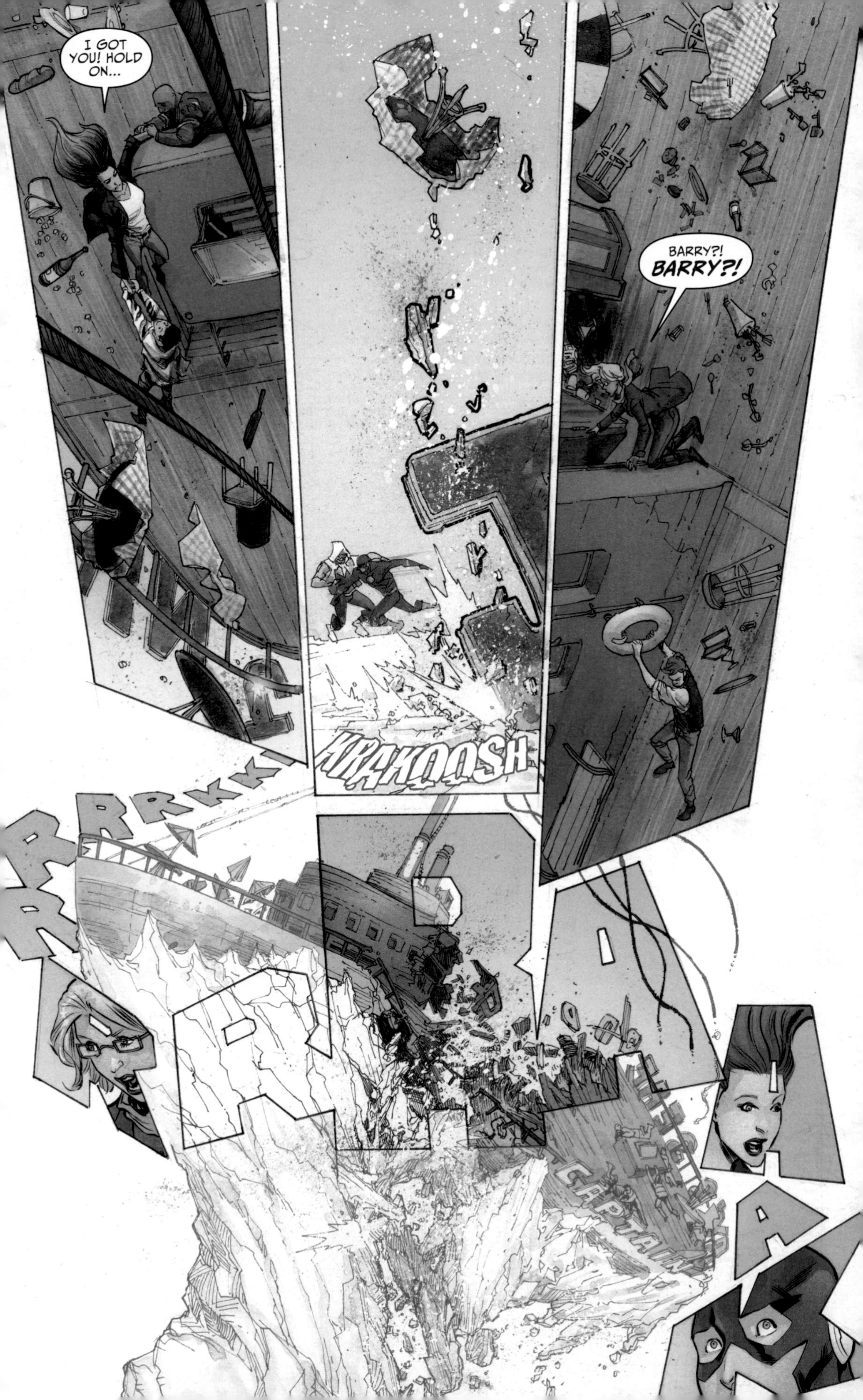
I GOT YOU! HOLD ON...
KRAKOOSH
BARRY?! BARRY?!

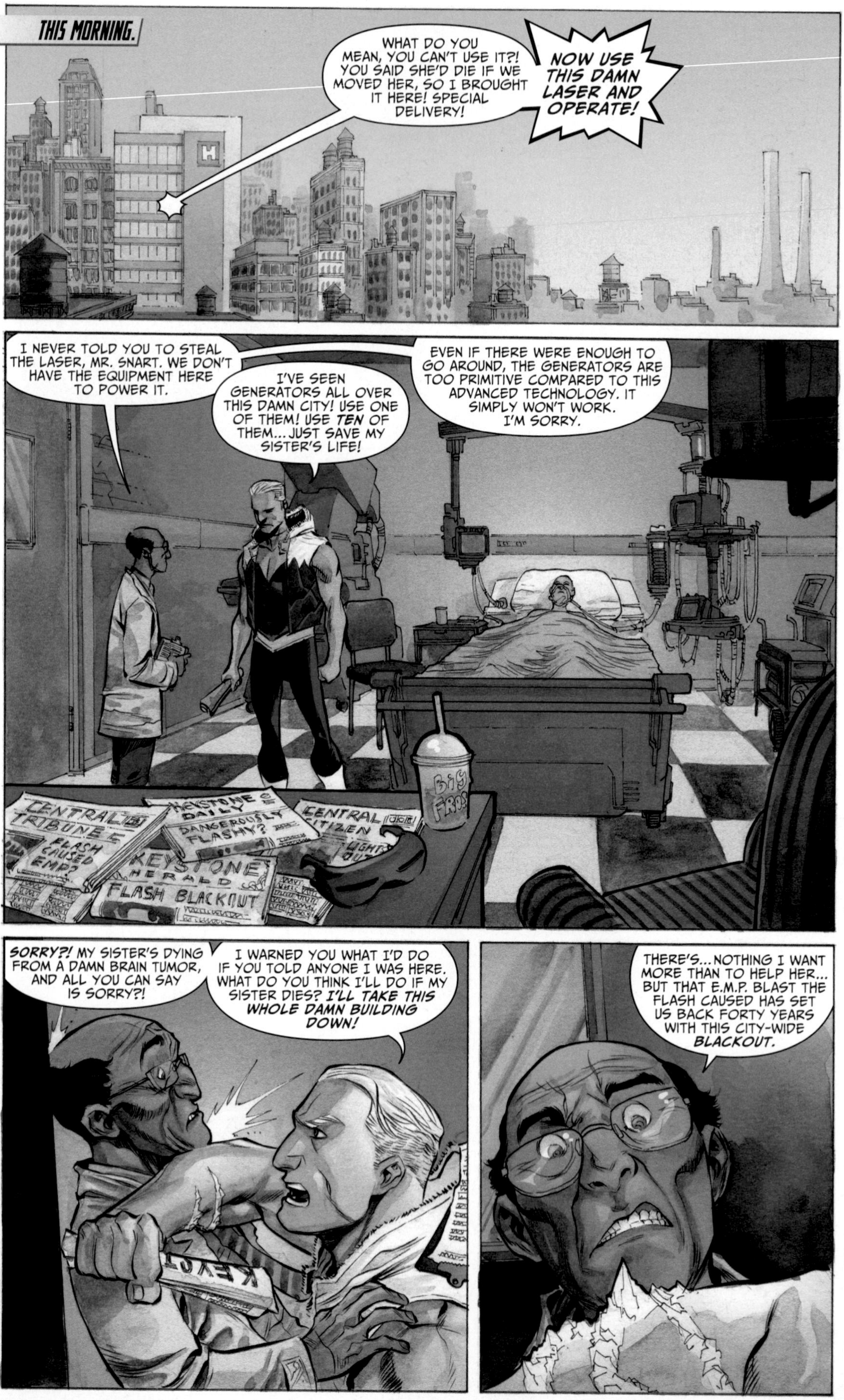
THIS MORNING.
WHAT DO YOU MEAN, YOU CAN'T USE IT?! YOU SAID SHE'D DIE IF WE MOVED HER, SO I BROUGHT IT HERE! SPECIAL DELIVERY!
NOW USE THIS DAMN LASER AND OPERATE!
I NEVER TOLD YOU TO STEAL THE LASER, MR. SNART. WE DON'T HAVE THE EQUIPMENT HERE TO POWER IT.
I'VE SEEN GENERATORS ALL OVER THIS DAMN CITY! USE ONE OF THEM! USE TEN OF THEM... JUST SAVE MY SISTER'S LIFE!
EVEN IF THERE WERE ENOUGH TO GO AROUND, THE GENERATORS ARE TOO PRIMITIVE COMPARED TO THIS ADVANCED TECHNOLOGY. IT SIMPLY WON'T WORK. I'M SORRY.
CENTRAL TRIBUNE
FLASH CAUSED EMP?
KEYSTONE DAILY
DANGEROUSLY FLASHY?
CENTRAL CITIZEN
KEYSTONE HERALD
FLASH BLACKOUT
SORRY?! MY SISTER'S DYING FROM A DAMN BRAIN TUMOR, AND ALL YOU CAN SAY IS SORRY?!
I WARNED YOU WHAT I'D DO IF YOU TOLD ANYONE I WAS HERE. WHAT DO YOU THINK I'LL DO IF MY SISTER DIES? I'LL TAKE THIS WHOLE DAMN BUILDING DOWN!
THERE'S... NOTHING I WANT MORE THAN TO HELP HER... BUT THAT E.M.P. BLAST THE FLASH CAUSED HAS SET US BACK FORTY YEARS WITH THIS CITY-WIDE BLACKOUT.

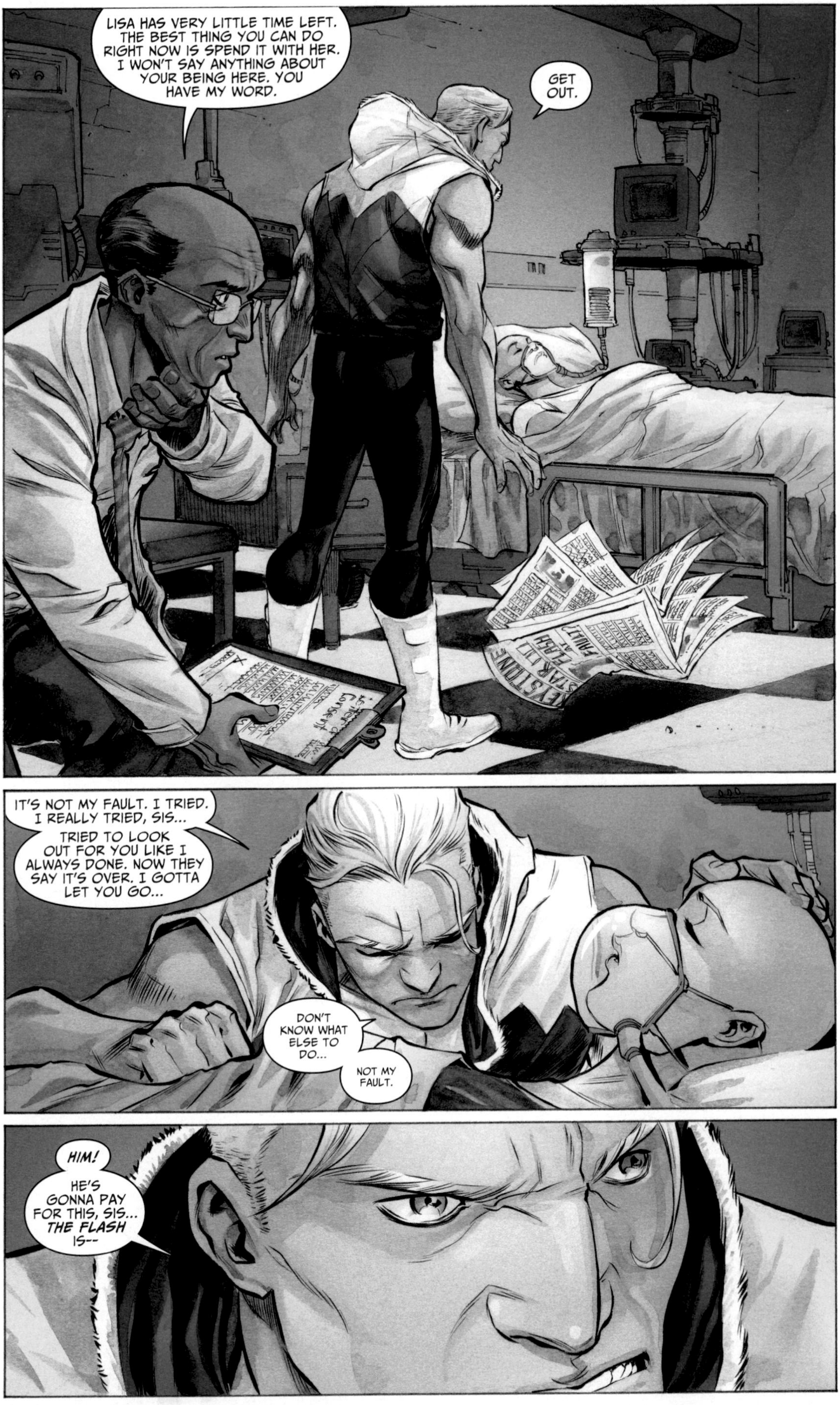
LISA HAS VERY LITTLE TIME LEFT. THE BEST THING YOU CAN DO RIGHT NOW IS SPEND IT WITH HER. I WON'T SAY ANYTHING ABOUT YOUR BEING HERE. YOU HAVE MY WORD.
GET OUT.
IT'S NOT MY FAULT. I TRIED. I REALLY TRIED, SIS...
TRIED TO LOOK OUT FOR YOU LIKE I ALWAYS DONE. NOW THEY SAY IT'S OVER. I GOTTA LET YOU GO...
DON'T KNOW WHAT ELSE TO DO...
NOT MY FAULT.
HIM!
HE'S GONNA PAY FOR THIS, SIS... THE FLASH IS--

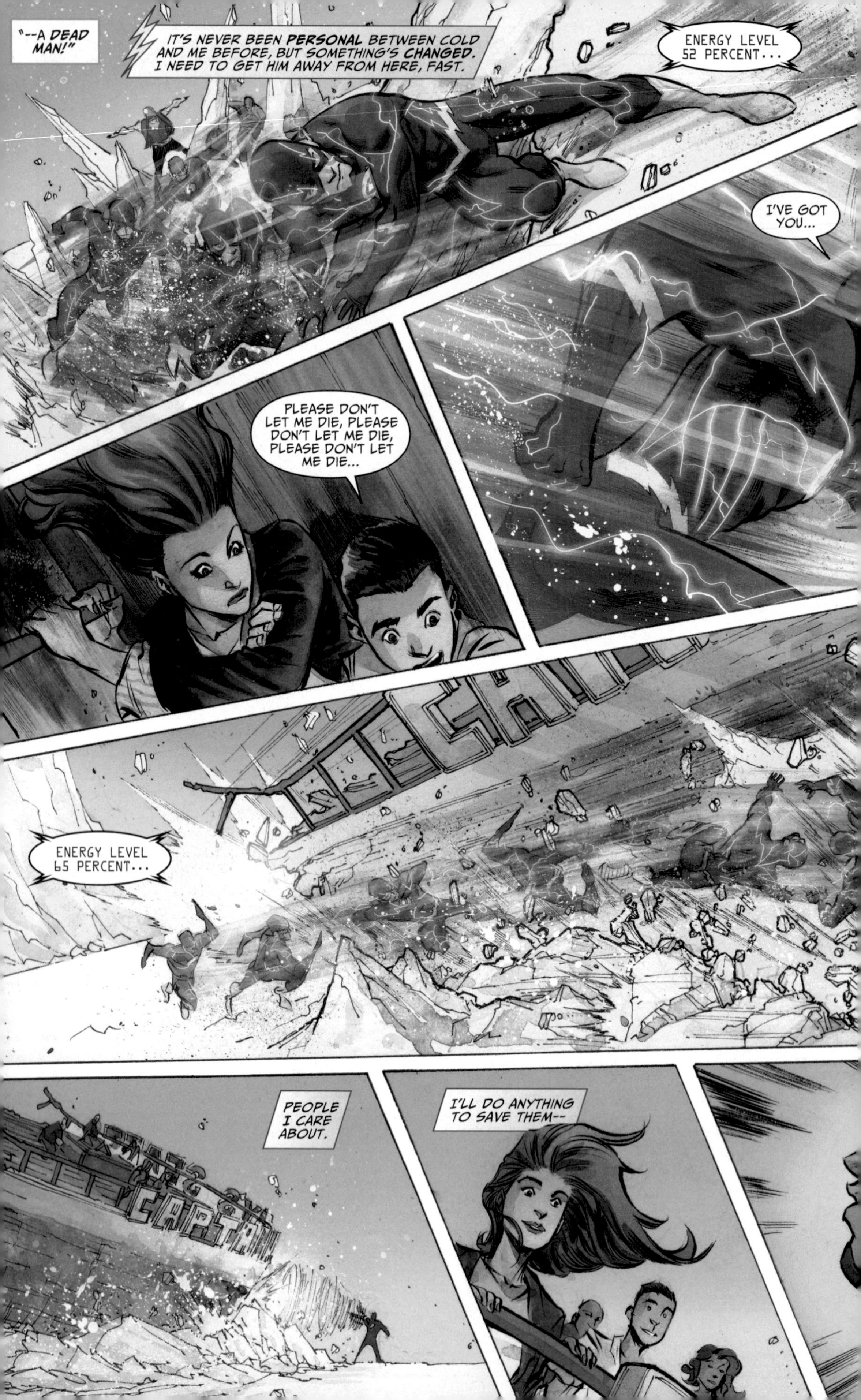
"--A DEAD MAN!"
IT'S NEVER BEEN PERSONAL BETWEEN COLD AND ME BEFORE, BUT SOMETHING'S CHANGED. I NEED TO GET HIM AWAY FROM HERE, FAST.
ENERGY LEVEL 52 PERCENT...
I'VE GOT YOU...
PLEASE DON'T LET ME DIE, PLEASE DON'T LET ME DIE, PLEASE DON'T LET ME DIE...
ENERGY LEVEL 65 PERCENT...
PEOPLE I CARE ABOUT.
I'LL DO ANYTHING TO SAVE THEM--

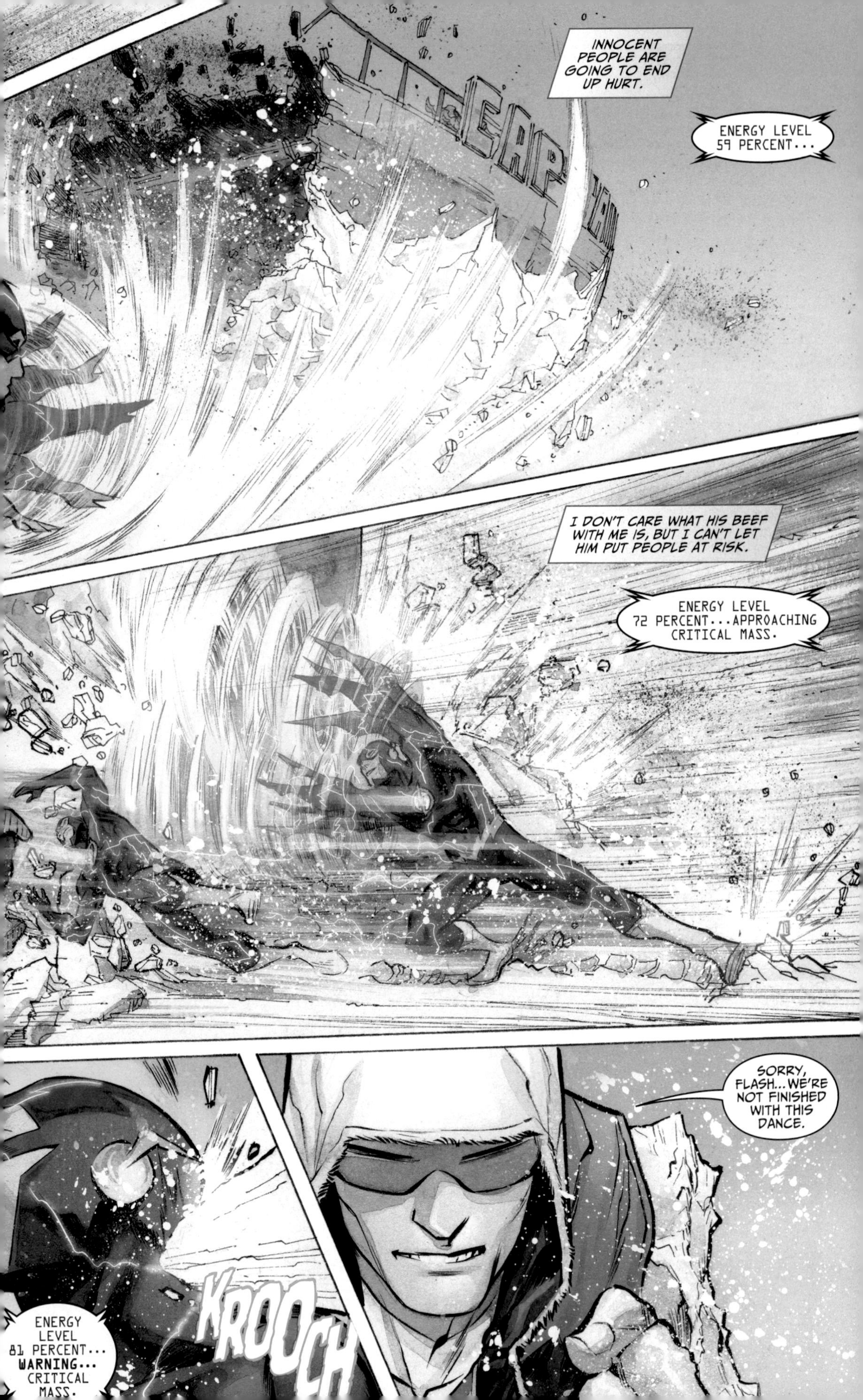
INNOCENT PEOPLE ARE GOING TO END UP HURT.
ENERGY LEVEL 59 PERCENT...
I DON'T CARE WHAT HIS BEEF WITH ME IS, BUT I CAN'T LET HIM PUT PEOPLE AT RISK.
ENERGY LEVEL 72 PERCENT...APPROACHING CRITICAL MASS.
SORRY, FLASH...WE'RE NOT FINISHED WITH THIS DANCE.
KROOCH
ENERGY LEVEL 81 PERCENT... **WARNING...** CRITICAL MASS.

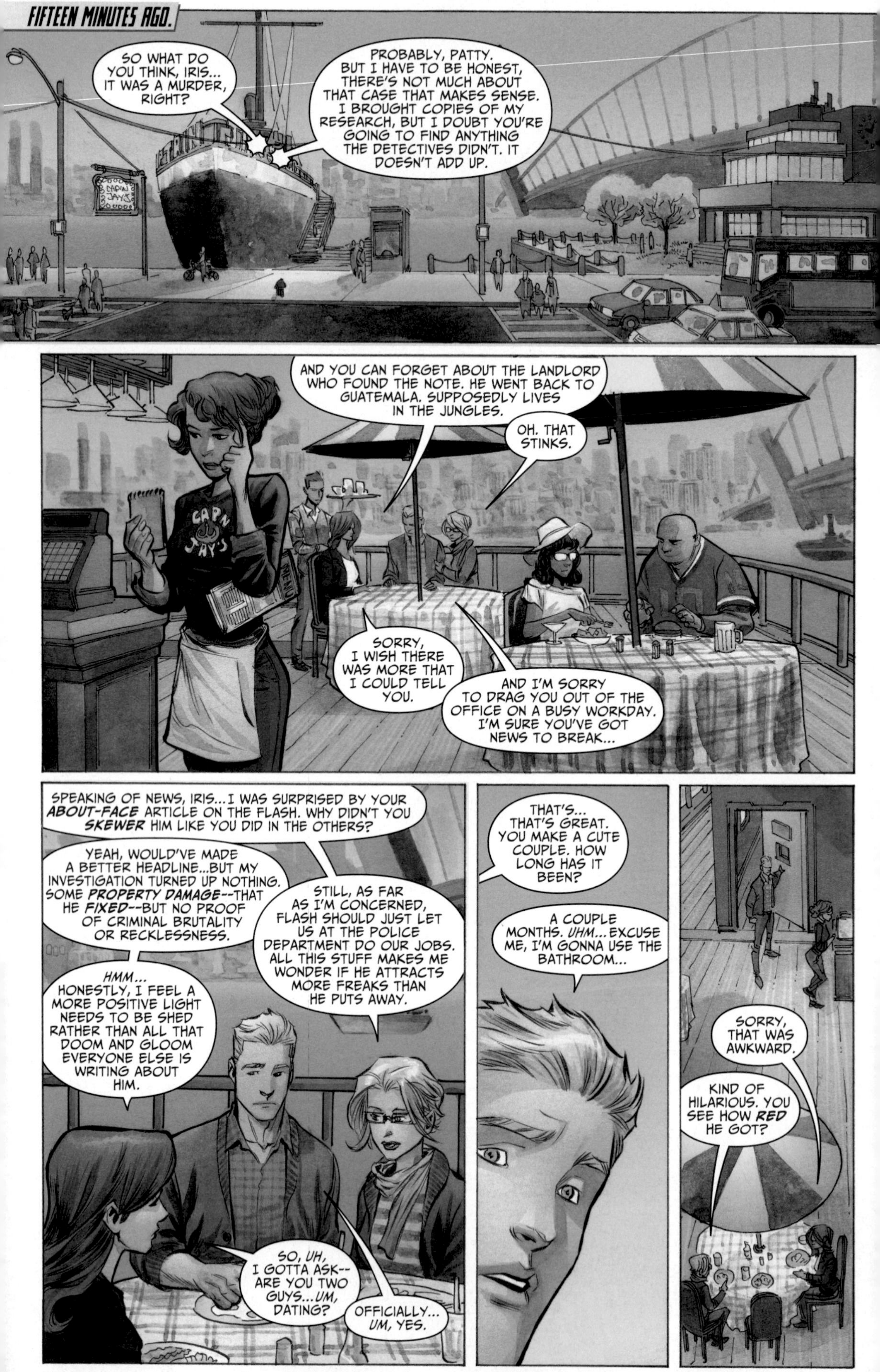
FIFTEEN MINUTES AGO.
SO WHAT DO YOU THINK, IRIS... IT WAS A MURDER, RIGHT?
PROBABLY, PATTY. BUT I HAVE TO BE HONEST, THERE'S NOT MUCH ABOUT THAT CASE THAT MAKES SENSE. I BROUGHT COPIES OF MY RESEARCH, BUT I DOUBT YOU'RE GOING TO FIND ANYTHING THE DETECTIVES DIDN'T. IT DOESN'T ADD UP.
AND YOU CAN FORGET ABOUT THE LANDLORD WHO FOUND THE NOTE. HE WENT BACK TO GUATEMALA. SUPPOSEDLY LIVES IN THE JUNGLES.
OH. THAT STINKS.
SORRY, I WISH THERE WAS MORE THAT I COULD TELL YOU.
AND I'M SORRY TO DRAG YOU OUT OF THE OFFICE ON A BUSY WORKDAY. I'M SURE YOU'VE GOT NEWS TO BREAK...
SPEAKING OF NEWS, IRIS... I WAS SURPRISED BY YOUR ABOUT-FACE ARTICLE ON THE FLASH. WHY DIDN'T YOU SKEWER HIM LIKE YOU DID IN THE OTHERS?
YEAH, WOULD'VE MADE A BETTER HEADLINE...BUT MY INVESTIGATION TURNED UP NOTHING. SOME PROPERTY DAMAGE--THAT HE FIXED--BUT NO PROOF OF CRIMINAL BRUTALITY OR RECKLESSNESS.
STILL, AS FAR AS I'M CONCERNED, FLASH SHOULD JUST LET US AT THE POLICE DEPARTMENT DO OUR JOBS. ALL THIS STUFF MAKES ME WONDER IF HE ATTRACTS MORE FREAKS THAN HE PUTS AWAY.
HMM... HONESTLY, I FEEL A MORE POSITIVE LIGHT NEEDS TO BE SHED RATHER THAN ALL THAT DOOM AND GLOOM EVERYONE ELSE IS WRITING ABOUT HIM.
SO, UH, I GOTTA ASK-- ARE YOU TWO GUYS...UM, DATING?
OFFICIALLY... UM, YES.
THAT'S... THAT'S GREAT. YOU MAKE A CUTE COUPLE. HOW LONG HAS IT BEEN?
A COUPLE MONTHS. UHM... EXCUSE ME, I'M GONNA USE THE BATHROOM...
SORRY, THAT WAS AWKWARD.
KIND OF HILARIOUS. YOU SEE HOW RED HE GOT?

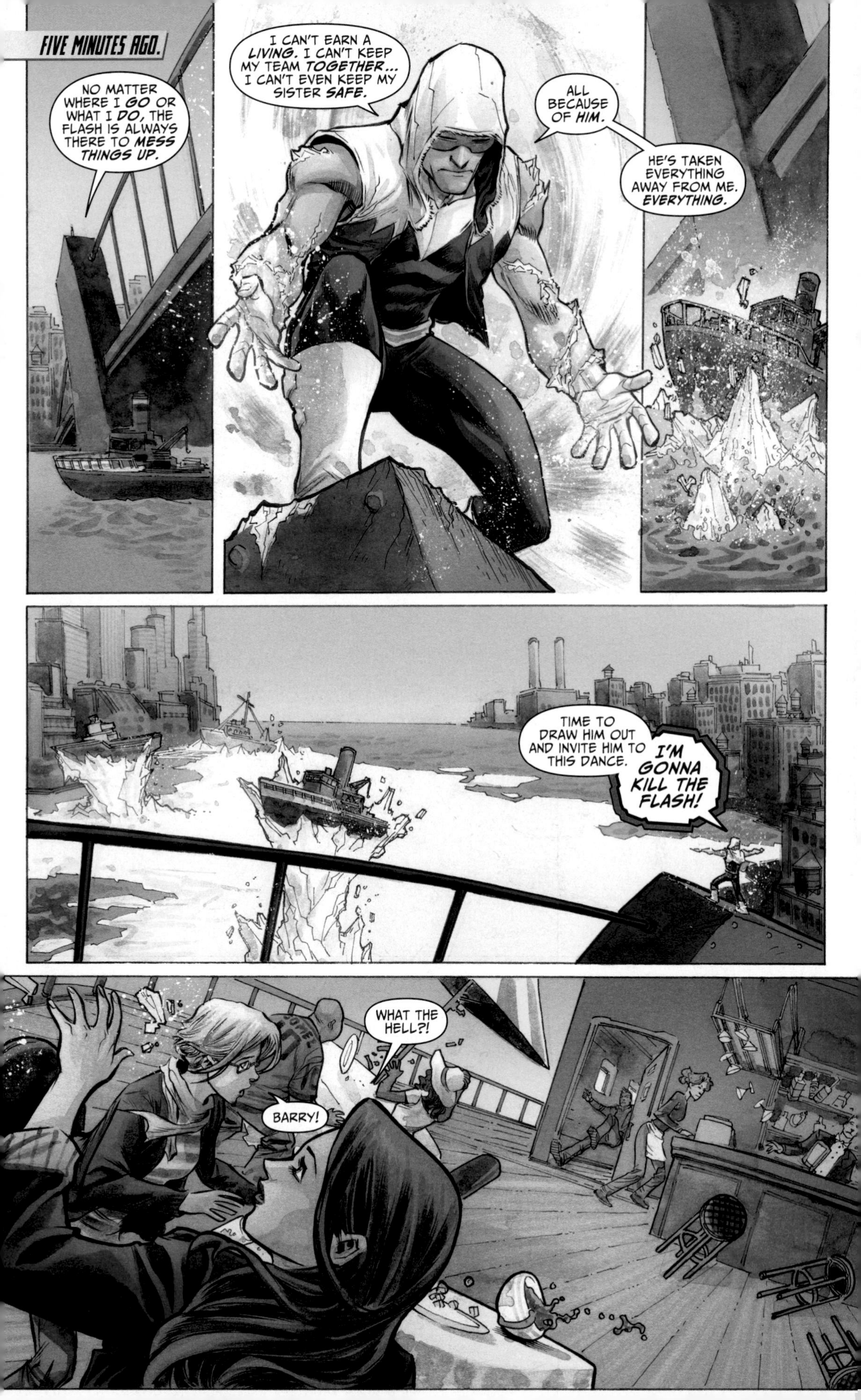
FIVE MINUTES AGO.
NO MATTER WHERE I GO OR WHAT I DO, THE FLASH IS ALWAYS THERE TO MESS THINGS UP.
I CAN'T EARN A LIVING. I CAN'T KEEP MY TEAM TOGETHER... I CAN'T EVEN KEEP MY SISTER SAFE.
ALL BECAUSE OF HIM.
HE'S TAKEN EVERYTHING AWAY FROM ME. EVERYTHING.
TIME TO DRAW HIM OUT AND INVITE HIM TO THIS DANCE.
I'M GONNA KILL THE FLASH!
WHAT THE HELL?!
BARRY!

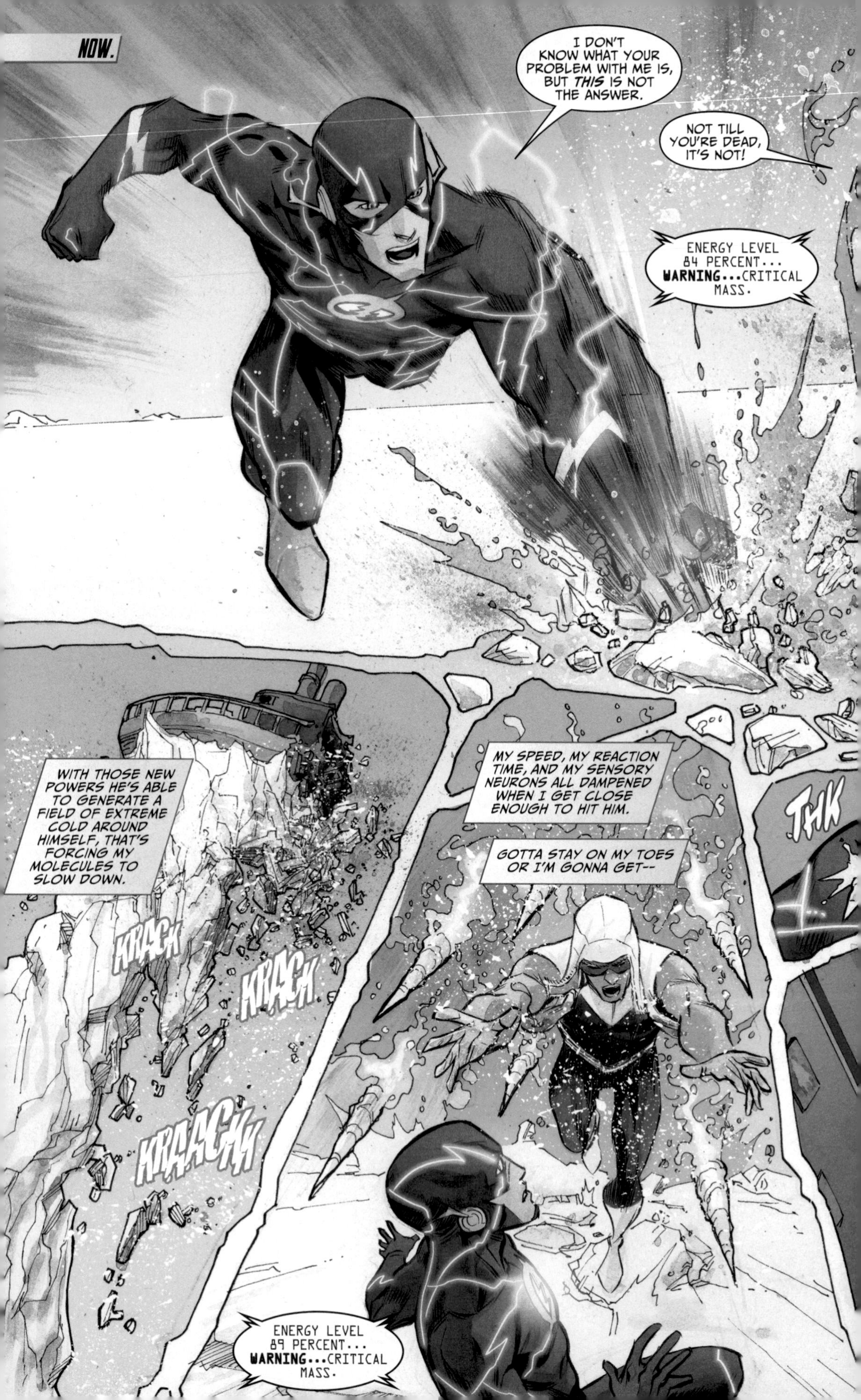
NOW.
I DON'T KNOW WHAT YOUR PROBLEM WITH ME IS, BUT *THIS* IS NOT THE ANSWER.
NOT TILL YOU'RE DEAD, IT'S NOT!
ENERGY LEVEL 84 PERCENT... **WARNING...**CRITICAL MASS.
WITH THOSE NEW POWERS HE'S ABLE TO GENERATE A FIELD OF EXTREME COLD AROUND HIMSELF, THAT'S FORCING MY MOLECULES TO SLOW DOWN.
KRACK
KRACK
KRAACKK
MY SPEED, MY REACTION TIME, AND MY SENSORY NEURONS ALL DAMPENED WHEN I GET CLOSE ENOUGH TO HIT HIM.
GOTTA STAY ON MY TOES OR I'M GONNA GET--
THK
ENERGY LEVEL 89 PERCENT... **WARNING...**CRITICAL MASS.

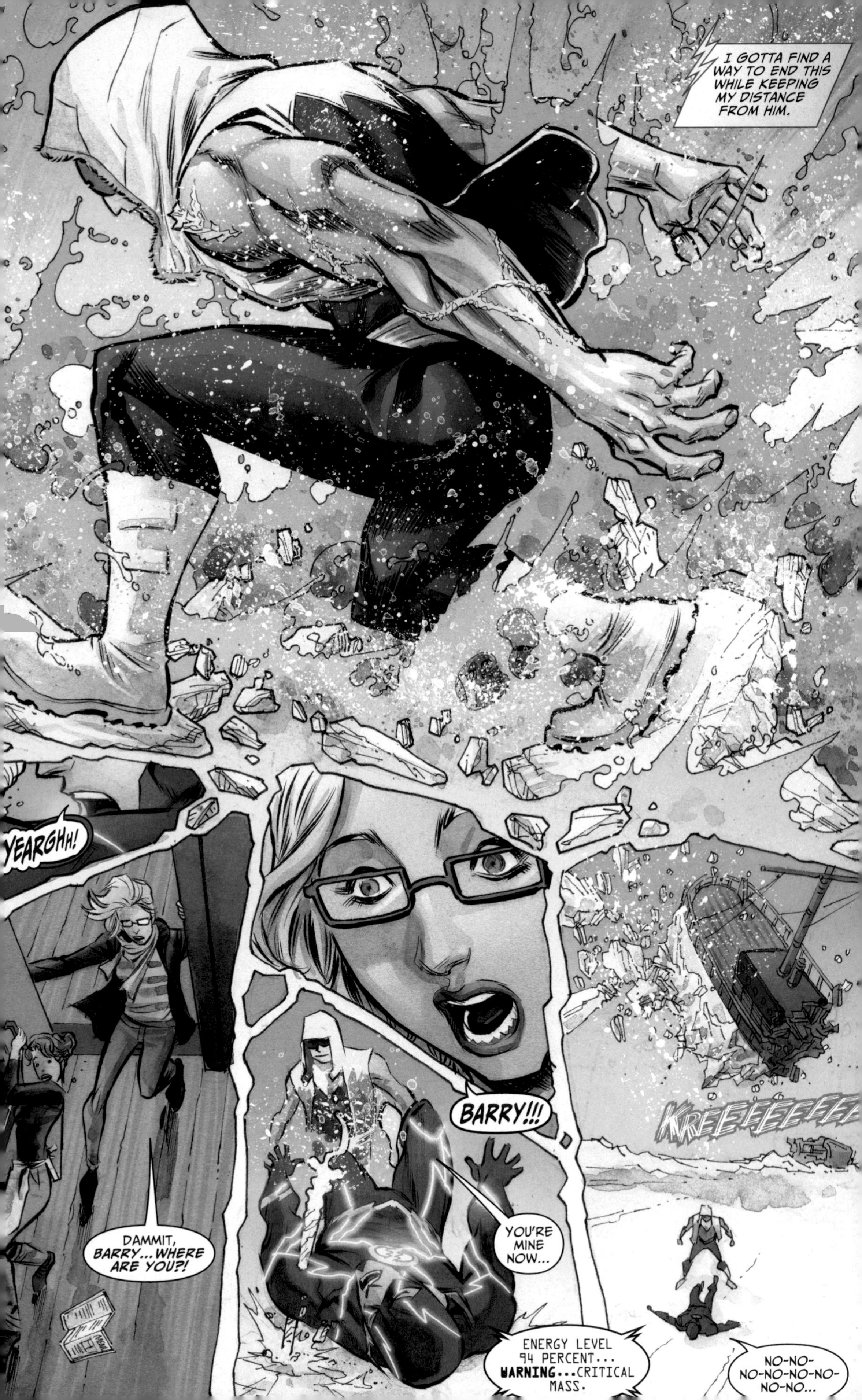
I GOTTA FIND A WAY TO END THIS WHILE KEEPING MY DISTANCE FROM HIM.
YEARGHH!
DAMMIT, BARRY...WHERE ARE YOU?!
BARRY!!!
YOU'RE MINE NOW...
ENERGY LEVEL 94 PERCENT... WARNING...CRITICAL MASS.
KREEEEEEEE
NO-NO-NO-NO-NO-NO-NO-NO...

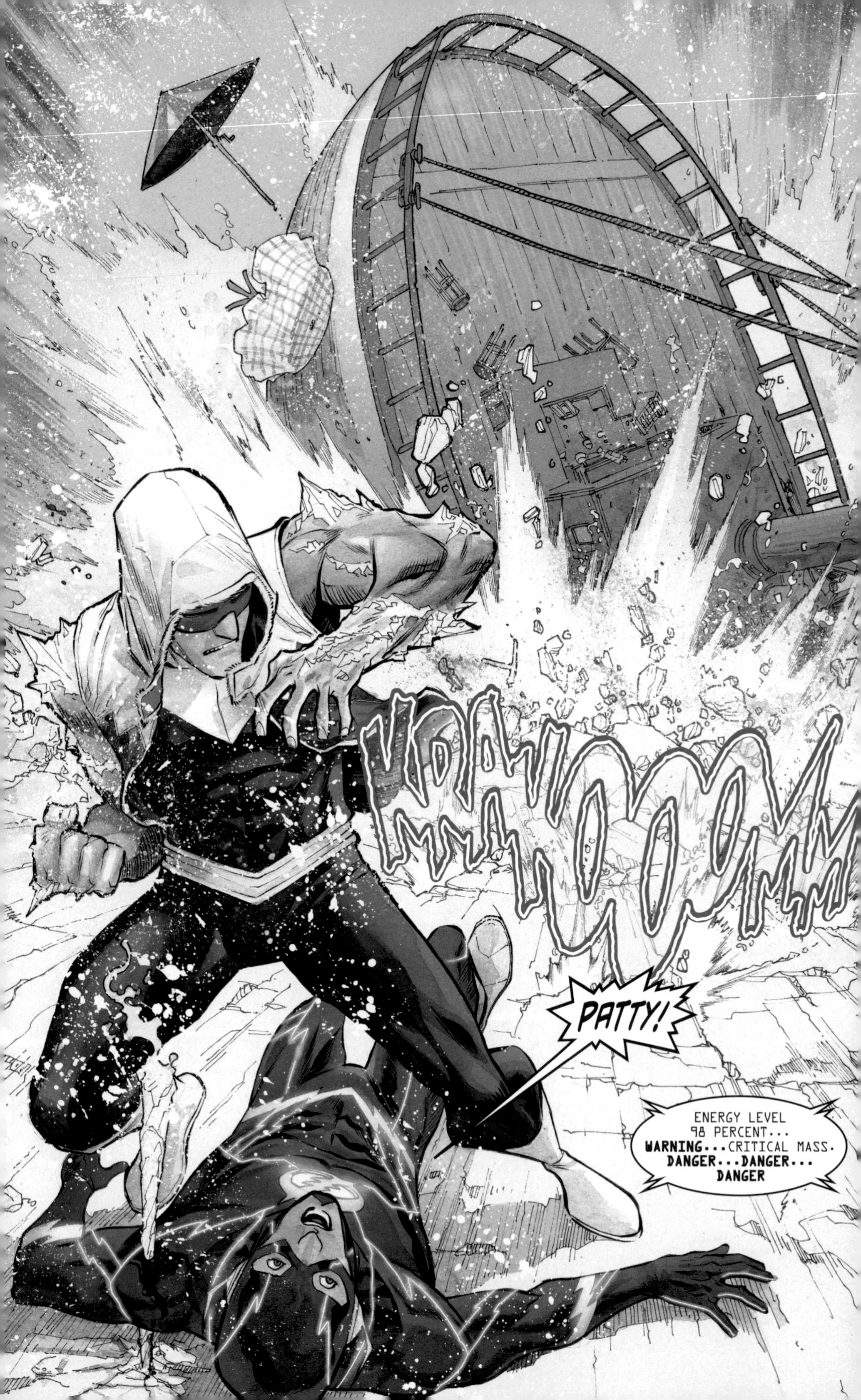
VRAWOOOOM
PATTY!
ENERGY LEVEL
98 PERCENT...
WARNING...CRITICAL MASS.
DANGER...DANGER...
DANGER

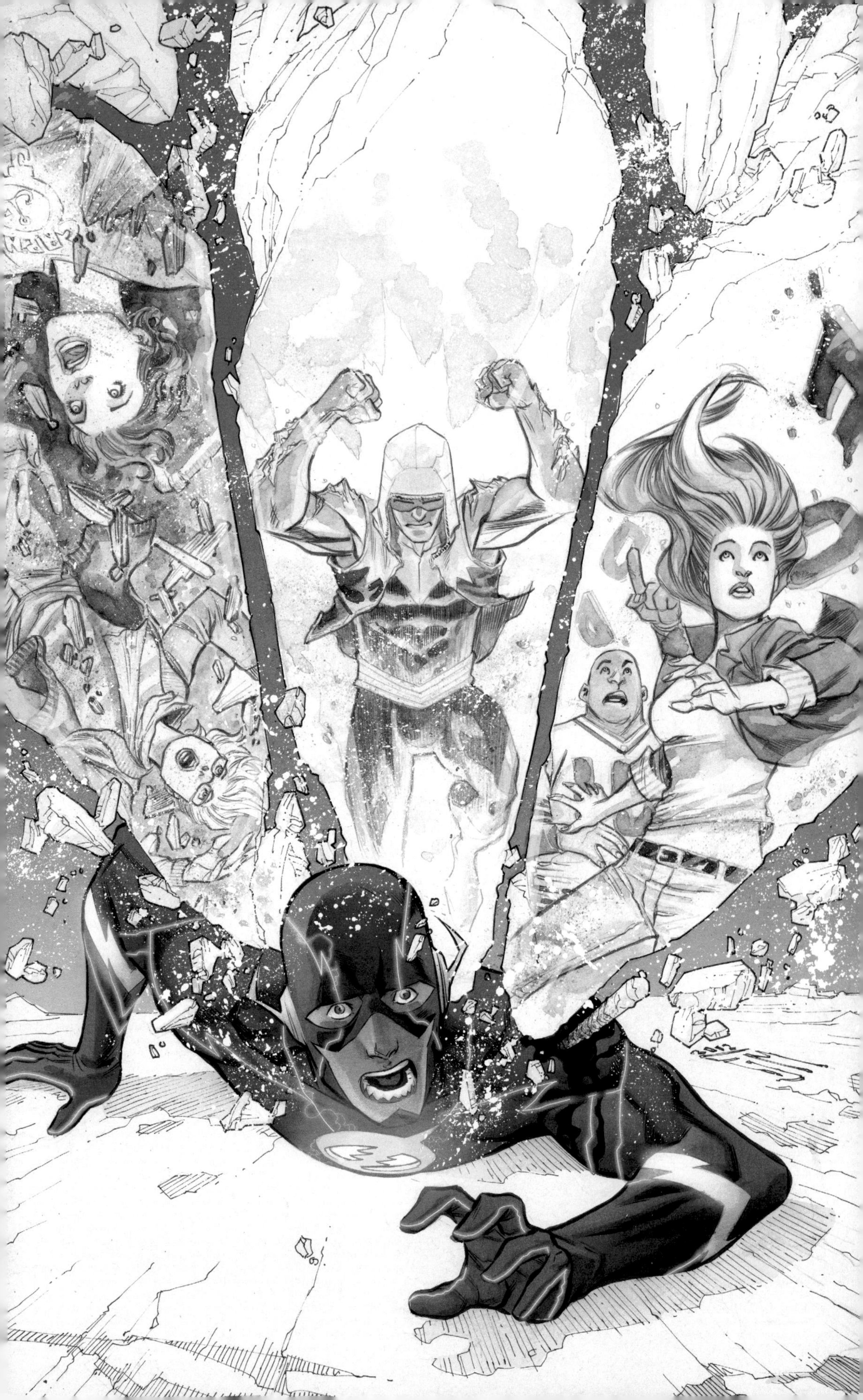

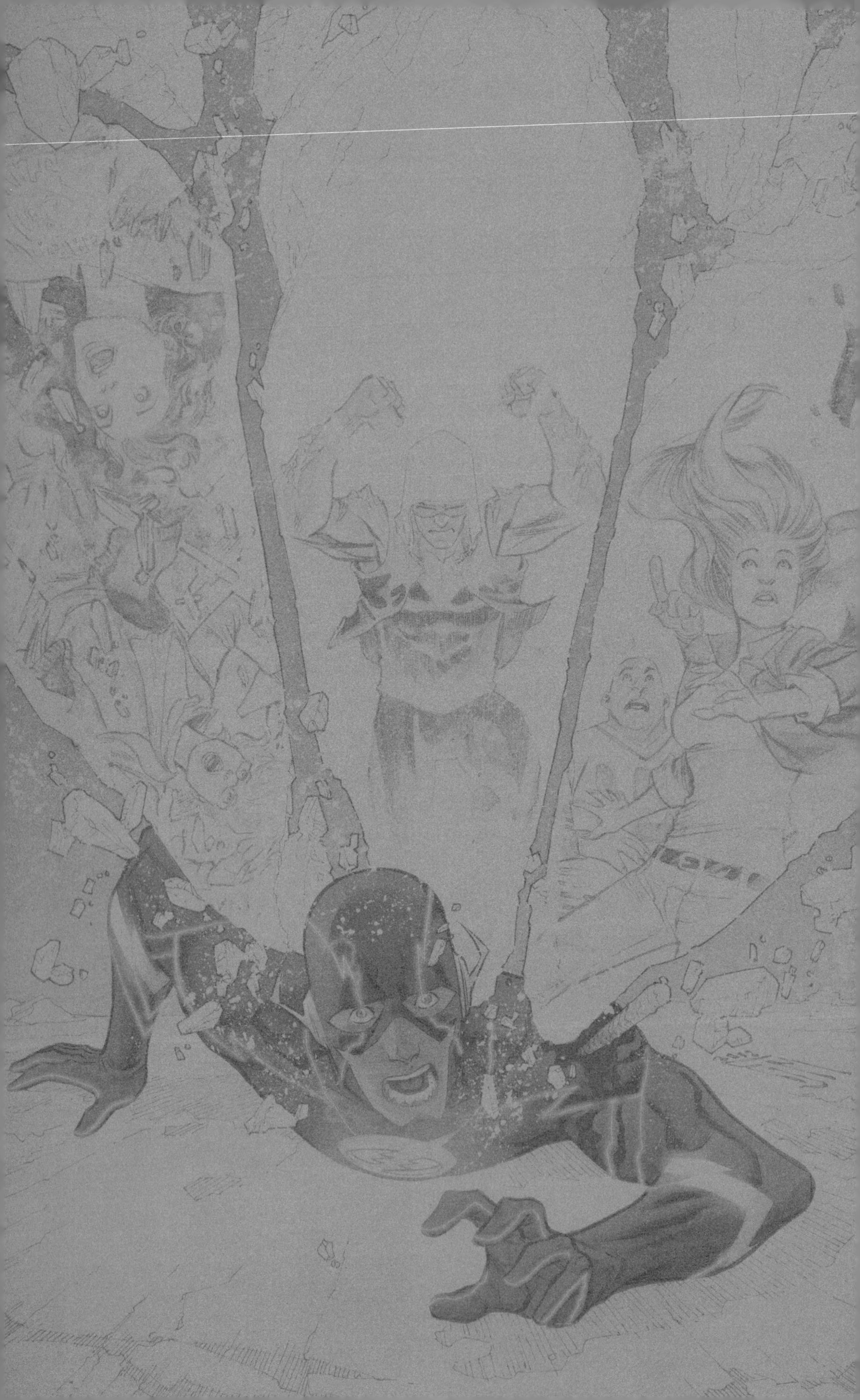

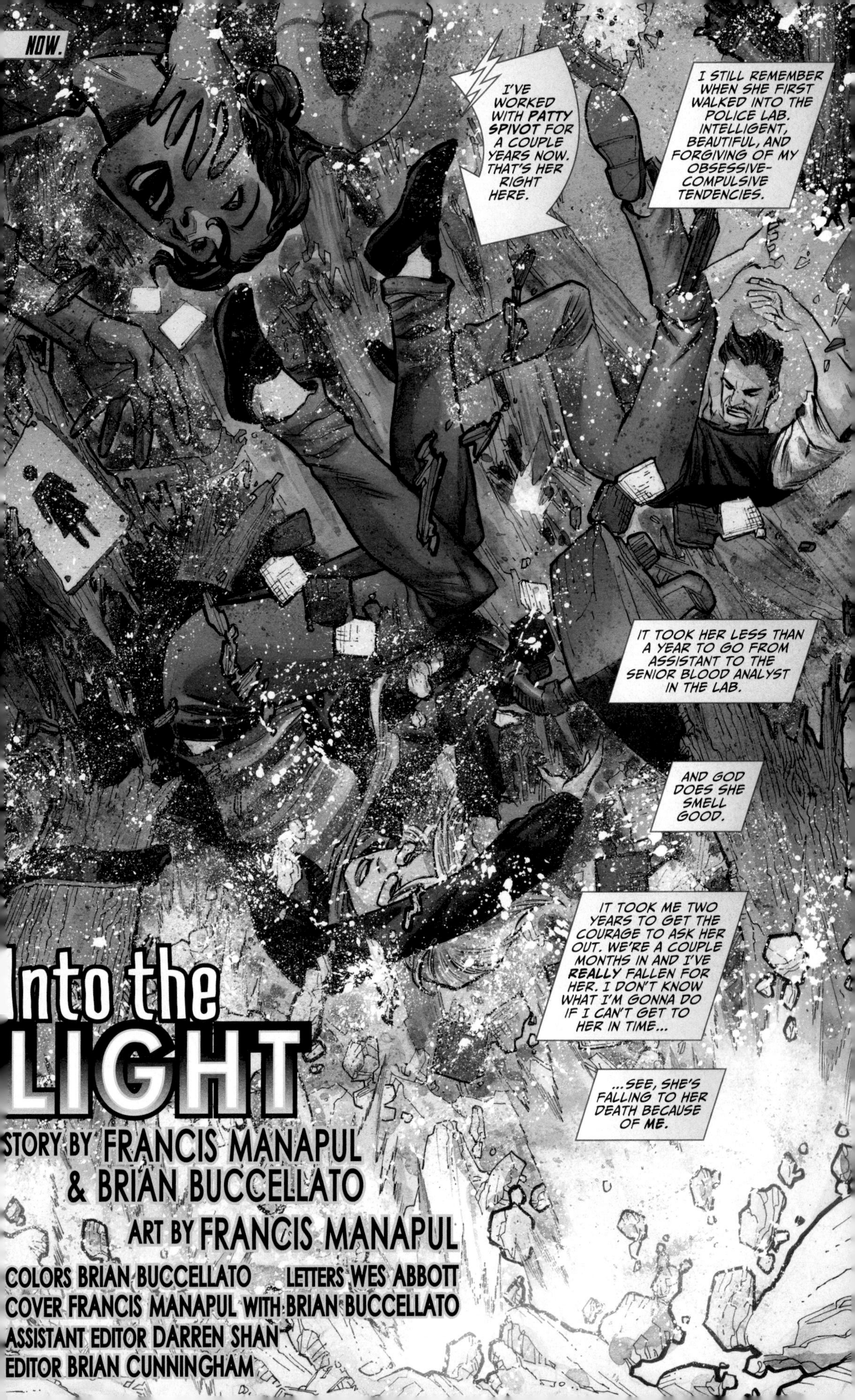
NOW.
I'VE WORKED WITH PATTY SPIVOT FOR A COUPLE YEARS NOW. THAT'S HER RIGHT HERE.
I STILL REMEMBER WHEN SHE FIRST WALKED INTO THE POLICE LAB. INTELLIGENT, BEAUTIFUL, AND FORGIVING OF MY OBSESSIVE-COMPULSIVE TENDENCIES.
IT TOOK HER LESS THAN A YEAR TO GO FROM ASSISTANT TO THE SENIOR BLOOD ANALYST IN THE LAB.
AND GOD DOES SHE SMELL GOOD.
IT TOOK ME TWO YEARS TO GET THE COURAGE TO ASK HER OUT. WE'RE A COUPLE MONTHS IN AND I'VE REALLY FALLEN FOR HER. I DON'T KNOW WHAT I'M GONNA DO IF I CAN'T GET TO HER IN TIME...
...SEE, SHE'S FALLING TO HER DEATH BECAUSE OF ME.
Into the LIGHT
STORY BY FRANCIS MANAPUL & BRIAN BUCCELLATO
ART BY FRANCIS MANAPUL
COLORS BRIAN BUCCELLATO LETTERS WES ABBOTT
COVER FRANCIS MANAPUL WITH BRIAN BUCCELLATO
ASSISTANT EDITOR DARREN SHAN
EDITOR BRIAN CUNNINGHAM

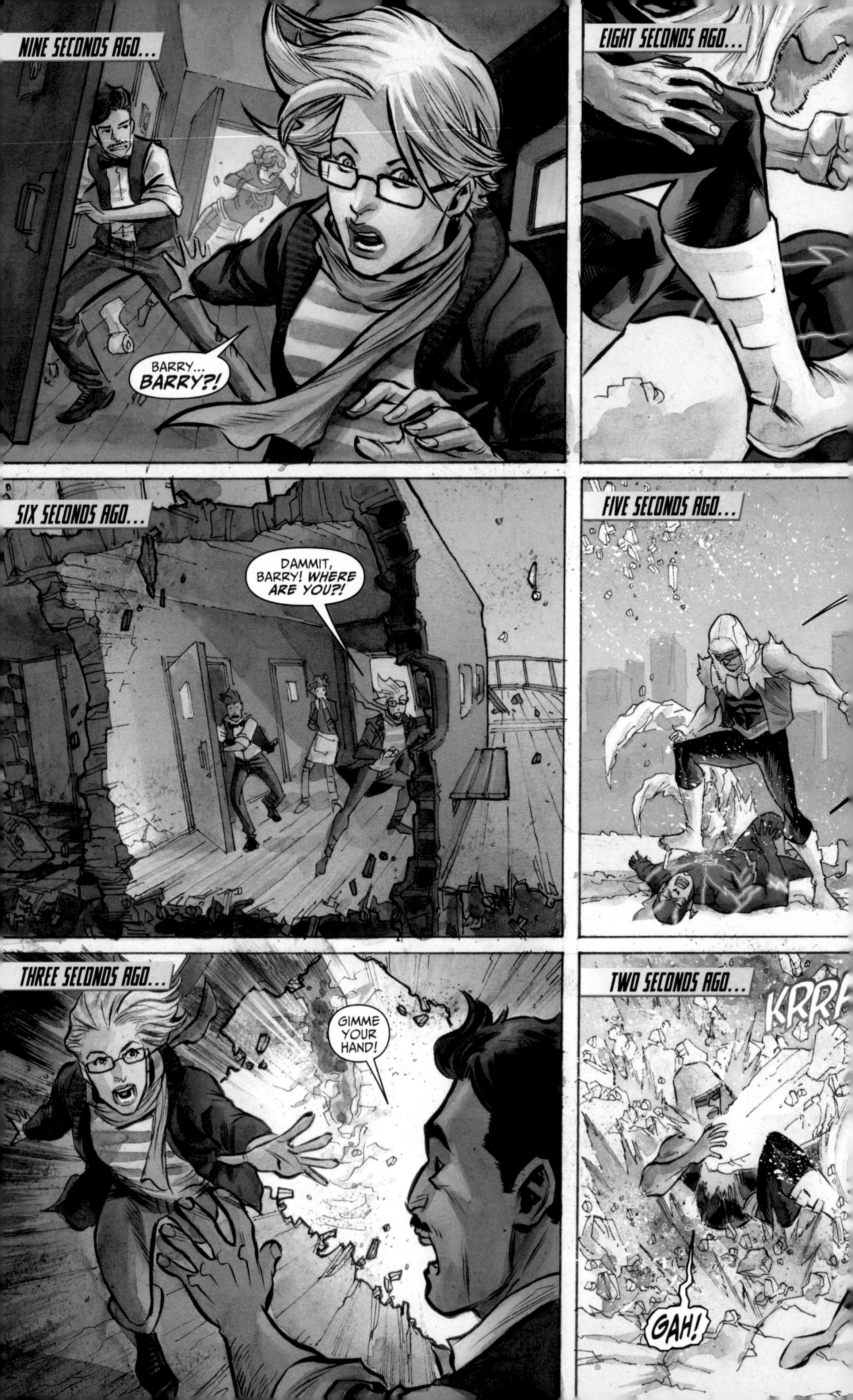
NINE SECONDS AGO...
BARRY... BARRY?!
EIGHT SECONDS AGO...
SIX SECONDS AGO...
DAMMIT, BARRY! WHERE ARE YOU?!
FIVE SECONDS AGO...
THREE SECONDS AGO...
GIMME YOUR HAND!
TWO SECONDS AGO...
GAH!

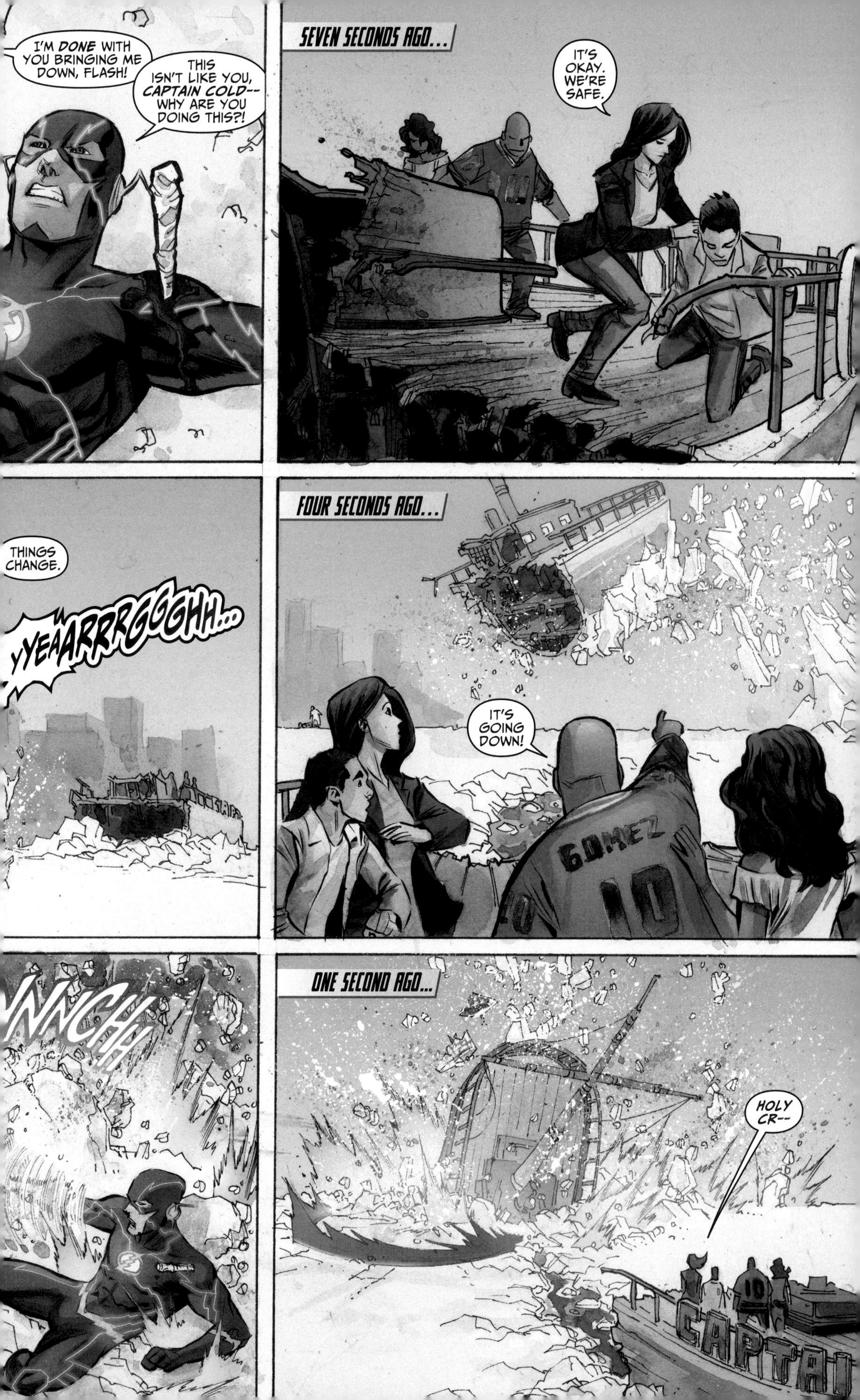

I'M DONE WITH YOU BRINGING ME DOWN, FLASH!
THIS ISN'T LIKE YOU, CAPTAIN COLD-- WHY ARE YOU DOING THIS?!
SEVEN SECONDS AGO...
IT'S OKAY. WE'RE SAFE.
THINGS CHANGE.
YYEAARRRGGGHH...
FOUR SECONDS AGO...
IT'S GOING DOWN!
GOMEZ
10
NNCHH
ONE SECOND AGO...
HOLY CR--
CAPTAI

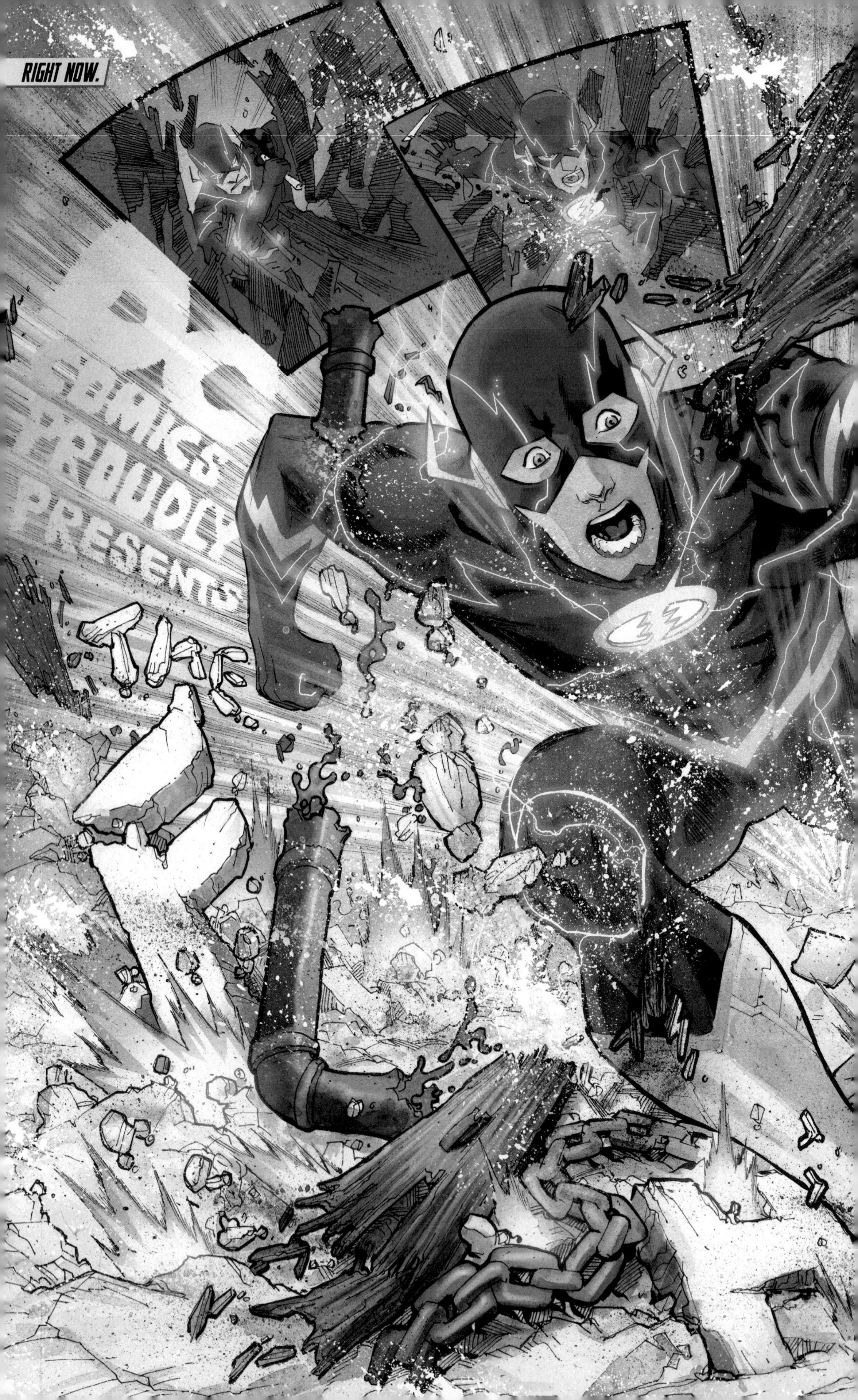
RIGHT NOW.
PROUDLY
PRESENTS
THE

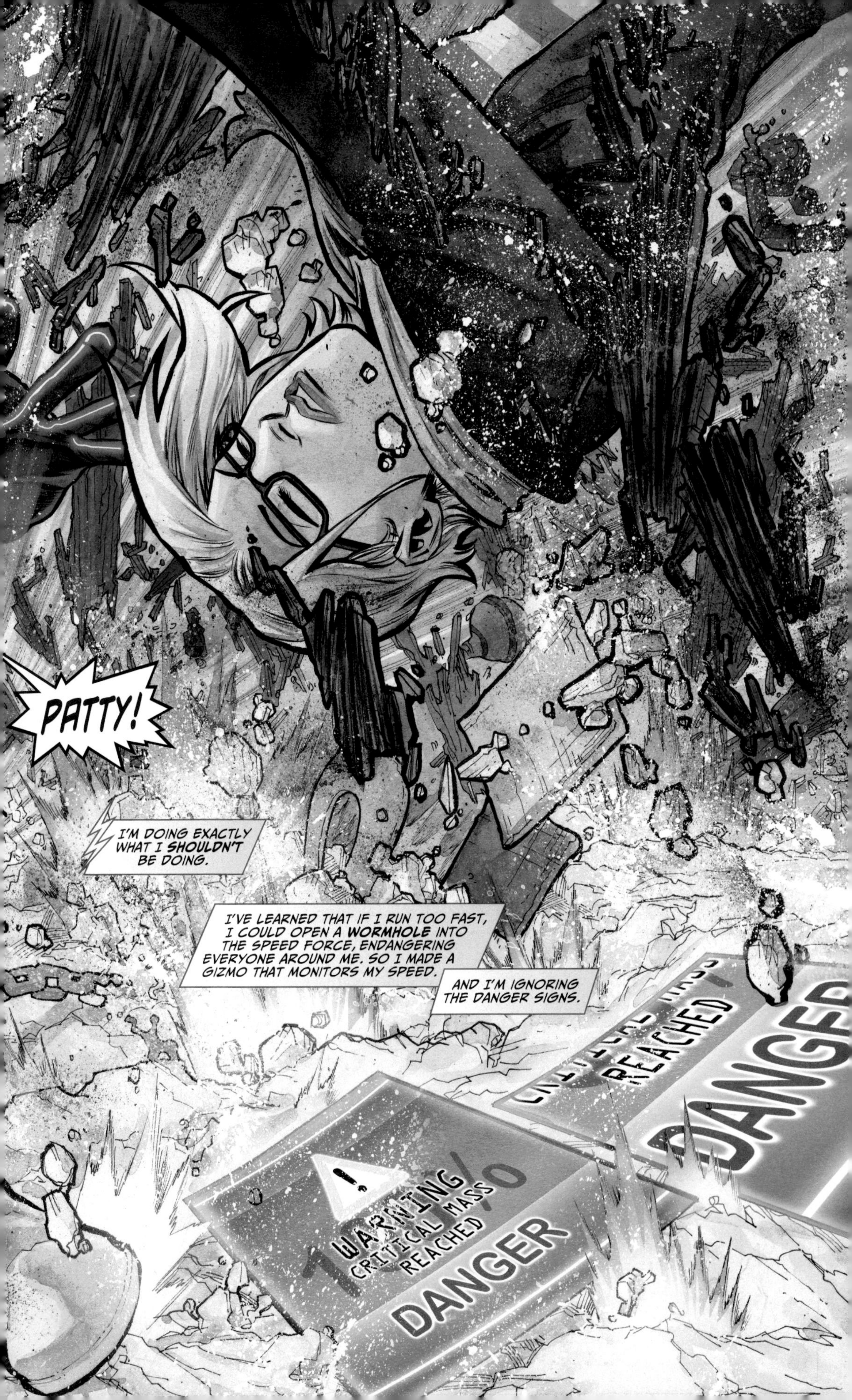
PATTY!
I'M DOING EXACTLY WHAT I SHOULDN'T BE DOING.
I'VE LEARNED THAT IF I RUN TOO FAST, I COULD OPEN A WORMHOLE INTO THE SPEED FORCE, ENDANGERING EVERYONE AROUND ME. SO I MADE A GIZMO THAT MONITORS MY SPEED.
AND I'M IGNORING THE DANGER SIGNS.
REACHED
WARNING
CRITICAL MASS
REACHED
DANGER

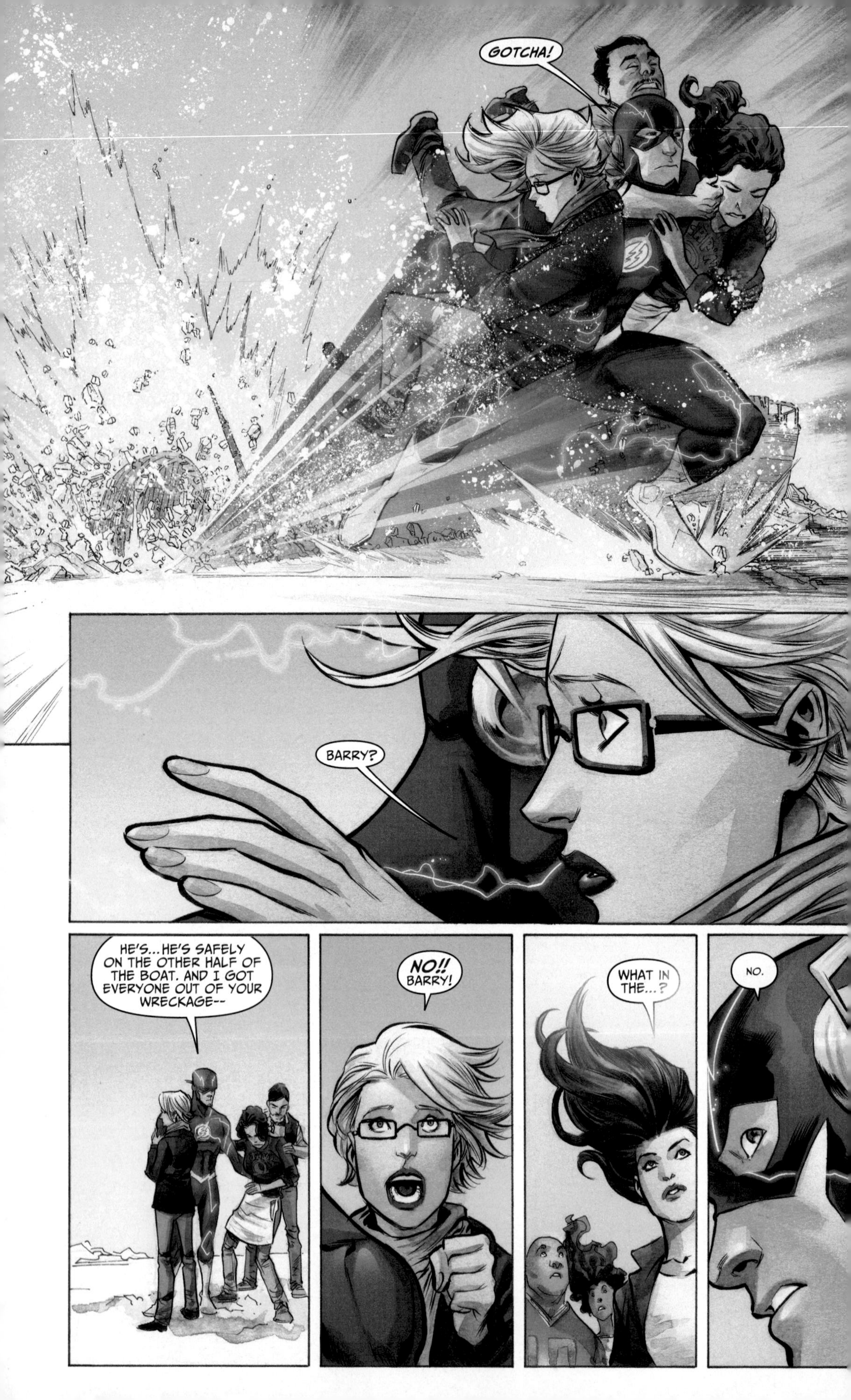
GOTCHA!
BARRY?
HE'S...HE'S SAFELY ON THE OTHER HALF OF THE BOAT. AND I GOT EVERYONE OUT OF YOUR WRECKAGE--
NO!! BARRY!
WHAT IN THE...?
NO.

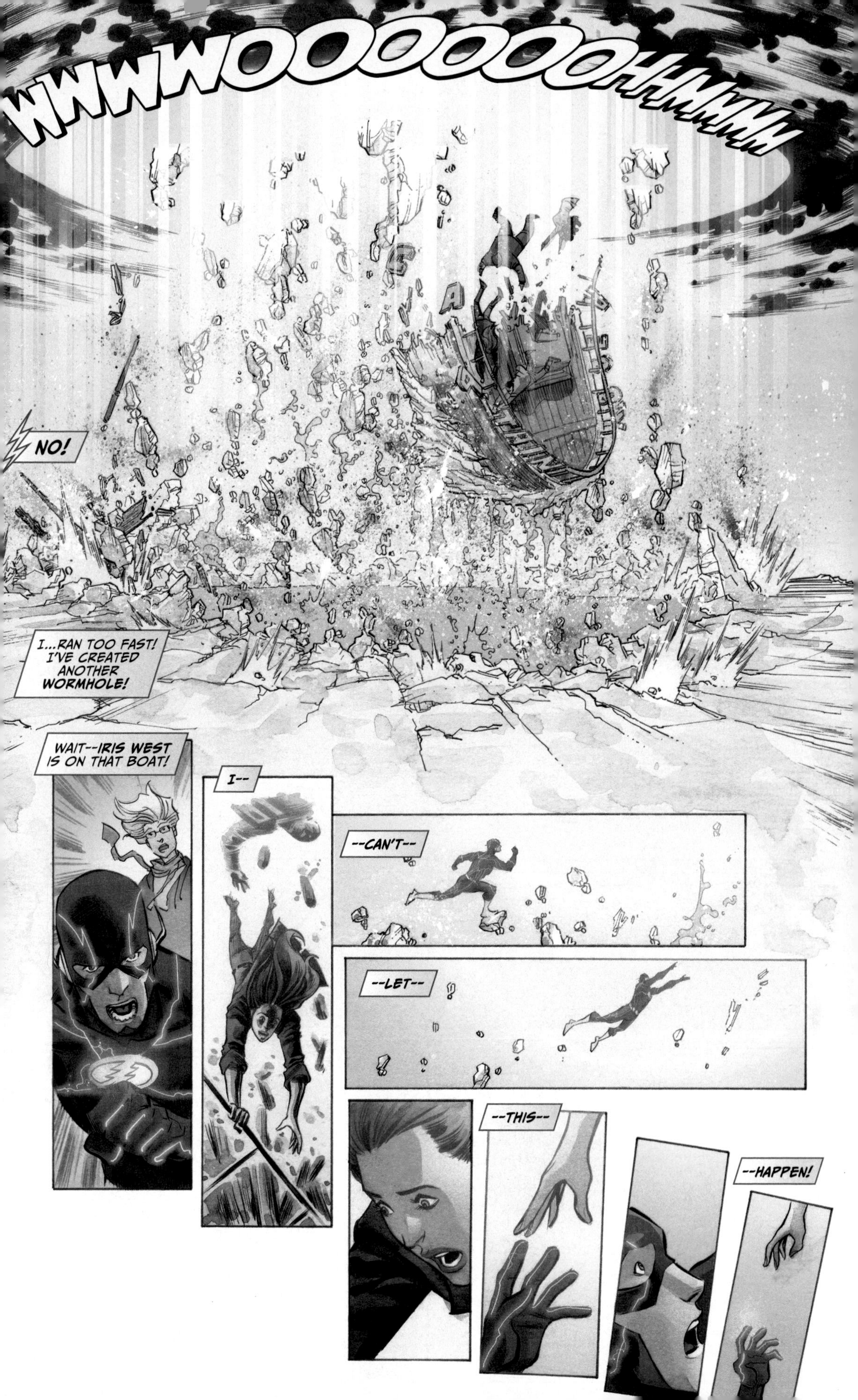
WWWWOOOOOOOOHMMMM
NO!
I...RAN TOO FAST! I'VE CREATED ANOTHER WORMHOLE!
WAIT--IRIS WEST IS ON THAT BOAT!
I--
--CAN'T--
--LET--
--THIS--
--HAPPEN!

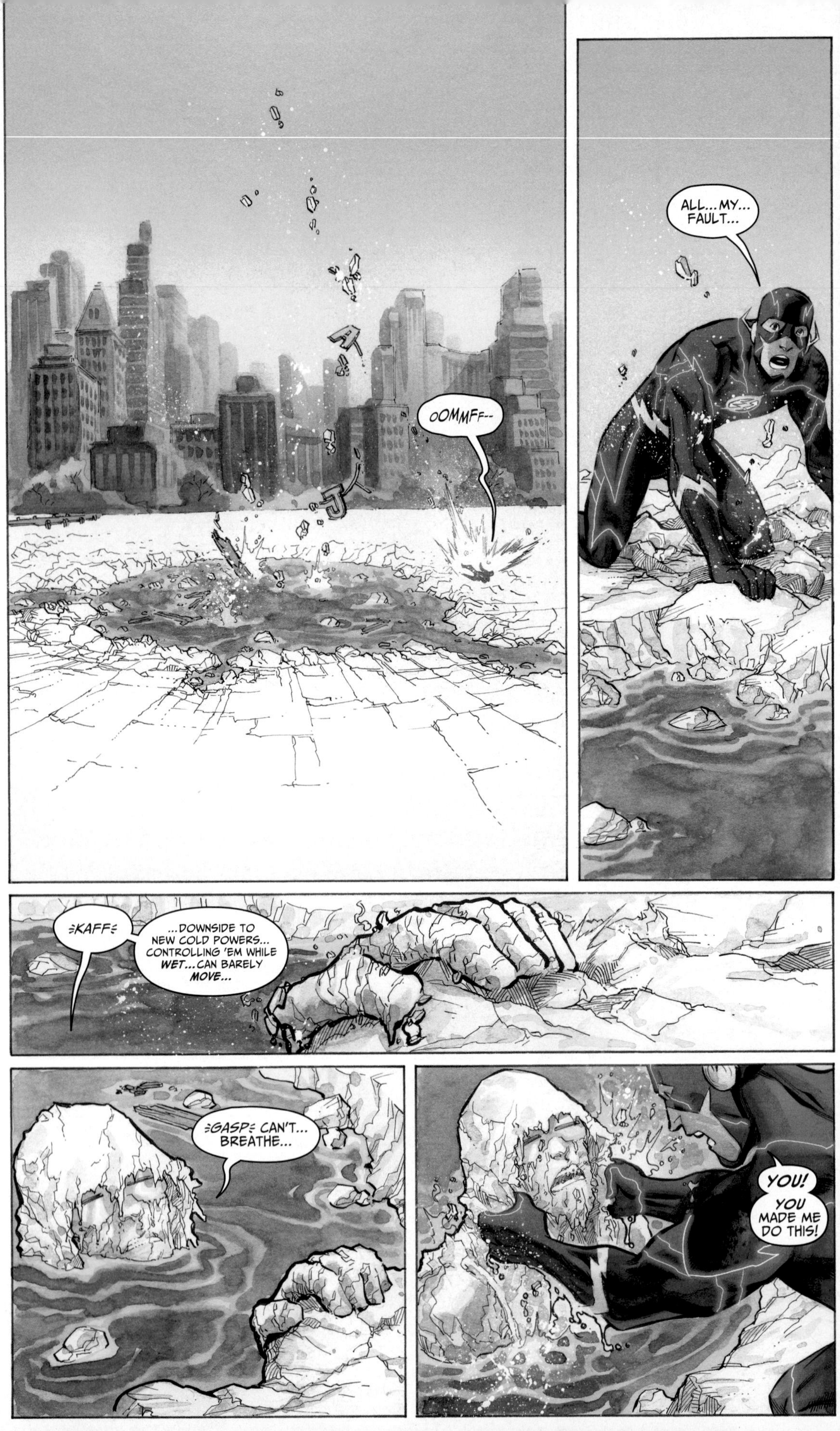
OOMMFF--
ALL...MY... FAULT...
KAFF
...DOWNSIDE TO NEW COLD POWERS... CONTROLLING 'EM WHILE WET...CAN BARELY MOVE...
GASP CAN'T... BREATHE...
YOU! YOU MADE ME DO THIS!

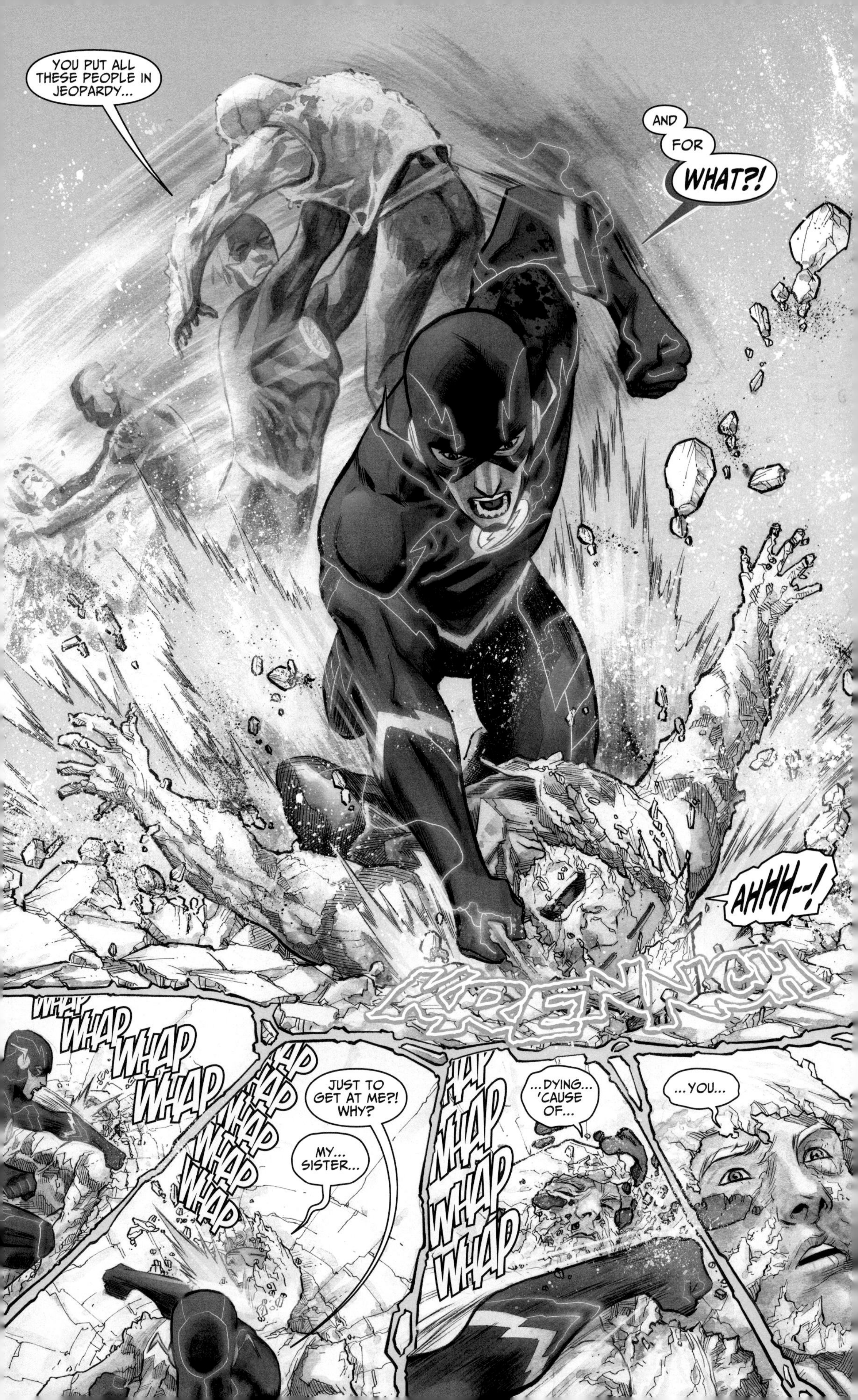
YOU PUT ALL THESE PEOPLE IN JEOPARDY...
AND FOR WHAT?!
AHHH--!
KRRENNCH
WHAP WHAP WHAP WHAP
WHAP WHAP WHAP WHAP WHAP
JUST TO GET AT ME?! WHY?
MY... SISTER...
WHAP WHAP WHAP WHAP
...DYING... 'CAUSE OF...
...YOU...

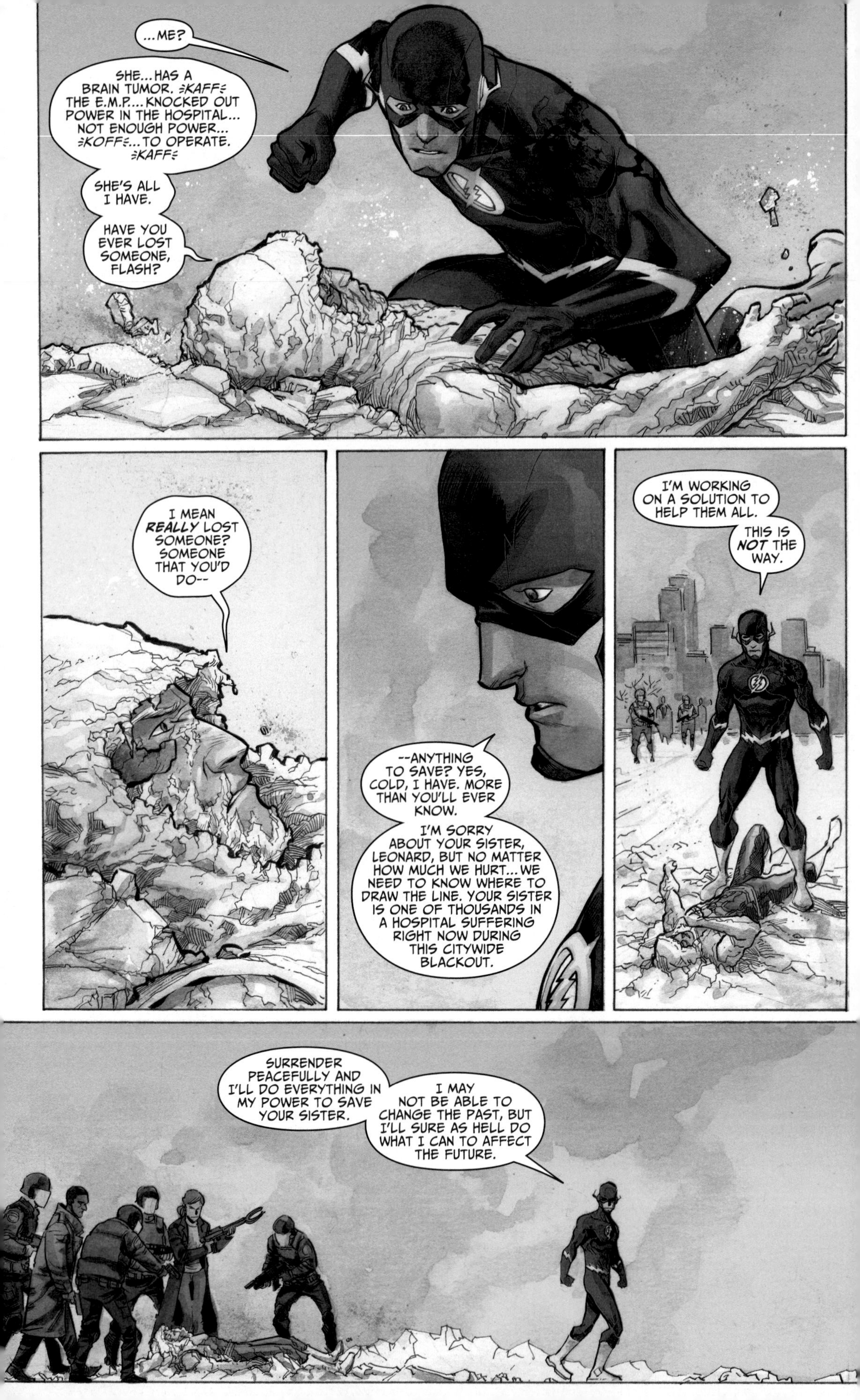
...ME?
SHE...HAS A BRAIN TUMOR. ≡KAFF≡ THE E.M.P....KNOCKED OUT POWER IN THE HOSPITAL... NOT ENOUGH POWER... ≡KOFF≡...TO OPERATE. ≡KAFF≡
SHE'S ALL I HAVE.
HAVE YOU EVER LOST SOMEONE, FLASH?
I MEAN *REALLY* LOST SOMEONE? SOMEONE THAT YOU'D DO--
--ANYTHING TO SAVE? YES, COLD, I HAVE. MORE THAN YOU'LL EVER KNOW.
I'M SORRY ABOUT YOUR SISTER, LEONARD, BUT NO MATTER HOW MUCH WE HURT...WE NEED TO KNOW WHERE TO DRAW THE LINE. YOUR SISTER IS ONE OF THOUSANDS IN A HOSPITAL SUFFERING RIGHT NOW DURING THIS CITYWIDE BLACKOUT.
I'M WORKING ON A SOLUTION TO HELP THEM ALL.
THIS IS *NOT* THE WAY.
SURRENDER PEACEFULLY AND I'LL DO EVERYTHING IN MY POWER TO SAVE YOUR SISTER.
I MAY NOT BE ABLE TO CHANGE THE PAST, BUT I'LL SURE AS HELL DO WHAT I CAN TO AFFECT THE FUTURE.

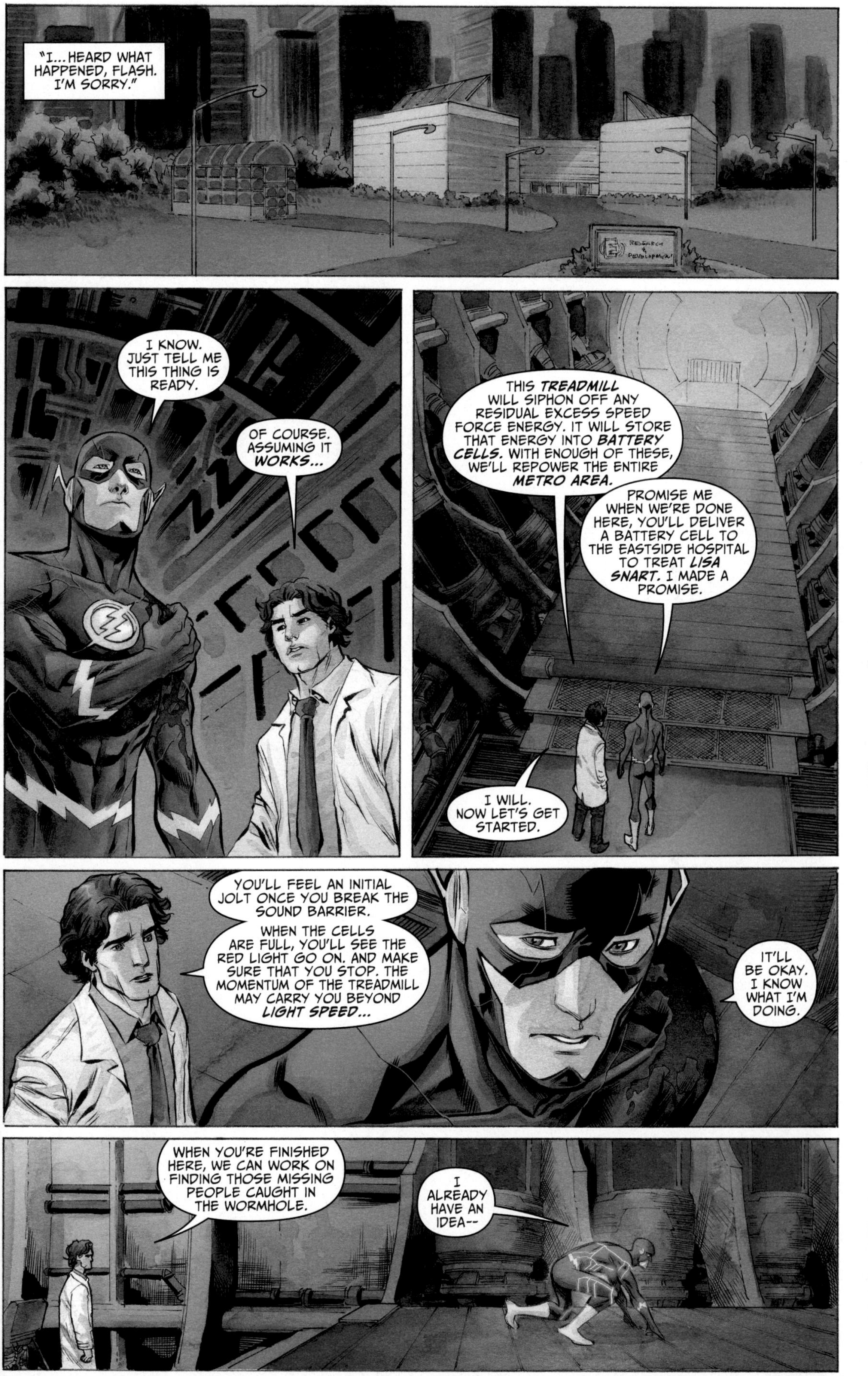
"I...HEARD WHAT HAPPENED, FLASH. I'M SORRY."
I KNOW. JUST TELL ME THIS THING IS READY.
OF COURSE. ASSUMING IT WORKS...
THIS TREADMILL WILL SIPHON OFF ANY RESIDUAL EXCESS SPEED FORCE ENERGY. IT WILL STORE THAT ENERGY INTO BATTERY CELLS. WITH ENOUGH OF THESE, WE'LL REPOWER THE ENTIRE METRO AREA.
PROMISE ME WHEN WE'RE DONE HERE, YOU'LL DELIVER A BATTERY CELL TO THE EASTSIDE HOSPITAL TO TREAT LISA SNART. I MADE A PROMISE.
I WILL. NOW LET'S GET STARTED.
YOU'LL FEEL AN INITIAL JOLT ONCE YOU BREAK THE SOUND BARRIER.
WHEN THE CELLS ARE FULL, YOU'LL SEE THE RED LIGHT GO ON. AND MAKE SURE THAT YOU STOP. THE MOMENTUM OF THE TREADMILL MAY CARRY YOU BEYOND LIGHT SPEED...
IT'LL BE OKAY. I KNOW WHAT I'M DOING.
WHEN YOU'RE FINISHED HERE, WE CAN WORK ON FINDING THOSE MISSING PEOPLE CAUGHT IN THE WORMHOLE.
I ALREADY HAVE AN IDEA--

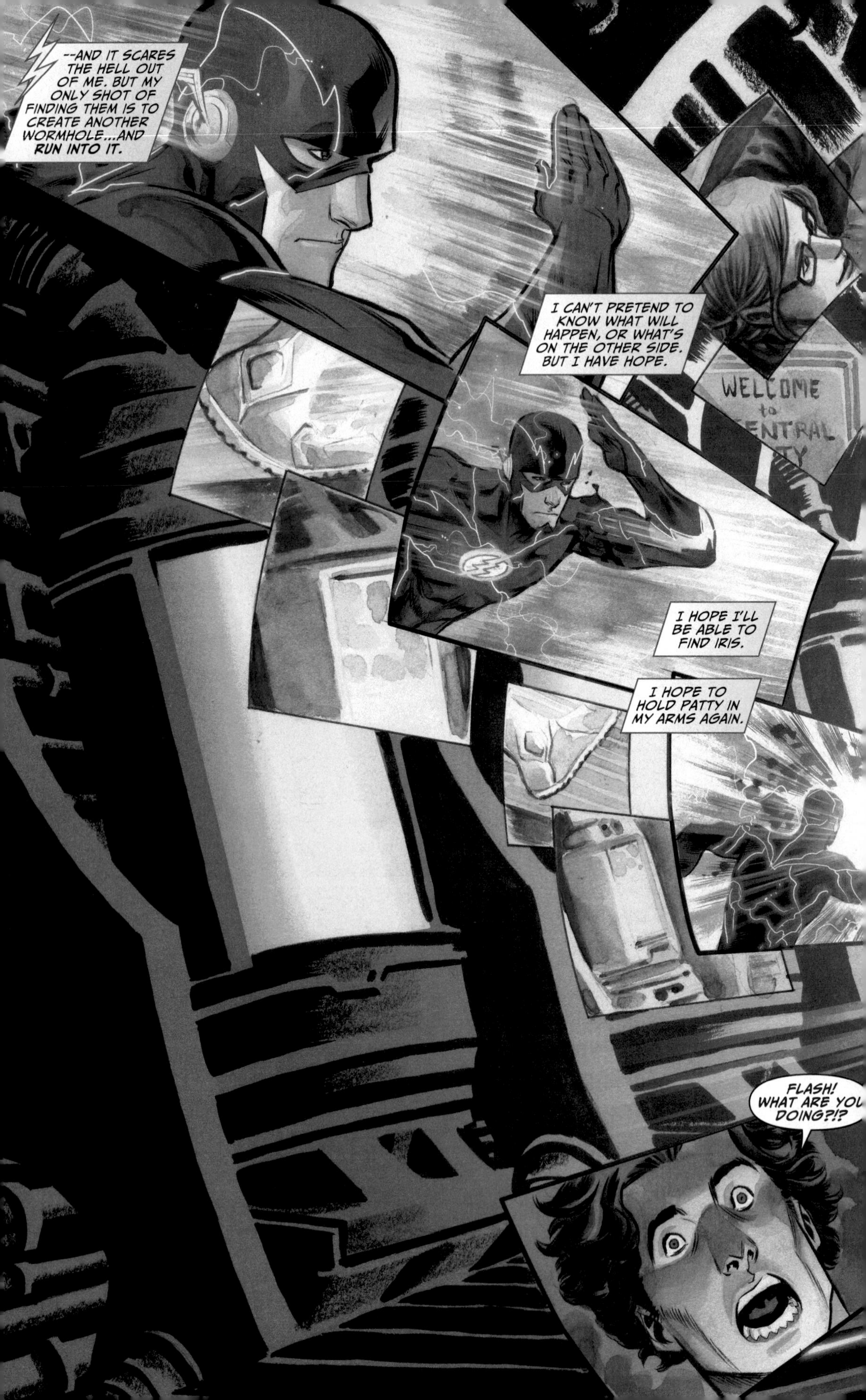
--AND IT SCARES THE HELL OUT OF ME. BUT MY ONLY SHOT OF FINDING THEM IS TO CREATE ANOTHER WORMHOLE...AND RUN INTO IT.
I CAN'T PRETEND TO KNOW WHAT WILL HAPPEN, OR WHAT'S ON THE OTHER SIDE. BUT I HAVE HOPE.
WELCOME to
I HOPE I'LL BE ABLE TO FIND IRIS.
I HOPE TO HOLD PATTY IN MY ARMS AGAIN.
FLASH! WHAT ARE YOU DOING?!?

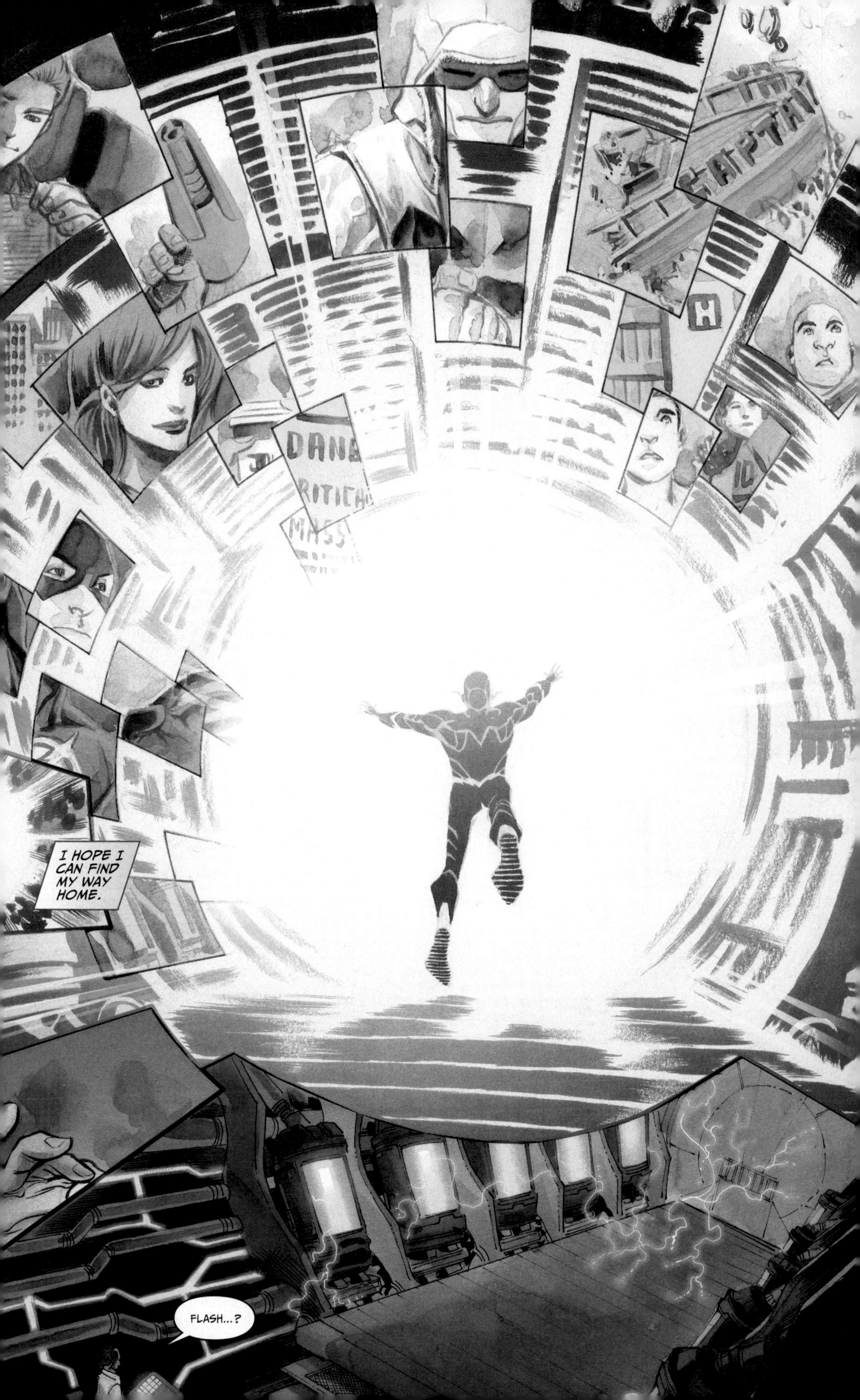

I HOPE I CAN FIND MY WAY HOME.
FLASH...?

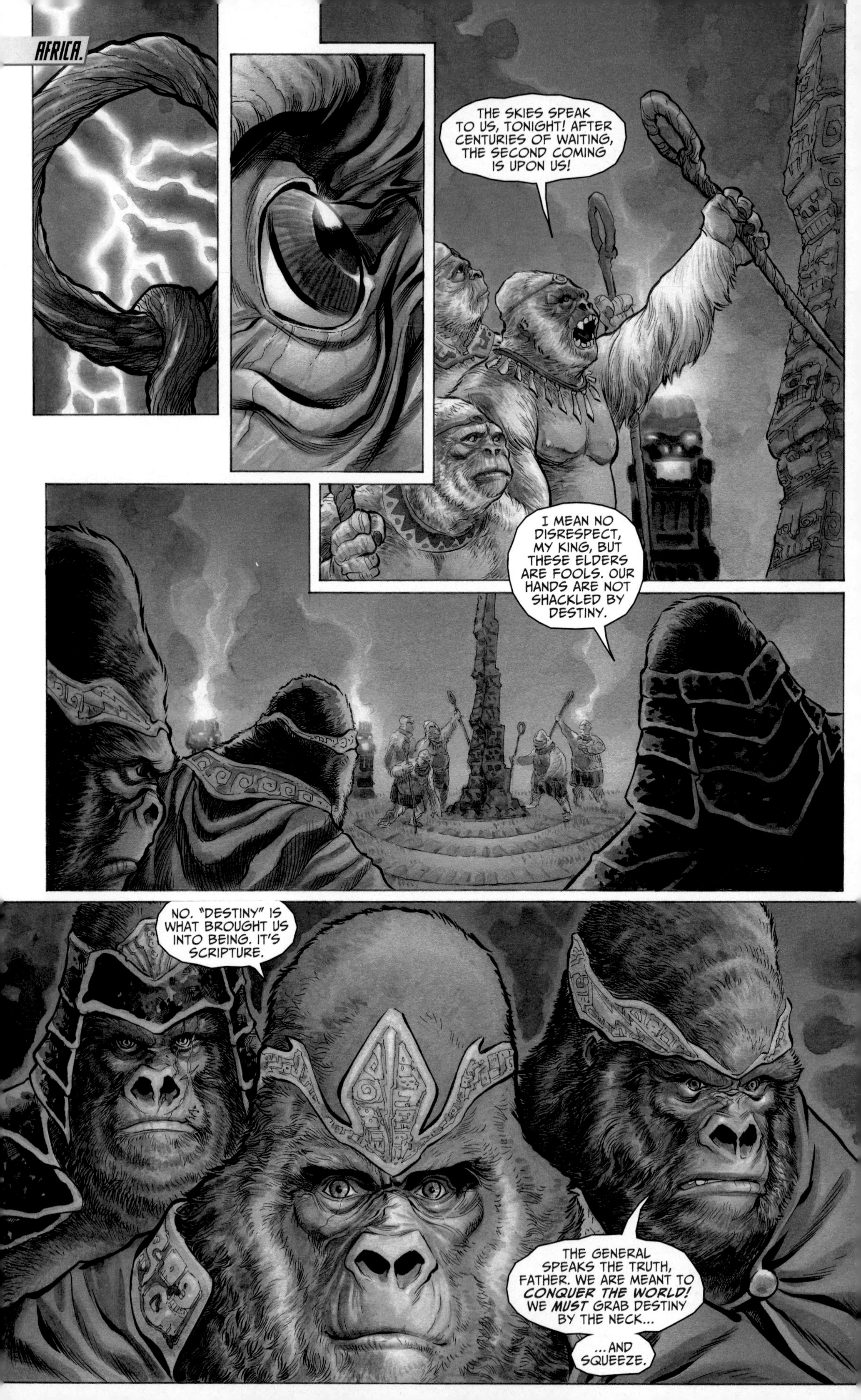
AFRICA.
THE SKIES SPEAK TO US, TONIGHT! AFTER CENTURIES OF WAITING, THE SECOND COMING IS UPON US!
I MEAN NO DISRESPECT, MY KING, BUT THESE ELDERS ARE FOOLS. OUR HANDS ARE NOT SHACKLED BY DESTINY.
NO. "DESTINY" IS WHAT BROUGHT US INTO BEING. IT'S SCRIPTURE.
THE GENERAL SPEAKS THE TRUTH, FATHER. WE ARE MEANT TO ***CONQUER THE WORLD!*** WE ***MUST*** GRAB DESTINY BY THE NECK...
...AND SQUEEZE.

"MY SISTER... SHE'S REALLY GONNA BE OKAY?"

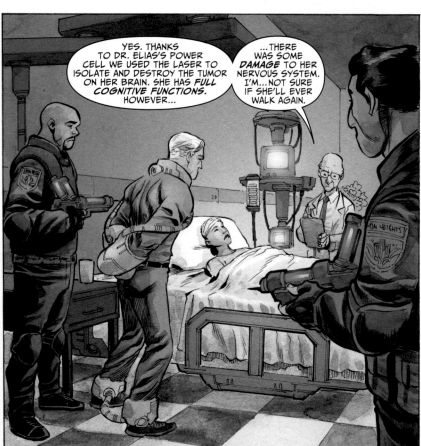

YES. THANKS TO DR. ELIAS'S POWER CELL WE USED THE LASER TO ISOLATE AND DESTROY THE TUMOR ON HER BRAIN. SHE HAS *FULL COGNITIVE FUNCTIONS.* HOWEVER...

...THERE WAS SOME *DAMAGE* TO HER NERVOUS SYSTEM. I'M...NOT SURE IF SHE'LL EVER WALK AGAIN.

UUUUHHH...

LISA! I'M HERE, SIS...I'M RIGHT HERE.

L...LE... LEN? IS THAT YOU?

IT'S ME, SIS... OH, GOD, I THOUGHT I LOST YOU...

YOU... AFTER WHAT YOU *DID* TO US...TO ME...

...YOU SHOULD'VE LET ME DIE.

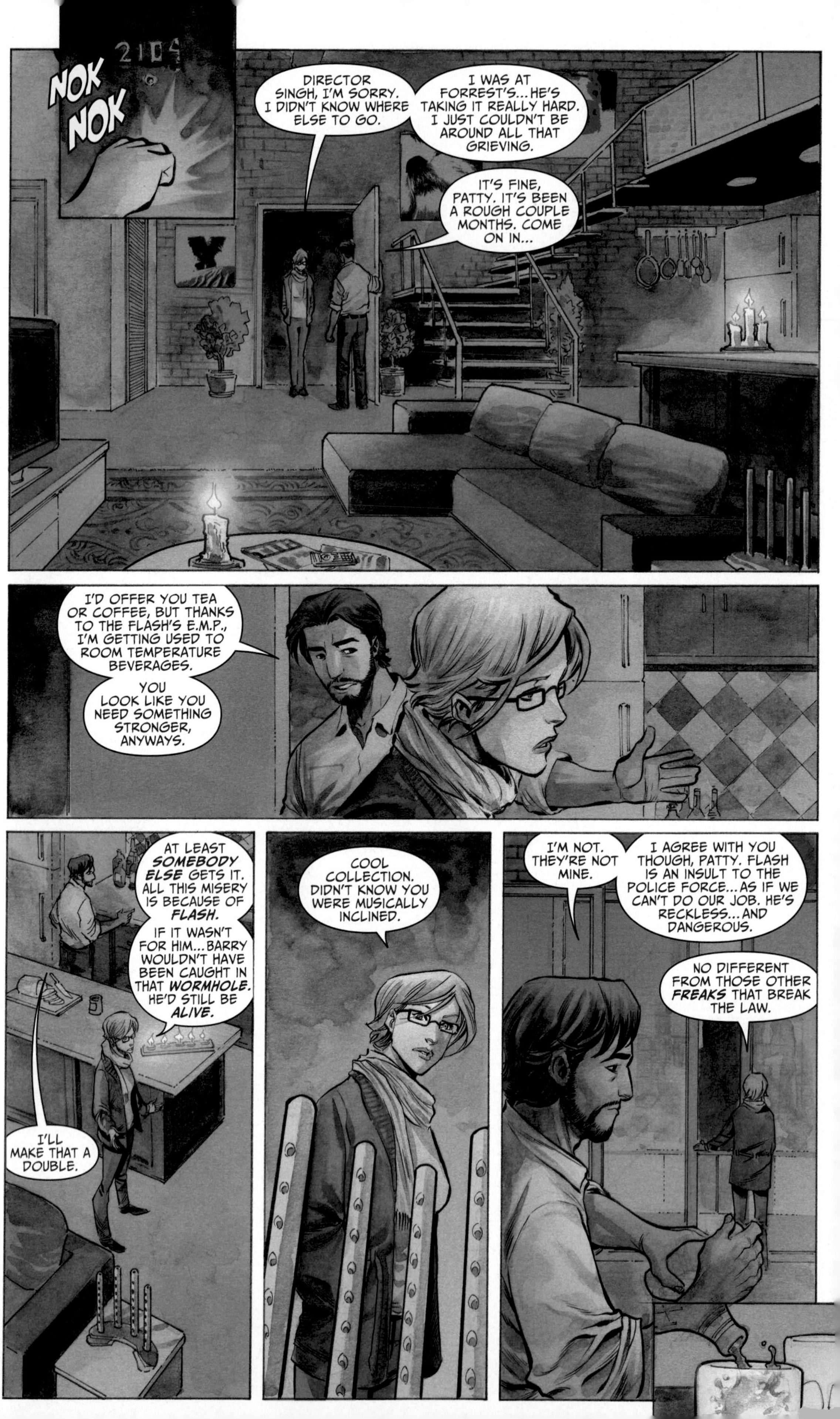
2104
NOK NOK
DIRECTOR SINGH, I'M SORRY. I DIDN'T KNOW WHERE ELSE TO GO.
I WAS AT FORREST'S... HE'S TAKING IT REALLY HARD. I JUST COULDN'T BE AROUND ALL THAT GRIEVING.
IT'S FINE, PATTY. IT'S BEEN A ROUGH COUPLE MONTHS. COME ON IN...
I'D OFFER YOU TEA OR COFFEE, BUT THANKS TO THE FLASH'S E.M.P., I'M GETTING USED TO ROOM TEMPERATURE BEVERAGES.
YOU LOOK LIKE YOU NEED SOMETHING STRONGER, ANYWAYS.
AT LEAST SOMEBODY ELSE GETS IT. ALL THIS MISERY IS BECAUSE OF FLASH.
IF IT WASN'T FOR HIM... BARRY WOULDN'T HAVE BEEN CAUGHT IN THAT WORMHOLE. HE'D STILL BE ALIVE.
I'LL MAKE THAT A DOUBLE.
COOL COLLECTION. DIDN'T KNOW YOU WERE MUSICALLY INCLINED.
I'M NOT. THEY'RE NOT MINE.
I AGREE WITH YOU THOUGH, PATTY. FLASH IS AN INSULT TO THE POLICE FORCE... AS IF WE CAN'T DO OUR JOB. HE'S RECKLESS... AND DANGEROUS.
NO DIFFERENT FROM THOSE OTHER FREAKS THAT BREAK THE LAW.

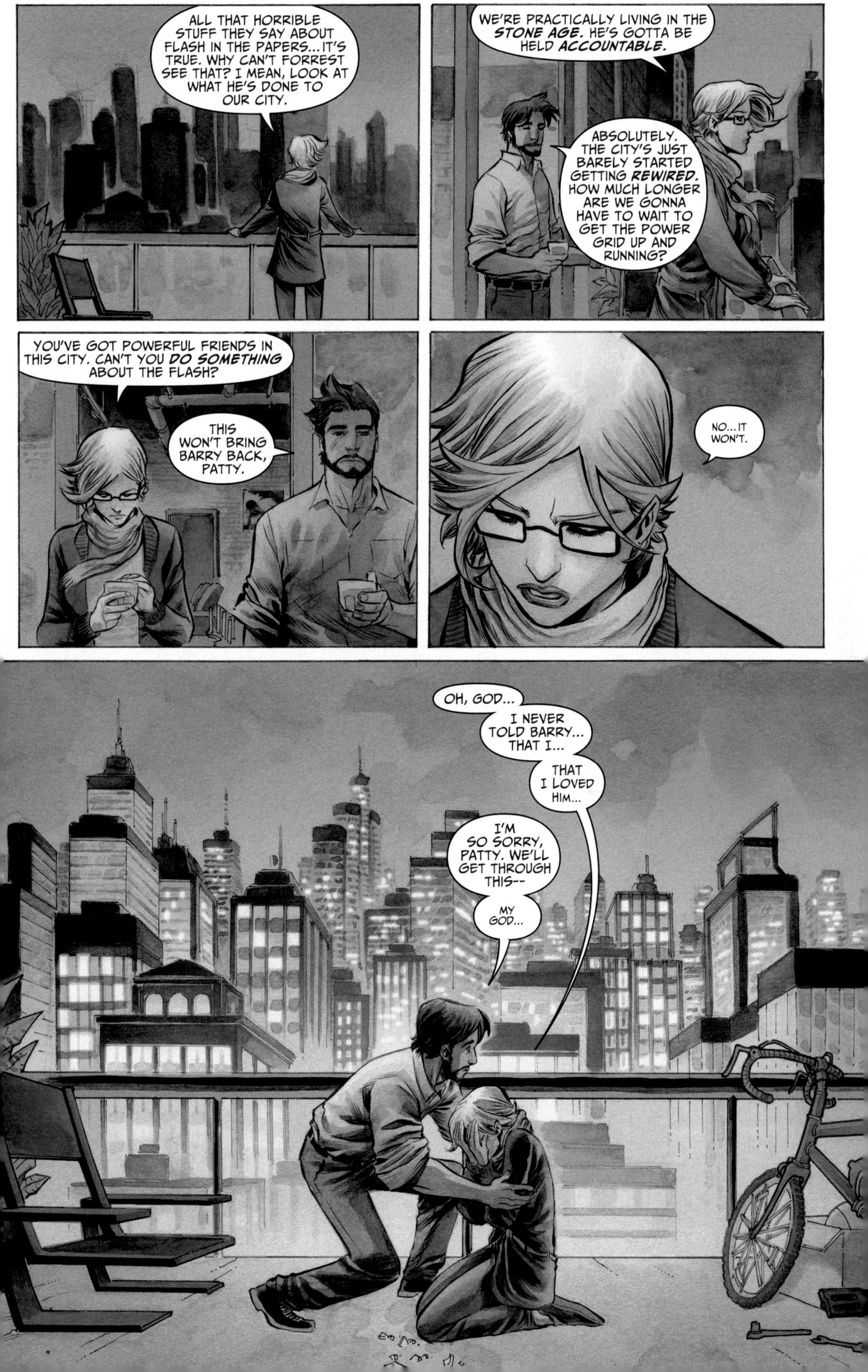
ALL THAT HORRIBLE STUFF THEY SAY ABOUT FLASH IN THE PAPERS...IT'S TRUE. WHY CAN'T FORREST SEE THAT? I MEAN, LOOK AT WHAT HE'S DONE TO OUR CITY.
WE'RE PRACTICALLY LIVING IN THE STONE AGE. HE'S GOTTA BE HELD ACCOUNTABLE.
ABSOLUTELY. THE CITY'S JUST BARELY STARTED GETTING REWIRED. HOW MUCH LONGER ARE WE GONNA HAVE TO WAIT TO GET THE POWER GRID UP AND RUNNING?
YOU'VE GOT POWERFUL FRIENDS IN THIS CITY. CAN'T YOU DO SOMETHING ABOUT THE FLASH?
THIS WON'T BRING BARRY BACK, PATTY.
NO...IT WON'T.
OH, GOD...
I NEVER TOLD BARRY... THAT I...
THAT I LOVED HIM...
I'M SO SORRY, PATTY. WE'LL GET THROUGH THIS--
MY GOD...

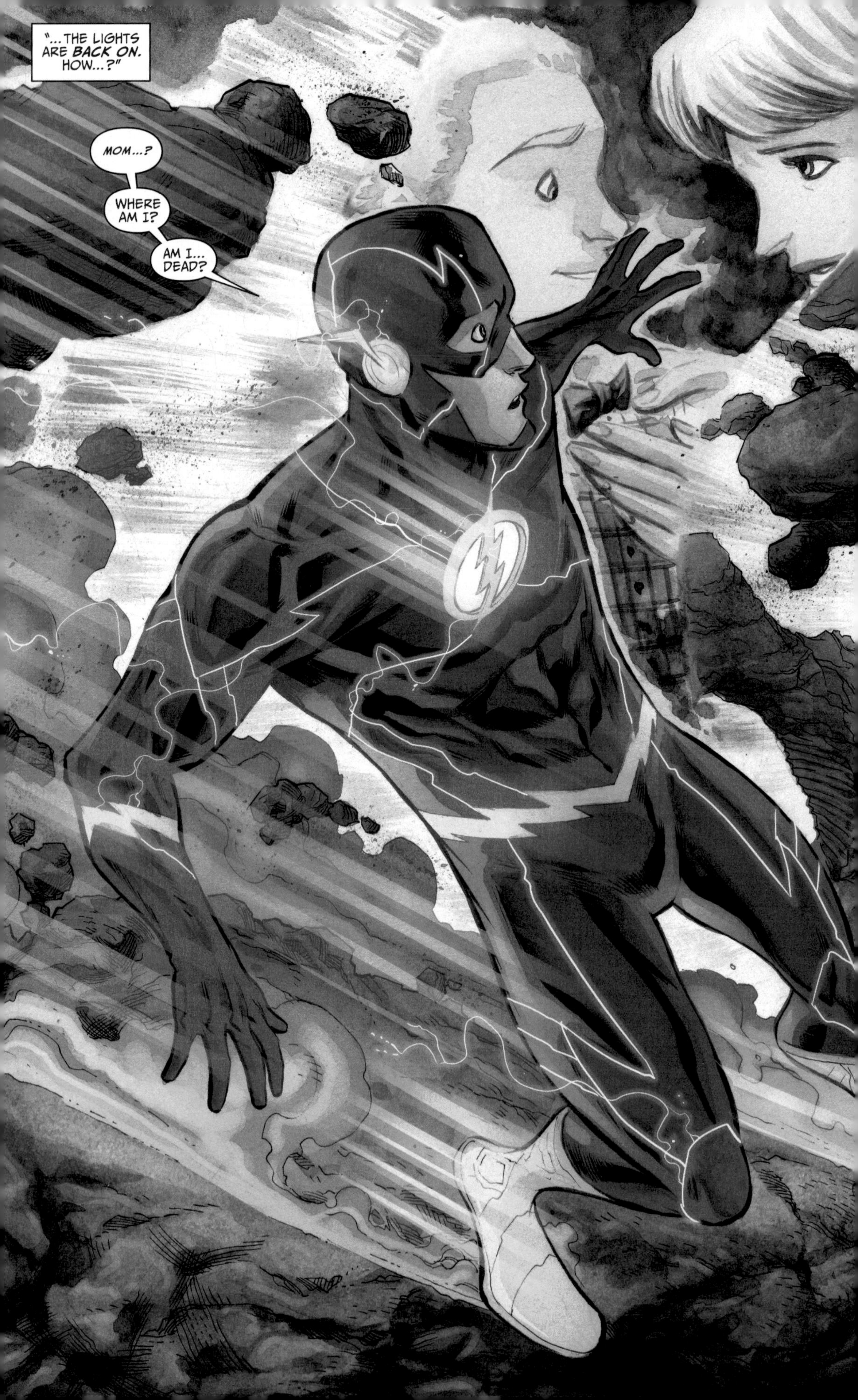
"...THE LIGHTS ARE BACK ON. HOW...?"
MOM...?
WHERE AM I?
AM I... DEAD?

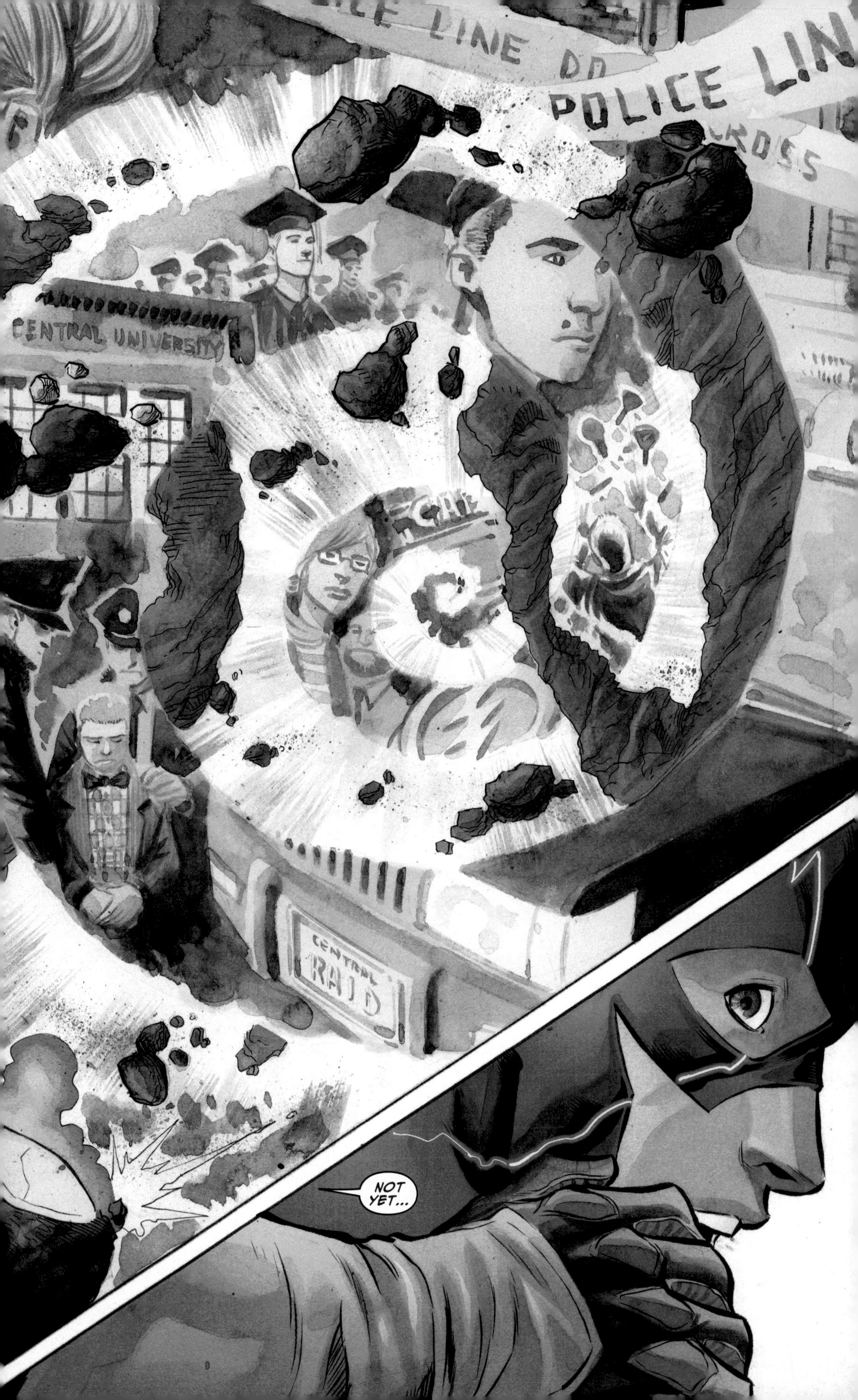
POLICE LINE DO
POLICE LINE
CROSS
CENTRAL UNIVERSITY
CENTRAL
NOT YET...

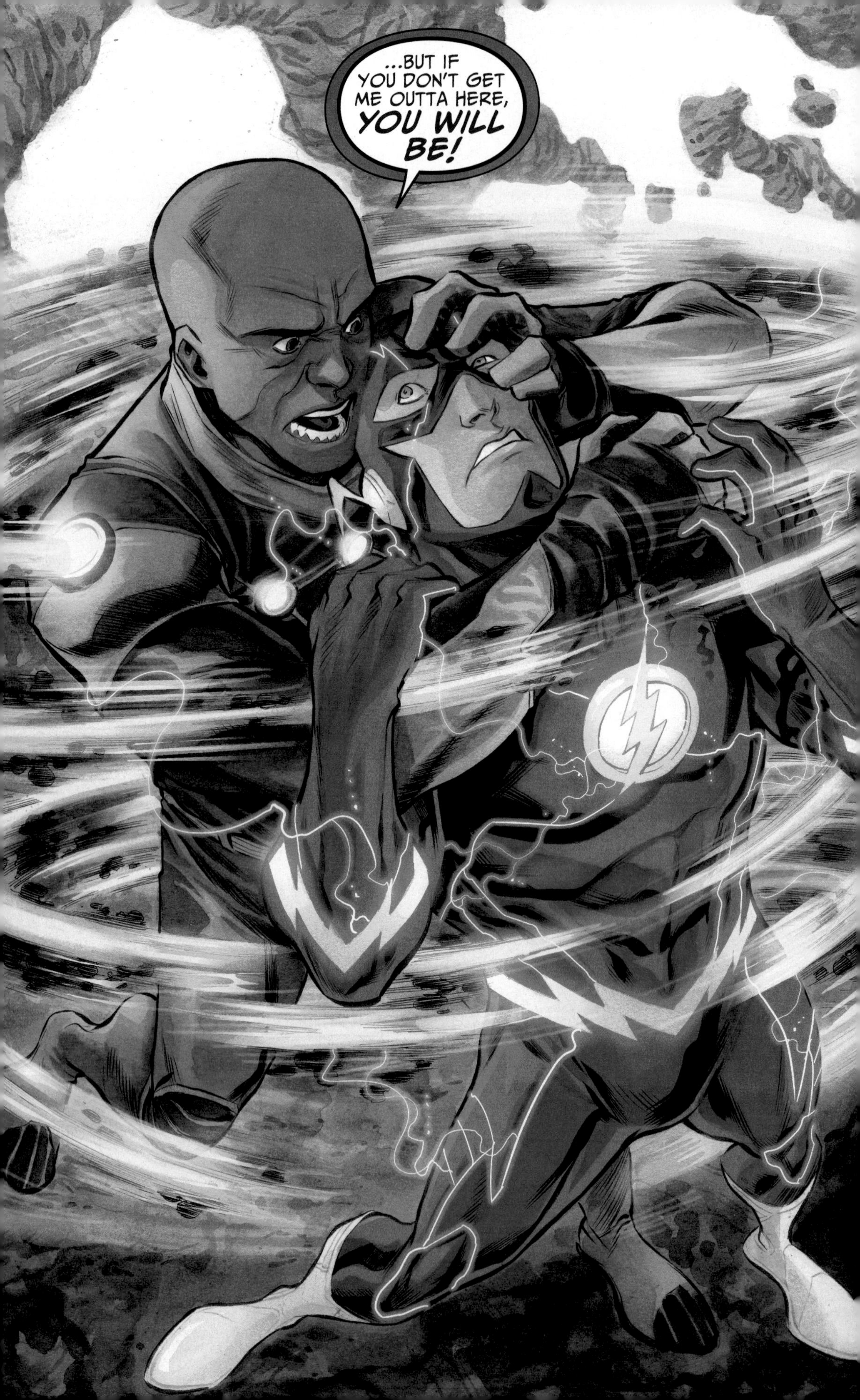
...BUT IF YOU DON'T GET ME OUTTA HERE, YOU WILL BE!

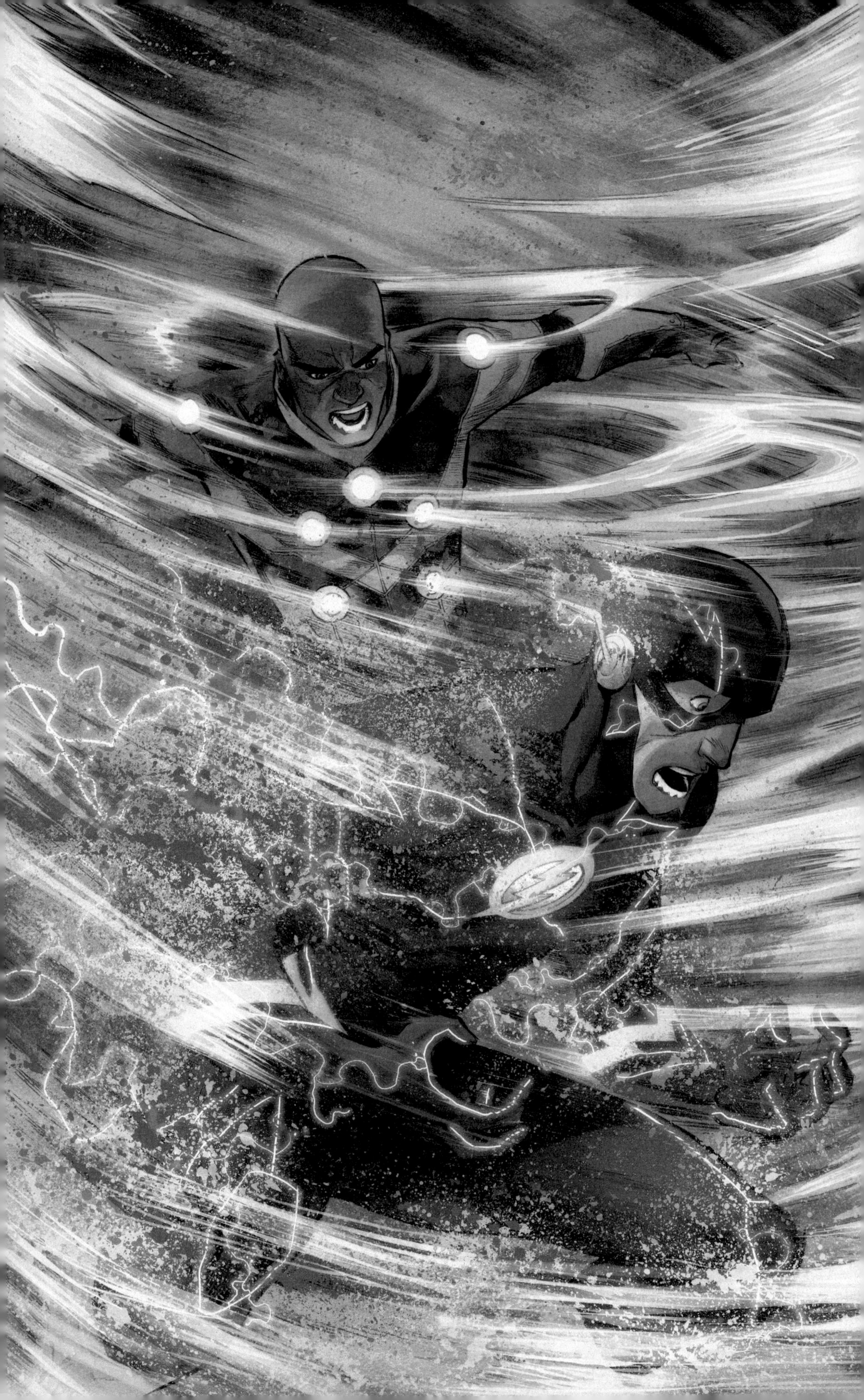

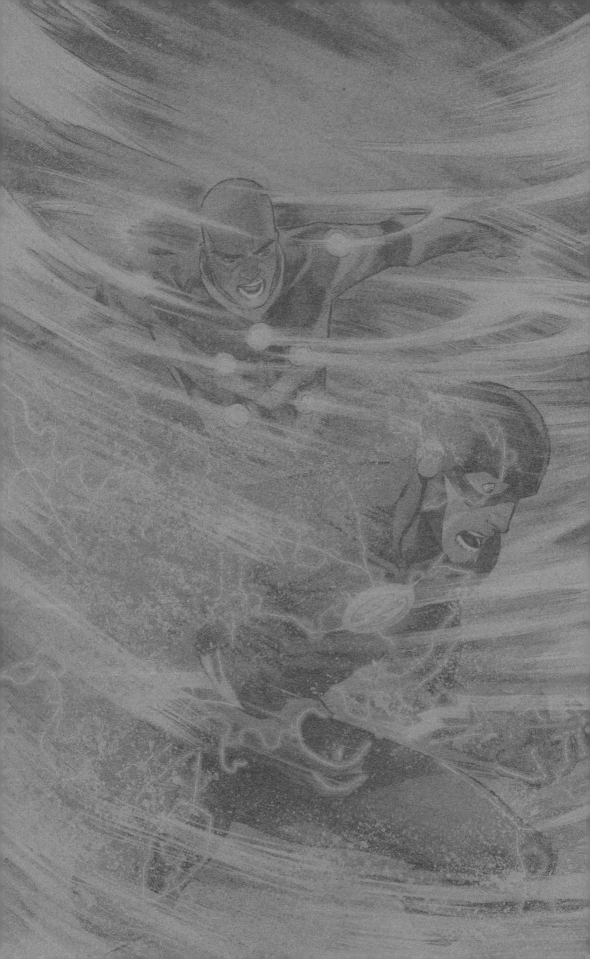

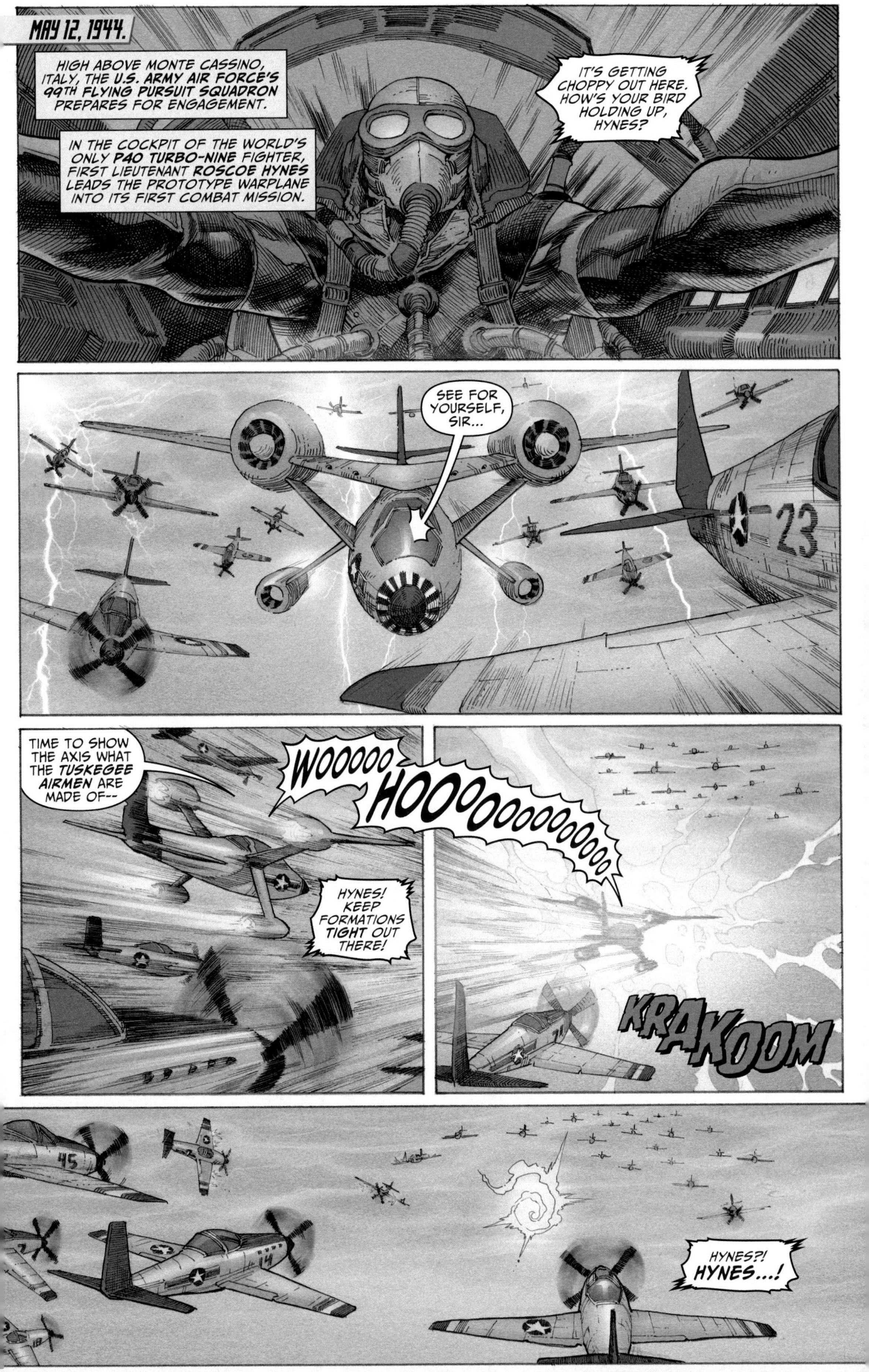
MAY 12, 1944.
HIGH ABOVE MONTE CASSINO, ITALY, THE U.S. ARMY AIR FORCE'S 99TH FLYING PURSUIT SQUADRON PREPARES FOR ENGAGEMENT.
IN THE COCKPIT OF THE WORLD'S ONLY P40 TURBO-NINE FIGHTER, FIRST LIEUTENANT ROSCOE HYNES LEADS THE PROTOTYPE WARPLANE INTO ITS FIRST COMBAT MISSION.
IT'S GETTING CHOPPY OUT HERE. HOW'S YOUR BIRD HOLDING UP, HYNES?
SEE FOR YOURSELF, SIR...
23
TIME TO SHOW THE AXIS WHAT THE TUSKEGEE AIRMEN ARE MADE OF--
WOOOOO HOOOOOOOOOOOOO
HYNES! KEEP FORMATIONS TIGHT OUT THERE!
KRAKOOM
45
14
HYNES?! HYNES...!

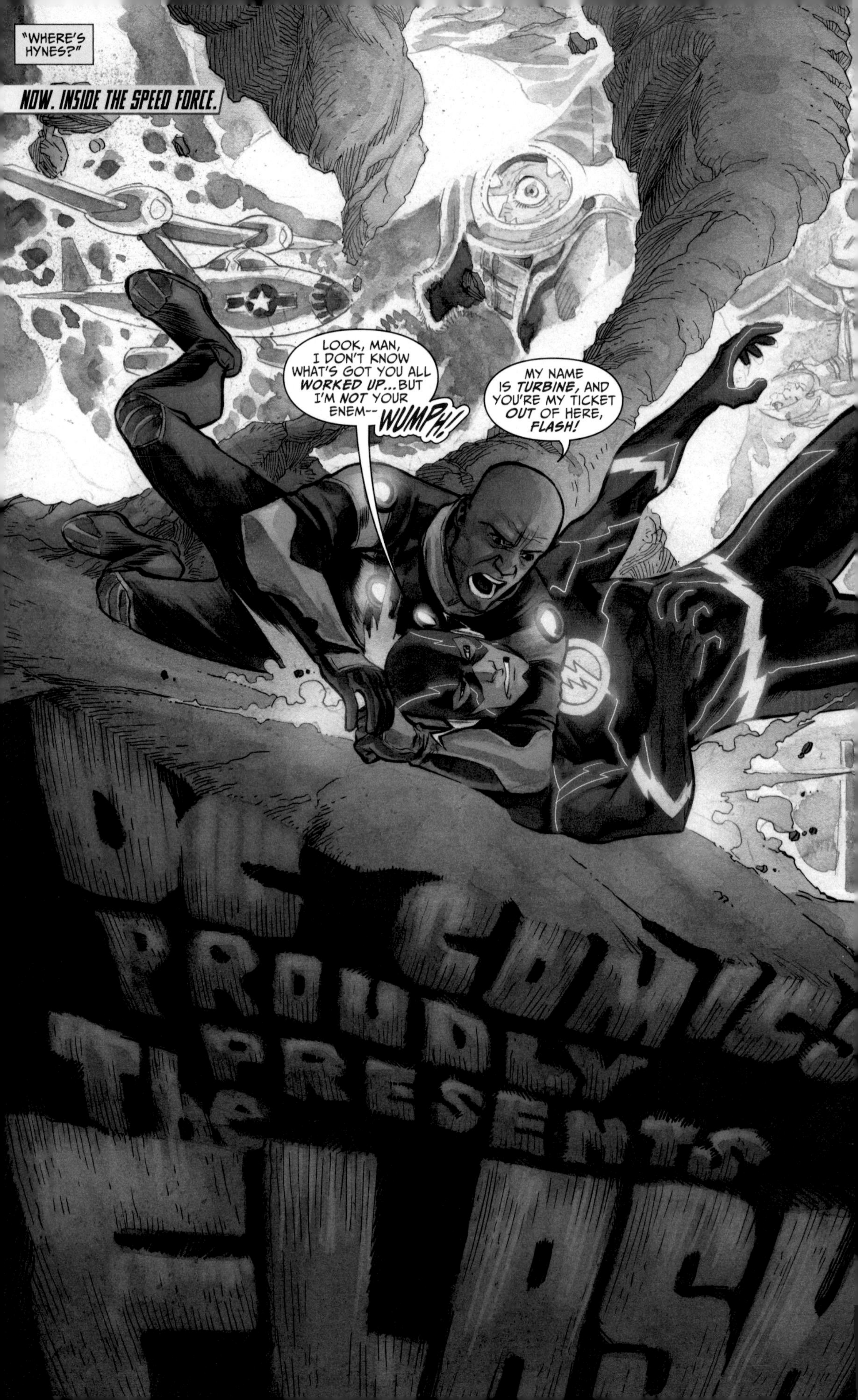
"WHERE'S HYNES?"
NOW. INSIDE THE SPEED FORCE.
LOOK, MAN, I DON'T KNOW WHAT'S GOT YOU ALL WORKED UP...BUT I'M NOT YOUR ENEM--
WUMPH!
MY NAME IS TURBINE, AND YOU'RE MY TICKET OUT OF HERE, FLASH!
PROUDLY PRESENTS
FLASH

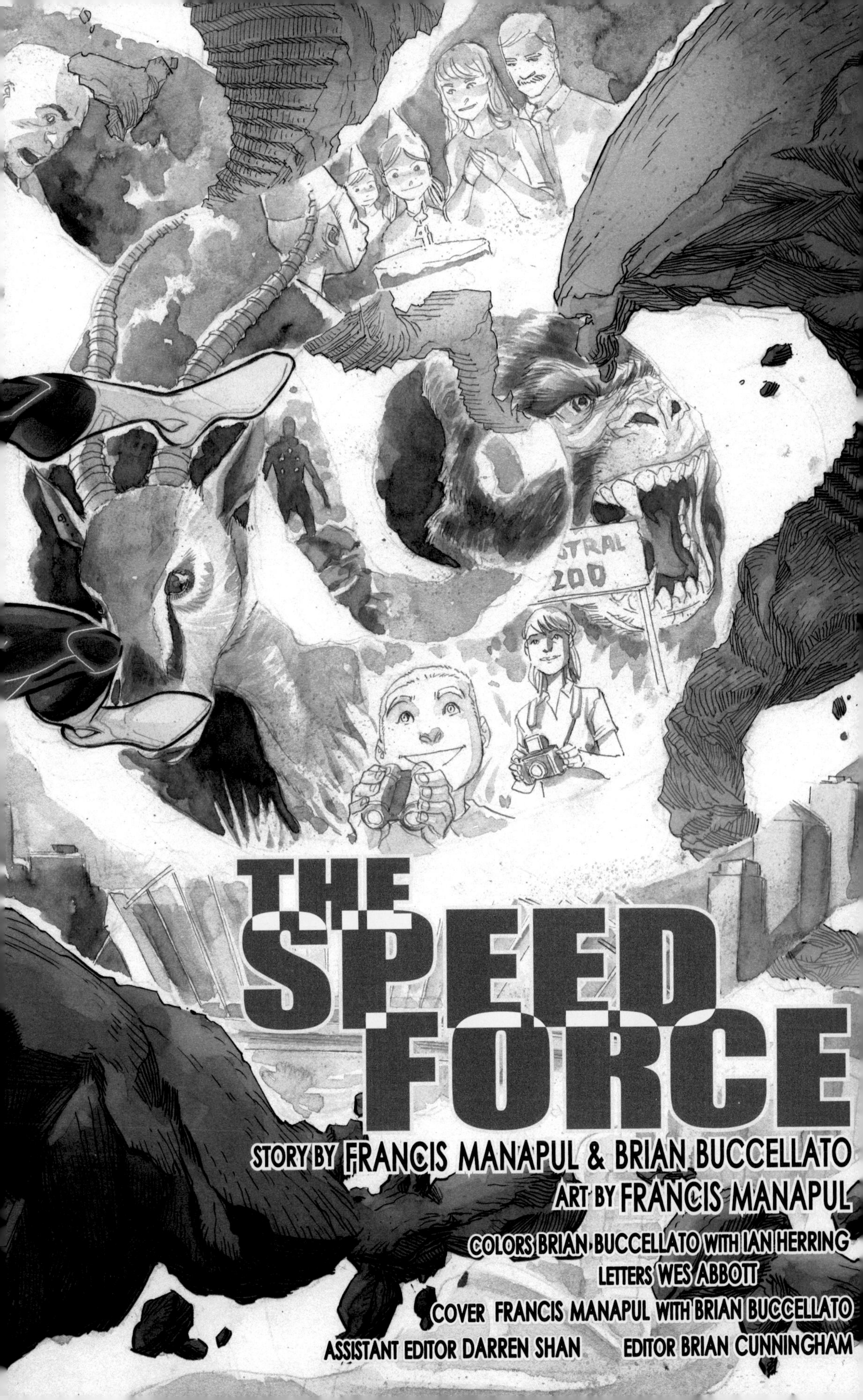
STRAL
ZOO
THE SPEED FORCE
STORY BY FRANCIS MANAPUL & BRIAN BUCCELLATO
ART BY FRANCIS MANAPUL
COLORS BRIAN BUCCELLATO WITH IAN HERRING
LETTERS WES ABBOTT
COVER FRANCIS MANAPUL WITH BRIAN BUCCELLATO
ASSISTANT EDITOR DARREN SHAN
EDITOR BRIAN CUNNINGHAM

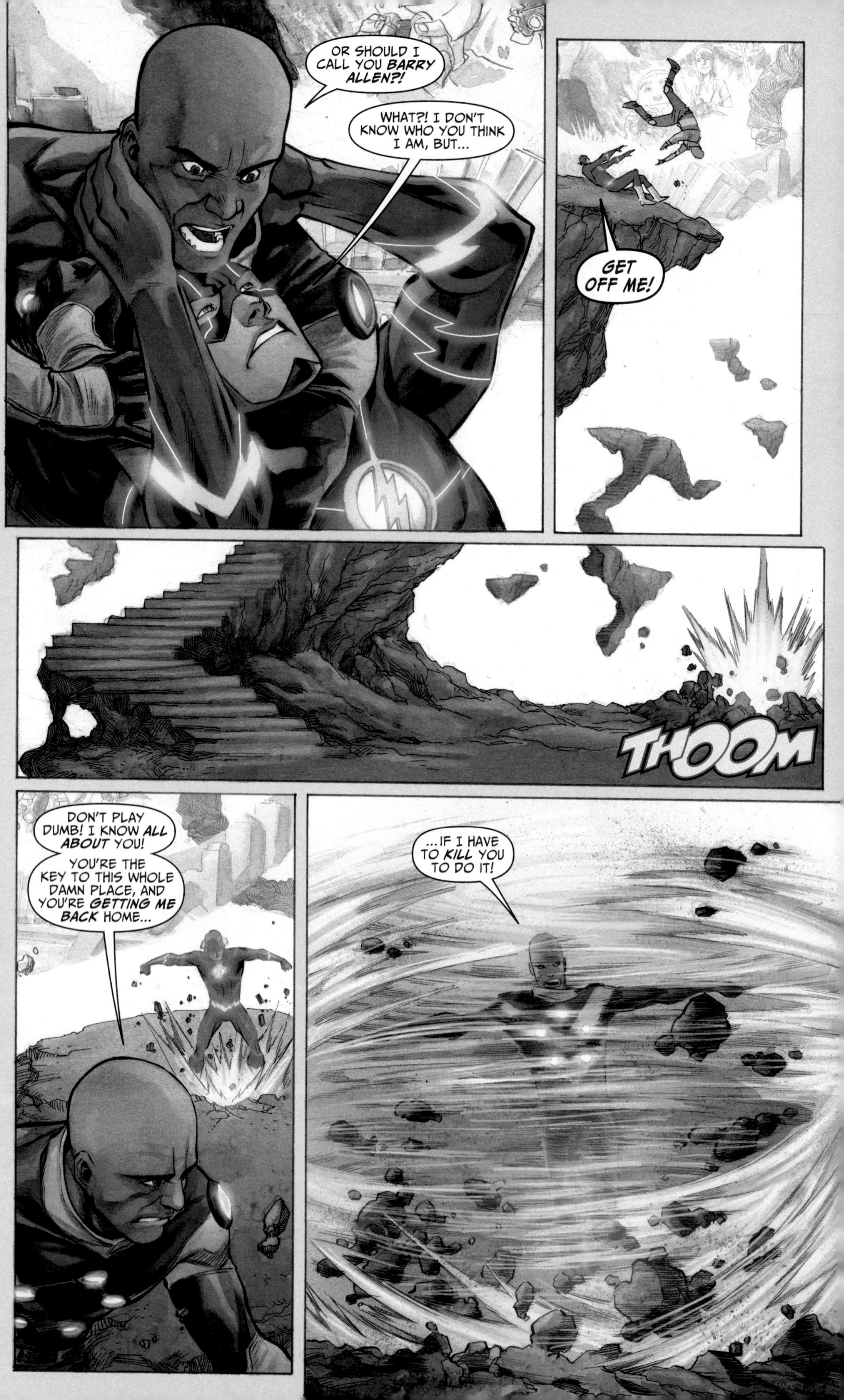
OR SHOULD I CALL YOU BARRY ALLEN?!
WHAT?! I DON'T KNOW WHO YOU THINK I AM, BUT...
GET OFF ME!
THOOM
DON'T PLAY DUMB! I KNOW ALL ABOUT YOU!
YOU'RE THE KEY TO THIS WHOLE DAMN PLACE, AND YOU'RE GETTING ME BACK HOME...
...IF I HAVE TO KILL YOU TO DO IT!

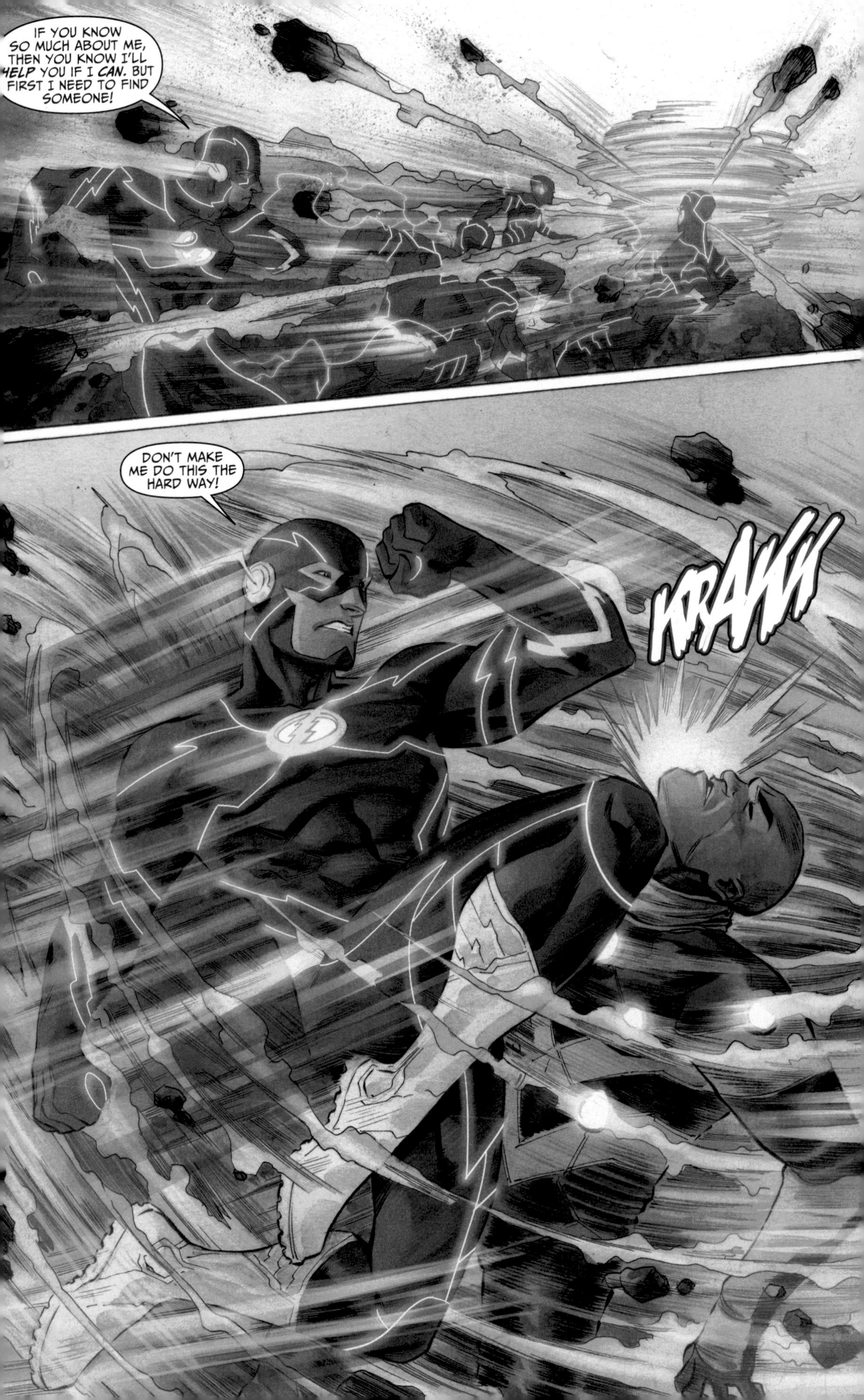
IF YOU KNOW SO MUCH ABOUT ME, THEN YOU KNOW I'LL HELP YOU IF I CAN. BUT FIRST I NEED TO FIND SOMEONE!
DON'T MAKE ME DO THIS THE HARD WAY!
KRANG

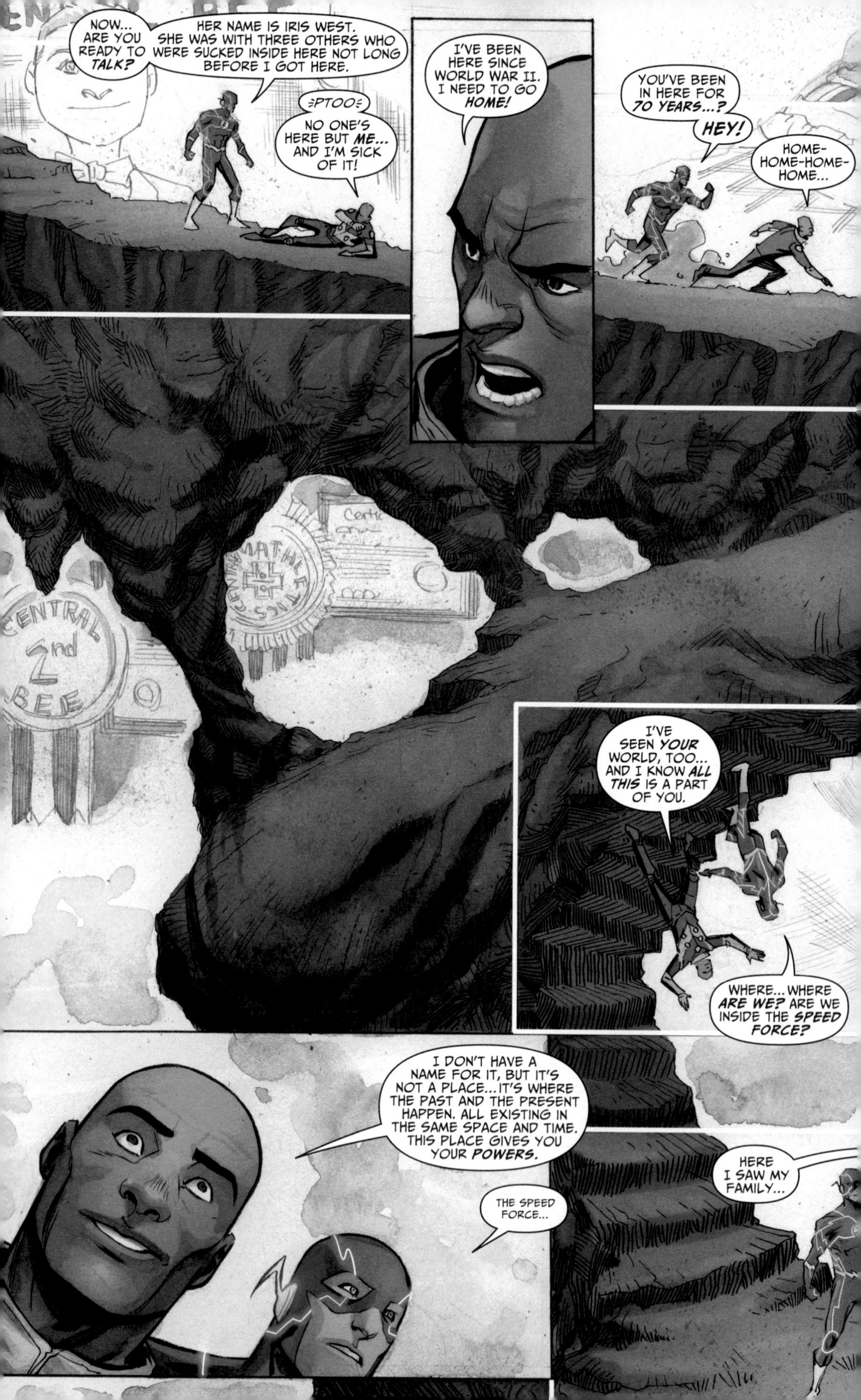
NOW... ARE YOU READY TO TALK?
HER NAME IS IRIS WEST. SHE WAS WITH THREE OTHERS WHO WERE SUCKED INSIDE HERE NOT LONG BEFORE I GOT HERE.
PTOO
NO ONE'S HERE BUT ME... AND I'M SICK OF IT!
I'VE BEEN HERE SINCE WORLD WAR II. I NEED TO GO HOME!
YOU'VE BEEN IN HERE FOR 70 YEARS...?
HEY!
HOME-HOME-HOME-HOME-HOME...
CENTRAL 2nd BEE
I'VE SEEN YOUR WORLD, TOO... AND I KNOW ALL THIS IS A PART OF YOU.
WHERE... WHERE ARE WE? ARE WE INSIDE THE SPEED FORCE?
I DON'T HAVE A NAME FOR IT, BUT IT'S NOT A PLACE... IT'S WHERE THE PAST AND THE PRESENT HAPPEN. ALL EXISTING IN THE SAME SPACE AND TIME. THIS PLACE GIVES YOU YOUR POWERS.
THE SPEED FORCE...
HERE I SAW MY FAMILY...

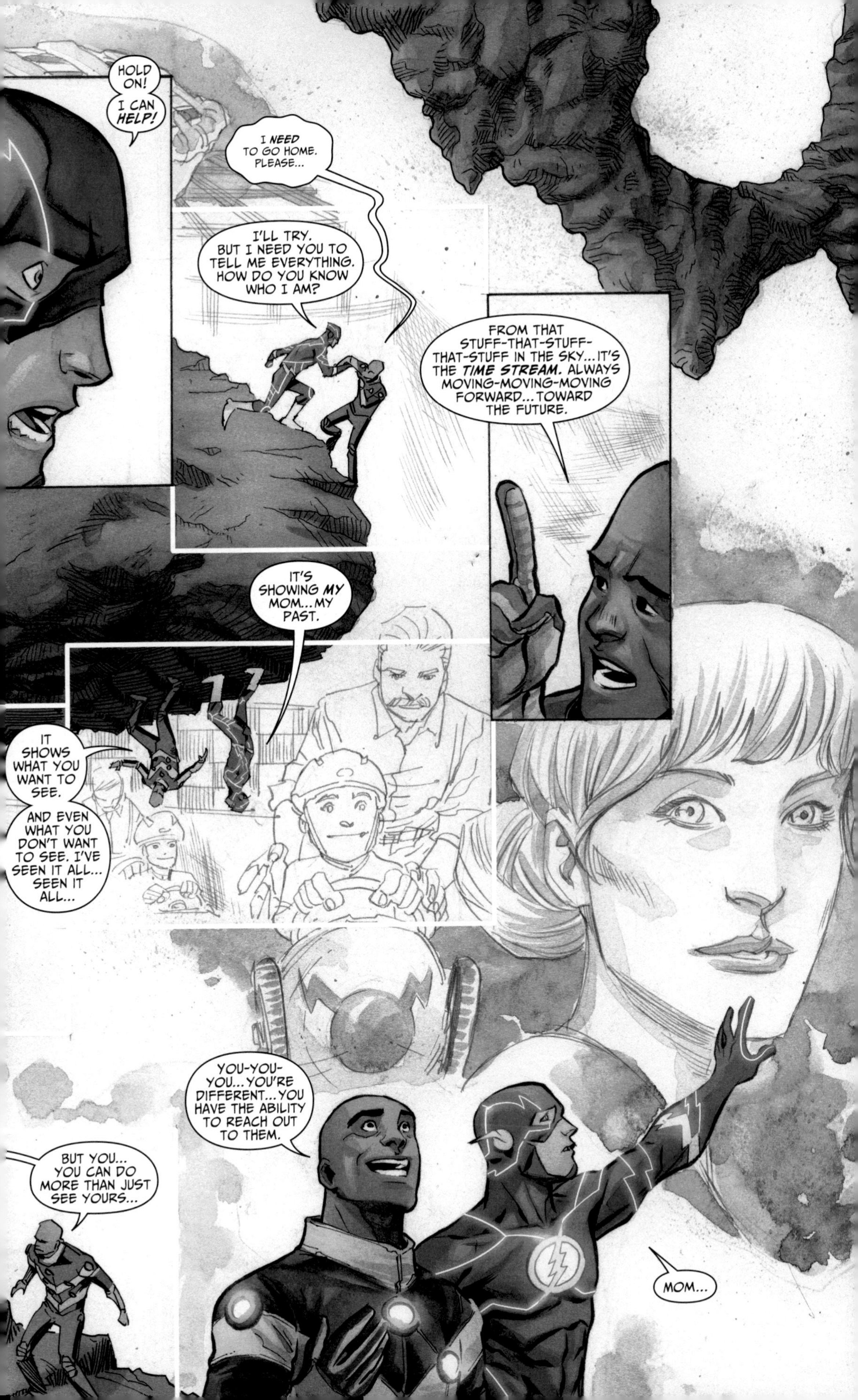
HOLD ON! I CAN HELP!
I NEED TO GO HOME. PLEASE...
I'LL TRY. BUT I NEED YOU TO TELL ME EVERYTHING. HOW DO YOU KNOW WHO I AM?
FROM THAT STUFF-THAT-STUFF-THAT-STUFF IN THE SKY... IT'S THE TIME STREAM. ALWAYS MOVING-MOVING-MOVING FORWARD... TOWARD THE FUTURE.
IT'S SHOWING MY MOM... MY PAST.
IT SHOWS WHAT YOU WANT TO SEE.
AND EVEN WHAT YOU DON'T WANT TO SEE. I'VE SEEN IT ALL... SEEN IT ALL...
BUT YOU... YOU CAN DO MORE THAN JUST SEE YOURS...
YOU-YOU-YOU... YOU'RE DIFFERENT... YOU HAVE THE ABILITY TO REACH OUT TO THEM.
MOM...

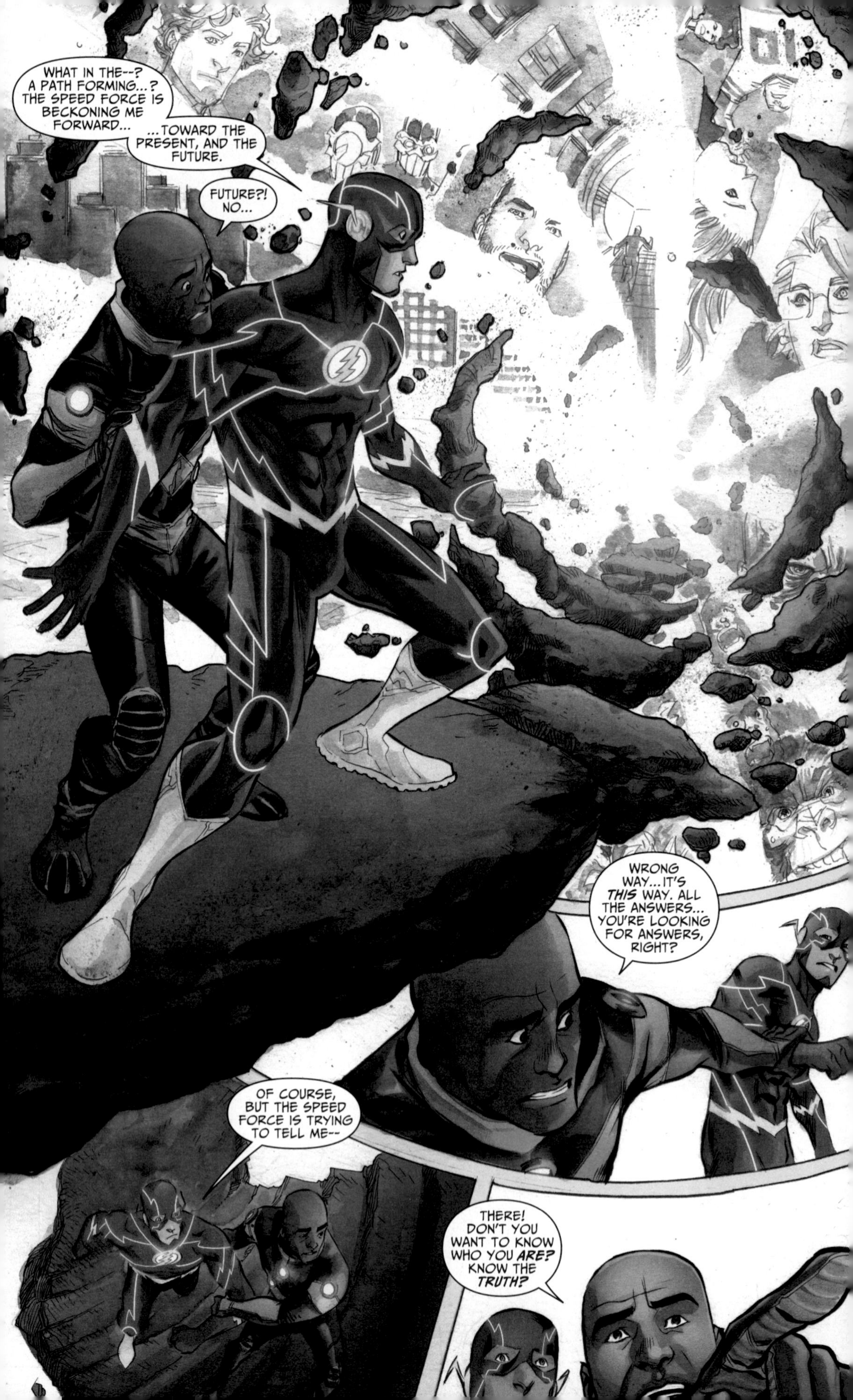
WHAT IN THE--? A PATH FORMING...? THE SPEED FORCE IS BECKONING ME FORWARD...
...TOWARD THE PRESENT, AND THE FUTURE.
FUTURE?! NO...
WRONG WAY...IT'S *THIS* WAY. ALL THE ANSWERS... YOU'RE LOOKING FOR ANSWERS, RIGHT?
OF COURSE, BUT THE SPEED FORCE IS TRYING TO TELL ME--
THERE! DON'T YOU WANT TO KNOW WHO YOU *ARE?* KNOW THE *TRUTH?*

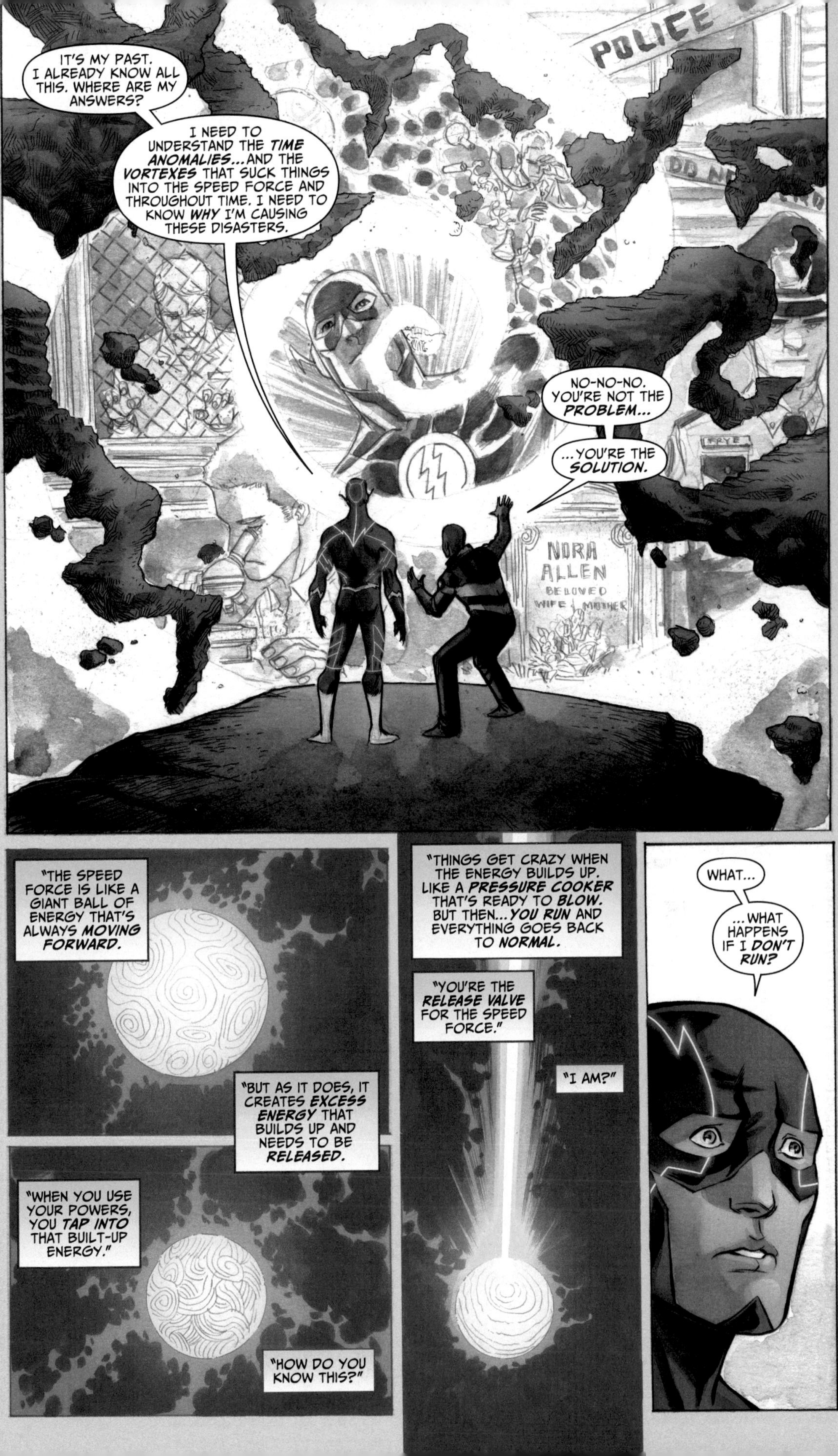

POLICE
IT'S MY PAST. I ALREADY KNOW ALL THIS. WHERE ARE MY ANSWERS?
I NEED TO UNDERSTAND THE *TIME ANOMALIES*...AND THE *VORTEXES* THAT SUCK THINGS INTO THE SPEED FORCE AND THROUGHOUT TIME. I NEED TO KNOW *WHY* I'M CAUSING THESE DISASTERS.
NO-NO-NO. YOU'RE NOT THE *PROBLEM*...
...YOU'RE THE *SOLUTION.*
FRYE
NORA ALLEN BELOVED WIFE & MOTHER
"THE SPEED FORCE IS LIKE A GIANT BALL OF ENERGY THAT'S ALWAYS *MOVING FORWARD.*
"BUT AS IT DOES, IT CREATES *EXCESS ENERGY* THAT BUILDS UP AND NEEDS TO BE *RELEASED.*
"WHEN YOU USE YOUR POWERS, YOU *TAP INTO* THAT BUILT-UP ENERGY."
"HOW DO YOU KNOW THIS?"
"THINGS GET CRAZY WHEN THE ENERGY BUILDS UP. LIKE A *PRESSURE COOKER* THAT'S READY TO *BLOW.* BUT THEN...*YOU RUN* AND EVERYTHING GOES BACK TO *NORMAL.*
"YOU'RE THE *RELEASE VALVE* FOR THE SPEED FORCE."
"I AM?"
WHAT...
...WHAT HAPPENS IF I *DON'T RUN?*

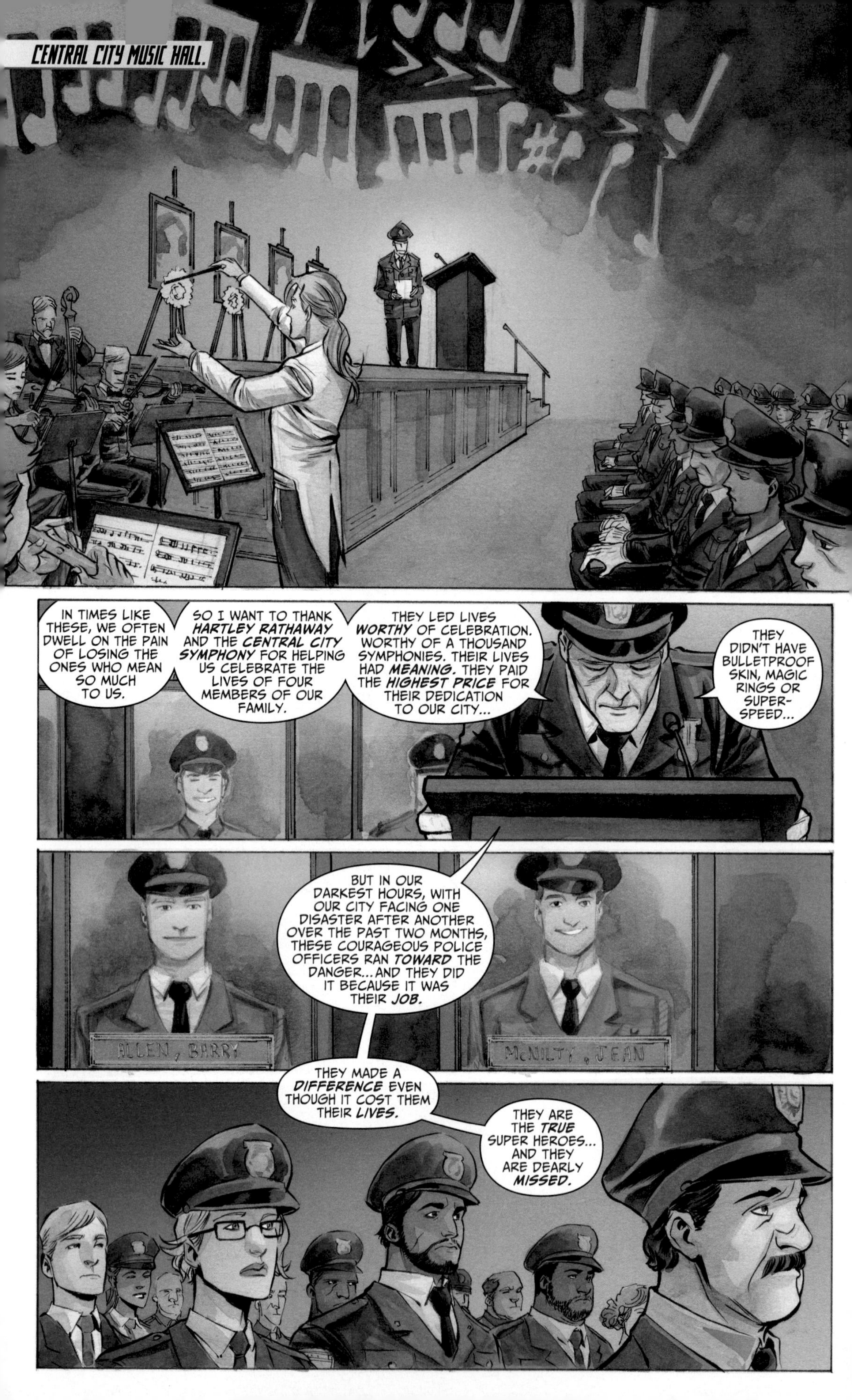
CENTRAL CITY MUSIC HALL.
IN TIMES LIKE THESE, WE OFTEN DWELL ON THE PAIN OF LOSING THE ONES WHO MEAN SO MUCH TO US.
SO I WANT TO THANK HARTLEY RATHAWAY AND THE CENTRAL CITY SYMPHONY FOR HELPING US CELEBRATE THE LIVES OF FOUR MEMBERS OF OUR FAMILY.
THEY LED LIVES WORTHY OF CELEBRATION. WORTHY OF A THOUSAND SYMPHONIES. THEIR LIVES HAD MEANING. THEY PAID THE HIGHEST PRICE FOR THEIR DEDICATION TO OUR CITY...
THEY DIDN'T HAVE BULLETPROOF SKIN, MAGIC RINGS OR SUPER-SPEED...
BUT IN OUR DARKEST HOURS, WITH OUR CITY FACING ONE DISASTER AFTER ANOTHER OVER THE PAST TWO MONTHS, THESE COURAGEOUS POLICE OFFICERS RAN TOWARD THE DANGER...AND THEY DID IT BECAUSE IT WAS THEIR JOB.
ALLEN, BARRY
McNILTY, JEAN
THEY MADE A DIFFERENCE EVEN THOUGH IT COST THEM THEIR LIVES.
THEY ARE THE TRUE SUPER HEROES... AND THEY ARE DEARLY MISSED.

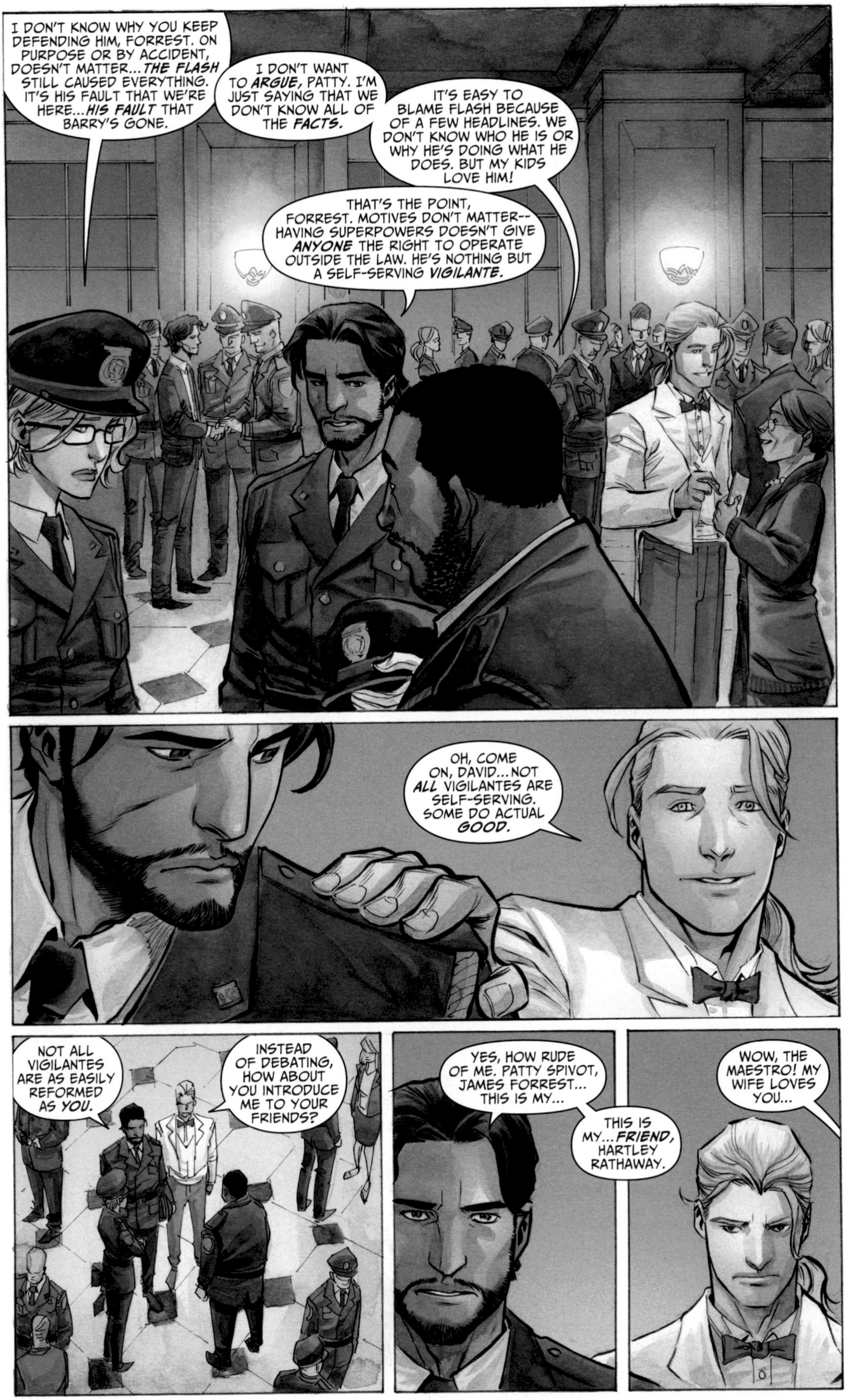
I DON'T KNOW WHY YOU KEEP DEFENDING HIM, FORREST. ON PURPOSE OR BY ACCIDENT, DOESN'T MATTER...THE FLASH STILL CAUSED EVERYTHING. IT'S HIS FAULT THAT WE'RE HERE...HIS FAULT THAT BARRY'S GONE.
I DON'T WANT TO ARGUE, PATTY. I'M JUST SAYING THAT WE DON'T KNOW ALL OF THE FACTS.
IT'S EASY TO BLAME FLASH BECAUSE OF A FEW HEADLINES. WE DON'T KNOW WHO HE IS OR WHY HE'S DOING WHAT HE DOES. BUT MY KIDS LOVE HIM!
THAT'S THE POINT, FORREST. MOTIVES DON'T MATTER--HAVING SUPERPOWERS DOESN'T GIVE ANYONE THE RIGHT TO OPERATE OUTSIDE THE LAW. HE'S NOTHING BUT A SELF-SERVING VIGILANTE.
OH, COME ON, DAVID...NOT ALL VIGILANTES ARE SELF-SERVING. SOME DO ACTUAL GOOD.
NOT ALL VIGILANTES ARE AS EASILY REFORMED AS YOU.
INSTEAD OF DEBATING, HOW ABOUT YOU INTRODUCE ME TO YOUR FRIENDS?
YES, HOW RUDE OF ME. PATTY SPIVOT, JAMES FORREST... THIS IS MY...
THIS IS MY...FRIEND, HARTLEY RATHAWAY.
WOW, THE MAESTRO! MY WIFE LOVES YOU...

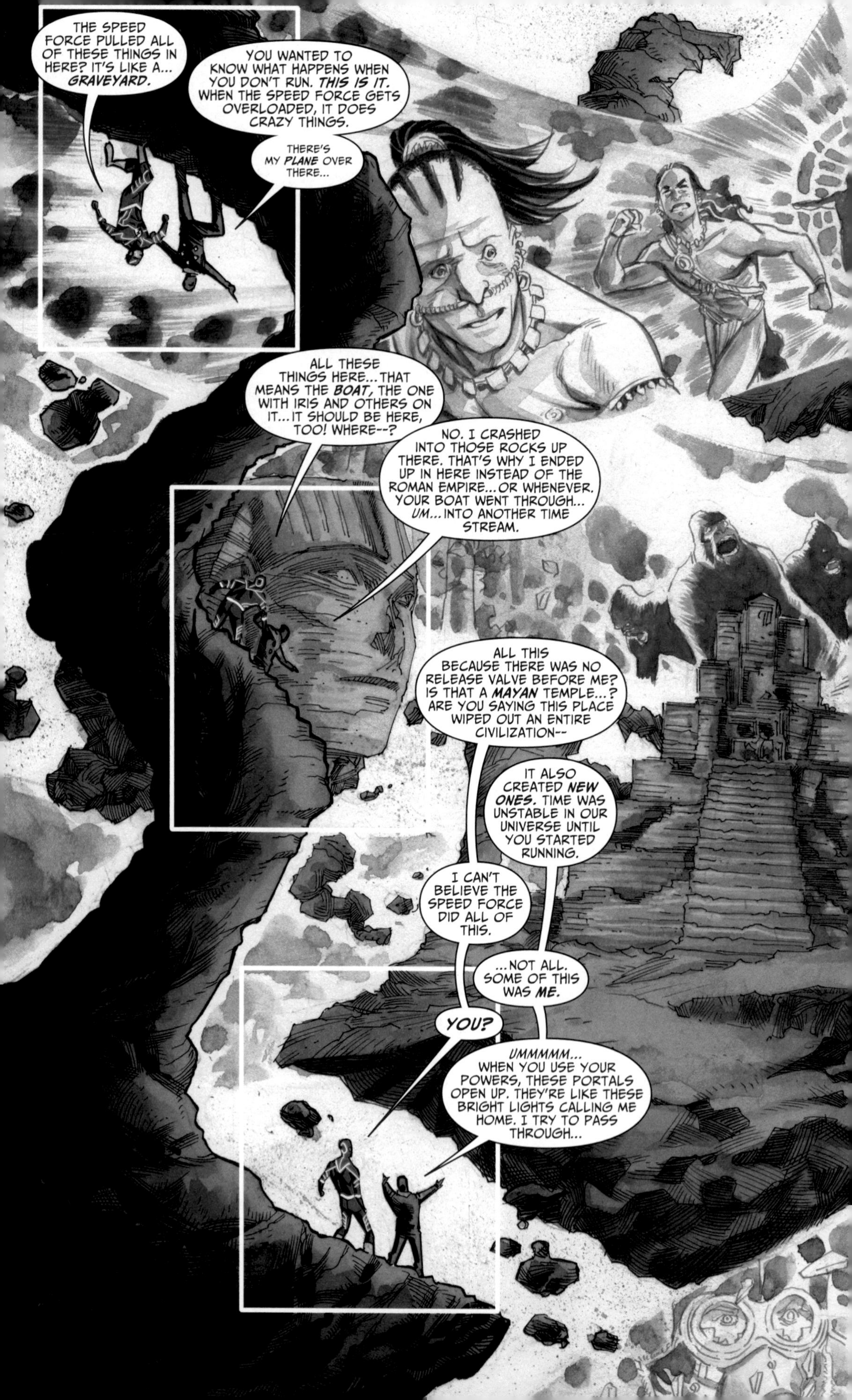
THE SPEED FORCE PULLED ALL OF THESE THINGS IN HERE? IT'S LIKE A... GRAVEYARD.
YOU WANTED TO KNOW WHAT HAPPENS WHEN YOU DON'T RUN. THIS IS IT. WHEN THE SPEED FORCE GETS OVERLOADED, IT DOES CRAZY THINGS.
THERE'S MY PLANE OVER THERE...
ALL THESE THINGS HERE... THAT MEANS THE BOAT, THE ONE WITH IRIS AND OTHERS ON IT... IT SHOULD BE HERE, TOO! WHERE--?
NO. I CRASHED INTO THOSE ROCKS UP THERE. THAT'S WHY I ENDED UP IN HERE INSTEAD OF THE ROMAN EMPIRE... OR WHENEVER. YOUR BOAT WENT THROUGH... UM... INTO ANOTHER TIME STREAM.
ALL THIS BECAUSE THERE WAS NO RELEASE VALVE BEFORE ME? IS THAT A MAYAN TEMPLE...? ARE YOU SAYING THIS PLACE WIPED OUT AN ENTIRE CIVILIZATION--
IT ALSO CREATED NEW ONES. TIME WAS UNSTABLE IN OUR UNIVERSE UNTIL YOU STARTED RUNNING.
I CAN'T BELIEVE THE SPEED FORCE DID ALL OF THIS.
...NOT ALL. SOME OF THIS WAS ME.
YOU?
UMMMMM... WHEN YOU USE YOUR POWERS, THESE PORTALS OPEN UP. THEY'RE LIKE THESE BRIGHT LIGHTS CALLING ME HOME. I TRY TO PASS THROUGH...

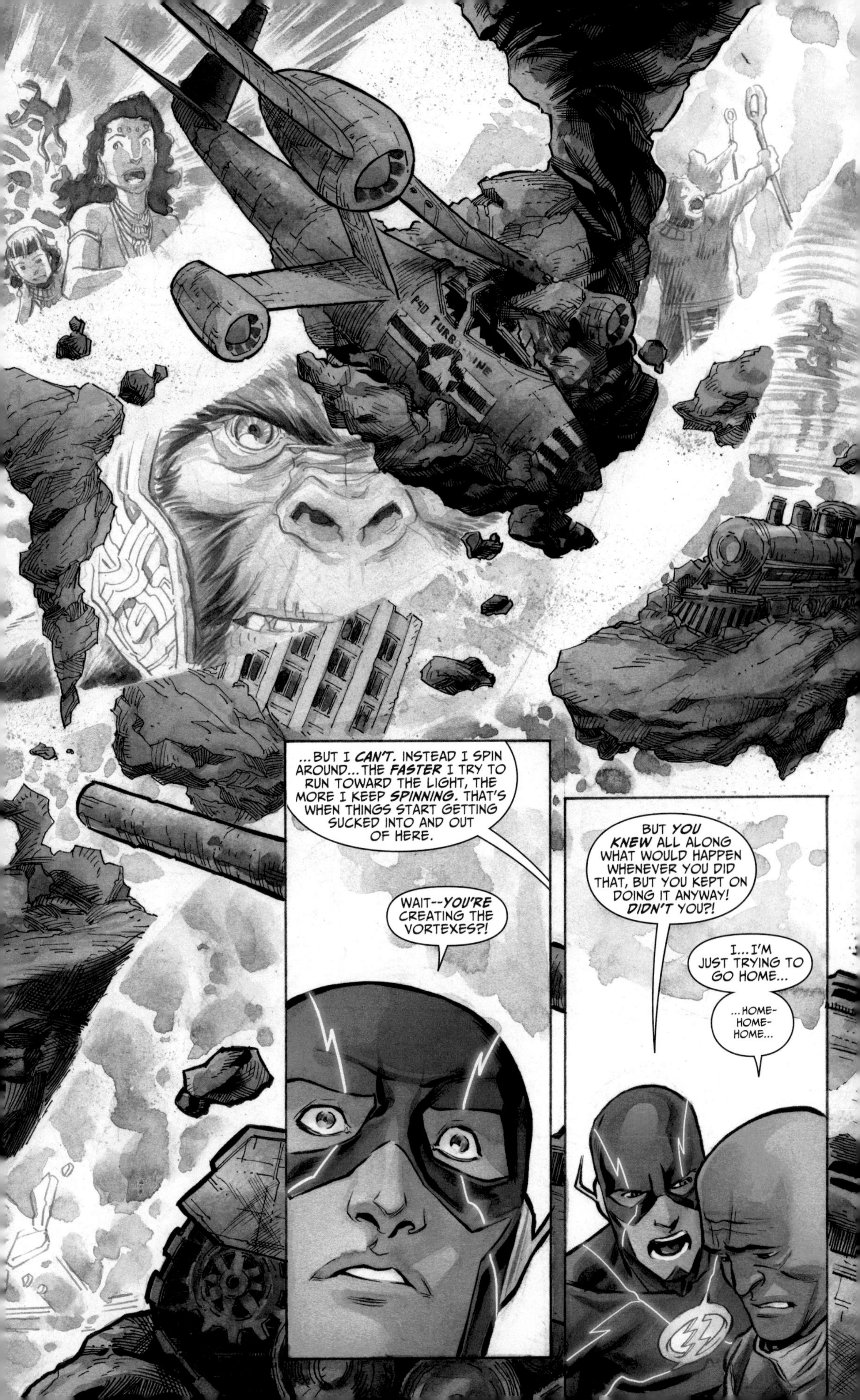
...BUT I CAN'T. INSTEAD I SPIN AROUND...THE FASTER I TRY TO RUN TOWARD THE LIGHT, THE MORE I KEEP SPINNING. THAT'S WHEN THINGS START GETTING SUCKED INTO AND OUT OF HERE.
WAIT--YOU'RE CREATING THE VORTEXES?!
BUT YOU KNEW ALL ALONG WHAT WOULD HAPPEN WHENEVER YOU DID THAT, BUT YOU KEPT ON DOING IT ANYWAY! DIDN'T YOU?!
I...I'M JUST TRYING TO GO HOME...
...HOME-HOME-HOME...

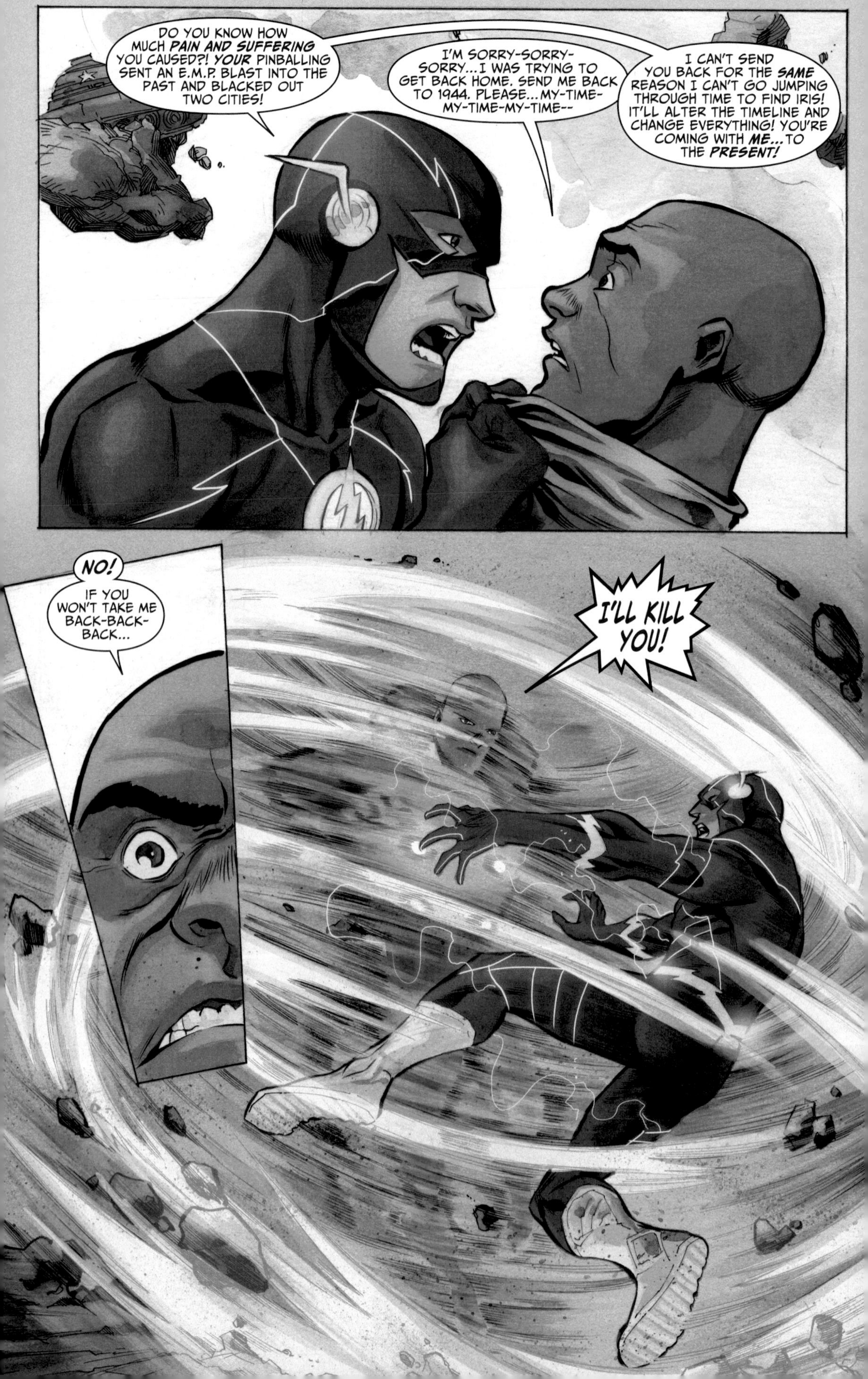
DO YOU KNOW HOW MUCH PAIN AND SUFFERING YOU CAUSED?! YOUR PINBALLING SENT AN E.M.P. BLAST INTO THE PAST AND BLACKED OUT TWO CITIES!
I'M SORRY-SORRY-SORRY...I WAS TRYING TO GET BACK HOME. SEND ME BACK TO 1944. PLEASE...MY-TIME-MY-TIME-MY-TIME--
I CAN'T SEND YOU BACK FOR THE SAME REASON I CAN'T GO JUMPING THROUGH TIME TO FIND IRIS! IT'LL ALTER THE TIMELINE AND CHANGE EVERYTHING! YOU'RE COMING WITH ME...TO THE PRESENT!
NO!
IF YOU WON'T TAKE ME BACK-BACK-BACK...
I'LL KILL YOU!

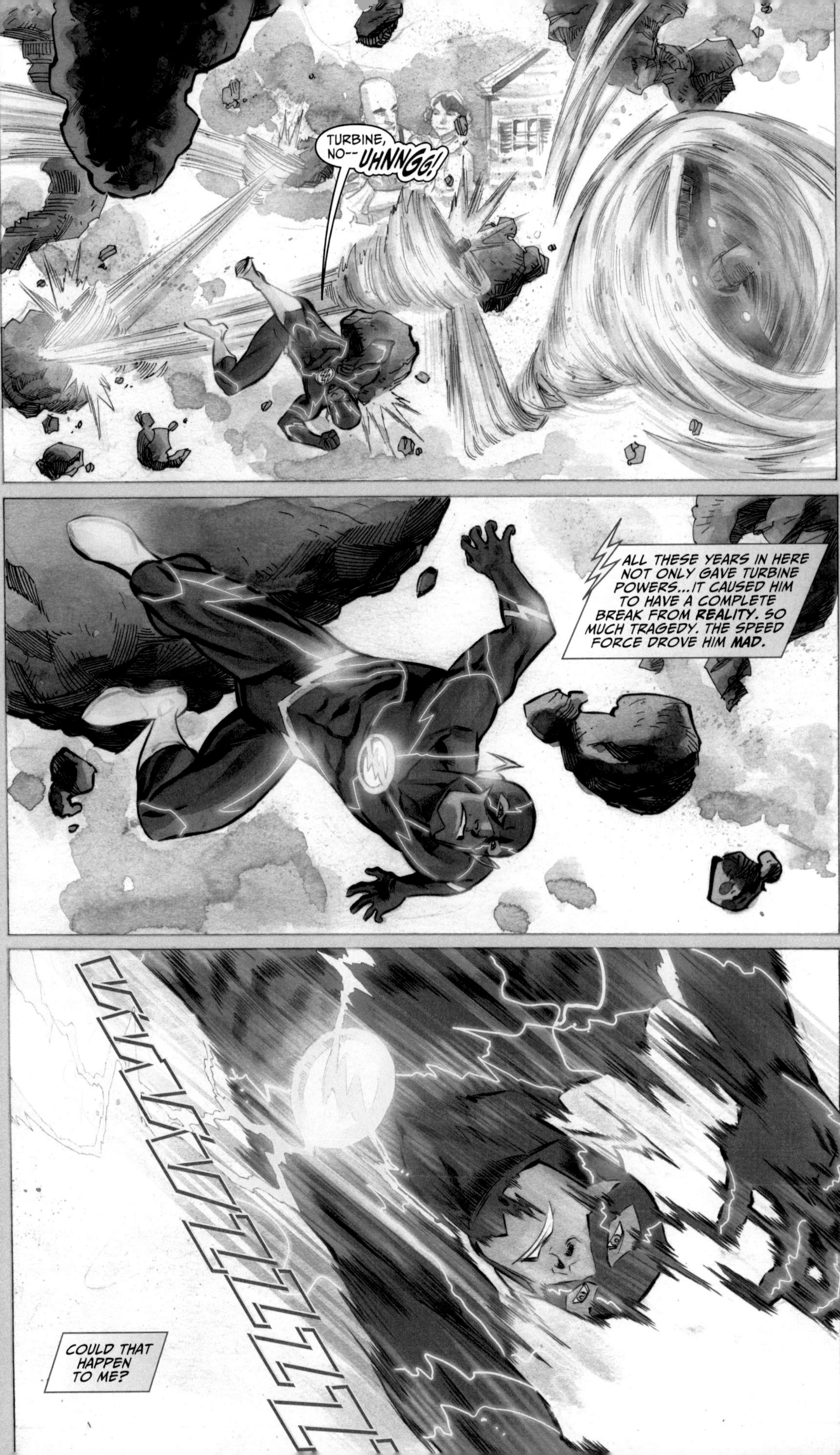
TURBINE, NO-- UHNNGG!
ALL THESE YEARS IN HERE NOT ONLY GAVE TURBINE POWERS...IT CAUSED HIM TO HAVE A COMPLETE BREAK FROM REALITY. SO MUCH TRAGEDY. THE SPEED FORCE DROVE HIM MAD.
COULD THAT HAPPEN TO ME?

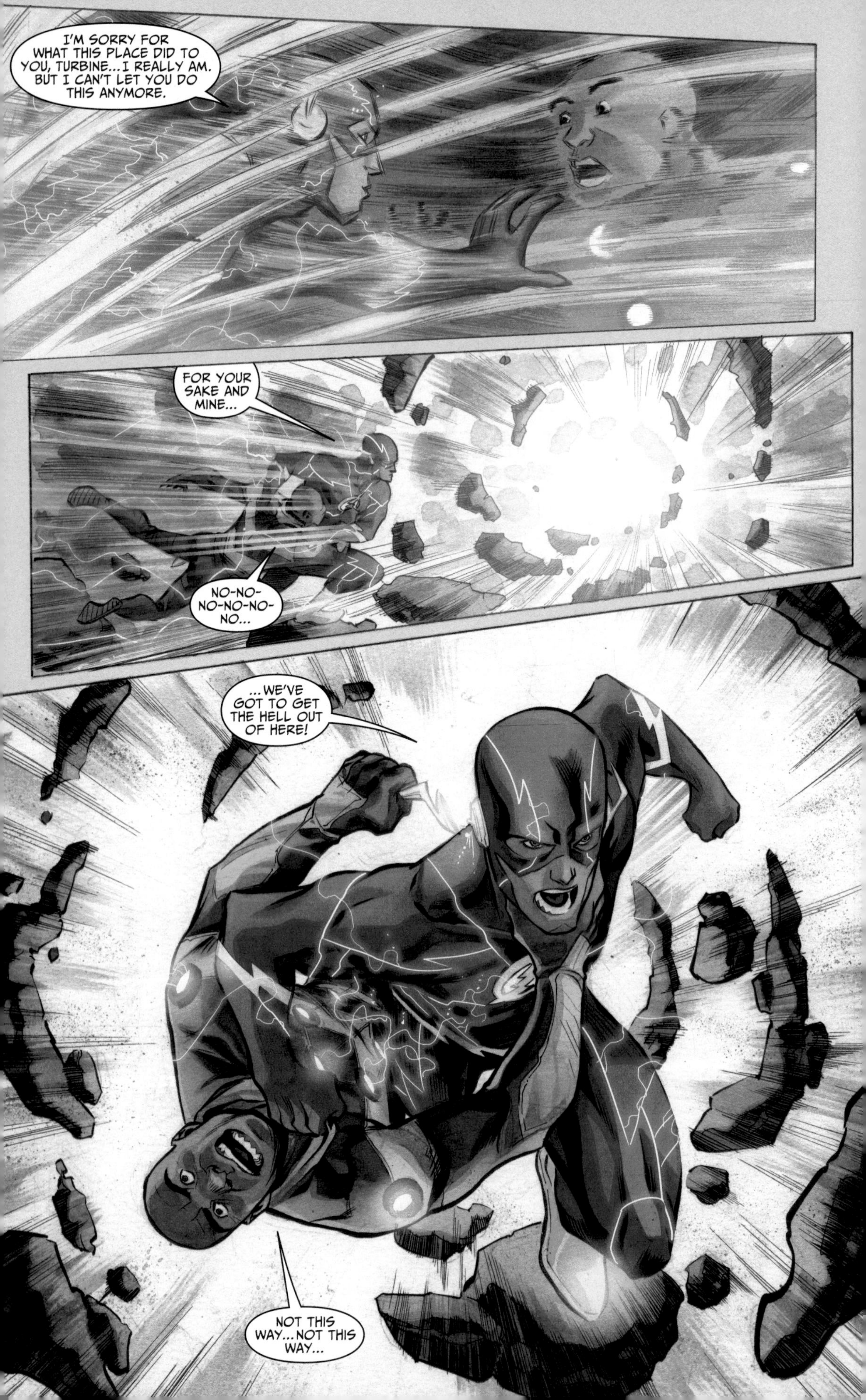
I'M SORRY FOR WHAT THIS PLACE DID TO YOU, TURBINE...I REALLY AM. BUT I CAN'T LET YOU DO THIS ANYMORE.
FOR YOUR SAKE AND MINE...
NO-NO-NO-NO-NO-NO...
...WE'VE GOT TO GET THE HELL OUT OF HERE!
NOT THIS WAY...NOT THIS WAY...

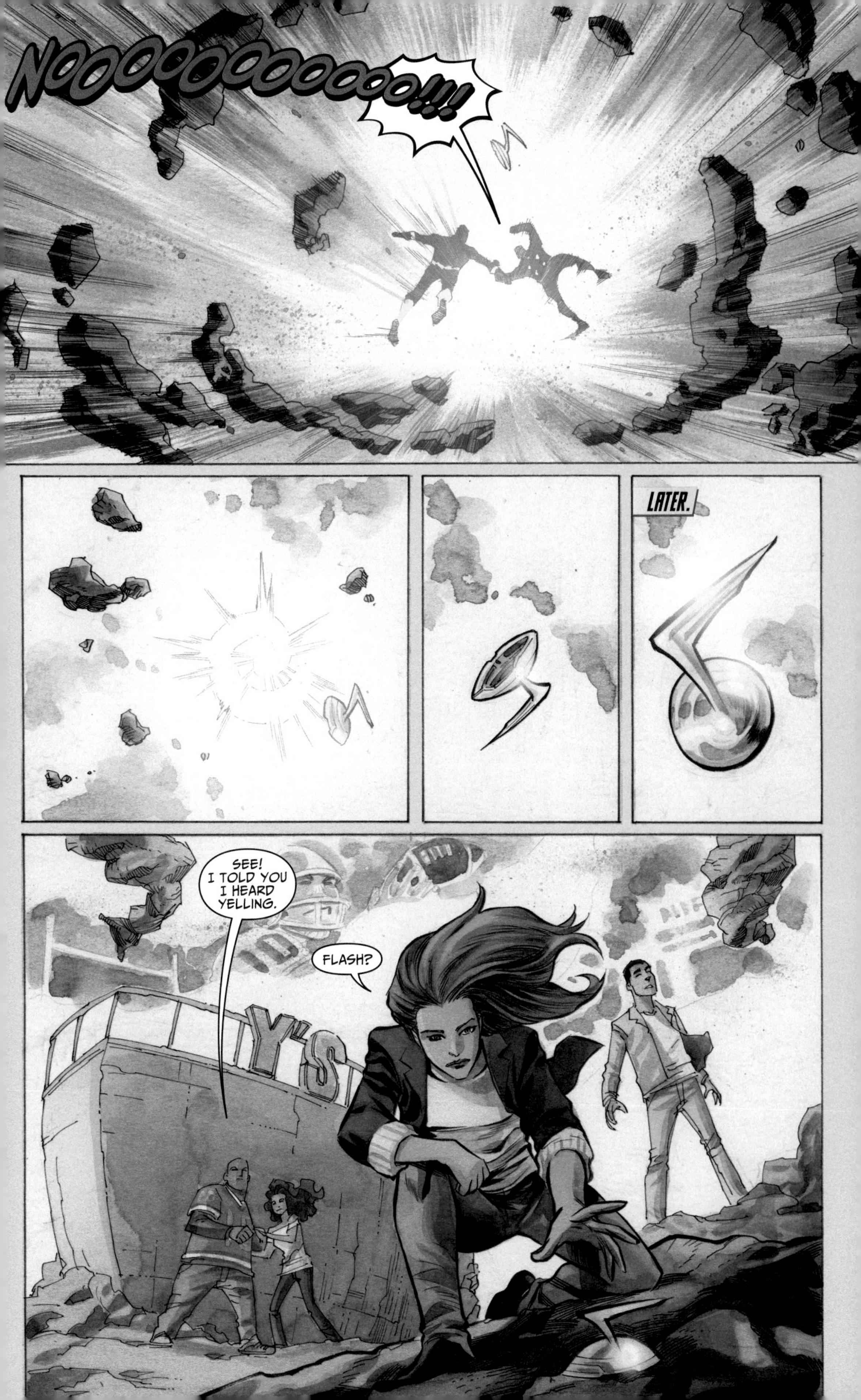
NOOOOOOOOOOOO!!!
LATER.
SEE! I TOLD YOU I HEARD YELLING.
FLASH?

GRODD! GRODD! GRODD! GRODD! GRODD!

IT IS TIME, GRODD-SON.

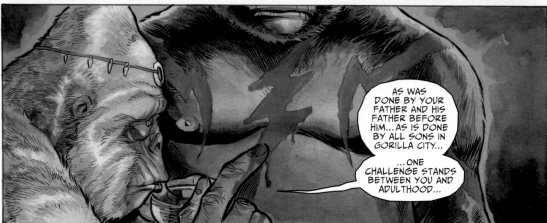

AS WAS DONE BY YOUR FATHER AND HIS FATHER BEFORE HIM... AS IS DONE BY ALL SONS IN GORILLA CITY...

...ONE CHALLENGE STANDS BETWEEN YOU AND ADULTHOOD...

YOU MUST FACE YOUR FATHER IN MORTAL COMBAT! A FIGHT TO THE DEATH TO STAKE YOUR CLAIM TO HIS NAME...HIS MEMORIES... HIS KNOWLEDGE...

AND HIS THRONE.

ENOUGH TALKING, LET'S GET ON WITH IT.

ARE YOU IN SUCH A HURRY TO DIE, MY SON?

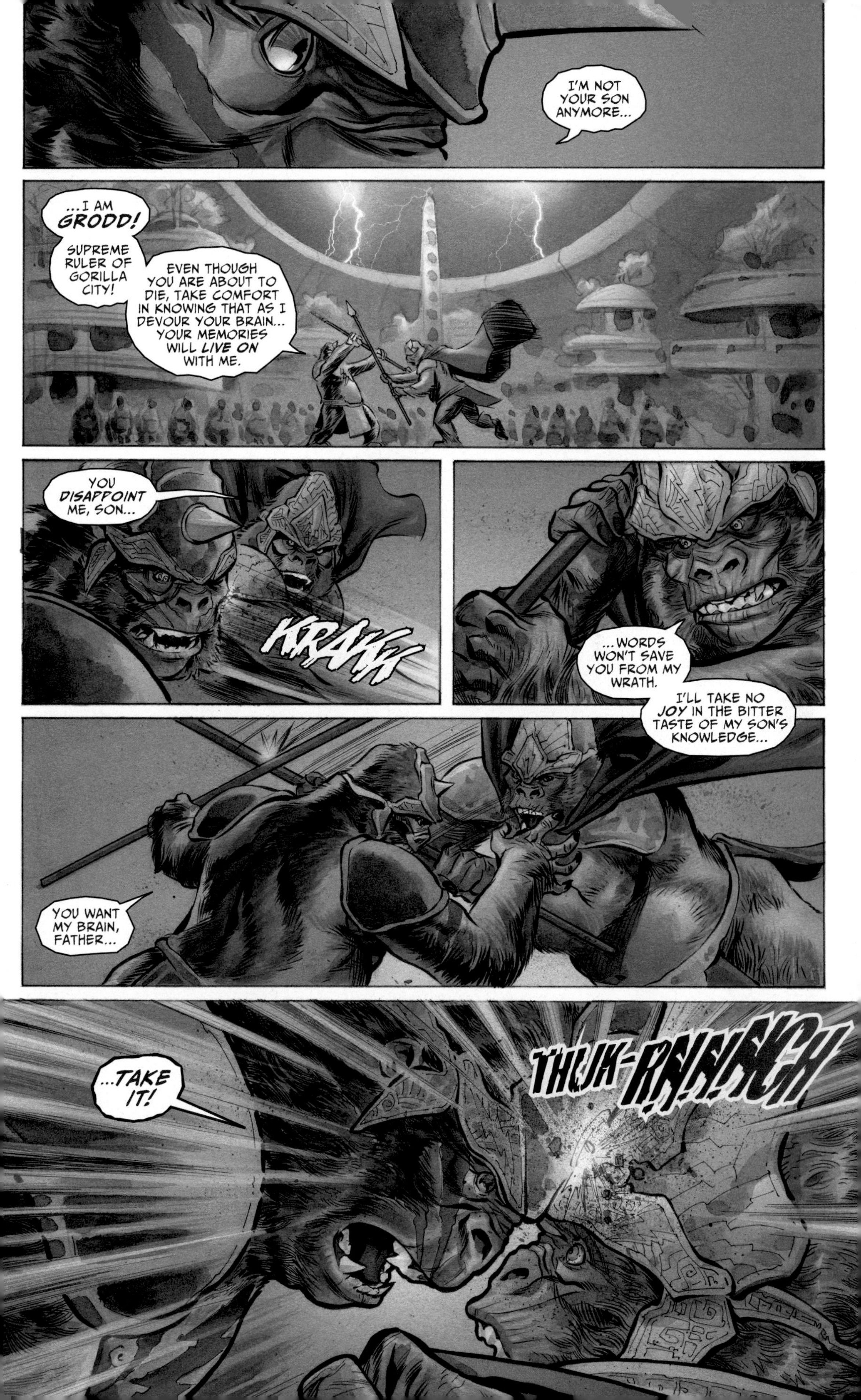
I'M NOT YOUR SON ANYMORE...
...I AM GRODD!
SUPREME RULER OF GORILLA CITY!
EVEN THOUGH YOU ARE ABOUT TO DIE, TAKE COMFORT IN KNOWING THAT AS I DEVOUR YOUR BRAIN... YOUR MEMORIES WILL LIVE ON WITH ME.
YOU DISAPPOINT ME, SON...
KRAKK
...WORDS WON'T SAVE YOU FROM MY WRATH.
I'LL TAKE NO JOY IN THE BITTER TASTE OF MY SON'S KNOWLEDGE...
YOU WANT MY BRAIN, FATHER...
...TAKE IT!
THUK-RRRUNCH

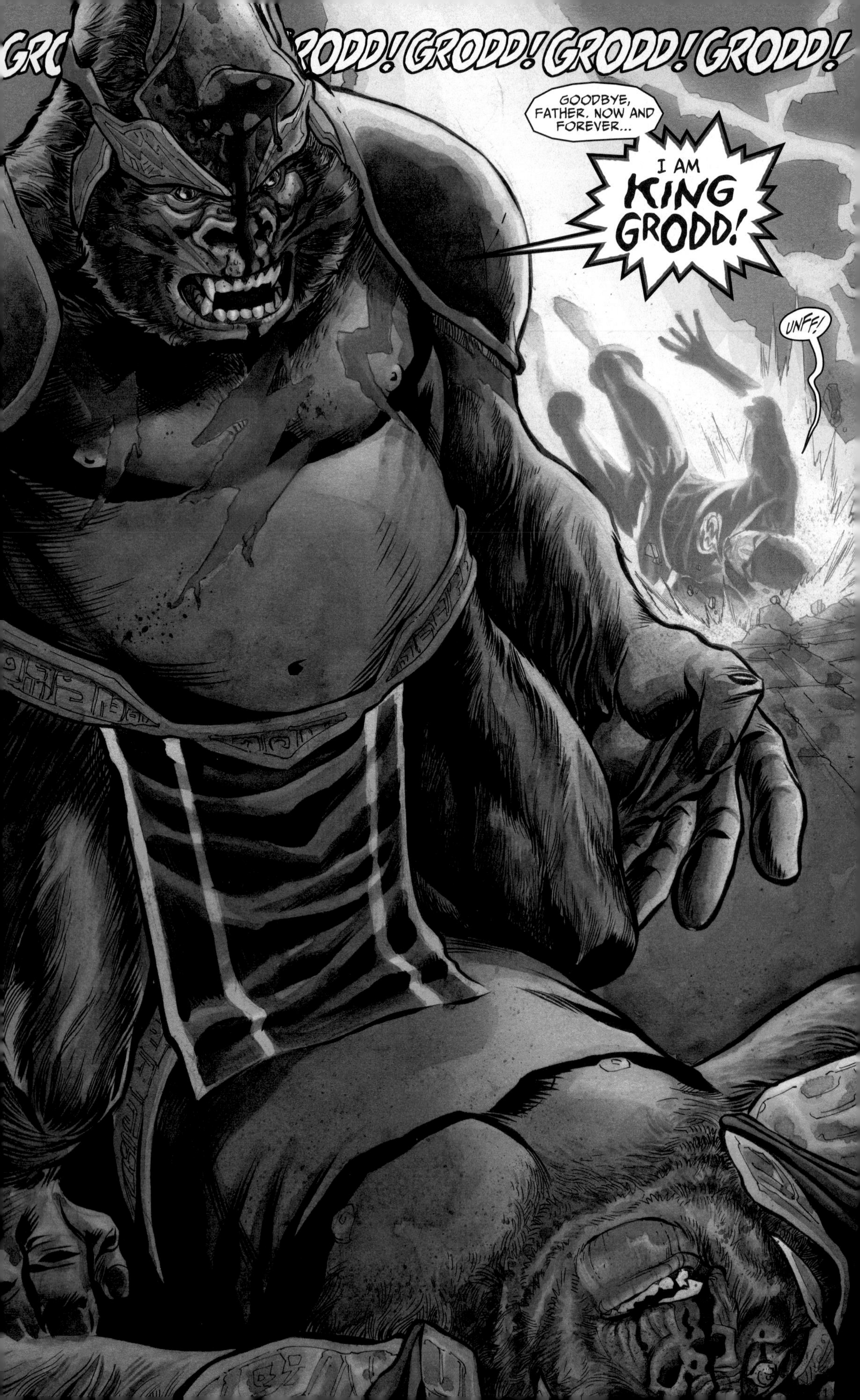
GRO... RODD! GRODD! GRODD! GRODD!
GOODBYE, FATHER. NOW AND FOREVER...
I AM KING GRODD!
UNFF!

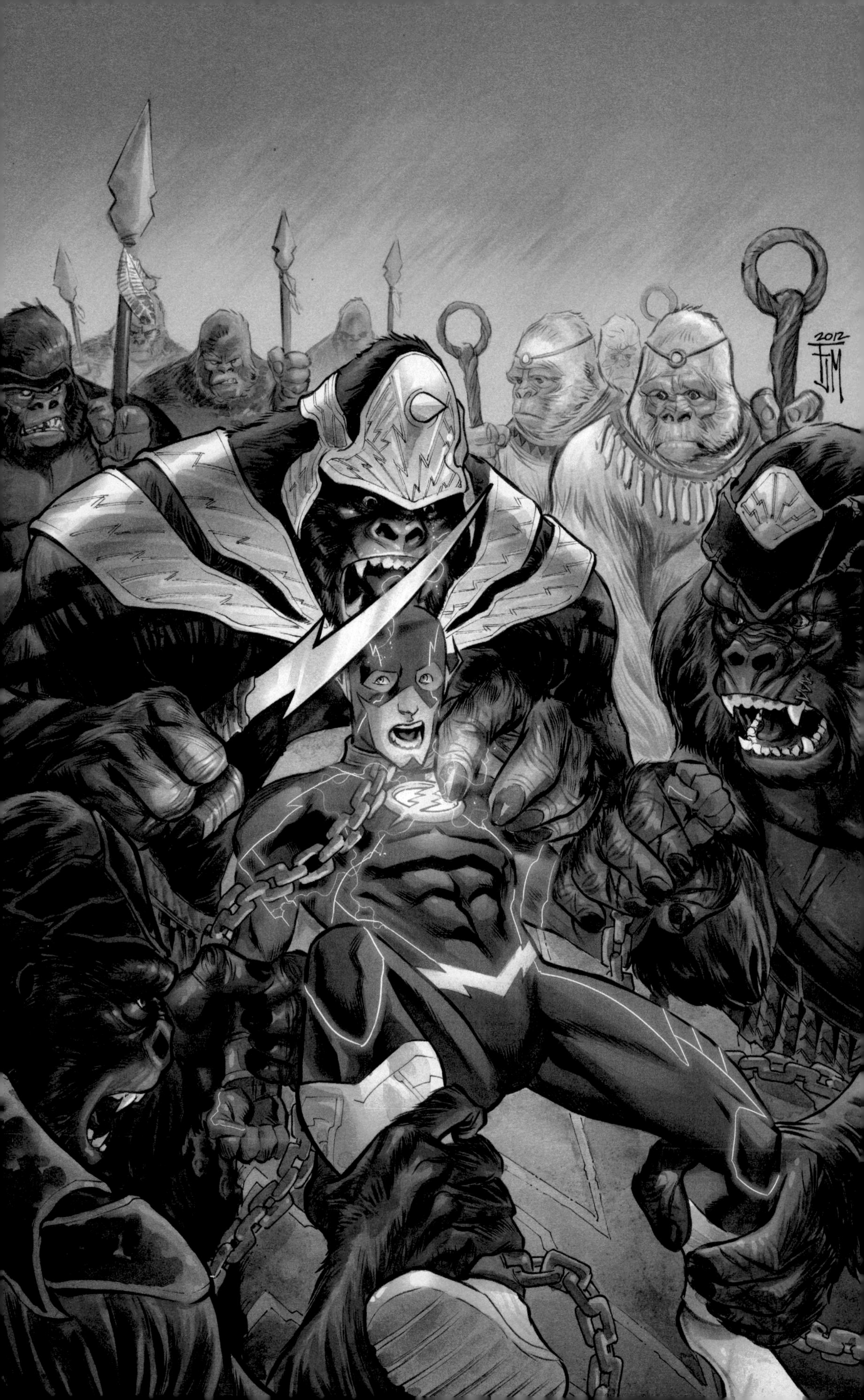
2012

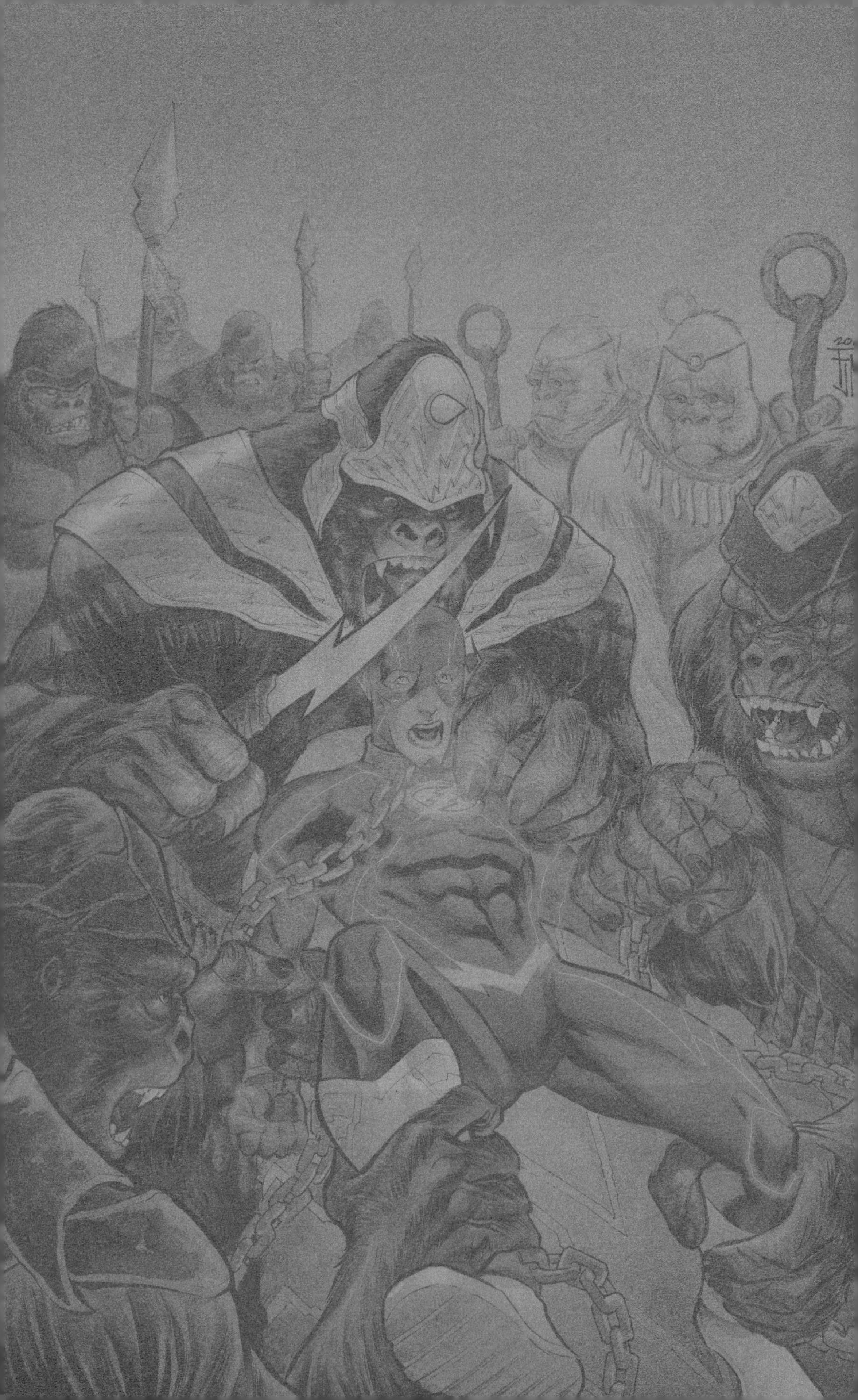

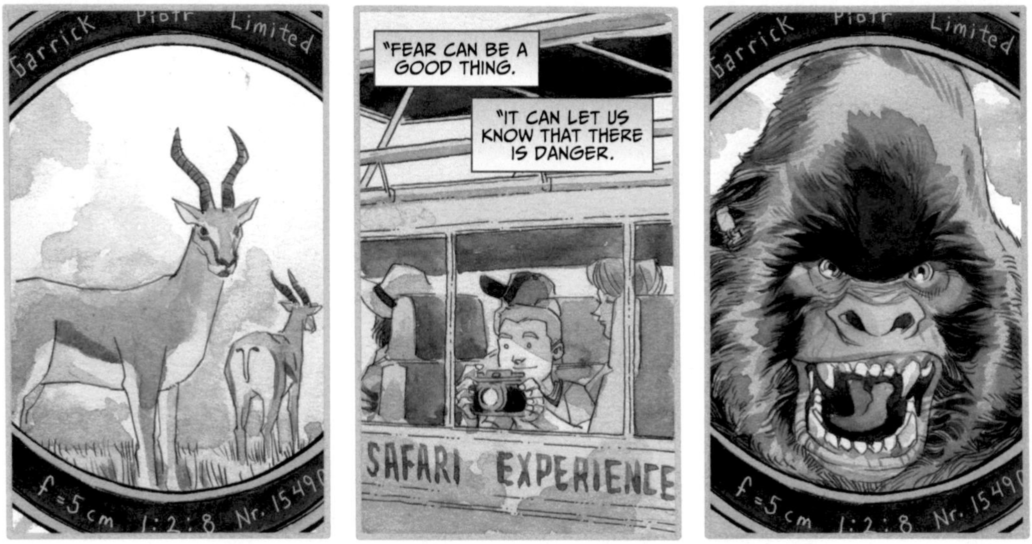
Garrick Piotr Limited
"FEAR CAN BE A GOOD THING.
"IT CAN LET US KNOW THAT THERE IS DANGER.
SAFARI EXPERIENCE
Garrick Piotr Limited

DC COMICS

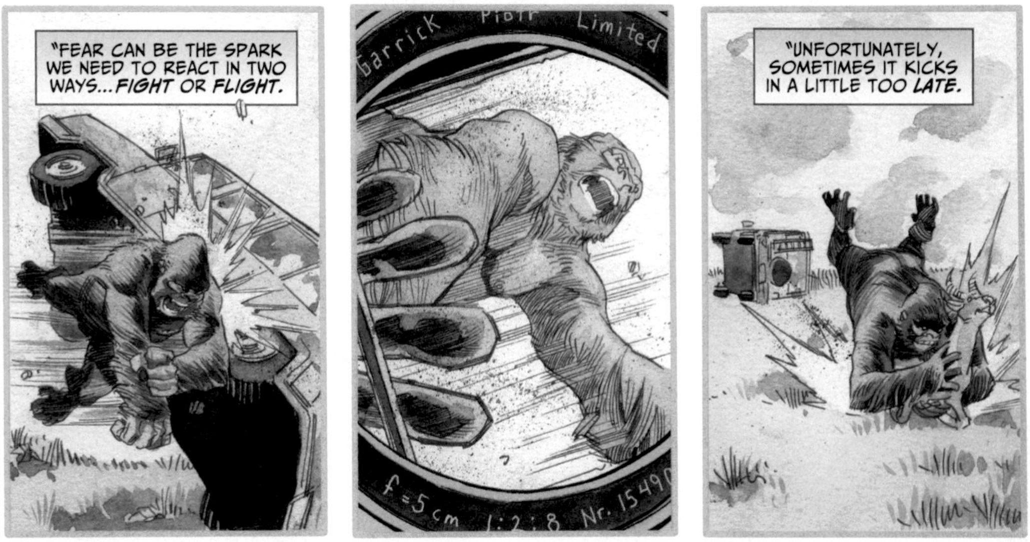
"FEAR CAN BE THE SPARK WE NEED TO REACT IN TWO WAYS...*FIGHT* OR *FLIGHT*.
Garrick Piotr Limited
"UNFORTUNATELY, SOMETIMES IT KICKS IN A LITTLE TOO *LATE*.

PROUDLY PRESENTS

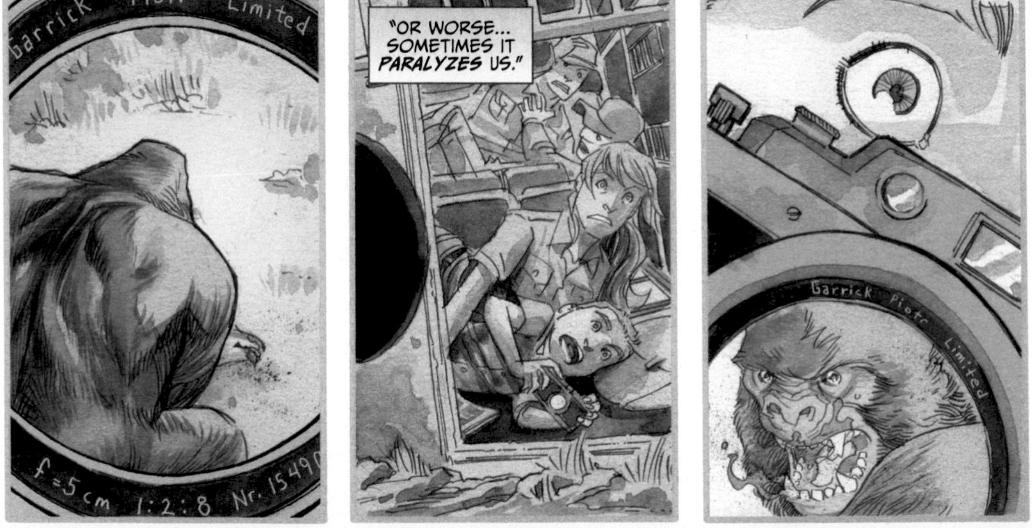
Garrick Piotr Limited
"OR WORSE... SOMETIMES IT *PARALYZES* US."
Garrick Piotr Limited

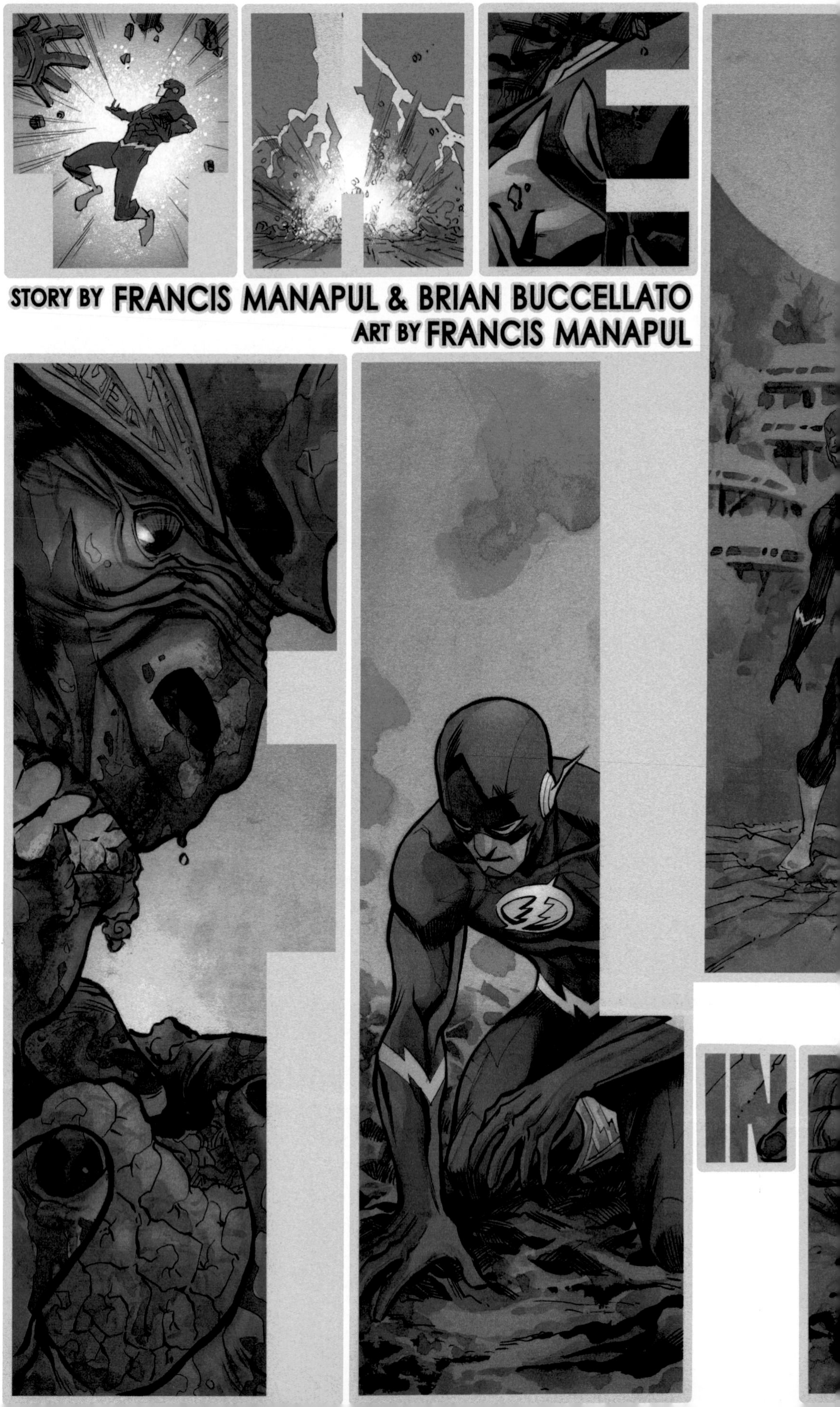
STORY BY FRANCIS MANAPUL & BRIAN BUCCELLATO
ART BY FRANCIS MANAPUL

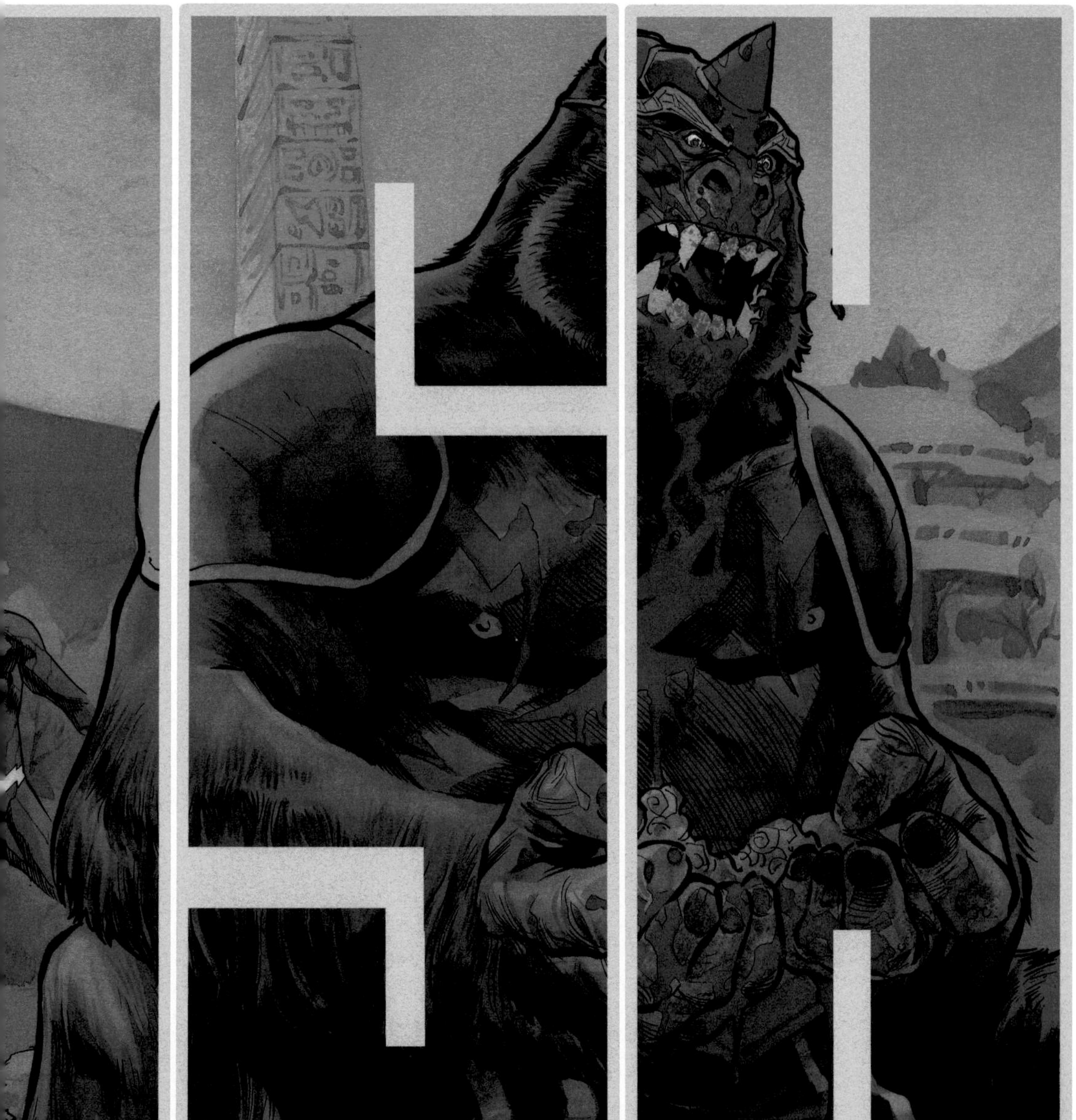

COLORS BRIAN BUCCELLATO • LETTERS WES ABBOTT
COVER MANAPUL WITH BUCCELLATO
ASSISTANT EDITOR DARREN SHAN • EDITOR BRIAN CUNNINGHAM

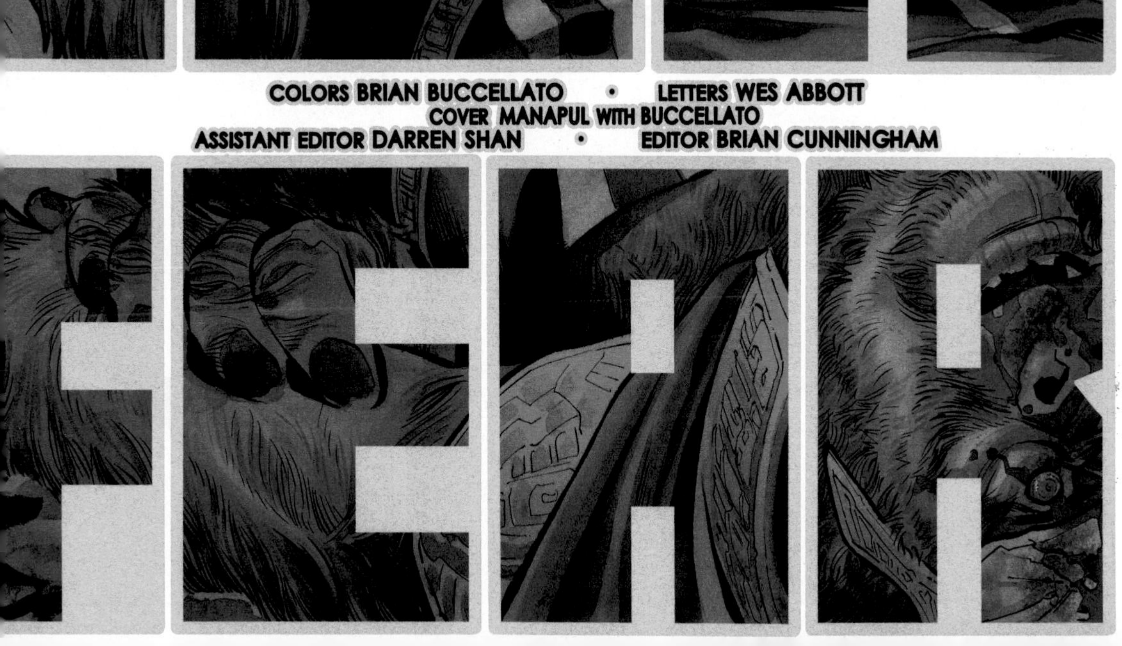
FEAR

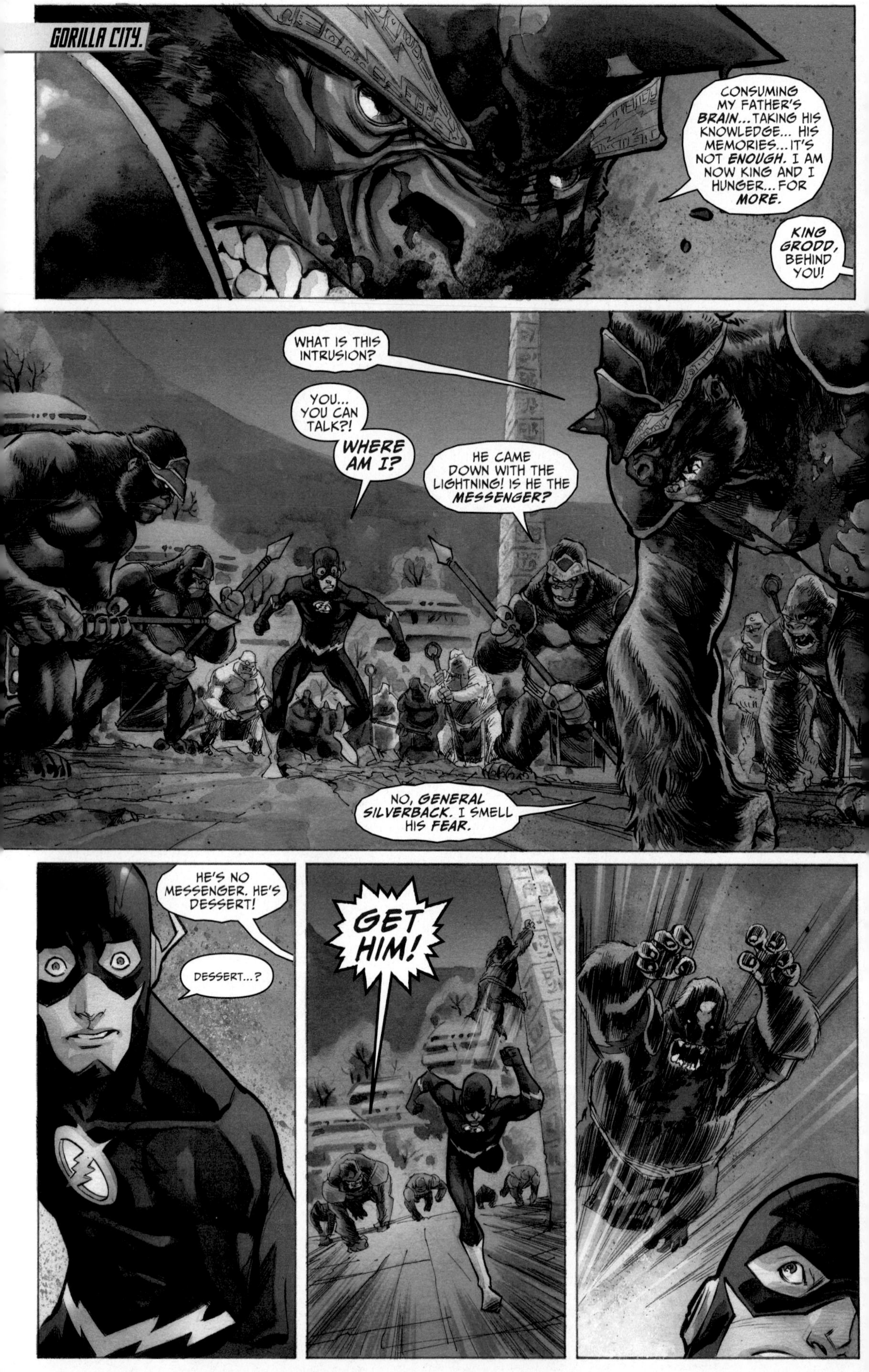
GORILLA CITY.
CONSUMING MY FATHER'S BRAIN... TAKING HIS KNOWLEDGE... HIS MEMORIES... IT'S NOT ENOUGH. I AM NOW KING AND I HUNGER... FOR MORE.
KING GRODD, BEHIND YOU!
WHAT IS THIS INTRUSION?
YOU... YOU CAN TALK?! WHERE AM I?
HE CAME DOWN WITH THE LIGHTNING! IS HE THE MESSENGER?
NO, GENERAL SILVERBACK. I SMELL HIS FEAR.
HE'S NO MESSENGER. HE'S DESSERT!
DESSERT...?
GET HIM!

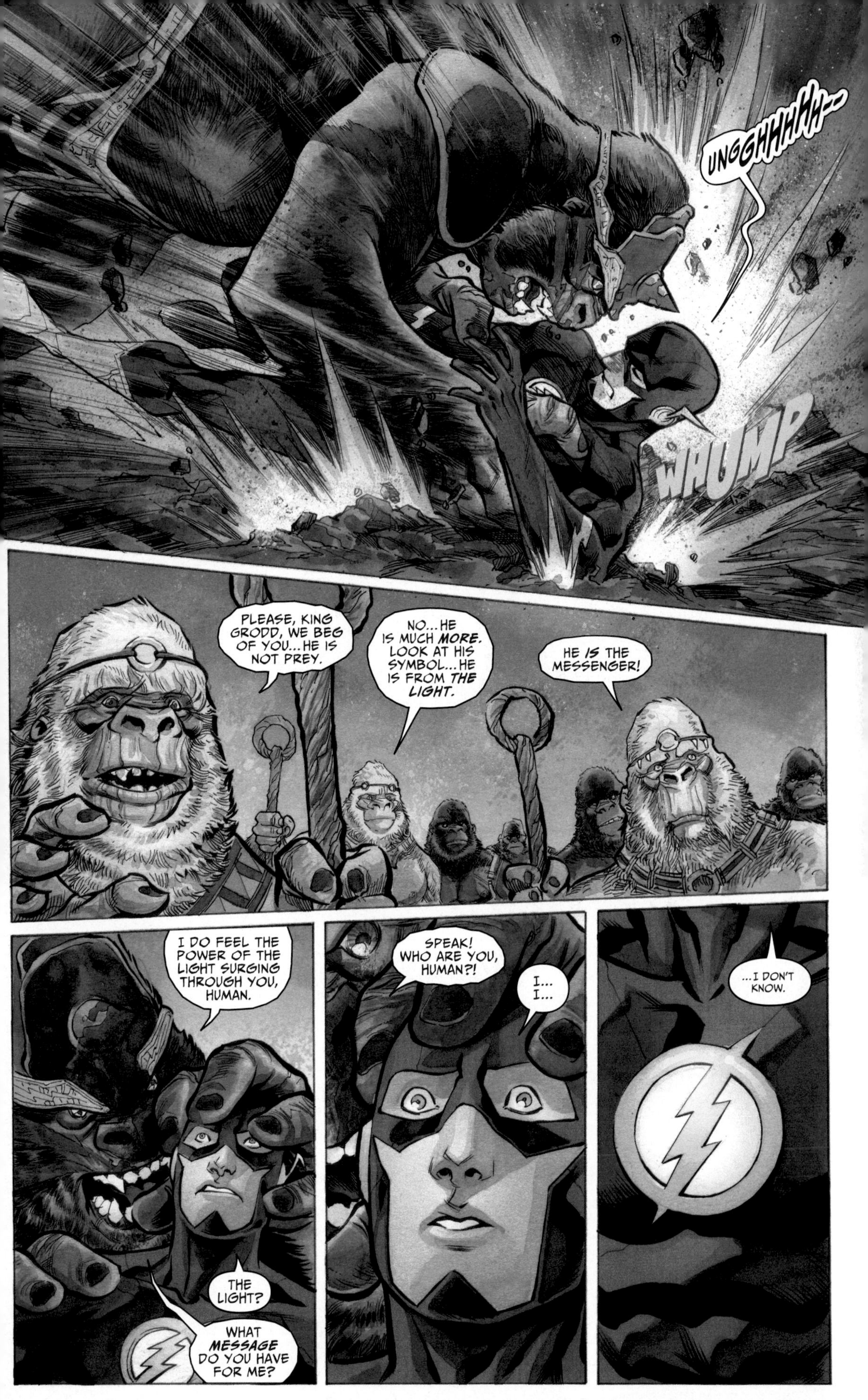
UNGGHHHHH--
WHUMP
PLEASE, KING GRODD, WE BEG OF YOU...HE IS NOT PREY.
NO...HE IS MUCH MORE. LOOK AT HIS SYMBOL...HE IS FROM THE LIGHT.
HE IS THE MESSENGER!
I DO FEEL THE POWER OF THE LIGHT SURGING THROUGH YOU, HUMAN.
THE LIGHT?
WHAT MESSAGE DO YOU HAVE FOR ME?
SPEAK! WHO ARE YOU, HUMAN?!
I... I...
...I DON'T KNOW.

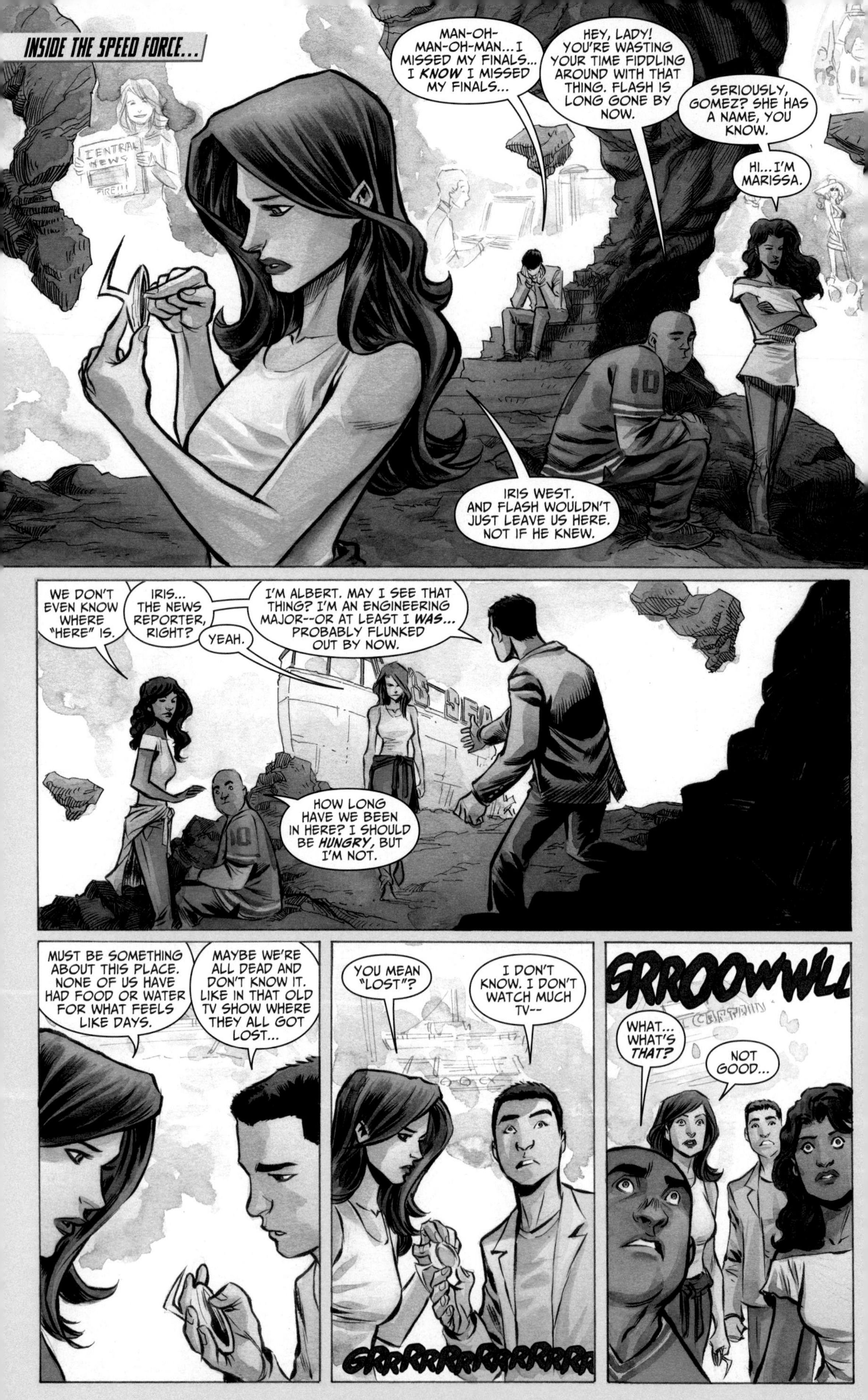
INSIDE THE SPEED FORCE...
MAN-OH-MAN-OH-MAN... I MISSED MY FINALS... I KNOW I MISSED MY FINALS...
HEY, LADY! YOU'RE WASTING YOUR TIME FIDDLING AROUND WITH THAT THING. FLASH IS LONG GONE BY NOW.
SERIOUSLY, GOMEZ? SHE HAS A NAME, YOU KNOW.
HI... I'M MARISSA.
IRIS WEST. AND FLASH WOULDN'T JUST LEAVE US HERE. NOT IF HE KNEW.
WE DON'T EVEN KNOW WHERE "HERE" IS.
IRIS... THE NEWS REPORTER, RIGHT?
YEAH.
I'M ALBERT. MAY I SEE THAT THING? I'M AN ENGINEERING MAJOR--OR AT LEAST I WAS... PROBABLY FLUNKED OUT BY NOW.
HOW LONG HAVE WE BEEN IN HERE? I SHOULD BE HUNGRY, BUT I'M NOT.
MUST BE SOMETHING ABOUT THIS PLACE. NONE OF US HAVE HAD FOOD OR WATER FOR WHAT FEELS LIKE DAYS.
MAYBE WE'RE ALL DEAD AND DON'T KNOW IT. LIKE IN THAT OLD TV SHOW WHERE THEY ALL GOT LOST...
YOU MEAN "LOST"?
I DON'T KNOW. I DON'T WATCH MUCH TV--
GRRRRRRRRRRRRRRRR
GRROOWWLL
WHAT... WHAT'S THAT?
NOT GOOD...

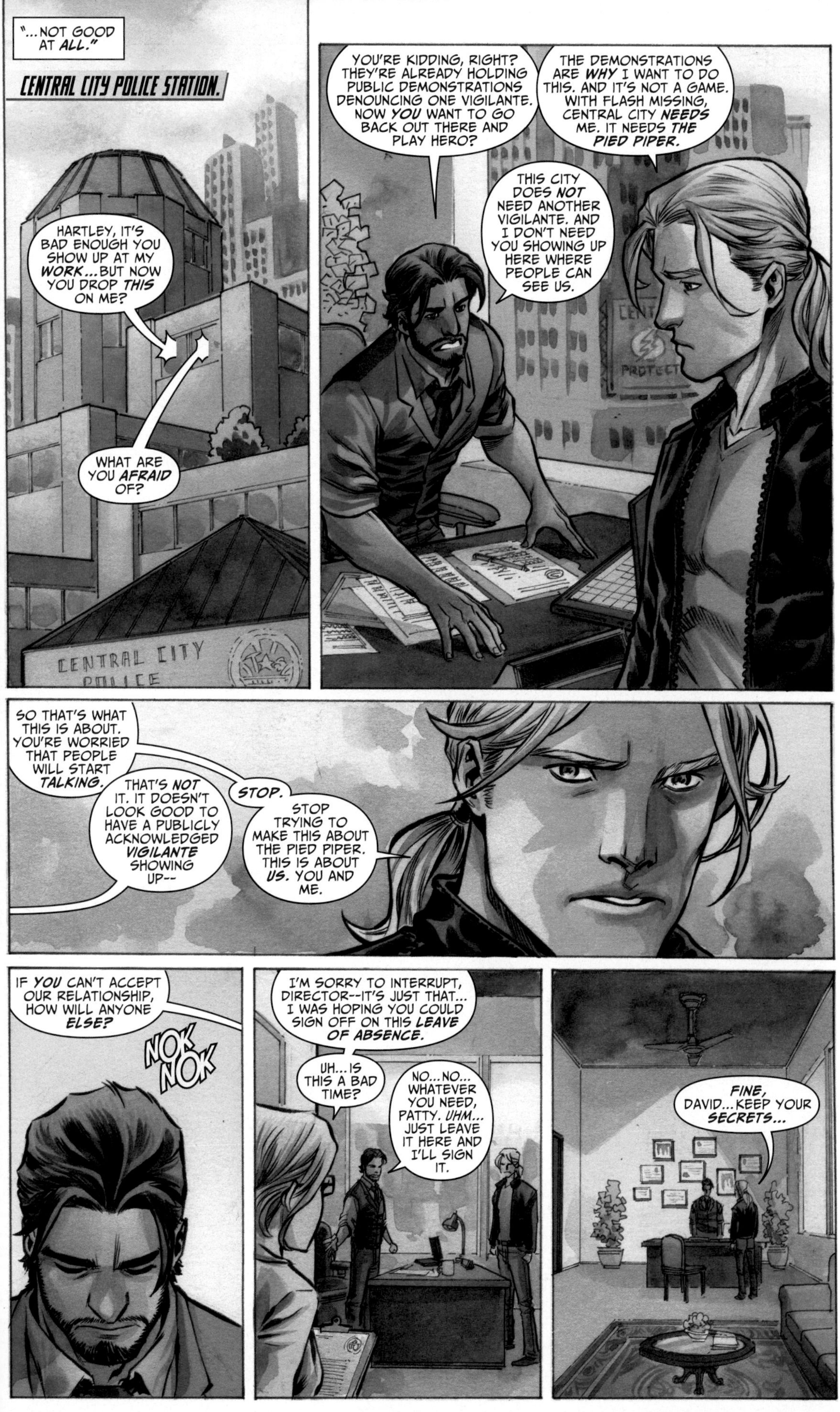
"...NOT GOOD AT ALL."
CENTRAL CITY POLICE STATION.
HARTLEY, IT'S BAD ENOUGH YOU SHOW UP AT MY WORK...BUT NOW YOU DROP THIS ON ME?
WHAT ARE YOU AFRAID OF?
CENTRAL CITY POLICE
YOU'RE KIDDING, RIGHT? THEY'RE ALREADY HOLDING PUBLIC DEMONSTRATIONS DENOUNCING ONE VIGILANTE. NOW YOU WANT TO GO BACK OUT THERE AND PLAY HERO?
THE DEMONSTRATIONS ARE WHY I WANT TO DO THIS. AND IT'S NOT A GAME. WITH FLASH MISSING, CENTRAL CITY NEEDS ME. IT NEEDS THE PIED PIPER.
THIS CITY DOES NOT NEED ANOTHER VIGILANTE. AND I DON'T NEED YOU SHOWING UP HERE WHERE PEOPLE CAN SEE US.
SO THAT'S WHAT THIS IS ABOUT. YOU'RE WORRIED THAT PEOPLE WILL START TALKING.
THAT'S NOT IT. IT DOESN'T LOOK GOOD TO HAVE A PUBLICLY ACKNOWLEDGED VIGILANTE SHOWING UP--
STOP.
STOP TRYING TO MAKE THIS ABOUT THE PIED PIPER. THIS IS ABOUT US. YOU AND ME.
IF YOU CAN'T ACCEPT OUR RELATIONSHIP, HOW WILL ANYONE ELSE?
NOK NOK
I'M SORRY TO INTERRUPT, DIRECTOR--IT'S JUST THAT... I WAS HOPING YOU COULD SIGN OFF ON THIS LEAVE OF ABSENCE.
UH...IS THIS A BAD TIME?
NO...NO... WHATEVER YOU NEED, PATTY. UHM... JUST LEAVE IT HERE AND I'LL SIGN IT.
FINE, DAVID...KEEP YOUR SECRETS...

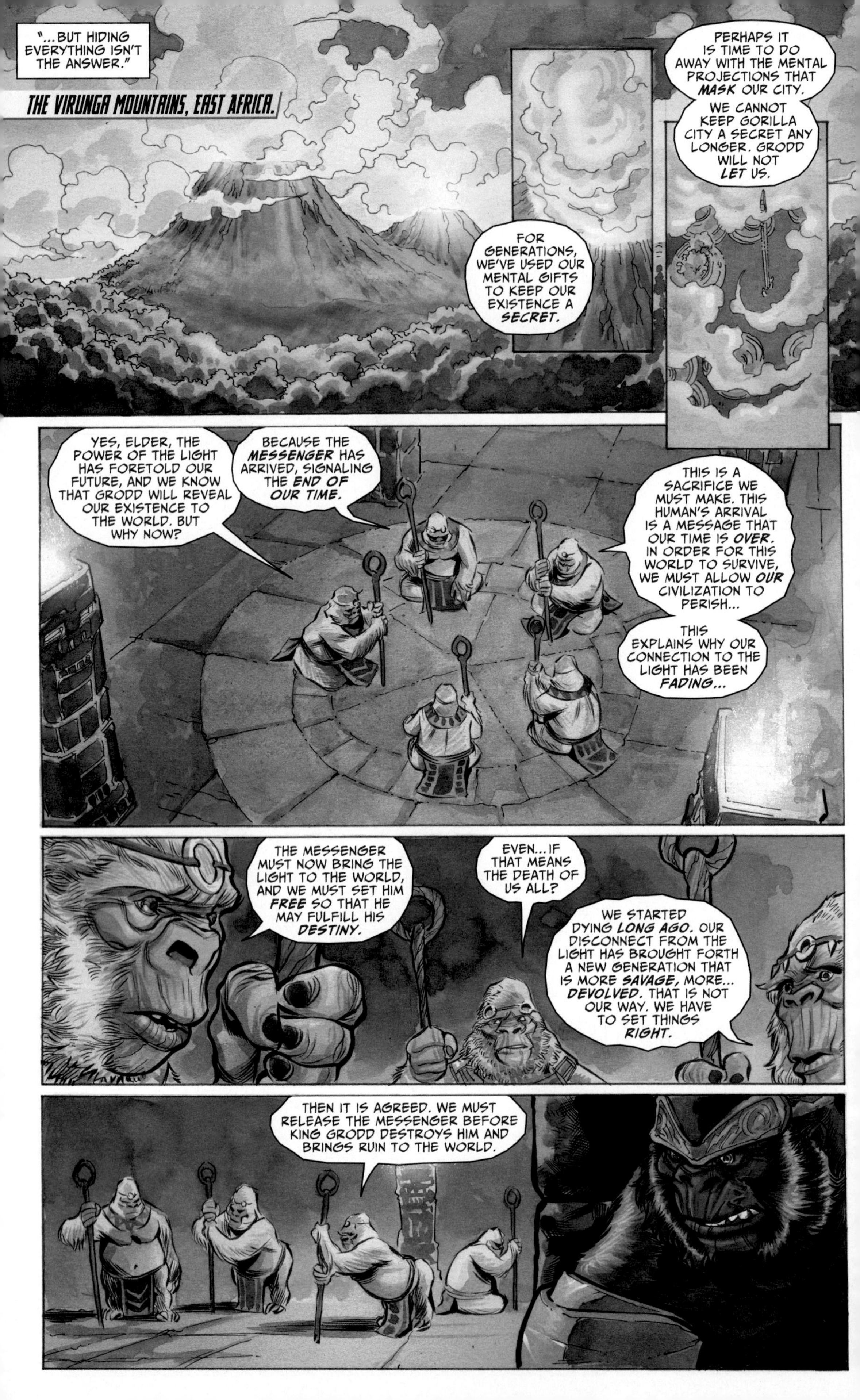
"...BUT HIDING EVERYTHING ISN'T THE ANSWER."
THE VIRUNGA MOUNTAINS, EAST AFRICA.
FOR GENERATIONS, WE'VE USED OUR MENTAL GIFTS TO KEEP OUR EXISTENCE A SECRET.
PERHAPS IT IS TIME TO DO AWAY WITH THE MENTAL PROJECTIONS THAT MASK OUR CITY.
WE CANNOT KEEP GORILLA CITY A SECRET ANY LONGER. GRODD WILL NOT LET US.
YES, ELDER, THE POWER OF THE LIGHT HAS FORETOLD OUR FUTURE, AND WE KNOW THAT GRODD WILL REVEAL OUR EXISTENCE TO THE WORLD. BUT WHY NOW?
BECAUSE THE MESSENGER HAS ARRIVED, SIGNALING THE END OF OUR TIME.
THIS IS A SACRIFICE WE MUST MAKE. THIS HUMAN'S ARRIVAL IS A MESSAGE THAT OUR TIME IS OVER. IN ORDER FOR THIS WORLD TO SURVIVE, WE MUST ALLOW OUR CIVILIZATION TO PERISH...
THIS EXPLAINS WHY OUR CONNECTION TO THE LIGHT HAS BEEN FADING...
THE MESSENGER MUST NOW BRING THE LIGHT TO THE WORLD, AND WE MUST SET HIM FREE SO THAT HE MAY FULFILL HIS DESTINY.
EVEN...IF THAT MEANS THE DEATH OF US ALL?
WE STARTED DYING LONG AGO. OUR DISCONNECT FROM THE LIGHT HAS BROUGHT FORTH A NEW GENERATION THAT IS MORE SAVAGE, MORE... DEVOLVED. THAT IS NOT OUR WAY. WE HAVE TO SET THINGS RIGHT.
THEN IT IS AGREED. WE MUST RELEASE THE MESSENGER BEFORE KING GRODD DESTROYS HIM AND BRINGS RUIN TO THE WORLD.

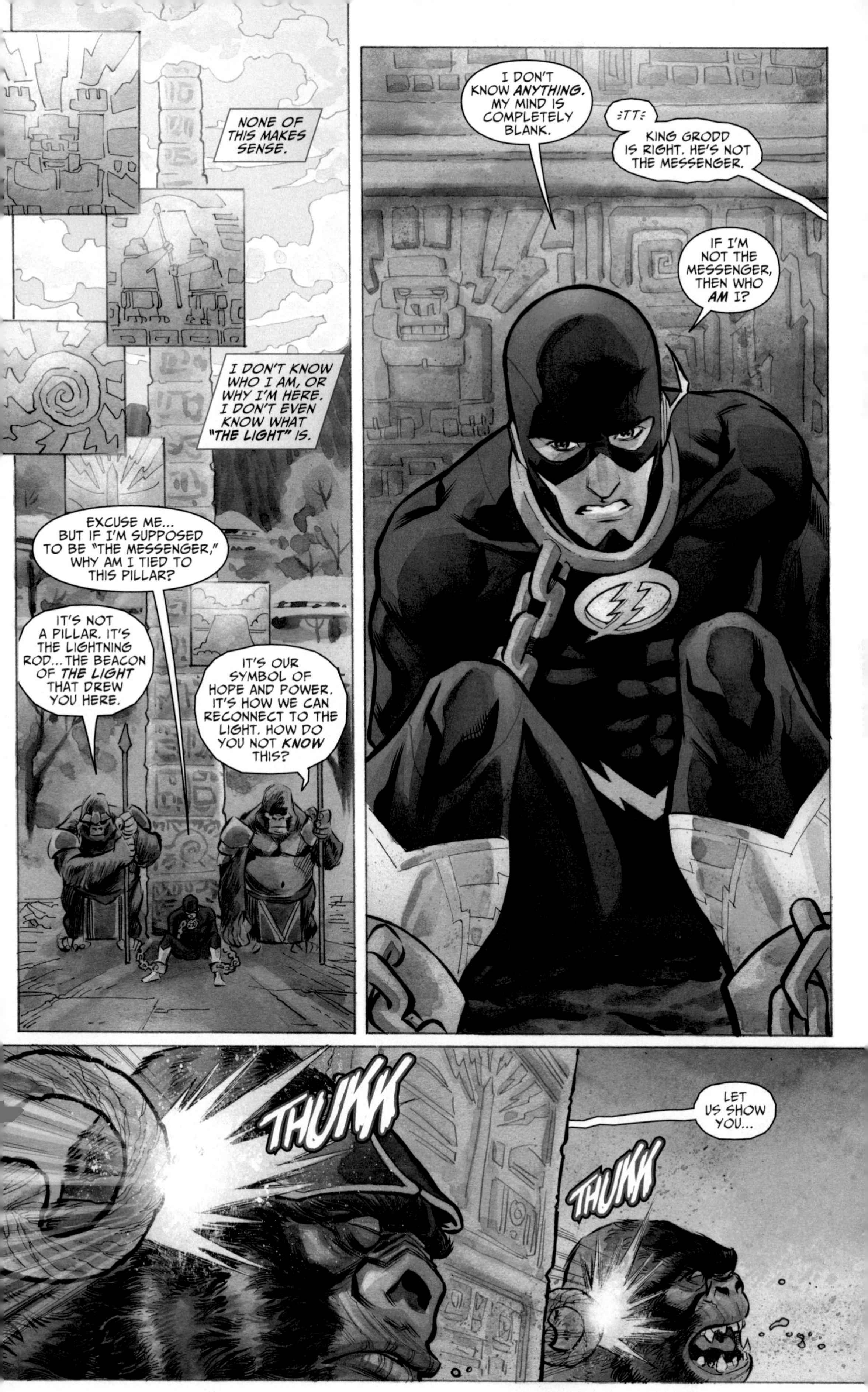
NONE OF THIS MAKES SENSE.
I DON'T KNOW WHO I AM, OR WHY I'M HERE. I DON'T EVEN KNOW WHAT "THE LIGHT" IS.
EXCUSE ME... BUT IF I'M SUPPOSED TO BE "THE MESSENGER," WHY AM I TIED TO THIS PILLAR?
IT'S NOT A PILLAR. IT'S THE LIGHTNING ROD...THE BEACON OF THE LIGHT THAT DREW YOU HERE.
IT'S OUR SYMBOL OF HOPE AND POWER. IT'S HOW WE CAN RECONNECT TO THE LIGHT. HOW DO YOU NOT KNOW THIS?
I DON'T KNOW ANYTHING. MY MIND IS COMPLETELY BLANK.
TT
KING GRODD IS RIGHT. HE'S NOT THE MESSENGER.
IF I'M NOT THE MESSENGER, THEN WHO AM I?
THUKK
LET US SHOW YOU...
THUKK

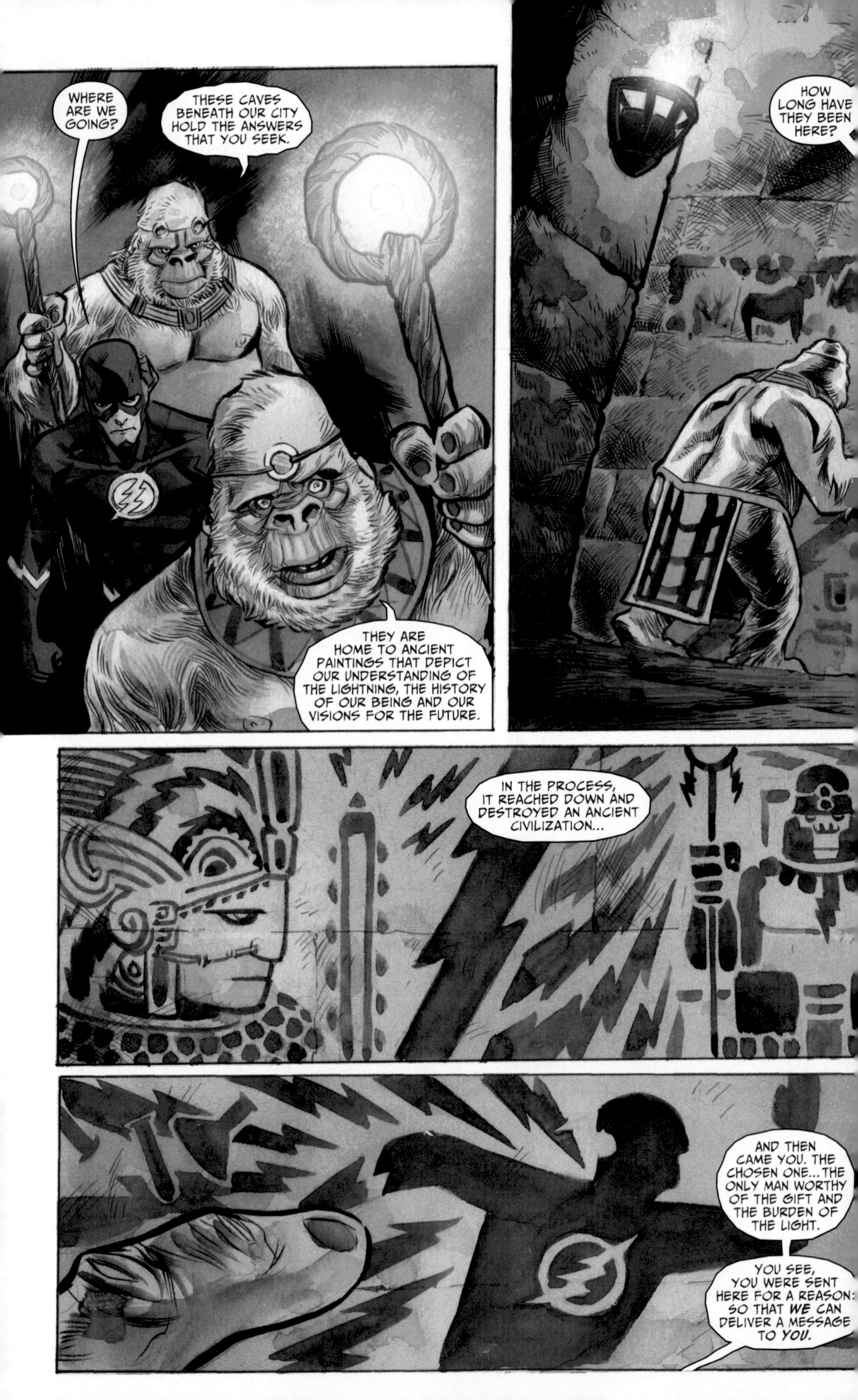
WHERE ARE WE GOING?
THESE CAVES BENEATH OUR CITY HOLD THE ANSWERS THAT YOU SEEK.
THEY ARE HOME TO ANCIENT PAINTINGS THAT DEPICT OUR UNDERSTANDING OF THE LIGHTNING, THE HISTORY OF OUR BEING AND OUR VISIONS FOR THE FUTURE.
HOW LONG HAVE THEY BEEN HERE?
IN THE PROCESS, IT REACHED DOWN AND DESTROYED AN ANCIENT CIVILIZATION...
AND THEN CAME YOU. THE CHOSEN ONE... THE ONLY MAN WORTHY OF THE GIFT AND THE BURDEN OF THE LIGHT.
YOU SEE, YOU WERE SENT HERE FOR A REASON: SO THAT *WE* CAN DELIVER A MESSAGE TO *YOU*.

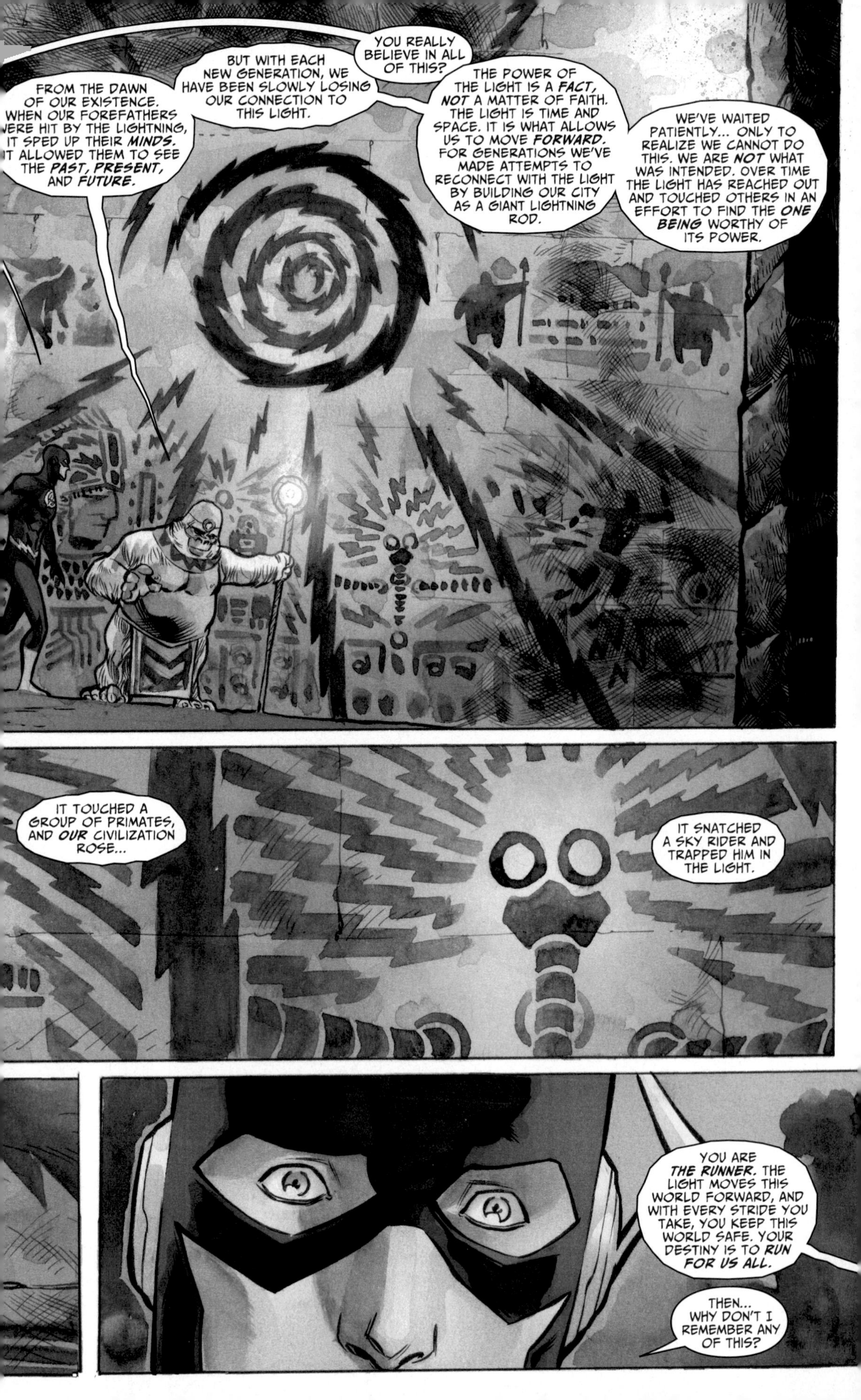
FROM THE DAWN OF OUR EXISTENCE. WHEN OUR FOREFATHERS WERE HIT BY THE LIGHTNING, IT SPED UP THEIR MINDS. IT ALLOWED THEM TO SEE THE PAST, PRESENT, AND FUTURE.
BUT WITH EACH NEW GENERATION, WE HAVE BEEN SLOWLY LOSING OUR CONNECTION TO THIS LIGHT.
YOU REALLY BELIEVE IN ALL OF THIS?
THE POWER OF THE LIGHT IS A FACT, NOT A MATTER OF FAITH. THE LIGHT IS TIME AND SPACE. IT IS WHAT ALLOWS US TO MOVE FORWARD. FOR GENERATIONS WE'VE MADE ATTEMPTS TO RECONNECT WITH THE LIGHT BY BUILDING OUR CITY AS A GIANT LIGHTNING ROD.
WE'VE WAITED PATIENTLY... ONLY TO REALIZE WE CANNOT DO THIS. WE ARE NOT WHAT WAS INTENDED. OVER TIME THE LIGHT HAS REACHED OUT AND TOUCHED OTHERS IN AN EFFORT TO FIND THE ONE BEING WORTHY OF ITS POWER.
IT TOUCHED A GROUP OF PRIMATES, AND OUR CIVILIZATION ROSE...
IT SNATCHED A SKY RIDER AND TRAPPED HIM IN THE LIGHT.
YOU ARE THE RUNNER. THE LIGHT MOVES THIS WORLD FORWARD, AND WITH EVERY STRIDE YOU TAKE, YOU KEEP THIS WORLD SAFE. YOUR DESTINY IS TO RUN FOR US ALL.
THEN... WHY DON'T I REMEMBER ANY OF THIS?

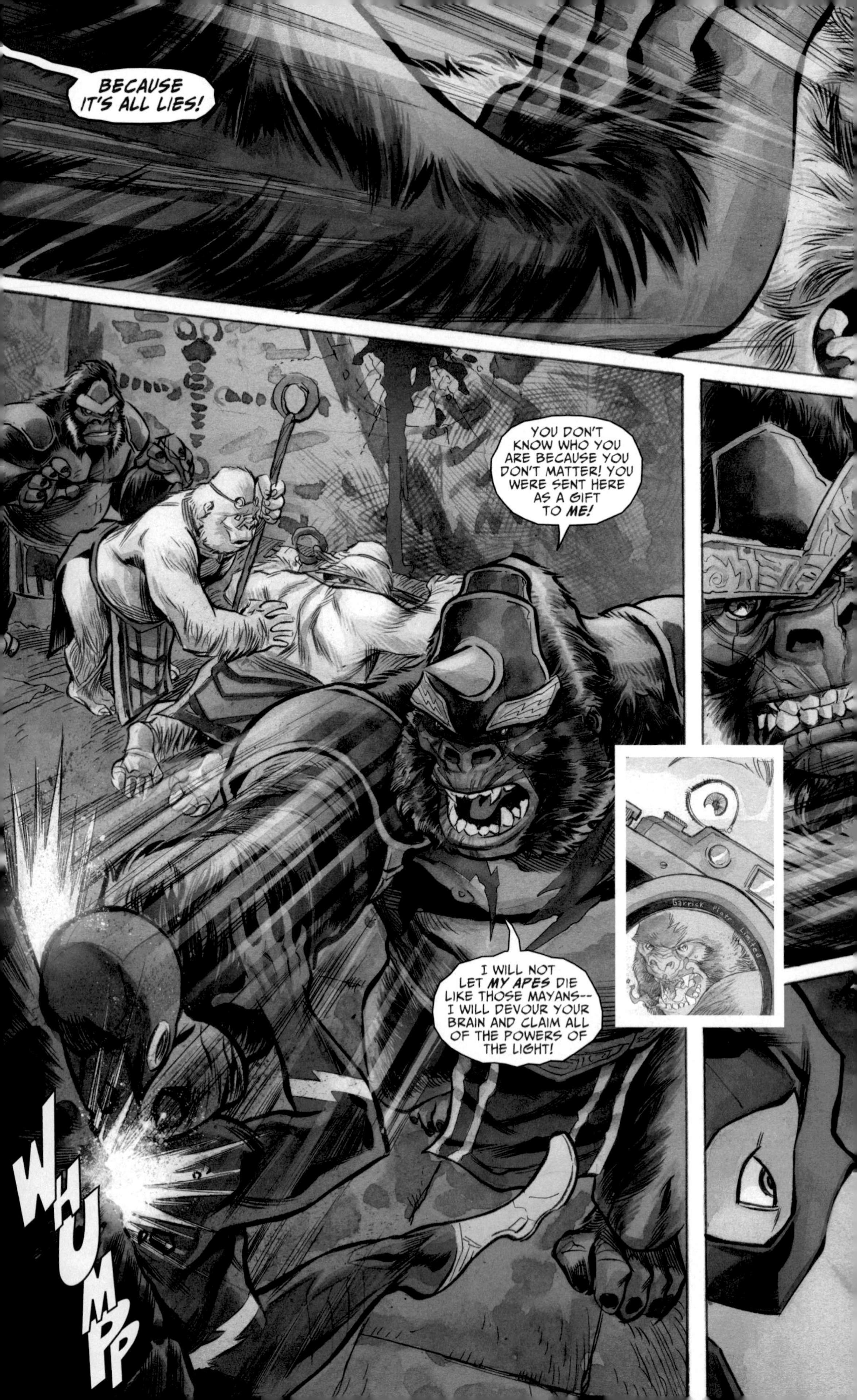
BECAUSE IT'S ALL LIES!
YOU DON'T KNOW WHO YOU ARE BECAUSE YOU DON'T MATTER! YOU WERE SENT HERE AS A GIFT TO ME!
I WILL NOT LET MY APES DIE LIKE THOSE MAYANS-- I WILL DEVOUR YOUR BRAIN AND CLAIM ALL OF THE POWERS OF THE LIGHT!
WHUMPP

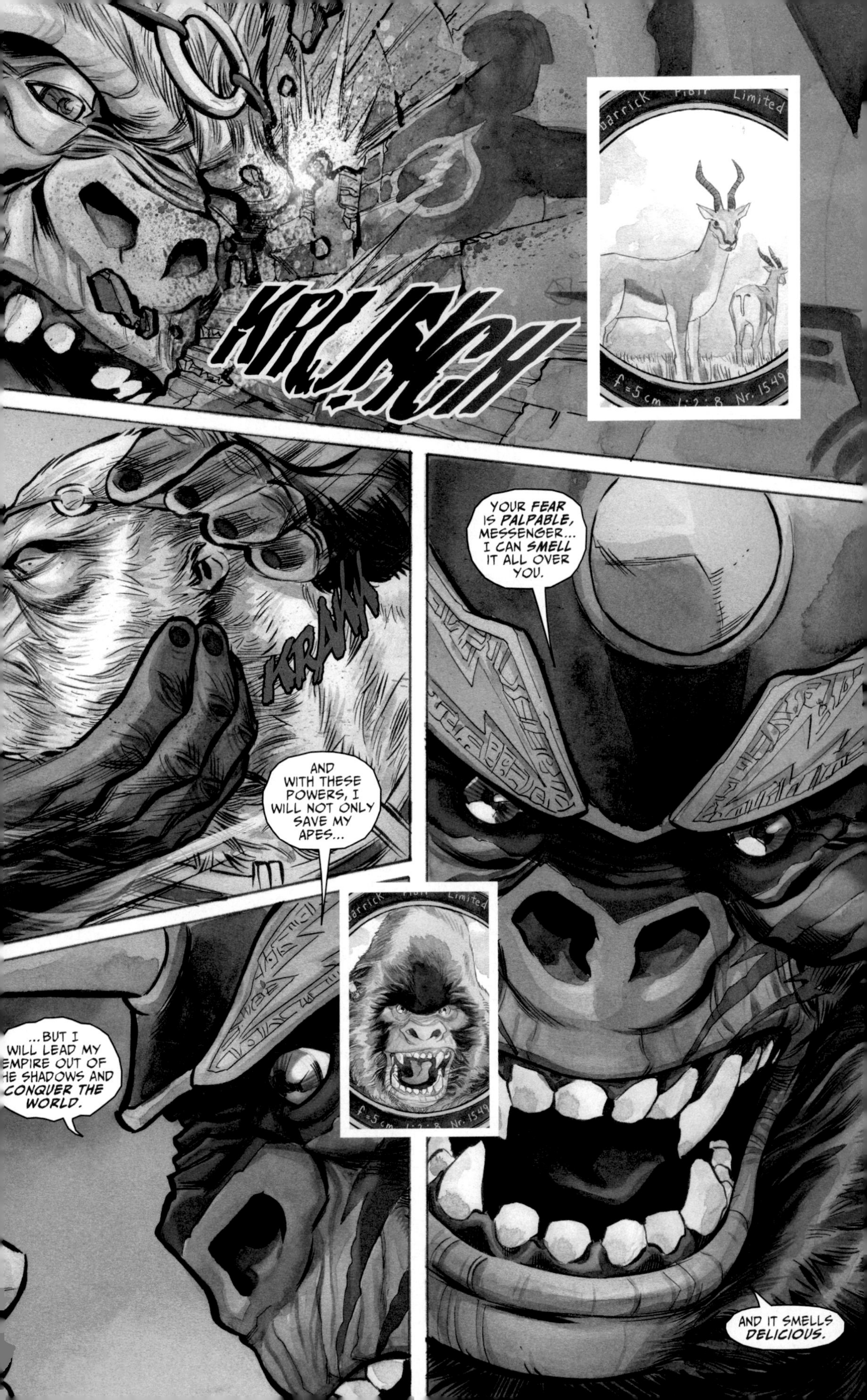
KRUNCH
KRAK
AND WITH THESE POWERS, I WILL NOT ONLY SAVE MY APES...
YOUR FEAR IS PALPABLE, MESSENGER... I CAN SMELL IT ALL OVER YOU.
...BUT I WILL LEAD MY EMPIRE OUT OF HE SHADOWS AND CONQUER THE WORLD.
AND IT SMELLS DELICIOUS.

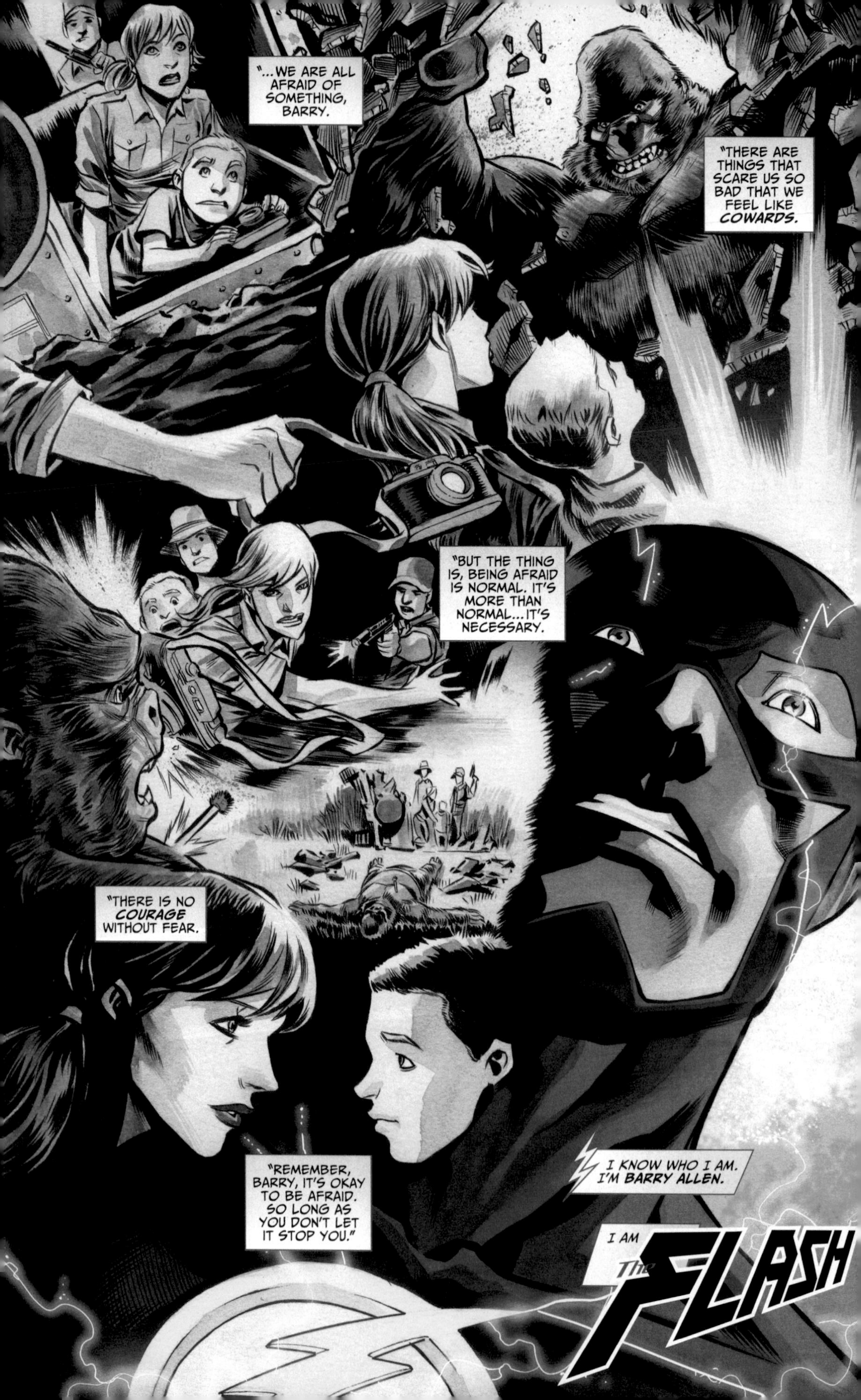
"...WE ARE ALL AFRAID OF SOMETHING, BARRY.
"THERE ARE THINGS THAT SCARE US SO BAD THAT WE FEEL LIKE COWARDS.
"BUT THE THING IS, BEING AFRAID IS NORMAL. IT'S MORE THAN NORMAL...IT'S NECESSARY.
"THERE IS NO COURAGE WITHOUT FEAR.
"REMEMBER, BARRY, IT'S OKAY TO BE AFRAID. SO LONG AS YOU DON'T LET IT STOP YOU."
I KNOW WHO I AM. I'M BARRY ALLEN.
I AM
The FLASH

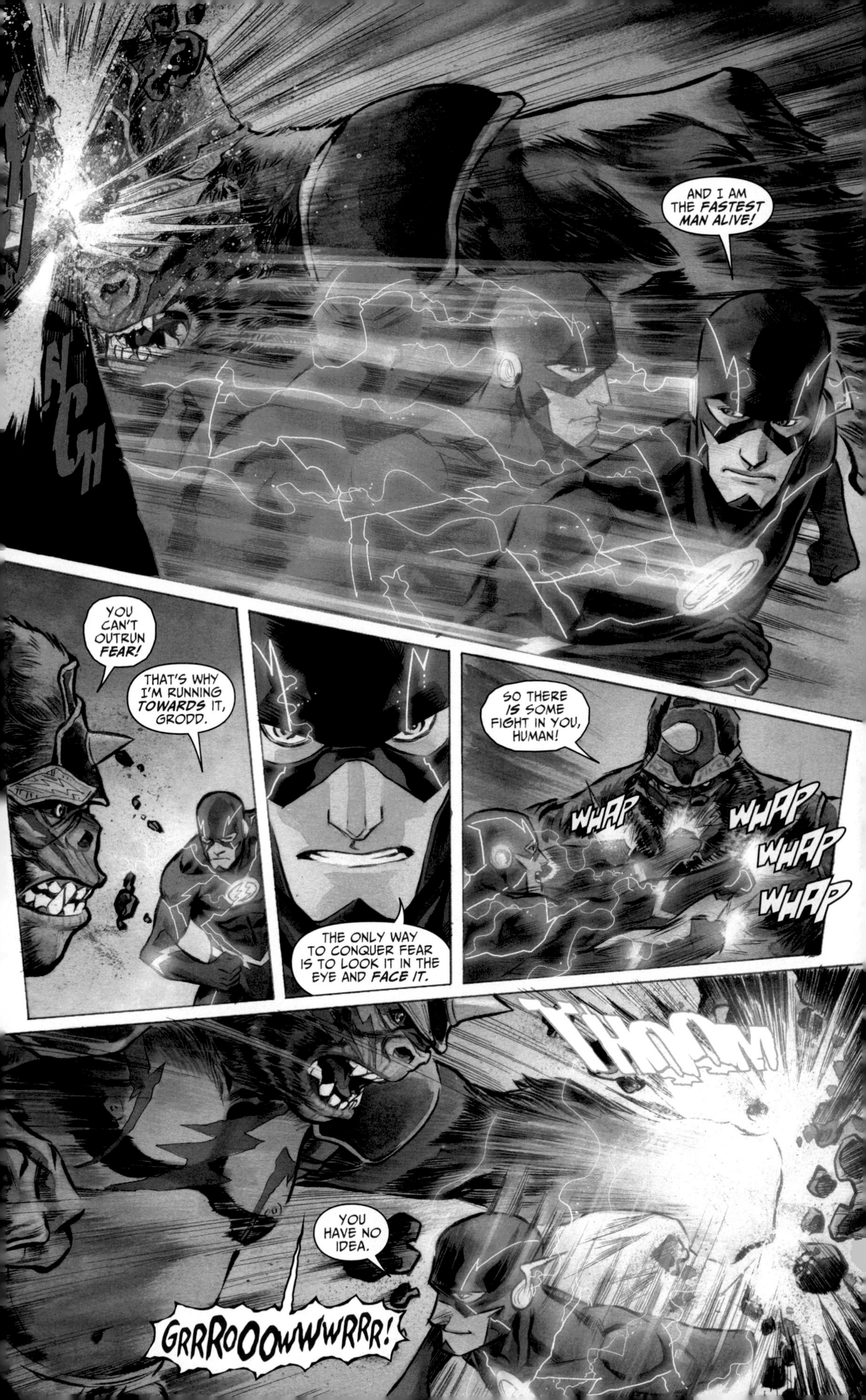
AND I AM THE FASTEST MAN ALIVE!
YOU CAN'T OUTRUN FEAR!
THAT'S WHY I'M RUNNING TOWARDS IT, GRODD.
THE ONLY WAY TO CONQUER FEAR IS TO LOOK IT IN THE EYE AND FACE IT.
SO THERE IS SOME FIGHT IN YOU, HUMAN!
WHAP
WHAP
WHAP
WHAP
THOOM
YOU HAVE NO IDEA.
GRRROOOWWWRRR!

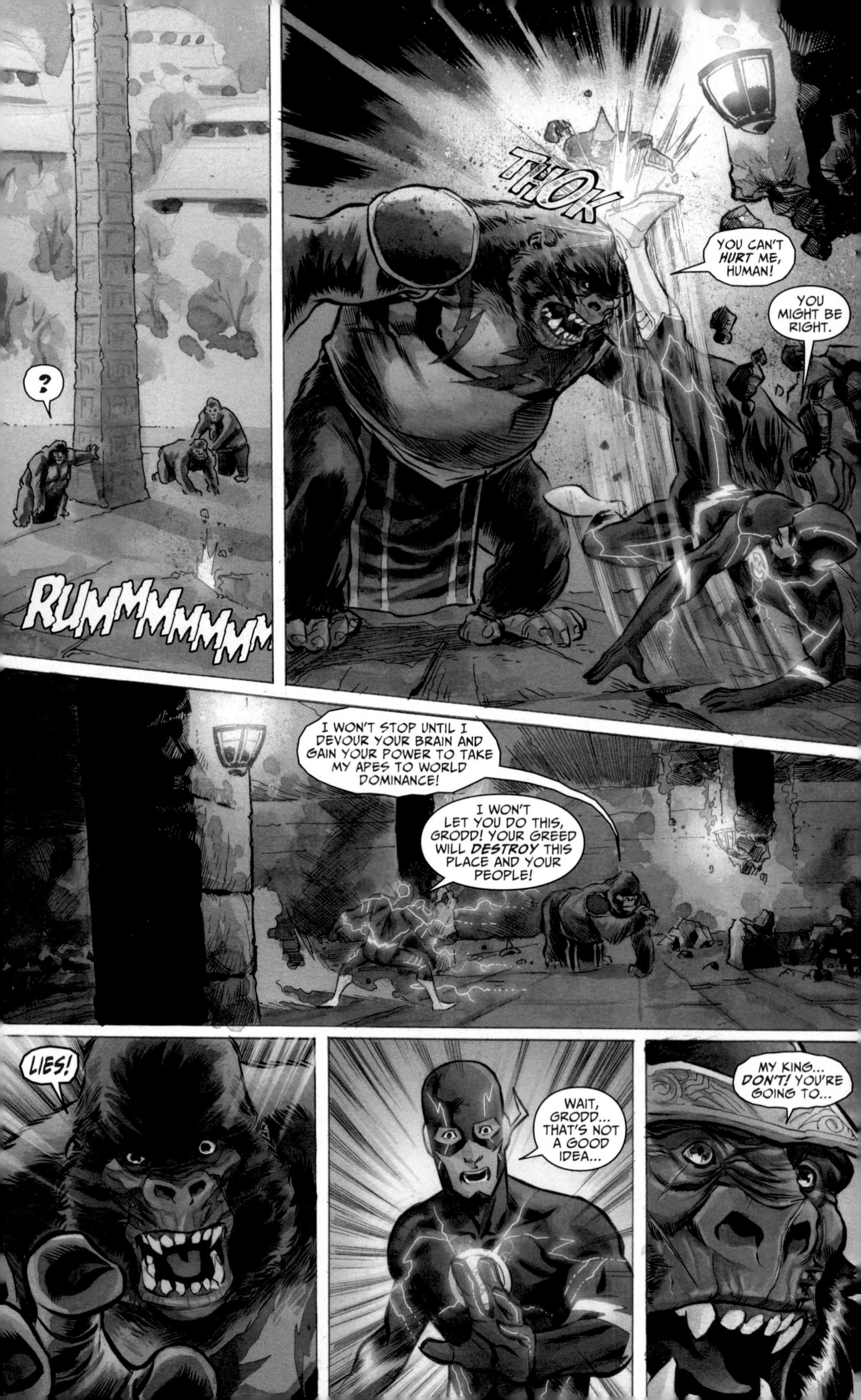
?
RUMMMMMMMM
THOK
YOU CAN'T HURT ME, HUMAN!
YOU MIGHT BE RIGHT.
I WON'T STOP UNTIL I DEVOUR YOUR BRAIN AND GAIN YOUR POWER TO TAKE MY APES TO WORLD DOMINANCE!
I WON'T LET YOU DO THIS, GRODD! YOUR GREED WILL DESTROY THIS PLACE AND YOUR PEOPLE!
LIES!
WAIT, GRODD... THAT'S NOT A GOOD IDEA...
MY KING... DON'T! YOU'RE GOING TO...

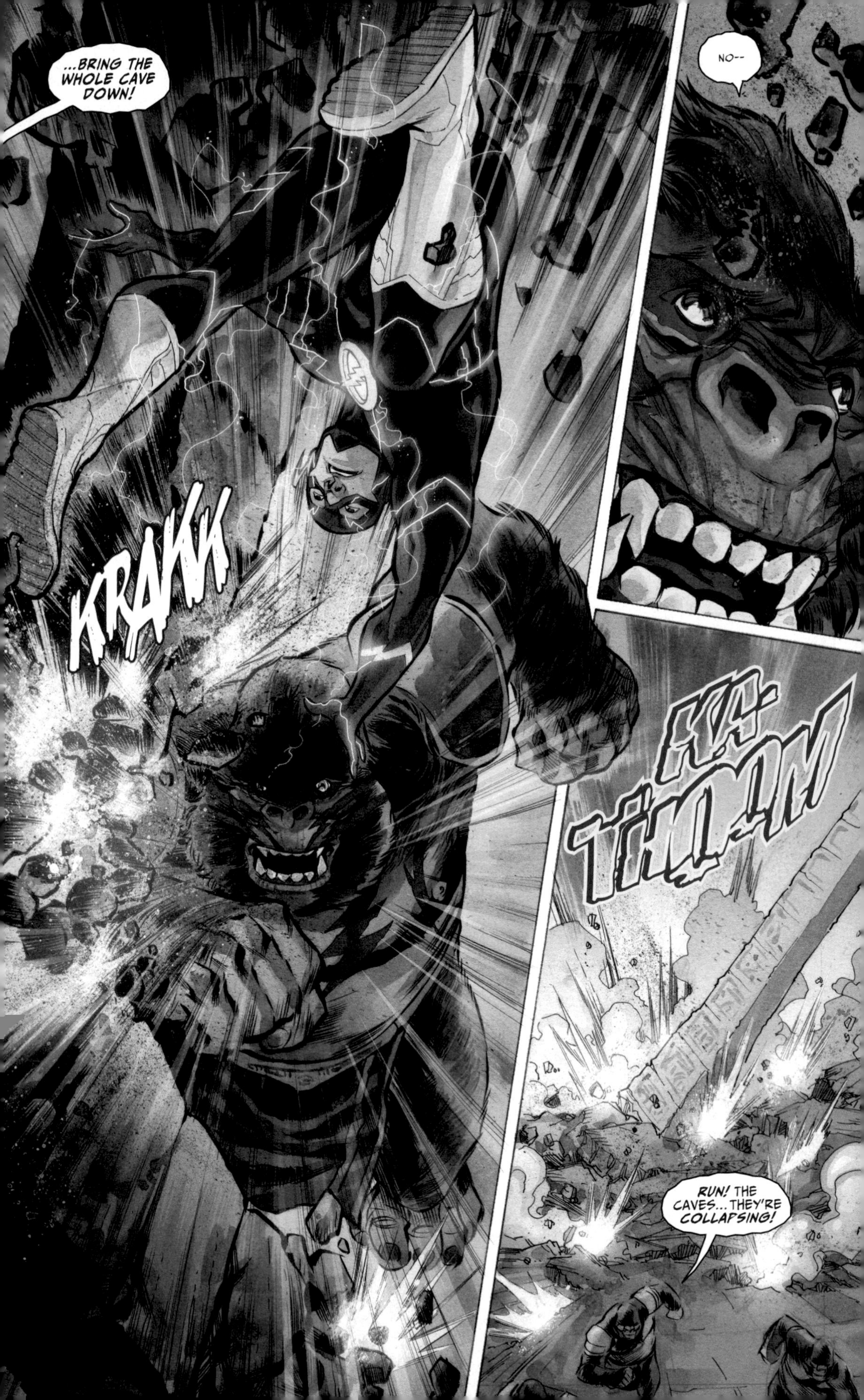
...BRING THE WHOLE CAVE DOWN!
KRAKK
NO--
KA-THOOM
RUN! THE CAVES... THEY'RE COLLAPSING!

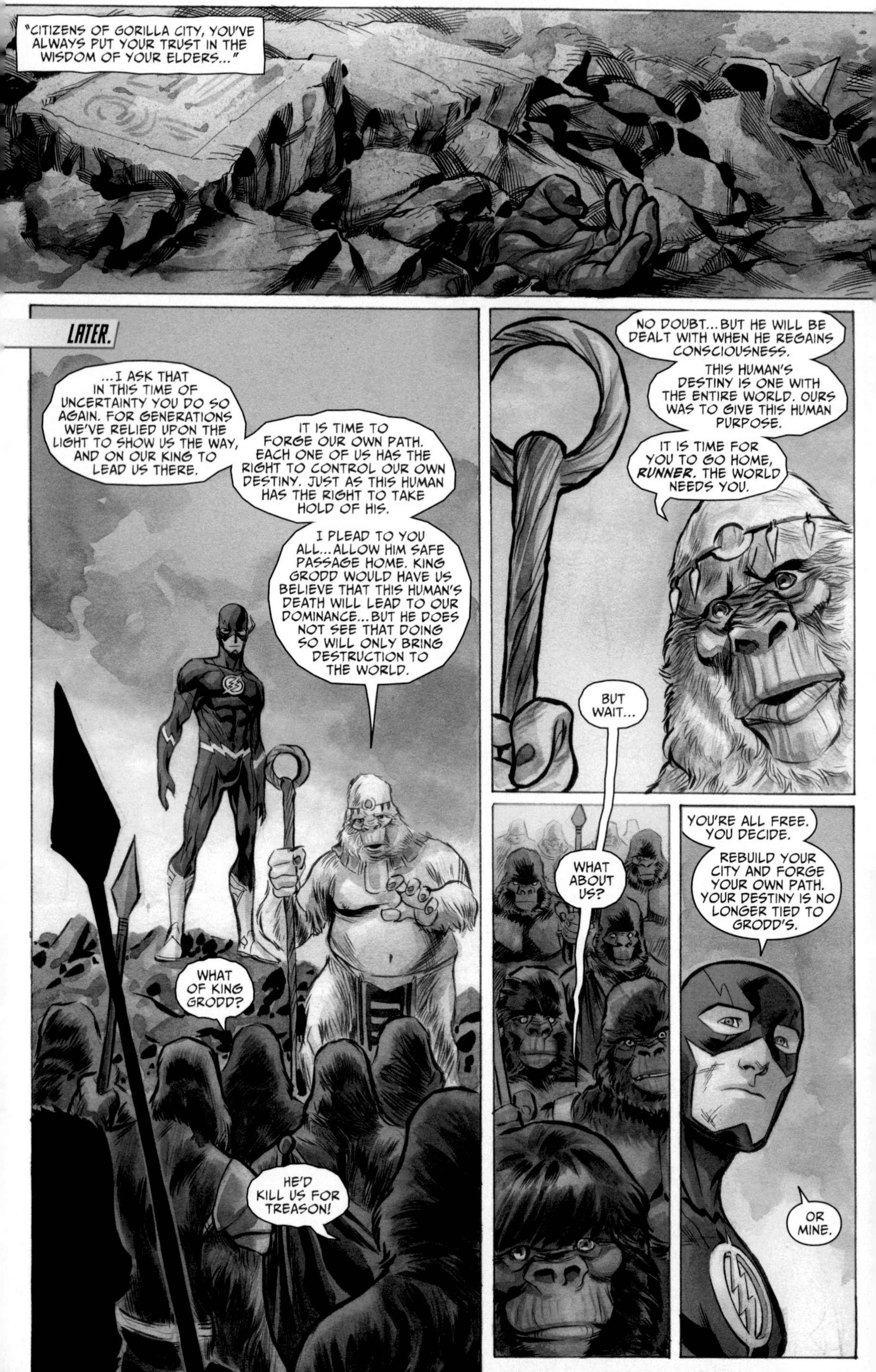
"CITIZENS OF GORILLA CITY, YOU'VE ALWAYS PUT YOUR TRUST IN THE WISDOM OF YOUR ELDERS..."
LATER.
...I ASK THAT IN THIS TIME OF UNCERTAINTY YOU DO SO AGAIN. FOR GENERATIONS WE'VE RELIED UPON THE LIGHT TO SHOW US THE WAY, AND ON OUR KING TO LEAD US THERE.
IT IS TIME TO FORGE OUR OWN PATH. EACH ONE OF US HAS THE RIGHT TO CONTROL OUR OWN DESTINY. JUST AS THIS HUMAN HAS THE RIGHT TO TAKE HOLD OF HIS.
I PLEAD TO YOU ALL...ALLOW HIM SAFE PASSAGE HOME. KING GRODD WOULD HAVE US BELIEVE THAT THIS HUMAN'S DEATH WILL LEAD TO OUR DOMINANCE...BUT HE DOES NOT SEE THAT DOING SO WILL ONLY BRING DESTRUCTION TO THE WORLD.
WHAT OF KING GRODD?
HE'D KILL US FOR TREASON!
NO DOUBT...BUT HE WILL BE DEALT WITH WHEN HE REGAINS CONSCIOUSNESS.
THIS HUMAN'S DESTINY IS ONE WITH THE ENTIRE WORLD. OURS WAS TO GIVE THIS HUMAN PURPOSE.
IT IS TIME FOR YOU TO GO HOME, *RUNNER*. THE WORLD NEEDS YOU.
BUT WAIT...
WHAT ABOUT US?
YOU'RE ALL FREE. YOU DECIDE.
REBUILD YOUR CITY AND FORGE YOUR OWN PATH. YOUR DESTINY IS NO LONGER TIED TO GRODD'S.
OR MINE.

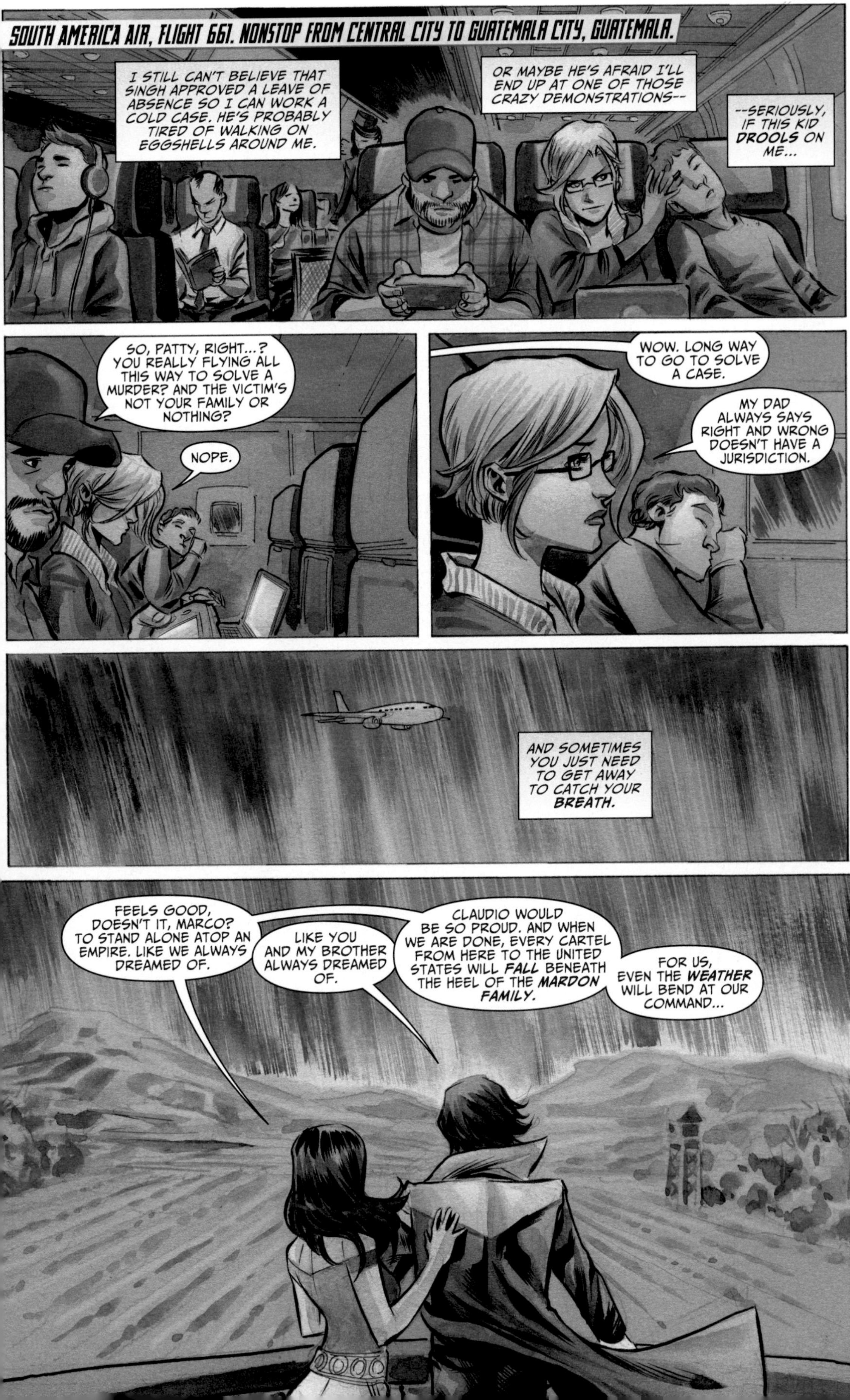
SOUTH AMERICA AIR, FLIGHT 661. NONSTOP FROM CENTRAL CITY TO GUATEMALA CITY, GUATEMALA.
I STILL CAN'T BELIEVE THAT SINGH APPROVED A LEAVE OF ABSENCE SO I CAN WORK A COLD CASE. HE'S PROBABLY TIRED OF WALKING ON EGGSHELLS AROUND ME.
OR MAYBE HE'S AFRAID I'LL END UP AT ONE OF THOSE CRAZY DEMONSTRATIONS--
--SERIOUSLY, IF THIS KID DROOLS ON ME...
SO, PATTY, RIGHT...? YOU REALLY FLYING ALL THIS WAY TO SOLVE A MURDER? AND THE VICTIM'S NOT YOUR FAMILY OR NOTHING?
NOPE.
WOW. LONG WAY TO GO TO SOLVE A CASE.
MY DAD ALWAYS SAYS RIGHT AND WRONG DOESN'T HAVE A JURISDICTION.
AND SOMETIMES YOU JUST NEED TO GET AWAY TO CATCH YOUR BREATH.
FEELS GOOD, DOESN'T IT, MARCO? TO STAND ALONE ATOP AN EMPIRE. LIKE WE ALWAYS DREAMED OF.
LIKE YOU AND MY BROTHER ALWAYS DREAMED OF.
CLAUDIO WOULD BE SO PROUD. AND WHEN WE ARE DONE, EVERY CARTEL FROM HERE TO THE UNITED STATES WILL FALL BENEATH THE HEEL OF THE MARDON FAMILY.
FOR US, EVEN THE WEATHER WILL BEND AT OUR COMMAND...

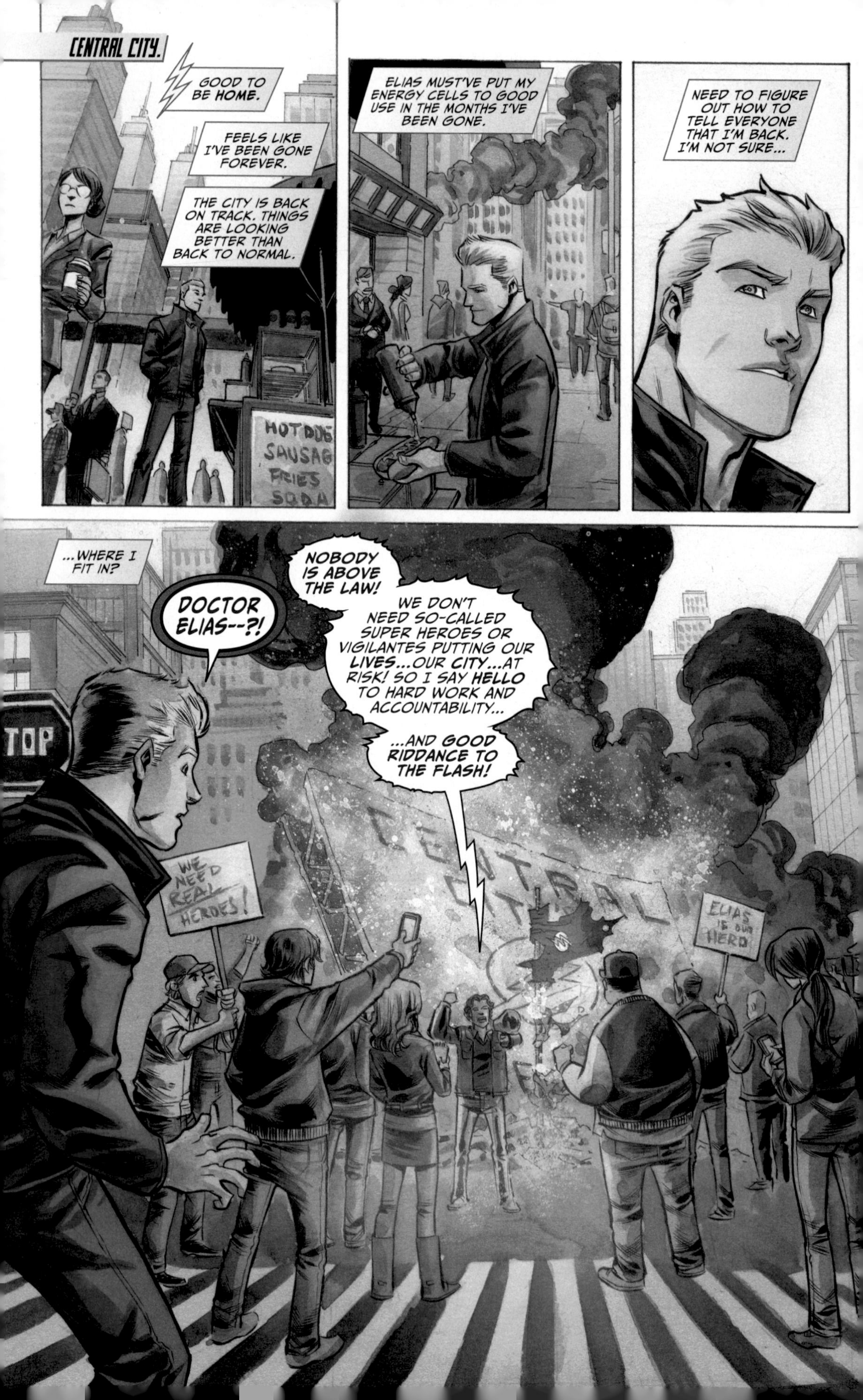
CENTRAL CITY.
GOOD TO BE HOME.
FEELS LIKE I'VE BEEN GONE FOREVER.
THE CITY IS BACK ON TRACK. THINGS ARE LOOKING BETTER THAN BACK TO NORMAL.
HOT DOG SAUSAG FRIES SODA
ELIAS MUST'VE PUT MY ENERGY CELLS TO GOOD USE IN THE MONTHS I'VE BEEN GONE.
NEED TO FIGURE OUT HOW TO TELL EVERYONE THAT I'M BACK. I'M NOT SURE...
...WHERE I FIT IN?
DOCTOR ELIAS--?!
NOBODY IS ABOVE THE LAW!
WE DON'T NEED SO-CALLED SUPER HEROES OR VIGILANTES PUTTING OUR LIVES...OUR CITY...AT RISK! SO I SAY HELLO TO HARD WORK AND ACCOUNTABILITY...
...AND GOOD RIDDANCE TO THE FLASH!
WE NEED REAL HEROES!
ELIAS IS OUR HERO

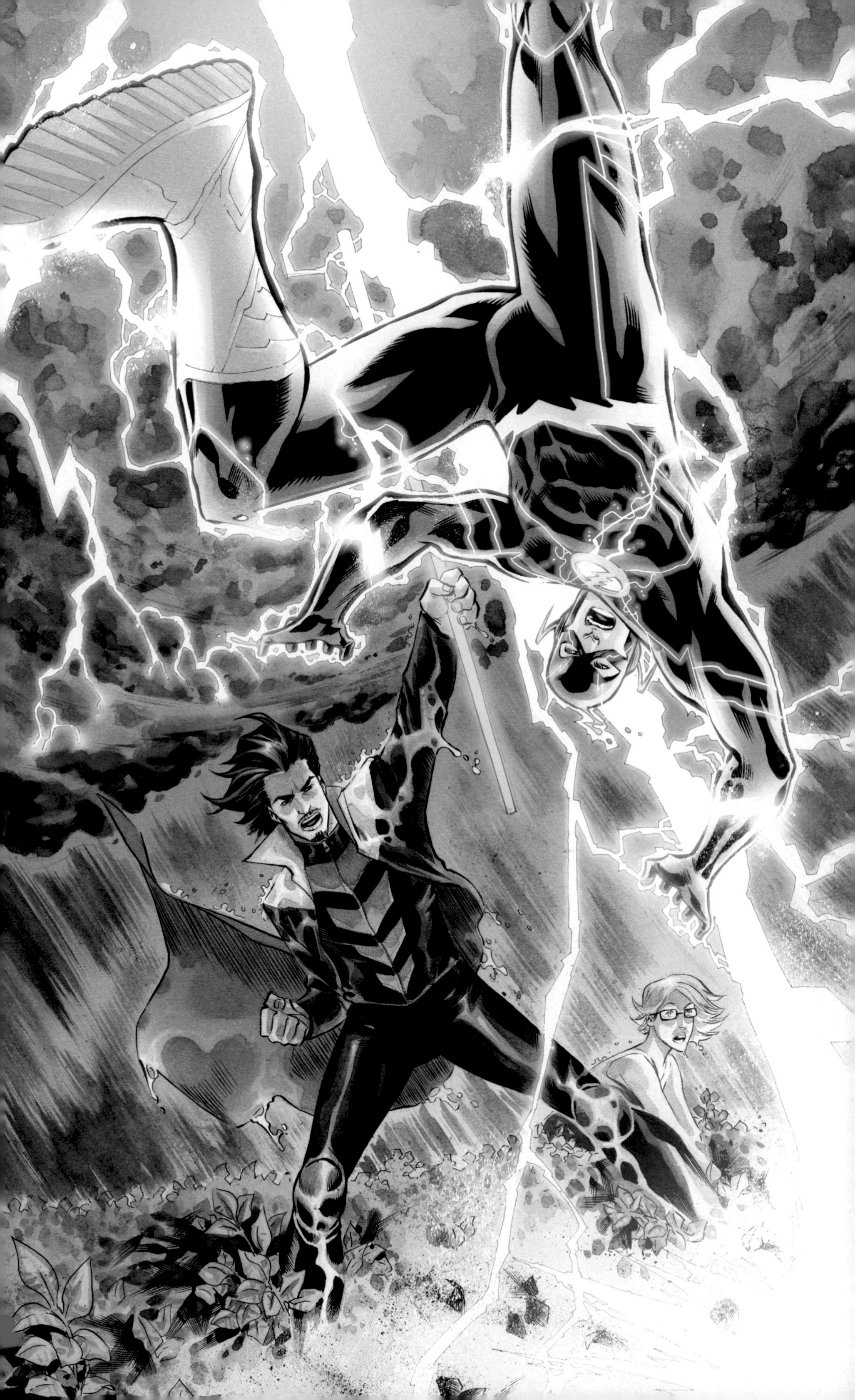

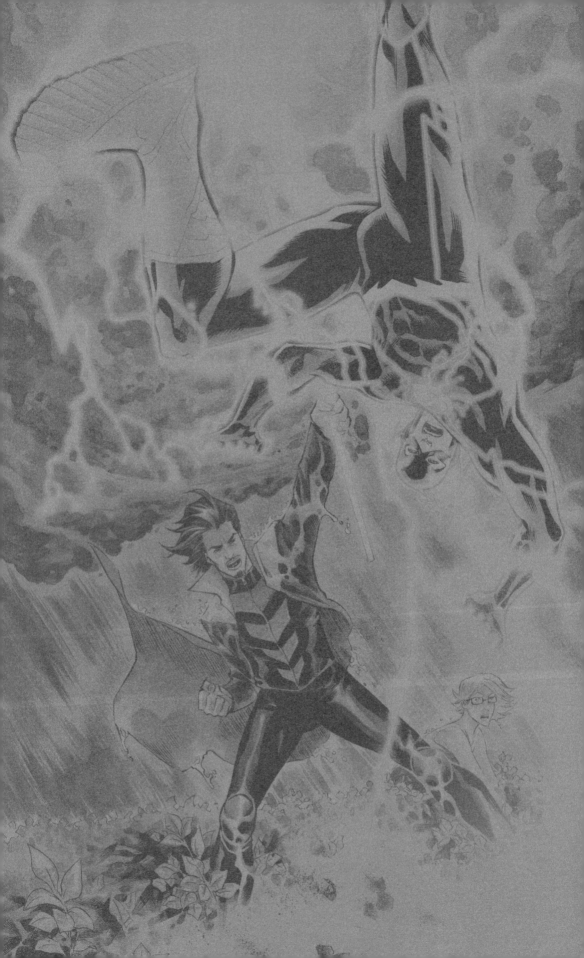

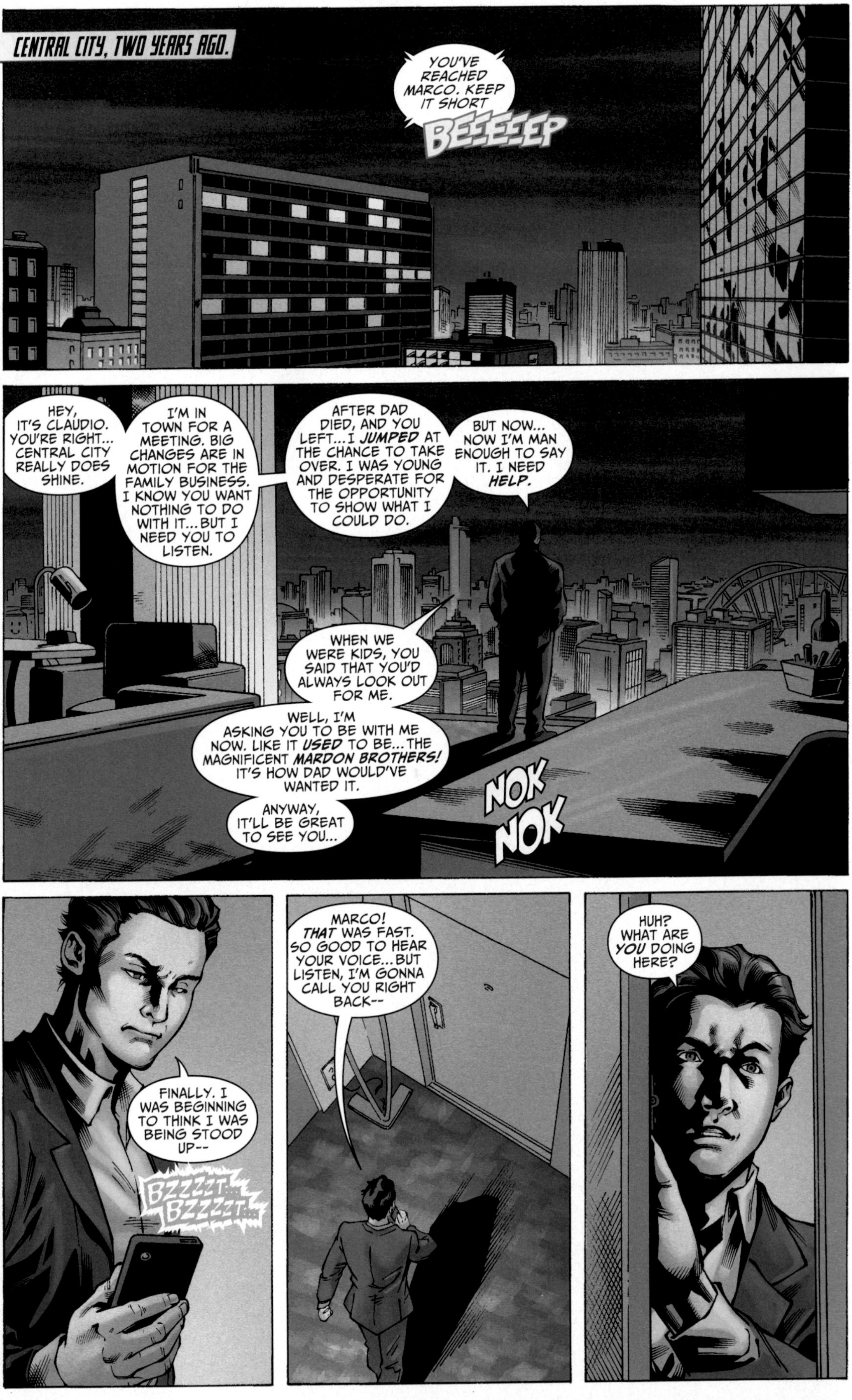
CENTRAL CITY, TWO YEARS AGO.
YOU'VE REACHED MARCO. KEEP IT SHORT
BEEEEEP
HEY, IT'S CLAUDIO. YOU'RE RIGHT... CENTRAL CITY REALLY DOES SHINE.
I'M IN TOWN FOR A MEETING. BIG CHANGES ARE IN MOTION FOR THE FAMILY BUSINESS. I KNOW YOU WANT NOTHING TO DO WITH IT... BUT I NEED YOU TO LISTEN.
AFTER DAD DIED, AND YOU LEFT... I JUMPED AT THE CHANCE TO TAKE OVER. I WAS YOUNG AND DESPERATE FOR THE OPPORTUNITY TO SHOW WHAT I COULD DO.
BUT NOW... NOW I'M MAN ENOUGH TO SAY IT. I NEED HELP.
WHEN WE WERE KIDS, YOU SAID THAT YOU'D ALWAYS LOOK OUT FOR ME.
WELL, I'M ASKING YOU TO BE WITH ME NOW. LIKE IT USED TO BE... THE MAGNIFICENT MARDON BROTHERS! IT'S HOW DAD WOULD'VE WANTED IT.
ANYWAY, IT'LL BE GREAT TO SEE YOU...
NOK NOK
FINALLY. I WAS BEGINNING TO THINK I WAS BEING STOOD UP--
BZZZZT... BZZZZT...
MARCO! THAT WAS FAST. SO GOOD TO HEAR YOUR VOICE... BUT LISTEN, I'M GONNA CALL YOU RIGHT BACK--
HUH? WHAT ARE YOU DOING HERE?

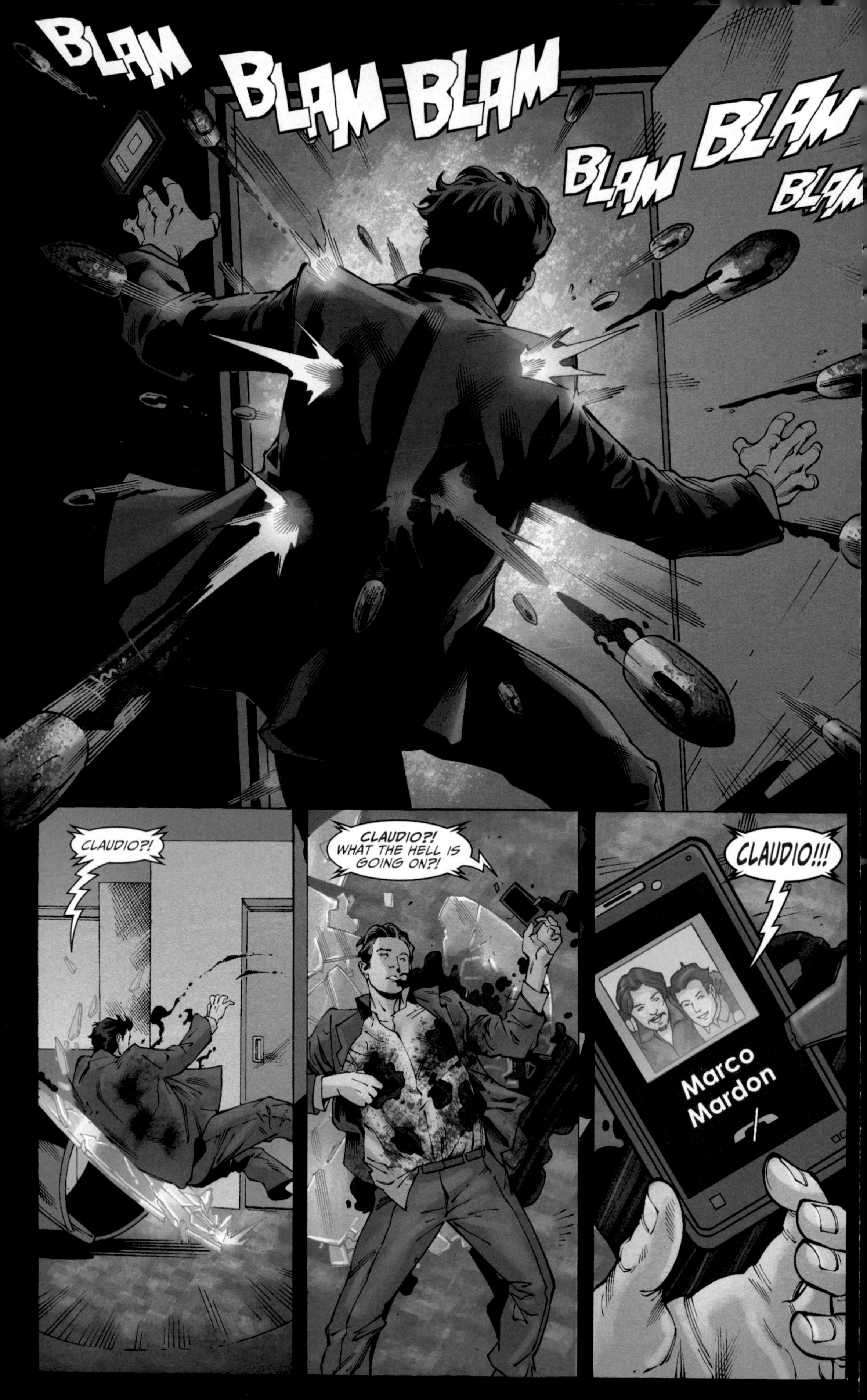
BLAM
BLAM BLAM
BLAM BLAM
BLAM
CLAUDIO?!
CLAUDIO?! WHAT THE HELL IS GOING ON?!
CLAUDIO!!!
Marco Mardon

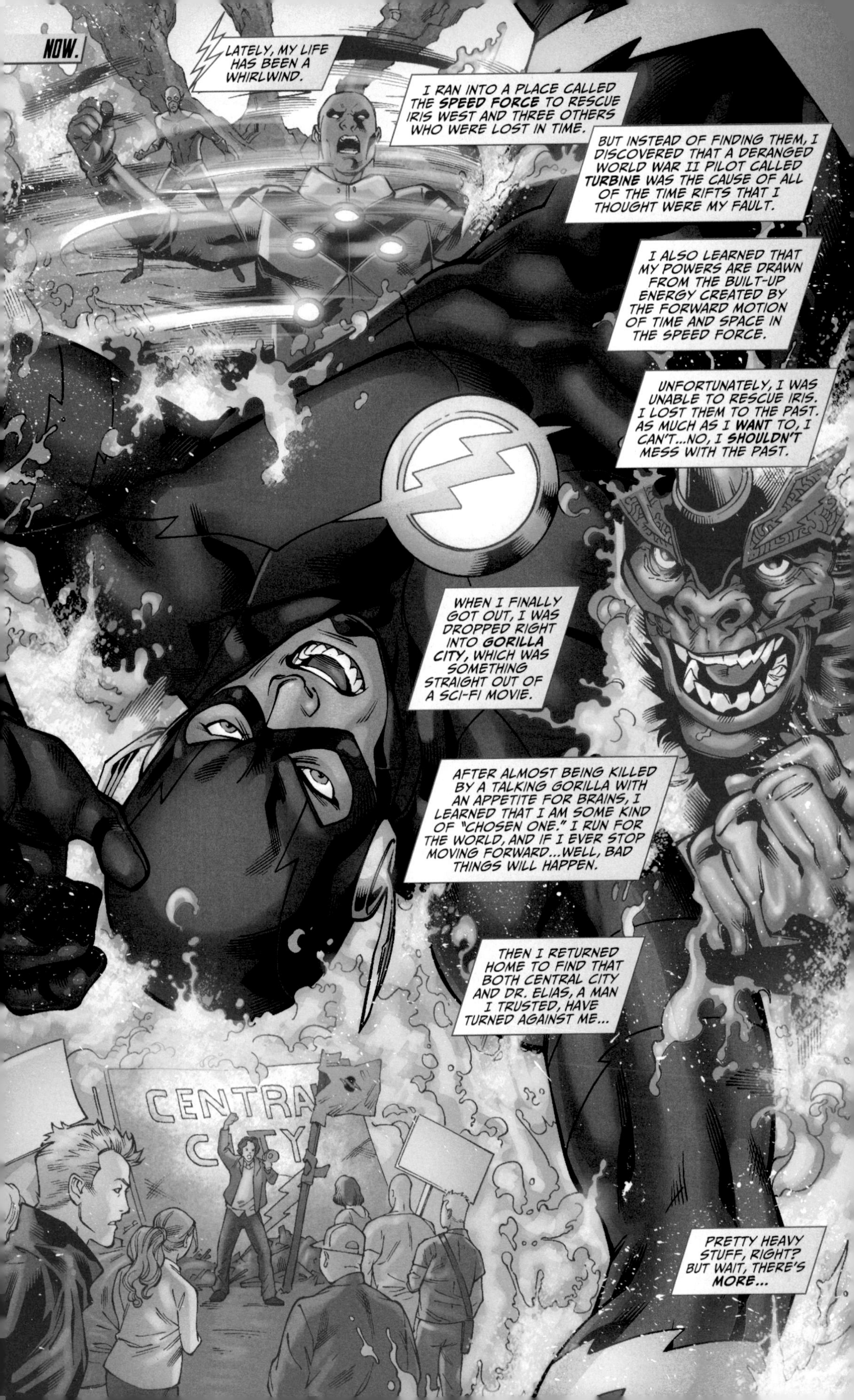
NOW.
LATELY, MY LIFE HAS BEEN A WHIRLWIND.
I RAN INTO A PLACE CALLED THE SPEED FORCE TO RESCUE IRIS WEST AND THREE OTHERS WHO WERE LOST IN TIME.
BUT INSTEAD OF FINDING THEM, I DISCOVERED THAT A DERANGED WORLD WAR II PILOT CALLED TURBINE WAS THE CAUSE OF ALL OF THE TIME RIFTS THAT I THOUGHT WERE MY FAULT.
I ALSO LEARNED THAT MY POWERS ARE DRAWN FROM THE BUILT-UP ENERGY CREATED BY THE FORWARD MOTION OF TIME AND SPACE IN THE SPEED FORCE.
UNFORTUNATELY, I WAS UNABLE TO RESCUE IRIS. I LOST THEM TO THE PAST. AS MUCH AS I WANT TO, I CAN'T...NO, I SHOULDN'T MESS WITH THE PAST.
WHEN I FINALLY GOT OUT, I WAS DROPPED RIGHT INTO GORILLA CITY, WHICH WAS SOMETHING STRAIGHT OUT OF A SCI-FI MOVIE.
AFTER ALMOST BEING KILLED BY A TALKING GORILLA WITH AN APPETITE FOR BRAINS, I LEARNED THAT I AM SOME KIND OF "CHOSEN ONE." I RUN FOR THE WORLD, AND IF I EVER STOP MOVING FORWARD...WELL, BAD THINGS WILL HAPPEN.
THEN I RETURNED HOME TO FIND THAT BOTH CENTRAL CITY AND DR. ELIAS, A MAN I TRUSTED, HAVE TURNED AGAINST ME...
PRETTY HEAVY STUFF, RIGHT? BUT WAIT, THERE'S MORE...

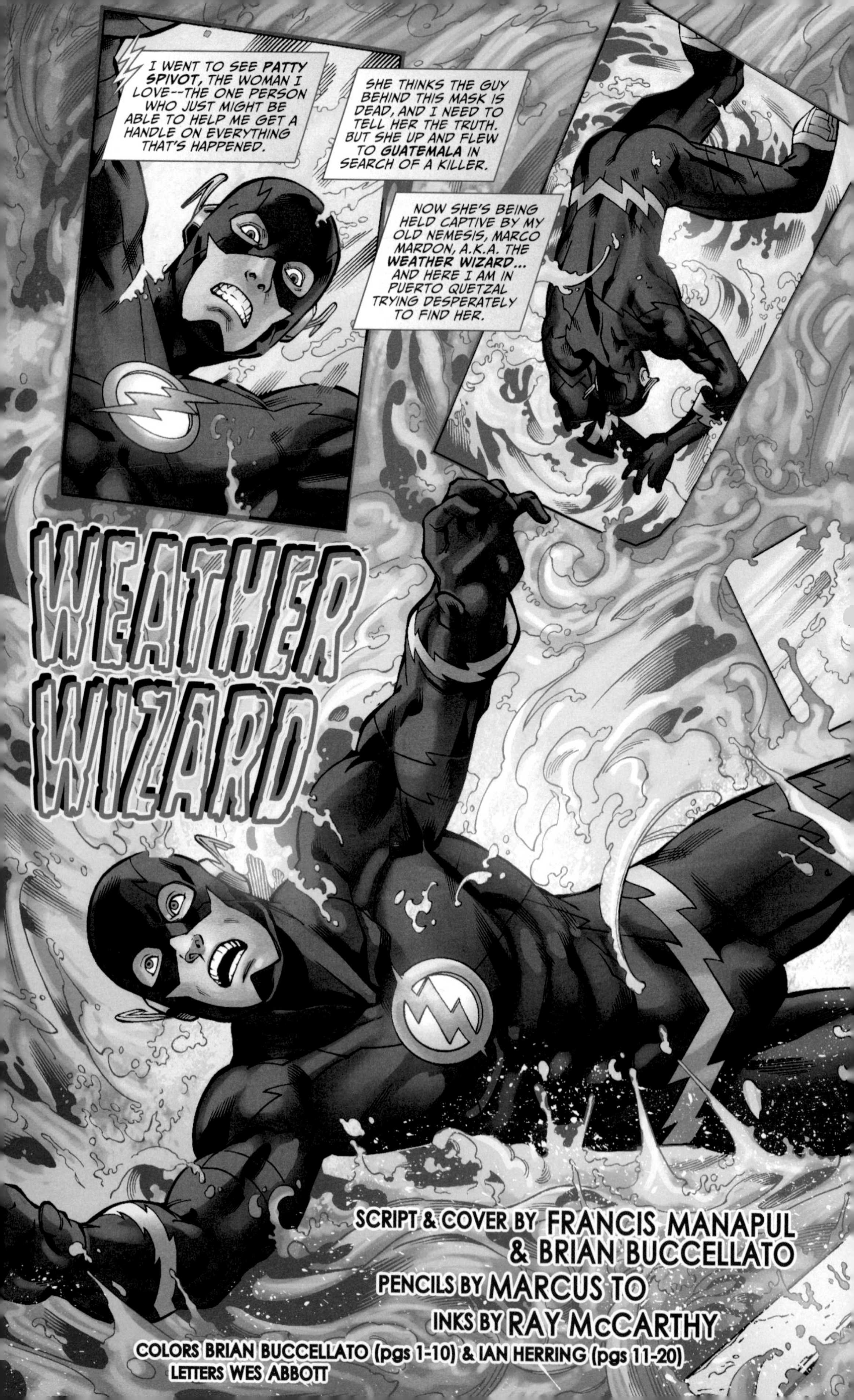
I WENT TO SEE PATTY SPIVOT, THE WOMAN I LOVE--THE ONE PERSON WHO JUST MIGHT BE ABLE TO HELP ME GET A HANDLE ON EVERYTHING THAT'S HAPPENED.
SHE THINKS THE GUY BEHIND THIS MASK IS DEAD, AND I NEED TO TELL HER THE TRUTH. BUT SHE UP AND FLEW TO GUATEMALA IN SEARCH OF A KILLER.
NOW SHE'S BEING HELD CAPTIVE BY MY OLD NEMESIS, MARCO MARDON, A.K.A. THE WEATHER WIZARD... AND HERE I AM IN PUERTO QUETZAL TRYING DESPERATELY TO FIND HER.
WEATHER WIZARD
SCRIPT & COVER BY FRANCIS MANAPUL & BRIAN BUCCELLATO
PENCILS BY MARCUS TO
INKS BY RAY McCARTHY
COLORS BRIAN BUCCELLATO (pgs 1-10) & IAN HERRING (pgs 11-20)
LETTERS WES ABBOTT

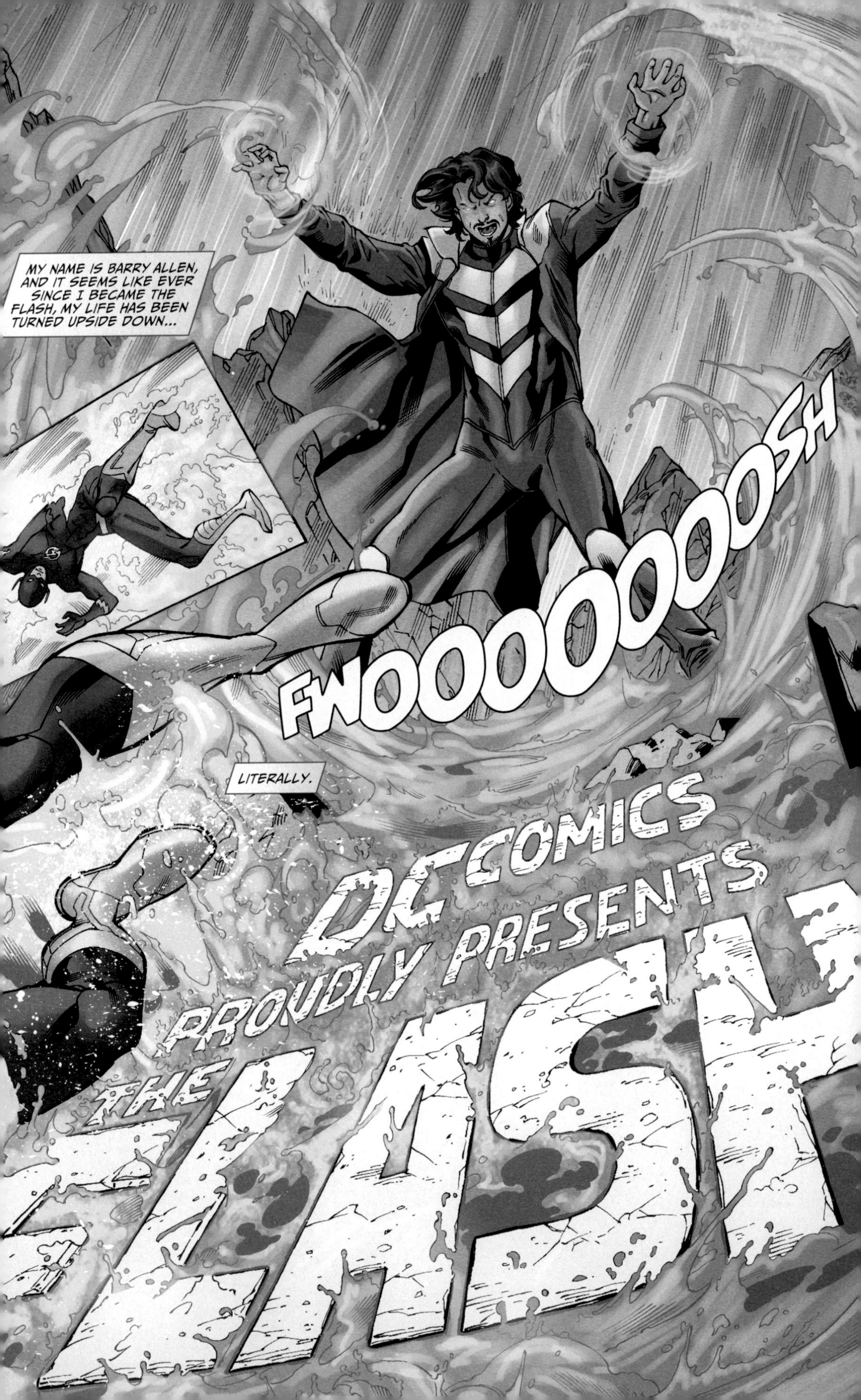

MY NAME IS BARRY ALLEN, AND IT SEEMS LIKE EVER SINCE I BECAME THE FLASH, MY LIFE HAS BEEN TURNED UPSIDE DOWN...
FWOOOOOOOOOSH
LITERALLY.
DC COMICS PROUDLY PRESENTS
THE FLASH

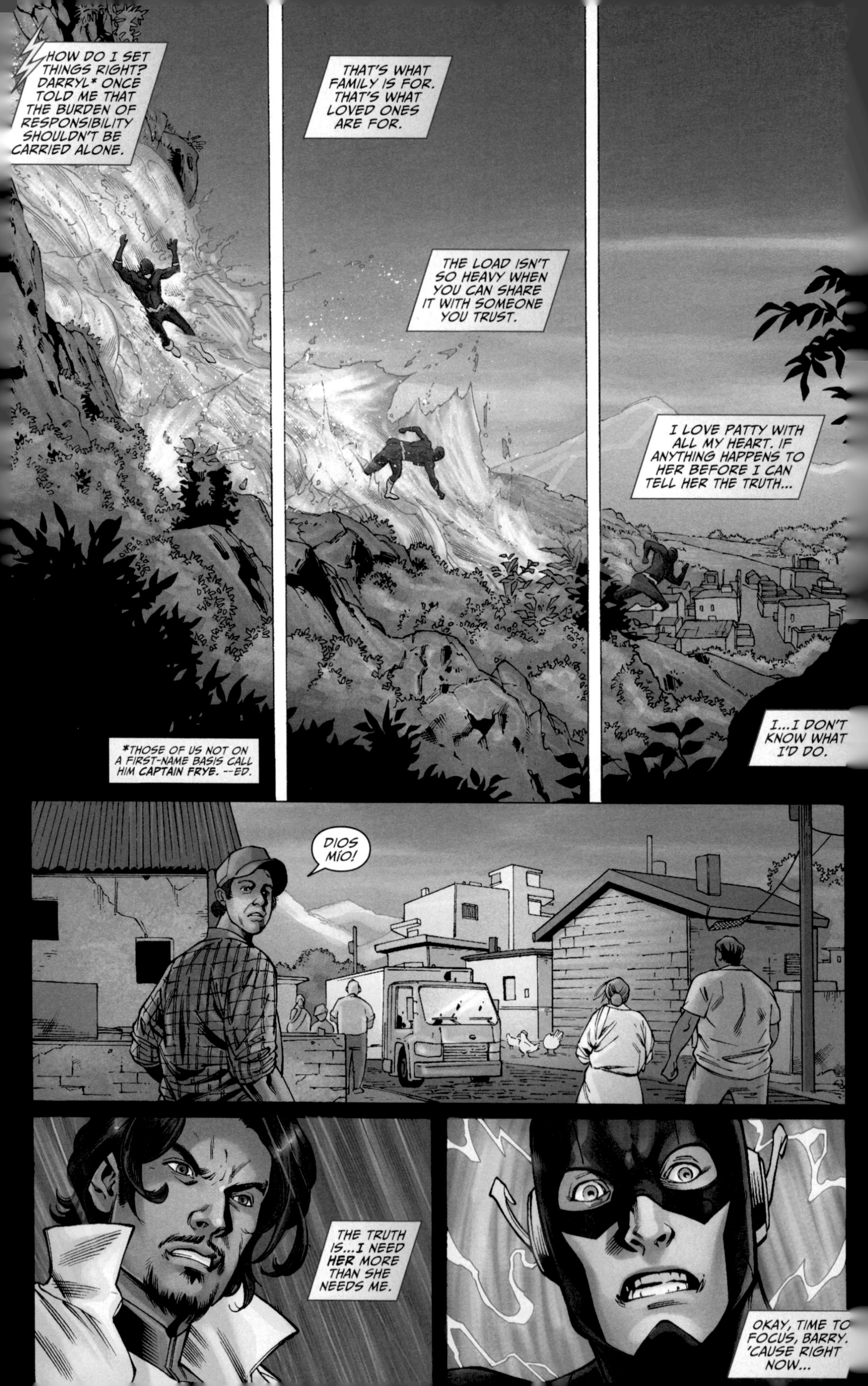
HOW DO I SET THINGS RIGHT? DARRYL* ONCE TOLD ME THAT THE BURDEN OF RESPONSIBILITY SHOULDN'T BE CARRIED ALONE.
*THOSE OF US NOT ON A FIRST-NAME BASIS CALL HIM CAPTAIN FRYE. --ED.
THAT'S WHAT FAMILY IS FOR. THAT'S WHAT LOVED ONES ARE FOR.
THE LOAD ISN'T SO HEAVY WHEN YOU CAN SHARE IT WITH SOMEONE YOU TRUST.
I LOVE PATTY WITH ALL MY HEART. IF ANYTHING HAPPENS TO HER BEFORE I CAN TELL HER THE TRUTH...
I...I DON'T KNOW WHAT I'D DO.
DIOS MÍO!
THE TRUTH IS...I NEED HER MORE THAN SHE NEEDS ME.
OKAY, TIME TO FOCUS, BARRY. 'CAUSE RIGHT NOW...

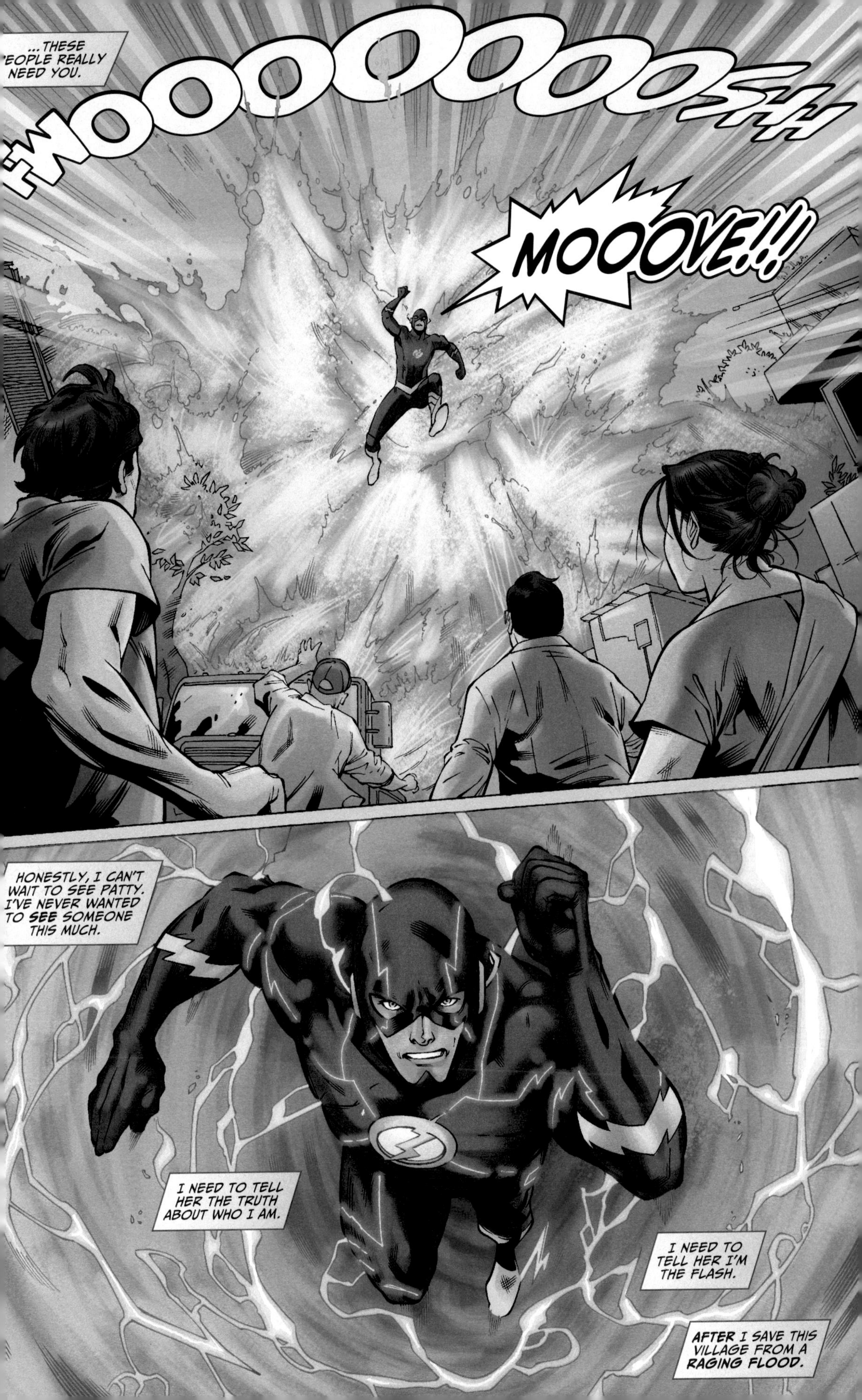
...THESE
PEOPLE REALLY NEED YOU.
WHOOOOOOOOSH
MOOOVE!!
HONESTLY, I CAN'T WAIT TO SEE PATTY. I'VE NEVER WANTED TO **SEE** SOMEONE THIS MUCH.
I NEED TO TELL HER THE TRUTH ABOUT WHO I AM.
I NEED TO TELL HER I'M THE FLASH.
AFTER I SAVE THIS VILLAGE FROM A **RAGING FLOOD.**

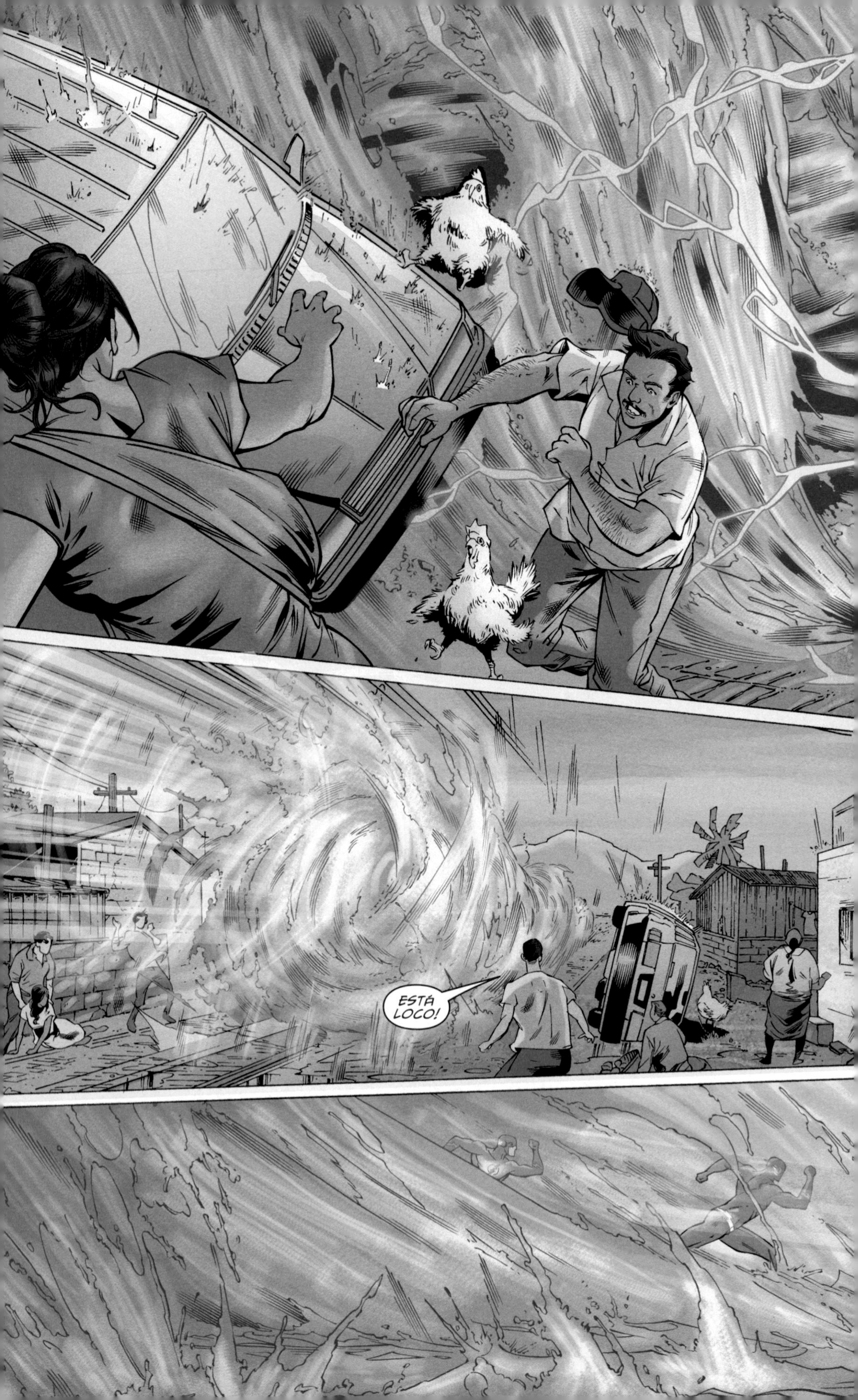
ESTÁ LOCO!

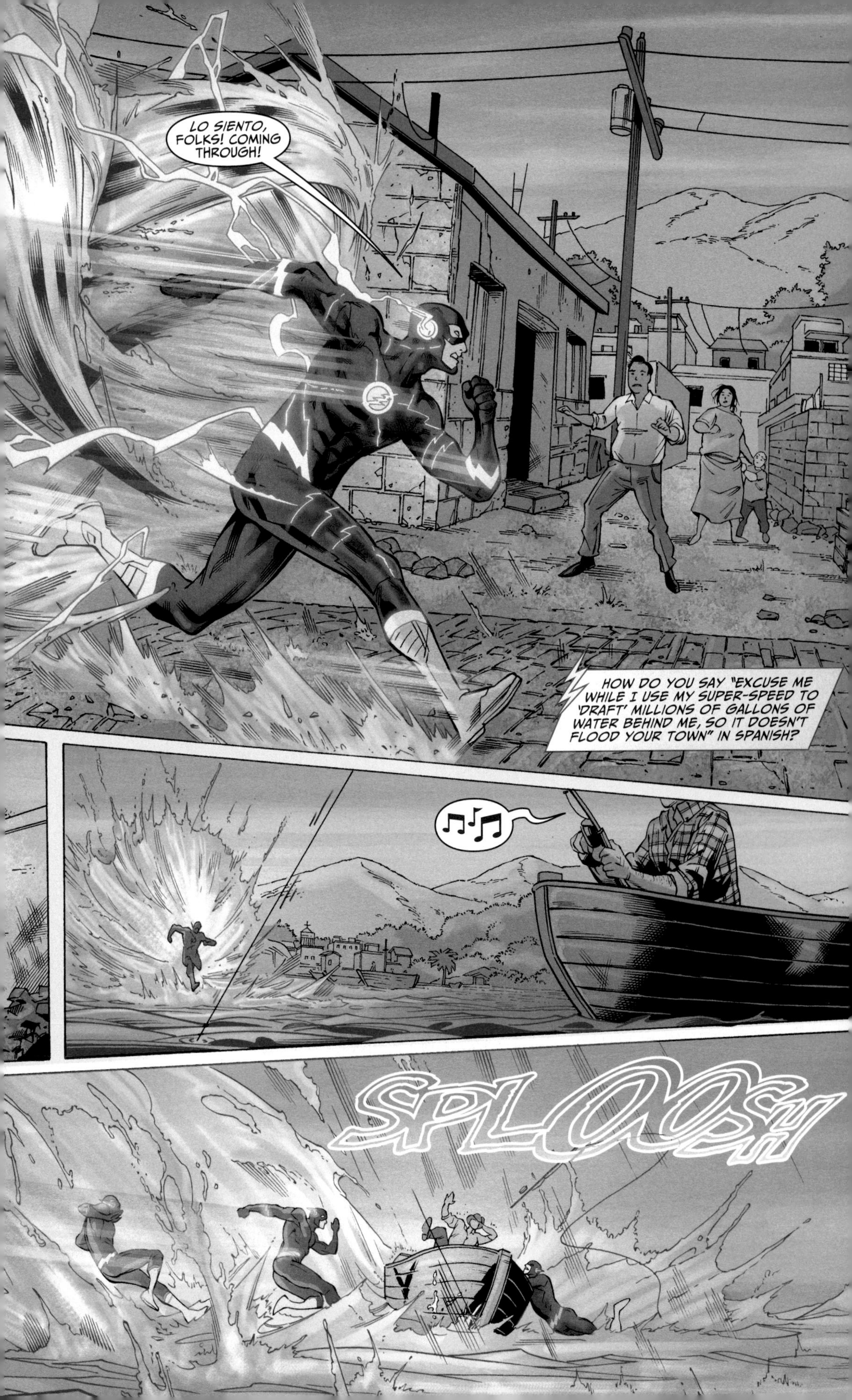
LO SIENTO, FOLKS! COMING THROUGH!
HOW DO YOU SAY "EXCUSE ME WHILE I USE MY SUPER-SPEED TO 'DRAFT' MILLIONS OF GALLONS OF WATER BEHIND ME, SO IT DOESN'T FLOOD YOUR TOWN" IN SPANISH?
SPLOOSH

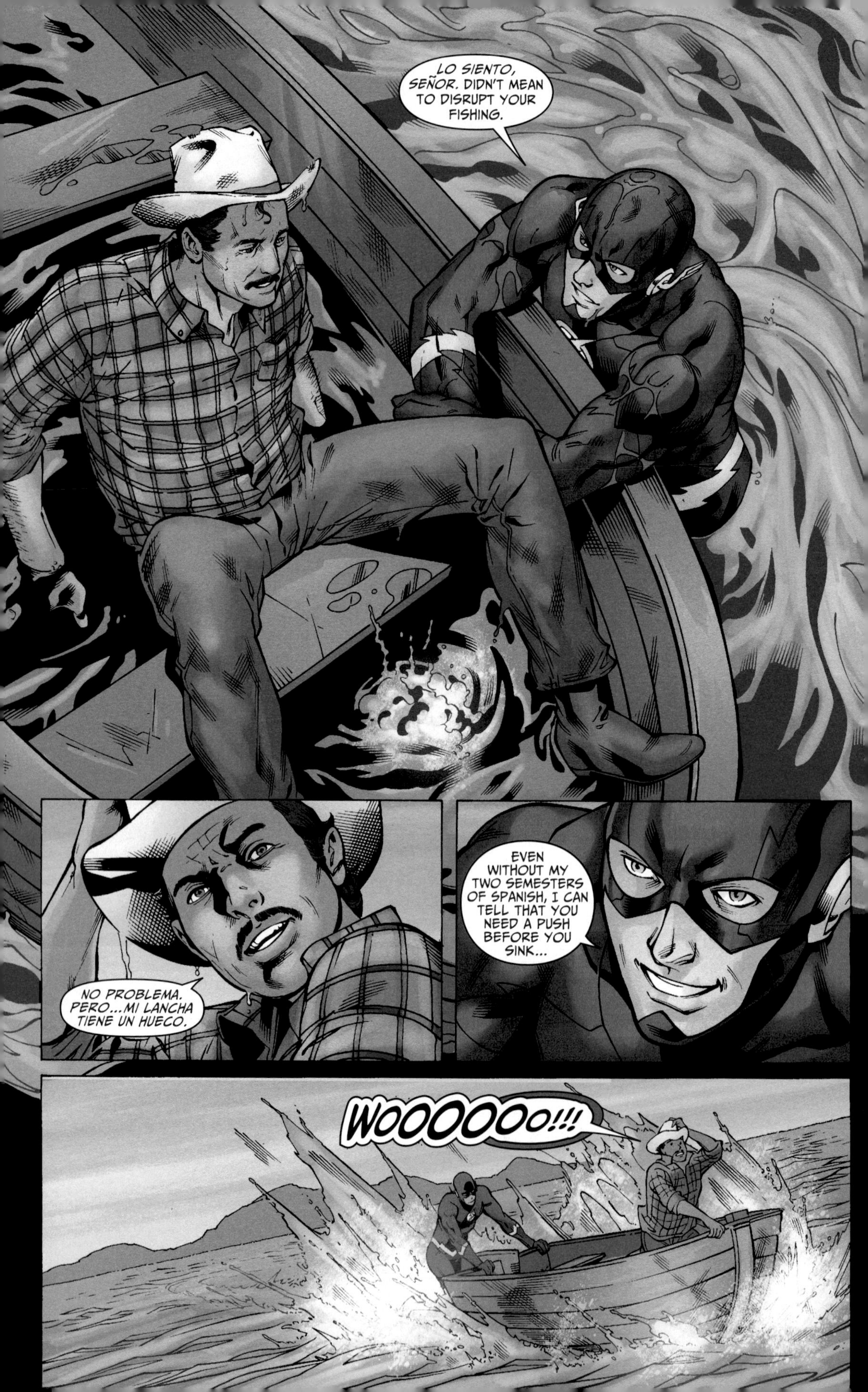
LO SIENTO, SEÑOR. DIDN'T MEAN TO DISRUPT YOUR FISHING.
NO PROBLEMA. PERO...MI LANCHA TIENE UN HUECO.
EVEN WITHOUT MY TWO SEMESTERS OF SPANISH, I CAN TELL THAT YOU NEED A PUSH BEFORE YOU SINK...
WOOOOOO!!!

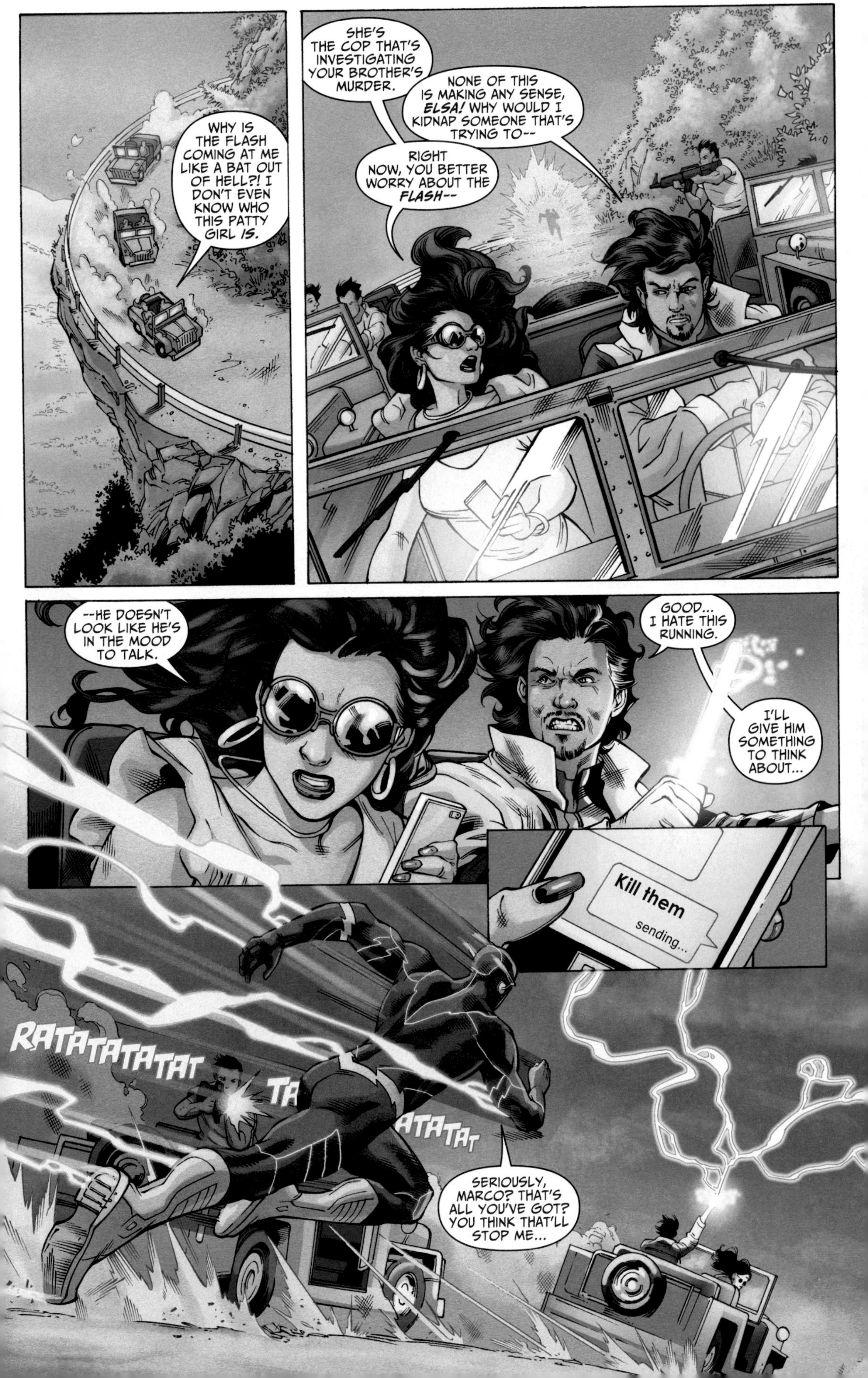
WHY IS THE FLASH COMING AT ME LIKE A BAT OUT OF HELL?! I DON'T EVEN KNOW WHO THIS PATTY GIRL IS.
SHE'S THE COP THAT'S INVESTIGATING YOUR BROTHER'S MURDER.
NONE OF THIS IS MAKING ANY SENSE, ELSA! WHY WOULD I KIDNAP SOMEONE THAT'S TRYING TO--
RIGHT NOW, YOU BETTER WORRY ABOUT THE FLASH--
--HE DOESN'T LOOK LIKE HE'S IN THE MOOD TO TALK.
GOOD... I HATE THIS RUNNING.
I'LL GIVE HIM SOMETHING TO THINK ABOUT...
Kill them
sending...
RATATATATAT
TA
ATATAT
SERIOUSLY, MARCO? THAT'S ALL YOU'VE GOT? YOU THINK THAT'LL STOP ME...

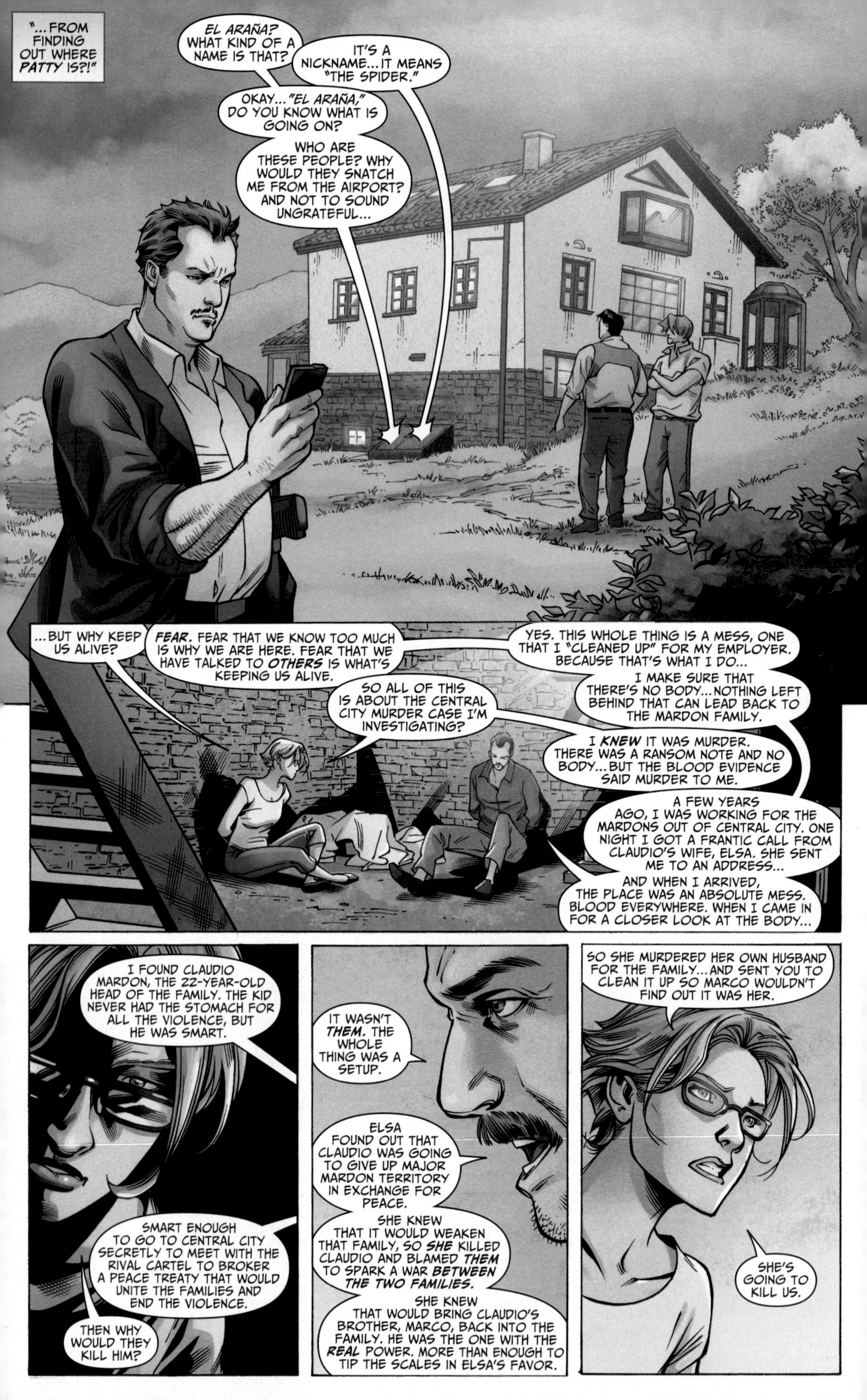
"...FROM FINDING OUT WHERE *PATTY* IS?!"
EL ARAÑA? WHAT KIND OF A NAME IS THAT?
IT'S A NICKNAME...IT MEANS "THE SPIDER."
OKAY... "*EL ARAÑA,*" DO YOU KNOW WHAT IS GOING ON?
WHO ARE THESE PEOPLE? WHY WOULD THEY SNATCH ME FROM THE AIRPORT? AND NOT TO SOUND UNGRATEFUL...
...BUT WHY KEEP US ALIVE?
FEAR. FEAR THAT WE KNOW TOO MUCH IS WHY WE ARE HERE. FEAR THAT WE HAVE TALKED TO *OTHERS* IS WHAT'S KEEPING US ALIVE.
SO ALL OF THIS IS ABOUT THE CENTRAL CITY MURDER CASE I'M INVESTIGATING?
YES. THIS WHOLE THING IS A MESS, ONE THAT I "CLEANED UP" FOR MY EMPLOYER. BECAUSE THAT'S WHAT I DO...
I MAKE SURE THAT THERE'S NO BODY...NOTHING LEFT BEHIND THAT CAN LEAD BACK TO THE MARDON FAMILY.
I *KNEW* IT WAS MURDER. THERE WAS A RANSOM NOTE AND NO BODY...BUT THE BLOOD EVIDENCE SAID MURDER TO ME.
A FEW YEARS AGO, I WAS WORKING FOR THE MARDONS OUT OF CENTRAL CITY. ONE NIGHT I GOT A FRANTIC CALL FROM CLAUDIO'S WIFE, ELSA. SHE SENT ME TO AN ADDRESS...
AND WHEN I ARRIVED, THE PLACE WAS AN ABSOLUTE MESS. BLOOD EVERYWHERE. WHEN I CAME IN FOR A CLOSER LOOK AT THE BODY...
I FOUND CLAUDIO MARDON, THE 22-YEAR-OLD HEAD OF THE FAMILY. THE KID NEVER HAD THE STOMACH FOR ALL THE VIOLENCE, BUT HE WAS SMART.
SMART ENOUGH TO GO TO CENTRAL CITY SECRETLY TO MEET WITH THE RIVAL CARTEL TO BROKER A PEACE TREATY THAT WOULD UNITE THE FAMILIES AND END THE VIOLENCE.
THEN WHY WOULD THEY KILL HIM?
IT WASN'T *THEM.* THE WHOLE THING WAS A SETUP.
ELSA FOUND OUT THAT CLAUDIO WAS GOING TO GIVE UP MAJOR MARDON TERRITORY IN EXCHANGE FOR PEACE.
SHE KNEW THAT IT WOULD WEAKEN THAT FAMILY, SO *SHE* KILLED CLAUDIO AND BLAMED *THEM* TO SPARK A WAR *BETWEEN THE TWO FAMILIES.*
SHE KNEW THAT WOULD BRING CLAUDIO'S BROTHER, MARCO, BACK INTO THE FAMILY. HE WAS THE ONE WITH THE *REAL* POWER. MORE THAN ENOUGH TO TIP THE SCALES IN ELSA'S FAVOR.
SO SHE MURDERED HER OWN HUSBAND FOR THE FAMILY...AND SENT YOU TO CLEAN IT UP SO MARCO WOULDN'T FIND OUT IT WAS HER.
SHE'S GOING TO KILL US.

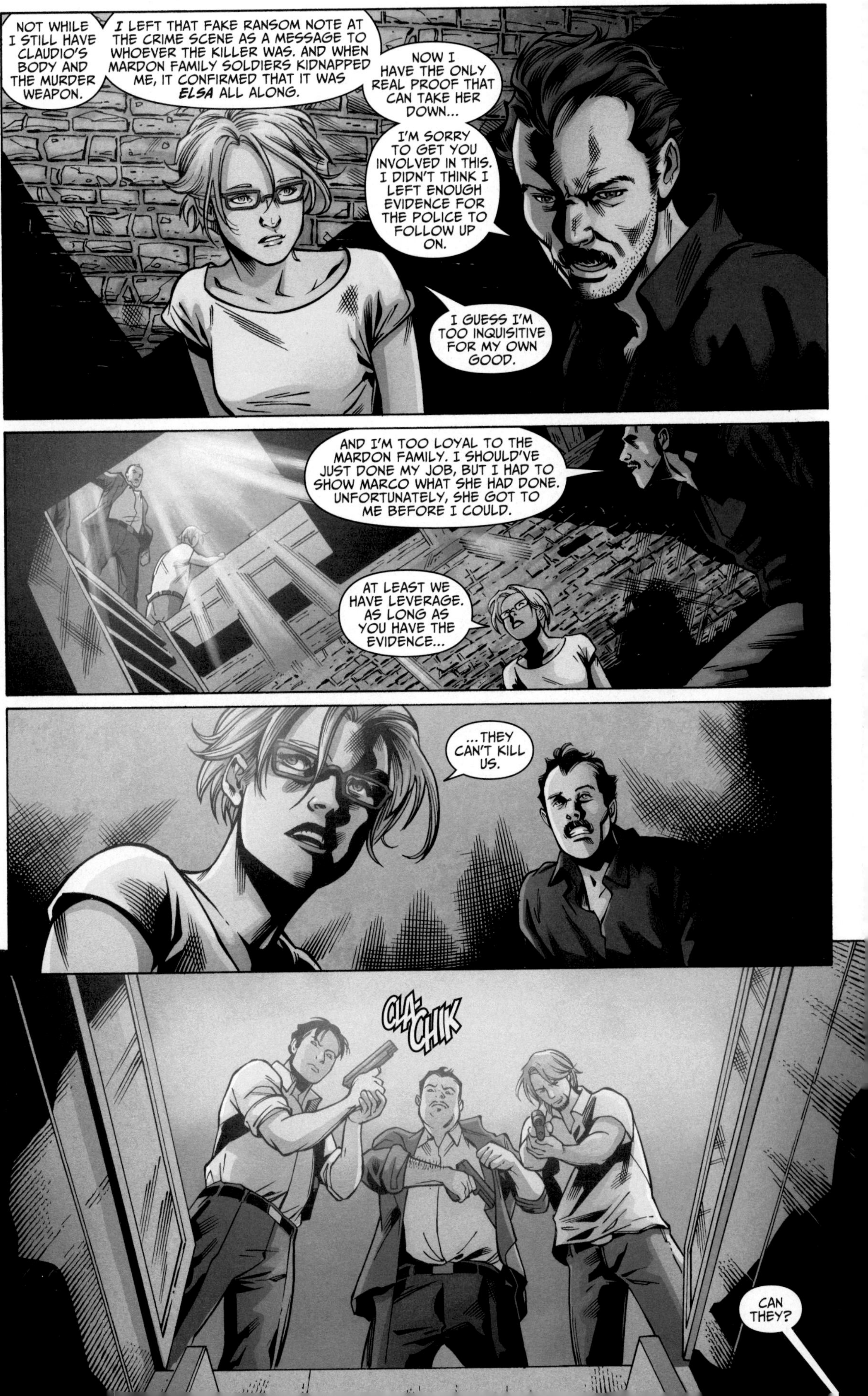
NOT WHILE I STILL HAVE CLAUDIO'S BODY AND THE MURDER WEAPON.
I LEFT THAT FAKE RANSOM NOTE AT THE CRIME SCENE AS A MESSAGE TO WHOEVER THE KILLER WAS. AND WHEN MARDON FAMILY SOLDIERS KIDNAPPED ME, IT CONFIRMED THAT IT WAS ELSA ALL ALONG.
NOW I HAVE THE ONLY REAL PROOF THAT CAN TAKE HER DOWN...
I'M SORRY TO GET YOU INVOLVED IN THIS. I DIDN'T THINK I LEFT ENOUGH EVIDENCE FOR THE POLICE TO FOLLOW UP ON.
I GUESS I'M TOO INQUISITIVE FOR MY OWN GOOD.
AND I'M TOO LOYAL TO THE MARDON FAMILY. I SHOULD'VE JUST DONE MY JOB, BUT I HAD TO SHOW MARCO WHAT SHE HAD DONE. UNFORTUNATELY, SHE GOT TO ME BEFORE I COULD.
AT LEAST WE HAVE LEVERAGE. AS LONG AS YOU HAVE THE EVIDENCE...
...THEY CAN'T KILL US.
CLA-CHIK
CAN THEY?

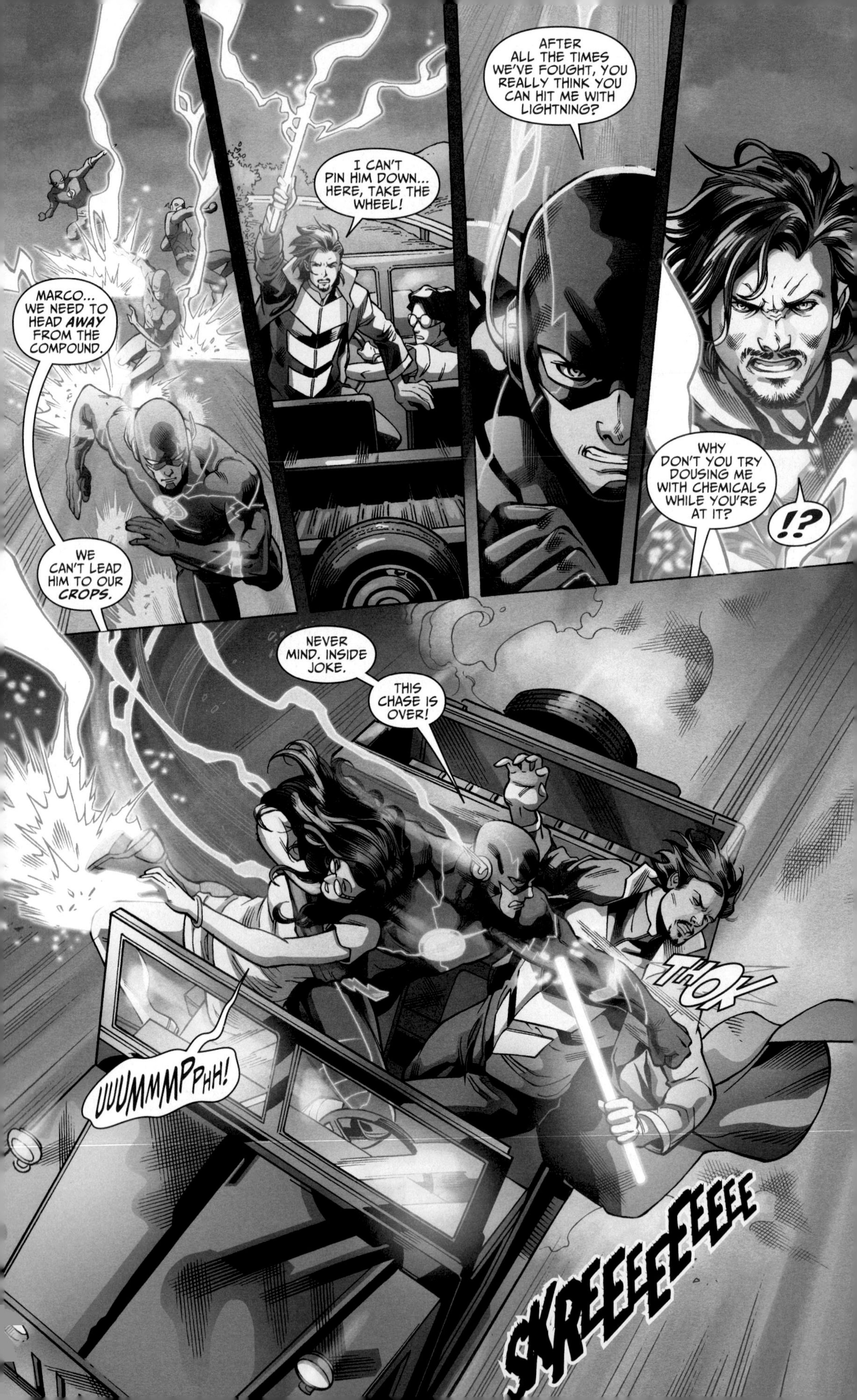

MARCO... WE NEED TO HEAD AWAY FROM THE COMPOUND.
WE CAN'T LEAD HIM TO OUR CROPS.
I CAN'T PIN HIM DOWN... HERE, TAKE THE WHEEL!
AFTER ALL THE TIMES WE'VE FOUGHT, YOU REALLY THINK YOU CAN HIT ME WITH LIGHTNING?
WHY DON'T YOU TRY DOUSING ME WITH CHEMICALS WHILE YOU'RE AT IT?
!?
NEVER MIND. INSIDE JOKE.
THIS CHASE IS OVER!
THOK
UUUMMMPPHH!
SKREEEEEEEEEE

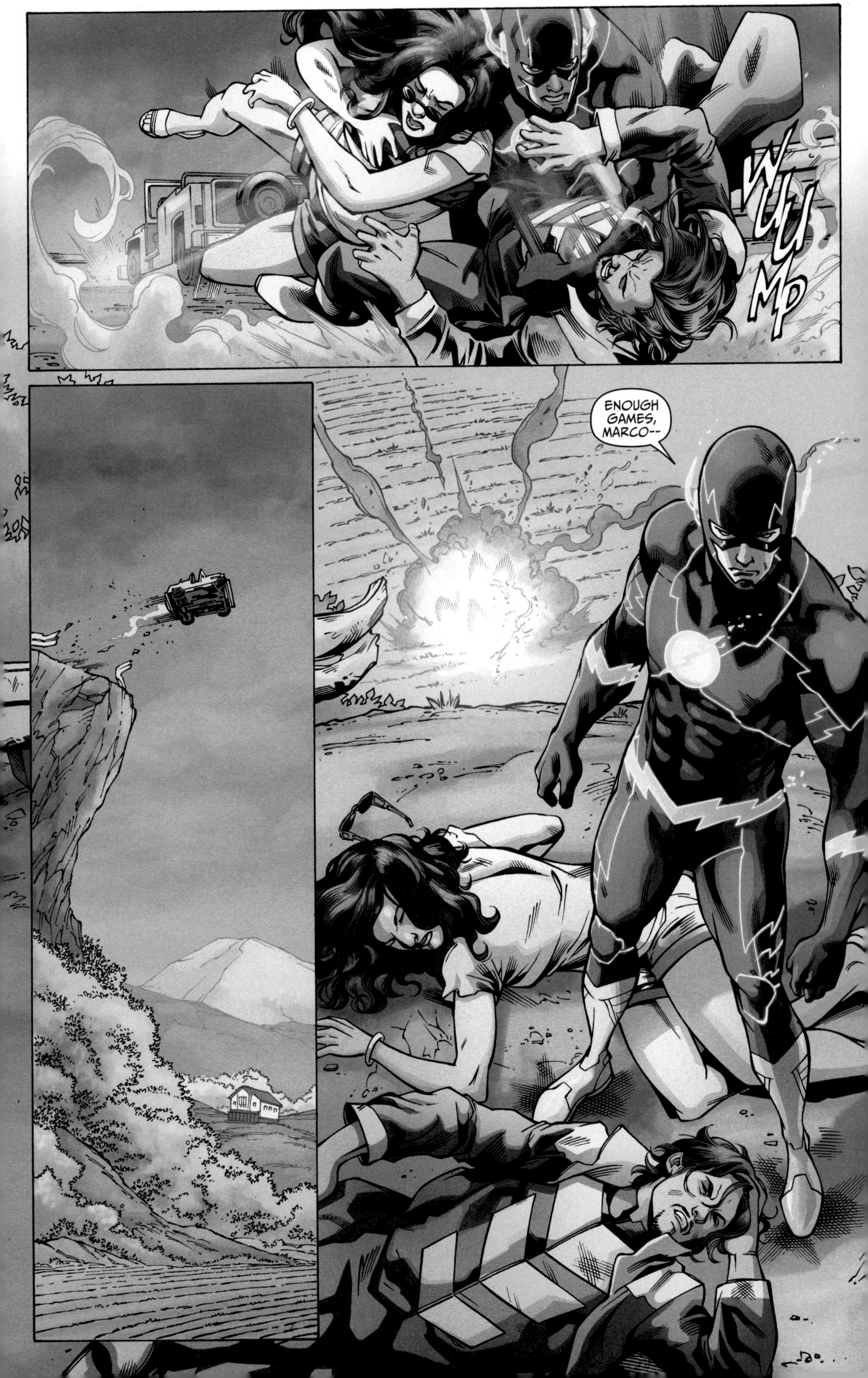
WUUMP
ENOUGH GAMES, MARCO--

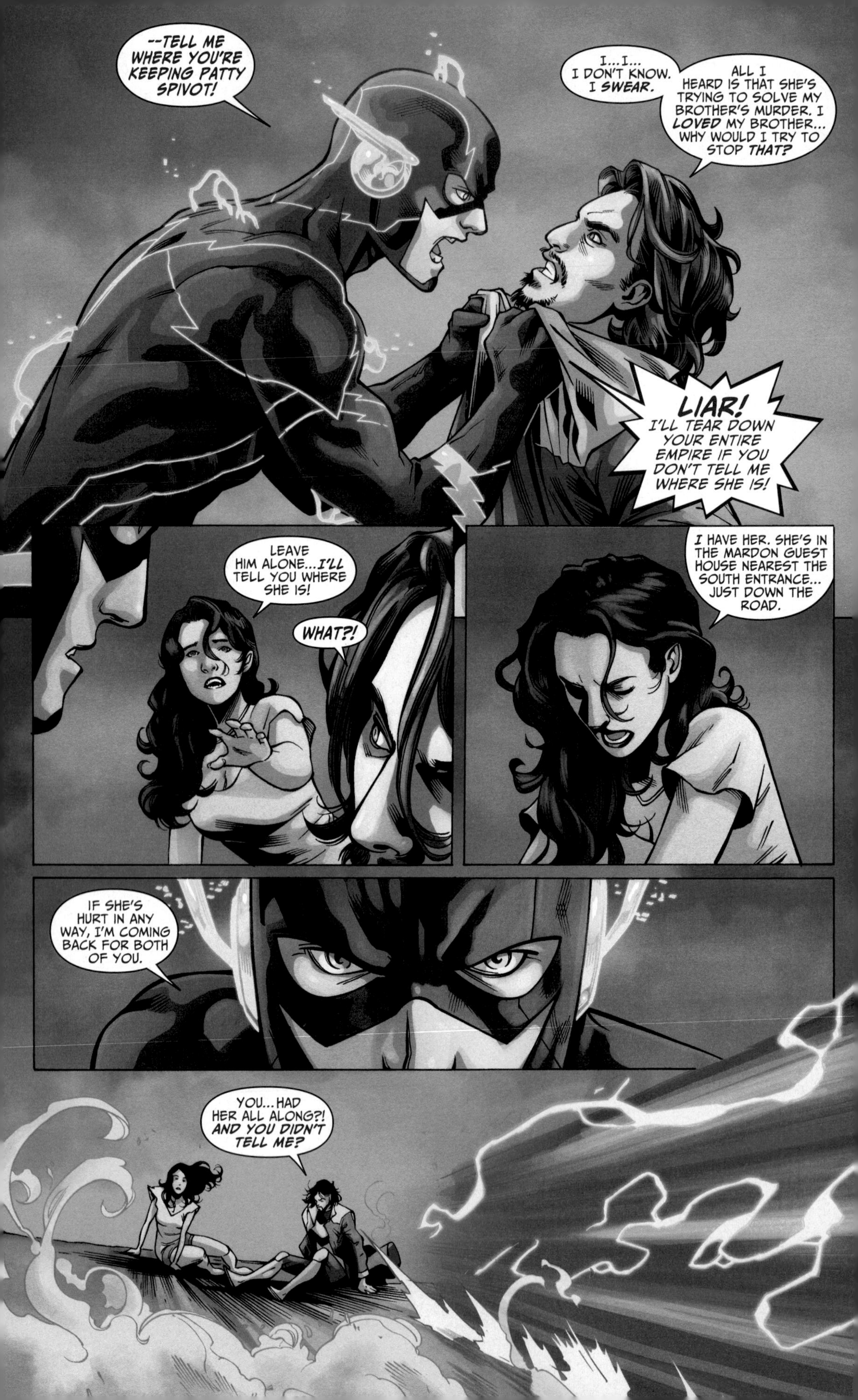
--TELL ME WHERE YOU'RE KEEPING PATTY SPIVOT!
I...I... I DON'T KNOW. I SWEAR.
ALL I HEARD IS THAT SHE'S TRYING TO SOLVE MY BROTHER'S MURDER. I LOVED MY BROTHER... WHY WOULD I TRY TO STOP THAT?
LIAR! I'LL TEAR DOWN YOUR ENTIRE EMPIRE IF YOU DON'T TELL ME WHERE SHE IS!
LEAVE HIM ALONE...I'LL TELL YOU WHERE SHE IS!
WHAT?!
I HAVE HER. SHE'S IN THE MARDON GUEST HOUSE NEAREST THE SOUTH ENTRANCE... JUST DOWN THE ROAD.
IF SHE'S HURT IN ANY WAY, I'M COMING BACK FOR BOTH OF YOU.
YOU...HAD HER ALL ALONG?! AND YOU DIDN'T TELL ME?

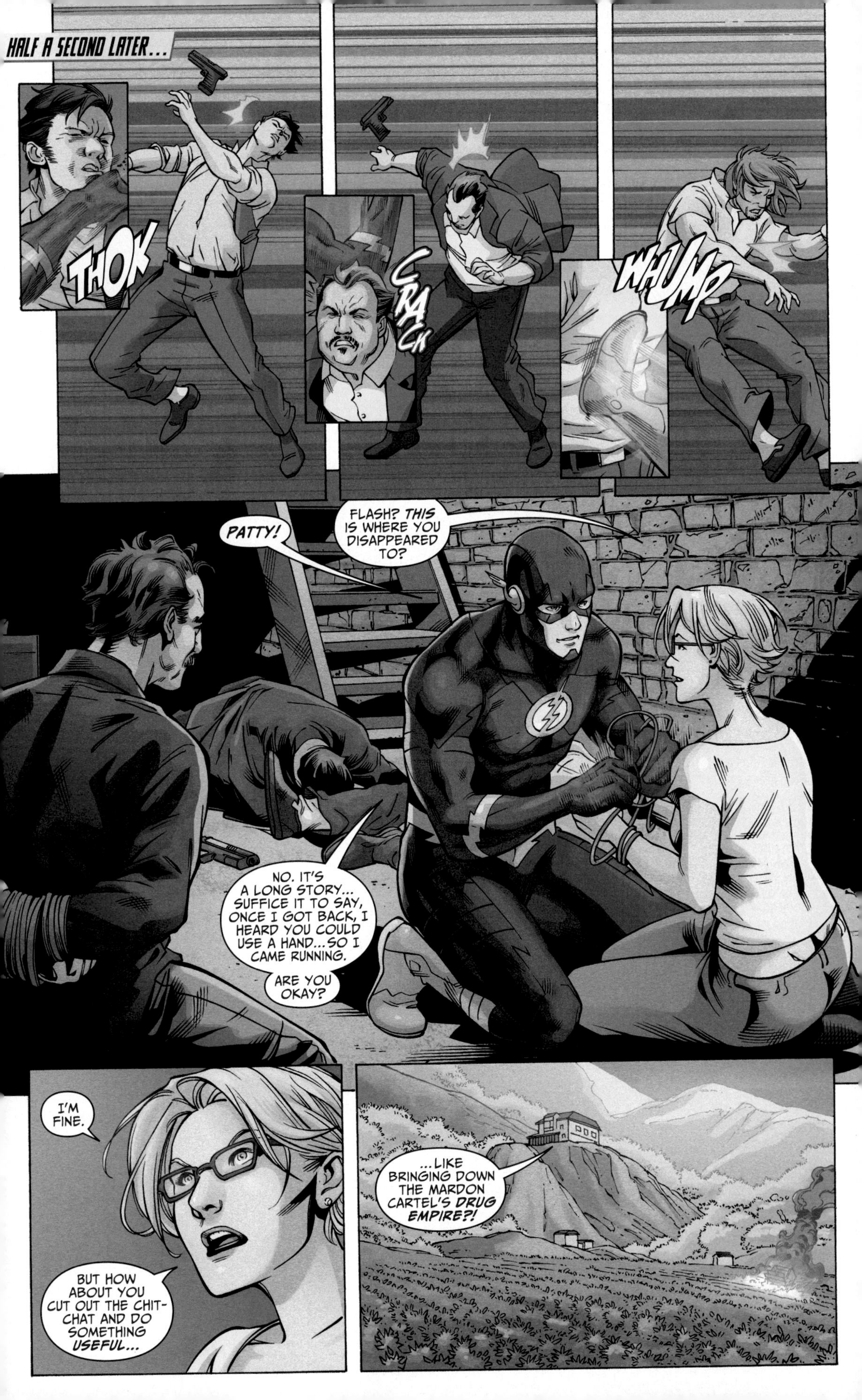
HALF A SECOND LATER...
THOK
CRACK
WHUMP
PATTY!
FLASH? THIS IS WHERE YOU DISAPPEARED TO?
NO. IT'S A LONG STORY... SUFFICE IT TO SAY, ONCE I GOT BACK, I HEARD YOU COULD USE A HAND...SO I CAME RUNNING.
ARE YOU OKAY?
I'M FINE.
BUT HOW ABOUT YOU CUT OUT THE CHIT-CHAT AND DO SOMETHING USEFUL...
...LIKE BRINGING DOWN THE MARDON CARTEL'S DRUG EMPIRE?!

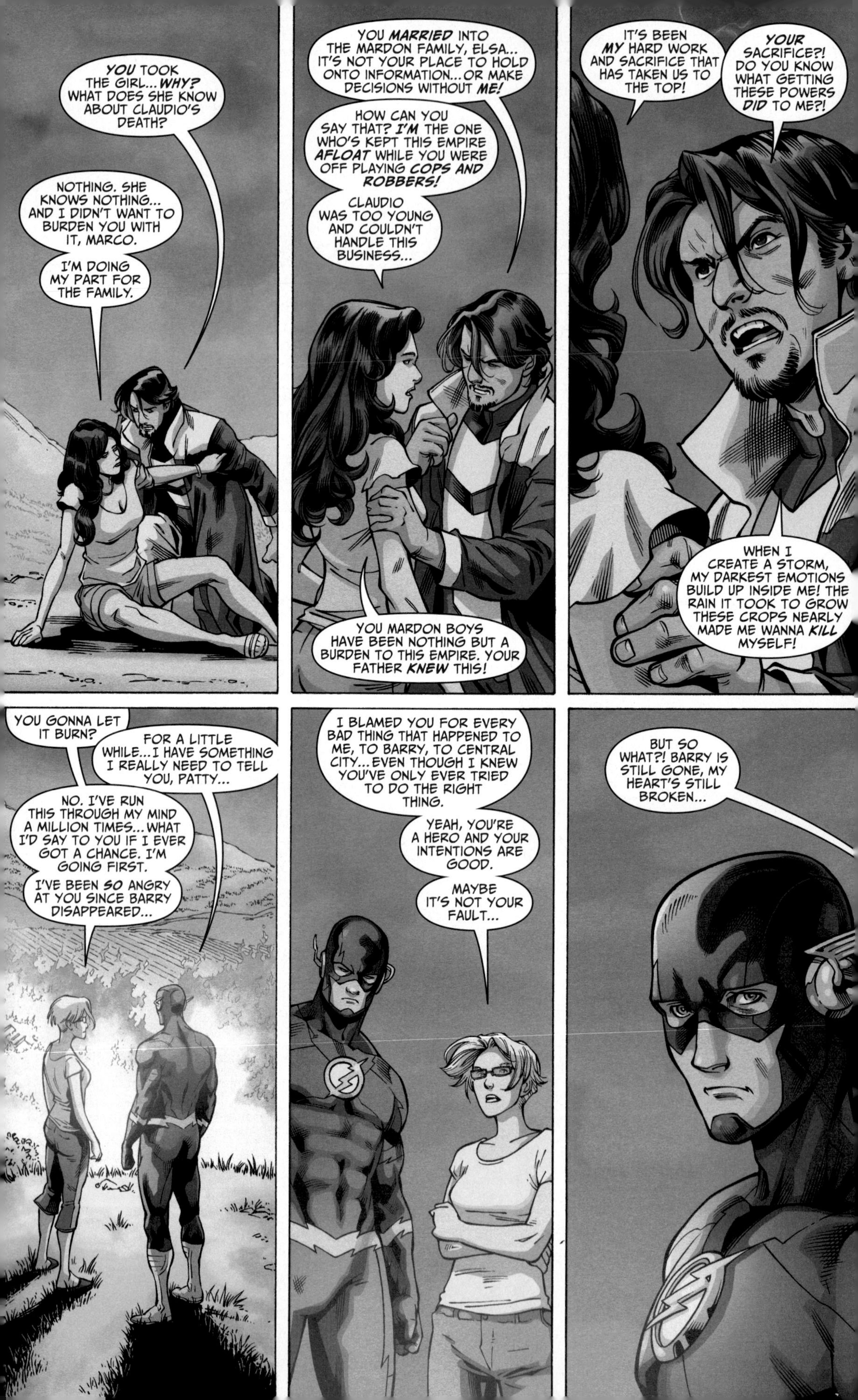
YOU TOOK THE GIRL... WHY? WHAT DOES SHE KNOW ABOUT CLAUDIO'S DEATH?
NOTHING. SHE KNOWS NOTHING... AND I DIDN'T WANT TO BURDEN YOU WITH IT, MARCO.
I'M DOING MY PART FOR THE FAMILY.
YOU MARRIED INTO THE MARDON FAMILY, ELSA... IT'S NOT YOUR PLACE TO HOLD ONTO INFORMATION...OR MAKE DECISIONS WITHOUT ME!
HOW CAN YOU SAY THAT? I'M THE ONE WHO'S KEPT THIS EMPIRE AFLOAT WHILE YOU WERE OFF PLAYING COPS AND ROBBERS!
CLAUDIO WAS TOO YOUNG AND COULDN'T HANDLE THIS BUSINESS...
YOU MARDON BOYS HAVE BEEN NOTHING BUT A BURDEN TO THIS EMPIRE. YOUR FATHER KNEW THIS!
IT'S BEEN MY HARD WORK AND SACRIFICE THAT HAS TAKEN US TO THE TOP!
YOUR SACRIFICE?! DO YOU KNOW WHAT GETTING THESE POWERS DID TO ME?!
WHEN I CREATE A STORM, MY DARKEST EMOTIONS BUILD UP INSIDE ME! THE RAIN IT TOOK TO GROW THESE CROPS NEARLY MADE ME WANNA KILL MYSELF!
YOU GONNA LET IT BURN?
FOR A LITTLE WHILE...I HAVE SOMETHING I REALLY NEED TO TELL YOU, PATTY...
NO. I'VE RUN THIS THROUGH MY MIND A MILLION TIMES...WHAT I'D SAY TO YOU IF I EVER GOT A CHANCE. I'M GOING FIRST.
I'VE BEEN SO ANGRY AT YOU SINCE BARRY DISAPPEARED...
I BLAMED YOU FOR EVERY BAD THING THAT HAPPENED TO ME, TO BARRY, TO CENTRAL CITY...EVEN THOUGH I KNEW YOU'VE ONLY EVER TRIED TO DO THE RIGHT THING.
YEAH, YOU'RE A HERO AND YOUR INTENTIONS ARE GOOD.
MAYBE IT'S NOT YOUR FAULT...
BUT SO WHAT?! BARRY IS STILL GONE, MY HEART'S STILL BROKEN...

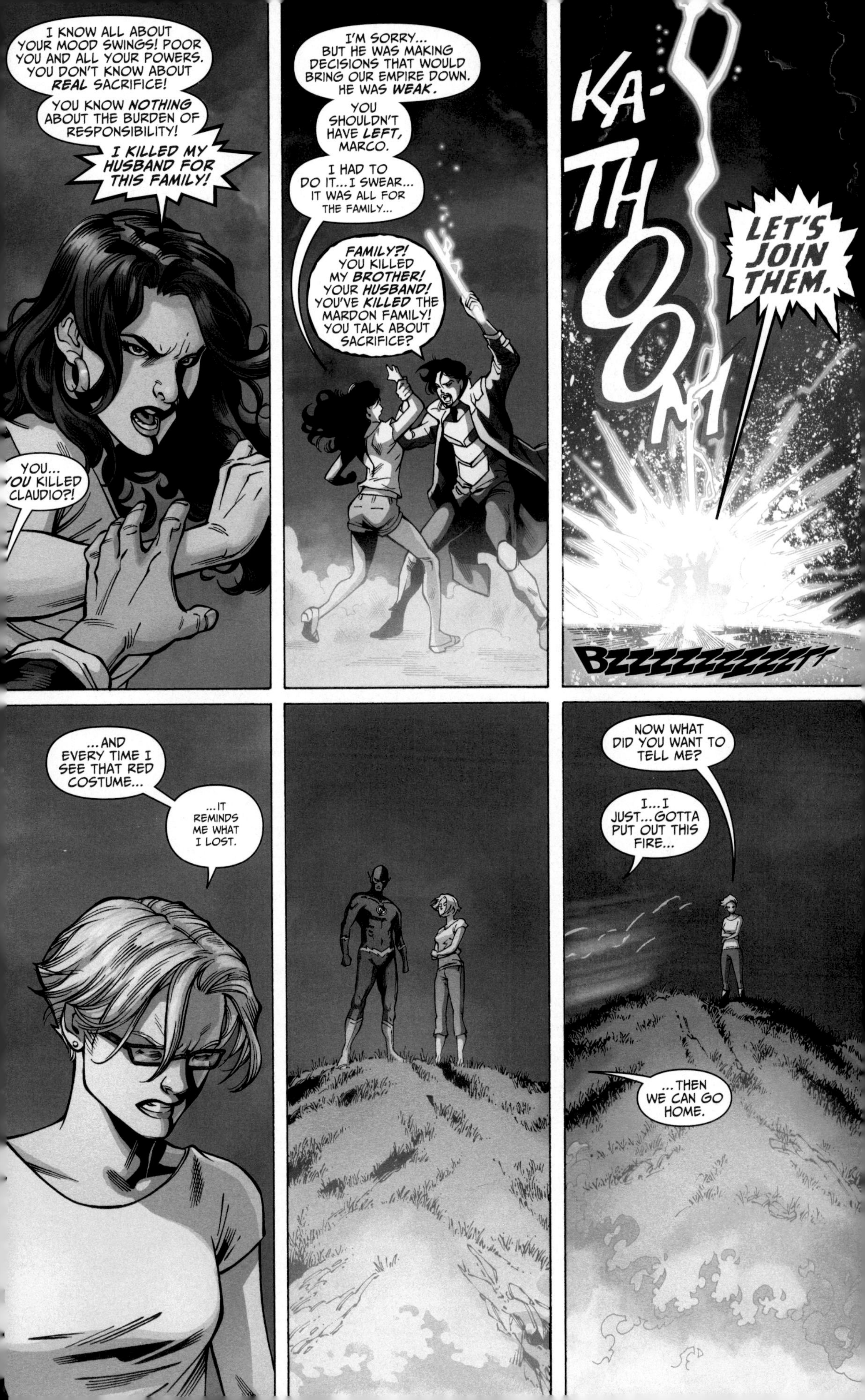

I KNOW ALL ABOUT YOUR MOOD SWINGS! POOR YOU AND ALL YOUR POWERS. YOU DON'T KNOW ABOUT REAL SACRIFICE!
YOU KNOW NOTHING ABOUT THE BURDEN OF RESPONSIBILITY!
I KILLED MY HUSBAND FOR THIS FAMILY!
YOU... YOU KILLED CLAUDIO?!
I'M SORRY... BUT HE WAS MAKING DECISIONS THAT WOULD BRING OUR EMPIRE DOWN. HE WAS WEAK.
YOU SHOULDN'T HAVE LEFT, MARCO.
I HAD TO DO IT... I SWEAR... IT WAS ALL FOR THE FAMILY...
FAMILY?! YOU KILLED MY BROTHER! YOUR HUSBAND! YOU'VE KILLED THE MARDON FAMILY! YOU TALK ABOUT SACRIFICE?
KA-THOOOM
LET'S JOIN THEM.
BZZZZZZZZZZZZT
...AND EVERY TIME I SEE THAT RED COSTUME...
...IT REMINDS ME WHAT I LOST.
NOW WHAT DID YOU WANT TO TELL ME?
I...I JUST...GOTTA PUT OUT THIS FIRE...
...THEN WE CAN GO HOME.

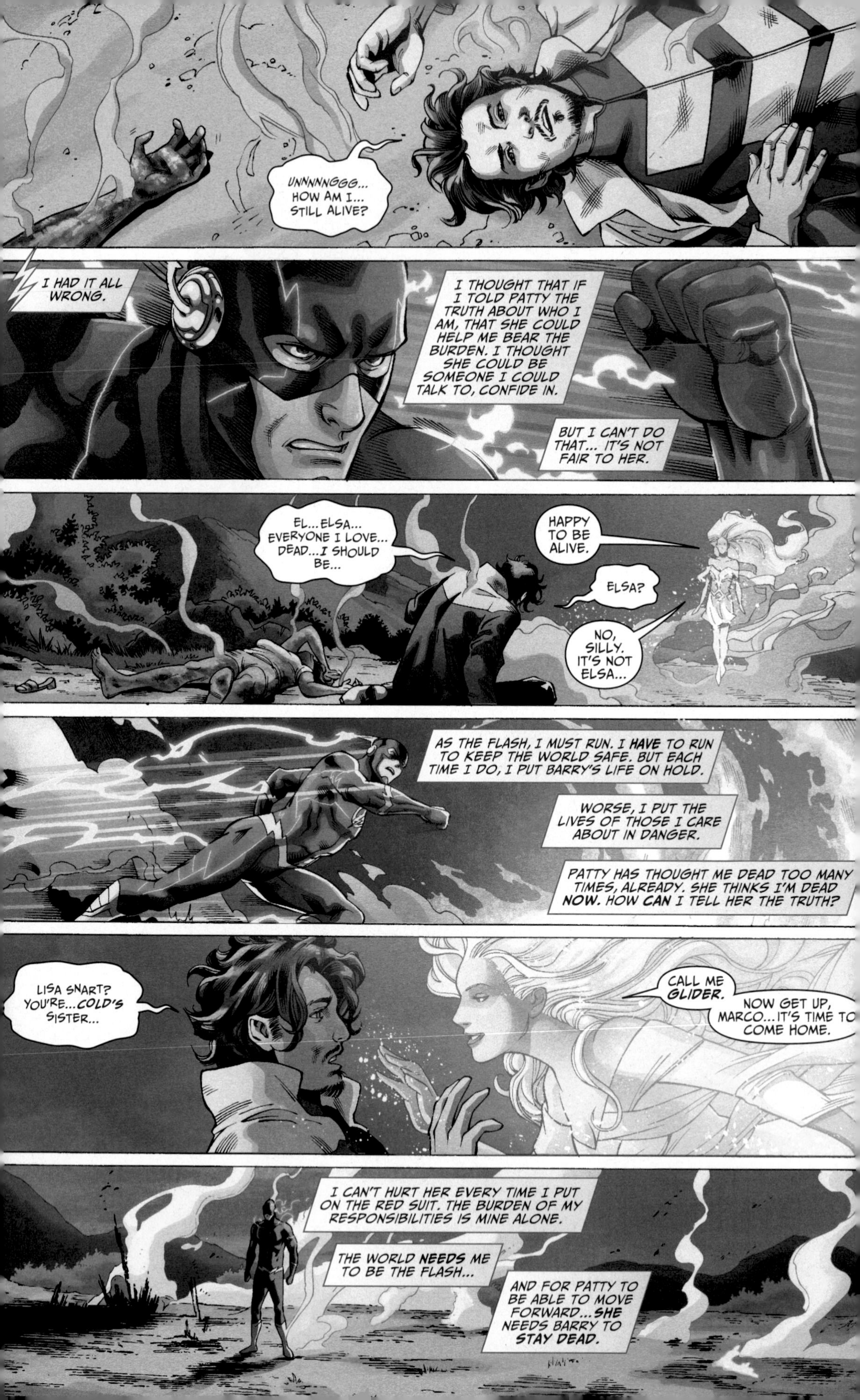
UNNNNNGGG... HOW AM I... STILL ALIVE?
I HAD IT ALL WRONG.
I THOUGHT THAT IF I TOLD PATTY THE TRUTH ABOUT WHO I AM, THAT SHE COULD HELP ME BEAR THE BURDEN. I THOUGHT SHE COULD BE SOMEONE I COULD TALK TO, CONFIDE IN.
BUT I CAN'T DO THAT... IT'S NOT FAIR TO HER.
EL...ELSA... EVERYONE I LOVE... DEAD...I SHOULD BE...
HAPPY TO BE ALIVE.
ELSA?
NO, SILLY. IT'S NOT ELSA...
AS THE FLASH, I MUST RUN. I **HAVE** TO RUN TO KEEP THE WORLD SAFE. BUT EACH TIME I DO, I PUT BARRY'S LIFE ON HOLD.
WORSE, I PUT THE LIVES OF THOSE I CARE ABOUT IN DANGER.
PATTY HAS THOUGHT ME DEAD TOO MANY TIMES, ALREADY. SHE THINKS I'M DEAD **NOW.** HOW **CAN** I TELL HER THE TRUTH?
LISA SNART? YOU'RE...**COLD'S** SISTER...
CALL ME **GLIDER.**
NOW GET UP, MARCO...IT'S TIME TO COME HOME.
I CAN'T HURT HER EVERY TIME I PUT ON THE RED SUIT. THE BURDEN OF MY RESPONSIBILITIES IS MINE ALONE.
THE WORLD **NEEDS** ME TO BE THE FLASH...
AND FOR PATTY TO BE ABLE TO MOVE FORWARD...**SHE** NEEDS BARRY TO **STAY DEAD.**

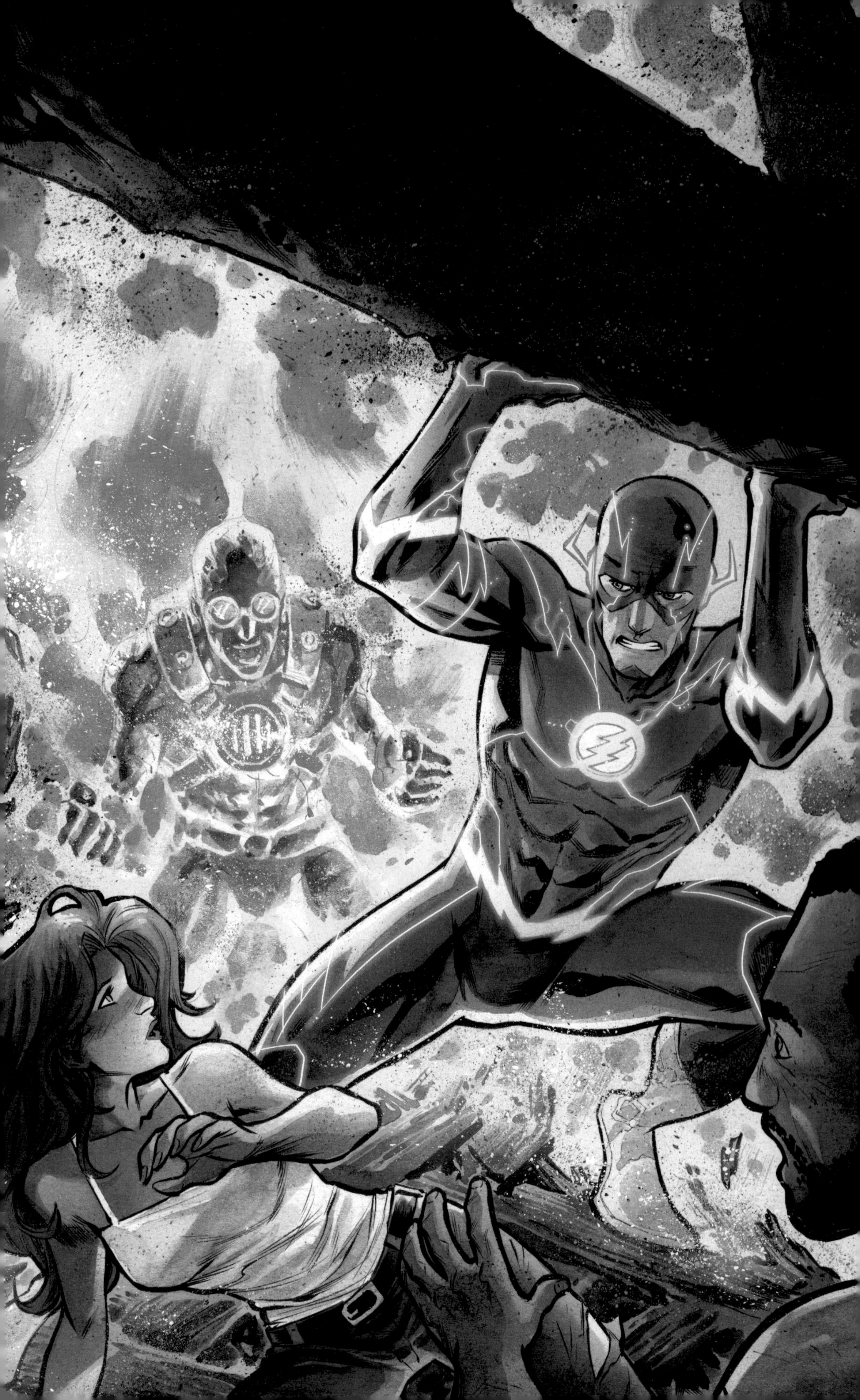

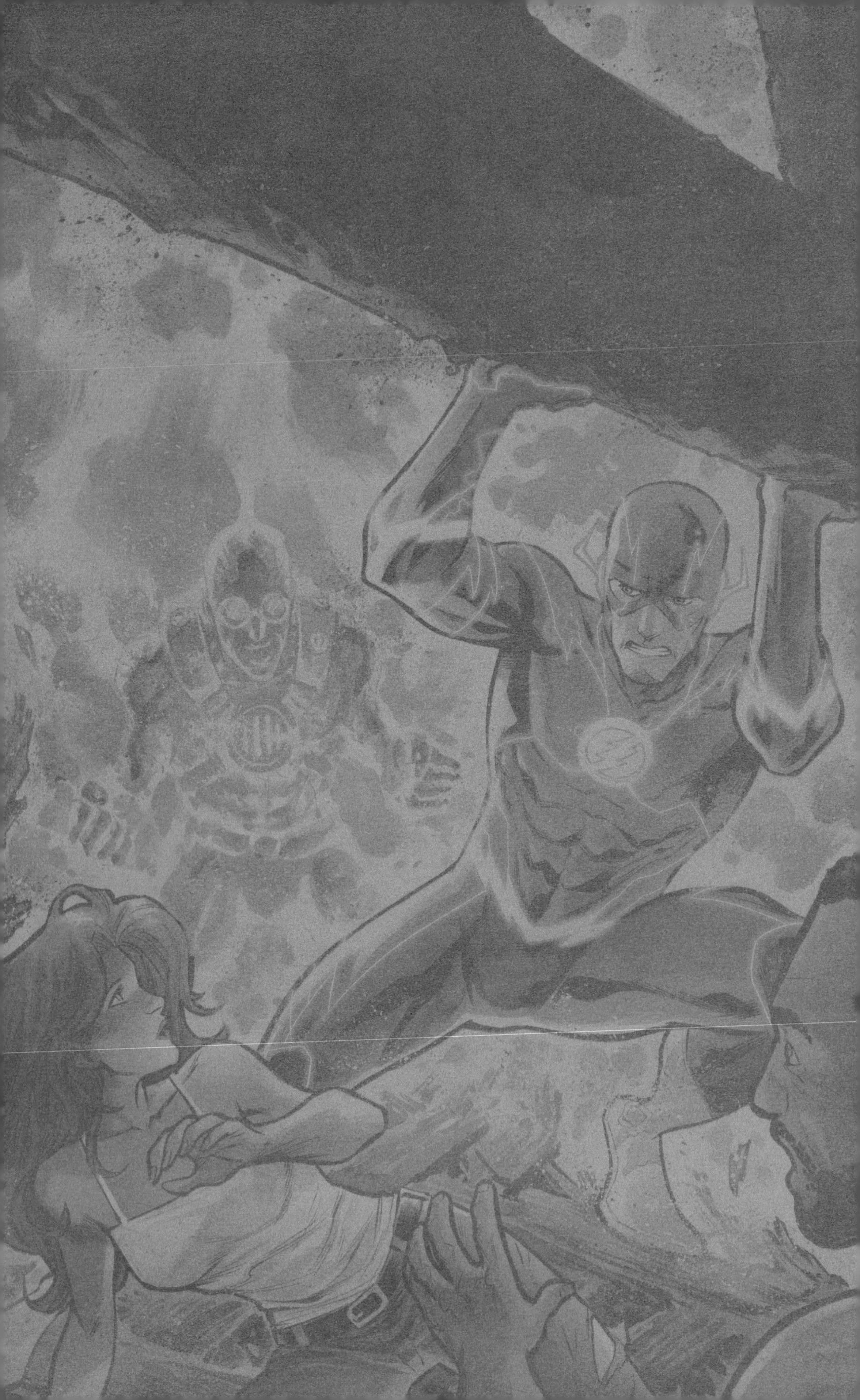

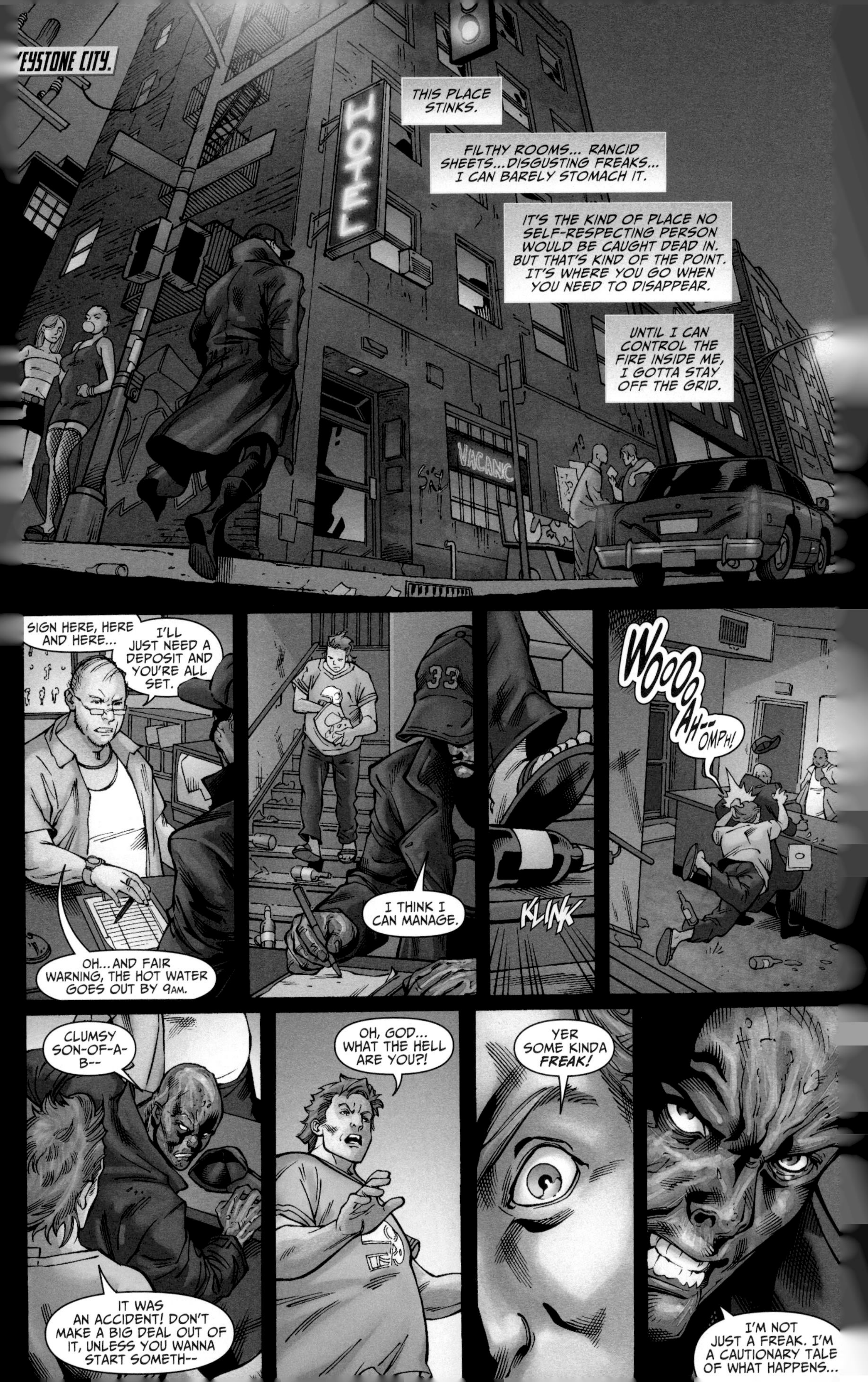
KEYSTONE CITY.
THIS PLACE STINKS.
FILTHY ROOMS... RANCID SHEETS...DISGUSTING FREAKS... I CAN BARELY STOMACH IT.
IT'S THE KIND OF PLACE NO SELF-RESPECTING PERSON WOULD BE CAUGHT DEAD IN. BUT THAT'S KIND OF THE POINT. IT'S WHERE YOU GO WHEN YOU NEED TO DISAPPEAR.
UNTIL I CAN CONTROL THE FIRE INSIDE ME, I GOTTA STAY OFF THE GRID.
HOTEL
VACANC
SIGN HERE, HERE AND HERE...
I'LL JUST NEED A DEPOSIT AND YOU'RE ALL SET.
OH...AND FAIR WARNING, THE HOT WATER GOES OUT BY 9AM.
I THINK I CAN MANAGE.
KLINK
WOOOOAH--OMPH!
CLUMSY SON-OF-A-B--
IT WAS AN ACCIDENT! DON'T MAKE A BIG DEAL OUT OF IT, UNLESS YOU WANNA START SOMETH--
OH, GOD... WHAT THE HELL ARE YOU?!
YER SOME KINDA FREAK!
I'M NOT JUST A FREAK. I'M A CAUTIONARY TALE OF WHAT HAPPENS...

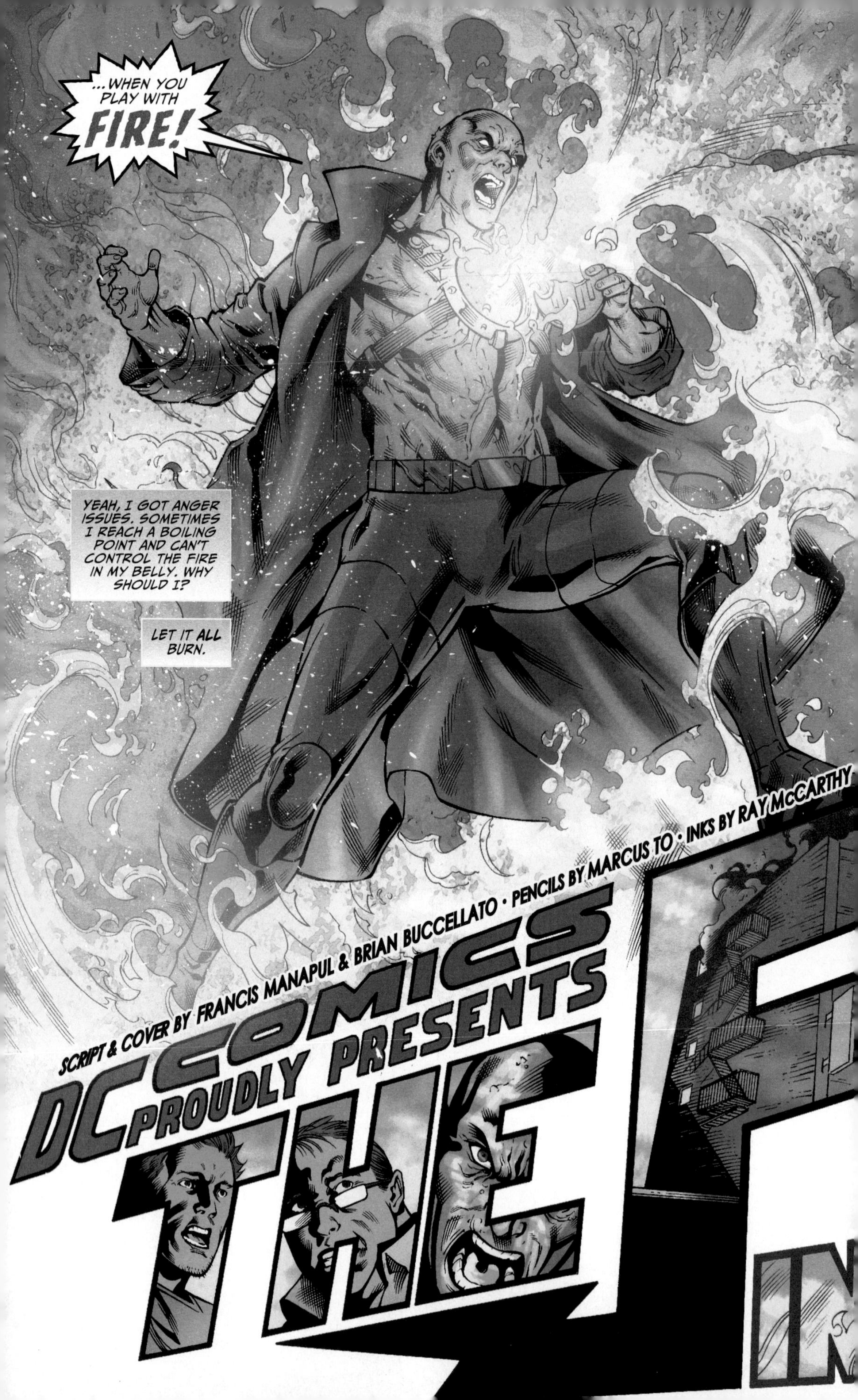
...WHEN YOU PLAY WITH FIRE!
YEAH, I GOT ANGER ISSUES. SOMETIMES I REACH A BOILING POINT AND CAN'T CONTROL THE FIRE IN MY BELLY. WHY SHOULD I?
LET IT ALL BURN.
SCRIPT & COVER BY FRANCIS MANAPUL & BRIAN BUCCELLATO · PENCILS BY MARCUS TO · INKS BY RAY McCARTHY
DC COMICS PROUDLY PRESENTS
THE

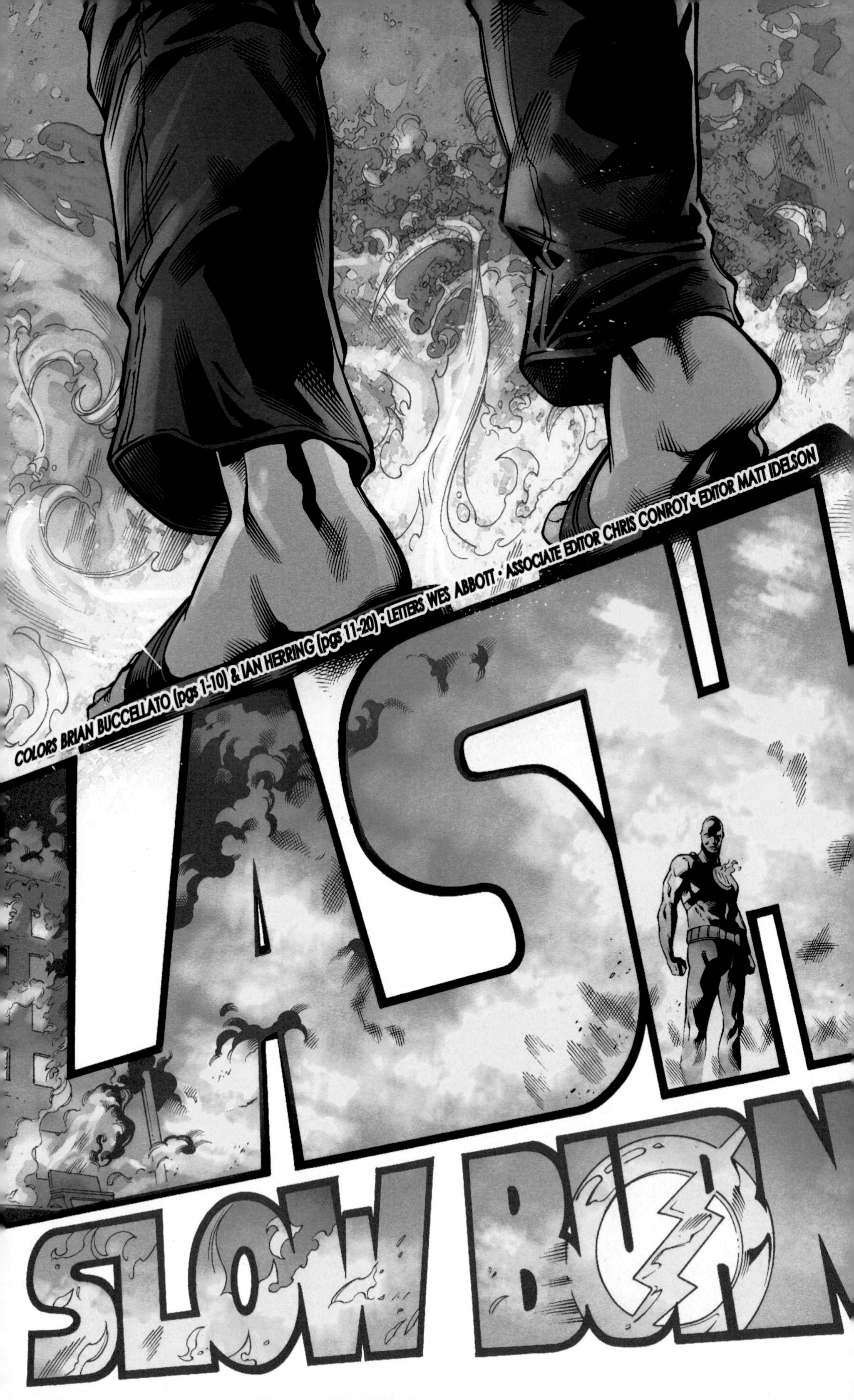
COLORS BRIAN BUCCELLATO (pgs 1-10) & IAN HERRING (pgs 11-20) • LETTERS WES ABBOTT • ASSOCIATE EDITOR CHRIS CONROY • EDITOR MATT IDELSON
SLOW BURN

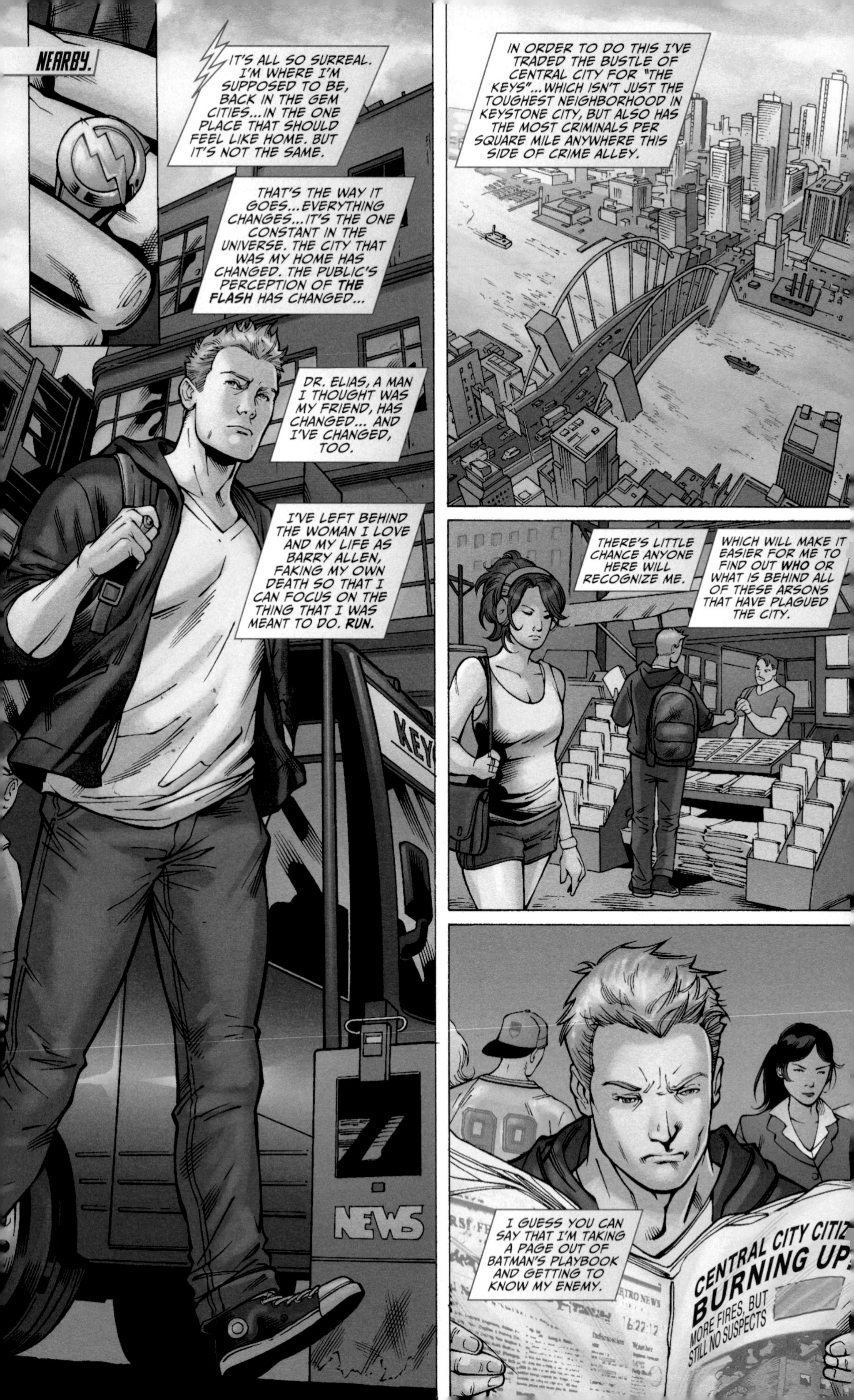
NEARBY.
IT'S ALL SO SURREAL. I'M WHERE I'M SUPPOSED TO BE, BACK IN THE GEM CITIES...IN THE ONE PLACE THAT SHOULD FEEL LIKE HOME. BUT IT'S NOT THE SAME.
THAT'S THE WAY IT GOES...EVERYTHING CHANGES...IT'S THE ONE CONSTANT IN THE UNIVERSE. THE CITY THAT WAS MY HOME HAS CHANGED. THE PUBLIC'S PERCEPTION OF THE FLASH HAS CHANGED...
DR. ELIAS, A MAN I THOUGHT WAS MY FRIEND, HAS CHANGED... AND I'VE CHANGED, TOO.
I'VE LEFT BEHIND THE WOMAN I LOVE AND MY LIFE AS BARRY ALLEN, FAKING MY OWN DEATH SO THAT I CAN FOCUS ON THE THING THAT I WAS MEANT TO DO. RUN.
NEWS
IN ORDER TO DO THIS I'VE TRADED THE BUSTLE OF CENTRAL CITY FOR "THE KEYS"...WHICH ISN'T JUST THE TOUGHEST NEIGHBORHOOD IN KEYSTONE CITY, BUT ALSO HAS THE MOST CRIMINALS PER SQUARE MILE ANYWHERE THIS SIDE OF CRIME ALLEY.
THERE'S LITTLE CHANCE ANYONE HERE WILL RECOGNIZE ME.
WHICH WILL MAKE IT EASIER FOR ME TO FIND OUT WHO OR WHAT IS BEHIND ALL OF THESE ARSONS THAT HAVE PLAGUED THE CITY.
I GUESS YOU CAN SAY THAT I'M TAKING A PAGE OUT OF BATMAN'S PLAYBOOK AND GETTING TO KNOW MY ENEMY.
CENTRAL CITY CITIZ
BURNING UP!
MORE FIRES, BUT STILL NO SUSPECTS

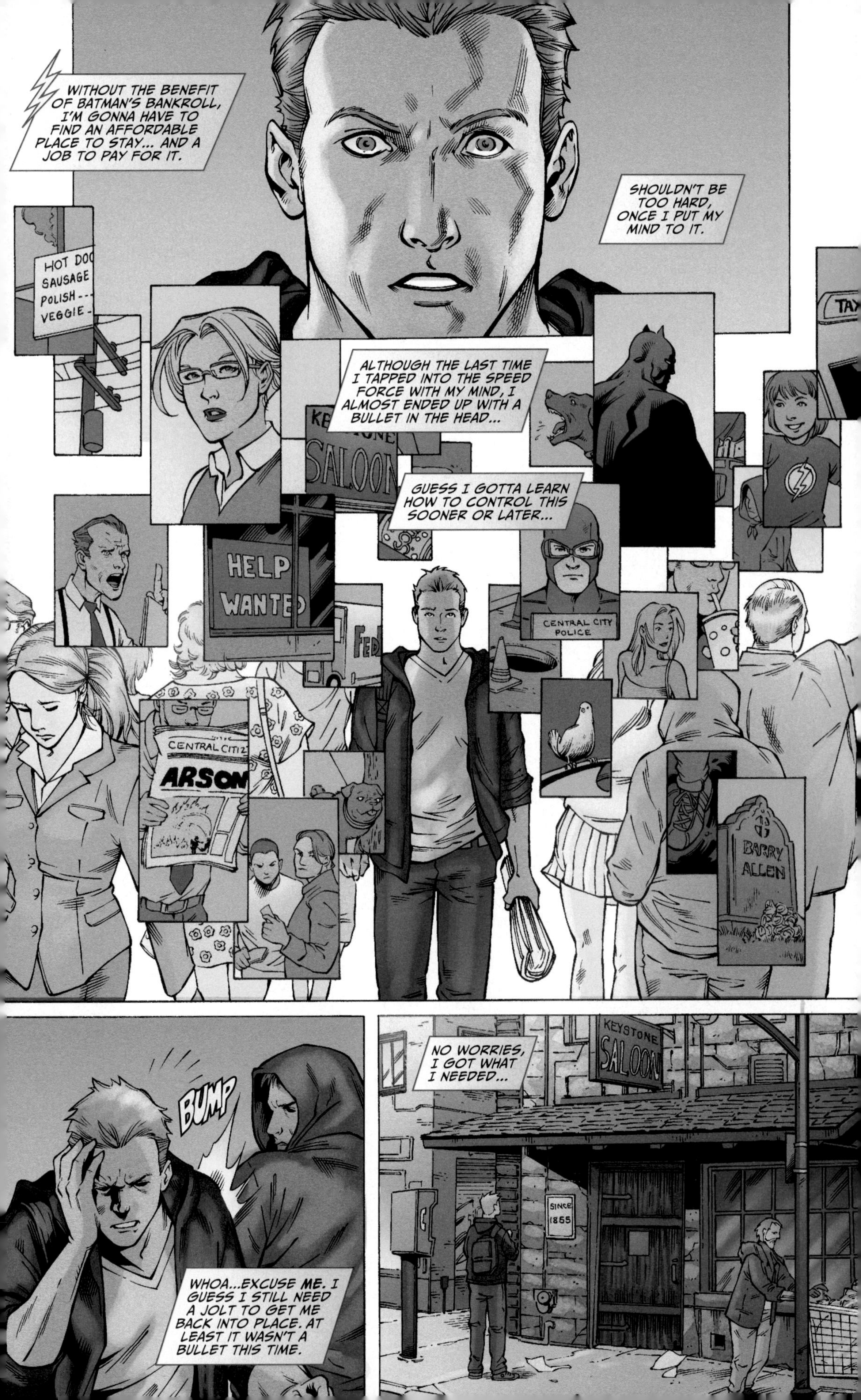
WITHOUT THE BENEFIT OF BATMAN'S BANKROLL, I'M GONNA HAVE TO FIND AN AFFORDABLE PLACE TO STAY... AND A JOB TO PAY FOR IT.
SHOULDN'T BE TOO HARD, ONCE I PUT MY MIND TO IT.
HOT DOG
SAUSAGE
POLISH
VEGGIE
ALTHOUGH THE LAST TIME I TAPPED INTO THE SPEED FORCE WITH MY MIND, I ALMOST ENDED UP WITH A BULLET IN THE HEAD...
SALOON
GUESS I GOTTA LEARN HOW TO CONTROL THIS SOONER OR LATER...
HELP WANTED
CENTRAL CITY POLICE
ARSON
BARRY ALLEN
BUMP
WHOA...EXCUSE ME. I GUESS I STILL NEED A JOLT TO GET ME BACK INTO PLACE. AT LEAST IT WASN'T A BULLET THIS TIME.
NO WORRIES, I GOT WHAT I NEEDED...
KEYSTONE SALOON
SINCE 1855

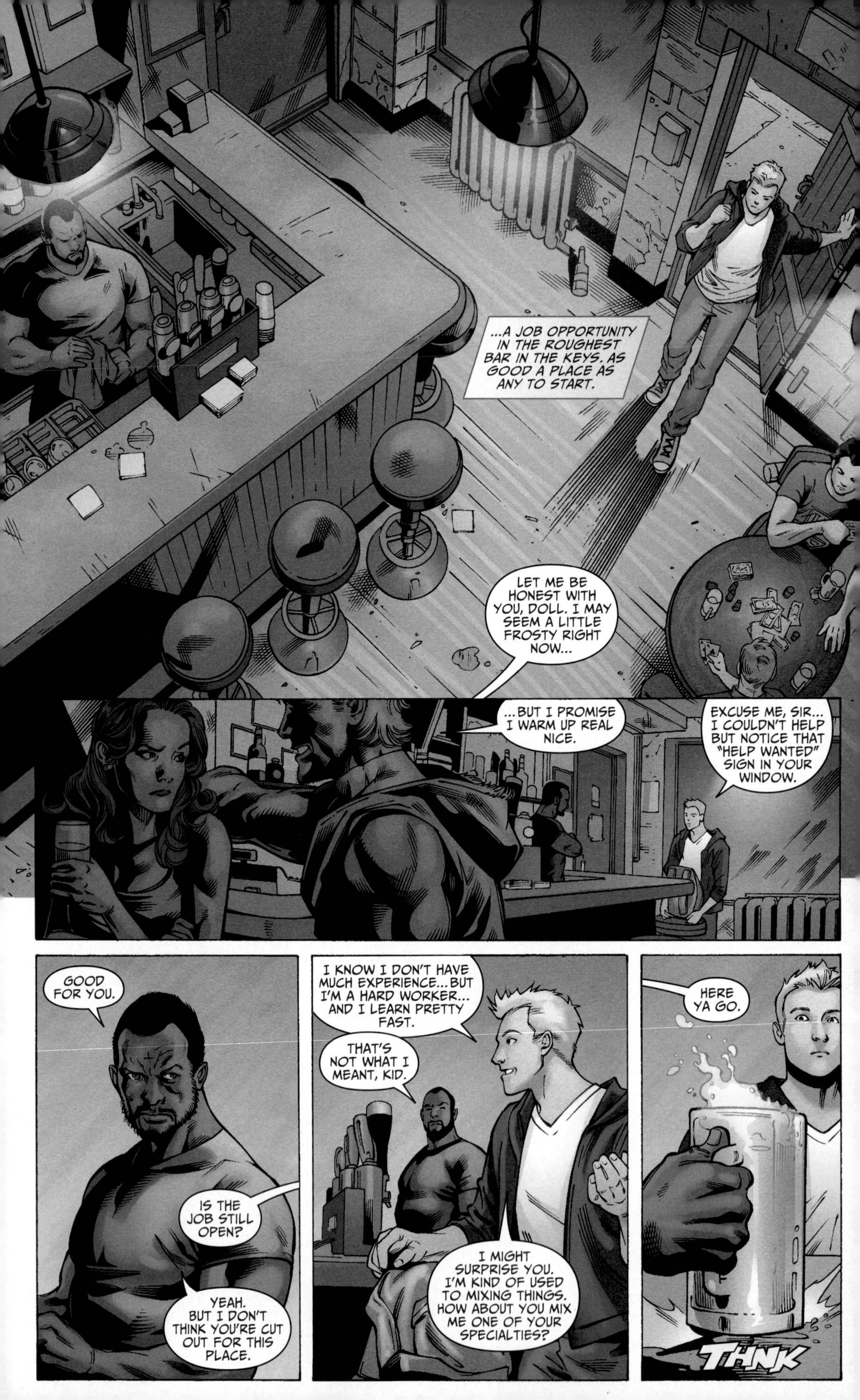
...A JOB OPPORTUNITY IN THE ROUGHEST BAR IN THE KEYS. AS GOOD A PLACE AS ANY TO START.
LET ME BE HONEST WITH YOU, DOLL. I MAY SEEM A LITTLE FROSTY RIGHT NOW...
...BUT I PROMISE I WARM UP REAL NICE.
EXCUSE ME, SIR... I COULDN'T HELP BUT NOTICE THAT "HELP WANTED" SIGN IN YOUR WINDOW.
GOOD FOR YOU.
IS THE JOB STILL OPEN?
YEAH. BUT I DON'T THINK YOU'RE CUT OUT FOR THIS PLACE.
I KNOW I DON'T HAVE MUCH EXPERIENCE... BUT I'M A HARD WORKER... AND I LEARN PRETTY FAST.
THAT'S NOT WHAT I MEANT, KID.
I MIGHT SURPRISE YOU. I'M KIND OF USED TO MIXING THINGS. HOW ABOUT YOU MIX ME ONE OF YOUR SPECIALTIES?
HERE YA GO.
THNK

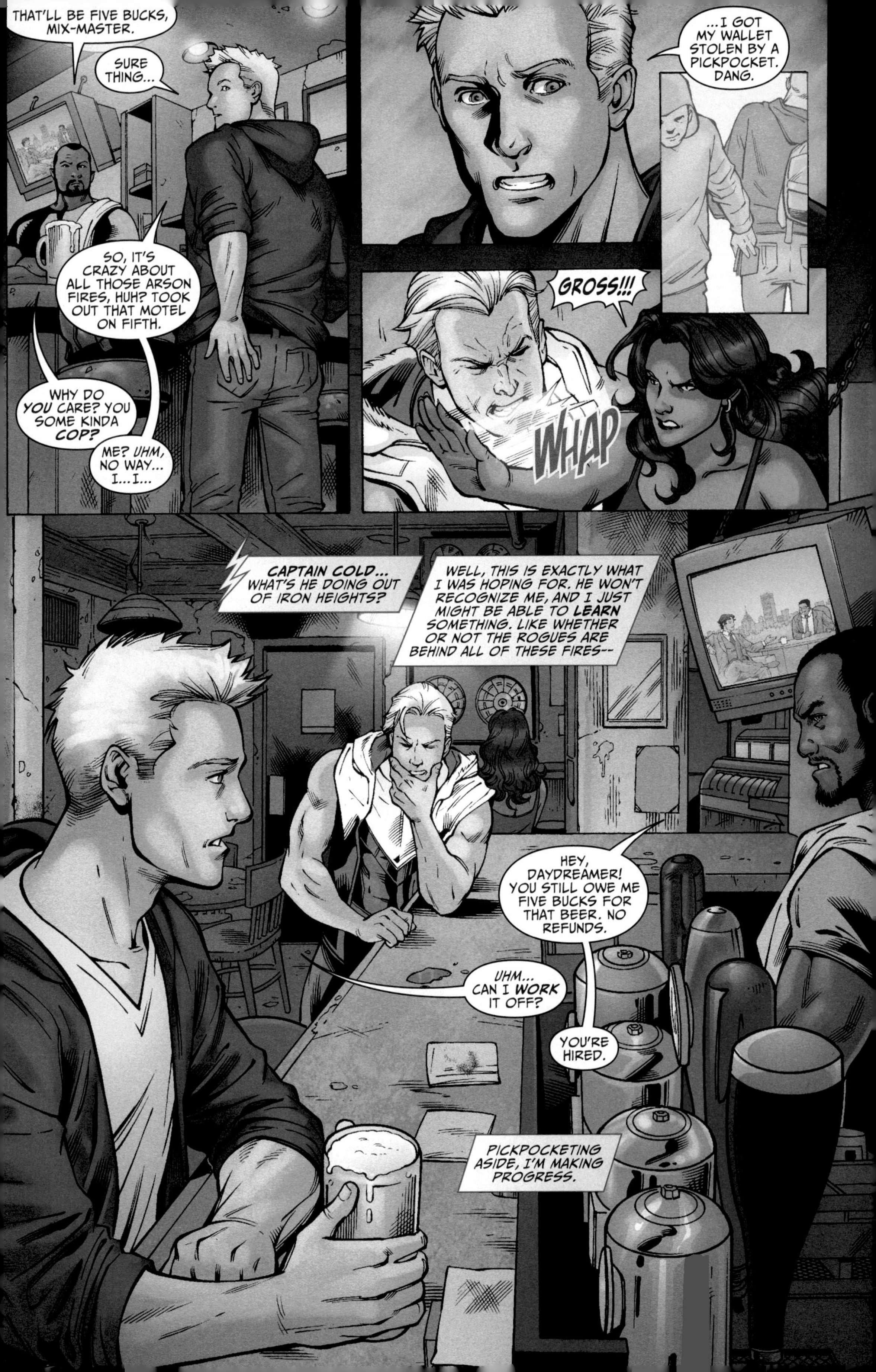
THAT'LL BE FIVE BUCKS, MIX-MASTER.
SURE THING...
SO, IT'S CRAZY ABOUT ALL THOSE ARSON FIRES, HUH? TOOK OUT THAT MOTEL ON FIFTH.
WHY DO YOU CARE? YOU SOME KINDA COP?
ME? UHM, NO WAY... I...I...
...I GOT MY WALLET STOLEN BY A PICKPOCKET. DANG.
GROSS!!!
WHAP
CAPTAIN COLD... WHAT'S HE DOING OUT OF IRON HEIGHTS?
WELL, THIS IS EXACTLY WHAT I WAS HOPING FOR. HE WON'T RECOGNIZE ME, AND I JUST MIGHT BE ABLE TO LEARN SOMETHING. LIKE WHETHER OR NOT THE ROGUES ARE BEHIND ALL OF THESE FIRES--
HEY, DAYDREAMER! YOU STILL OWE ME FIVE BUCKS FOR THAT BEER. NO REFUNDS.
UHM... CAN I WORK IT OFF?
YOU'RE HIRED.
PICKPOCKETING ASIDE, I'M MAKING PROGRESS.

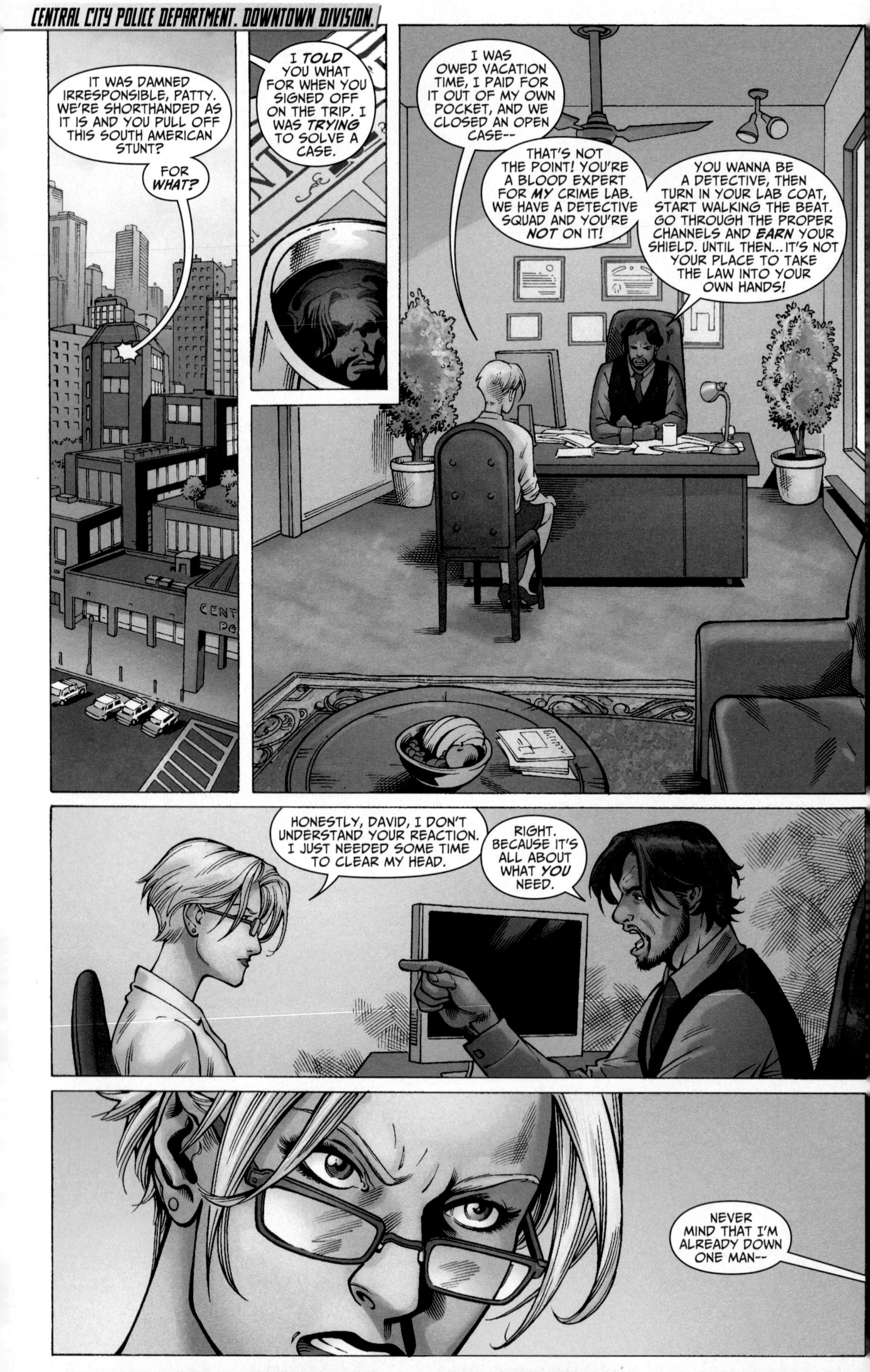
CENTRAL CITY POLICE DEPARTMENT. DOWNTOWN DIVISION.
IT WAS DAMNED IRRESPONSIBLE, PATTY. WE'RE SHORTHANDED AS IT IS AND YOU PULL OFF THIS SOUTH AMERICAN STUNT?
FOR WHAT?
I TOLD YOU WHAT FOR WHEN YOU SIGNED OFF ON THE TRIP. I WAS TRYING TO SOLVE A CASE.
I WAS OWED VACATION TIME, I PAID FOR IT OUT OF MY OWN POCKET, AND WE CLOSED AN OPEN CASE--
THAT'S NOT THE POINT! YOU'RE A BLOOD EXPERT FOR MY CRIME LAB. WE HAVE A DETECTIVE SQUAD AND YOU'RE NOT ON IT!
YOU WANNA BE A DETECTIVE, THEN TURN IN YOUR LAB COAT, START WALKING THE BEAT. GO THROUGH THE PROPER CHANNELS AND EARN YOUR SHIELD. UNTIL THEN... IT'S NOT YOUR PLACE TO TAKE THE LAW INTO YOUR OWN HANDS!
HONESTLY, DAVID, I DON'T UNDERSTAND YOUR REACTION. I JUST NEEDED SOME TIME TO CLEAR MY HEAD.
RIGHT. BECAUSE IT'S ALL ABOUT WHAT YOU NEED.
NEVER MIND THAT I'M ALREADY DOWN ONE MAN--

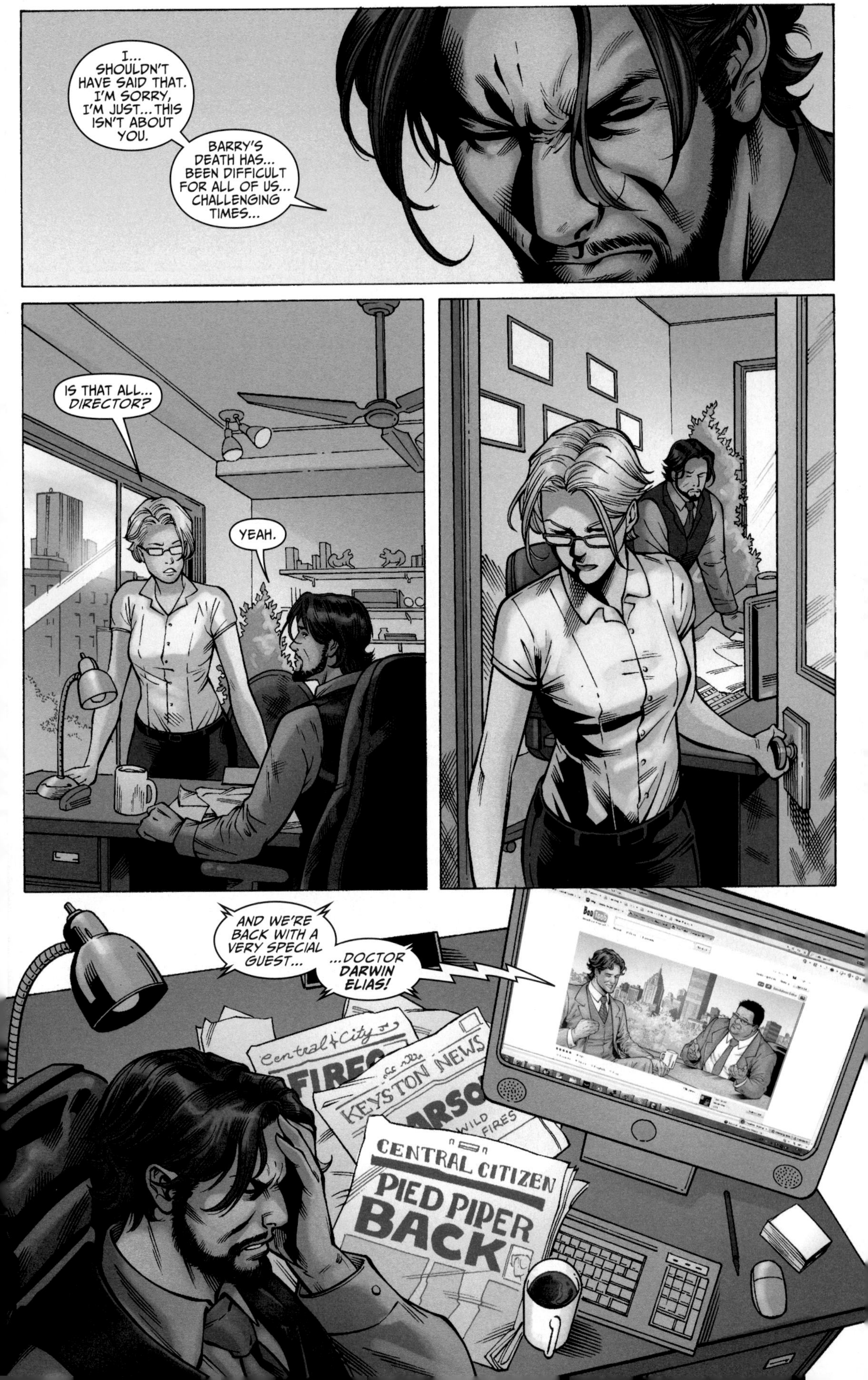
I... SHOULDN'T HAVE SAID THAT. I'M SORRY, I'M JUST...THIS ISN'T ABOUT YOU.
BARRY'S DEATH HAS... BEEN DIFFICULT FOR ALL OF US... CHALLENGING TIMES...
IS THAT ALL... DIRECTOR?
YEAH.
AND WE'RE BACK WITH A VERY SPECIAL GUEST...
...DOCTOR DARWIN ELIAS!
Central City
FIRE
KEYSTON NEWS
ARSO
WILD FIRES
CENTRAL CITIZEN
PIED PIPER BACK

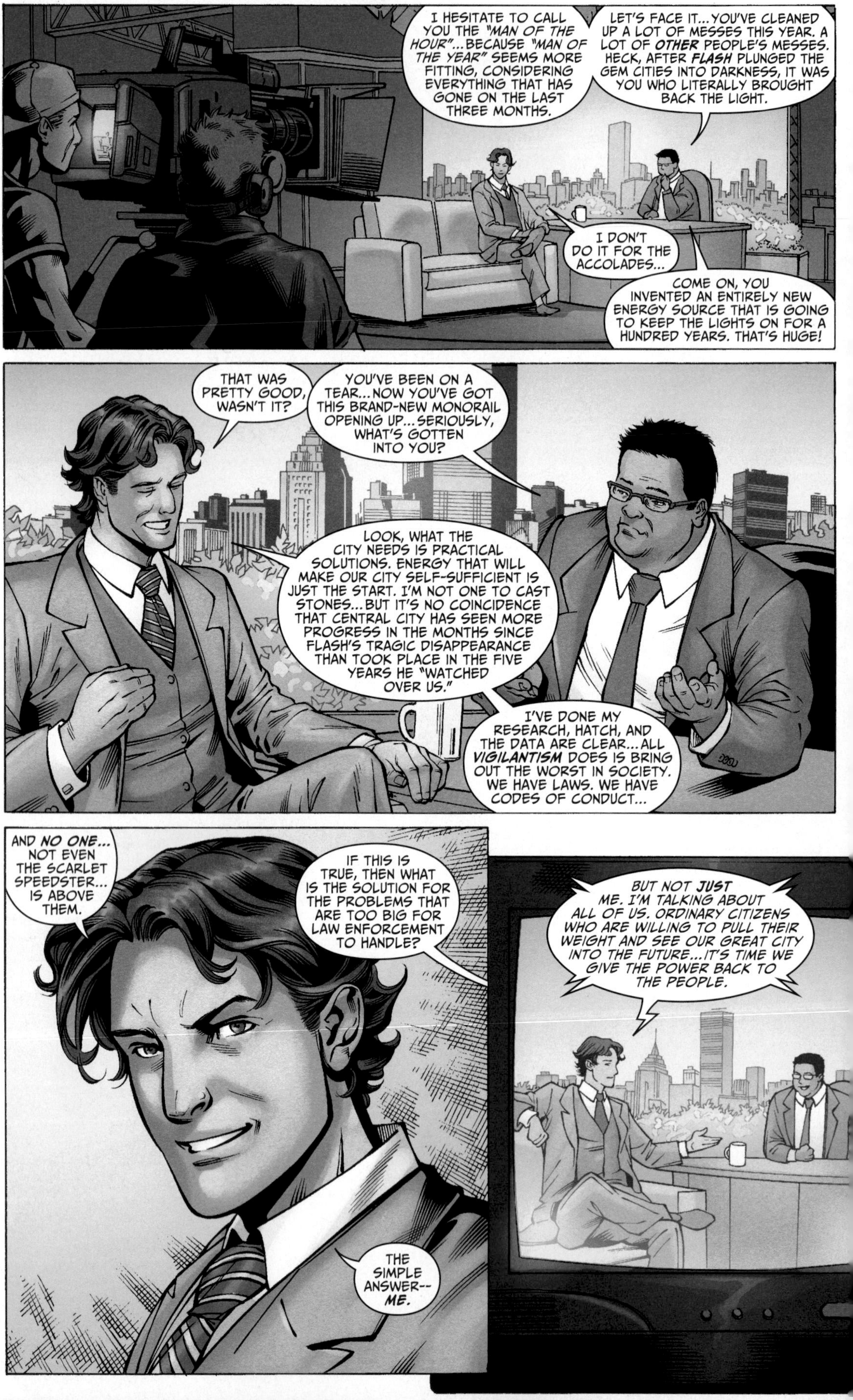
I HESITATE TO CALL YOU THE "MAN OF THE HOUR"...BECAUSE "MAN OF THE YEAR" SEEMS MORE FITTING, CONSIDERING EVERYTHING THAT HAS GONE ON THE LAST THREE MONTHS.
LET'S FACE IT...YOU'VE CLEANED UP A LOT OF MESSES THIS YEAR. A LOT OF OTHER PEOPLE'S MESSES. HECK, AFTER FLASH PLUNGED THE GEM CITIES INTO DARKNESS, IT WAS YOU WHO LITERALLY BROUGHT BACK THE LIGHT.
I DON'T DO IT FOR THE ACCOLADES...
COME ON, YOU INVENTED AN ENTIRELY NEW ENERGY SOURCE THAT IS GOING TO KEEP THE LIGHTS ON FOR A HUNDRED YEARS. THAT'S HUGE!
THAT WAS PRETTY GOOD, WASN'T IT?
YOU'VE BEEN ON A TEAR...NOW YOU'VE GOT THIS BRAND-NEW MONORAIL OPENING UP...SERIOUSLY, WHAT'S GOTTEN INTO YOU?
LOOK, WHAT THE CITY NEEDS IS PRACTICAL SOLUTIONS. ENERGY THAT WILL MAKE OUR CITY SELF-SUFFICIENT IS JUST THE START. I'M NOT ONE TO CAST STONES...BUT IT'S NO COINCIDENCE THAT CENTRAL CITY HAS SEEN MORE PROGRESS IN THE MONTHS SINCE FLASH'S TRAGIC DISAPPEARANCE THAN TOOK PLACE IN THE FIVE YEARS HE "WATCHED OVER US."
I'VE DONE MY RESEARCH, HATCH, AND THE DATA ARE CLEAR...ALL VIGILANTISM DOES IS BRING OUT THE WORST IN SOCIETY. WE HAVE LAWS. WE HAVE CODES OF CONDUCT...
AND NO ONE... NOT EVEN THE SCARLET SPEEDSTER... IS ABOVE THEM.
IF THIS IS TRUE, THEN WHAT IS THE SOLUTION FOR THE PROBLEMS THAT ARE TOO BIG FOR LAW ENFORCEMENT TO HANDLE?
THE SIMPLE ANSWER-- ME.
BUT NOT JUST ME. I'M TALKING ABOUT ALL OF US. ORDINARY CITIZENS WHO ARE WILLING TO PULL THEIR WEIGHT AND SEE OUR GREAT CITY INTO THE FUTURE...IT'S TIME WE GIVE THE POWER BACK TO THE PEOPLE.

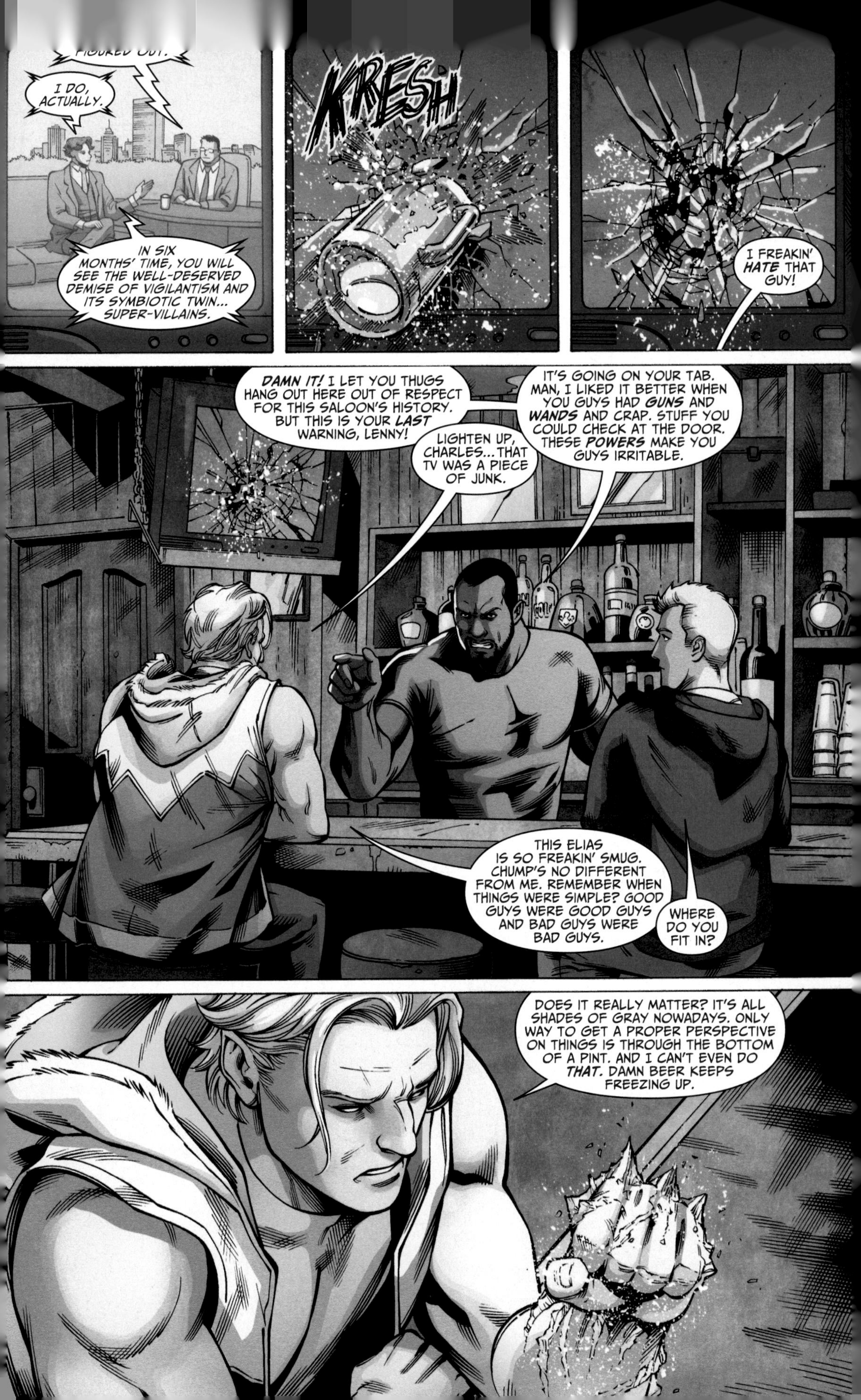
I DO, ACTUALLY.
IN SIX MONTHS' TIME, YOU WILL SEE THE WELL-DESERVED DEMISE OF VIGILANTISM AND ITS SYMBIOTIC TWIN... SUPER-VILLAINS.
KRESH
I FREAKIN' HATE THAT GUY!
DAMN IT! I LET YOU THUGS HANG OUT HERE OUT OF RESPECT FOR THIS SALOON'S HISTORY. BUT THIS IS YOUR LAST WARNING, LENNY!
LIGHTEN UP, CHARLES... THAT TV WAS A PIECE OF JUNK.
IT'S GOING ON YOUR TAB. MAN, I LIKED IT BETTER WHEN YOU GUYS HAD GUNS AND WANDS AND CRAP. STUFF YOU COULD CHECK AT THE DOOR. THESE POWERS MAKE YOU GUYS IRRITABLE.
THIS ELIAS IS SO FREAKIN' SMUG. CHUMP'S NO DIFFERENT FROM ME. REMEMBER WHEN THINGS WERE SIMPLE? GOOD GUYS WERE GOOD GUYS AND BAD GUYS WERE BAD GUYS.
WHERE DO YOU FIT IN?
DOES IT REALLY MATTER? IT'S ALL SHADES OF GRAY NOWADAYS. ONLY WAY TO GET A PROPER PERSPECTIVE ON THINGS IS THROUGH THE BOTTOM OF A PINT. AND I CAN'T EVEN DO THAT. DAMN BEER KEEPS FREEZING UP.

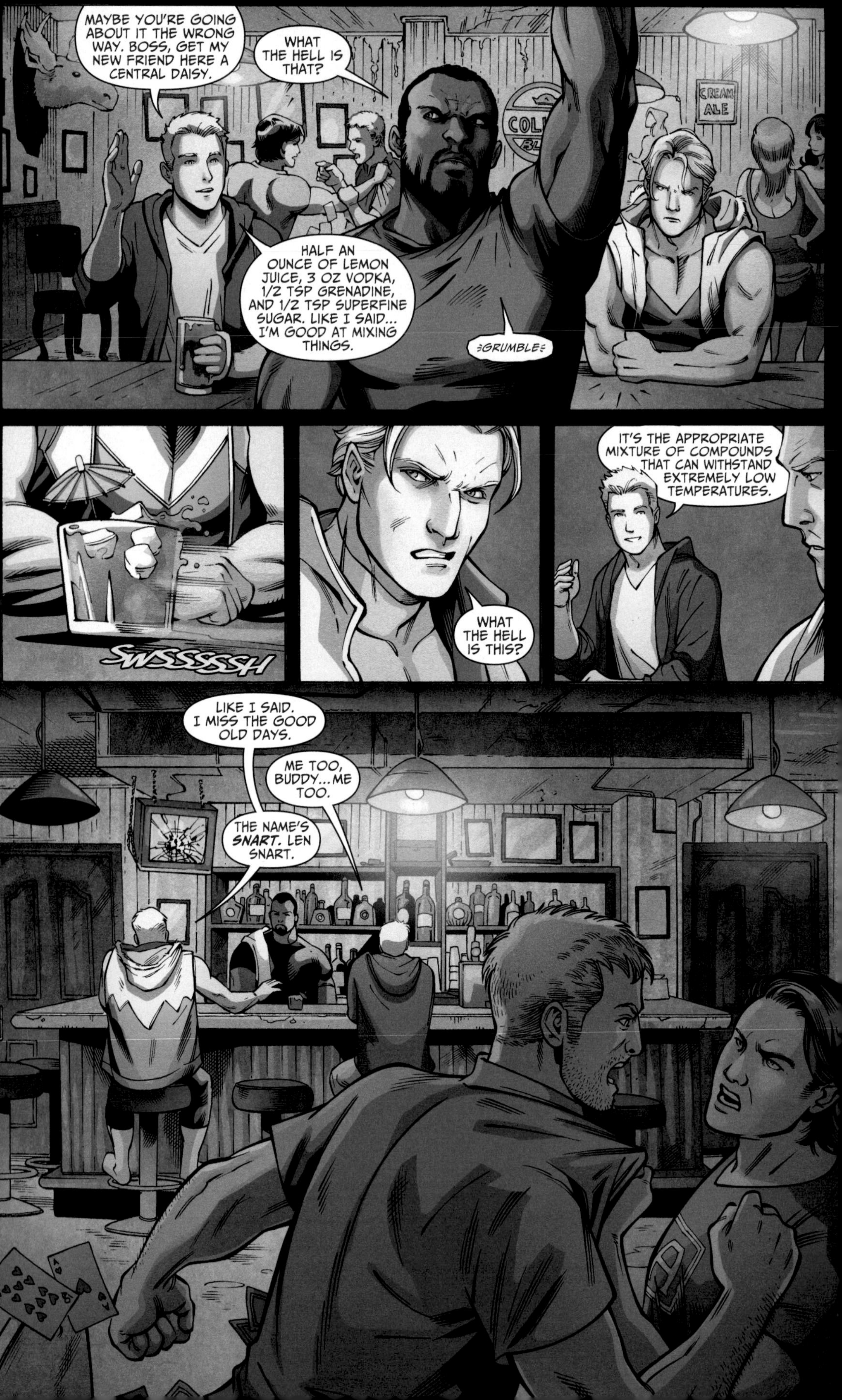
MAYBE YOU'RE GOING ABOUT IT THE WRONG WAY. BOSS, GET MY NEW FRIEND HERE A CENTRAL DAISY.
WHAT THE HELL IS THAT?
HALF AN OUNCE OF LEMON JUICE, 3 OZ VODKA, 1/2 TSP GRENADINE, AND 1/2 TSP SUPERFINE SUGAR. LIKE I SAID... I'M GOOD AT MIXING THINGS.
GRUMBLE
SWSSSSSH
WHAT THE HELL IS THIS?
IT'S THE APPROPRIATE MIXTURE OF COMPOUNDS THAT CAN WITHSTAND EXTREMELY LOW TEMPERATURES.
LIKE I SAID. I MISS THE GOOD OLD DAYS.
ME TOO, BUDDY...ME TOO.
THE NAME'S SNART. LEN SNART.

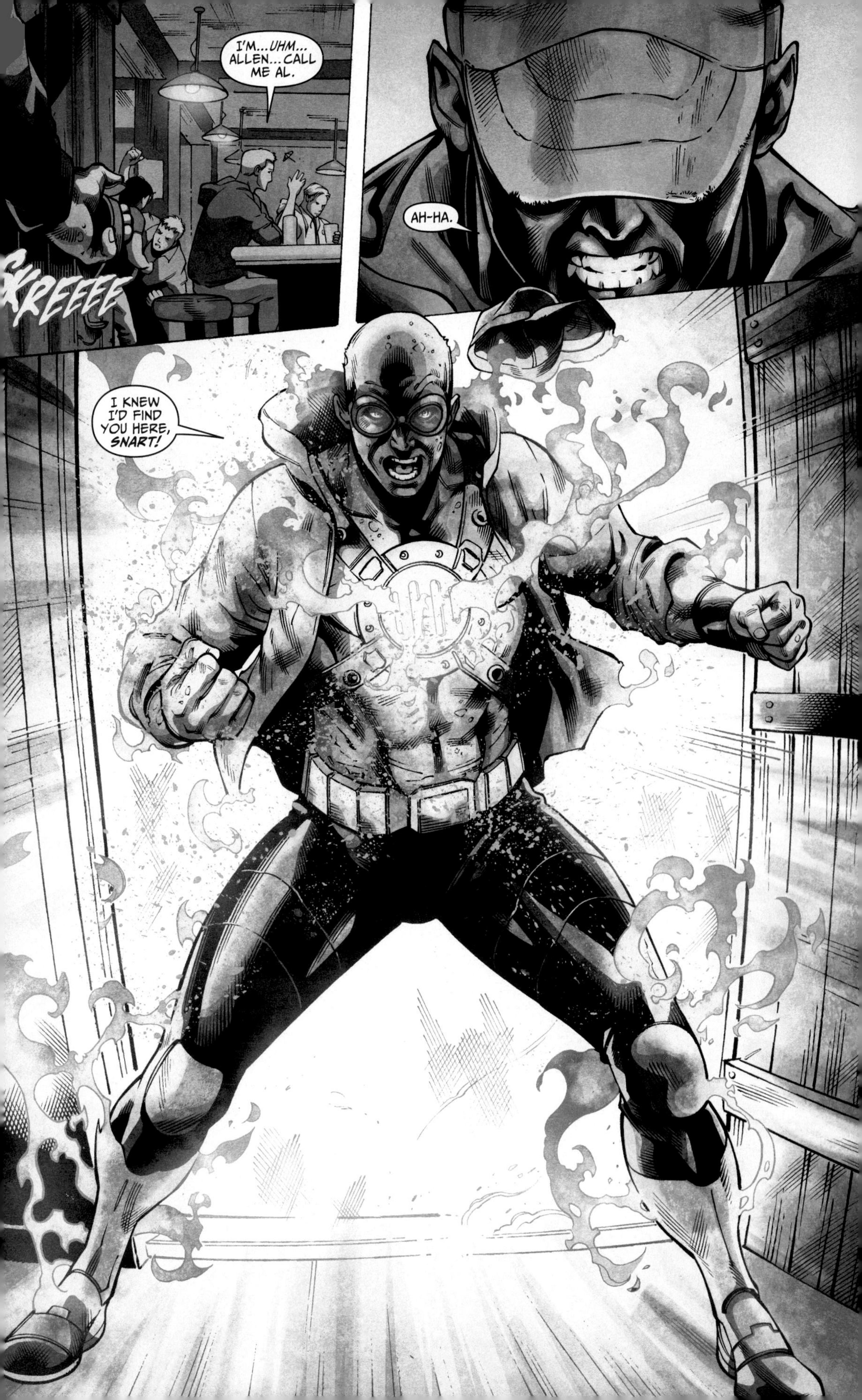
I'M...UHM... ALLEN...CALL ME AL.
AH-HA.
I KNEW I'D FIND YOU HERE, SNART!

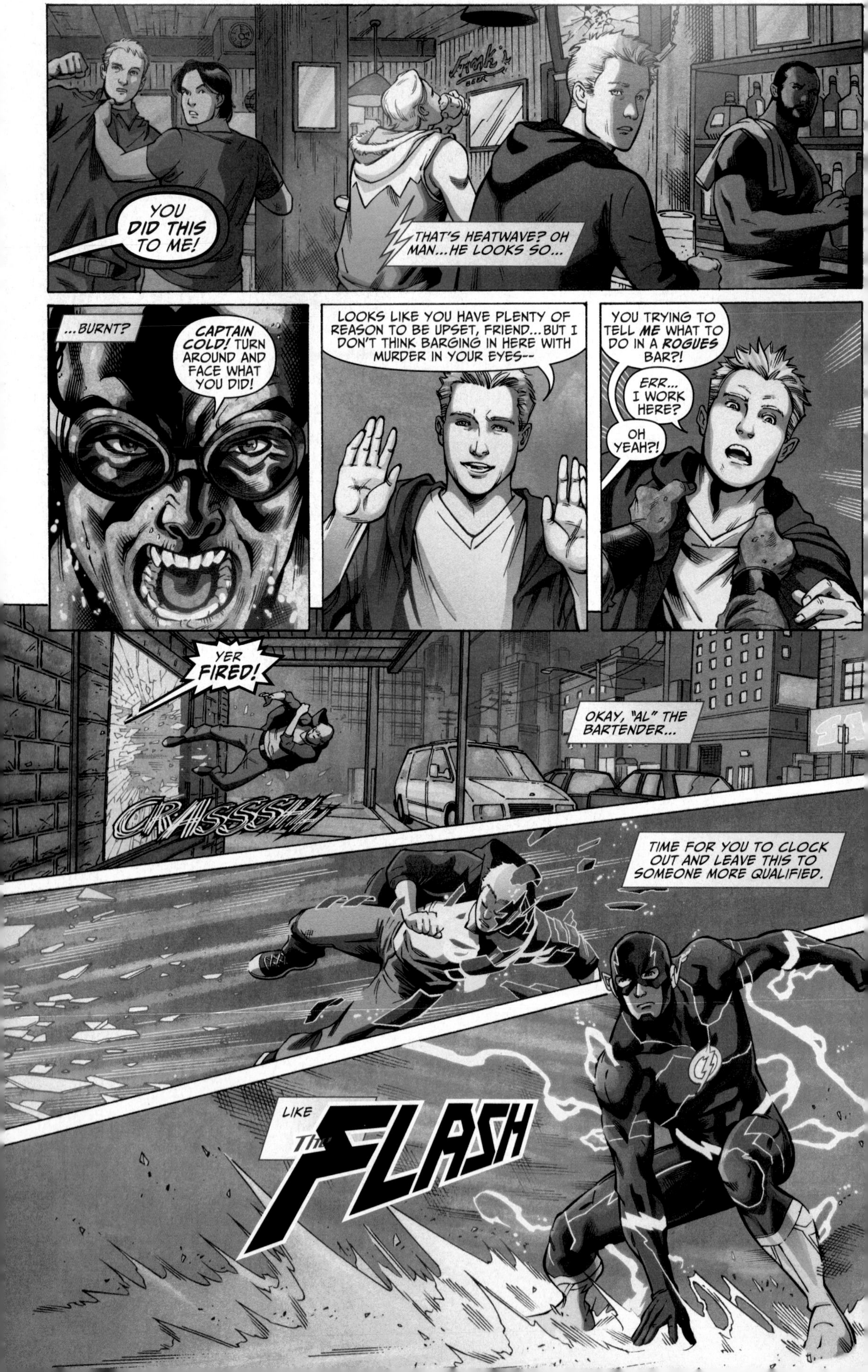
YOU DID THIS TO ME!
THAT'S HEATWAVE? OH MAN...HE LOOKS SO...
...BURNT?
CAPTAIN COLD! TURN AROUND AND FACE WHAT YOU DID!
LOOKS LIKE YOU HAVE PLENTY OF REASON TO BE UPSET, FRIEND...BUT I DON'T THINK BARGING IN HERE WITH MURDER IN YOUR EYES--
YOU TRYING TO TELL ME WHAT TO DO IN A ROGUES BAR?!
ERR... I WORK HERE?
OH YEAH?!
YER FIRED!
CRASSSSH
OKAY, "AL" THE BARTENDER...
TIME FOR YOU TO CLOCK OUT AND LEAVE THIS TO SOMEONE MORE QUALIFIED.
LIKE THE FLASH

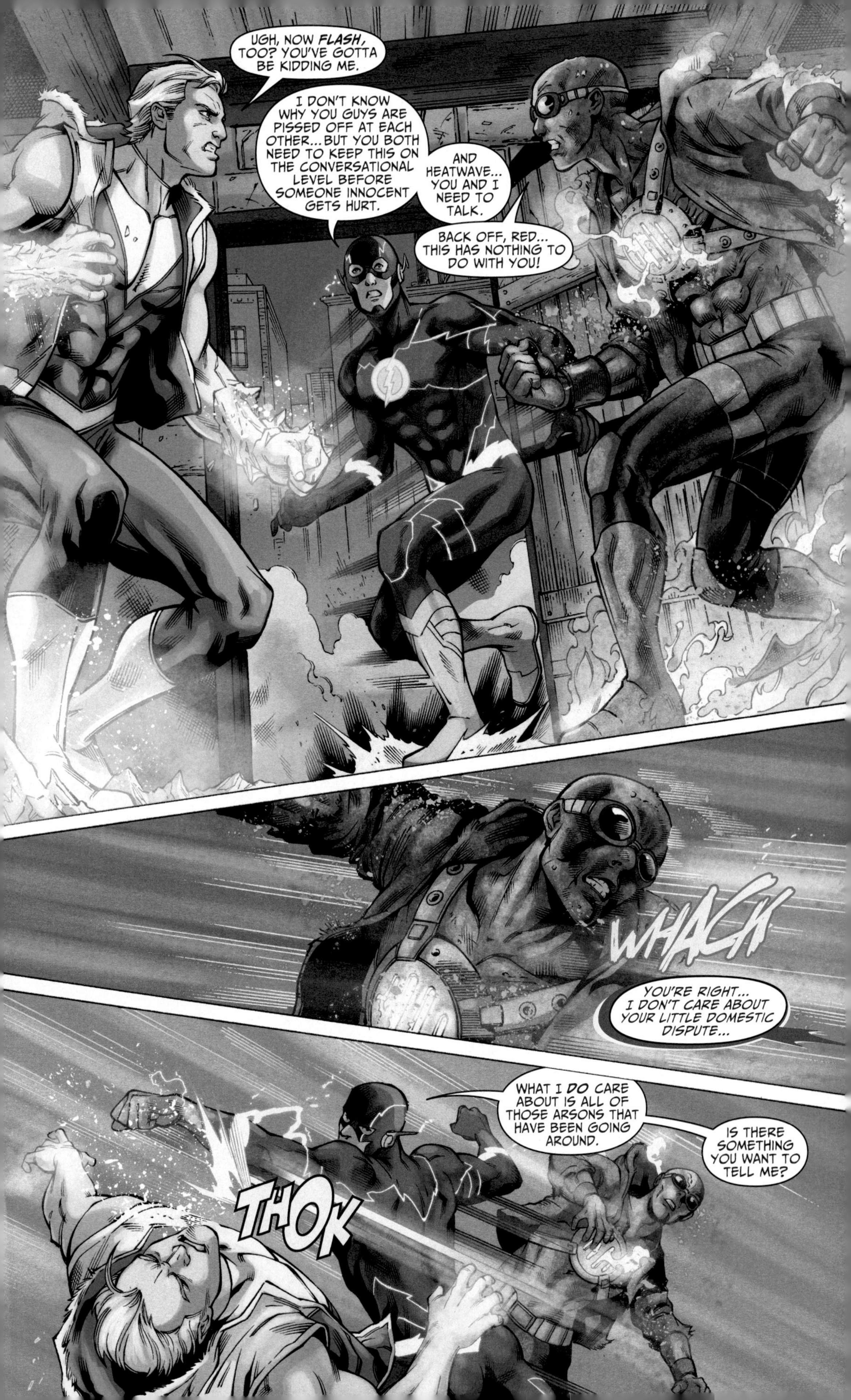
UGH, NOW FLASH, TOO? YOU'VE GOTTA BE KIDDING ME.
I DON'T KNOW WHY YOU GUYS ARE PISSED OFF AT EACH OTHER... BUT YOU BOTH NEED TO KEEP THIS ON THE CONVERSATIONAL LEVEL BEFORE SOMEONE INNOCENT GETS HURT.
AND HEATWAVE... YOU AND I NEED TO TALK.
BACK OFF, RED... THIS HAS NOTHING TO DO WITH YOU!
WHACK
YOU'RE RIGHT... I DON'T CARE ABOUT YOUR LITTLE DOMESTIC DISPUTE...
WHAT I DO CARE ABOUT IS ALL OF THOSE ARSONS THAT HAVE BEEN GOING AROUND.
IS THERE SOMETHING YOU WANT TO TELL ME?
THOK

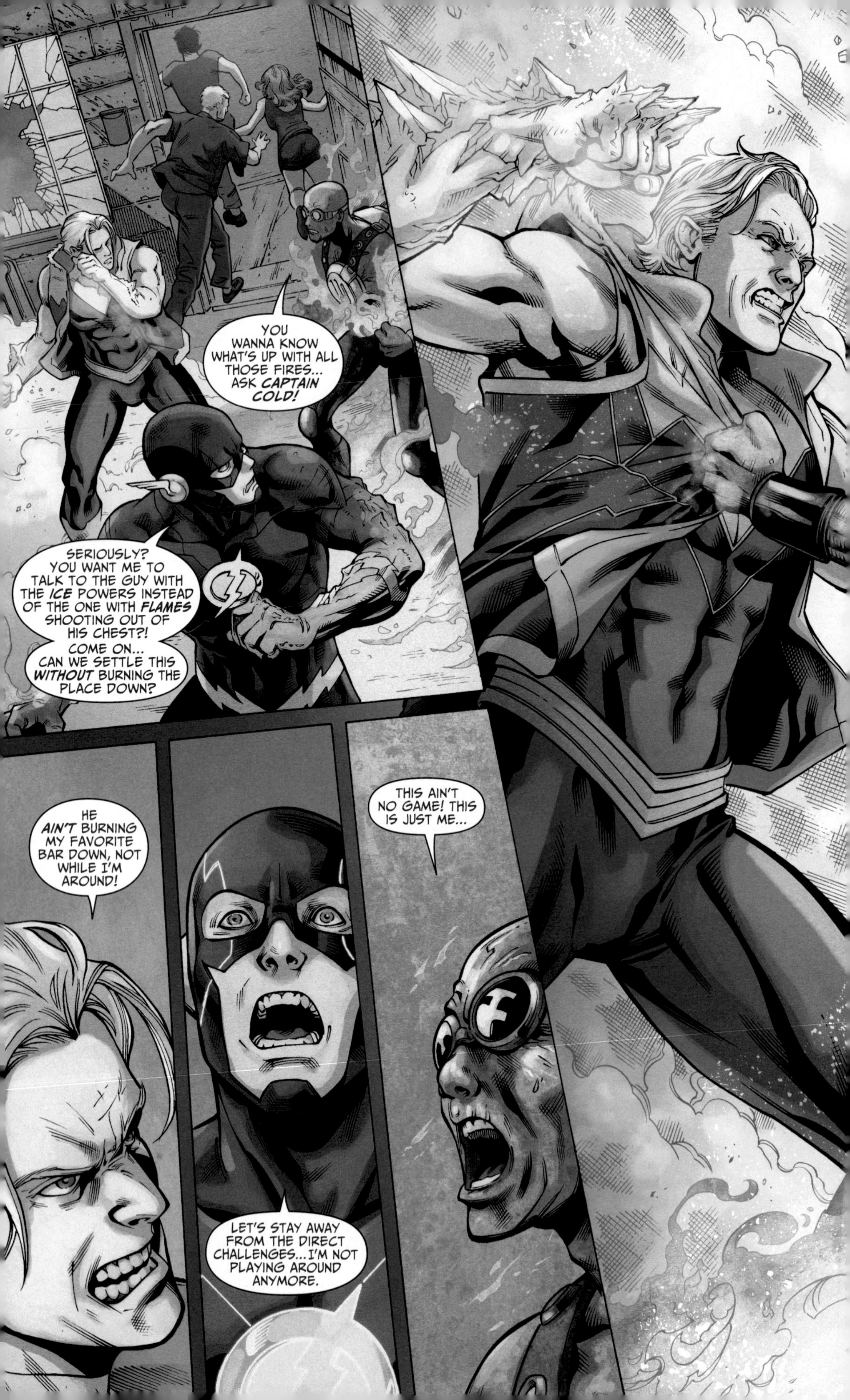
YOU WANNA KNOW WHAT'S UP WITH ALL THOSE FIRES... ASK CAPTAIN COLD!
SERIOUSLY? YOU WANT ME TO TALK TO THE GUY WITH THE ICE POWERS INSTEAD OF THE ONE WITH FLAMES SHOOTING OUT OF HIS CHEST?!
COME ON... CAN WE SETTLE THIS WITHOUT BURNING THE PLACE DOWN?
HE AIN'T BURNING MY FAVORITE BAR DOWN, NOT WHILE I'M AROUND!
LET'S STAY AWAY FROM THE DIRECT CHALLENGES...I'M NOT PLAYING AROUND ANYMORE.
THIS AIN'T NO GAME! THIS IS JUST ME...

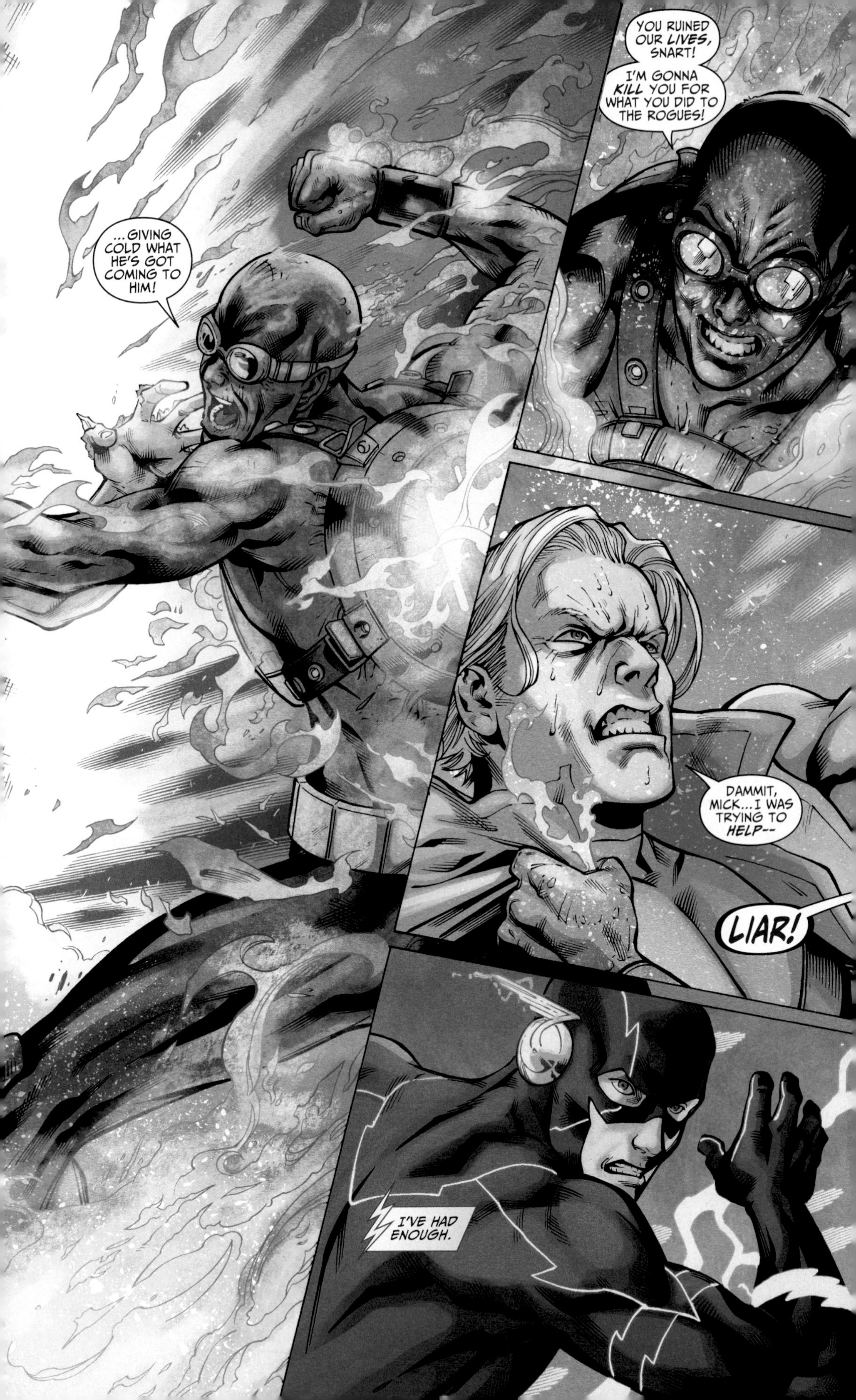

...GIVING COLD WHAT HE'S GOT COMING TO HIM!
YOU RUINED OUR *LIVES*, SNART!
I'M GONNA *KILL* YOU FOR WHAT YOU DID TO THE ROGUES!
DAMMIT, MICK...I WAS TRYING TO *HELP*--
LIAR!
I'VE HAD ENOUGH.

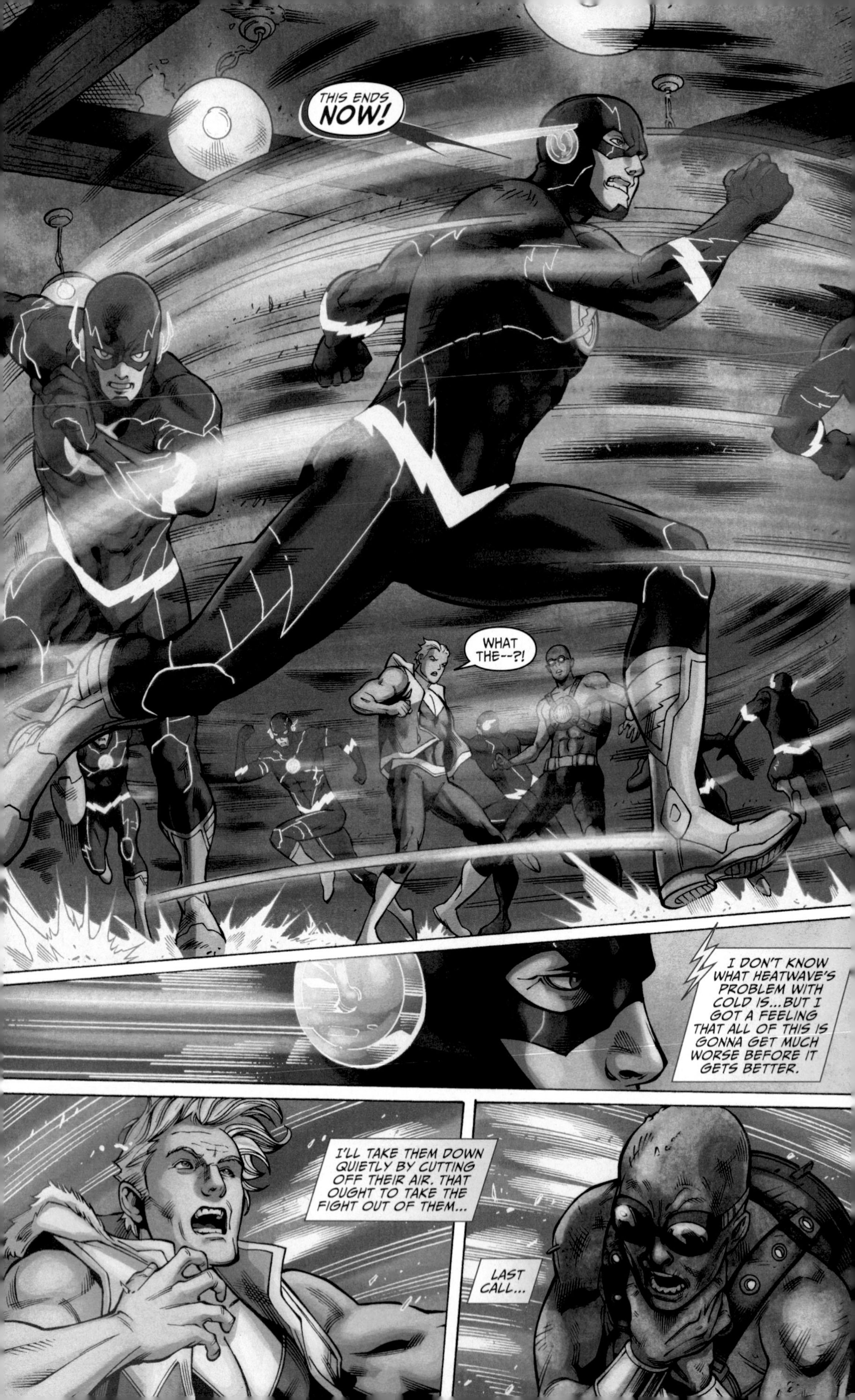
THIS ENDS NOW!
WHAT THE--?!
I DON'T KNOW WHAT HEATWAVE'S PROBLEM WITH COLD IS...BUT I GOT A FEELING THAT ALL OF THIS IS GONNA GET MUCH WORSE BEFORE IT GETS BETTER.
I'LL TAKE THEM DOWN QUIETLY BY CUTTING OFF THEIR AIR. THAT OUGHT TO TAKE THE FIGHT OUT OF THEM...
LAST CALL...

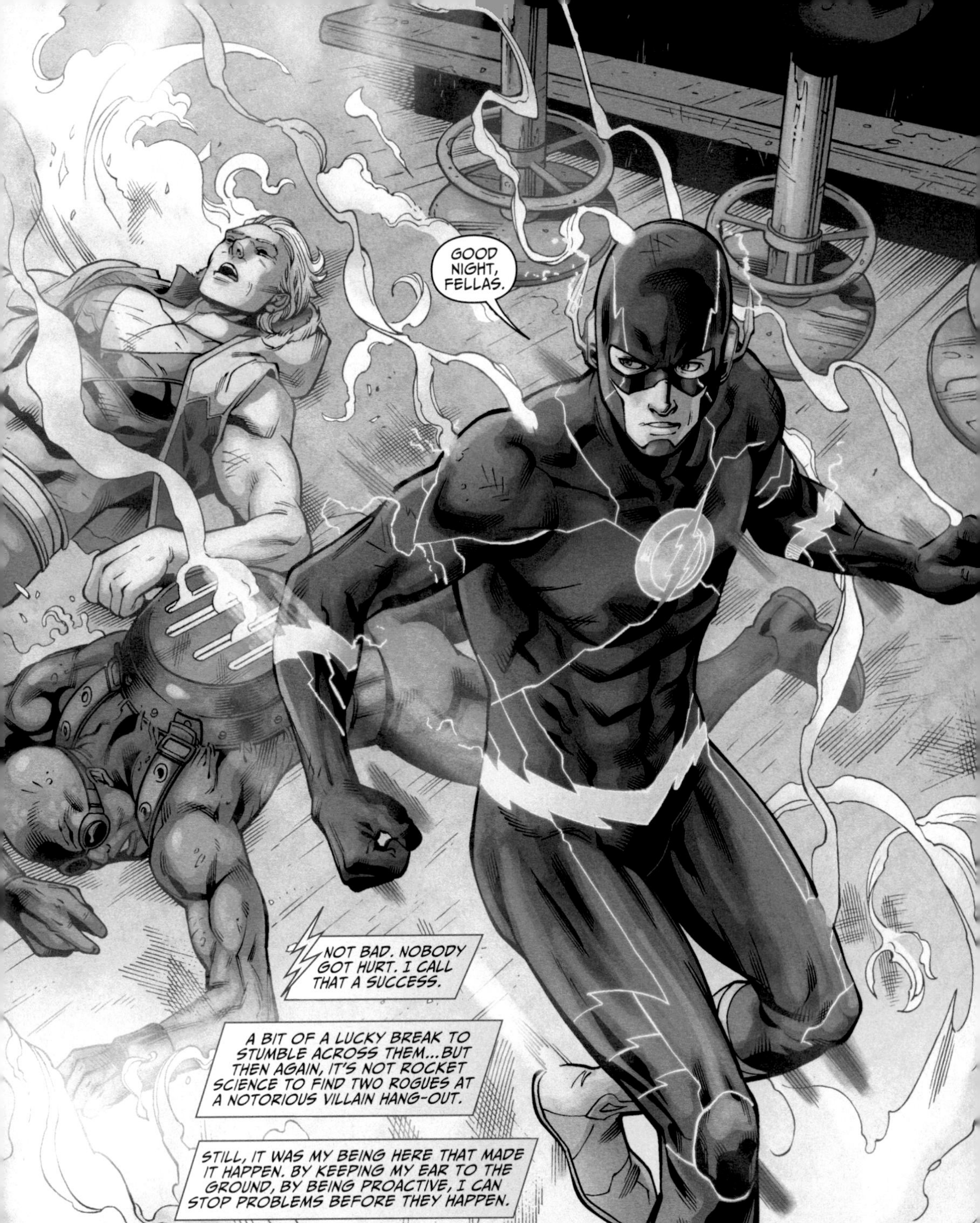
GOOD NIGHT, FELLAS.
NOT BAD. NOBODY GOT HURT. I CALL THAT A SUCCESS.
A BIT OF A LUCKY BREAK TO STUMBLE ACROSS THEM...BUT THEN AGAIN, IT'S NOT ROCKET SCIENCE TO FIND TWO ROGUES AT A NOTORIOUS VILLAIN HANG-OUT.
STILL, IT WAS MY BEING HERE THAT MADE IT HAPPEN. BY KEEPING MY EAR TO THE GROUND, BY BEING PROACTIVE, I CAN STOP PROBLEMS BEFORE THEY HAPPEN.

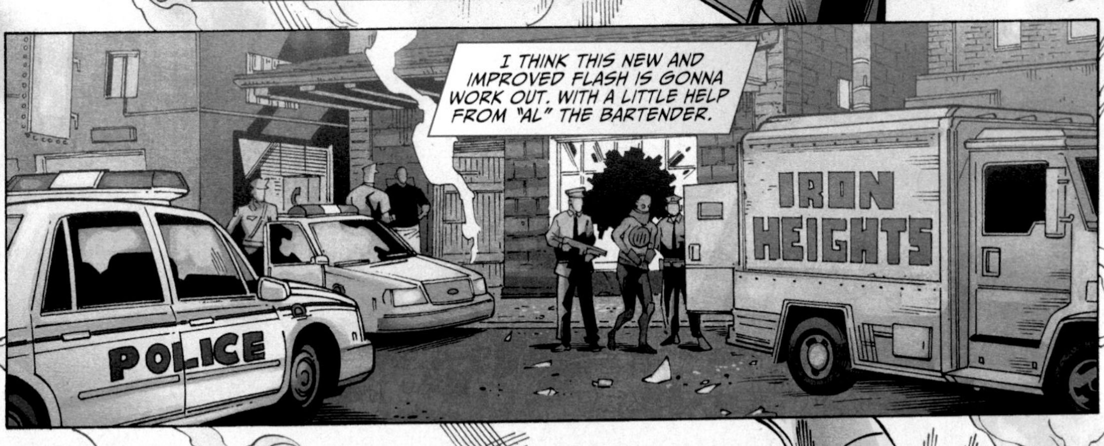
I THINK THIS NEW AND IMPROVED FLASH IS GONNA WORK OUT. WITH A LITTLE HELP FROM "AL" THE BARTENDER.
IRON HEIGHTS
POLICE

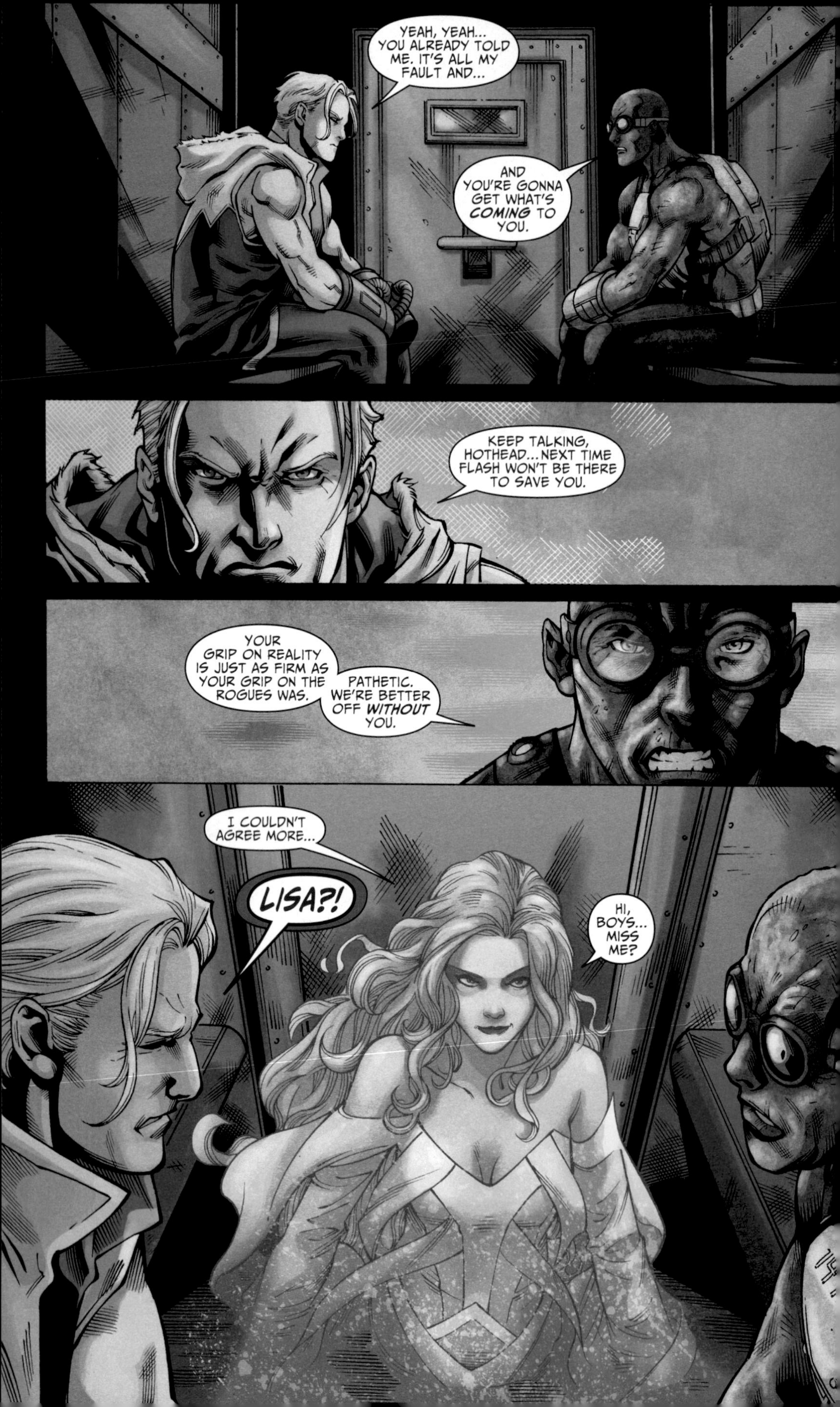
YEAH, YEAH... YOU ALREADY TOLD ME. IT'S ALL MY FAULT AND...
AND YOU'RE GONNA GET WHAT'S *COMING* TO YOU.
KEEP TALKING, HOTHEAD...NEXT TIME FLASH WON'T BE THERE TO SAVE YOU.
YOUR GRIP ON REALITY IS JUST AS FIRM AS YOUR GRIP ON THE ROGUES WAS.
PATHETIC. WE'RE BETTER OFF *WITHOUT* YOU.
I COULDN'T AGREE MORE...
LISA?!
HI, BOYS... MISS ME?

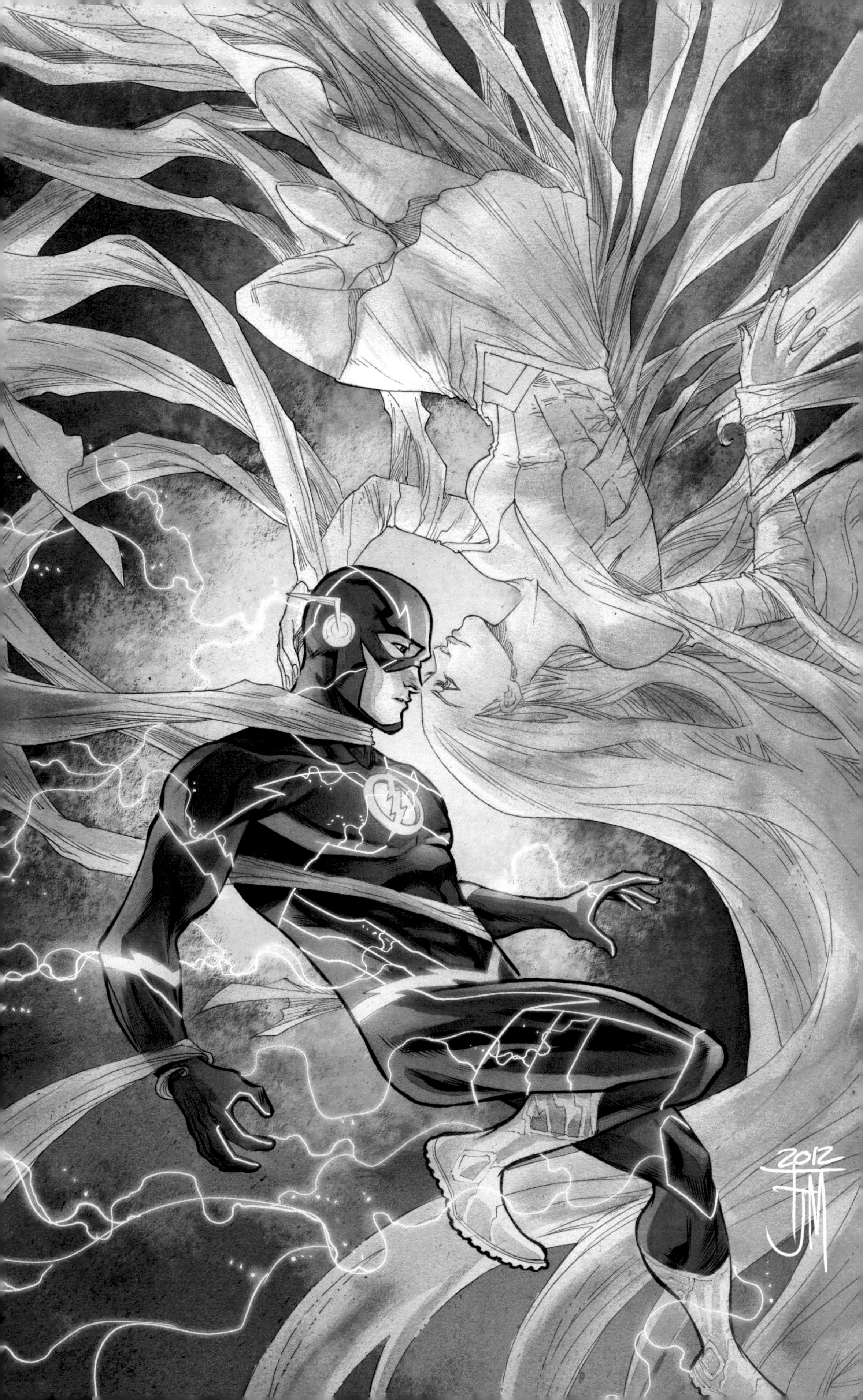
2012

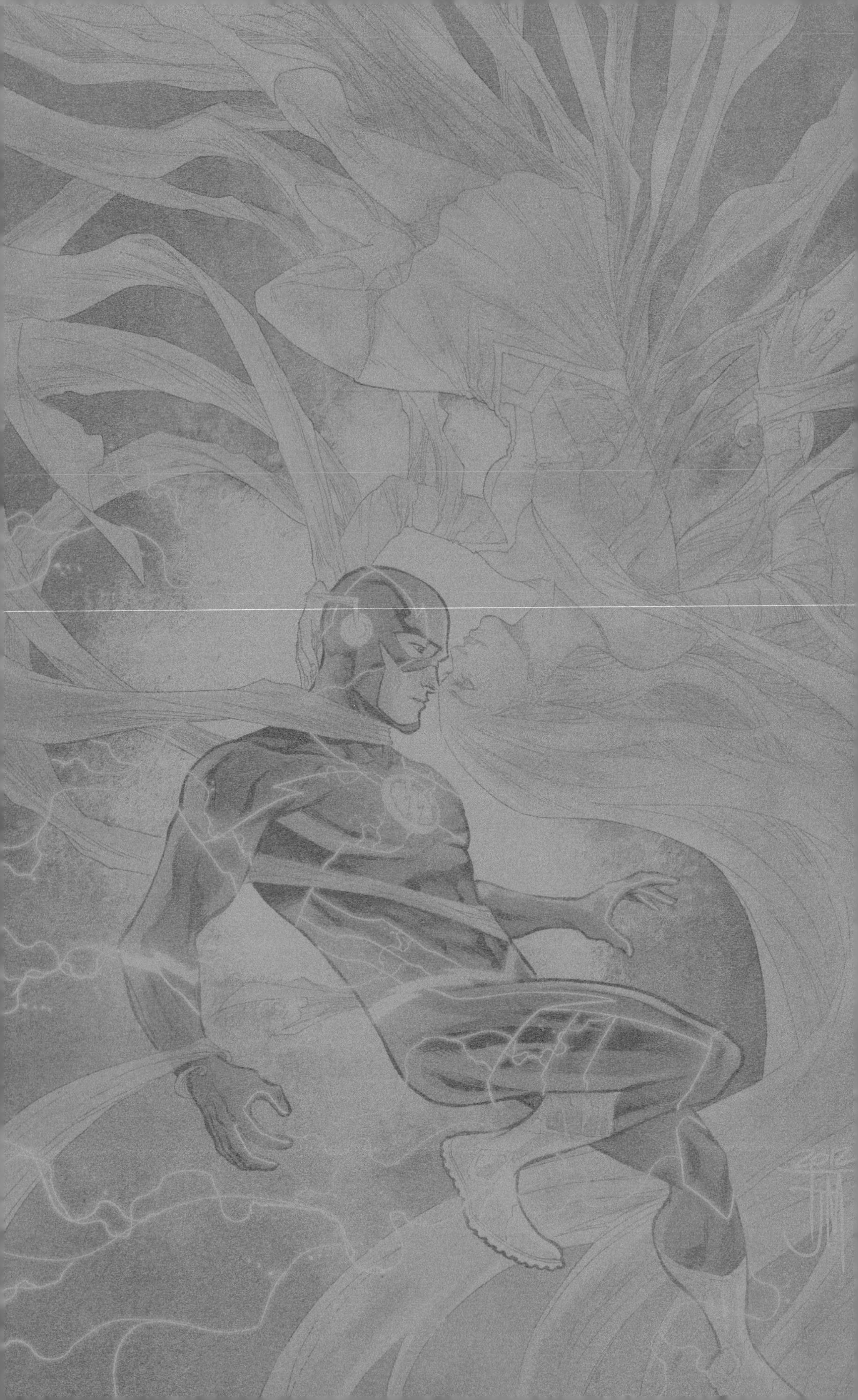

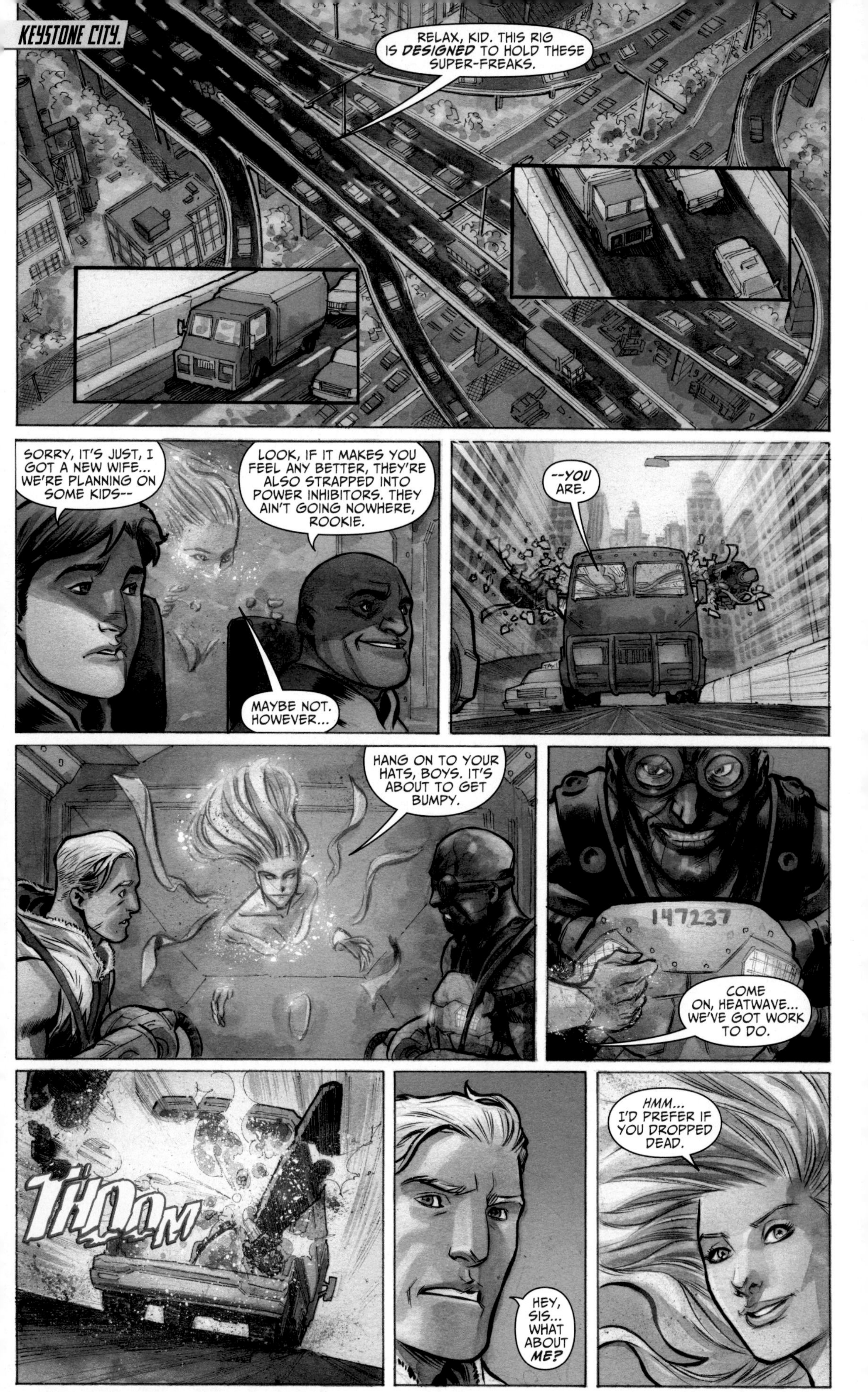
KEYSTONE CITY.
RELAX, KID. THIS RIG IS DESIGNED TO HOLD THESE SUPER-FREAKS.
SORRY, IT'S JUST, I GOT A NEW WIFE... WE'RE PLANNING ON SOME KIDS--
LOOK, IF IT MAKES YOU FEEL ANY BETTER, THEY'RE ALSO STRAPPED INTO POWER INHIBITORS. THEY AIN'T GOING NOWHERE, ROOKIE.
MAYBE NOT. HOWEVER...
--YOU ARE.
HANG ON TO YOUR HATS, BOYS. IT'S ABOUT TO GET BUMPY.
147237
COME ON, HEATWAVE... WE'VE GOT WORK TO DO.
THOOM
HEY, SIS... WHAT ABOUT ME?
HMM... I'D PREFER IF YOU DROPPED DEAD.

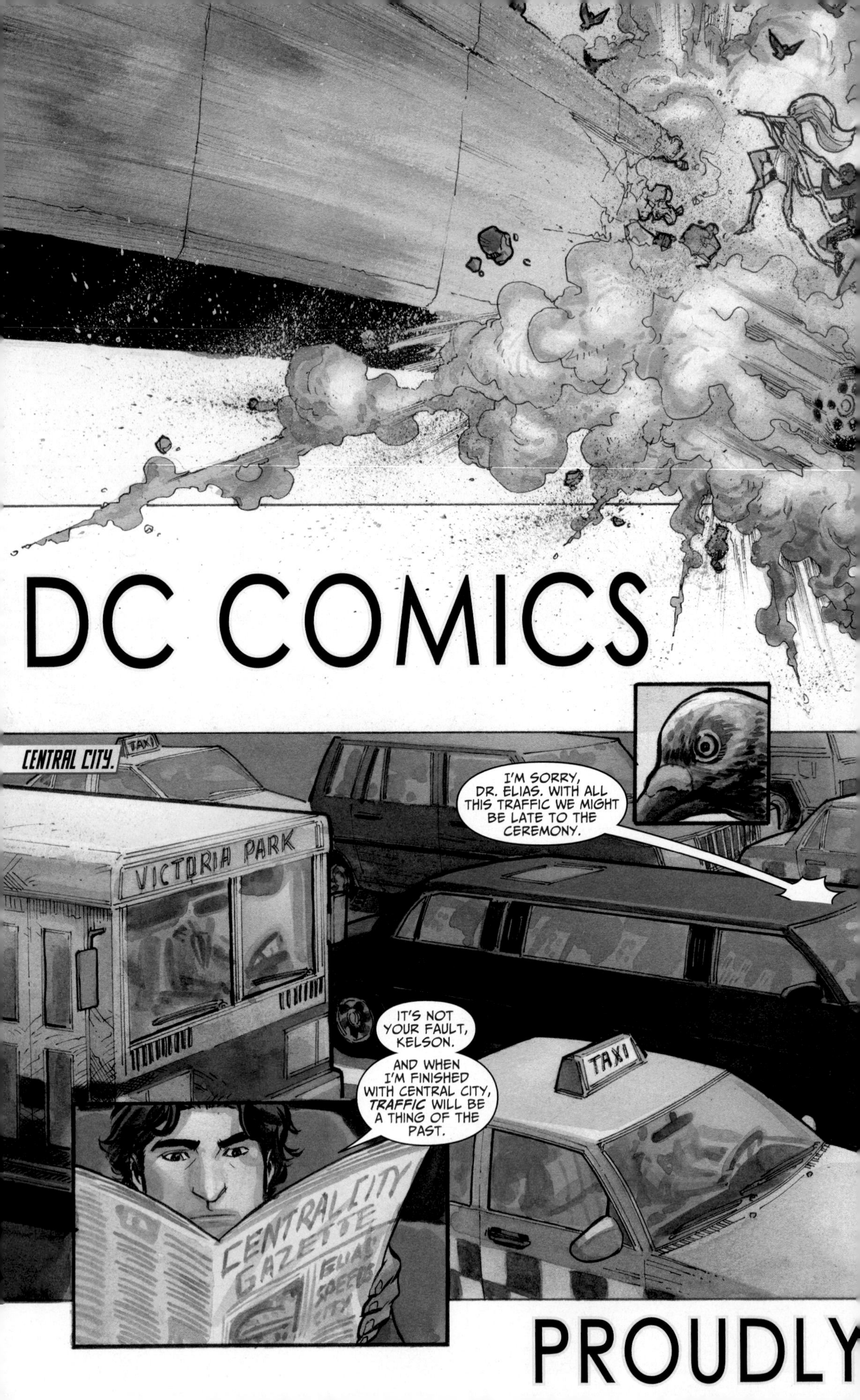

DC COMICS
CENTRAL CITY.
TAXI
VICTORIA PARK
I'M SORRY, DR. ELIAS. WITH ALL THIS TRAFFIC WE MIGHT BE LATE TO THE CEREMONY.
IT'S NOT YOUR FAULT, KELSON.
AND WHEN I'M FINISHED WITH CENTRAL CITY, *TRAFFIC* WILL BE A THING OF THE PAST.
TAXI
CENTRAL CITY GAZETTE
PROUDLY

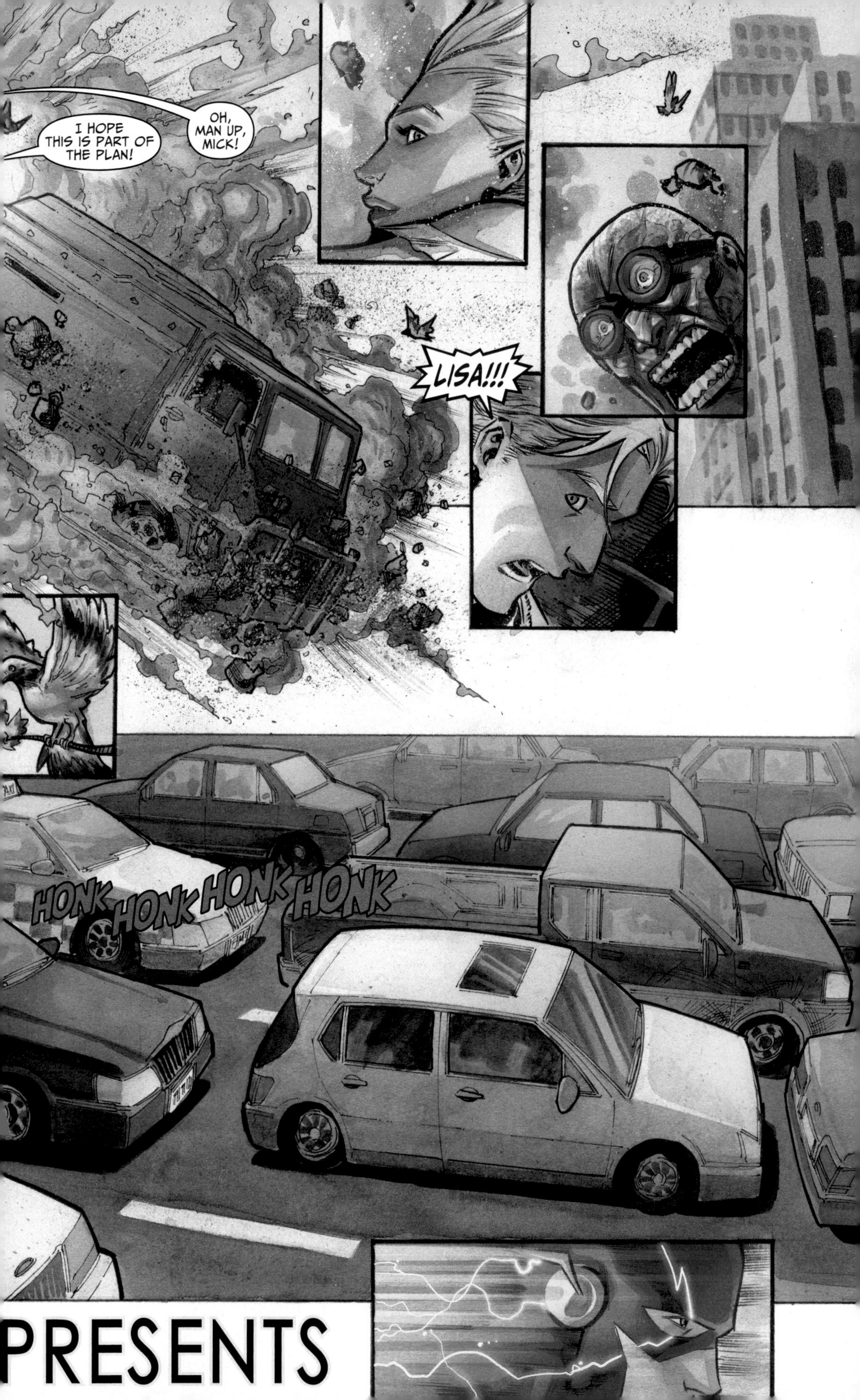
I HOPE THIS IS PART OF THE PLAN!
OH, MAN UP, MICK!
LISA!!!
HONK HONK HONK HONK
PRESENTS

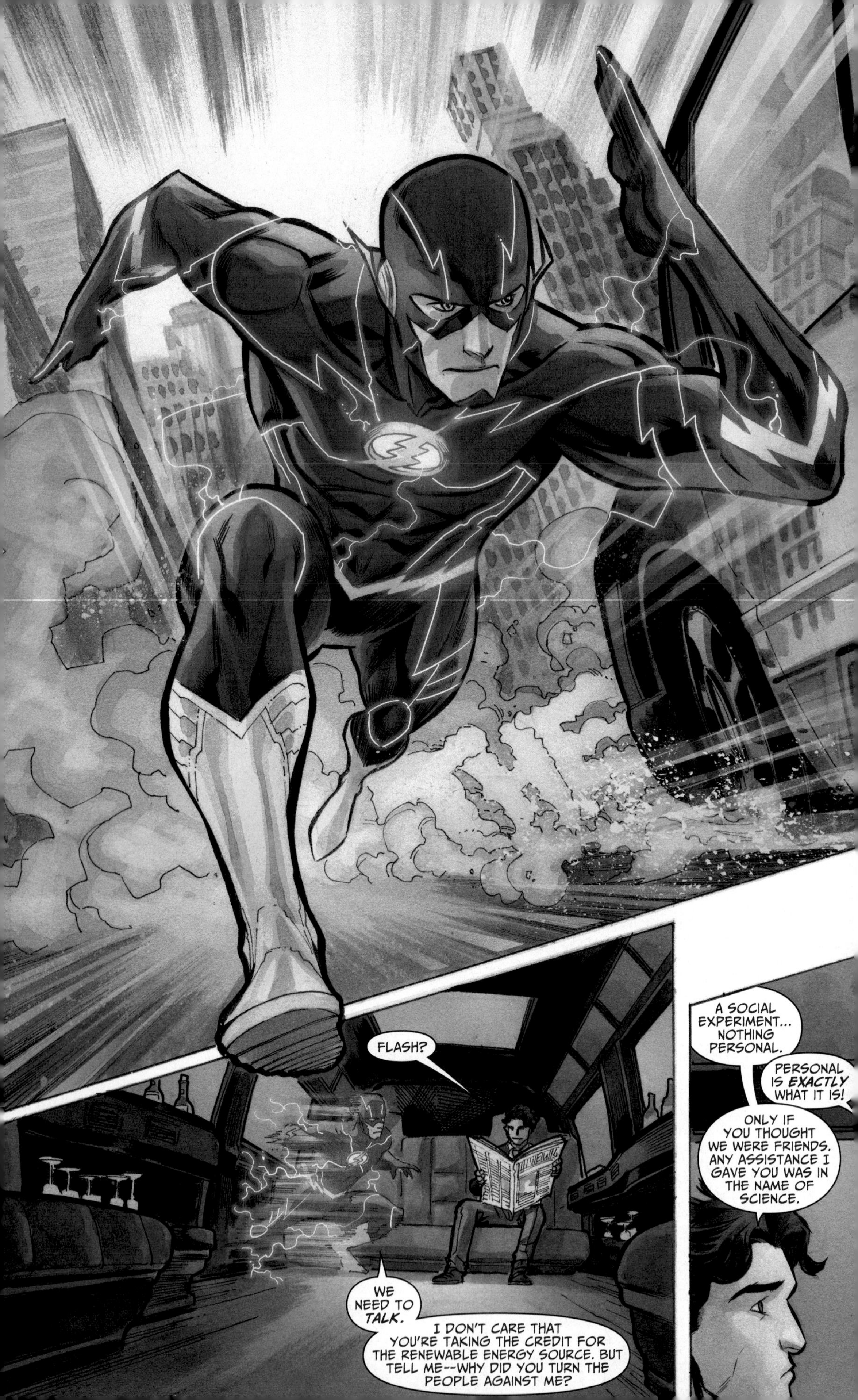
FLASH?
WE NEED TO TALK.
I DON'T CARE THAT YOU'RE TAKING THE CREDIT FOR THE RENEWABLE ENERGY SOURCE. BUT TELL ME--WHY DID YOU TURN THE PEOPLE AGAINST ME?
A SOCIAL EXPERIMENT... NOTHING PERSONAL.
PERSONAL IS EXACTLY WHAT IT IS!
ONLY IF YOU THOUGHT WE WERE FRIENDS. ANY ASSISTANCE I GAVE YOU WAS IN THE NAME OF SCIENCE.

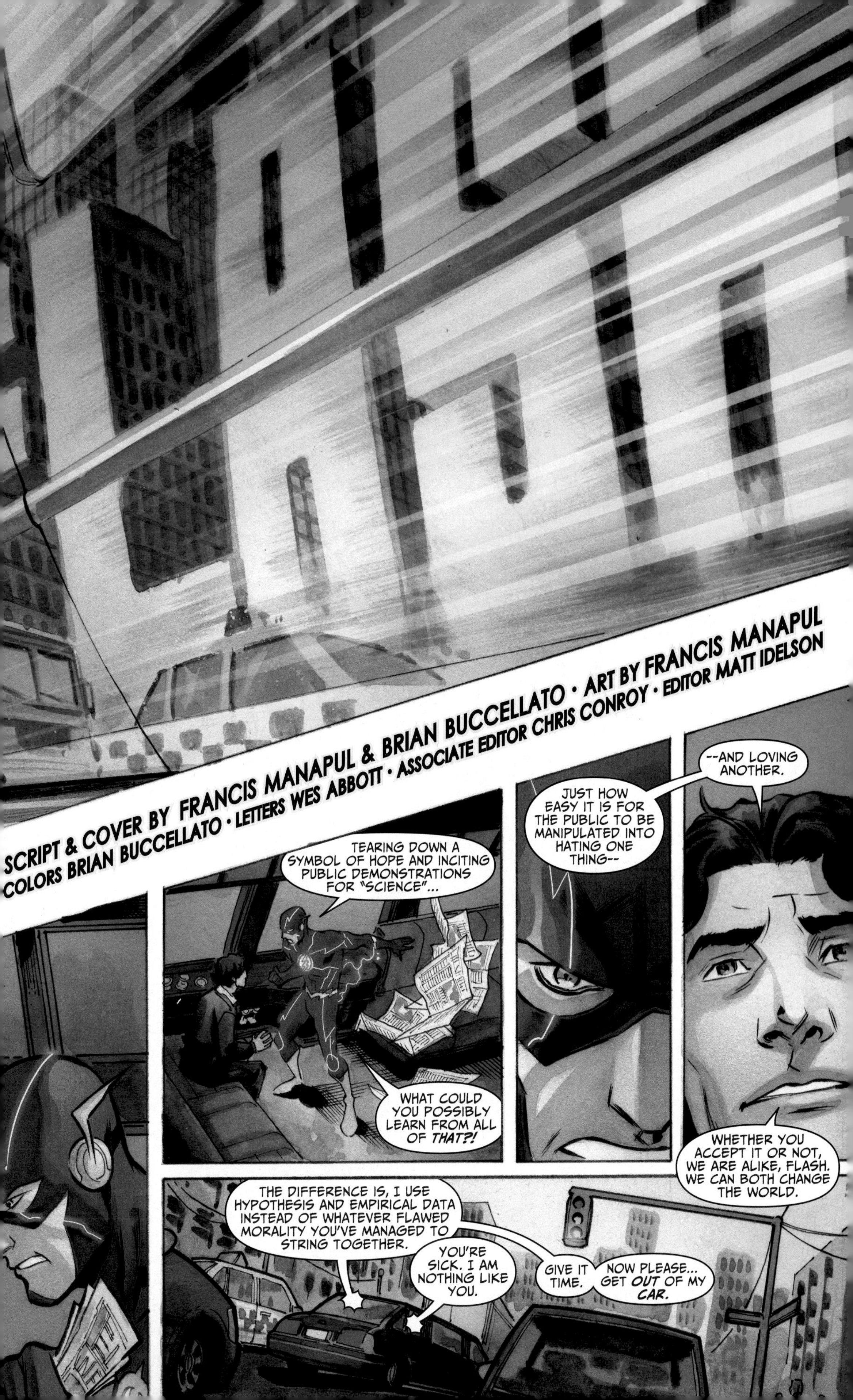
SCRIPT & COVER BY FRANCIS MANAPUL & BRIAN BUCCELLATO · ART BY FRANCIS MANAPUL
COLORS BRIAN BUCCELLATO · LETTERS WES ABBOTT · ASSOCIATE EDITOR CHRIS CONROY · EDITOR MATT IDELSON
TEARING DOWN A SYMBOL OF HOPE AND INCITING PUBLIC DEMONSTRATIONS FOR "SCIENCE"...
WHAT COULD YOU POSSIBLY LEARN FROM ALL OF THAT?!
JUST HOW EASY IT IS FOR THE PUBLIC TO BE MANIPULATED INTO HATING ONE THING--
--AND LOVING ANOTHER.
WHETHER YOU ACCEPT IT OR NOT, WE ARE ALIKE, FLASH. WE CAN BOTH CHANGE THE WORLD.
THE DIFFERENCE IS, I USE HYPOTHESIS AND EMPIRICAL DATA INSTEAD OF WHATEVER FLAWED MORALITY YOU'VE MANAGED TO STRING TOGETHER.
YOU'RE SICK. I AM NOTHING LIKE YOU.
GIVE IT TIME.
NOW PLEASE... GET OUT OF MY CAR.

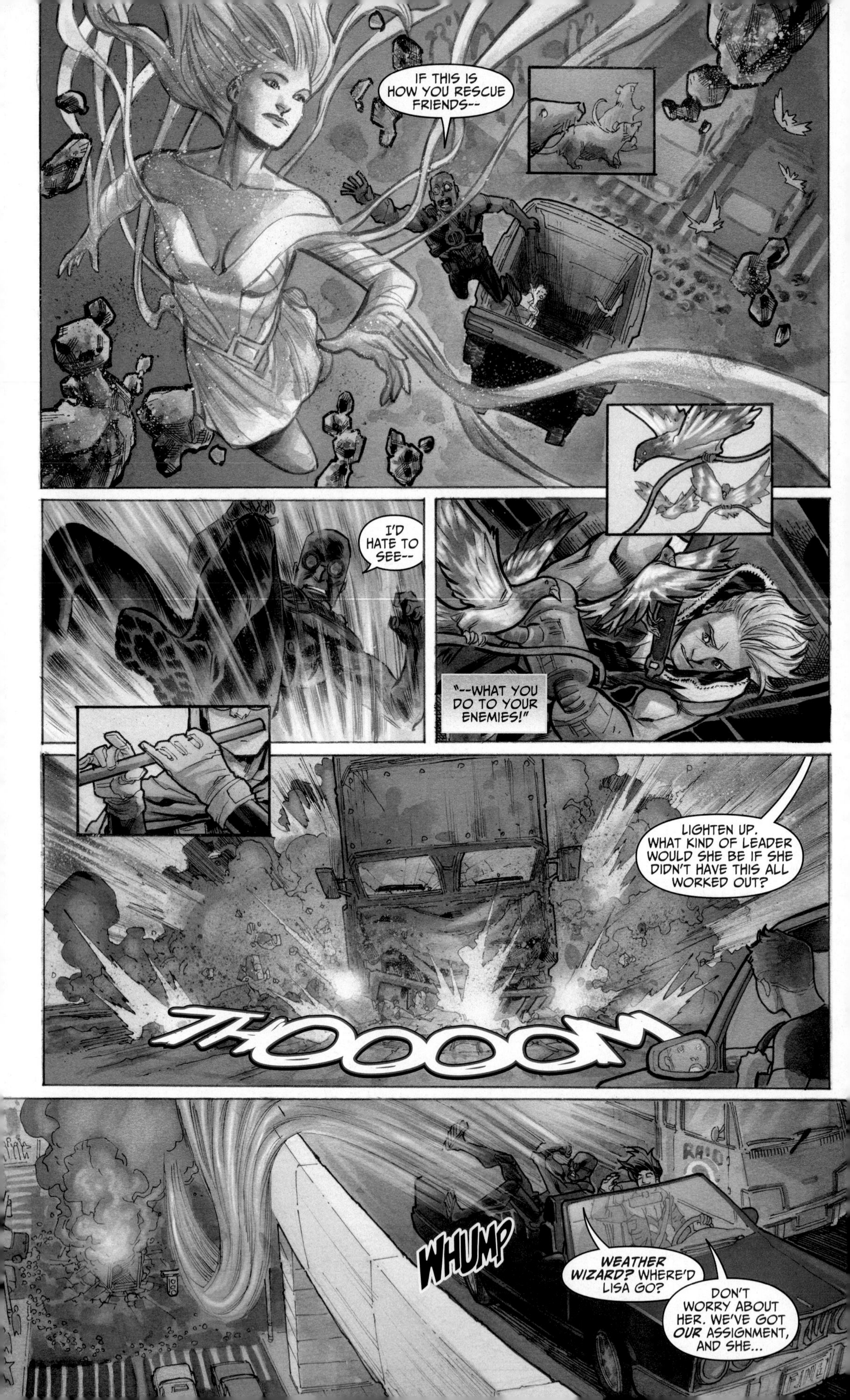
IF THIS IS HOW YOU RESCUE FRIENDS--
I'D HATE TO SEE--
"--WHAT YOU DO TO YOUR ENEMIES!"
LIGHTEN UP. WHAT KIND OF LEADER WOULD SHE BE IF SHE DIDN'T HAVE THIS ALL WORKED OUT?
THOOOOM
WHUMP
WEATHER WIZARD? WHERE'D LISA GO?
DON'T WORRY ABOUT HER. WE'VE GOT *OUR* ASSIGNMENT, AND SHE...

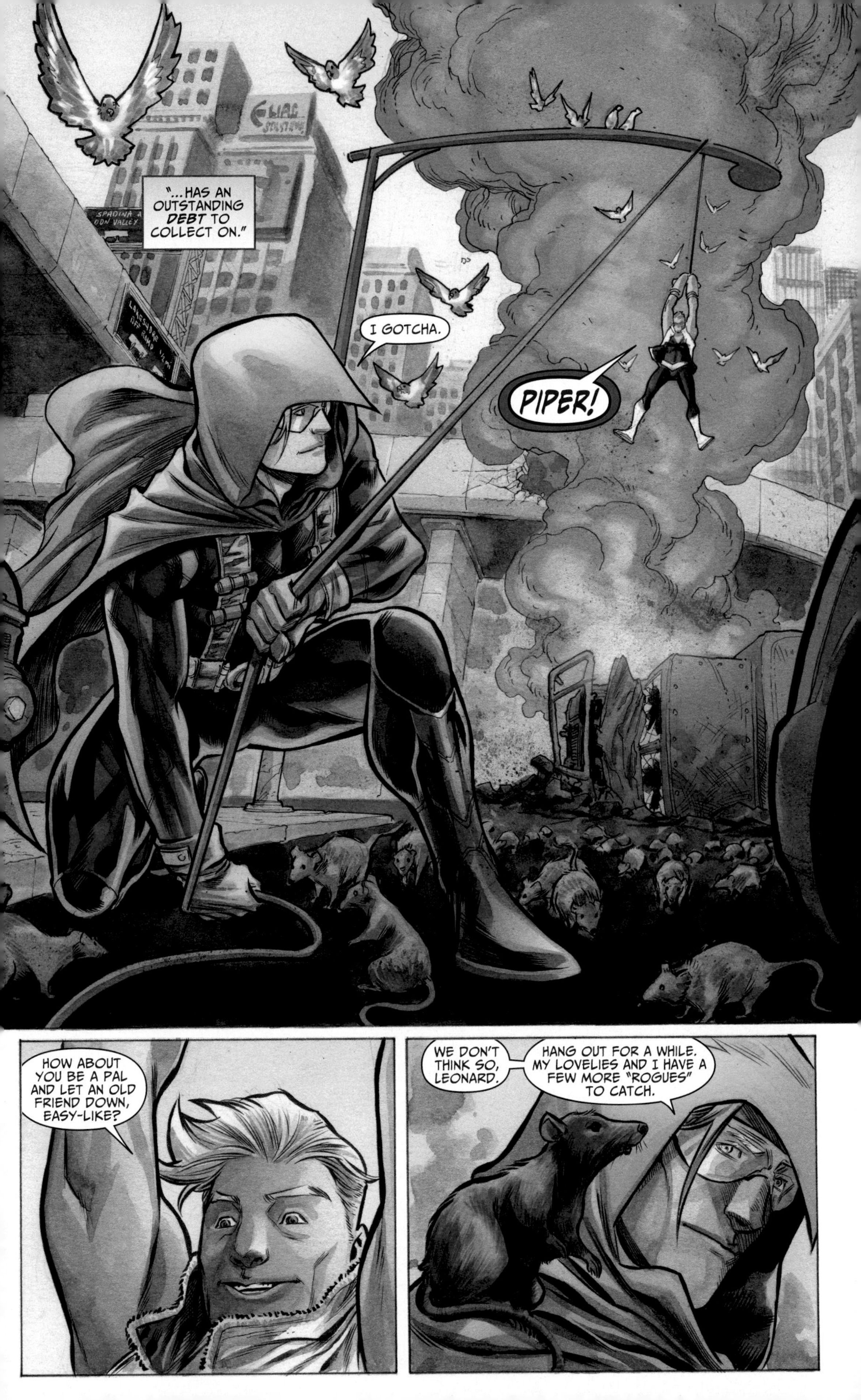
"...HAS AN OUTSTANDING DEBT TO COLLECT ON."
I GOTCHA.
PIPER!
HOW ABOUT YOU BE A PAL AND LET AN OLD FRIEND DOWN, EASY-LIKE?
WE DON'T THINK SO, LEONARD.
HANG OUT FOR A WHILE. MY LOVELIES AND I HAVE A FEW MORE "ROGUES" TO CATCH.

TODAY, CENTRAL CITY USHERS IN A NEW ERA! DR. DARWIN ELIAS HELPED BRING LIGHT TO THE CITY WHEN WE WERE PLUNGED INTO DARKNESS.

TODAY HE BRINGS US ONE GIANT LEAP INTO THE FUTURE, WITH THE NATION'S *FIRST* STATE OF THE ART *GREEN-ENERGY* MONORAIL SYSTEM!

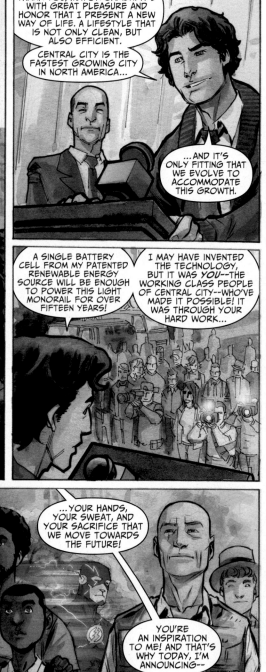

THANK YOU, MAYOR GAMEN. IT'S WITH GREAT PLEASURE AND HONOR THAT I PRESENT A NEW WAY OF LIFE. A LIFESTYLE THAT IS NOT ONLY CLEAN, BUT ALSO EFFICIENT.

CENTRAL CITY IS THE FASTEST GROWING CITY IN NORTH AMERICA...

...AND IT'S ONLY FITTING THAT WE EVOLVE TO ACCOMMODATE THIS GROWTH.

A SINGLE BATTERY CELL FROM MY PATENTED RENEWABLE ENERGY SOURCE WILL BE ENOUGH TO POWER THIS LIGHT MONORAIL FOR OVER FIFTEEN YEARS!

I MAY HAVE INVENTED THE TECHNOLOGY, BUT IT WAS *YOU*--THE WORKING CLASS PEOPLE OF CENTRAL CITY--WHO'VE MADE IT POSSIBLE! IT WAS THROUGH YOUR HARD WORK...

...YOUR HANDS, YOUR SWEAT, AND YOUR SACRIFICE THAT WE MOVE TOWARDS THE FUTURE!

YOU'RE AN INSPIRATION TO ME! AND THAT'S WHY TODAY, I'M ANNOUNCING--

WHOA...

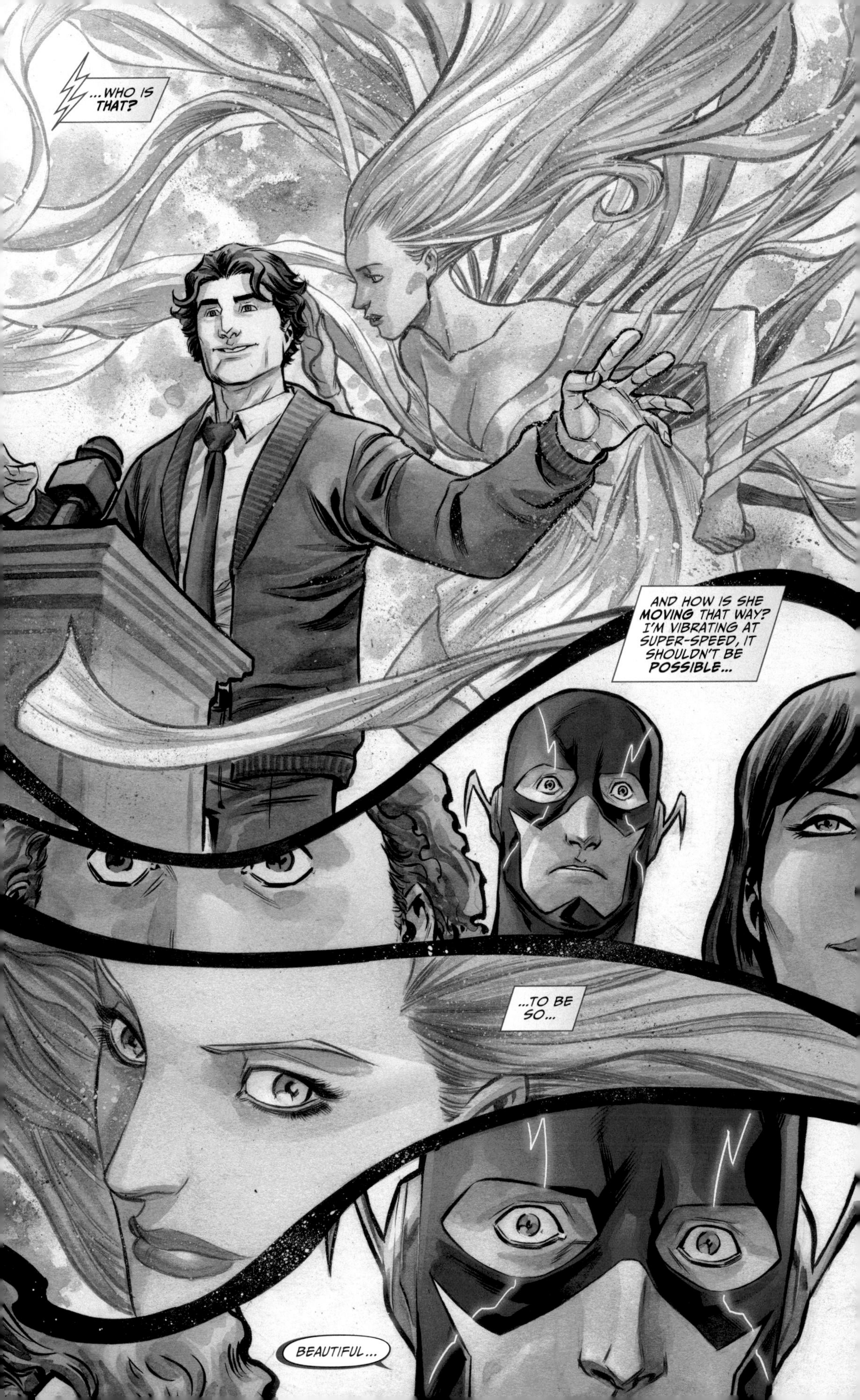
...WHO IS THAT?
AND HOW IS SHE MOVING THAT WAY? I'M VIBRATING AT SUPER-SPEED, IT SHOULDN'T BE POSSIBLE...
...TO BE SO...
BEAUTIFUL...

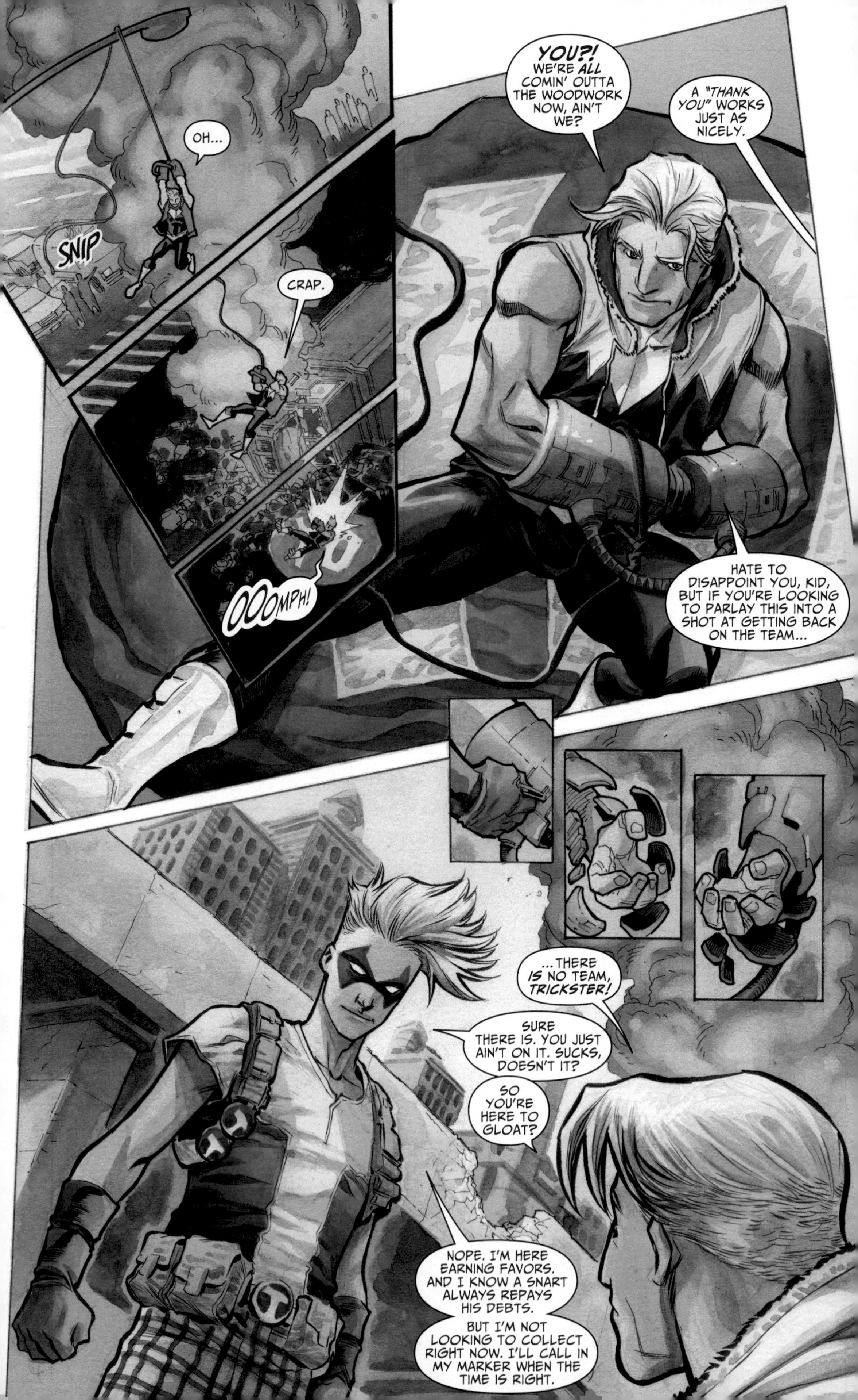
OH...
SNIP
CRAP.
OOOMPH!
YOU?! WE'RE ALL COMIN' OUTTA THE WOODWORK NOW, AIN'T WE?
A "THANK YOU" WORKS JUST AS NICELY.
HATE TO DISAPPOINT YOU, KID, BUT IF YOU'RE LOOKING TO PARLAY THIS INTO A SHOT AT GETTING BACK ON THE TEAM...
...THERE IS NO TEAM, TRICKSTER!
SURE THERE IS. YOU JUST AIN'T ON IT. SUCKS, DOESN'T IT?
SO YOU'RE HERE TO GLOAT?
NOPE. I'M HERE EARNING FAVORS. AND I KNOW A SNART ALWAYS REPAYS HIS DEBTS.
BUT I'M NOT LOOKING TO COLLECT RIGHT NOW. I'LL CALL IN MY MARKER WHEN THE TIME IS RIGHT.

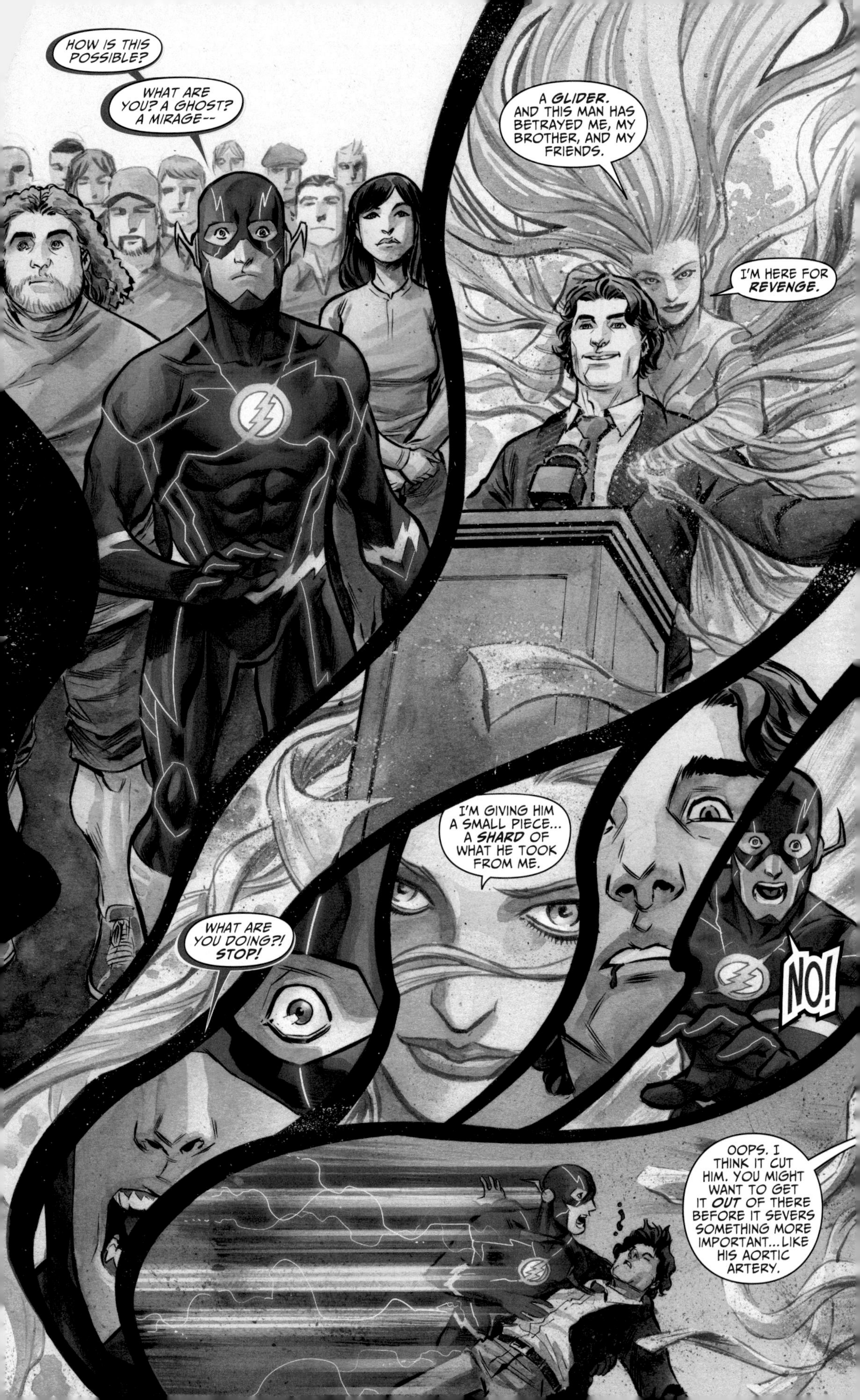
HOW IS THIS POSSIBLE?
WHAT ARE YOU? A GHOST? A MIRAGE--
A GLIDER. AND THIS MAN HAS BETRAYED ME, MY BROTHER, AND MY FRIENDS.
I'M HERE FOR REVENGE.
I'M GIVING HIM A SMALL PIECE... A SHARD OF WHAT HE TOOK FROM ME.
WHAT ARE YOU DOING?! STOP!
NO!
OOPS. I THINK IT CUT HIM. YOU MIGHT WANT TO GET IT OUT OF THERE BEFORE IT SEVERS SOMETHING MORE IMPORTANT...LIKE HIS AORTIC ARTERY.

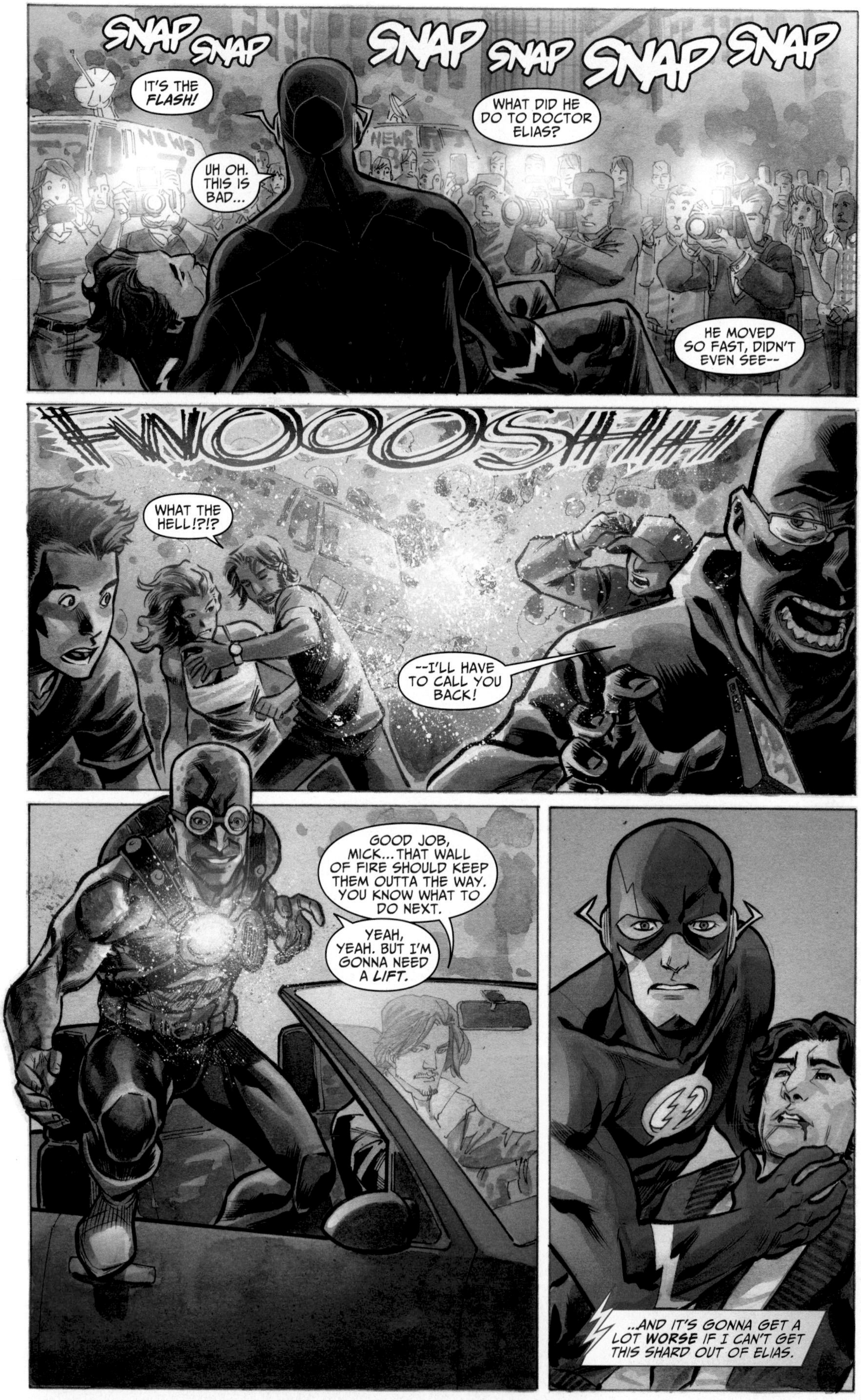
SNAP SNAP SNAP SNAP SNAP SNAP
IT'S THE FLASH!
UH OH. THIS IS BAD...
WHAT DID HE DO TO DOCTOR ELIAS?
HE MOVED SO FAST, DIDN'T EVEN SEE--
FWOOOSHHH
WHAT THE HELL!?!?
--I'LL HAVE TO CALL YOU BACK!
GOOD JOB, MICK...THAT WALL OF FIRE SHOULD KEEP THEM OUTTA THE WAY. YOU KNOW WHAT TO DO NEXT.
YEAH, YEAH. BUT I'M GONNA NEED A LIFT.
...AND IT'S GONNA GET A LOT WORSE IF I CAN'T GET THIS SHARD OUT OF ELIAS.

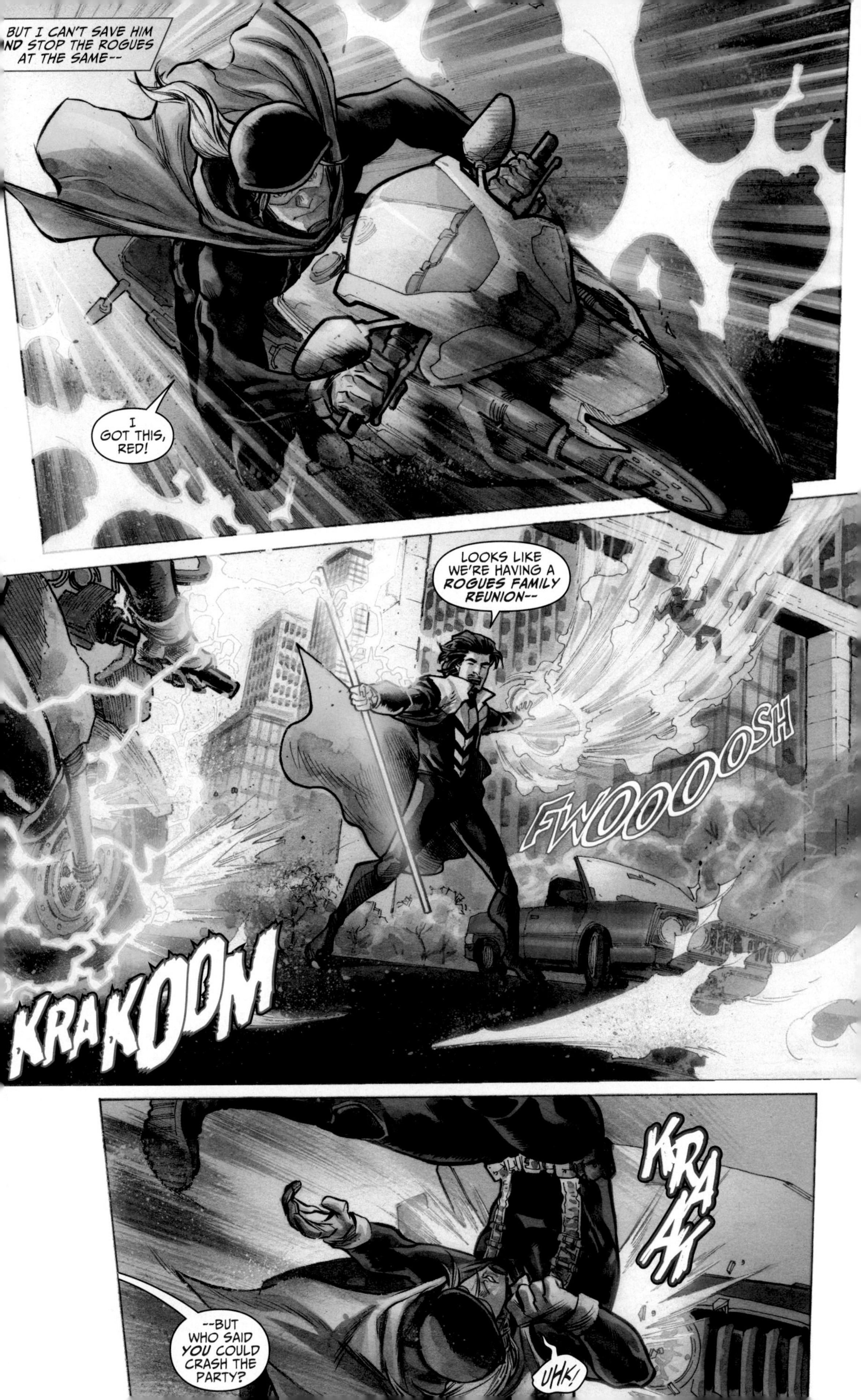

BUT I CAN'T SAVE HIM ND STOP THE ROGUES AT THE SAME--
I GOT THIS, RED!
LOOKS LIKE WE'RE HAVING A *ROGUES FAMILY* REUNION--
FWOOOOOOSH
KRAKOOM
KRAAK
--BUT WHO SAID *YOU* COULD CRASH THE PARTY?
UHK!

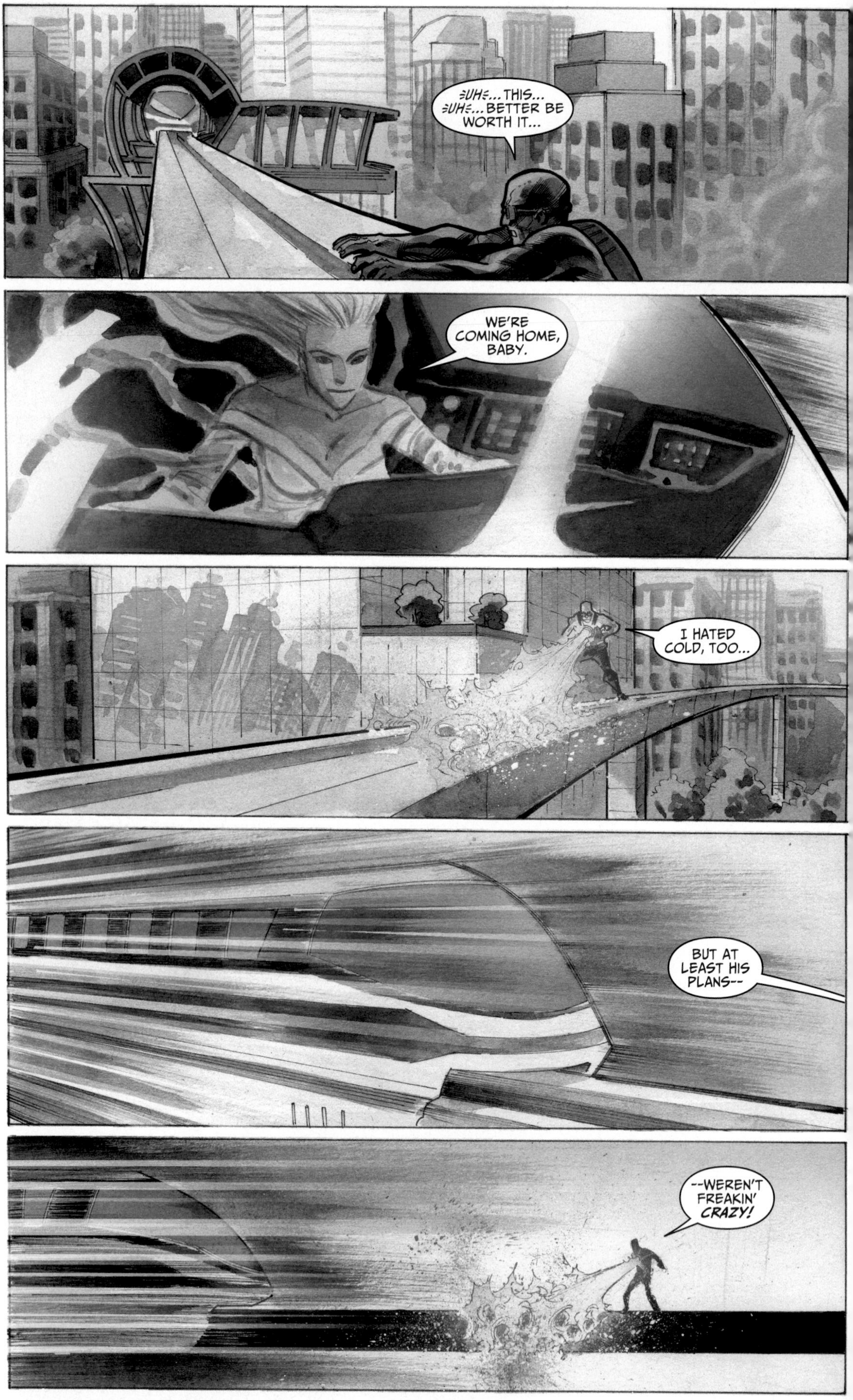
UHF... THIS...
UHF... BETTER BE WORTH IT...
WE'RE COMING HOME, BABY.
I HATED COLD, TOO...
BUT AT LEAST HIS PLANS--
--WEREN'T FREAKIN' *CRAZY!*

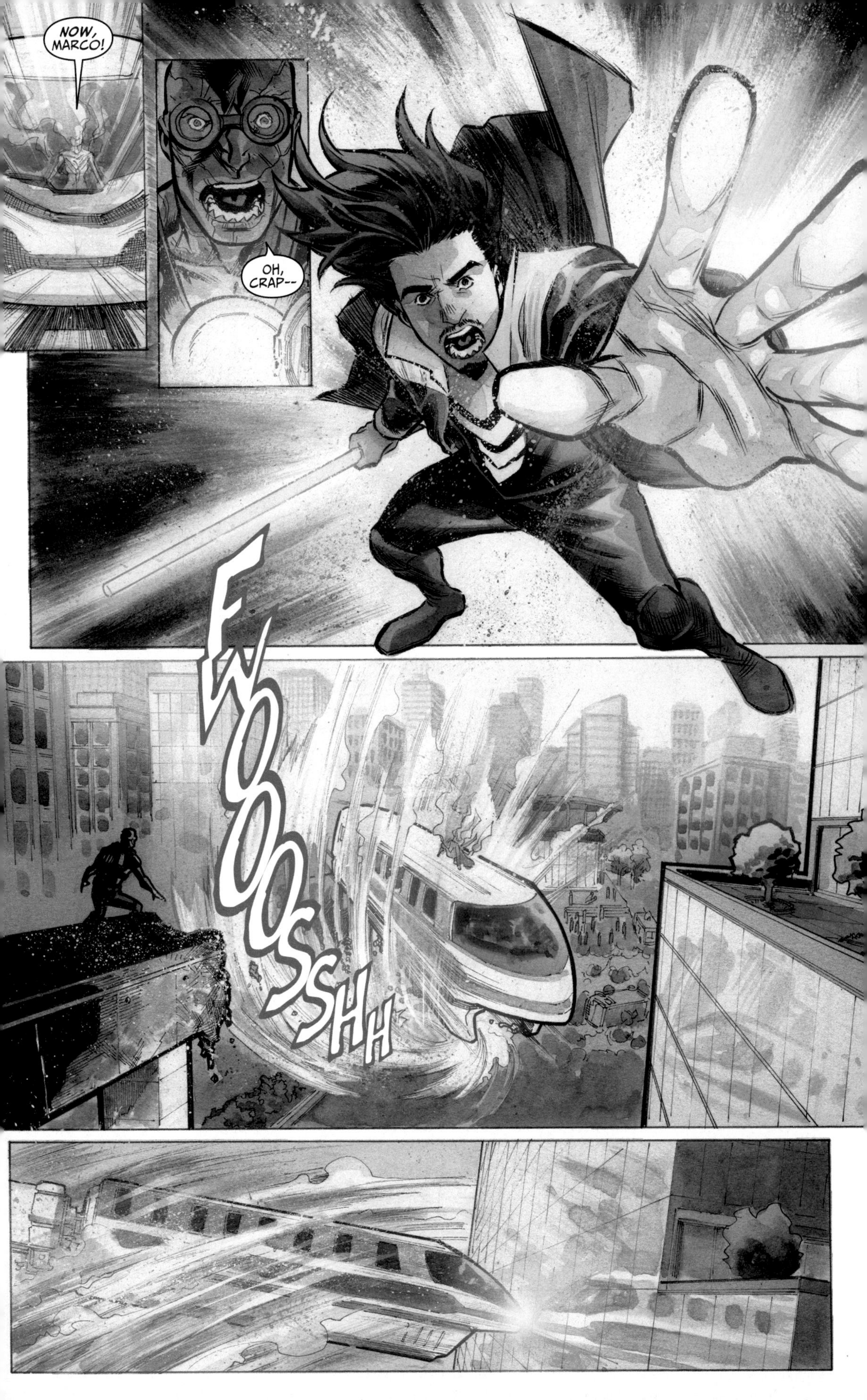
NOW, MARCO!
OH, CRAP--
FWOOOSSHH

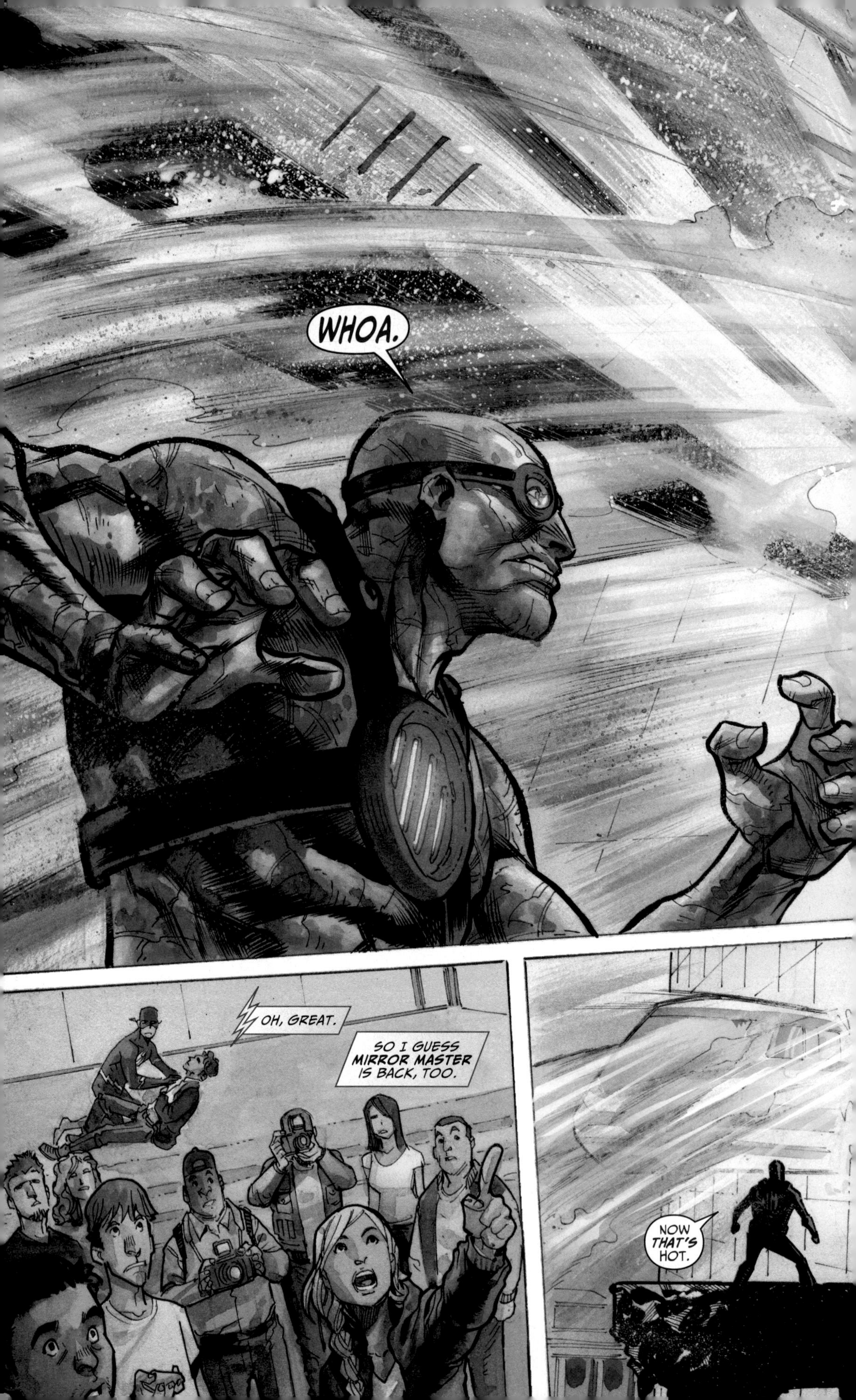
WHOA.
OH, GREAT.
SO I GUESS MIRROR MASTER IS BACK, TOO.
NOW THAT'S HOT.

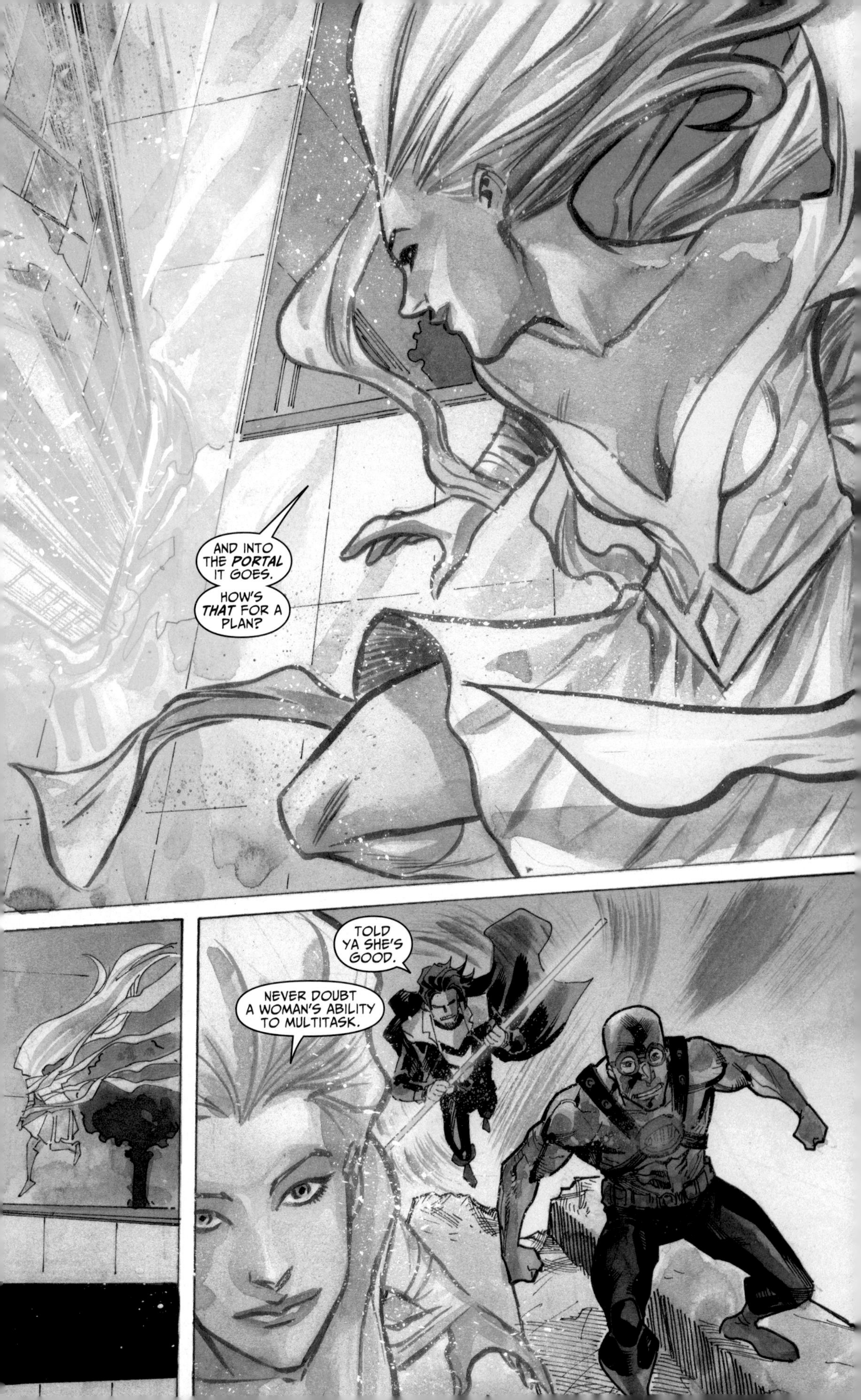
AND INTO THE PORTAL IT GOES.
HOW'S THAT FOR A PLAN?
TOLD YA SHE'S GOOD.
NEVER DOUBT A WOMAN'S ABILITY TO MULTITASK.

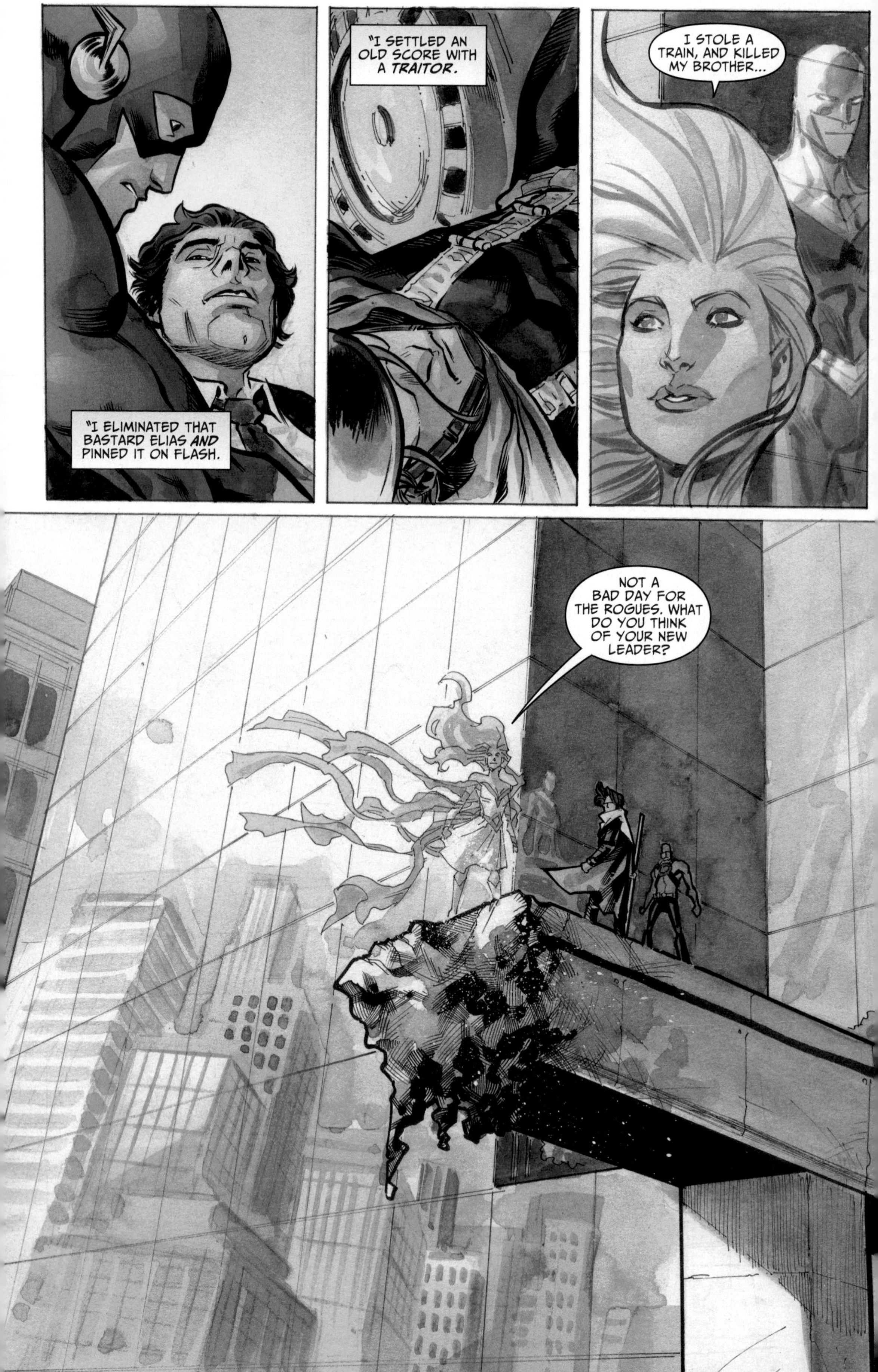
"I ELIMINATED THAT BASTARD ELIAS *AND* PINNED IT ON FLASH.
"I SETTLED AN OLD SCORE WITH A *TRAITOR*.
I STOLE A TRAIN, AND KILLED MY BROTHER...
NOT A BAD DAY FOR THE ROGUES. WHAT DO YOU THINK OF YOUR NEW LEADER?

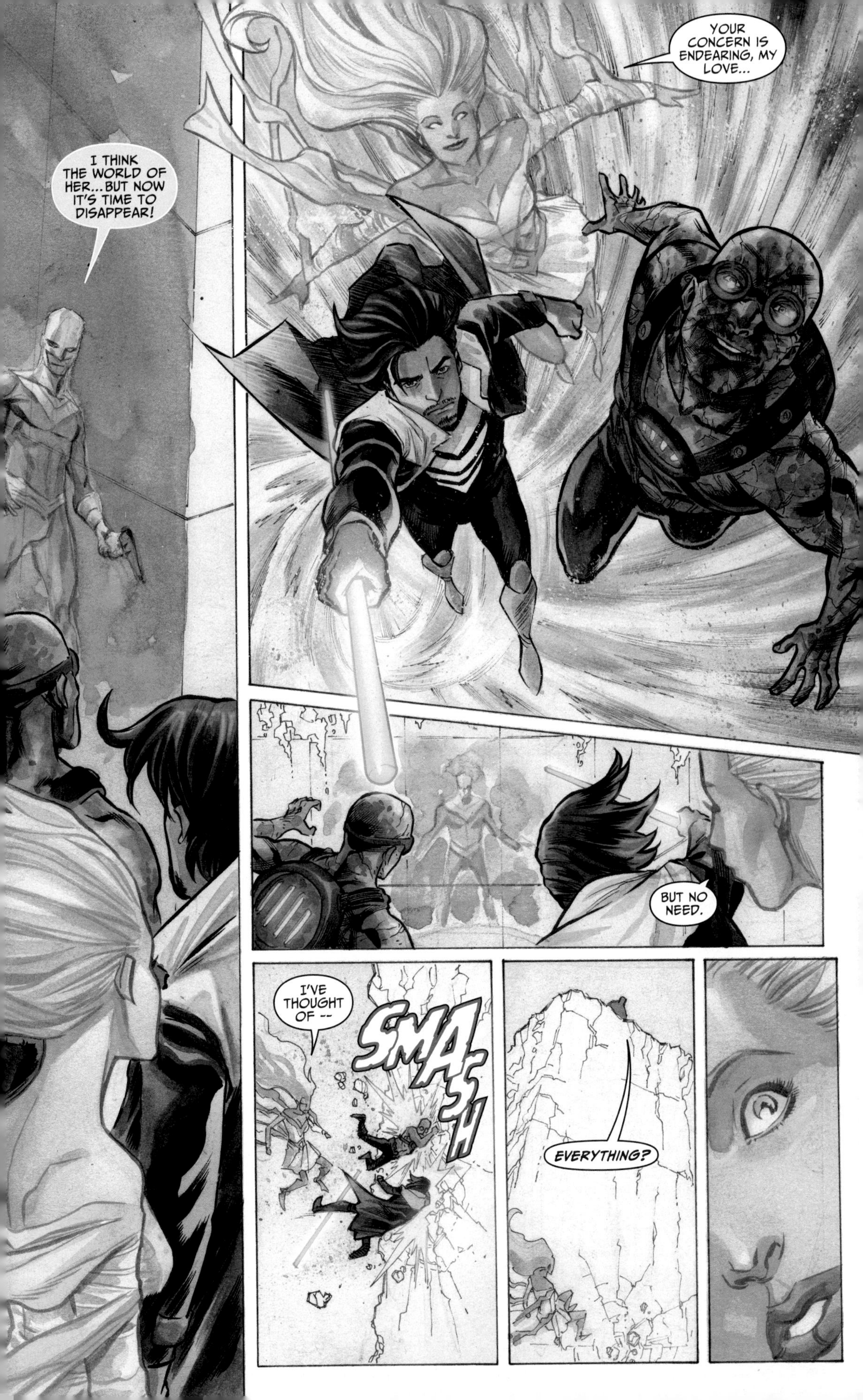
YOUR CONCERN IS ENDEARING, MY LOVE...
I THINK THE WORLD OF HER...BUT NOW IT'S TIME TO DISAPPEAR!
BUT NO NEED.
I'VE THOUGHT OF --
SMASH
EVERYTHING?

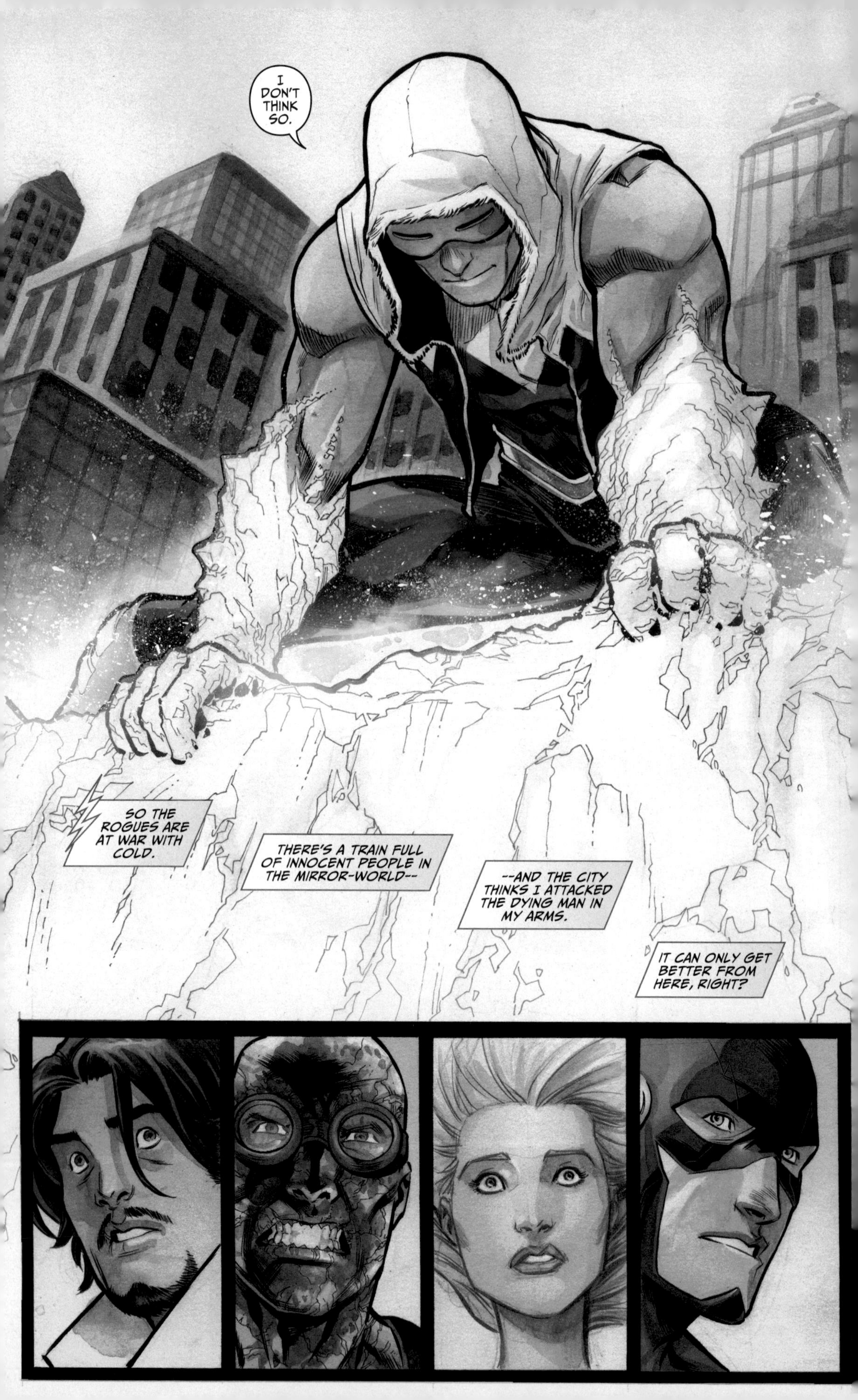
I DON'T THINK SO.
SO THE ROGUES ARE AT WAR WITH COLD.
THERE'S A TRAIN FULL OF INNOCENT PEOPLE IN THE MIRROR-WORLD--
--AND THE CITY THINKS I ATTACKED THE DYING MAN IN MY ARMS.
IT CAN ONLY GET BETTER FROM HERE, RIGHT?

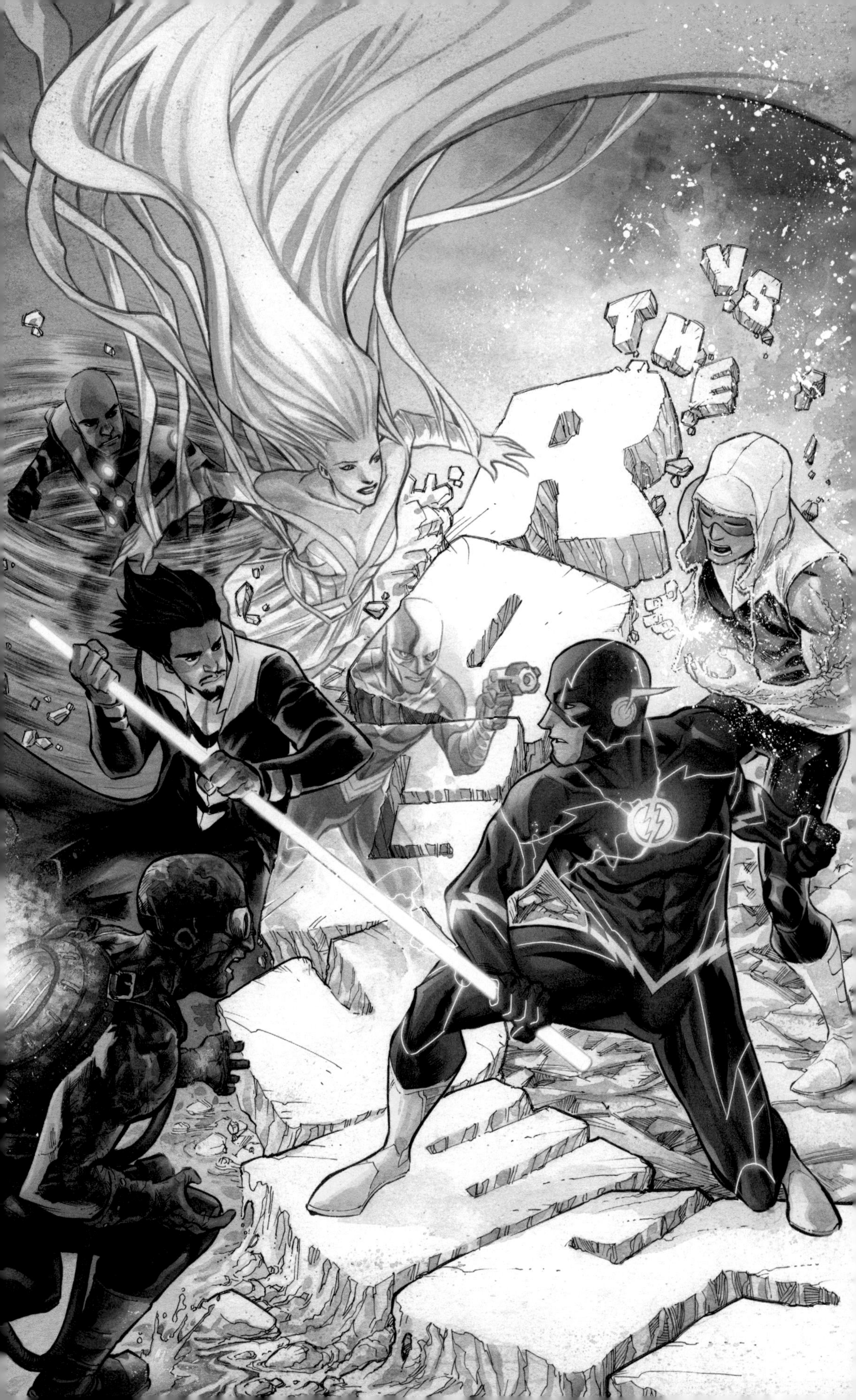
VS
THE

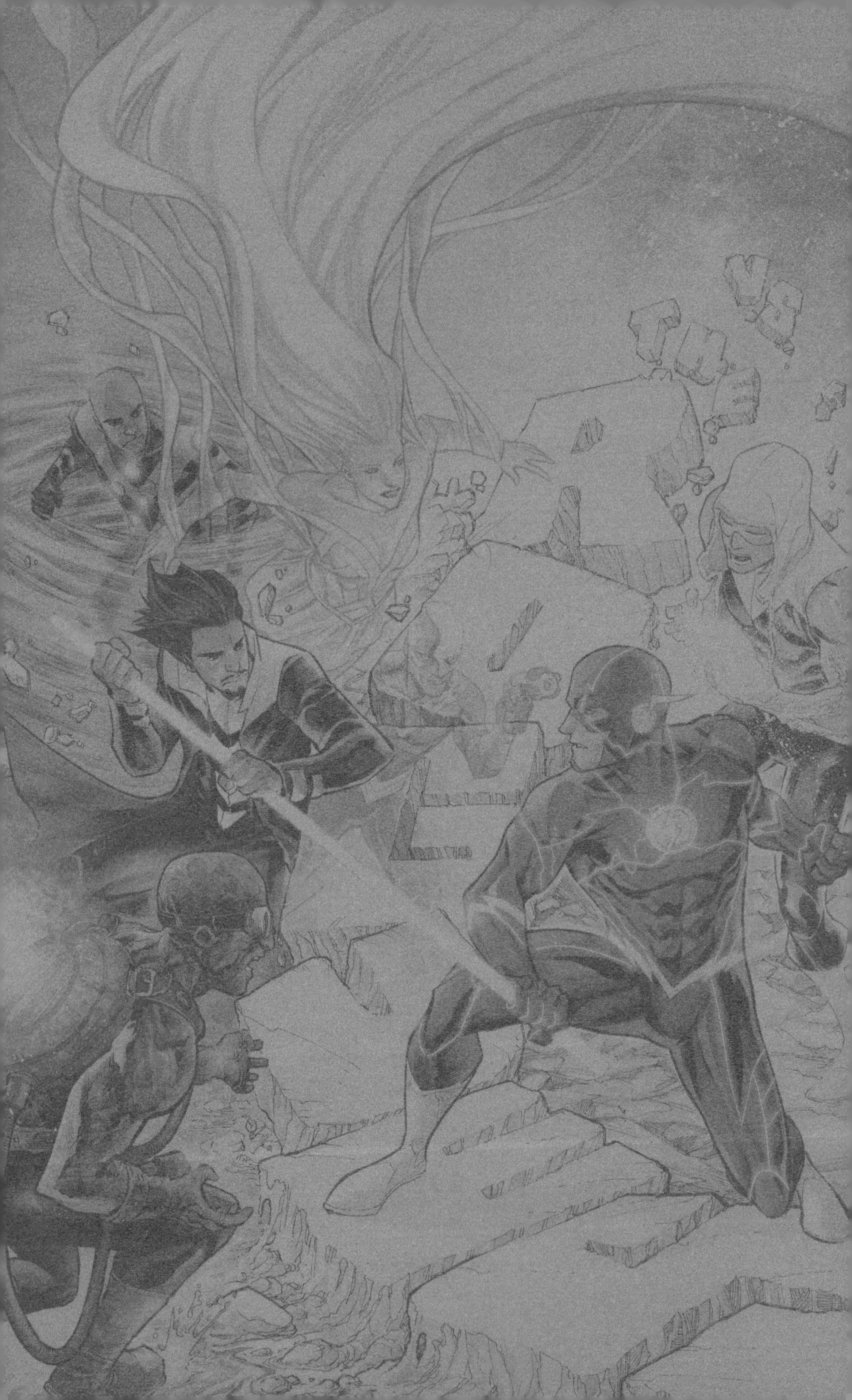

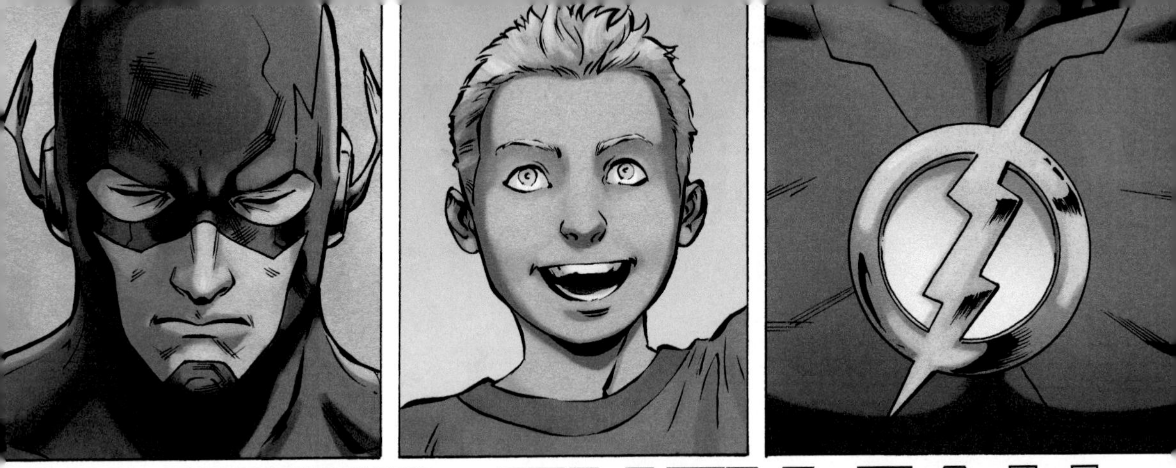

UNITED THEY FALL

FRANCIS MANAPUL & BRIAN BUCCELLATO-STORY & COVER
CHRIS CONROY-ASSOCIATE EDITOR MATT IDELSON-EDITOR

CHAPTER 1: THE FLATS

FRANCIS MANAPUL-BREAKDOWNS MARCUS TO-PENCILS & INKS
IAN HERRING-COLORS CARLOS M. MANGUAL-LETTERS

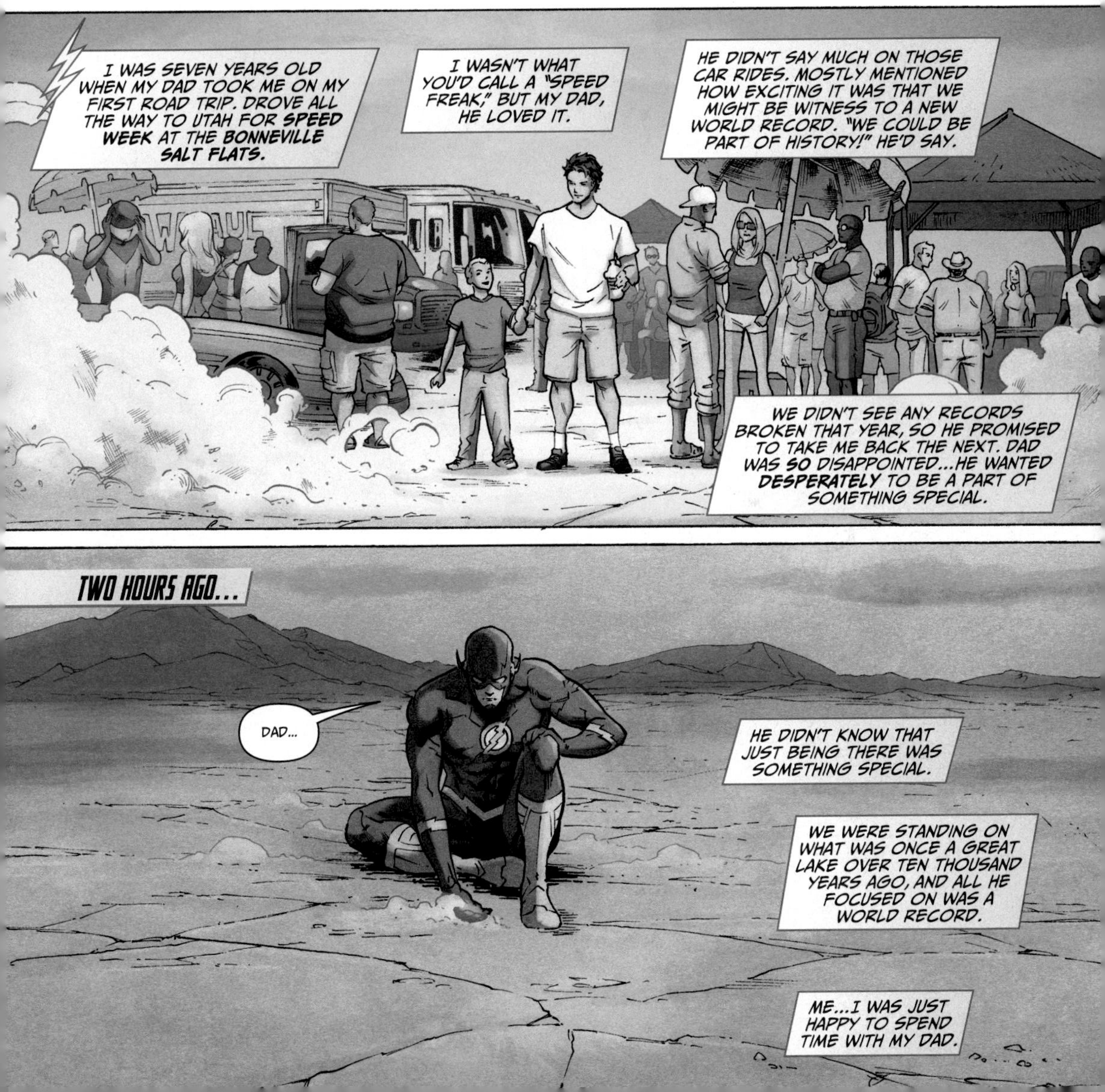
I WAS SEVEN YEARS OLD WHEN MY DAD TOOK ME ON MY FIRST ROAD TRIP. DROVE ALL THE WAY TO UTAH FOR SPEED WEEK AT THE BONNEVILLE SALT FLATS.
I WASN'T WHAT YOU'D CALL A "SPEED FREAK," BUT MY DAD, HE LOVED IT.
HE DIDN'T SAY MUCH ON THOSE CAR RIDES. MOSTLY MENTIONED HOW EXCITING IT WAS THAT WE MIGHT BE WITNESS TO A NEW WORLD RECORD. "WE COULD BE PART OF HISTORY!" HE'D SAY.
WE DIDN'T SEE ANY RECORDS BROKEN THAT YEAR, SO HE PROMISED TO TAKE ME BACK THE NEXT. DAD WAS SO DISAPPOINTED...HE WANTED DESPERATELY TO BE A PART OF SOMETHING SPECIAL.
TWO HOURS AGO...
DAD...
HE DIDN'T KNOW THAT JUST BEING THERE WAS SOMETHING SPECIAL.
WE WERE STANDING ON WHAT WAS ONCE A GREAT LAKE OVER TEN THOUSAND YEARS AGO, AND ALL HE FOCUSED ON WAS A WORLD RECORD.
ME...I WAS JUST HAPPY TO SPEND TIME WITH MY DAD.

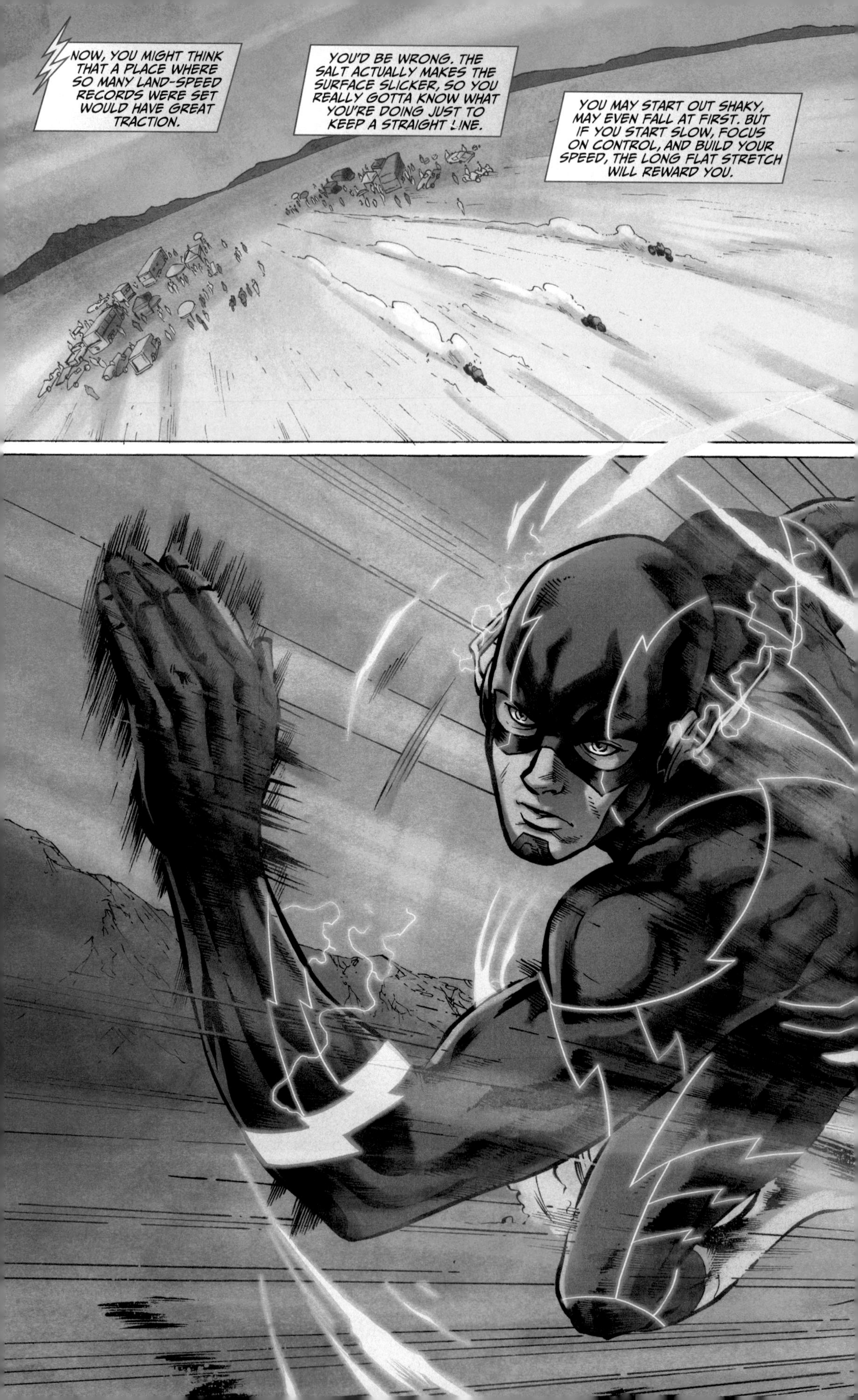
NOW, YOU MIGHT THINK THAT A PLACE WHERE SO MANY LAND-SPEED RECORDS WERE SET WOULD HAVE GREAT TRACTION.
YOU'D BE WRONG. THE SALT ACTUALLY MAKES THE SURFACE SLICKER, SO YOU REALLY GOTTA KNOW WHAT YOU'RE DOING JUST TO KEEP A STRAIGHT LINE.
YOU MAY START OUT SHAKY, MAY EVEN FALL AT FIRST. BUT IF YOU START SLOW, FOCUS ON CONTROL, AND BUILD YOUR SPEED, THE LONG FLAT STRETCH WILL REWARD YOU.

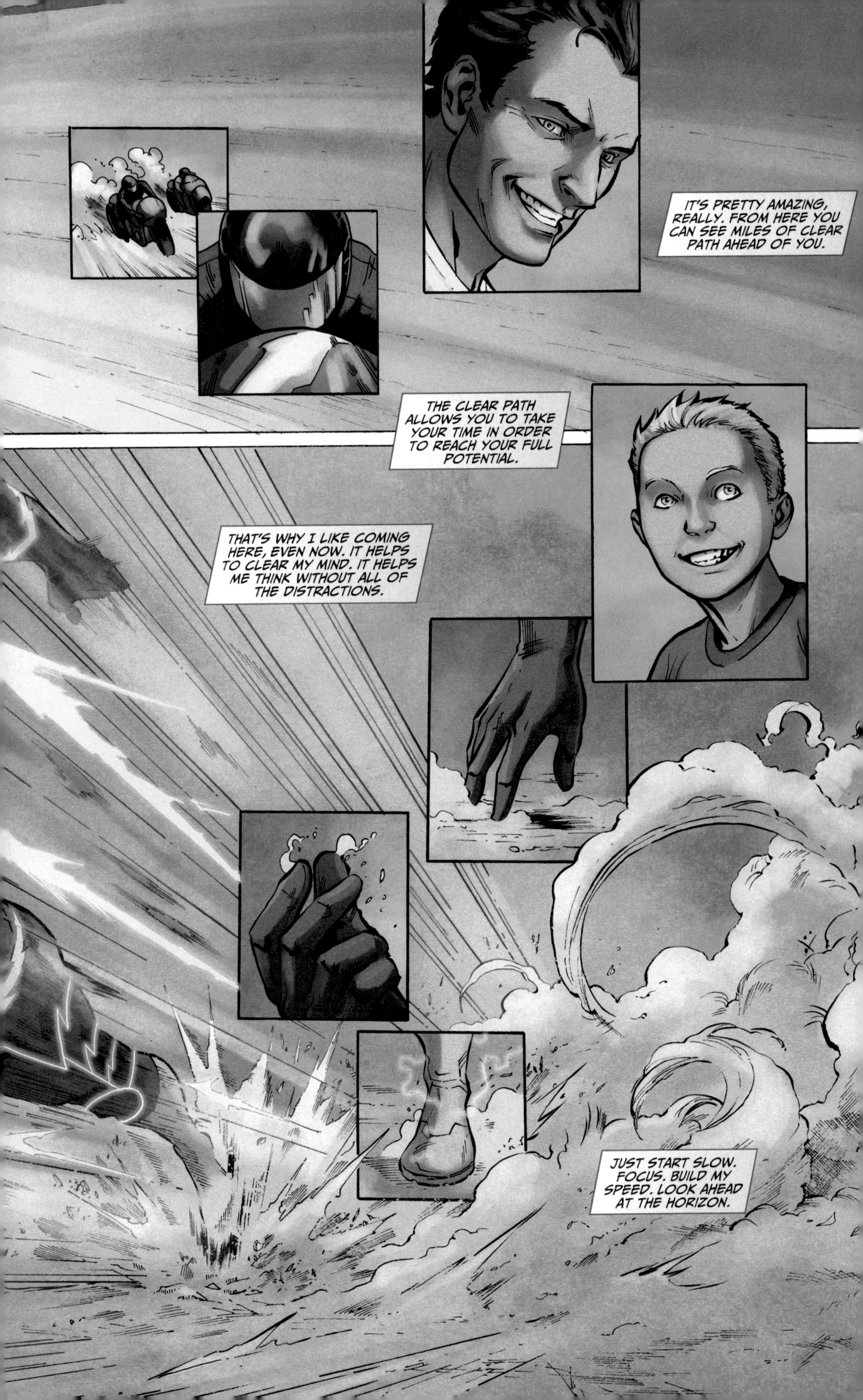
IT'S PRETTY AMAZING, REALLY. FROM HERE YOU CAN SEE MILES OF CLEAR PATH AHEAD OF YOU.
THE CLEAR PATH ALLOWS YOU TO TAKE YOUR TIME IN ORDER TO REACH YOUR FULL POTENTIAL.
THAT'S WHY I LIKE COMING HERE, EVEN NOW. IT HELPS TO CLEAR MY MIND. IT HELPS ME THINK WITHOUT ALL OF THE DISTRACTIONS.
JUST START SLOW. FOCUS. BUILD MY SPEED. LOOK AHEAD AT THE HORIZON.

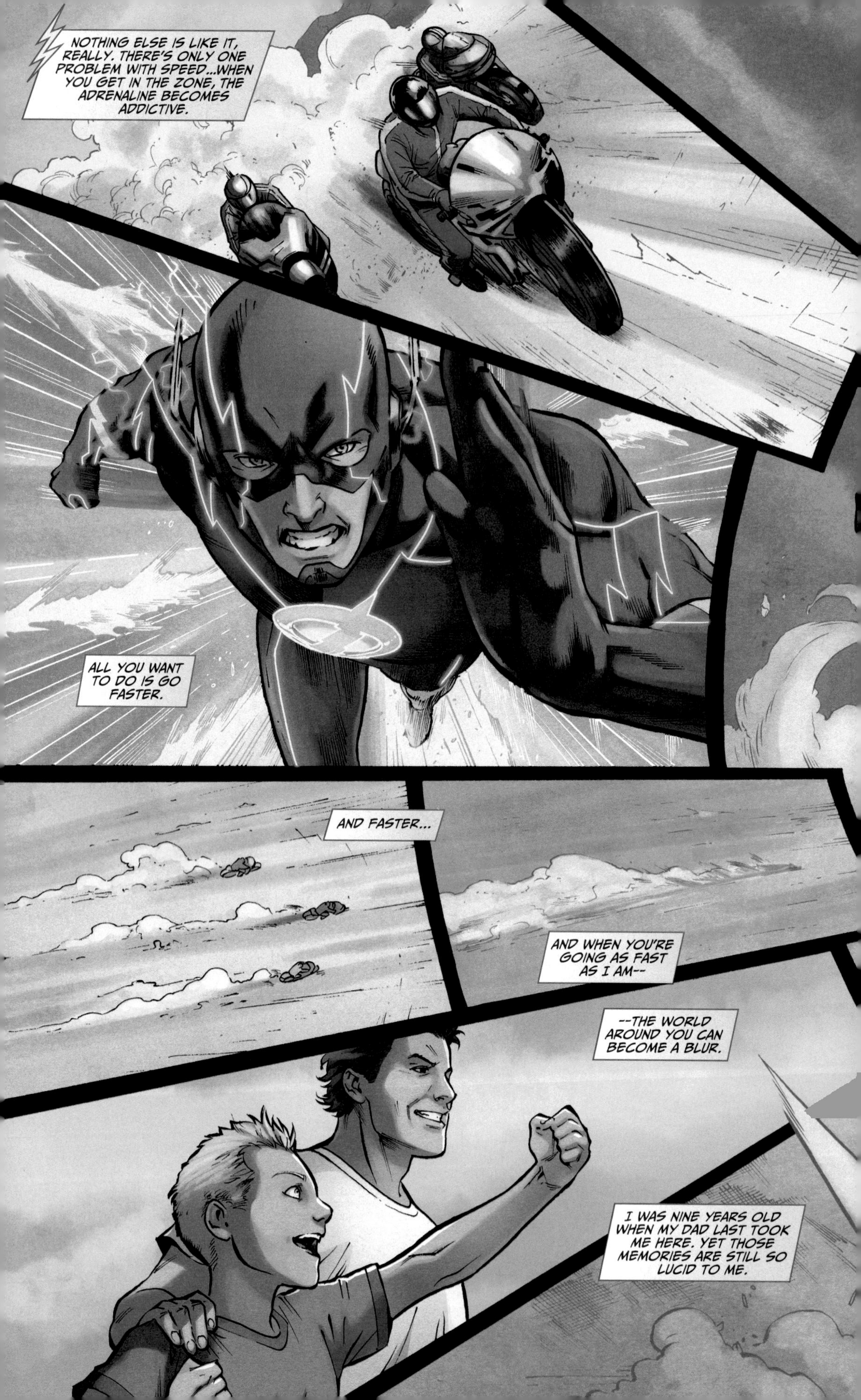
NOTHING ELSE IS LIKE IT, REALLY. THERE'S ONLY ONE PROBLEM WITH SPEED...WHEN YOU GET IN THE ZONE, THE ADRENALINE BECOMES ADDICTIVE.
ALL YOU WANT TO DO IS GO FASTER.
AND FASTER...
AND WHEN YOU'RE GOING AS FAST AS I AM--
--THE WORLD AROUND YOU CAN BECOME A BLUR.
I WAS NINE YEARS OLD WHEN MY DAD LAST TOOK ME HERE. YET THOSE MEMORIES ARE STILL SO LUCID TO ME.

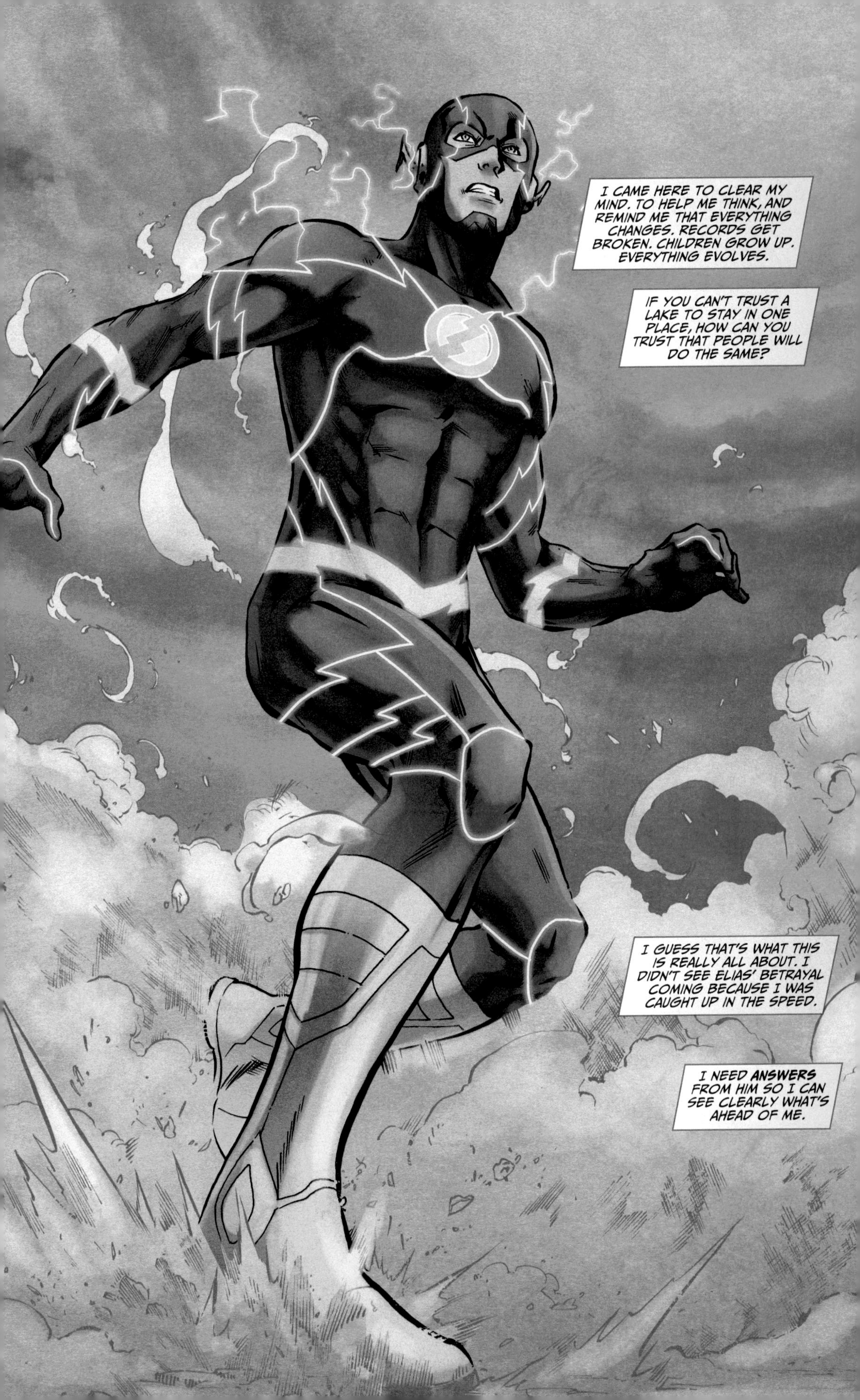
I CAME HERE TO CLEAR MY MIND. TO HELP ME THINK, AND REMIND ME THAT EVERYTHING CHANGES. RECORDS GET BROKEN. CHILDREN GROW UP. EVERYTHING EVOLVES.
IF YOU CAN'T TRUST A LAKE TO STAY IN ONE PLACE, HOW CAN YOU TRUST THAT PEOPLE WILL DO THE SAME?
I GUESS THAT'S WHAT THIS IS REALLY ALL ABOUT. I DIDN'T SEE ELIAS' BETRAYAL COMING BECAUSE I WAS CAUGHT UP IN THE SPEED.
I NEED **ANSWERS** FROM HIM SO I CAN SEE CLEARLY WHAT'S AHEAD OF ME.

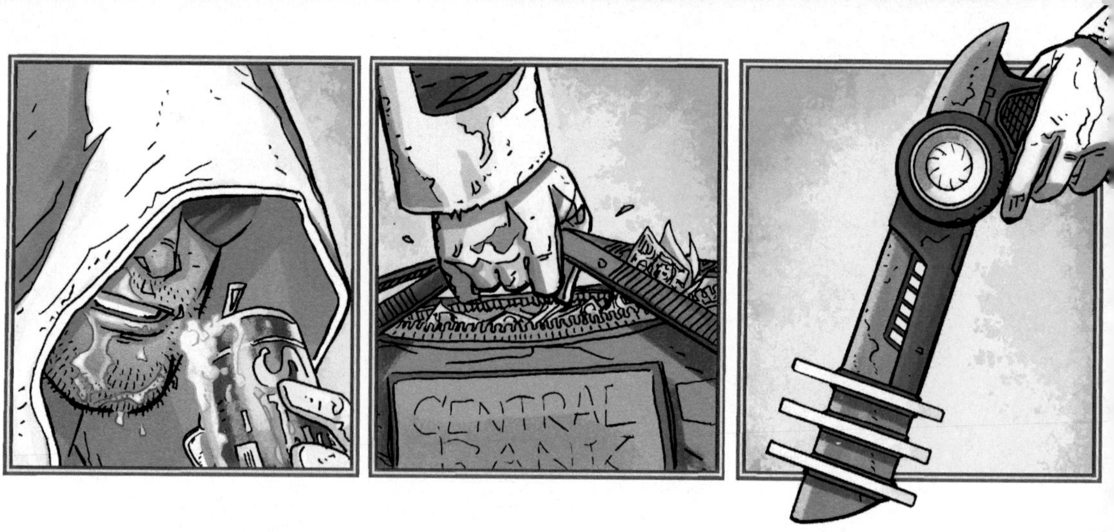
CENTRAL

CHAPTER 2: THE OPPORTUNITY

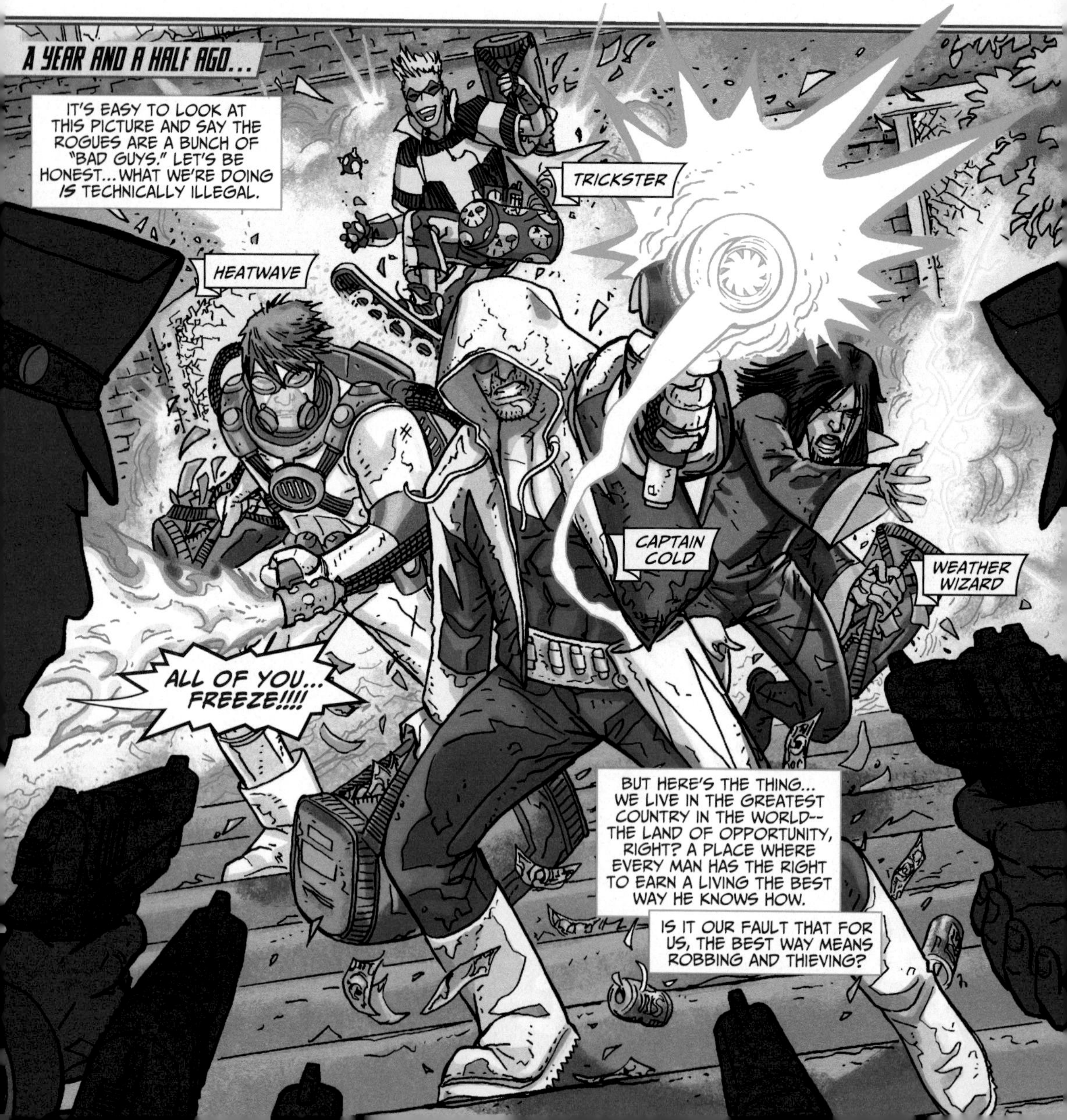
A YEAR AND A HALF AGO...
IT'S EASY TO LOOK AT THIS PICTURE AND SAY THE ROGUES ARE A BUNCH OF "BAD GUYS." LET'S BE HONEST...WHAT WE'RE DOING IS TECHNICALLY ILLEGAL.
TRICKSTER
HEATWAVE
CAPTAIN COLD
WEATHER WIZARD
ALL OF YOU... FREEZE!!!!
BUT HERE'S THE THING... WE LIVE IN THE GREATEST COUNTRY IN THE WORLD-- THE LAND OF OPPORTUNITY, RIGHT? A PLACE WHERE EVERY MAN HAS THE RIGHT TO EARN A LIVING THE BEST WAY HE KNOWS HOW.
IS IT OUR FAULT THAT FOR US, THE BEST WAY MEANS ROBBING AND THIEVING?

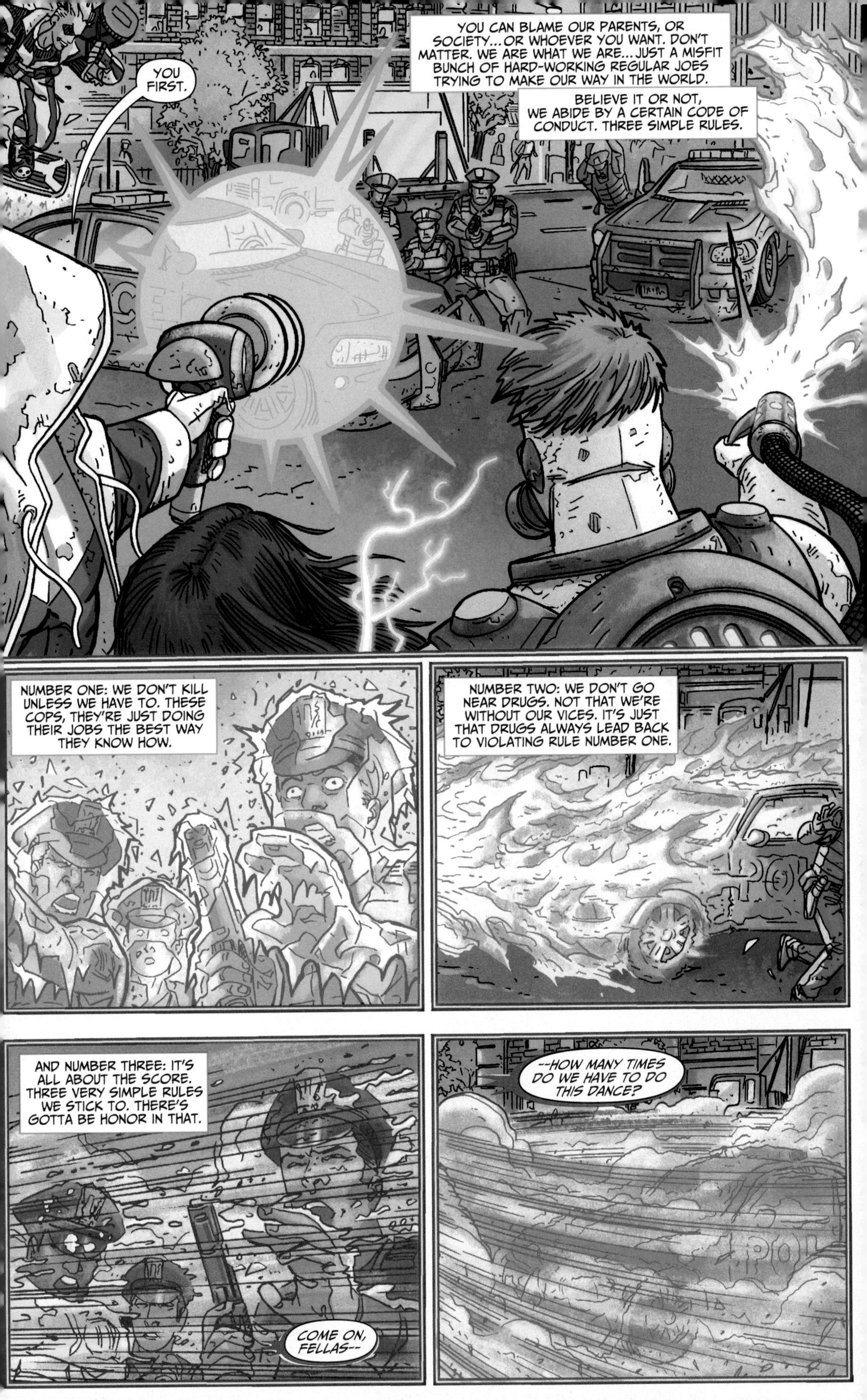
YOU CAN BLAME OUR PARENTS, OR SOCIETY... OR WHOEVER YOU WANT. DON'T MATTER. WE ARE WHAT WE ARE... JUST A MISFIT BUNCH OF HARD-WORKING REGULAR JOES TRYING TO MAKE OUR WAY IN THE WORLD.
YOU FIRST.
BELIEVE IT OR NOT, WE ABIDE BY A CERTAIN CODE OF CONDUCT. THREE SIMPLE RULES.
NUMBER ONE: WE DON'T KILL UNLESS WE HAVE TO. THESE COPS, THEY'RE JUST DOING THEIR JOBS THE BEST WAY THEY KNOW HOW.
NUMBER TWO: WE DON'T GO NEAR DRUGS. NOT THAT WE'RE WITHOUT OUR VICES. IT'S JUST THAT DRUGS ALWAYS LEAD BACK TO VIOLATING RULE NUMBER ONE.
AND NUMBER THREE: IT'S ALL ABOUT THE SCORE. THREE VERY SIMPLE RULES WE STICK TO. THERE'S GOTTA BE HONOR IN THAT.
COME ON, FELLAS--
--HOW MANY TIMES DO WE HAVE TO DO THIS DANCE?

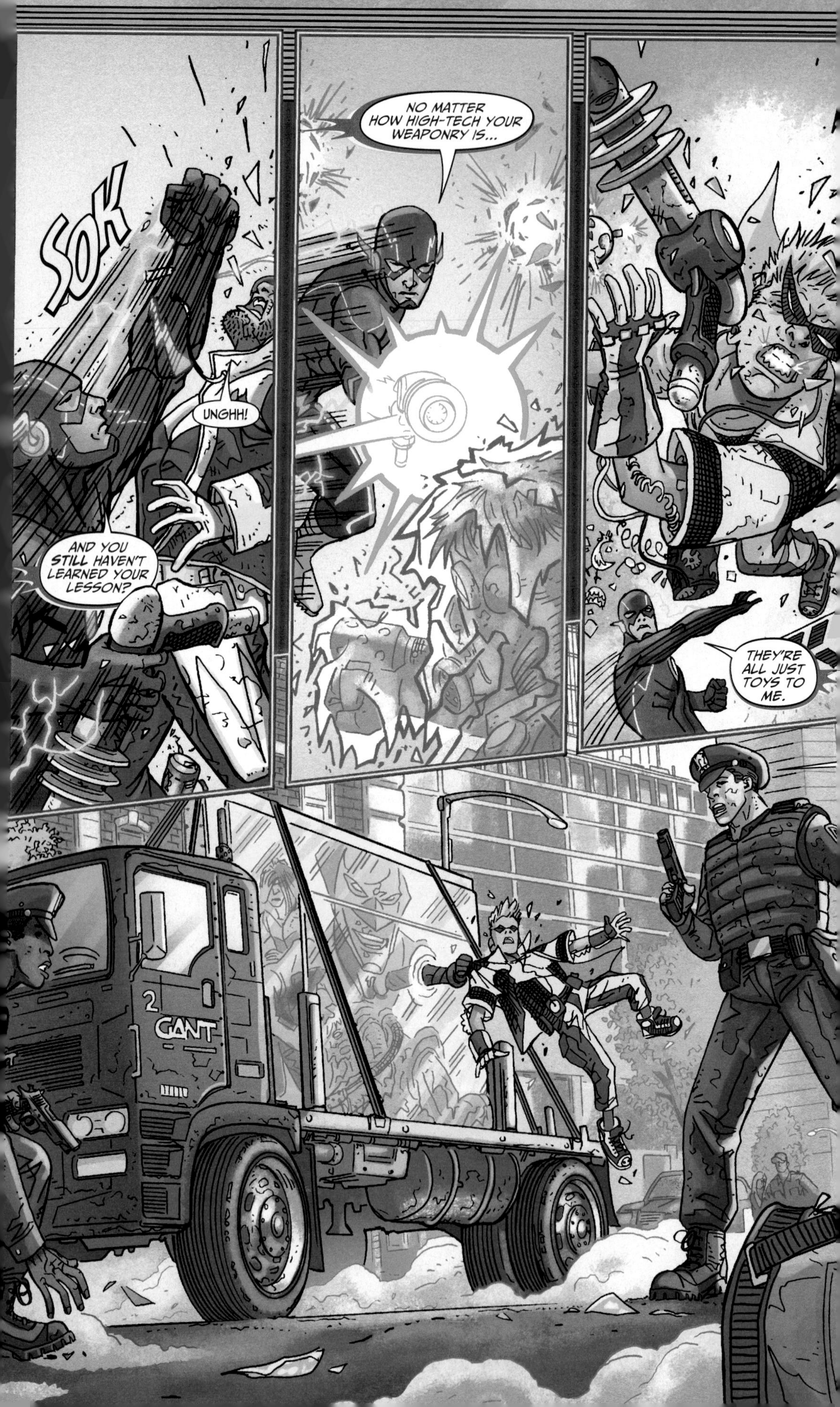
SOK
UNGHH!
AND YOU STILL HAVEN'T LEARNED YOUR LESSON?
NO MATTER HOW HIGH-TECH YOUR WEAPONRY IS...
THEY'RE ALL JUST TOYS TO ME.
2
GANT

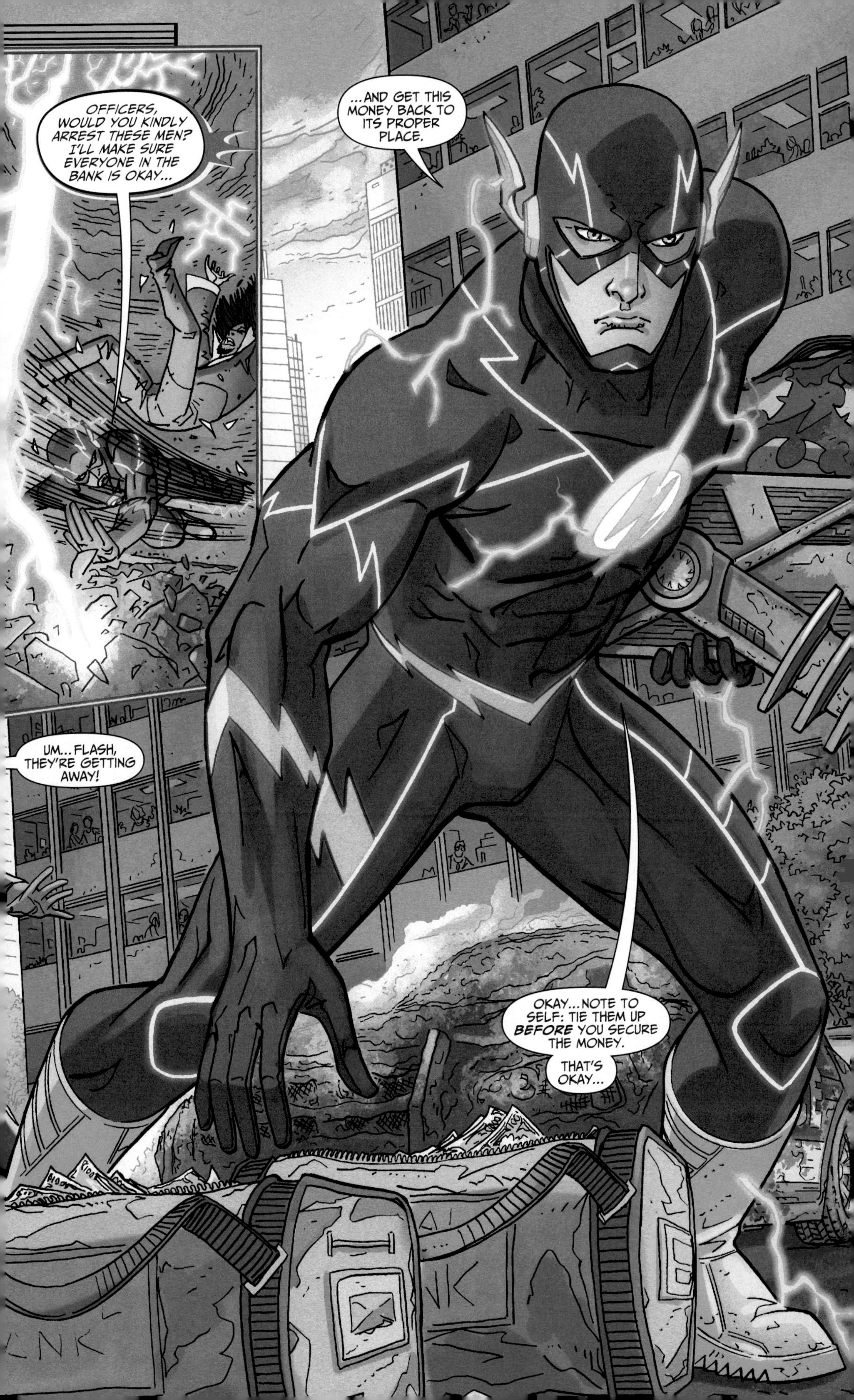
OFFICERS, WOULD YOU KINDLY ARREST THESE MEN? I'LL MAKE SURE EVERYONE IN THE BANK IS OKAY...
...AND GET THIS MONEY BACK TO ITS PROPER PLACE.
UM...FLASH, THEY'RE GETTING AWAY!
OKAY...NOTE TO SELF: TIE THEM UP **BEFORE** YOU SECURE THE MONEY.
THAT'S OKAY...

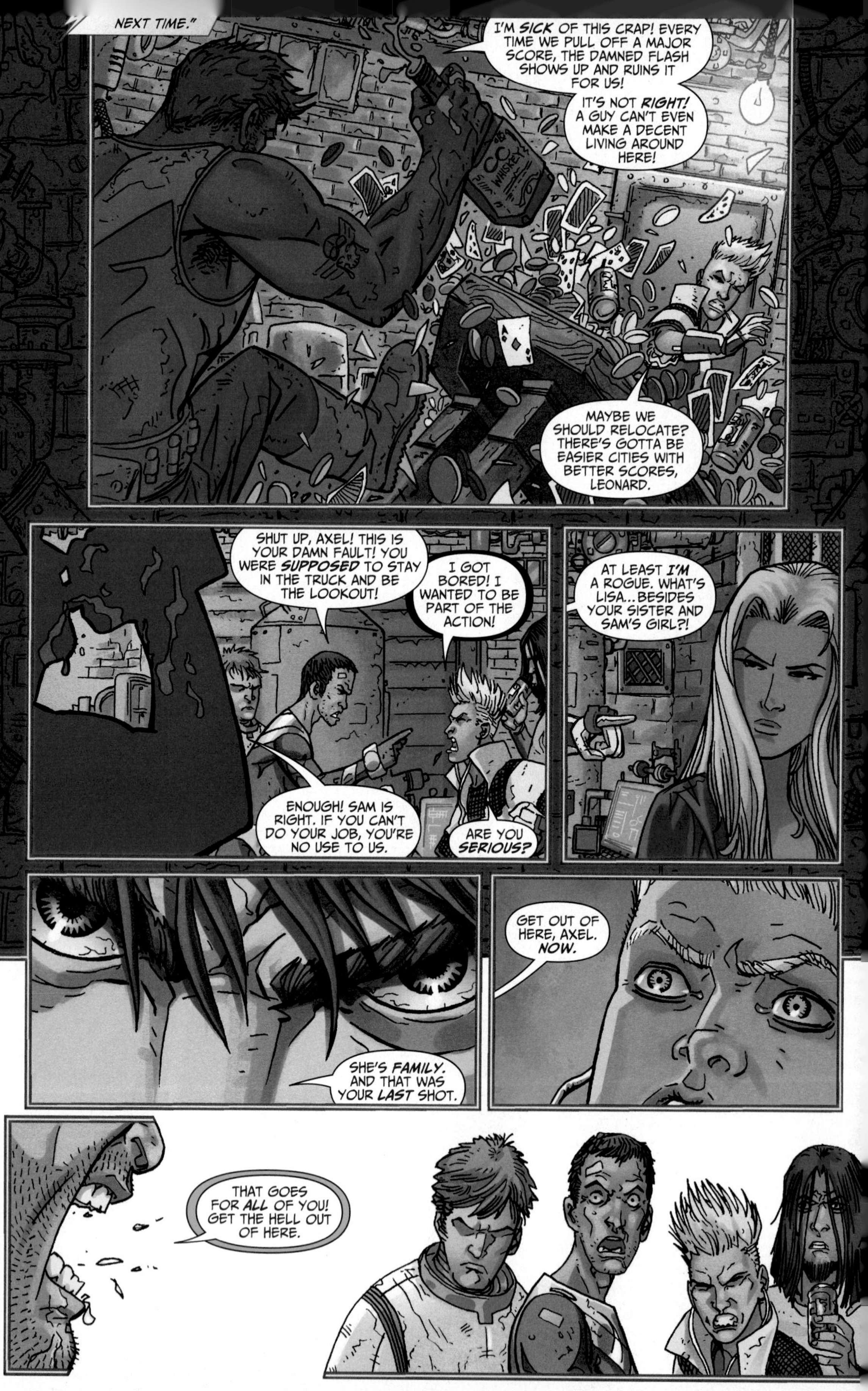
NEXT TIME."
I'M SICK OF THIS CRAP! EVERY TIME WE PULL OFF A MAJOR SCORE, THE DAMNED FLASH SHOWS UP AND RUINS IT FOR US!
IT'S NOT RIGHT! A GUY CAN'T EVEN MAKE A DECENT LIVING AROUND HERE!
WHISKEY
MAYBE WE SHOULD RELOCATE? THERE'S GOTTA BE EASIER CITIES WITH BETTER SCORES, LEONARD.
SHUT UP, AXEL! THIS IS YOUR DAMN FAULT! YOU WERE SUPPOSED TO STAY IN THE TRUCK AND BE THE LOOKOUT!
I GOT BORED! I WANTED TO BE PART OF THE ACTION!
ENOUGH! SAM IS RIGHT. IF YOU CAN'T DO YOUR JOB, YOU'RE NO USE TO US.
ARE YOU SERIOUS?
AT LEAST I'M A ROGUE. WHAT'S LISA...BESIDES YOUR SISTER AND SAM'S GIRL?!
SHE'S FAMILY. AND THAT WAS YOUR LAST SHOT.
GET OUT OF HERE, AXEL. NOW.
THAT GOES FOR ALL OF YOU! GET THE HELL OUT OF HERE.

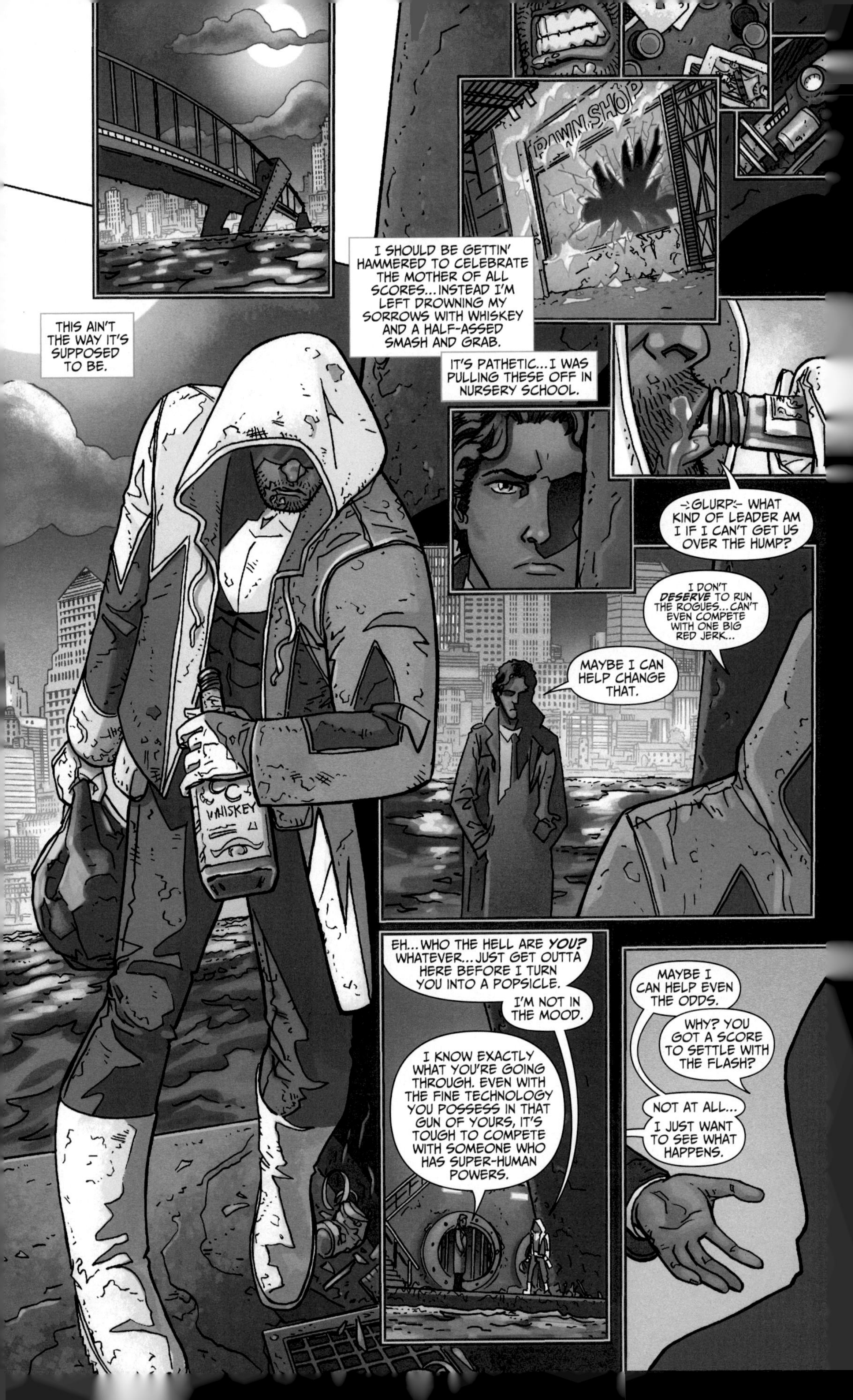
PAWN SHOP
I SHOULD BE GETTIN' HAMMERED TO CELEBRATE THE MOTHER OF ALL SCORES... INSTEAD I'M LEFT DROWNING MY SORROWS WITH WHISKEY AND A HALF-ASSED SMASH AND GRAB.
THIS AIN'T THE WAY IT'S SUPPOSED TO BE.
IT'S PATHETIC... I WAS PULLING THESE OFF IN NURSERY SCHOOL.
WHISKEY
-GLURP- WHAT KIND OF LEADER AM I IF I CAN'T GET US OVER THE HUMP?
I DON'T DESERVE TO RUN THE ROGUES... CAN'T EVEN COMPETE WITH ONE BIG RED JERK...
MAYBE I CAN HELP CHANGE THAT.
EH... WHO THE HELL ARE YOU? WHATEVER... JUST GET OUTTA HERE BEFORE I TURN YOU INTO A POPSICLE.
I'M NOT IN THE MOOD.
I KNOW EXACTLY WHAT YOU'RE GOING THROUGH. EVEN WITH THE FINE TECHNOLOGY YOU POSSESS IN THAT GUN OF YOURS, IT'S TOUGH TO COMPETE WITH SOMEONE WHO HAS SUPER-HUMAN POWERS.
MAYBE I CAN HELP EVEN THE ODDS.
WHY? YOU GOT A SCORE TO SETTLE WITH THE FLASH?
NOT AT ALL...
I JUST WANT TO SEE WHAT HAPPENS.

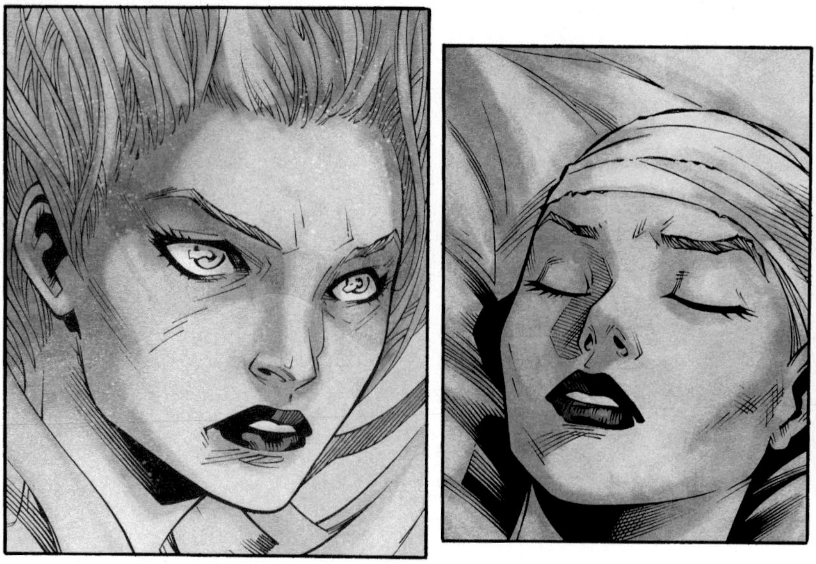

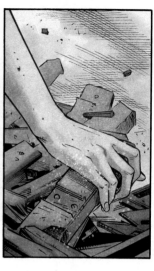

CHAPTER 3: THE PRICE

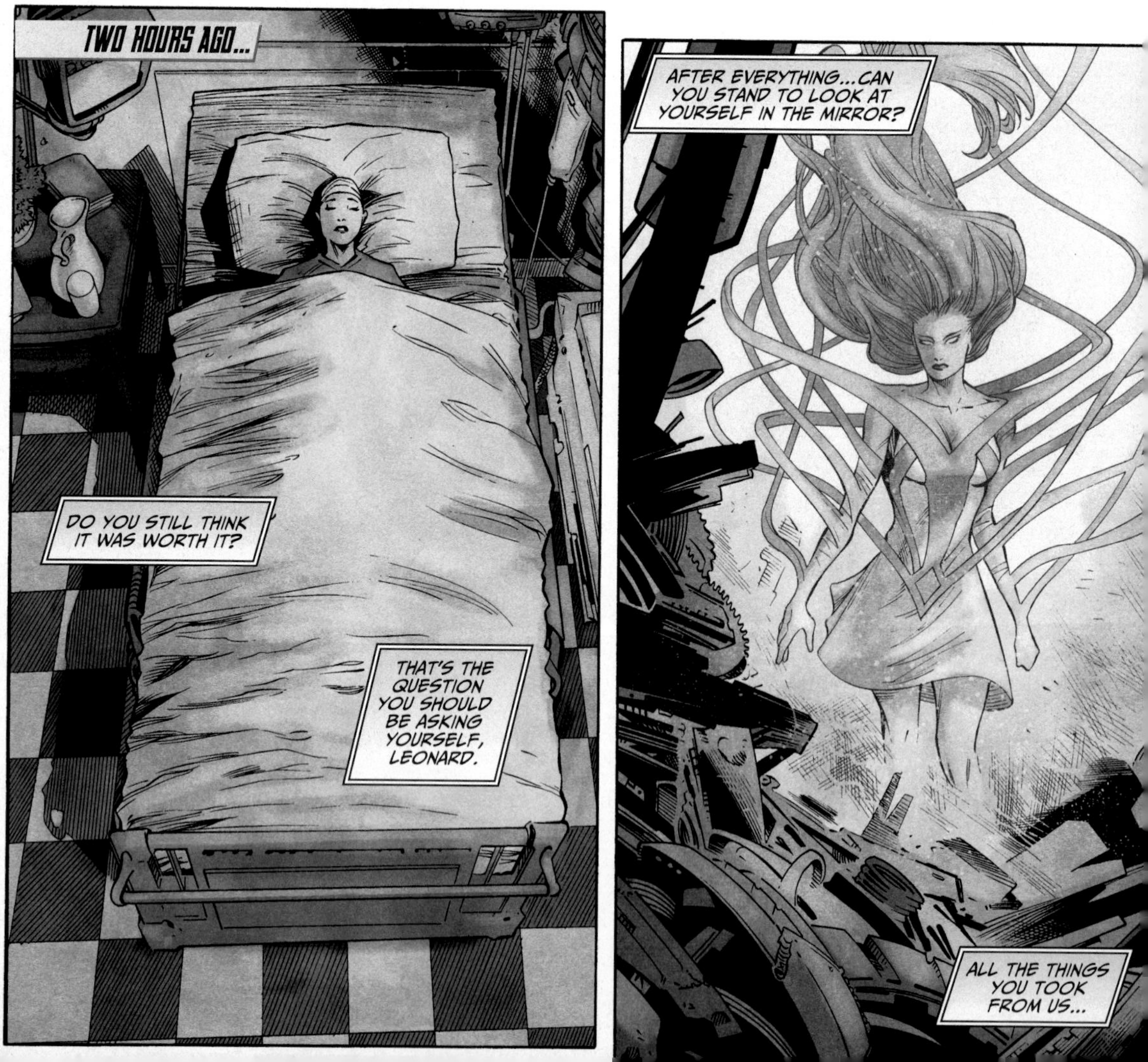
TWO HOURS AGO...
DO YOU STILL THINK IT WAS WORTH IT?
THAT'S THE QUESTION YOU SHOULD BE ASKING YOURSELF, LEONARD.
AFTER EVERYTHING...CAN YOU STAND TO LOOK AT YOURSELF IN THE MIRROR?
ALL THE THINGS YOU TOOK FROM US...

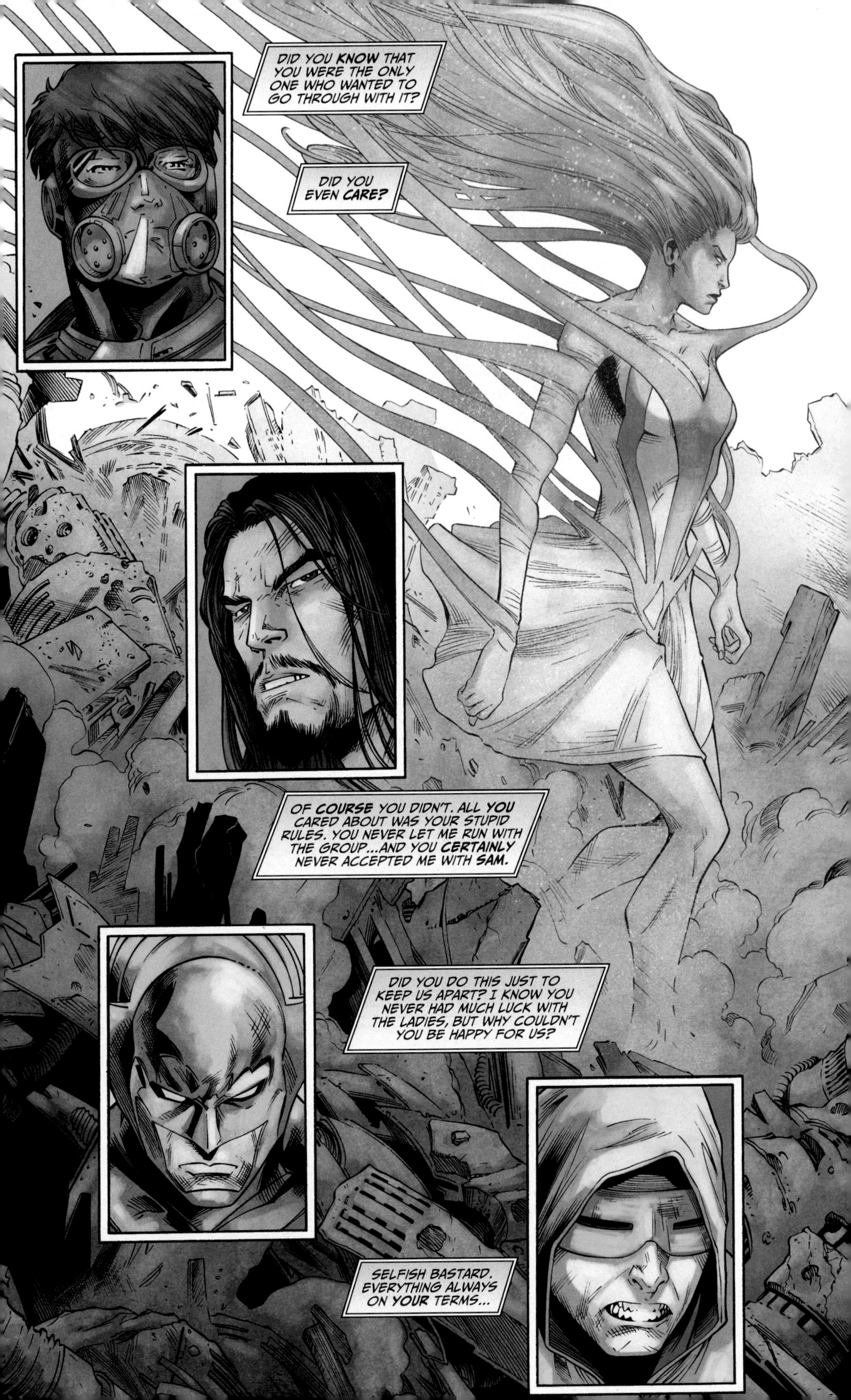
DID YOU KNOW THAT YOU WERE THE ONLY ONE WHO WANTED TO GO THROUGH WITH IT?
DID YOU EVEN CARE?
OF COURSE YOU DIDN'T. ALL YOU CARED ABOUT WAS YOUR STUPID RULES. YOU NEVER LET ME RUN WITH THE GROUP...AND YOU CERTAINLY NEVER ACCEPTED ME WITH SAM.
DID YOU DO THIS JUST TO KEEP US APART? I KNOW YOU NEVER HAD MUCH LUCK WITH THE LADIES, BUT WHY COULDN'T YOU BE HAPPY FOR US?
SELFISH BASTARD. EVERYTHING ALWAYS ON YOUR TERMS...

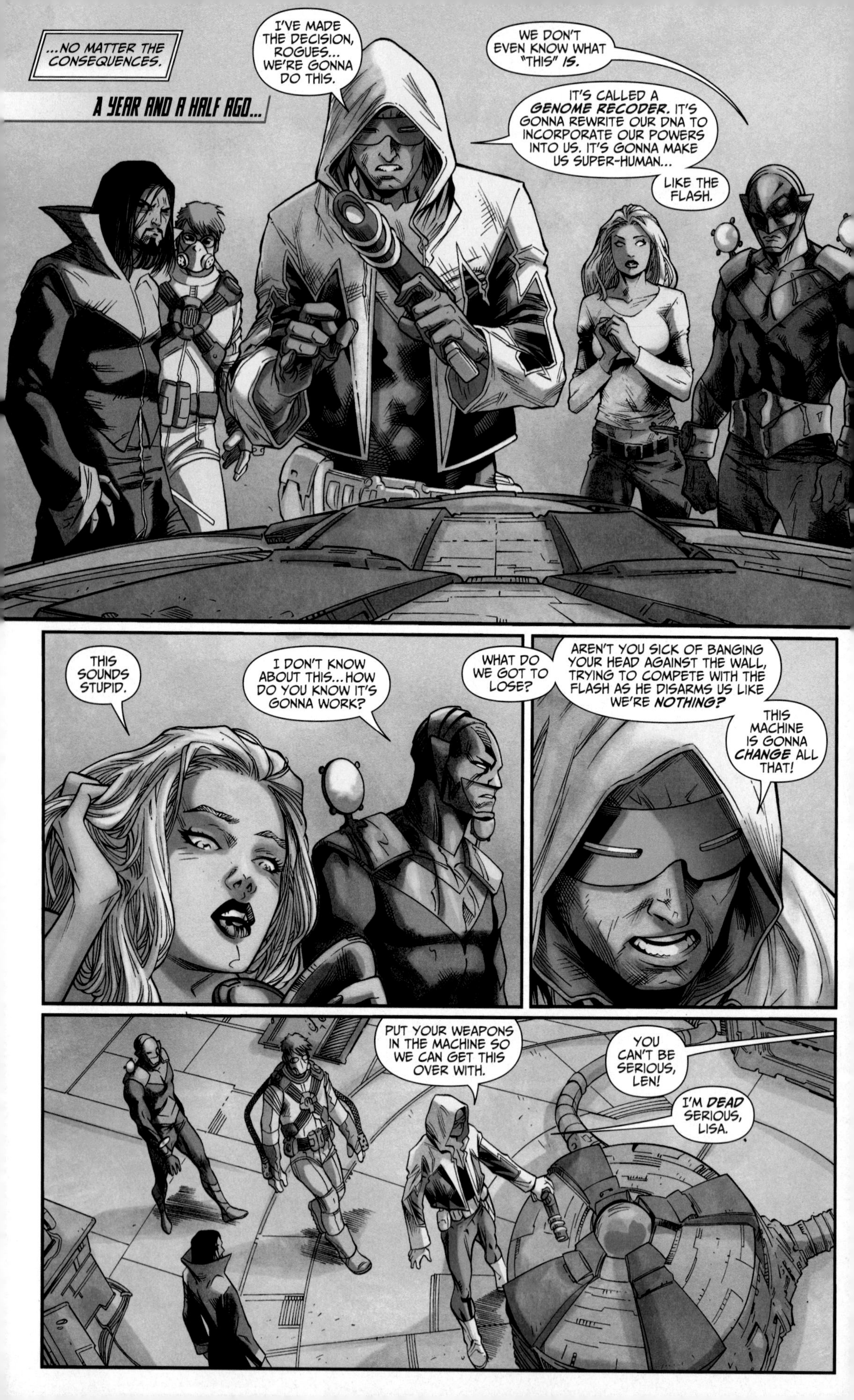
...NO MATTER THE CONSEQUENCES.
A YEAR AND A HALF AGO...
I'VE MADE THE DECISION, ROGUES... WE'RE GONNA DO THIS.
WE DON'T EVEN KNOW WHAT "THIS" IS.
IT'S CALLED A GENOME RECODER. IT'S GONNA REWRITE OUR DNA TO INCORPORATE OUR POWERS INTO US. IT'S GONNA MAKE US SUPER-HUMAN...
LIKE THE FLASH.
THIS SOUNDS STUPID.
I DON'T KNOW ABOUT THIS...HOW DO YOU KNOW IT'S GONNA WORK?
WHAT DO WE GOT TO LOSE?
AREN'T YOU SICK OF BANGING YOUR HEAD AGAINST THE WALL, TRYING TO COMPETE WITH THE FLASH AS HE DISARMS US LIKE WE'RE NOTHING?
THIS MACHINE IS GONNA CHANGE ALL THAT!
PUT YOUR WEAPONS IN THE MACHINE SO WE CAN GET THIS OVER WITH.
YOU CAN'T BE SERIOUS, LEN!
I'M DEAD SERIOUS, LISA.

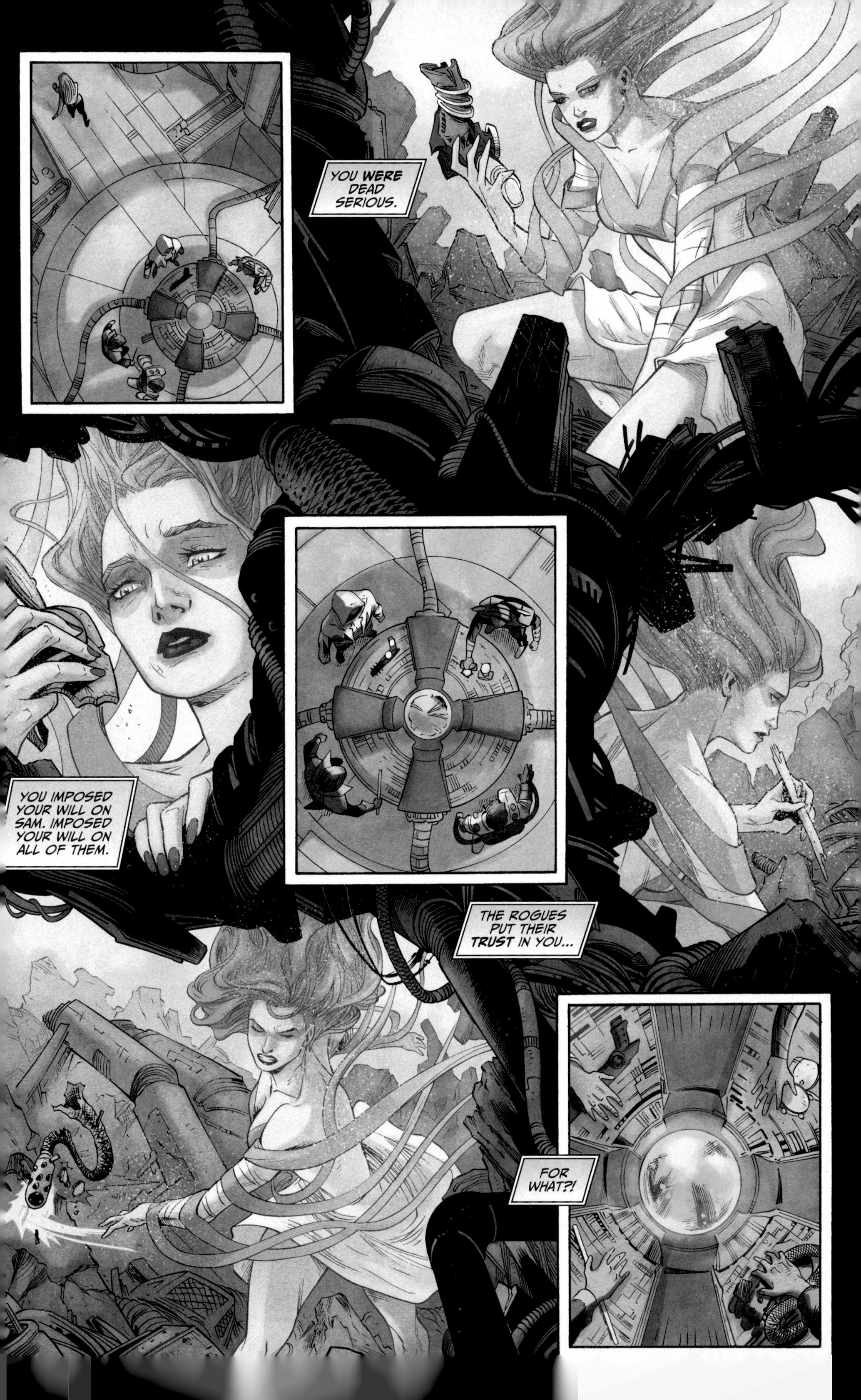
YOU WERE DEAD SERIOUS.
YOU IMPOSED YOUR WILL ON SAM. IMPOSED YOUR WILL ON ALL OF THEM.
THE ROGUES PUT THEIR TRUST IN YOU...
FOR WHAT?!

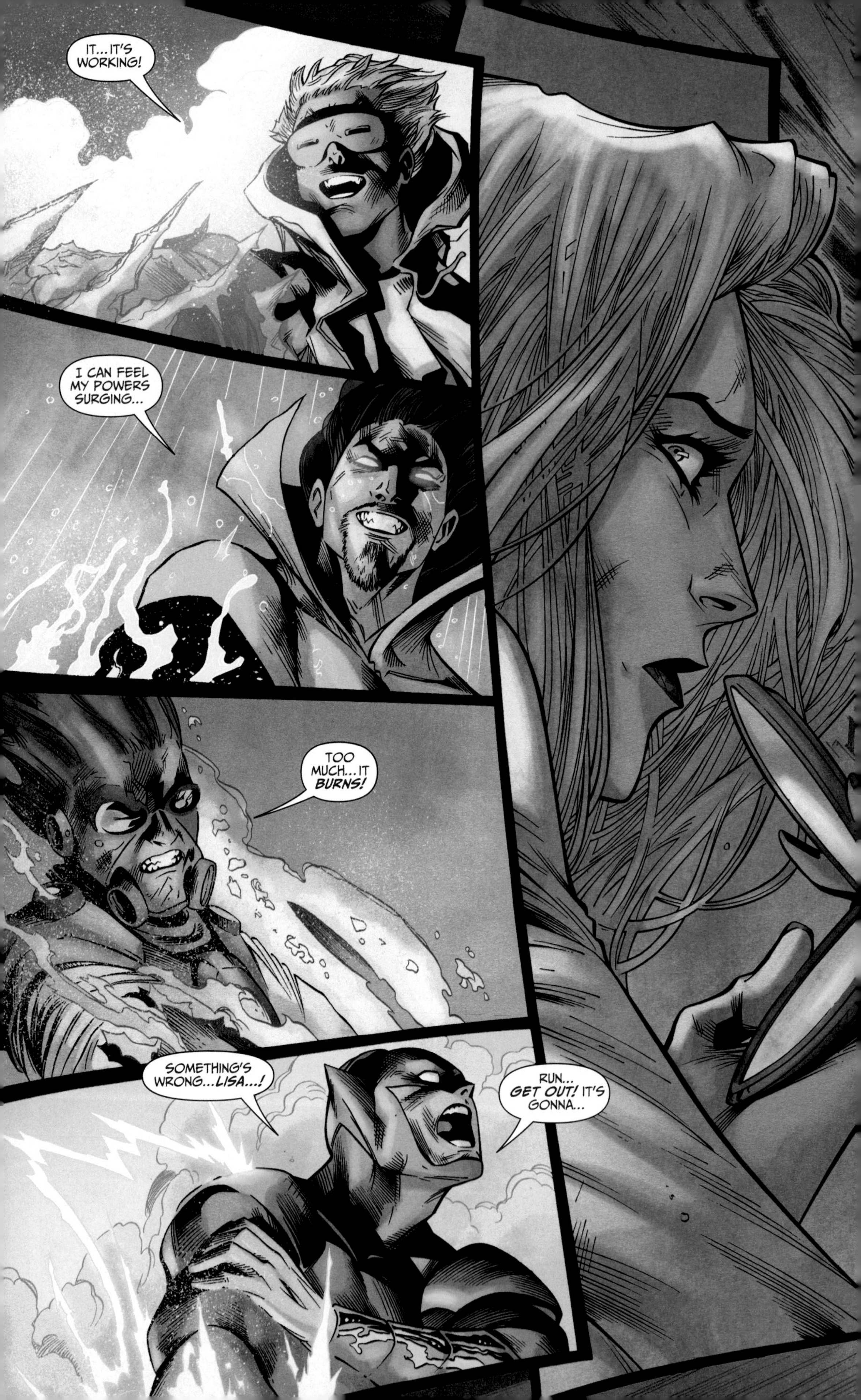
IT...IT'S WORKING!
I CAN FEEL MY POWERS SURGING...
TOO MUCH...IT BURNS!
SOMETHING'S WRONG...LISA...!
RUN... GET OUT! IT'S GONNA...

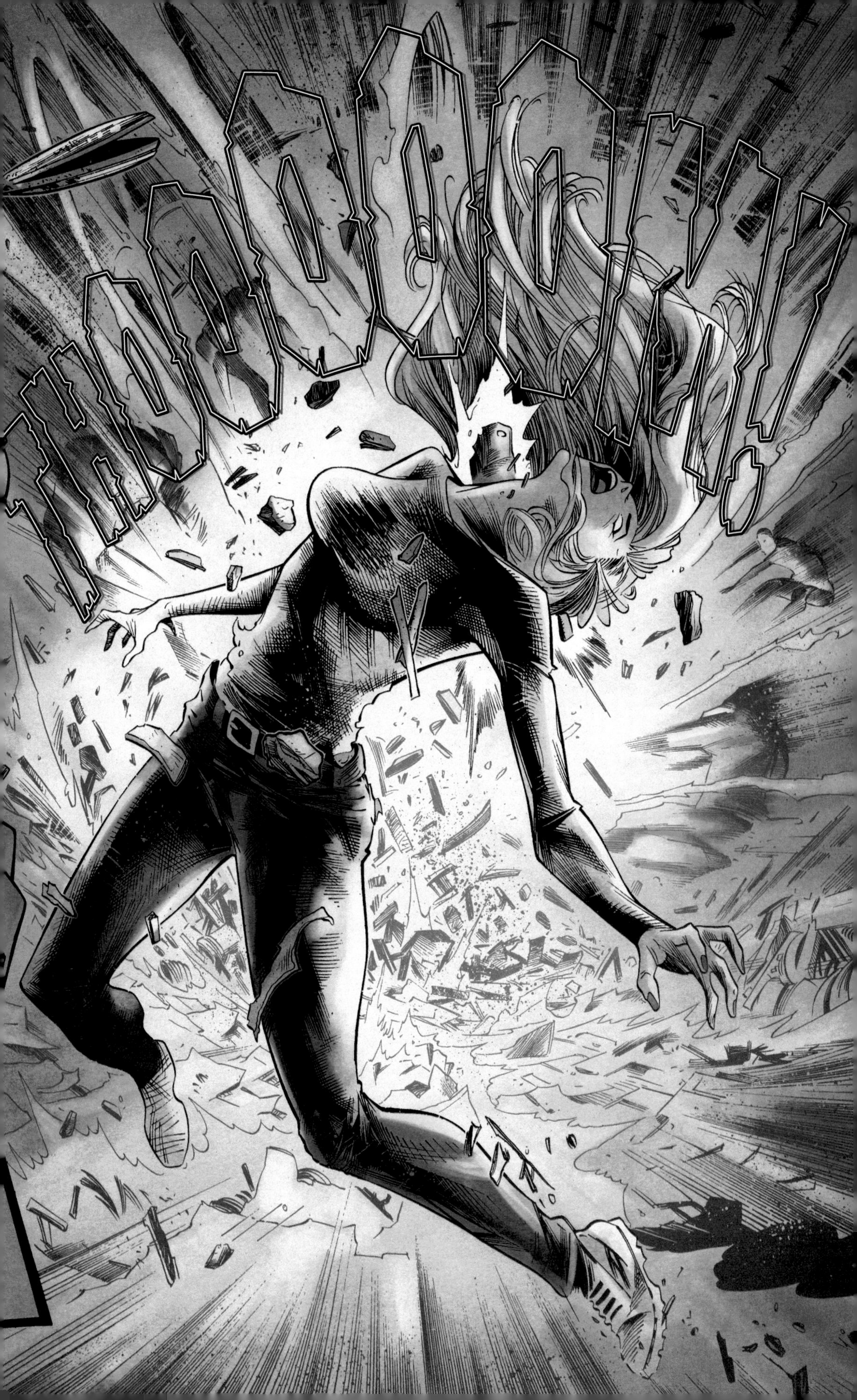
THOOOOOM!

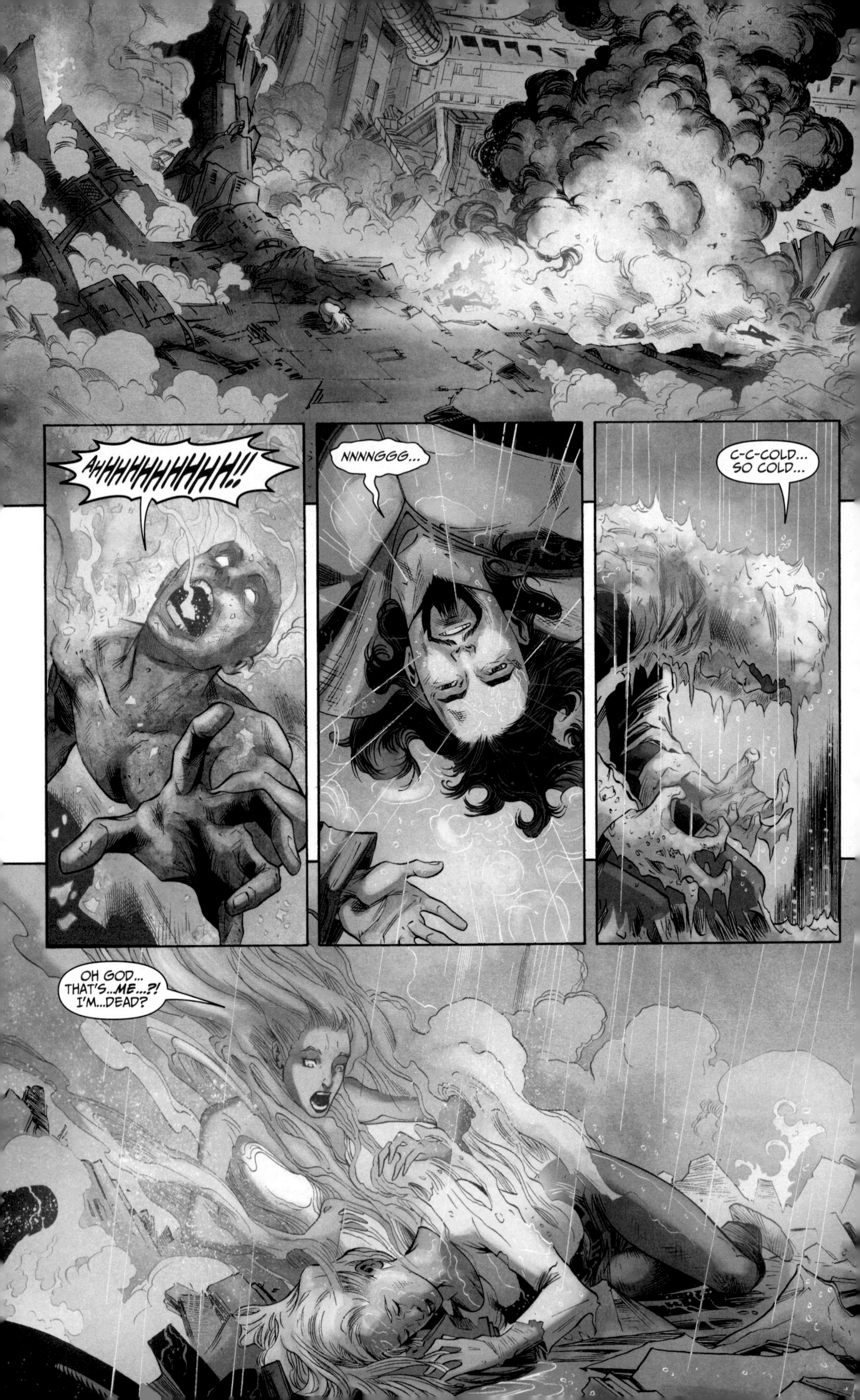
AHHHHHHHHHH!!
NNNNGGG...
C-C-COLD...
SO COLD...
OH GOD...
THAT'S...ME...?!
I'M...DEAD?

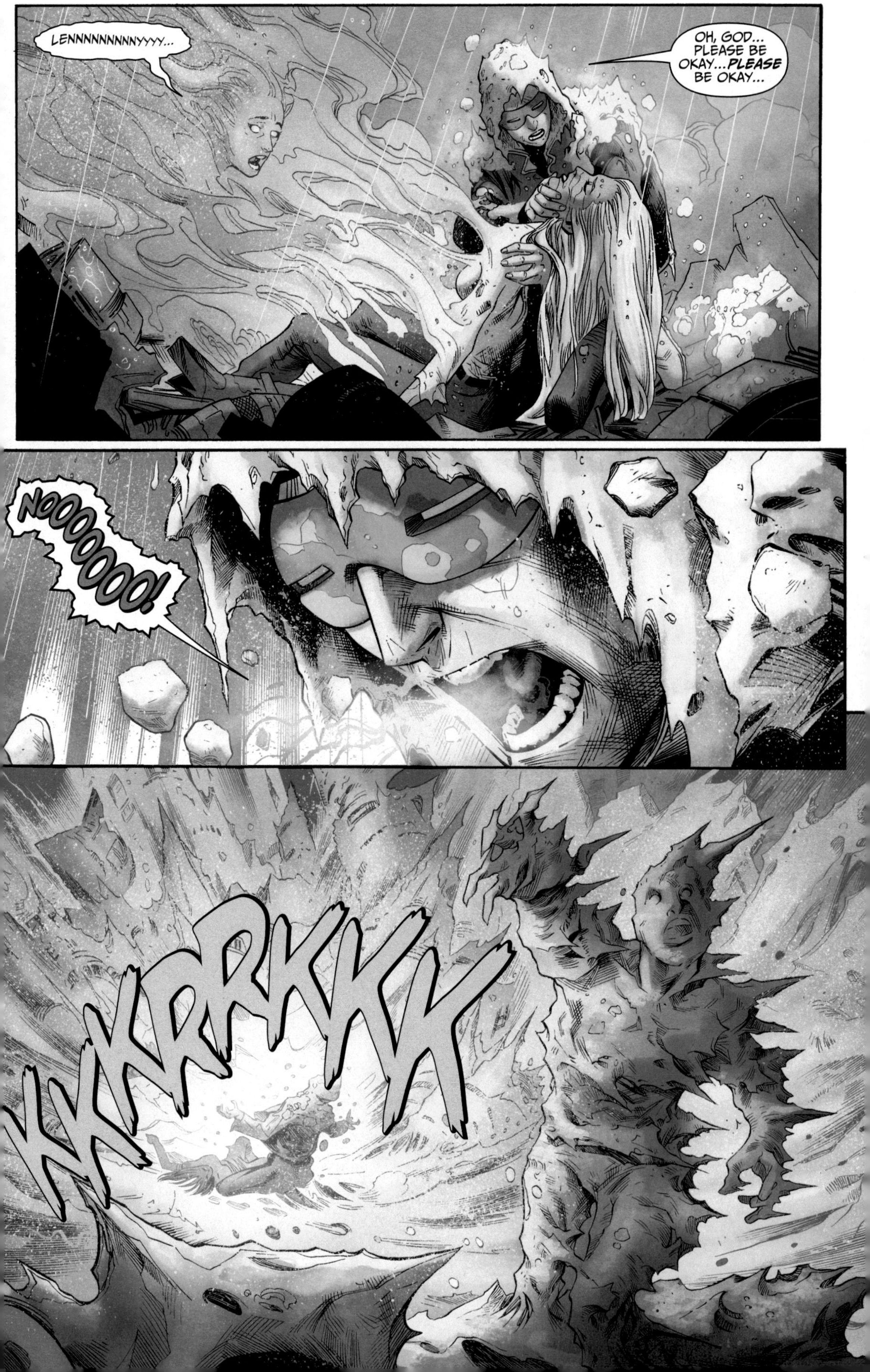
LENNNNNNNNNYYYY...
OH, GOD... PLEASE BE OKAY... PLEASE BE OKAY...
NOOOOOOOO!
KKKRKKK

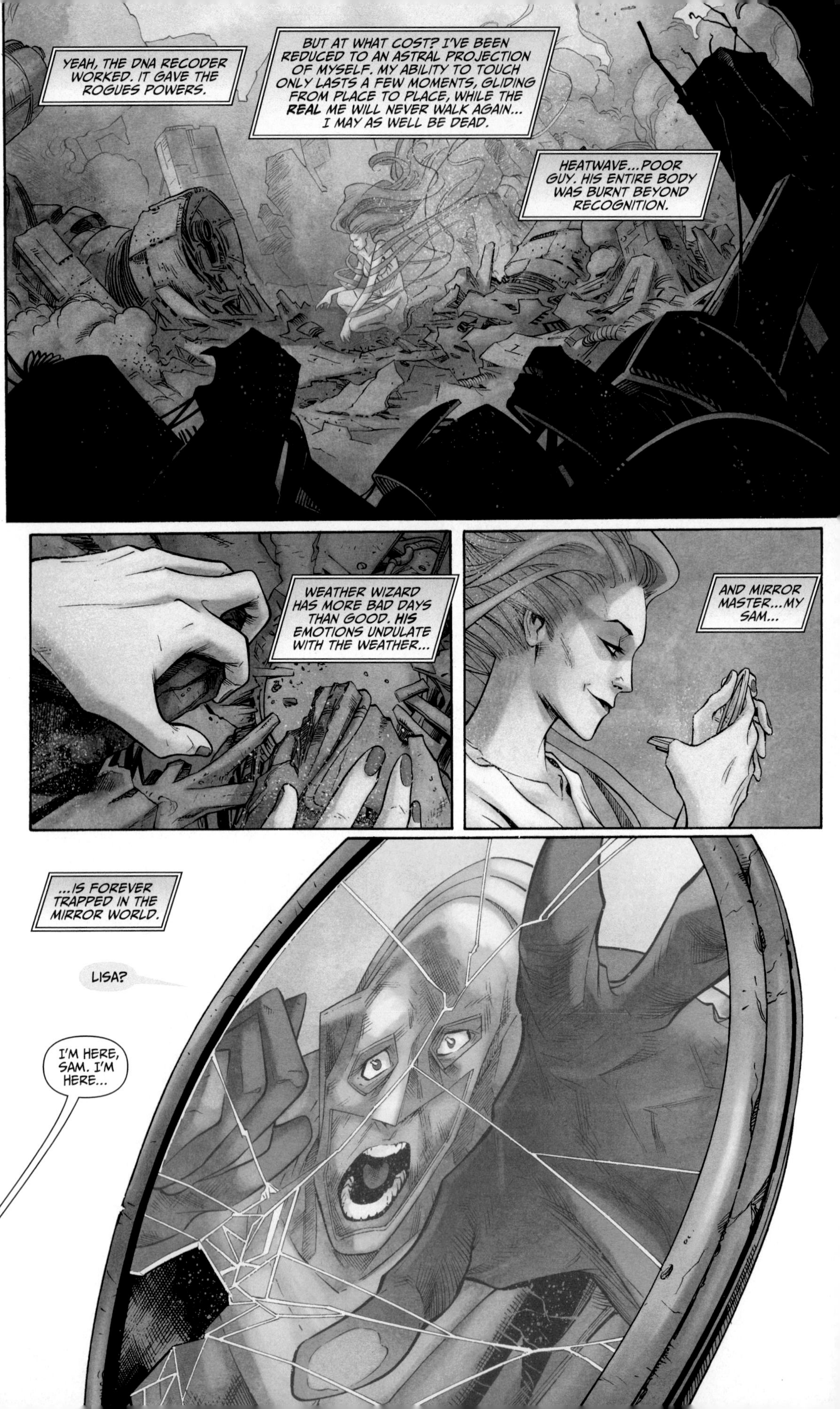
YEAH, THE DNA RECODER WORKED. IT GAVE THE ROGUES POWERS.
BUT AT WHAT COST? I'VE BEEN REDUCED TO AN ASTRAL PROJECTION OF MYSELF. MY ABILITY TO TOUCH ONLY LASTS A FEW MOMENTS, GLIDING FROM PLACE TO PLACE, WHILE THE **REAL** ME WILL NEVER WALK AGAIN... I MAY AS WELL BE DEAD.
HEATWAVE...POOR GUY. HIS ENTIRE BODY WAS BURNT BEYOND RECOGNITION.
WEATHER WIZARD HAS MORE BAD DAYS THAN GOOD. **HIS** EMOTIONS UNDULATE WITH THE WEATHER...
AND MIRROR MASTER...MY SAM...
...IS FOREVER TRAPPED IN THE MIRROR WORLD.
LISA?
I'M HERE, SAM. I'M HERE...

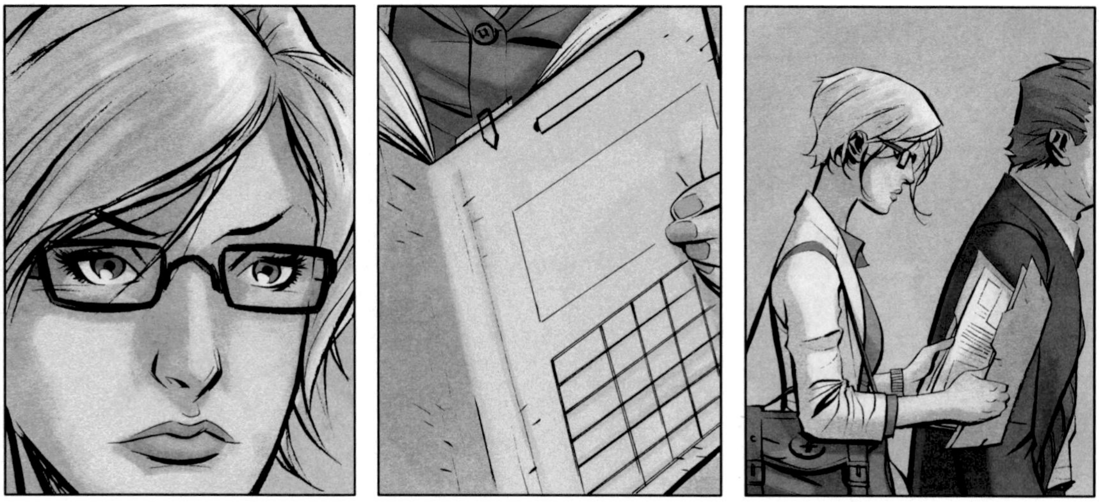

CHAPTER 4: THE SECRET

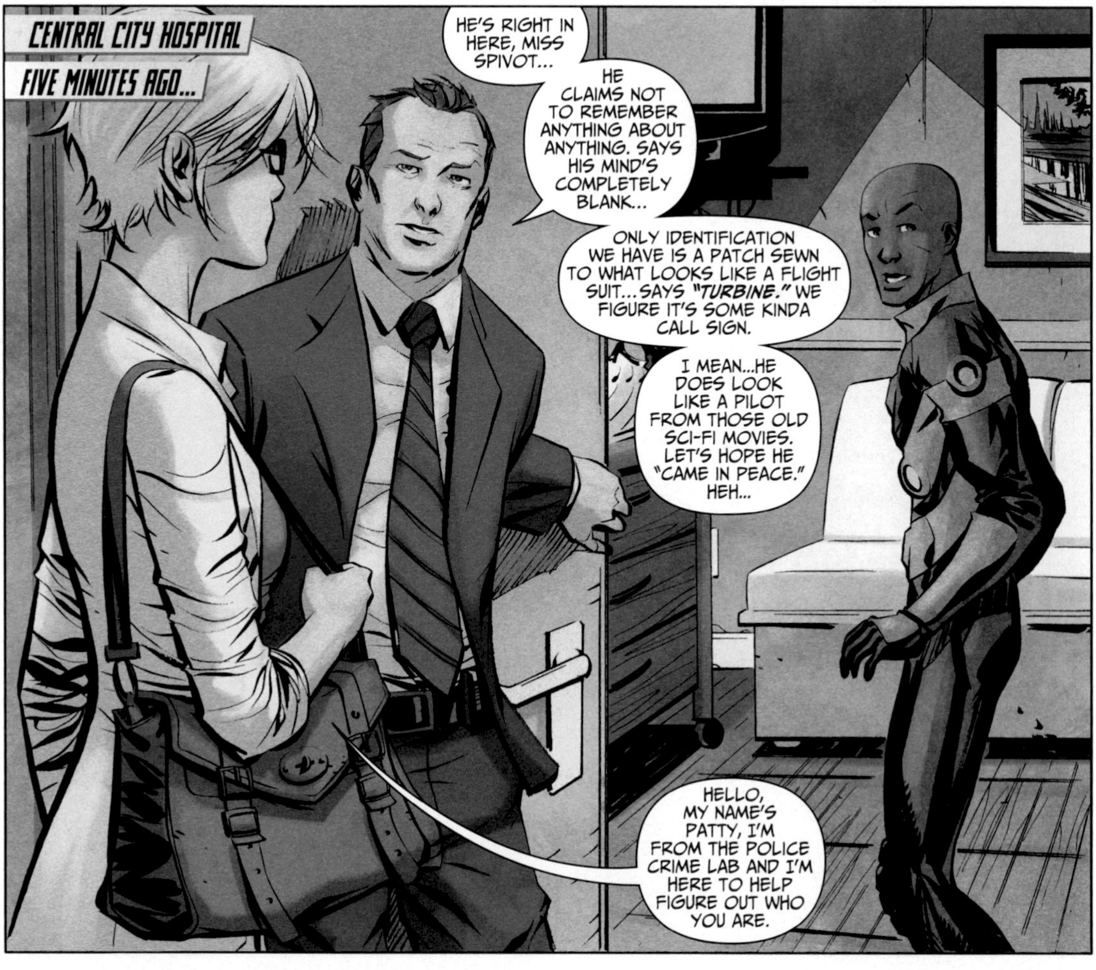
CENTRAL CITY HOSPITAL
FIVE MINUTES AGO...
HE'S RIGHT IN HERE, MISS SPIVOT...
HE CLAIMS NOT TO REMEMBER ANYTHING ABOUT ANYTHING. SAYS HIS MIND'S COMPLETELY BLANK...
ONLY IDENTIFICATION WE HAVE IS A PATCH SEWN TO WHAT LOOKS LIKE A FLIGHT SUIT...SAYS "TURBINE." WE FIGURE IT'S SOME KINDA CALL SIGN.
I MEAN...HE DOES LOOK LIKE A PILOT FROM THOSE OLD SCI-FI MOVIES. LET'S HOPE HE "CAME IN PEACE." HEH...
HELLO, MY NAME'S PATTY, I'M FROM THE POLICE CRIME LAB AND I'M HERE TO HELP FIGURE OUT WHO YOU ARE.

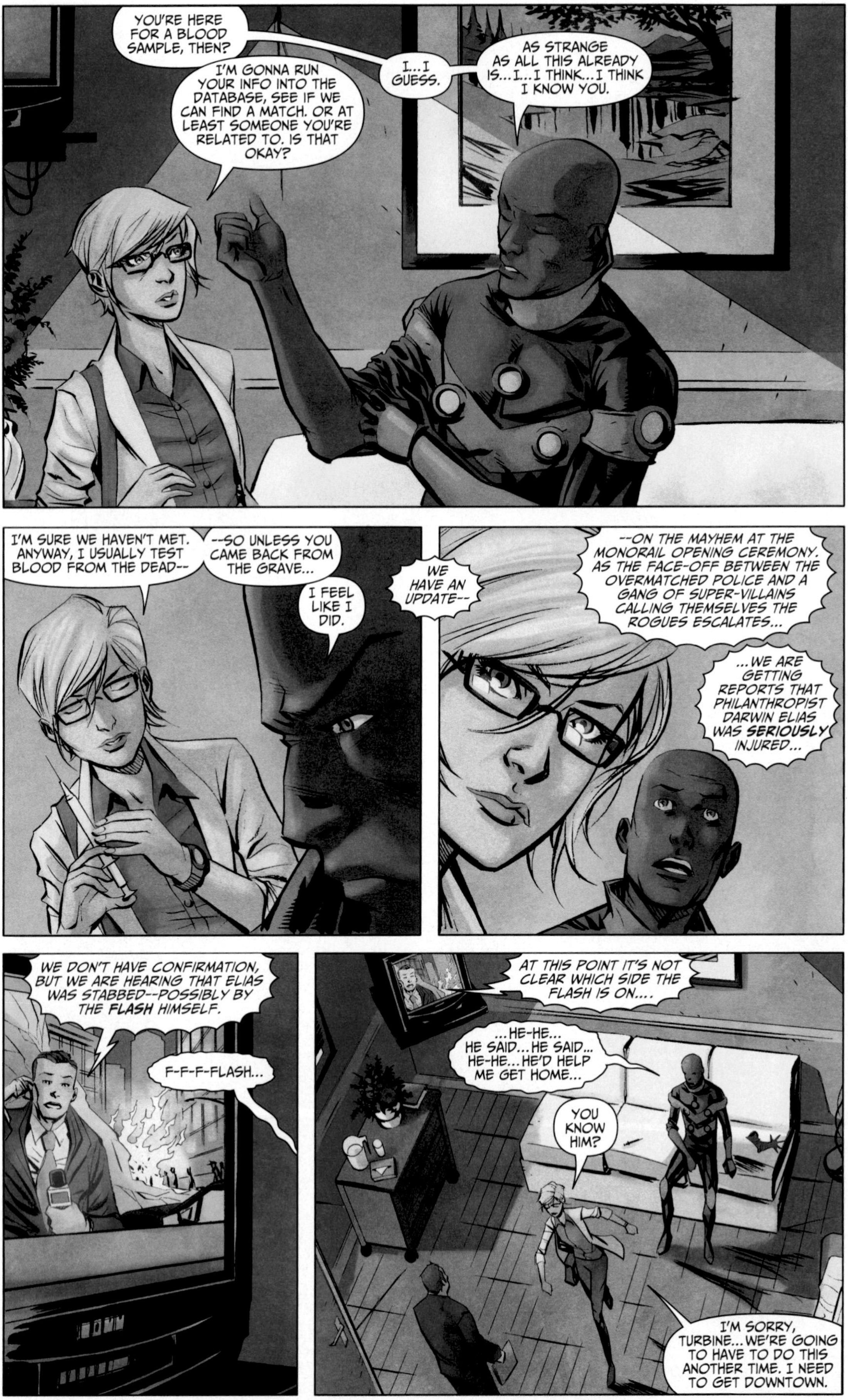
YOU'RE HERE FOR A BLOOD SAMPLE, THEN?
I'M GONNA RUN YOUR INFO INTO THE DATABASE, SEE IF WE CAN FIND A MATCH. OR AT LEAST SOMEONE YOU'RE RELATED TO. IS THAT OKAY?
I...I GUESS.
AS STRANGE AS ALL THIS ALREADY IS...I...I THINK...I THINK I KNOW YOU.
I'M SURE WE HAVEN'T MET. ANYWAY, I USUALLY TEST BLOOD FROM THE DEAD--
--SO UNLESS YOU CAME BACK FROM THE GRAVE...
I FEEL LIKE I DID.
WE HAVE AN UPDATE--
--ON THE MAYHEM AT THE MONORAIL OPENING CEREMONY. AS THE FACE-OFF BETWEEN THE OVERMATCHED POLICE AND A GANG OF SUPER-VILLAINS CALLING THEMSELVES THE ROGUES ESCALATES...
...WE ARE GETTING REPORTS THAT PHILANTHROPIST DARWIN ELIAS WAS SERIOUSLY INJURED...
WE DON'T HAVE CONFIRMATION, BUT WE ARE HEARING THAT ELIAS WAS STABBED--POSSIBLY BY THE FLASH HIMSELF.
F-F-F-FLASH...
AT THIS POINT IT'S NOT CLEAR WHICH SIDE THE FLASH IS ON....
...HE-HE... HE SAID...HE SAID... HE-HE...HE'D HELP ME GET HOME...
YOU KNOW HIM?
I'M SORRY, TURBINE...WE'RE GOING TO HAVE TO DO THIS ANOTHER TIME. I NEED TO GET DOWNTOWN.

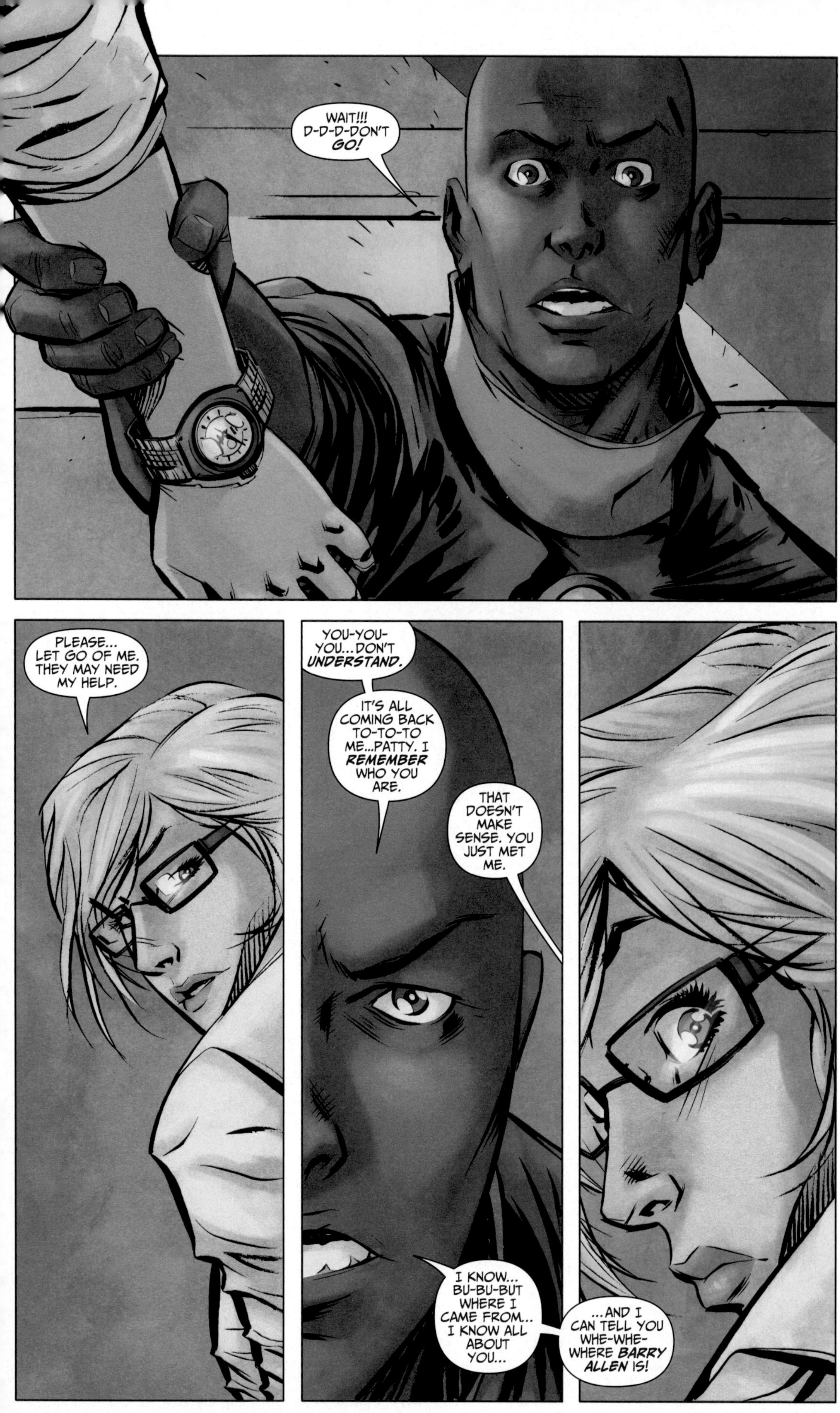
WAIT!!! D-D-D-DON'T *GO!*
PLEASE... LET GO OF ME. THEY MAY NEED MY HELP.
YOU-YOU-YOU...DON'T **UNDERSTAND.**
IT'S ALL COMING BACK TO-TO-TO ME...PATTY. I ***REMEMBER*** WHO YOU ARE.
THAT DOESN'T MAKE SENSE. YOU JUST MET ME.
I KNOW... BU-BU-BUT WHERE I CAME FROM... I KNOW ALL ABOUT YOU...
...AND I CAN TELL YOU WHE-WHE-WHERE ***BARRY ALLEN*** IS!

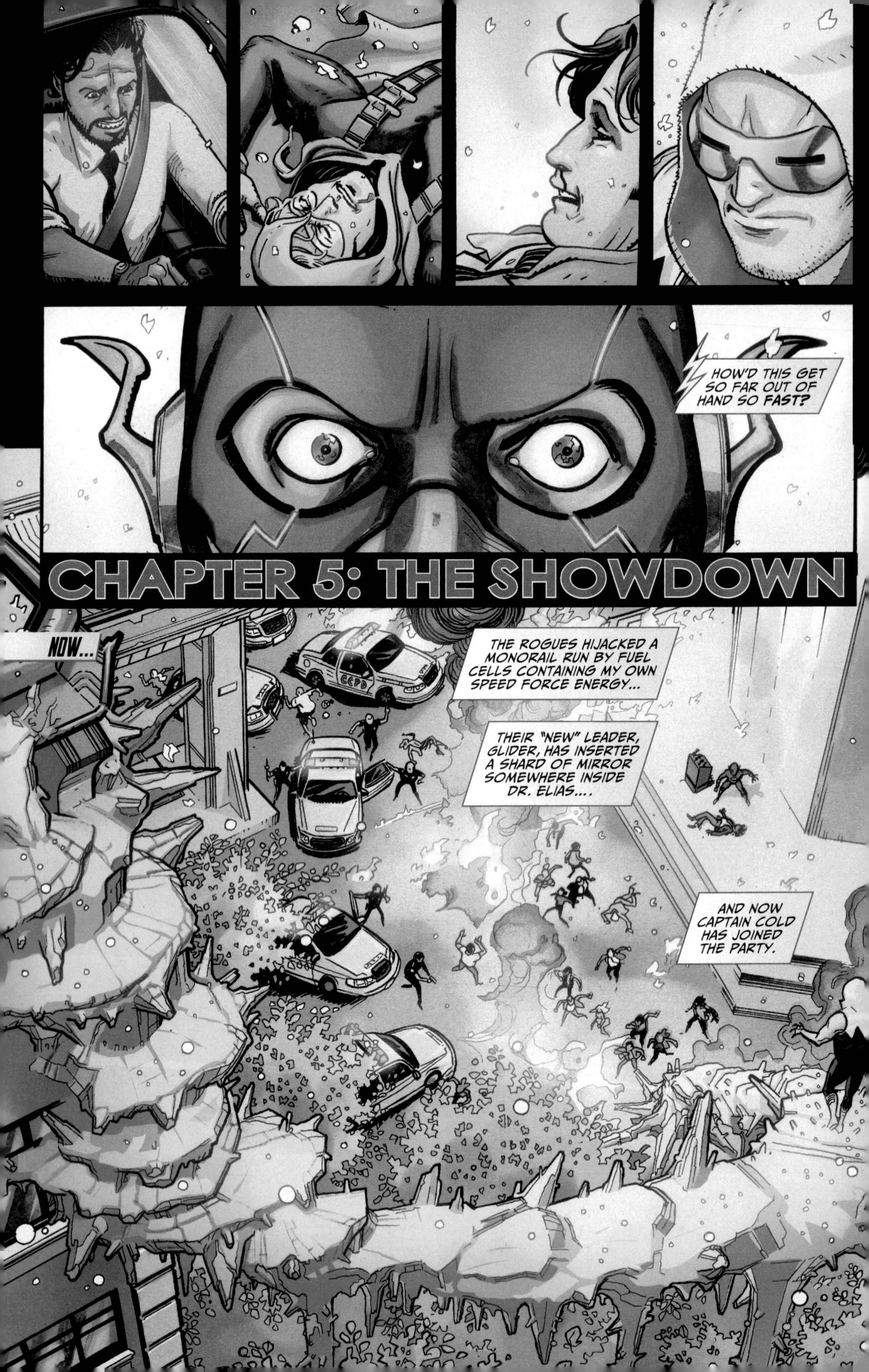
HOW'D THIS GET SO FAR OUT OF HAND SO FAST?
CHAPTER 5: THE SHOWDOWN
NOW...
THE ROGUES HIJACKED A MONORAIL RUN BY FUEL CELLS CONTAINING MY OWN SPEED FORCE ENERGY...
THEIR "NEW" LEADER, GLIDER, HAS INSERTED A SHARD OF MIRROR SOMEWHERE INSIDE DR. ELIAS....
AND NOW CAPTAIN COLD HAS JOINED THE PARTY.
CCPD

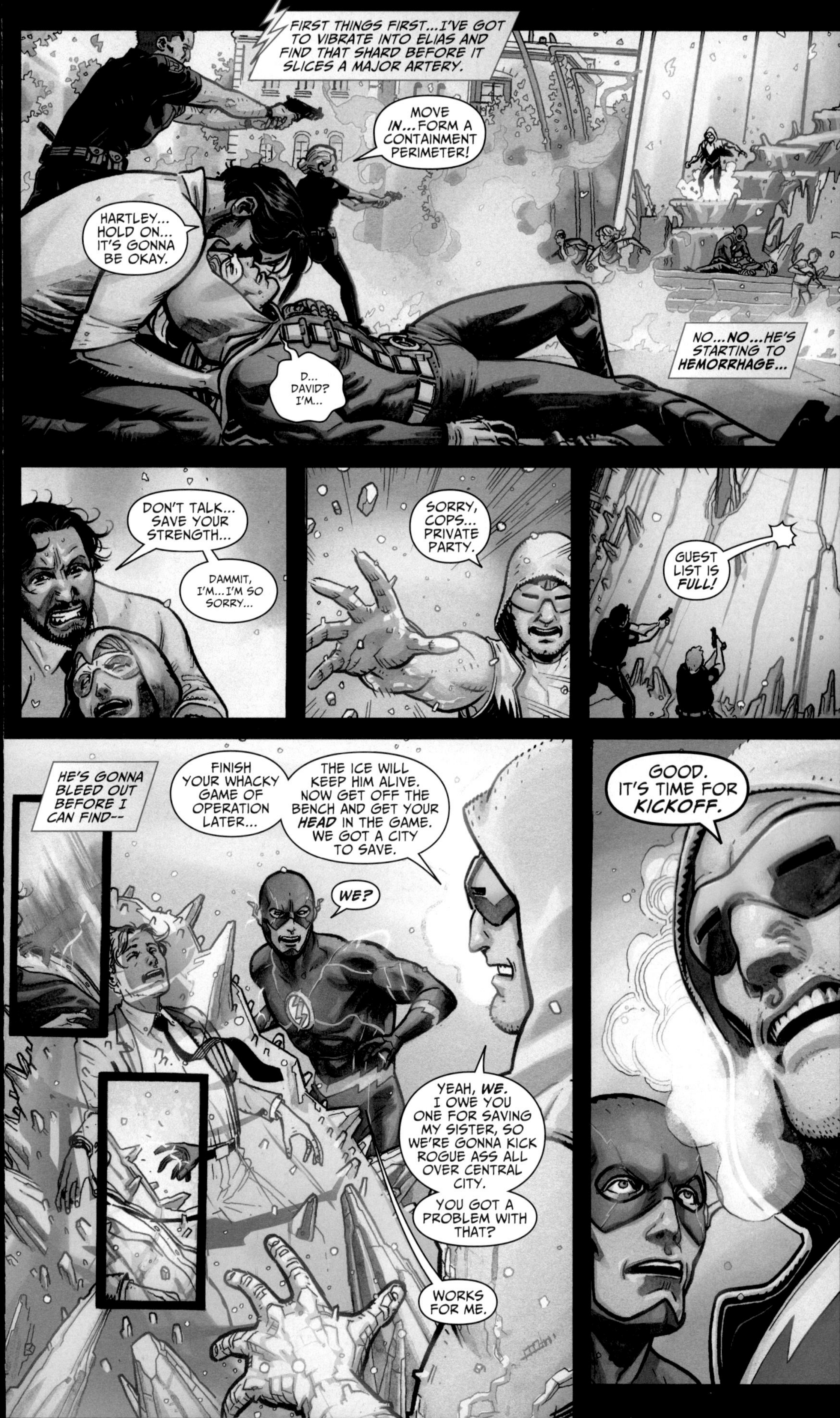
FIRST THINGS FIRST...I'VE GOT TO VIBRATE INTO ELIAS AND FIND THAT SHARD BEFORE IT SLICES A MAJOR ARTERY.
MOVE IN...FORM A CONTAINMENT PERIMETER!
HARTLEY... HOLD ON... IT'S GONNA BE OKAY.
D... DAVID? I'M...
NO...NO...HE'S STARTING TO HEMORRHAGE...
DON'T TALK... SAVE YOUR STRENGTH...
DAMMIT, I'M...I'M SO SORRY...
SORRY, COPS... PRIVATE PARTY.
GUEST LIST IS FULL!
HE'S GONNA BLEED OUT BEFORE I CAN FIND--
FINISH YOUR WHACKY GAME OF OPERATION LATER...
THE ICE WILL KEEP HIM ALIVE. NOW GET OFF THE BENCH AND GET YOUR HEAD IN THE GAME. WE GOT A CITY TO SAVE.
WE?
YEAH, WE. I OWE YOU ONE FOR SAVING MY SISTER, SO WE'RE GONNA KICK ROGUE ASS ALL OVER CENTRAL CITY.
YOU GOT A PROBLEM WITH THAT?
WORKS FOR ME.
GOOD. IT'S TIME FOR KICKOFF.

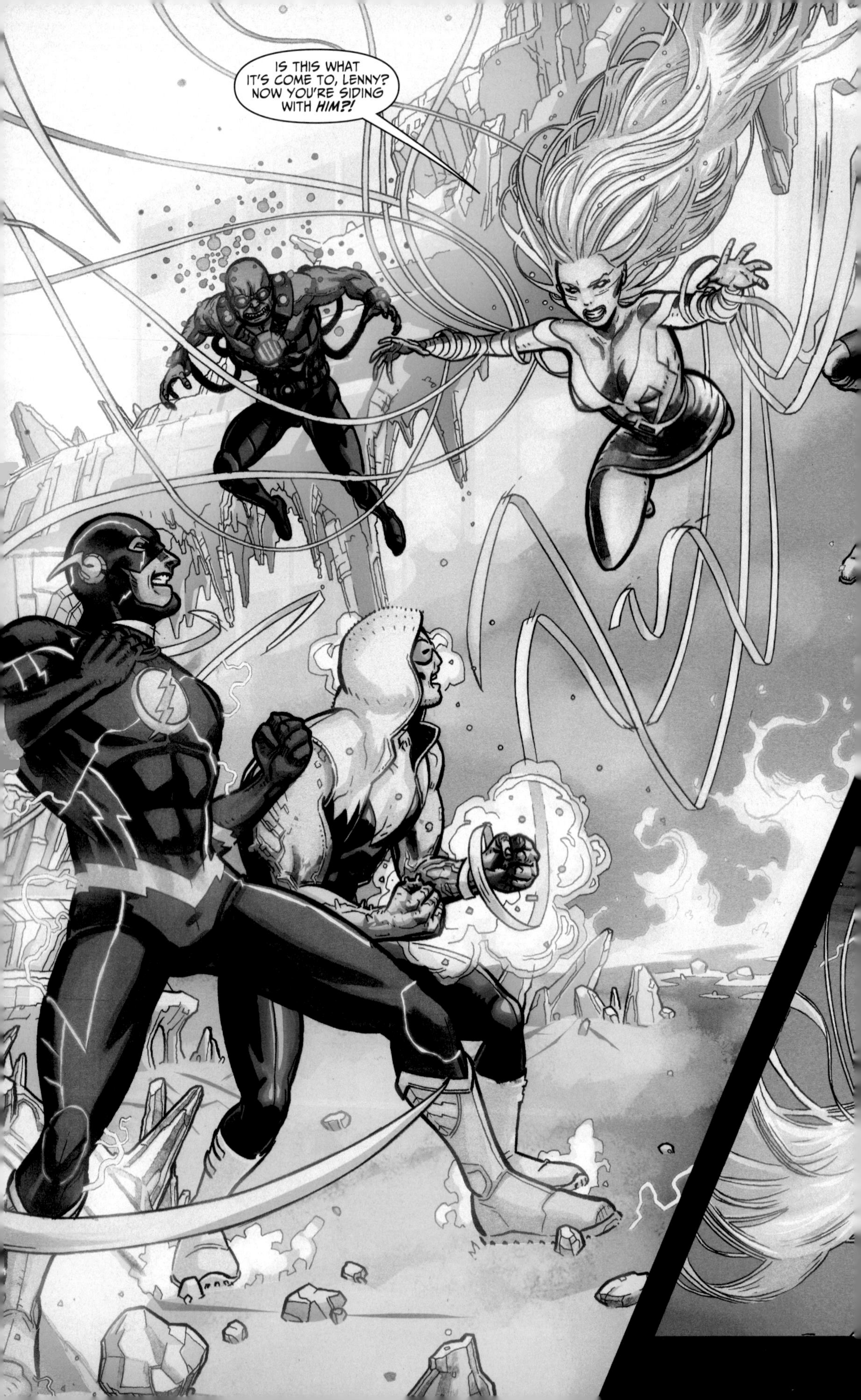
IS THIS WHAT IT'S COME TO, LENNY? NOW YOU'RE SIDING WITH *HIM?!*

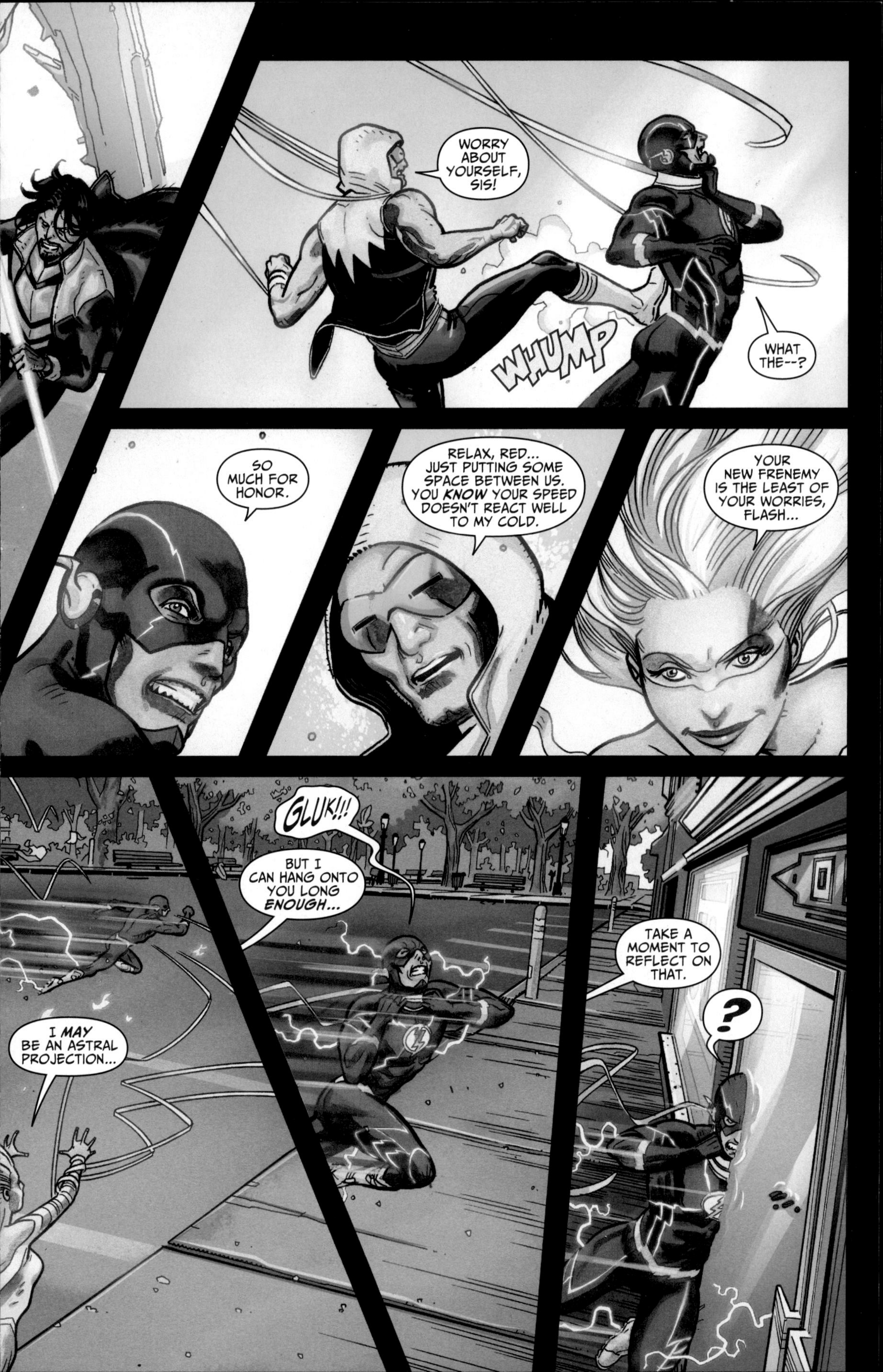
WORRY ABOUT YOURSELF, SIS!
WHUMP
WHAT THE--?
SO MUCH FOR HONOR.
RELAX, RED... JUST PUTTING SOME SPACE BETWEEN US. YOU KNOW YOUR SPEED DOESN'T REACT WELL TO MY COLD.
YOUR NEW FRENEMY IS THE LEAST OF YOUR WORRIES, FLASH...
I MAY BE AN ASTRAL PROJECTION...
GLUK!!!
BUT I CAN HANG ONTO YOU LONG ENOUGH...
TAKE A MOMENT TO REFLECT ON THAT.
?

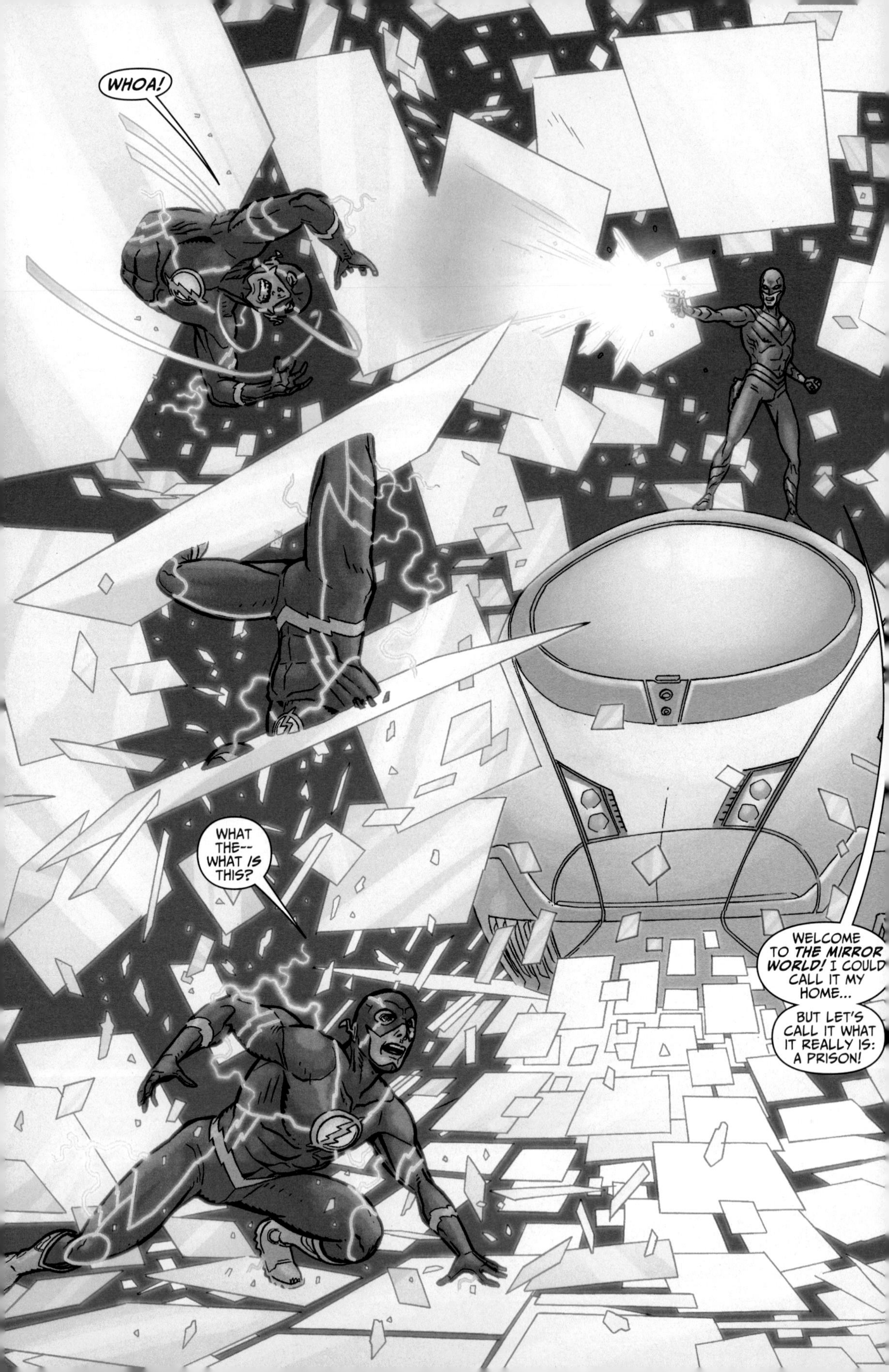
WHOA!
WHAT THE-- WHAT *IS* THIS?
WELCOME TO ***THE MIRROR WORLD!*** I COULD CALL IT MY HOME...
BUT LET'S CALL IT WHAT IT REALLY IS: A PRISON!

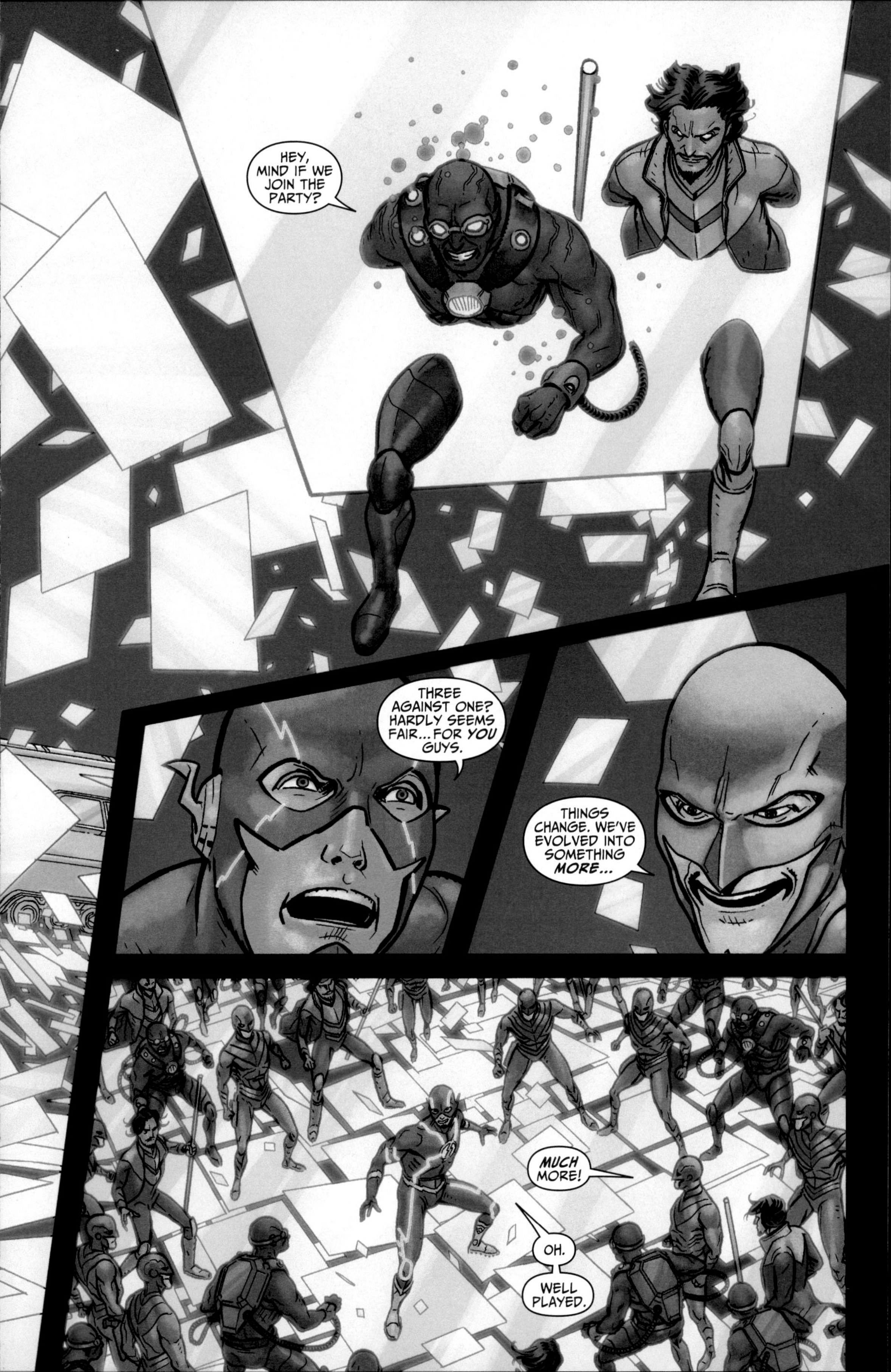
HEY, MIND IF WE JOIN THE PARTY?
THREE AGAINST ONE? HARDLY SEEMS FAIR...FOR *YOU* GUYS.
THINGS CHANGE. WE'VE EVOLVED INTO SOMETHING *MORE...*
MUCH MORE!
OH.
WELL PLAYED.

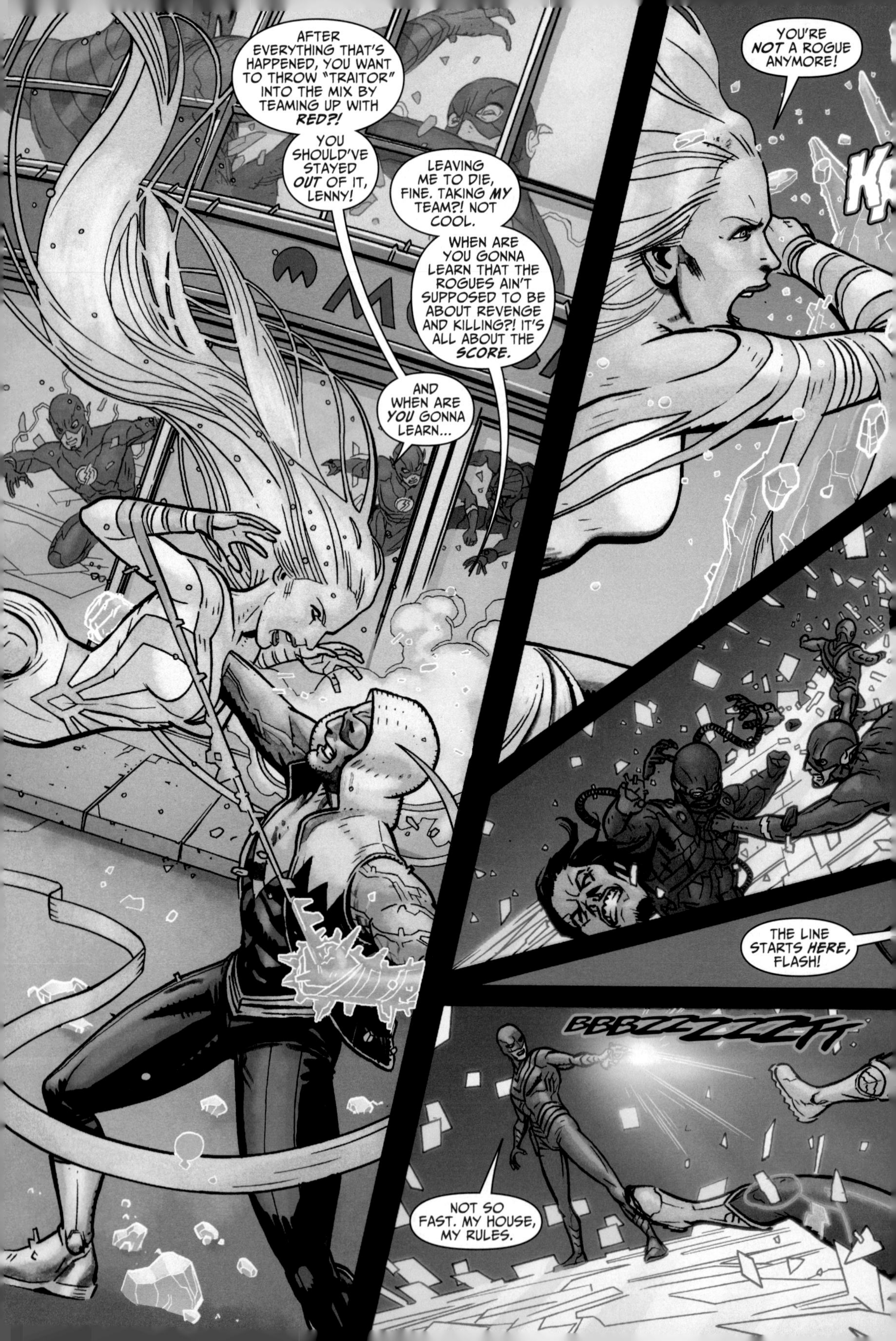
AFTER EVERYTHING THAT'S HAPPENED, YOU WANT TO THROW "TRAITOR" INTO THE MIX BY TEAMING UP WITH RED?!
YOU SHOULD'VE STAYED OUT OF IT, LENNY!
LEAVING ME TO DIE, FINE. TAKING MY TEAM?! NOT COOL.
WHEN ARE YOU GONNA LEARN THAT THE ROGUES AIN'T SUPPOSED TO BE ABOUT REVENGE AND KILLING?! IT'S ALL ABOUT THE SCORE.
AND WHEN ARE YOU GONNA LEARN...
YOU'RE NOT A ROGUE ANYMORE!
THE LINE STARTS HERE, FLASH!
BBBZZZZZZZZT
NOT SO FAST. MY HOUSE, MY RULES.

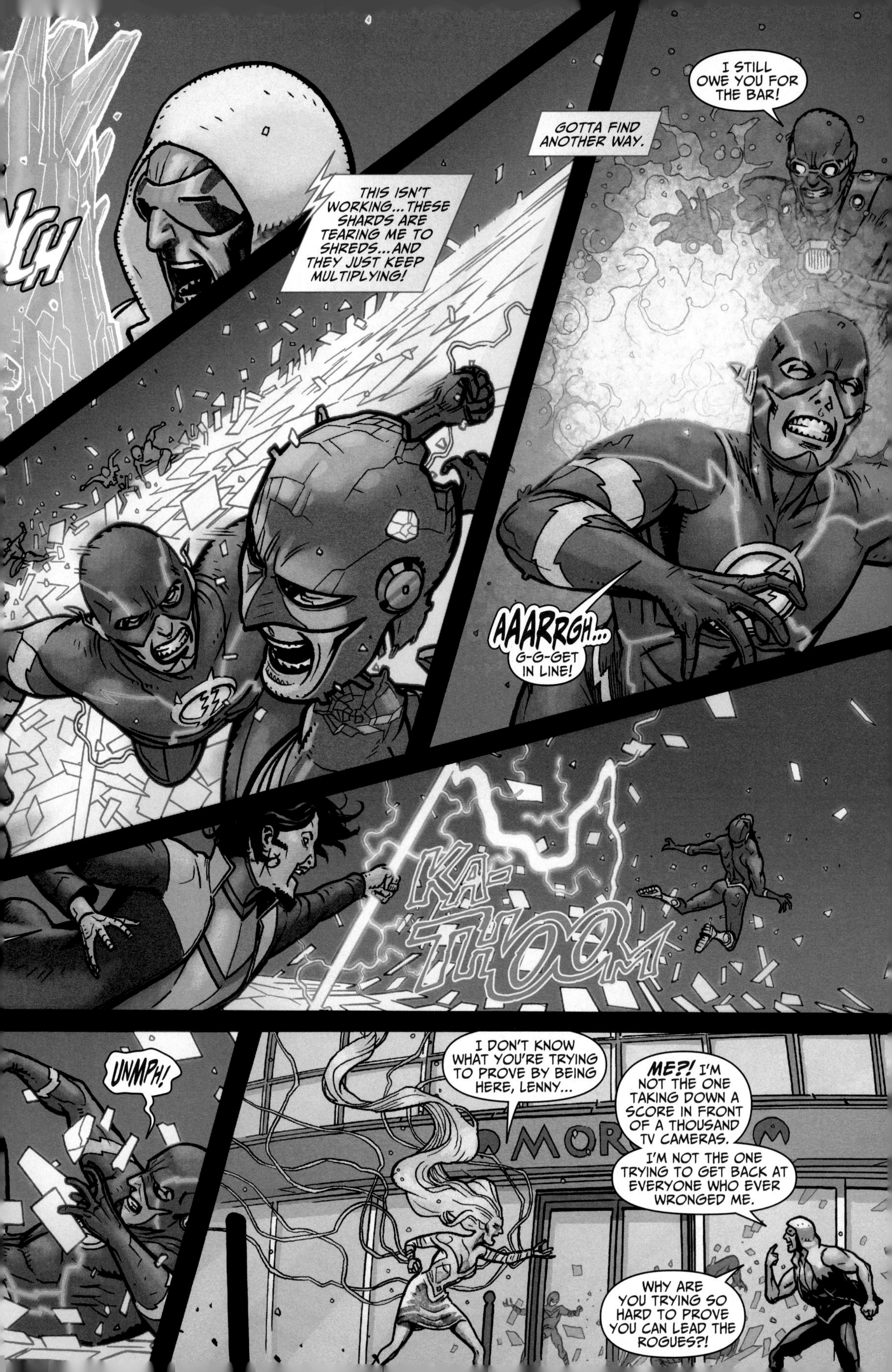

NCH
THIS ISN'T WORKING...THESE SHARDS ARE TEARING ME TO SHREDS...AND THEY JUST KEEP MULTIPLYING!
GOTTA FIND ANOTHER WAY.
I STILL OWE YOU FOR THE BAR!
AAARRGH... G-G-GET IN LINE!
KA-THOOM
UNMPH!
I DON'T KNOW WHAT YOU'RE TRYING TO PROVE BY BEING HERE, LENNY...
ME?! I'M NOT THE ONE TAKING DOWN A SCORE IN FRONT OF A THOUSAND TV CAMERAS.
I'M NOT THE ONE TRYING TO GET BACK AT EVERYONE WHO EVER WRONGED ME.
WHY ARE YOU TRYING SO HARD TO PROVE YOU CAN LEAD THE ROGUES?!

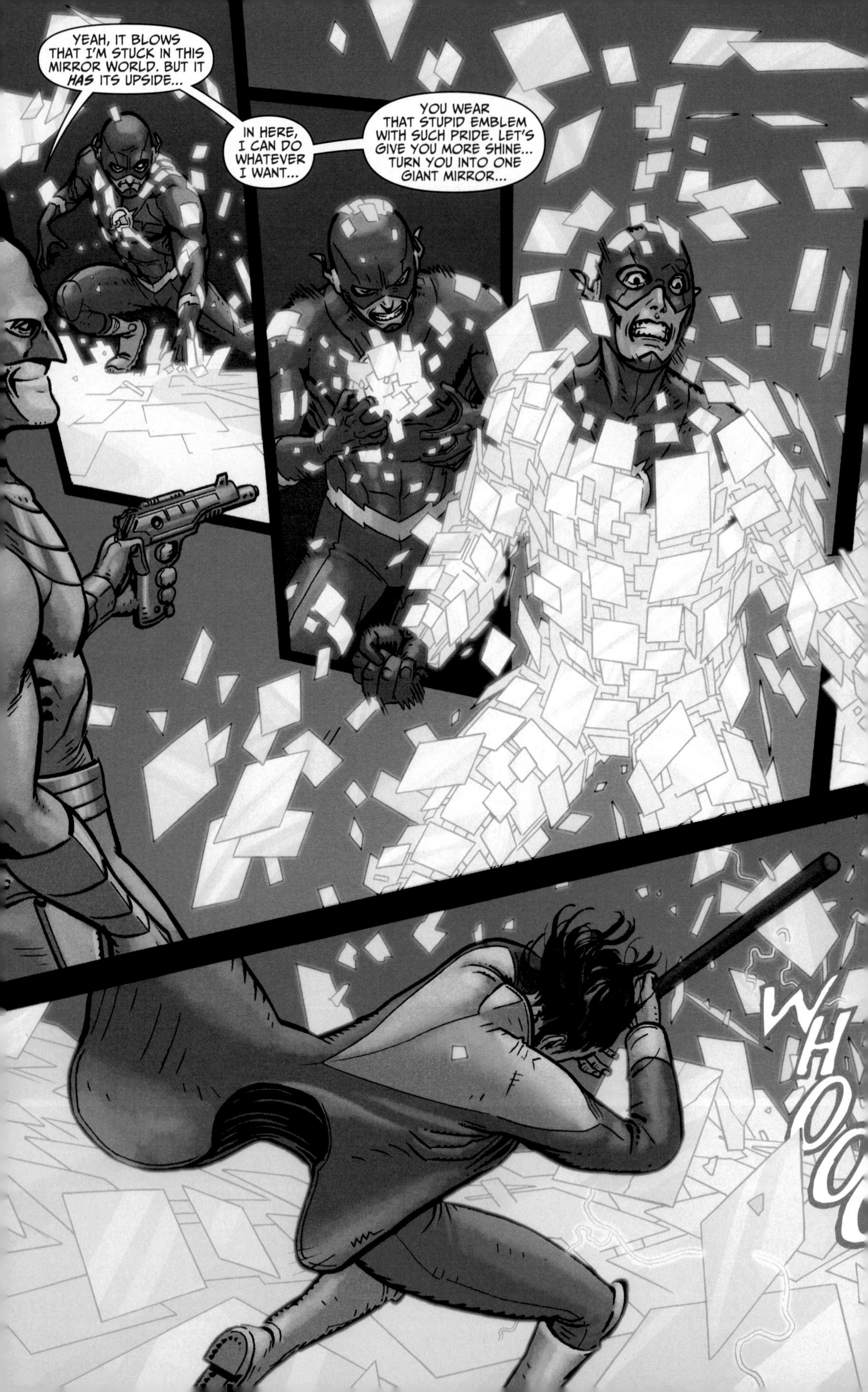
YEAH, IT BLOWS THAT I'M STUCK IN THIS MIRROR WORLD. BUT IT *HAS* ITS UPSIDE...
IN HERE, I CAN DO WHATEVER I WANT...
YOU WEAR THAT STUPID EMBLEM WITH SUCH PRIDE. LET'S GIVE YOU MORE SHINE... TURN YOU INTO ONE GIANT MIRROR...
WHOOO

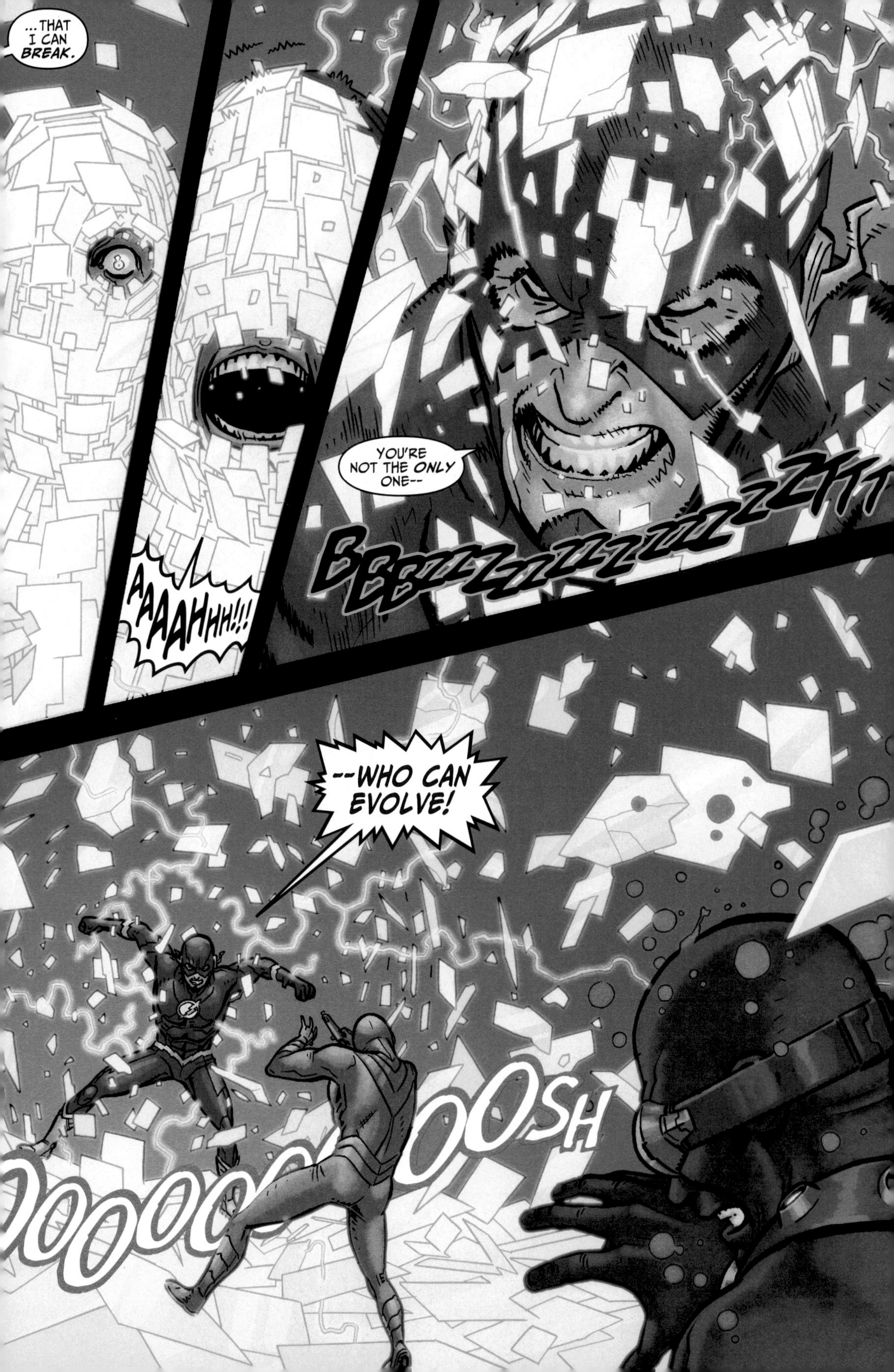
...THAT I CAN BREAK.
AAAAHHH!!!
YOU'RE NOT THE ONLY ONE--
BBBZZZZZZZZZZZZZZZZZTTT
--WHO CAN EVOLVE!
OOOOOOOOOOSH

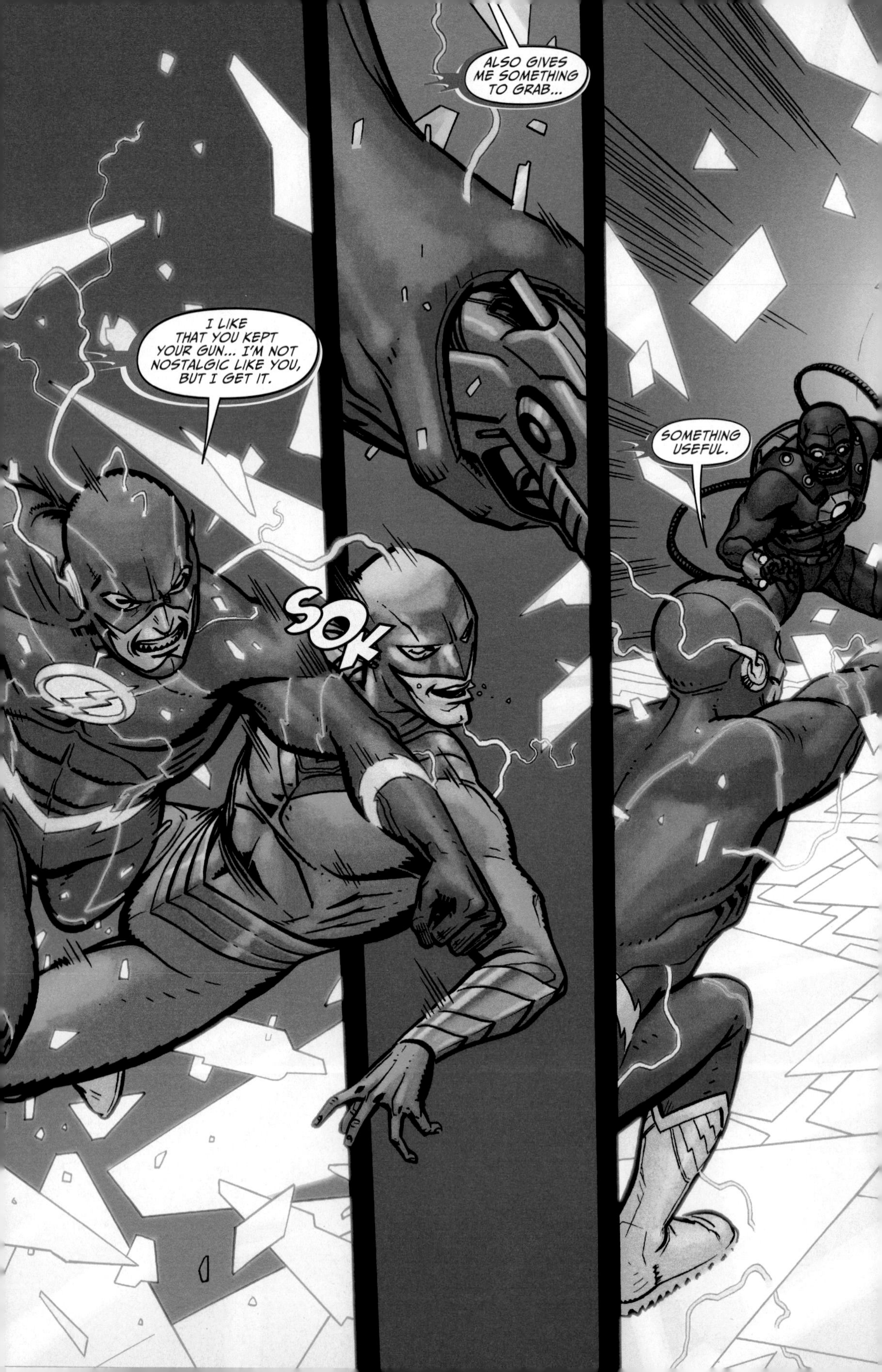
I LIKE THAT YOU KEPT YOUR GUN... I'M NOT NOSTALGIC LIKE YOU, BUT I GET IT.
SOK
ALSO GIVES ME SOMETHING TO GRAB...
SOMETHING USEFUL.

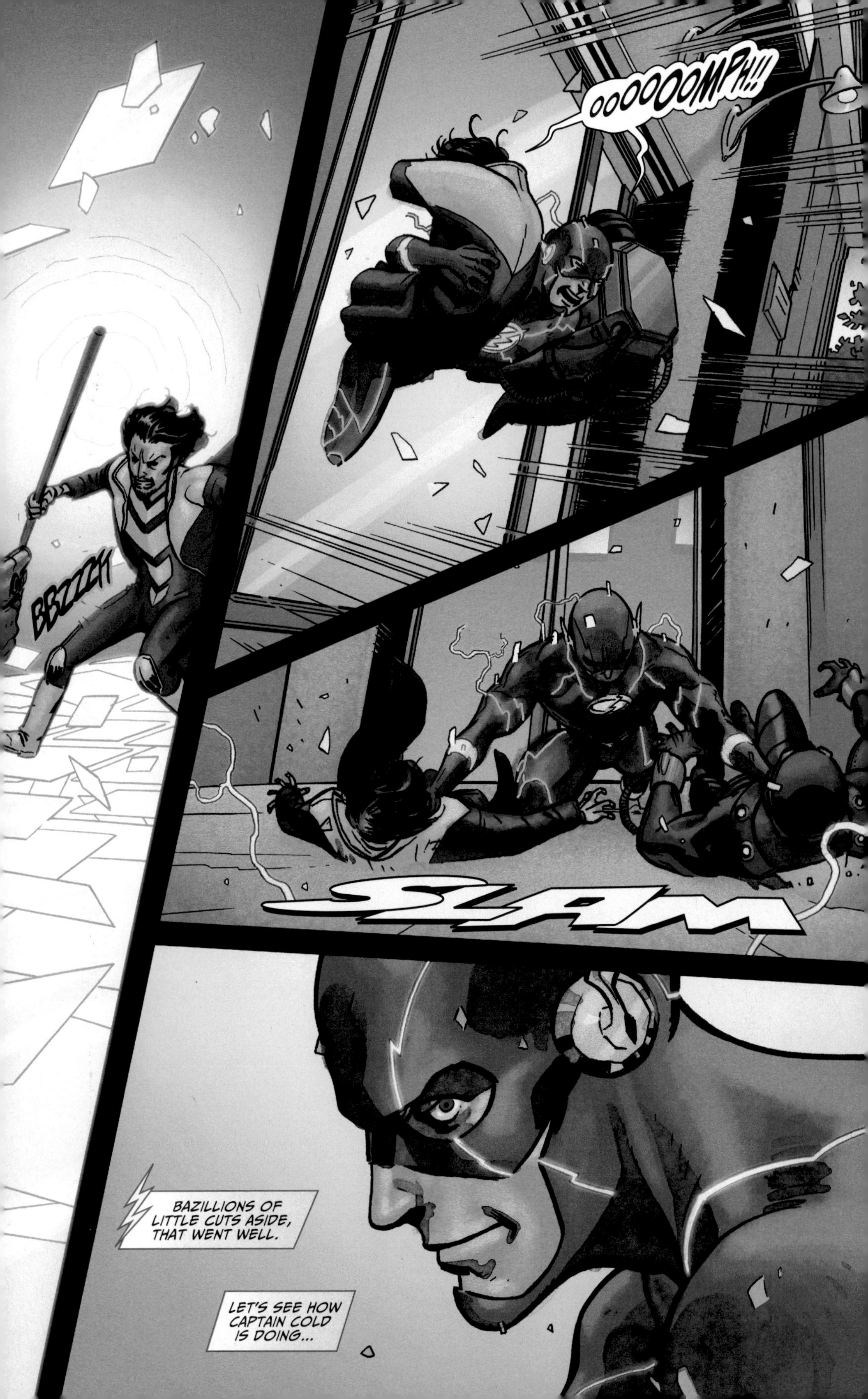

OOOOOOOMPH!!
BBZZZZT
SLAM
BAZILLIONS OF LITTLE CUTS ASIDE, THAT WENT WELL.
LET'S SEE HOW CAPTAIN COLD IS DOING...

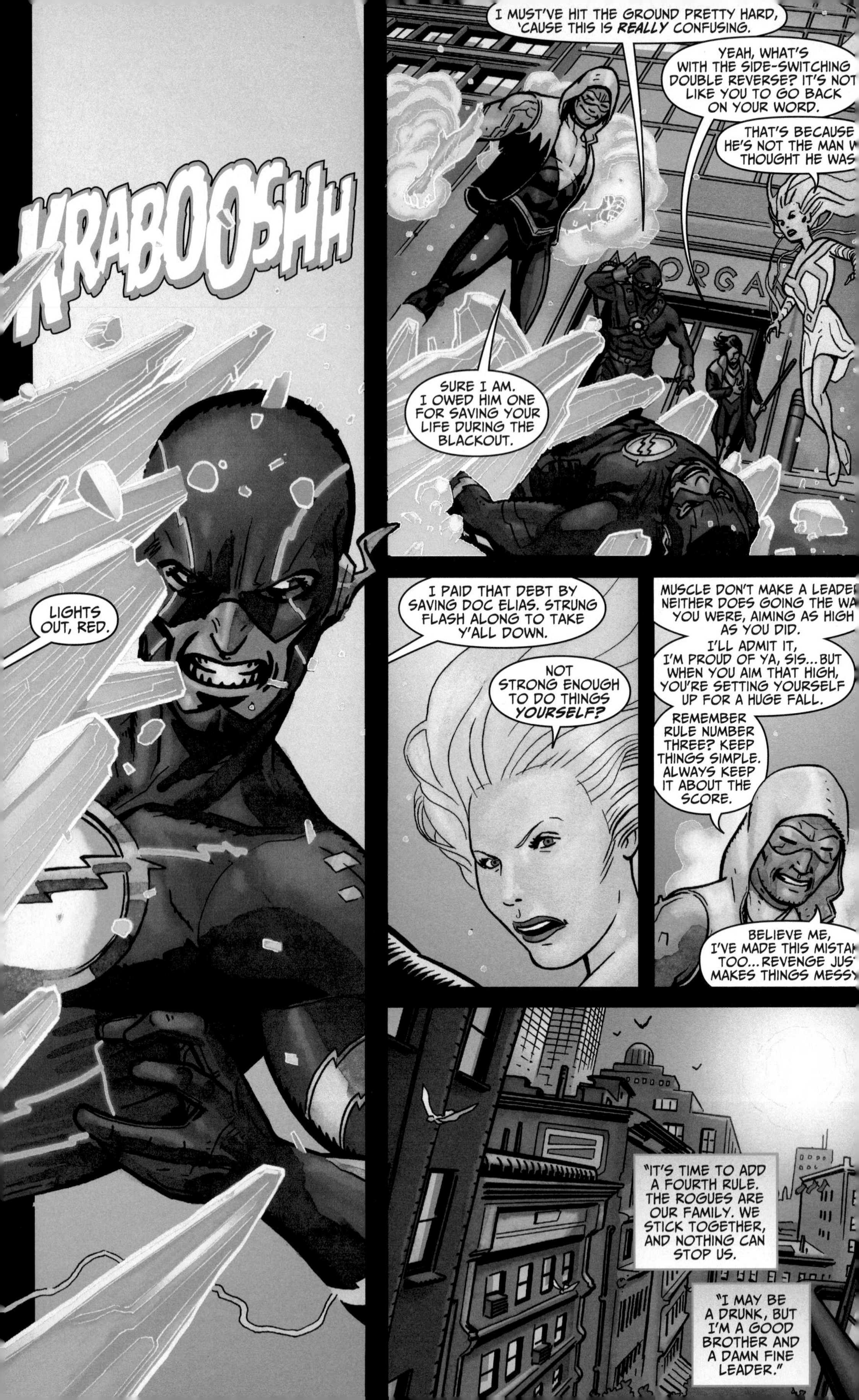
KRABOOSHH
LIGHTS OUT, RED.
I MUST'VE HIT THE GROUND PRETTY HARD, 'CAUSE THIS IS *REALLY* CONFUSING.
YEAH, WHAT'S WITH THE SIDE-SWITCHING DOUBLE REVERSE? IT'S NOT LIKE YOU TO GO BACK ON YOUR WORD.
THAT'S BECAUSE HE'S NOT THE MAN W THOUGHT HE WAS
SURE I AM. I OWED HIM ONE FOR SAVING YOUR LIFE DURING THE BLACKOUT.
I PAID THAT DEBT BY SAVING DOC ELIAS. STRUNG FLASH ALONG TO TAKE Y'ALL DOWN.
NOT STRONG ENOUGH TO DO THINGS *YOURSELF?*
MUSCLE DON'T MAKE A LEADE NEITHER DOES GOING THE WA YOU WERE, AIMING AS HIGH AS YOU DID.
I'LL ADMIT IT, I'M PROUD OF YA, SIS... BUT WHEN YOU AIM THAT HIGH, YOU'RE SETTING YOURSELF UP FOR A HUGE FALL.
REMEMBER RULE NUMBER THREE? KEEP THINGS SIMPLE. ALWAYS KEEP IT ABOUT THE SCORE.
BELIEVE ME, I'VE MADE THIS MISTA TOO... REVENGE JUS MAKES THINGS MESS
"IT'S TIME TO ADD A FOURTH RULE. THE ROGUES ARE OUR FAMILY. WE STICK TOGETHER, AND NOTHING CAN STOP US.
"I MAY BE A DRUNK, BUT I'M A GOOD BROTHER AND A DAMN FINE LEADER."

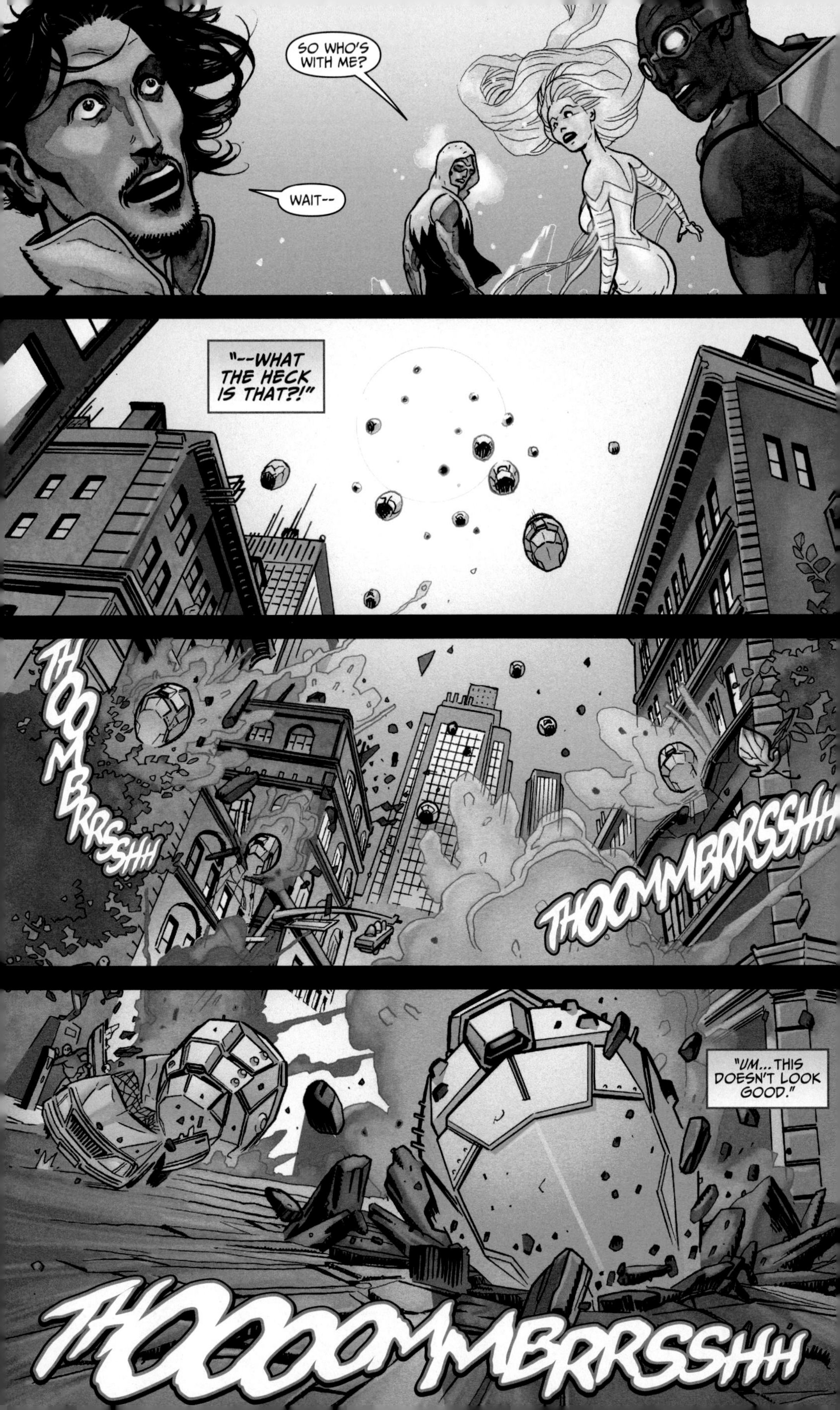
SO WHO'S WITH ME?
WAIT--
"--WHAT THE HECK IS THAT?!"
THOOMBRRSHH
THOOMMBRRSSHH
"UM... THIS DOESN'T LOOK GOOD."
THOOOOMMBRRSSHH

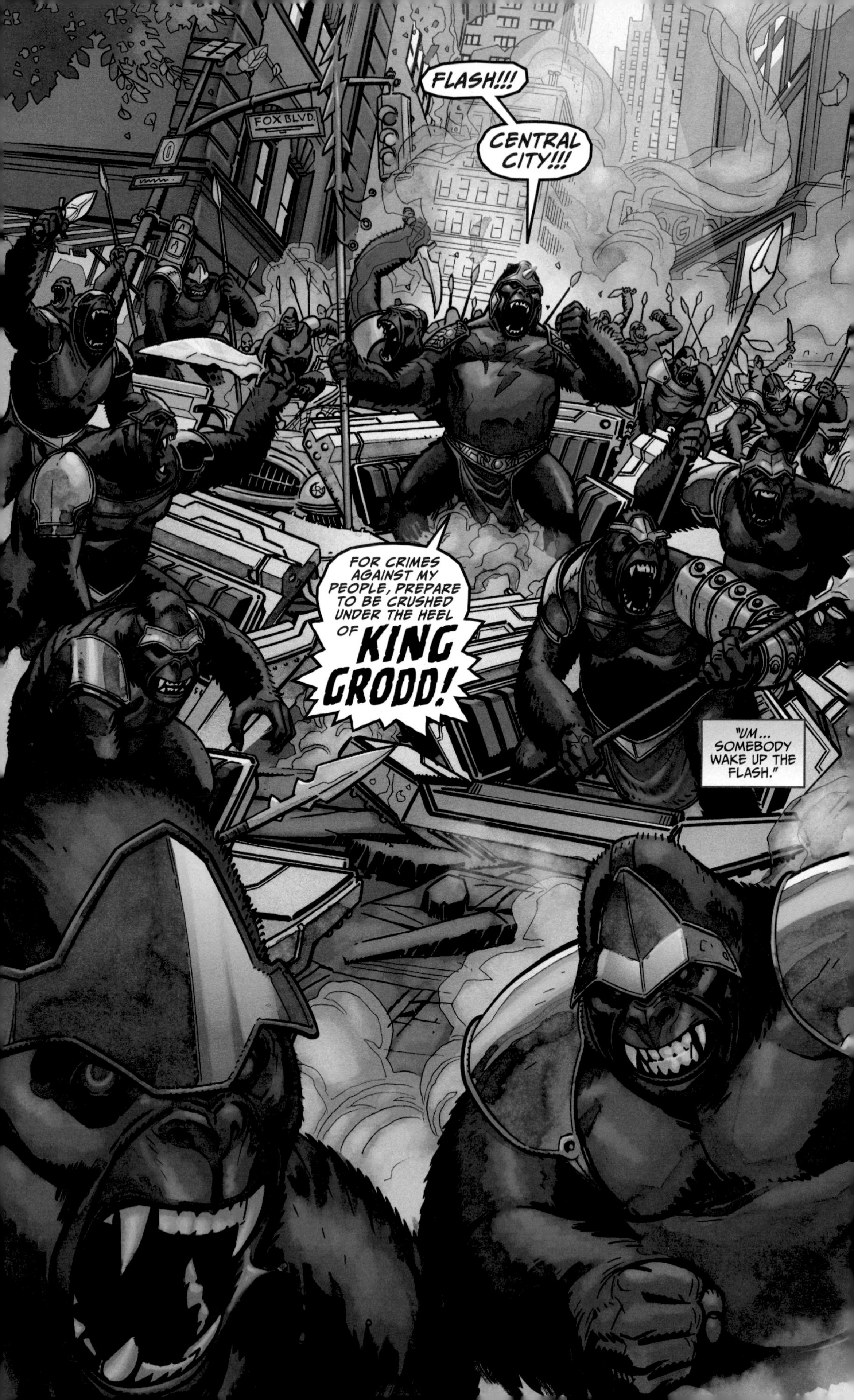
FOX BLVD.
FLASH!!!
CENTRAL CITY!!!
FOR CRIMES AGAINST MY PEOPLE, PREPARE TO BE CRUSHED UNDER THE HEEL OF KING GRODD!
"UM... SOMEBODY WAKE UP THE FLASH."

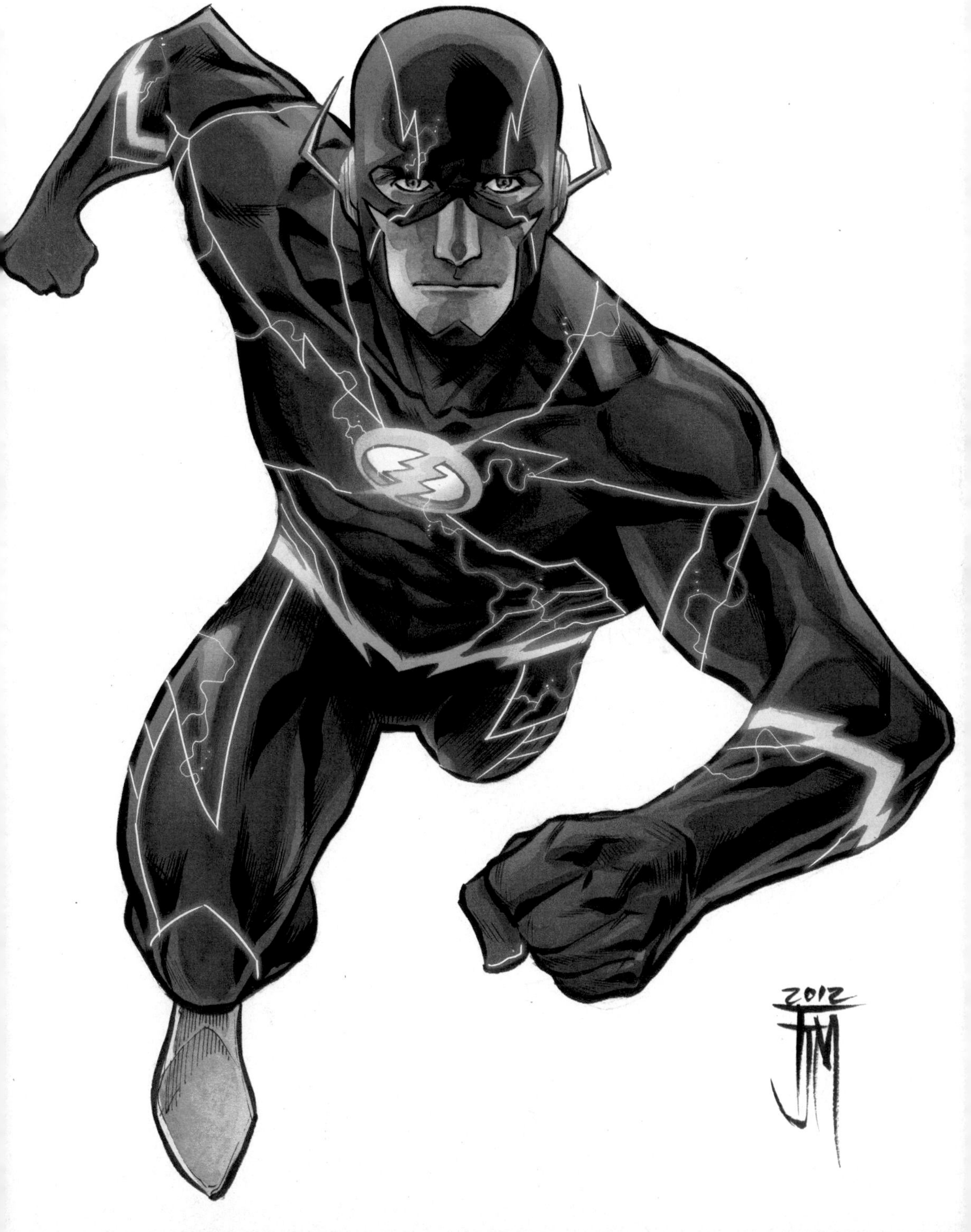
2012

FRANCIS MANAPUL and BRIAN BUCCELLATO
cover art

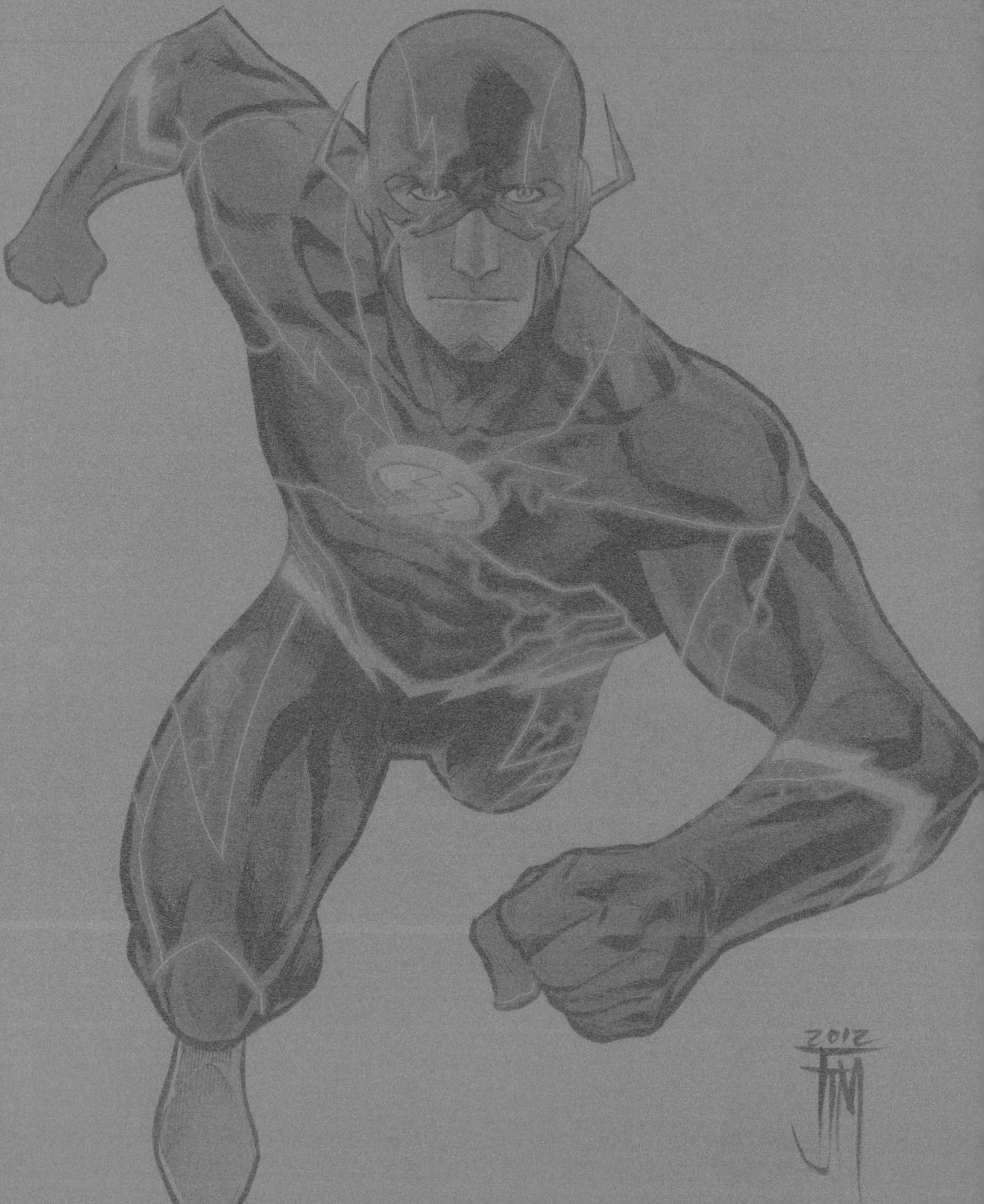
2012
FM

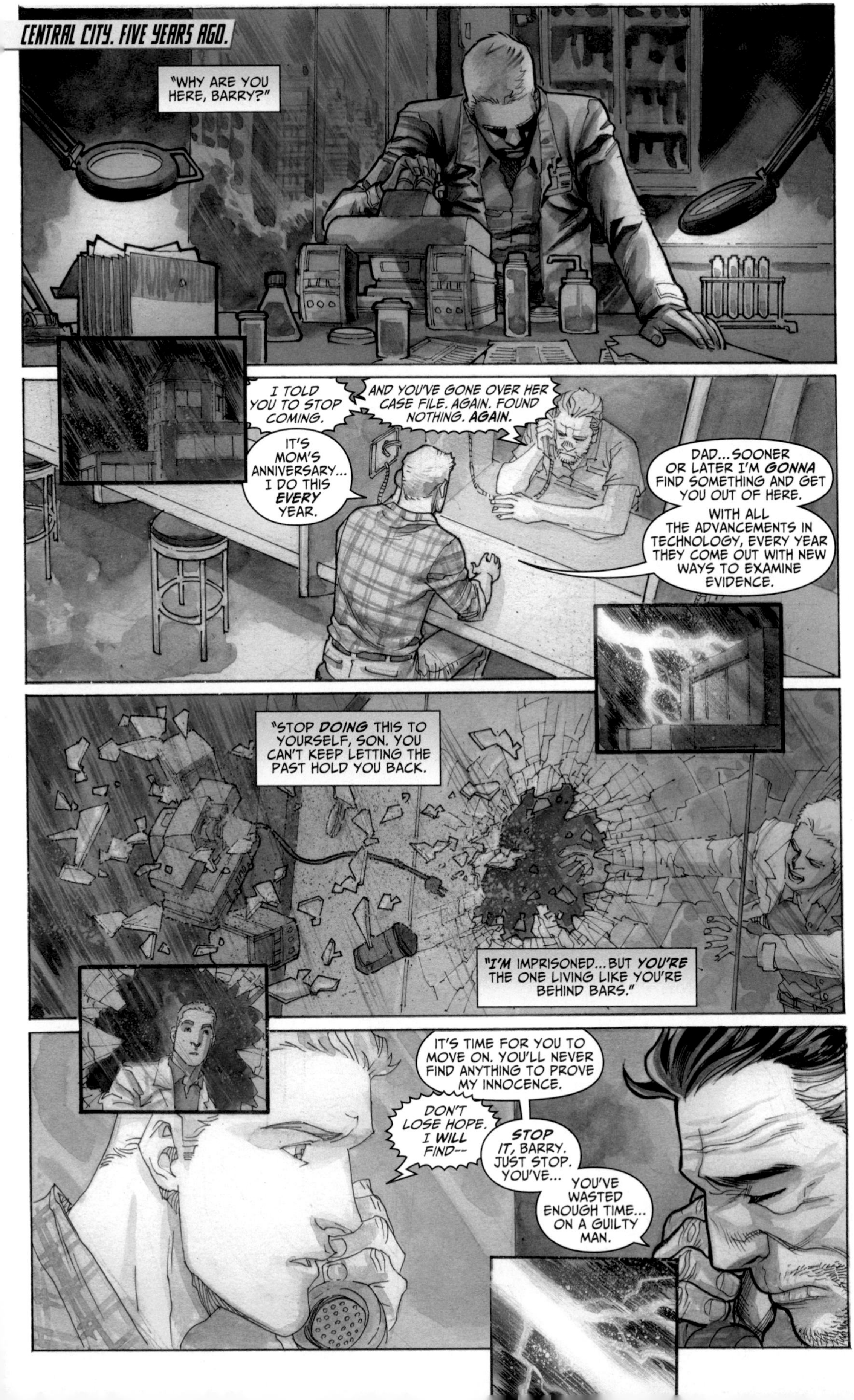
CENTRAL CITY. FIVE YEARS AGO.
"WHY ARE YOU HERE, BARRY?"
I TOLD YOU TO STOP COMING.
AND YOU'VE GONE OVER HER CASE FILE. AGAIN. FOUND NOTHING. AGAIN.
IT'S MOM'S ANNIVERSARY... I DO THIS EVERY YEAR.
DAD... SOONER OR LATER I'M GONNA FIND SOMETHING AND GET YOU OUT OF HERE.
WITH ALL THE ADVANCEMENTS IN TECHNOLOGY, EVERY YEAR THEY COME OUT WITH NEW WAYS TO EXAMINE EVIDENCE.
"STOP DOING THIS TO YOURSELF, SON. YOU CAN'T KEEP LETTING THE PAST HOLD YOU BACK.
"I'M IMPRISONED... BUT YOU'RE THE ONE LIVING LIKE YOU'RE BEHIND BARS."
IT'S TIME FOR YOU TO MOVE ON. YOU'LL NEVER FIND ANYTHING TO PROVE MY INNOCENCE.
DON'T LOSE HOPE. I WILL FIND--
STOP IT, BARRY. JUST STOP. YOU'VE...
YOU'VE WASTED ENOUGH TIME... ON A GUILTY MAN.

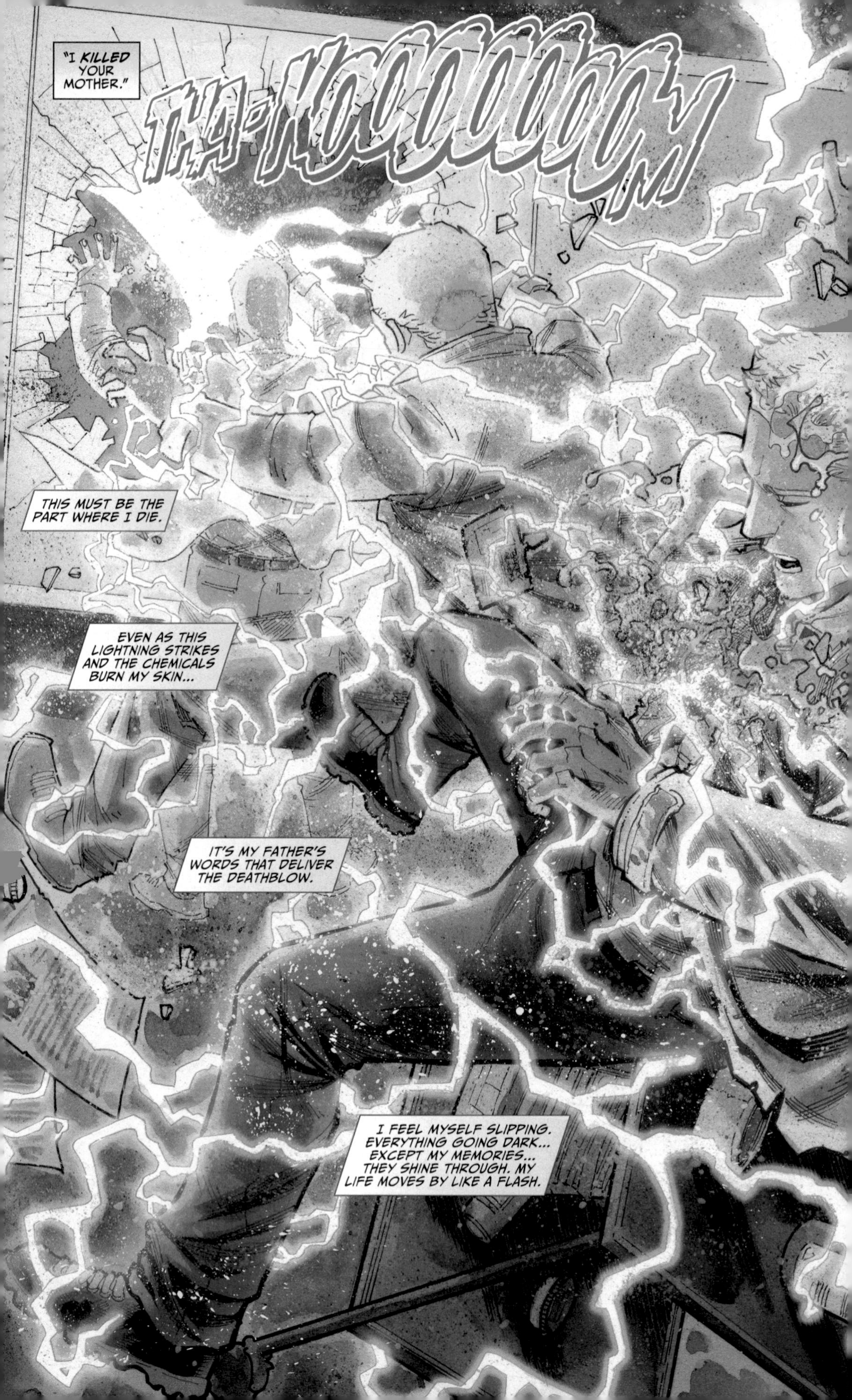
"I KILLED YOUR MOTHER."
KA-KOOOOOOOM
THIS MUST BE THE PART WHERE I DIE.
EVEN AS THIS LIGHTNING STRIKES AND THE CHEMICALS BURN MY SKIN...
IT'S MY FATHER'S WORDS THAT DELIVER THE DEATHBLOW.
I FEEL MYSELF SLIPPING. EVERYTHING GOING DARK... EXCEPT MY MEMORIES... THEY SHINE THROUGH. MY LIFE MOVES BY LIKE A FLASH.

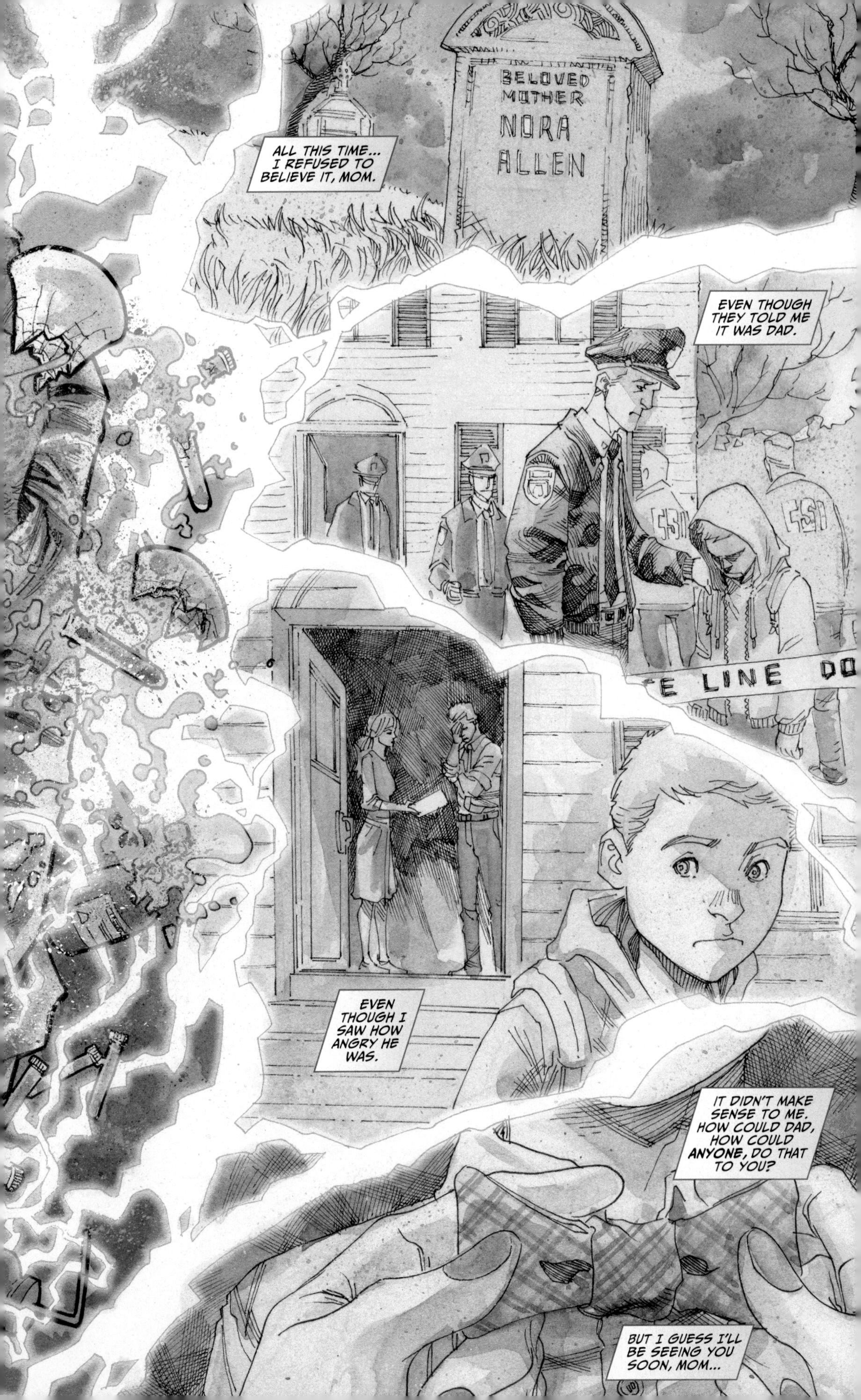
BELOVED
MOTHER
NORA
ALLEN
ALL THIS TIME... I REFUSED TO BELIEVE IT, MOM.
EVEN THOUGH THEY TOLD ME IT WAS DAD.
CSI
CSI
E LINE DO
EVEN THOUGH I SAW HOW ANGRY HE WAS.
IT DIDN'T MAKE SENSE TO ME. HOW COULD DAD, HOW COULD ANYONE, DO THAT TO YOU?
BUT I GUESS I'LL BE SEEING YOU SOON, MOM...

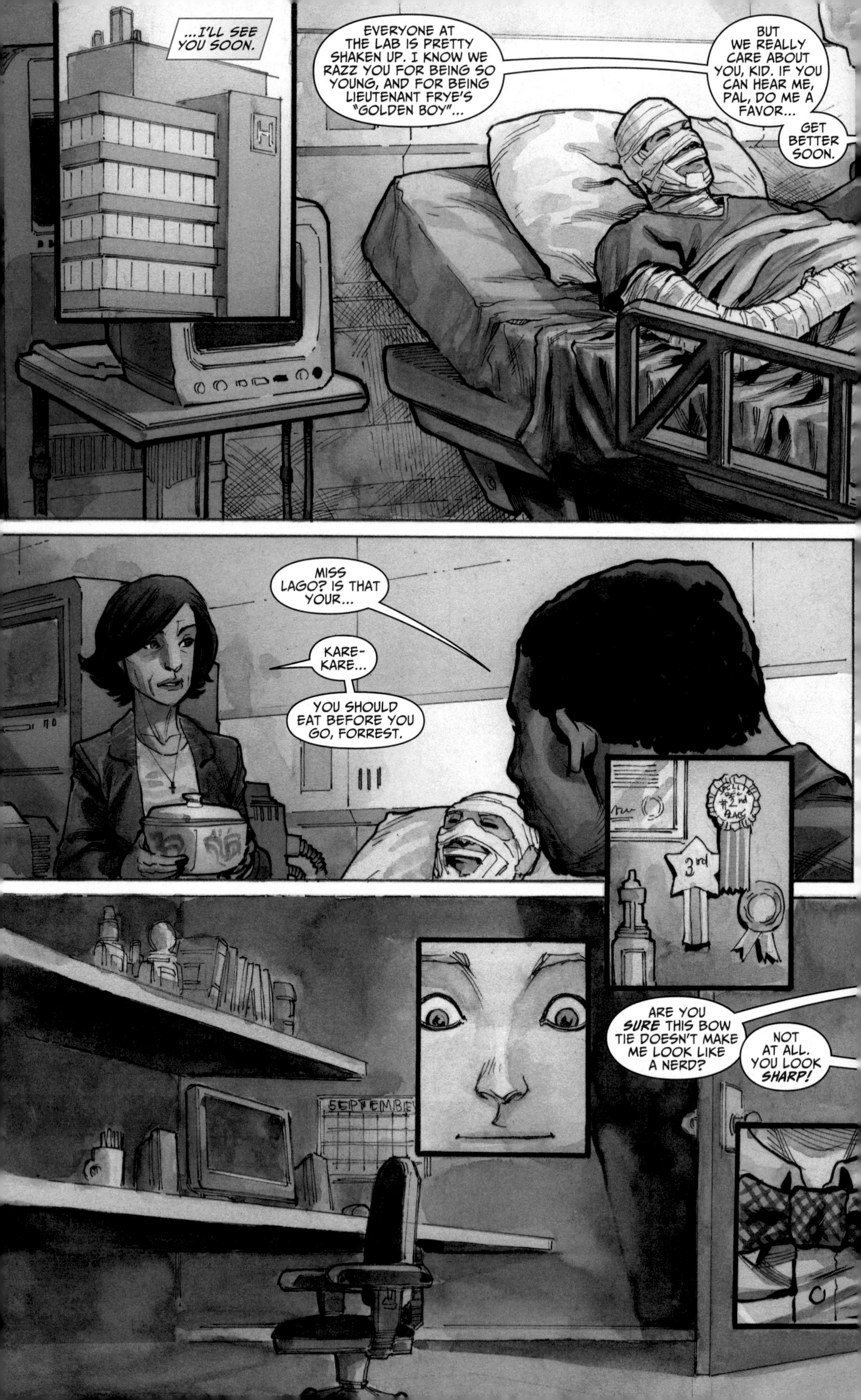
...I'LL SEE YOU SOON.
EVERYONE AT THE LAB IS PRETTY SHAKEN UP. I KNOW WE RAZZ YOU FOR BEING SO YOUNG, AND FOR BEING LIEUTENANT FRYE'S "GOLDEN BOY"...
BUT WE REALLY CARE ABOUT YOU, KID. IF YOU CAN HEAR ME, PAL, DO ME A FAVOR...
GET BETTER SOON.
MISS LAGO? IS THAT YOUR...
KARE-KARE...
YOU SHOULD EAT BEFORE YOU GO, FORREST.
ARE YOU **SURE** THIS BOW TIE DOESN'T MAKE ME LOOK LIKE A NERD?
NOT AT ALL. YOU LOOK **SHARP!**

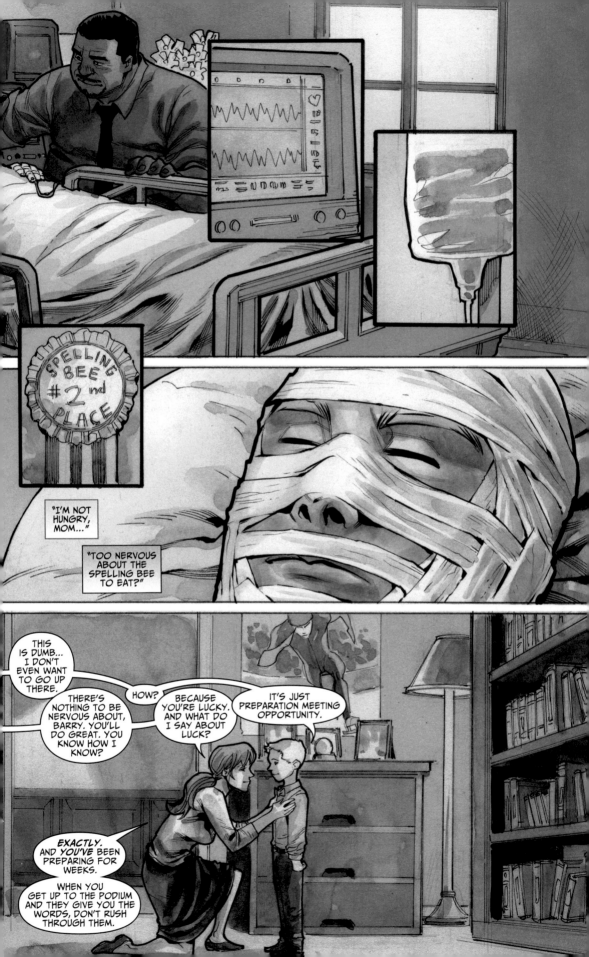

"I'M NOT HUNGRY, MOM..."

"TOO NERVOUS ABOUT THE SPELLING BEE TO EAT?"

THIS IS DUMB... I DON'T EVEN WANT TO GO UP THERE.

THERE'S NOTHING TO BE NERVOUS ABOUT, BARRY. YOU'LL DO GREAT. YOU KNOW HOW I KNOW?

HOW?

BECAUSE YOU'RE LUCKY. AND WHAT DO I SAY ABOUT LUCK?

IT'S JUST PREPARATION MEETING OPPORTUNITY.

EXACTLY. AND YOU'VE BEEN PREPARING FOR WEEKS.

WHEN YOU GET UP TO THE PODIUM AND THEY GIVE YOU THE WORDS, DON'T RUSH THROUGH THEM.

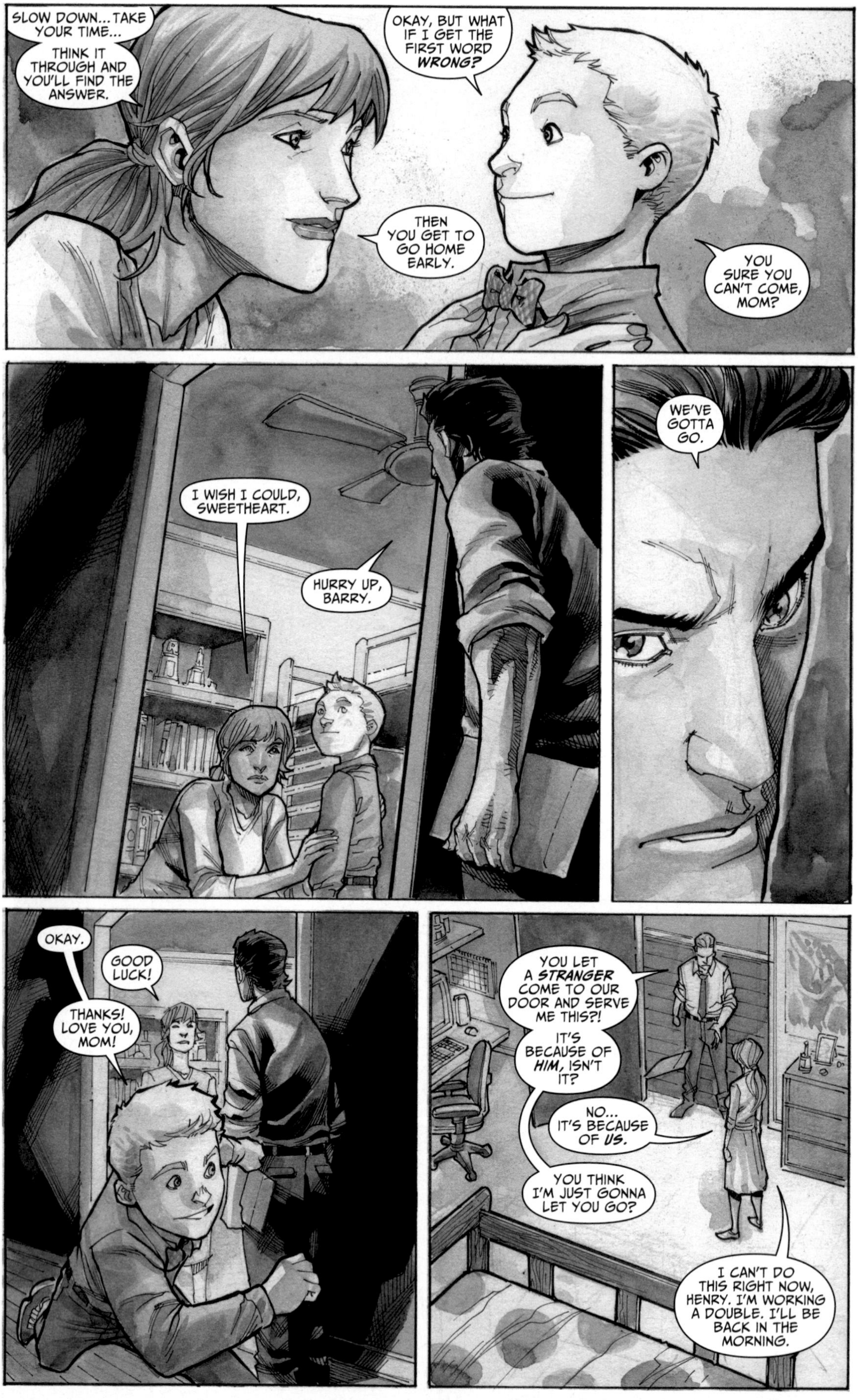
SLOW DOWN...TAKE YOUR TIME...
THINK IT THROUGH AND YOU'LL FIND THE ANSWER.
OKAY, BUT WHAT IF I GET THE FIRST WORD WRONG?
THEN YOU GET TO GO HOME EARLY.
YOU SURE YOU CAN'T COME, MOM?
I WISH I COULD, SWEETHEART.
HURRY UP, BARRY.
WE'VE GOTTA GO.
OKAY.
GOOD LUCK!
THANKS! LOVE YOU, MOM!
YOU LET A STRANGER COME TO OUR DOOR AND SERVE ME THIS?!
IT'S BECAUSE OF HIM, ISN'T IT?
NO... IT'S BECAUSE OF US.
YOU THINK I'M JUST GONNA LET YOU GO?
I CAN'T DO THIS RIGHT NOW, HENRY. I'M WORKING A DOUBLE. I'LL BE BACK IN THE MORNING.

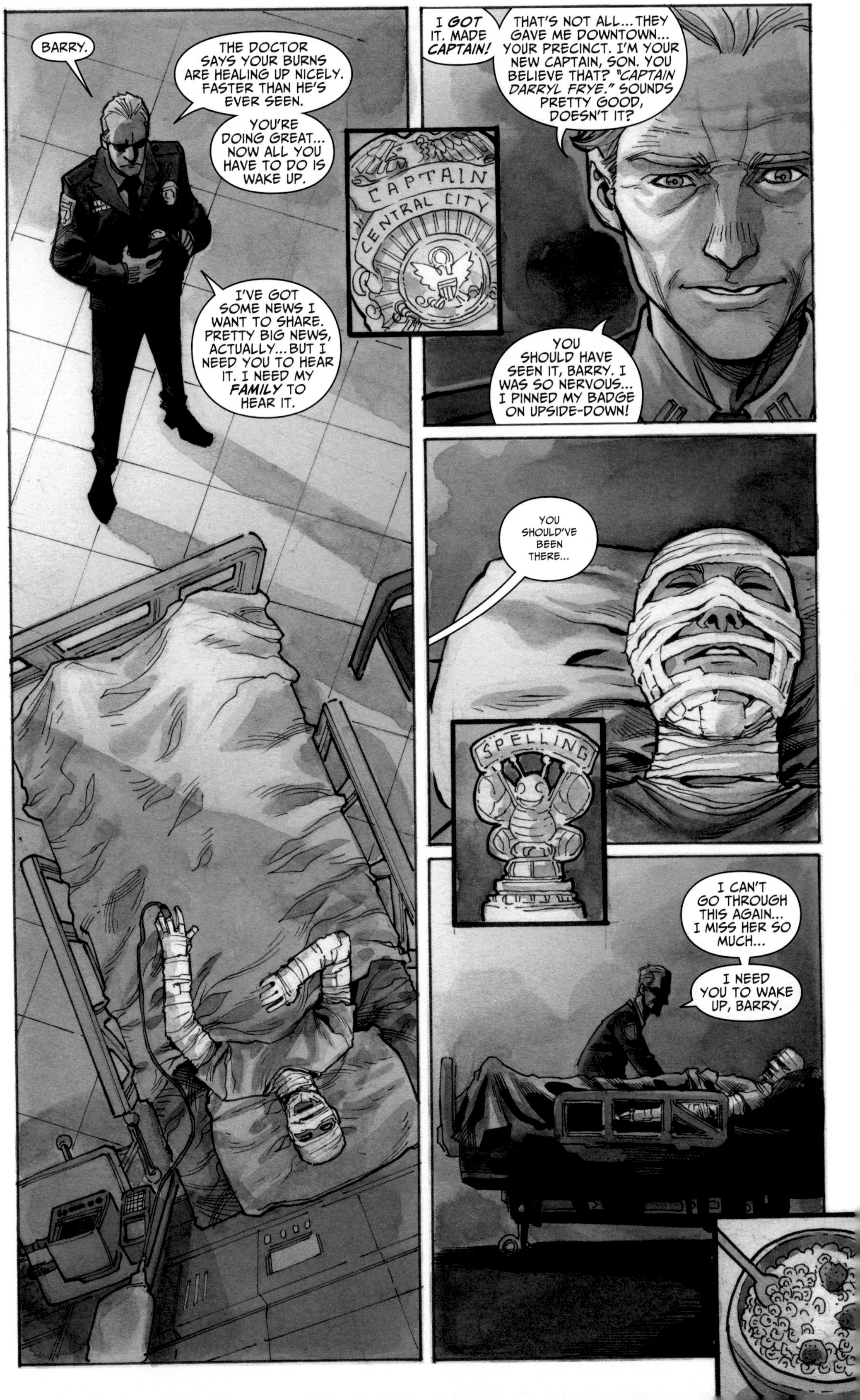
BARRY.
THE DOCTOR SAYS YOUR BURNS ARE HEALING UP NICELY. FASTER THAN HE'S EVER SEEN.
YOU'RE DOING GREAT... NOW ALL YOU HAVE TO DO IS WAKE UP.
I'VE GOT SOME NEWS I WANT TO SHARE. PRETTY BIG NEWS, ACTUALLY... BUT I NEED YOU TO HEAR IT. I NEED MY *FAMILY* TO HEAR IT.
CAPTAIN
CENTRAL CITY
I *GOT* IT. MADE *CAPTAIN!*
THAT'S NOT ALL... THEY GAVE ME DOWNTOWN... YOUR PRECINCT. I'M YOUR NEW CAPTAIN, SON. YOU BELIEVE THAT? *"CAPTAIN DARRYL FRYE."* SOUNDS PRETTY GOOD, DOESN'T IT?
YOU SHOULD HAVE SEEN IT, BARRY. I WAS SO NERVOUS... I PINNED MY BADGE ON UPSIDE-DOWN!
YOU SHOULD'VE BEEN THERE...
SPELLING
I CAN'T GO THROUGH THIS AGAIN... I MISS HER SO MUCH...
I NEED YOU TO WAKE UP, BARRY.

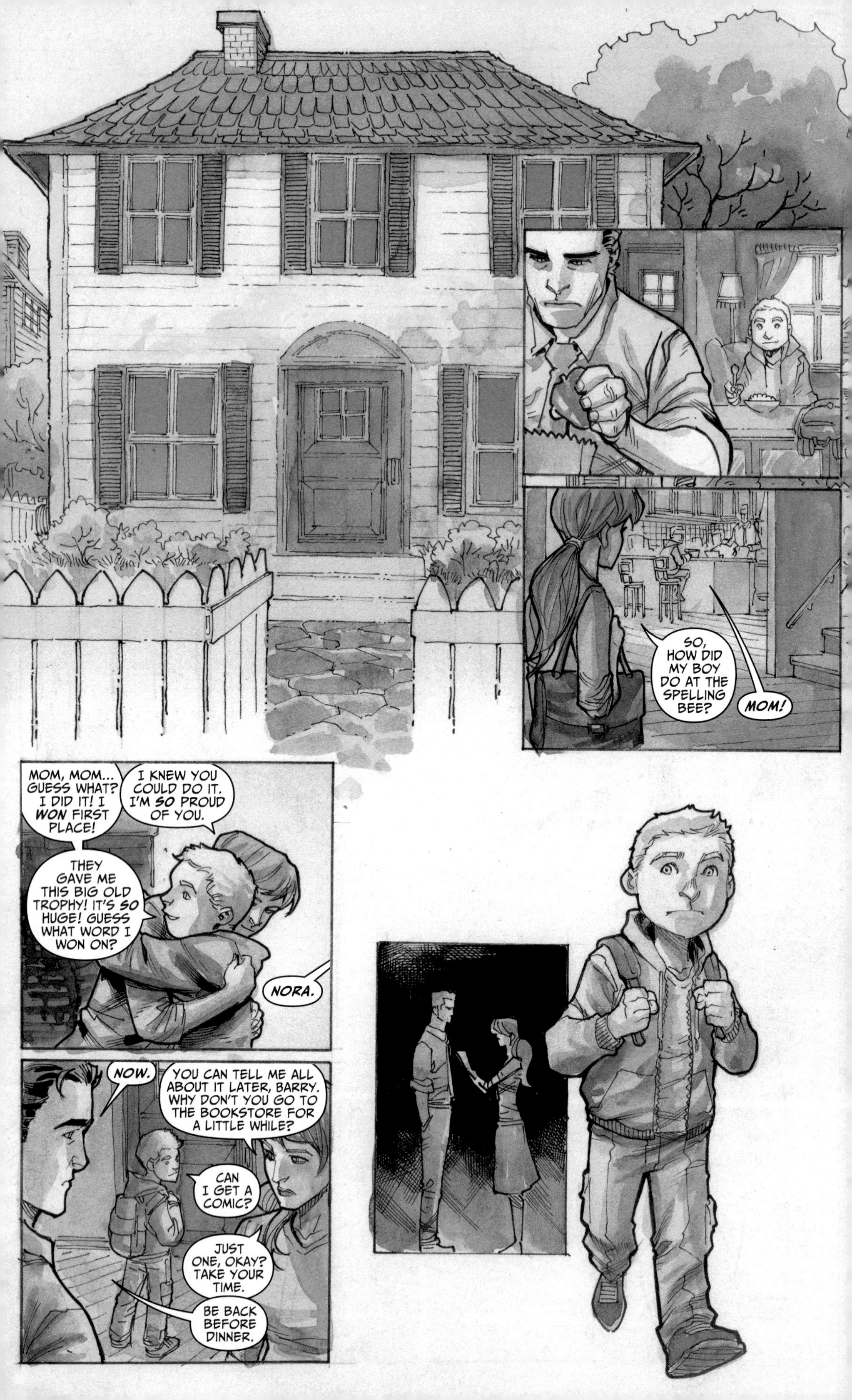

SO, HOW DID MY BOY DO AT THE SPELLING BEE?
MOM!
MOM, MOM... GUESS WHAT? I DID IT! I WON FIRST PLACE!
I KNEW YOU COULD DO IT. I'M SO PROUD OF YOU.
THEY GAVE ME THIS BIG OLD TROPHY! IT'S SO HUGE! GUESS WHAT WORD I WON ON?
NORA.
NOW.
YOU CAN TELL ME ALL ABOUT IT LATER, BARRY. WHY DON'T YOU GO TO THE BOOKSTORE FOR A LITTLE WHILE?
CAN I GET A COMIC?
JUST ONE, OKAY? TAKE YOUR TIME.
BE BACK BEFORE DINNER.

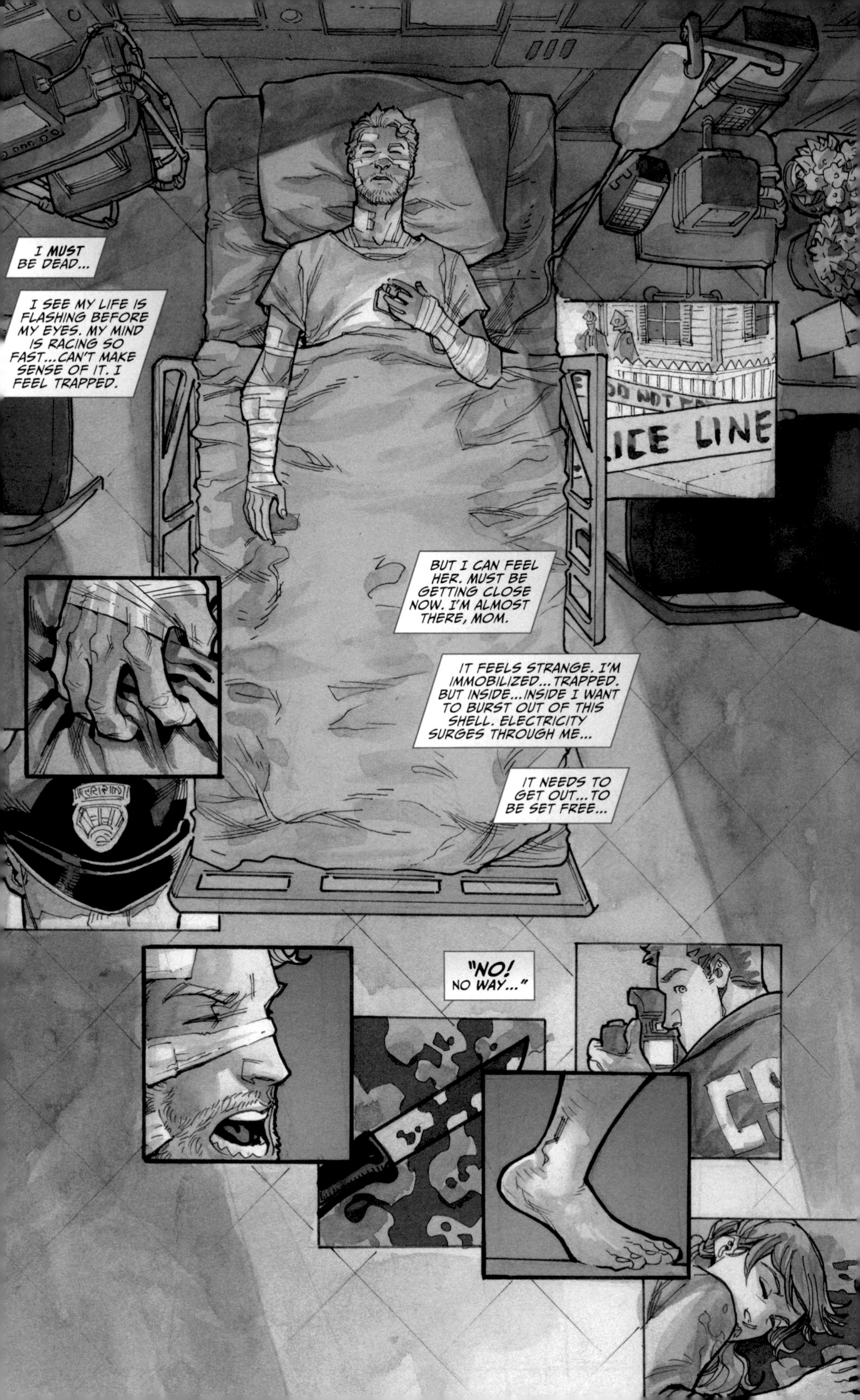
I MUST BE DEAD...
I SEE MY LIFE IS FLASHING BEFORE MY EYES. MY MIND IS RACING SO FAST...CAN'T MAKE SENSE OF IT. I FEEL TRAPPED.
BUT I CAN FEEL HER. MUST BE GETTING CLOSE NOW. I'M ALMOST THERE, MOM.
IT FEELS STRANGE. I'M IMMOBILIZED...TRAPPED. BUT INSIDE...INSIDE I WANT TO BURST OUT OF THIS SHELL. ELECTRICITY SURGES THROUGH ME...
IT NEEDS TO GET OUT...TO BE SET FREE...
"NO! NO WAY..."

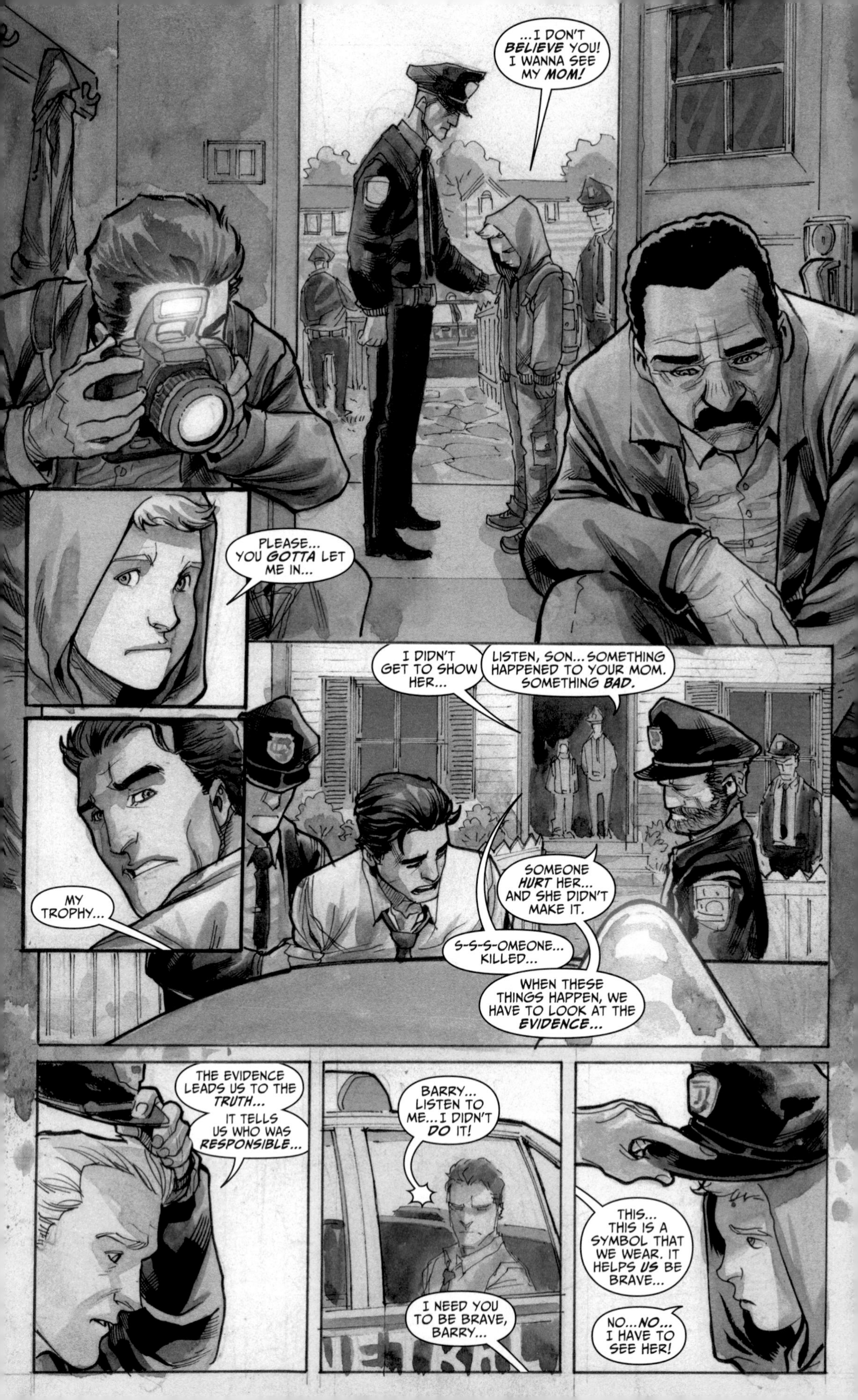

...I DON'T BELIEVE YOU! I WANNA SEE MY MOM!
PLEASE... YOU GOTTA LET ME IN...
I DIDN'T GET TO SHOW HER...
LISTEN, SON...SOMETHING HAPPENED TO YOUR MOM. SOMETHING BAD.
MY TROPHY...
SOMEONE HURT HER... AND SHE DIDN'T MAKE IT.
S-S-S-OMEONE... KILLED...
WHEN THESE THINGS HAPPEN, WE HAVE TO LOOK AT THE EVIDENCE...
THE EVIDENCE LEADS US TO THE TRUTH...
IT TELLS US WHO WAS RESPONSIBLE...
BARRY... LISTEN TO ME...I DIDN'T DO IT!
I NEED YOU TO BE BRAVE, BARRY...
THIS... THIS IS A SYMBOL THAT WE WEAR. IT HELPS US BE BRAVE...
NO...NO... I HAVE TO SEE HER!

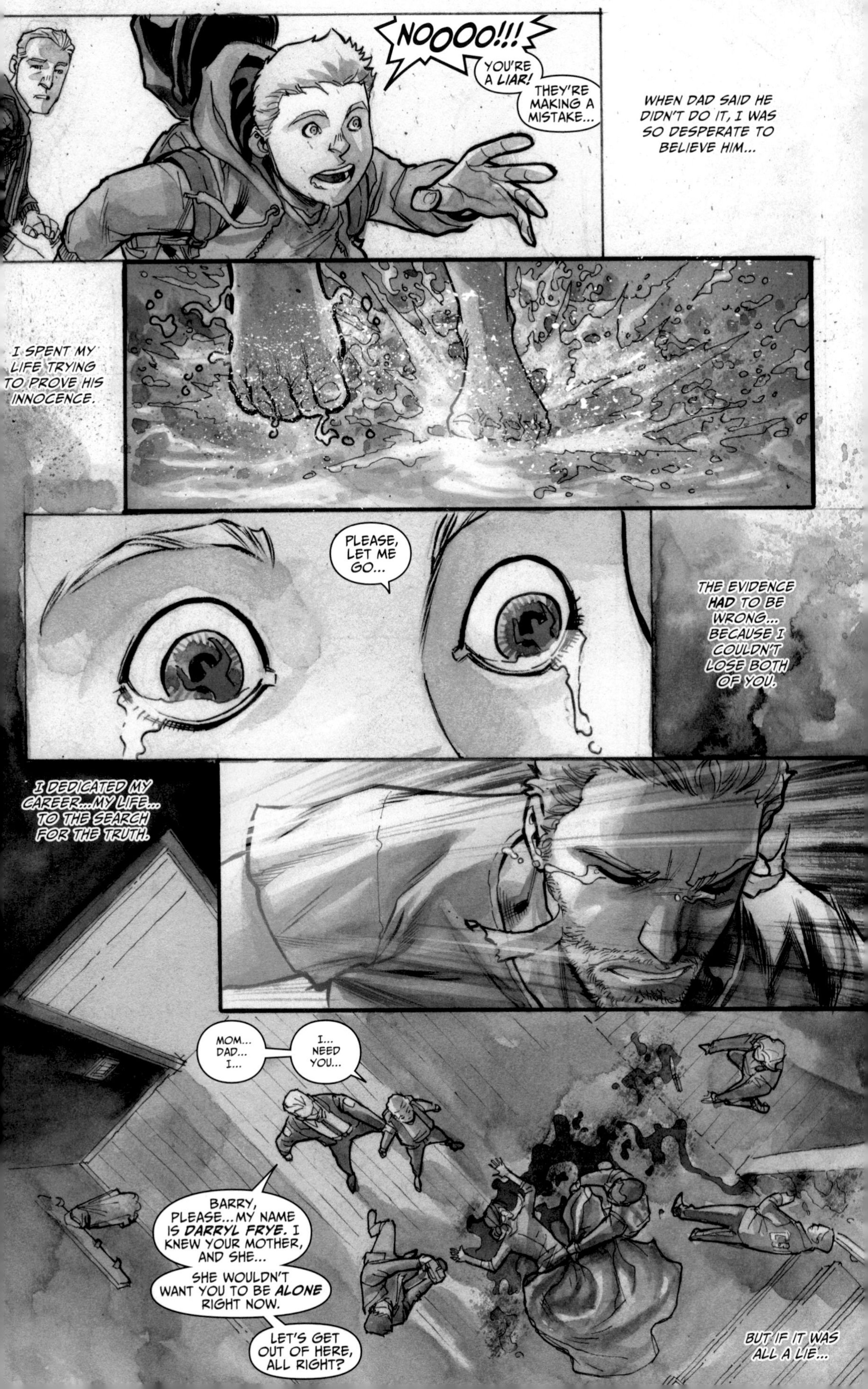
NOOOO!!!
YOU'RE A LIAR!
THEY'RE MAKING A MISTAKE...
WHEN DAD SAID HE DIDN'T DO IT, I WAS SO DESPERATE TO BELIEVE HIM...
I SPENT MY LIFE TRYING TO PROVE HIS INNOCENCE.
PLEASE, LET ME GO...
THE EVIDENCE HAD TO BE WRONG... BECAUSE I COULDN'T LOSE BOTH OF YOU.
I DEDICATED MY CAREER...MY LIFE... TO THE SEARCH FOR THE TRUTH.
MOM... DAD... I...
I... NEED YOU...
BARRY, PLEASE...MY NAME IS DARRYL FRYE. I KNEW YOUR MOTHER, AND SHE...
SHE WOULDN'T WANT YOU TO BE ALONE RIGHT NOW.
LET'S GET OUT OF HERE, ALL RIGHT?
BUT IF IT WAS ALL A LIE...

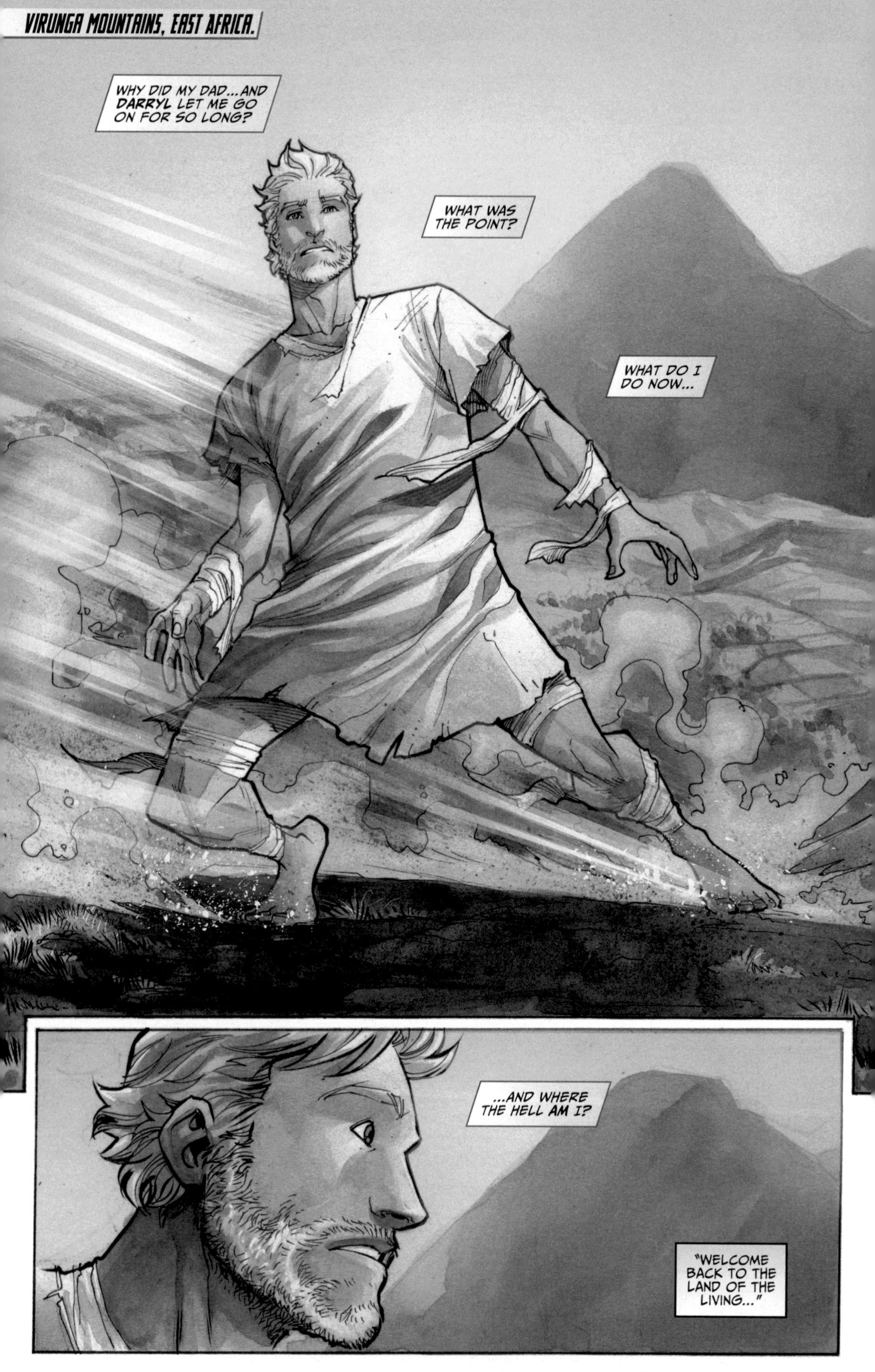
VIRUNGA MOUNTAINS, EAST AFRICA.
WHY DID MY DAD...AND DARRYL LET ME GO ON FOR SO LONG?
WHAT WAS THE POINT?
WHAT DO I DO NOW...
...AND WHERE THE HELL AM I?
"WELCOME BACK TO THE LAND OF THE LIVING..."

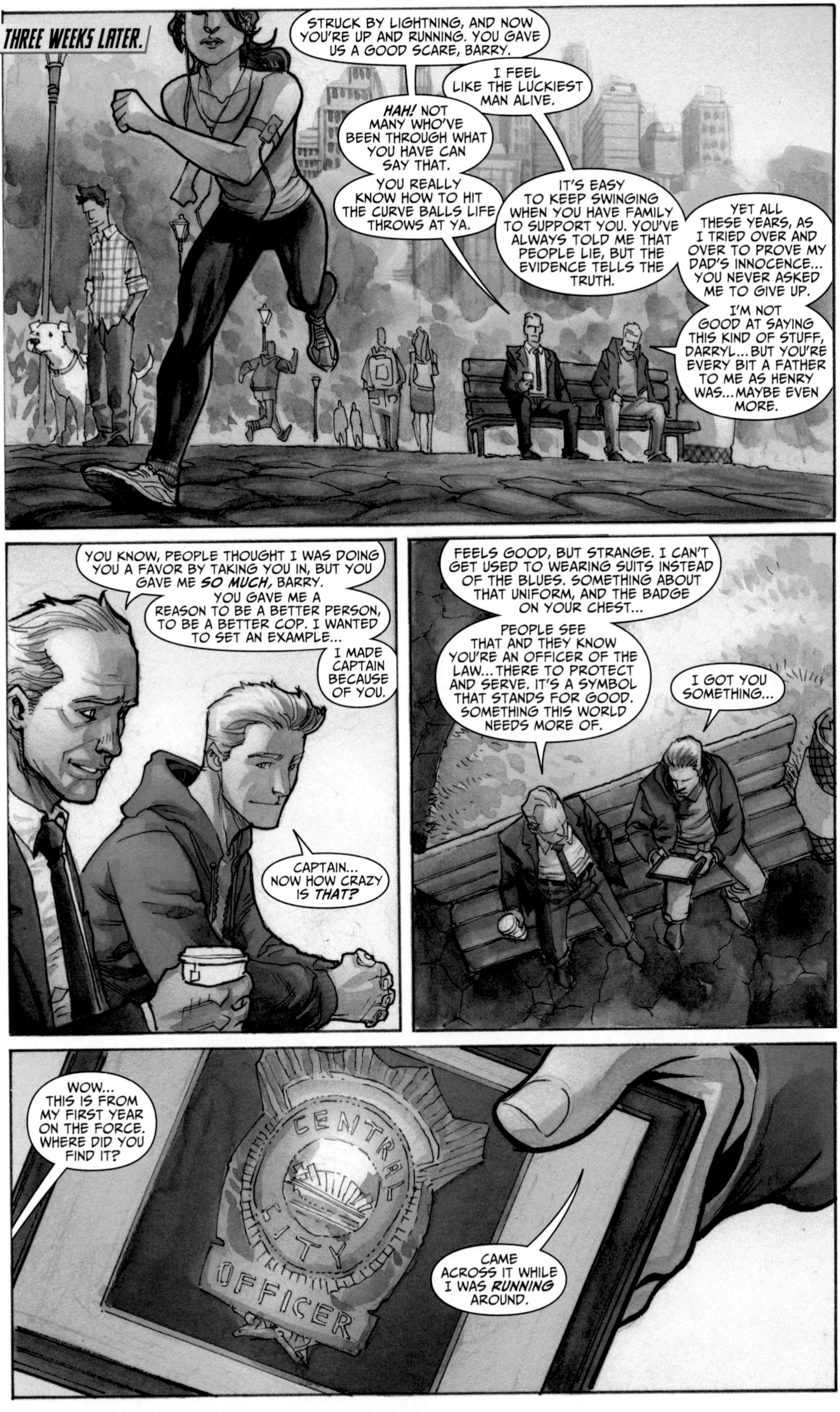
THREE WEEKS LATER.
STRUCK BY LIGHTNING, AND NOW YOU'RE UP AND RUNNING. YOU GAVE US A GOOD SCARE, BARRY.
I FEEL LIKE THE LUCKIEST MAN ALIVE.
HAH! NOT MANY WHO'VE BEEN THROUGH WHAT YOU HAVE CAN SAY THAT.
YOU REALLY KNOW HOW TO HIT THE CURVE BALLS LIFE THROWS AT YA.
IT'S EASY TO KEEP SWINGING WHEN YOU HAVE FAMILY TO SUPPORT YOU. YOU'VE ALWAYS TOLD ME THAT PEOPLE LIE, BUT THE EVIDENCE TELLS THE TRUTH.
YET ALL THESE YEARS, AS I TRIED OVER AND OVER TO PROVE MY DAD'S INNOCENCE... YOU NEVER ASKED ME TO GIVE UP.
I'M NOT GOOD AT SAYING THIS KIND OF STUFF, DARRYL... BUT YOU'RE EVERY BIT A FATHER TO ME AS HENRY WAS... MAYBE EVEN MORE.
YOU KNOW, PEOPLE THOUGHT I WAS DOING YOU A FAVOR BY TAKING YOU IN, BUT YOU GAVE ME SO MUCH, BARRY.
YOU GAVE ME A REASON TO BE A BETTER PERSON, TO BE A BETTER COP. I WANTED TO SET AN EXAMPLE...
I MADE CAPTAIN BECAUSE OF YOU.
CAPTAIN... NOW HOW CRAZY IS THAT?
FEELS GOOD, BUT STRANGE. I CAN'T GET USED TO WEARING SUITS INSTEAD OF THE BLUES. SOMETHING ABOUT THAT UNIFORM, AND THE BADGE ON YOUR CHEST...
PEOPLE SEE THAT AND THEY KNOW YOU'RE AN OFFICER OF THE LAW... THERE TO PROTECT AND SERVE. IT'S A SYMBOL THAT STANDS FOR GOOD. SOMETHING THIS WORLD NEEDS MORE OF.
I GOT YOU SOMETHING...
WOW... THIS IS FROM MY FIRST YEAR ON THE FORCE. WHERE DID YOU FIND IT?
CENTRAL CITY OFFICER
CAME ACROSS IT WHILE I WAS RUNNING AROUND.

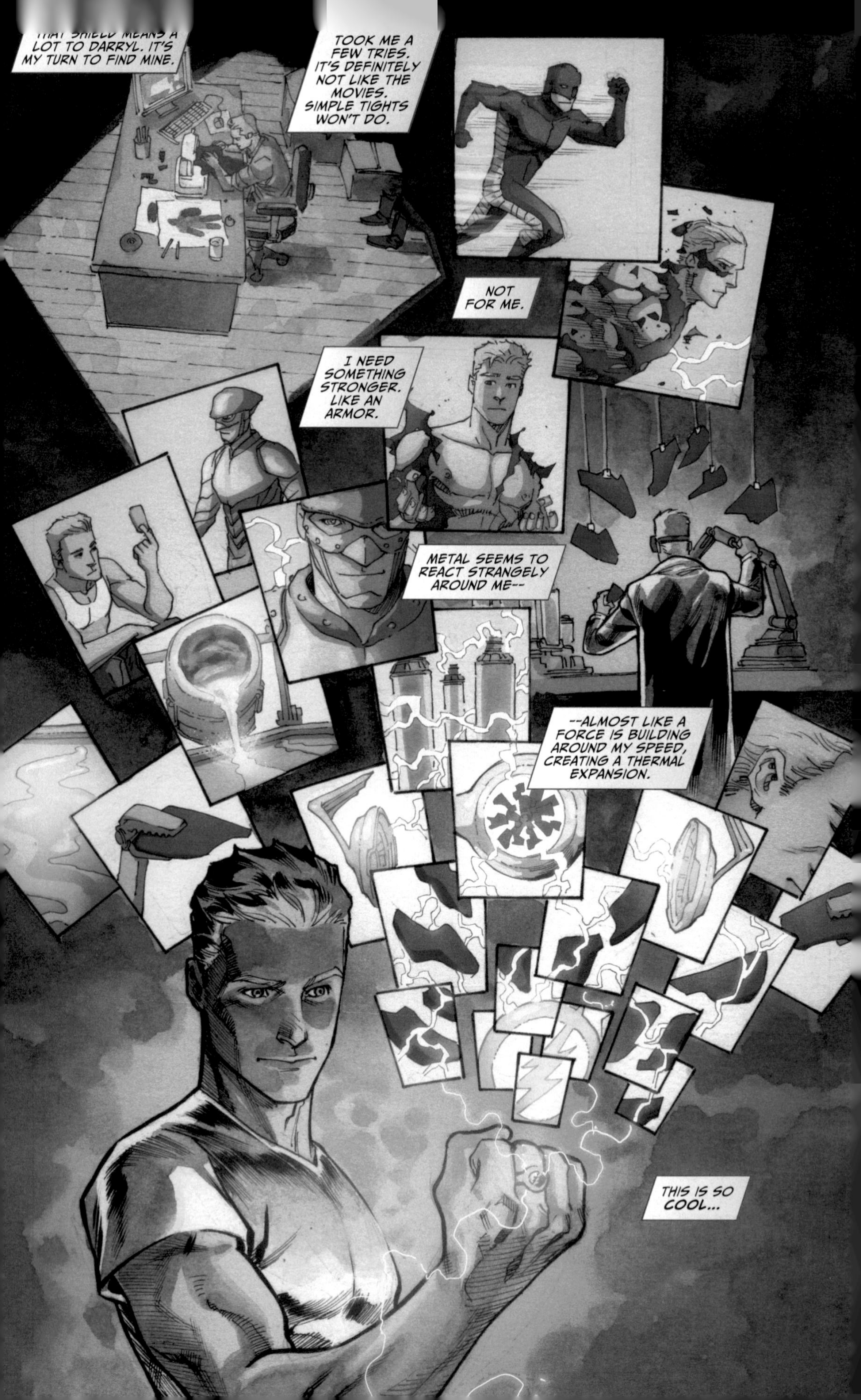
THAT SHIELD MEANS A LOT TO DARRYL. IT'S MY TURN TO FIND MINE.
TOOK ME A FEW TRIES. IT'S DEFINITELY NOT LIKE THE MOVIES. SIMPLE TIGHTS WON'T DO.
NOT FOR ME.
I NEED SOMETHING STRONGER. LIKE AN ARMOR.
METAL SEEMS TO REACT STRANGELY AROUND ME--
--ALMOST LIKE A FORCE IS BUILDING AROUND MY SPEED, CREATING A THERMAL EXPANSION.
THIS IS SO COOL...

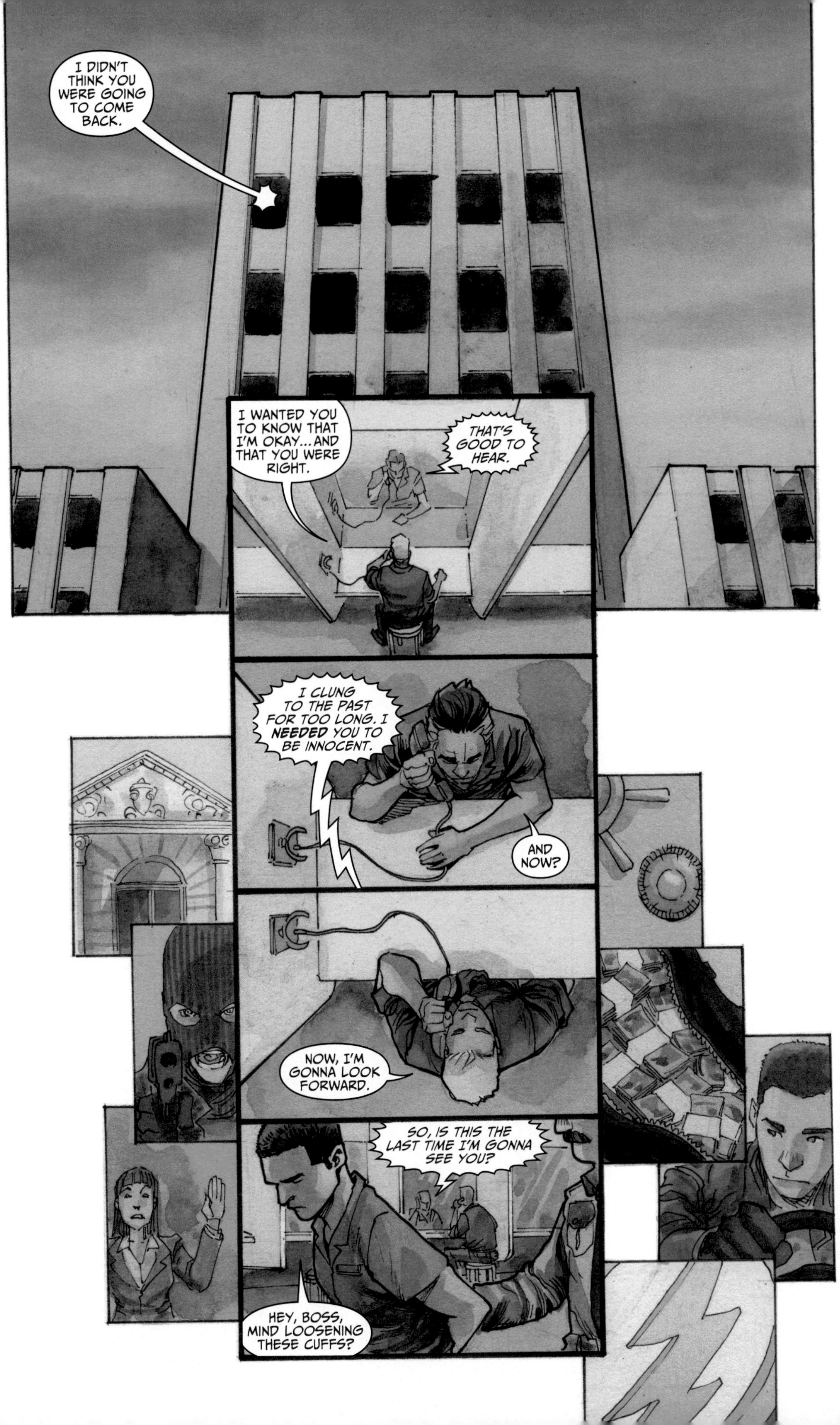
I DIDN'T THINK YOU WERE GOING TO COME BACK.
I WANTED YOU TO KNOW THAT I'M OKAY...AND THAT YOU WERE RIGHT.
THAT'S GOOD TO HEAR.
I CLUNG TO THE PAST FOR TOO LONG. I NEEDED YOU TO BE INNOCENT.
AND NOW?
NOW, I'M GONNA LOOK FORWARD.
SO, IS THIS THE LAST TIME I'M GONNA SEE YOU?
HEY, BOSS, MIND LOOSENING THESE CUFFS?

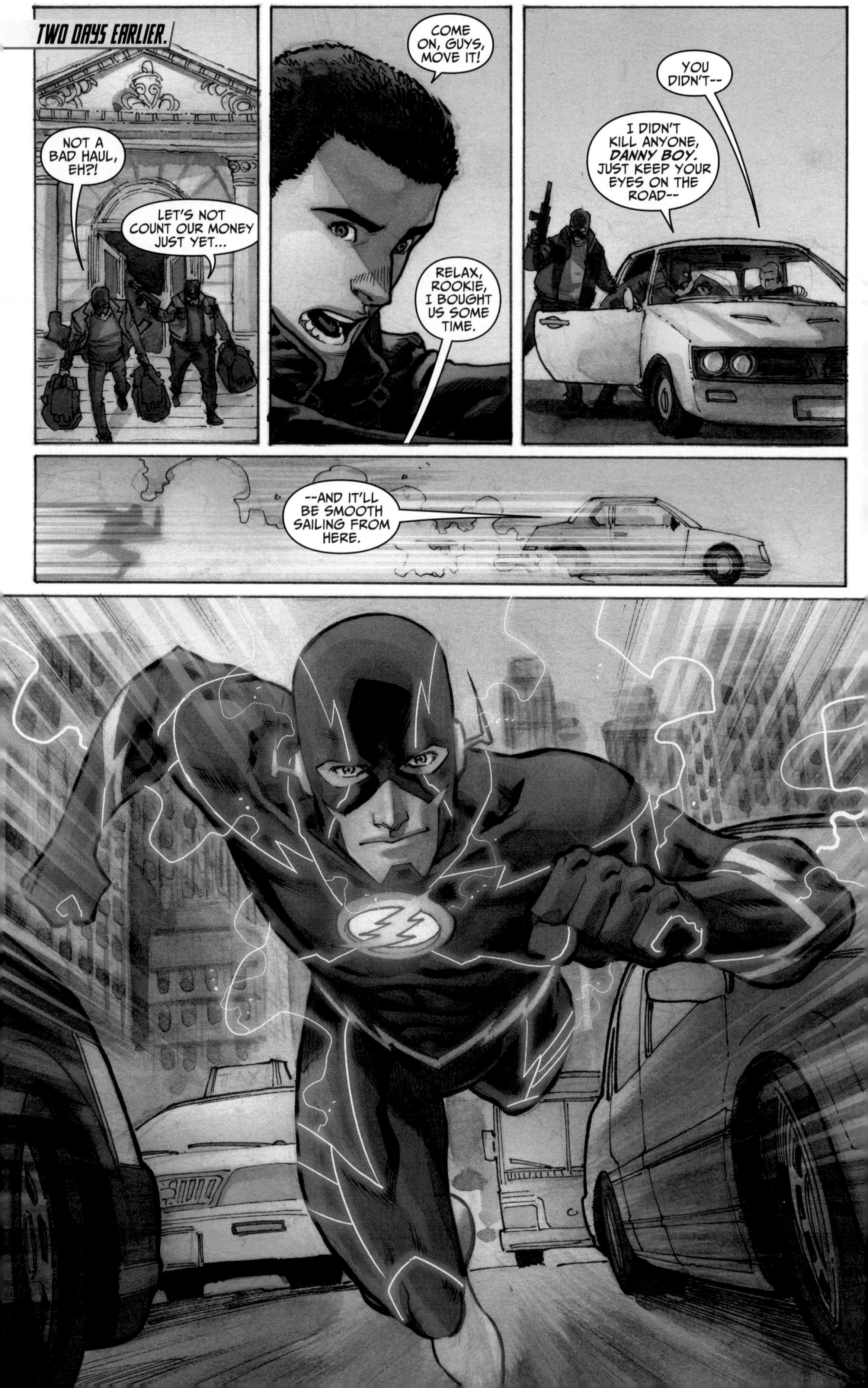

TWO DAYS EARLIER.
NOT A BAD HAUL, EH?!
LET'S NOT COUNT OUR MONEY JUST YET...
COME ON, GUYS, MOVE IT!
RELAX, ROOKIE, I BOUGHT US SOME TIME.
YOU DIDN'T--
I DIDN'T KILL ANYONE, DANNY BOY. JUST KEEP YOUR EYES ON THE ROAD--
--AND IT'LL BE SMOOTH SAILING FROM HERE.

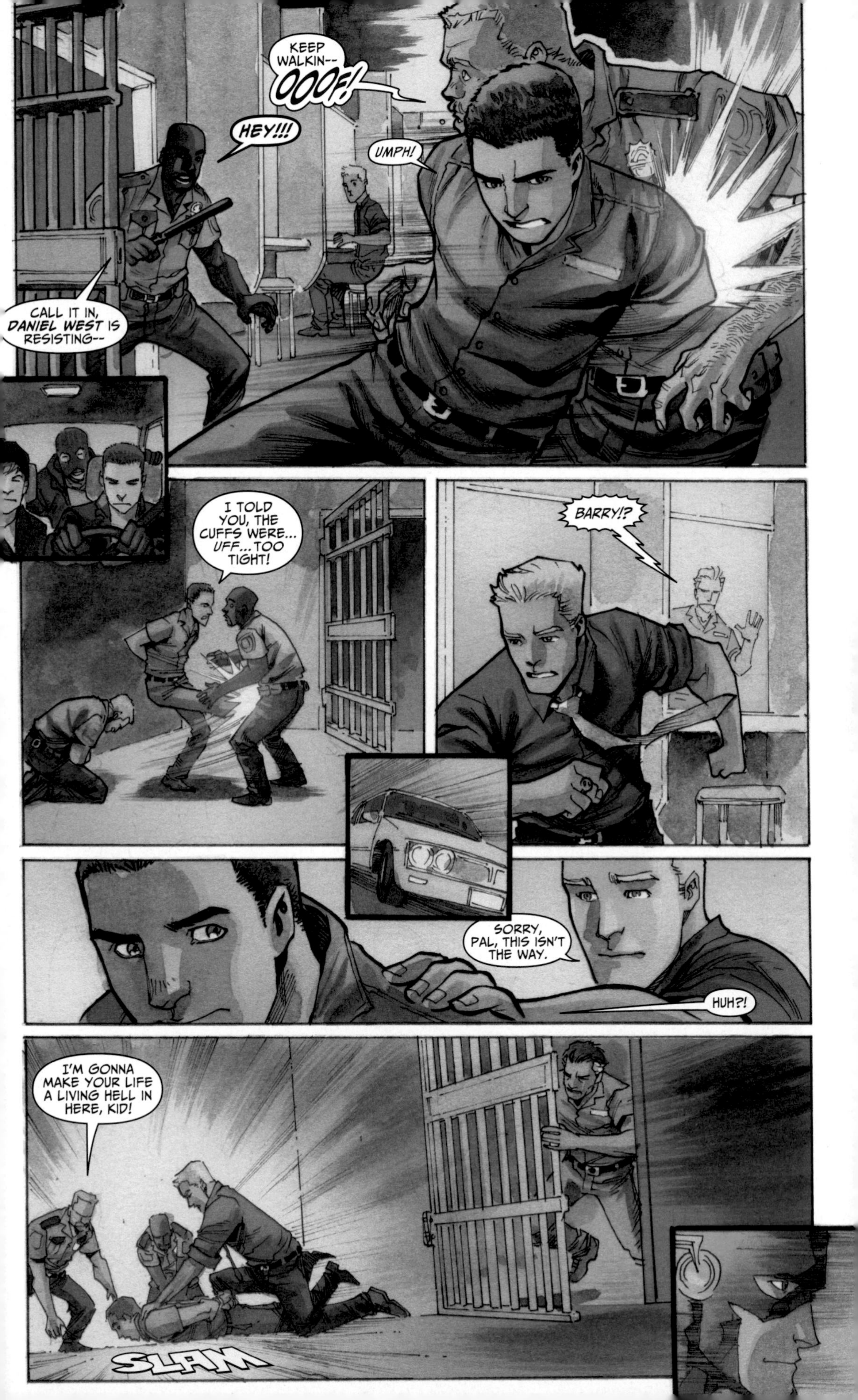
KEEP WALKIN-- OOOF!
HEY!!!
UMPH!
CALL IT IN, DANIEL WEST IS RESISTING--
I TOLD YOU, THE CUFFS WERE... UFF... TOO TIGHT!
BARRY!?
SORRY, PAL, THIS ISN'T THE WAY.
HUH?!
I'M GONNA MAKE YOUR LIFE A LIVING HELL IN HERE, KID!
SLAM

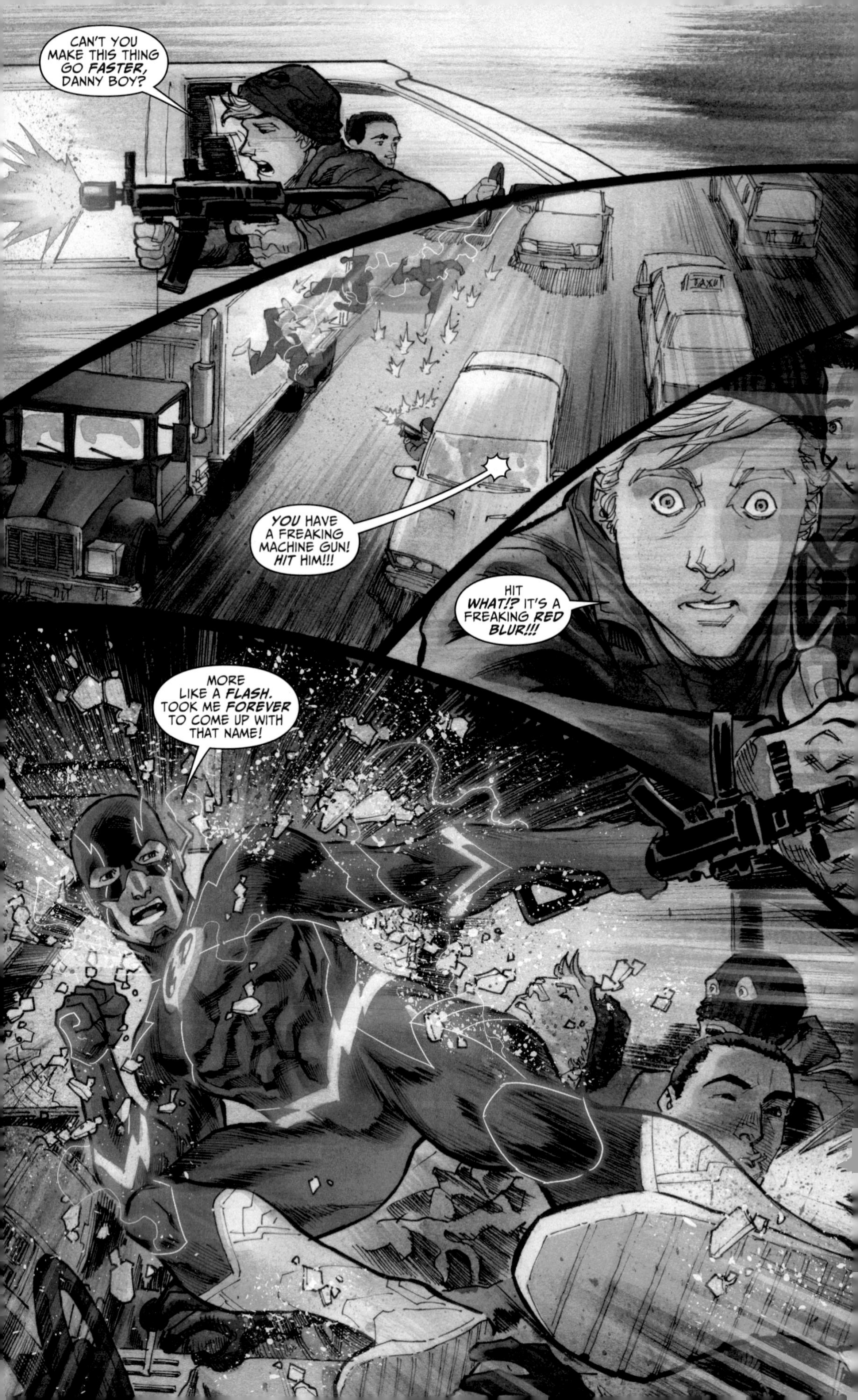
CAN'T YOU MAKE THIS THING GO *FASTER,* DANNY BOY?
YOU HAVE A FREAKING MACHINE GUN! *HIT* HIM!!!
HIT *WHAT!?* IT'S A FREAKING *RED BLUR!!!*
MORE LIKE A *FLASH.* TOOK ME *FOREVER* TO COME UP WITH THAT NAME!
TAXI

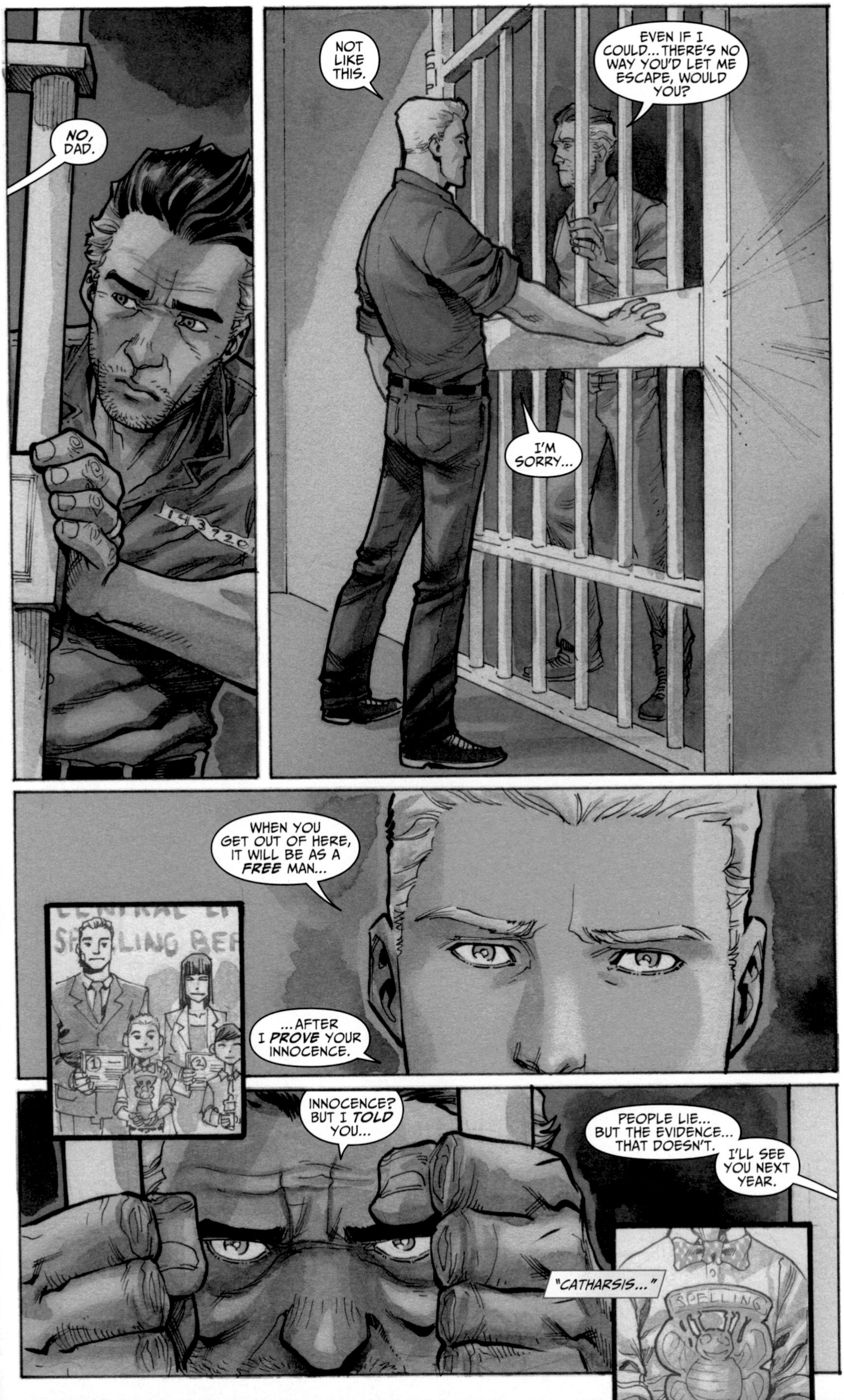
NO, DAD.
NOT LIKE THIS.
EVEN IF I COULD... THERE'S NO WAY YOU'D LET ME ESCAPE, WOULD YOU?
I'M SORRY...
WHEN YOU GET OUT OF HERE, IT WILL BE AS A *FREE* MAN...
...AFTER I *PROVE* YOUR INNOCENCE.
INNOCENCE? BUT I *TOLD* YOU...
PEOPLE LIE... BUT THE EVIDENCE... THAT DOESN'T.
I'LL SEE YOU NEXT YEAR.
"CATHARSIS..."

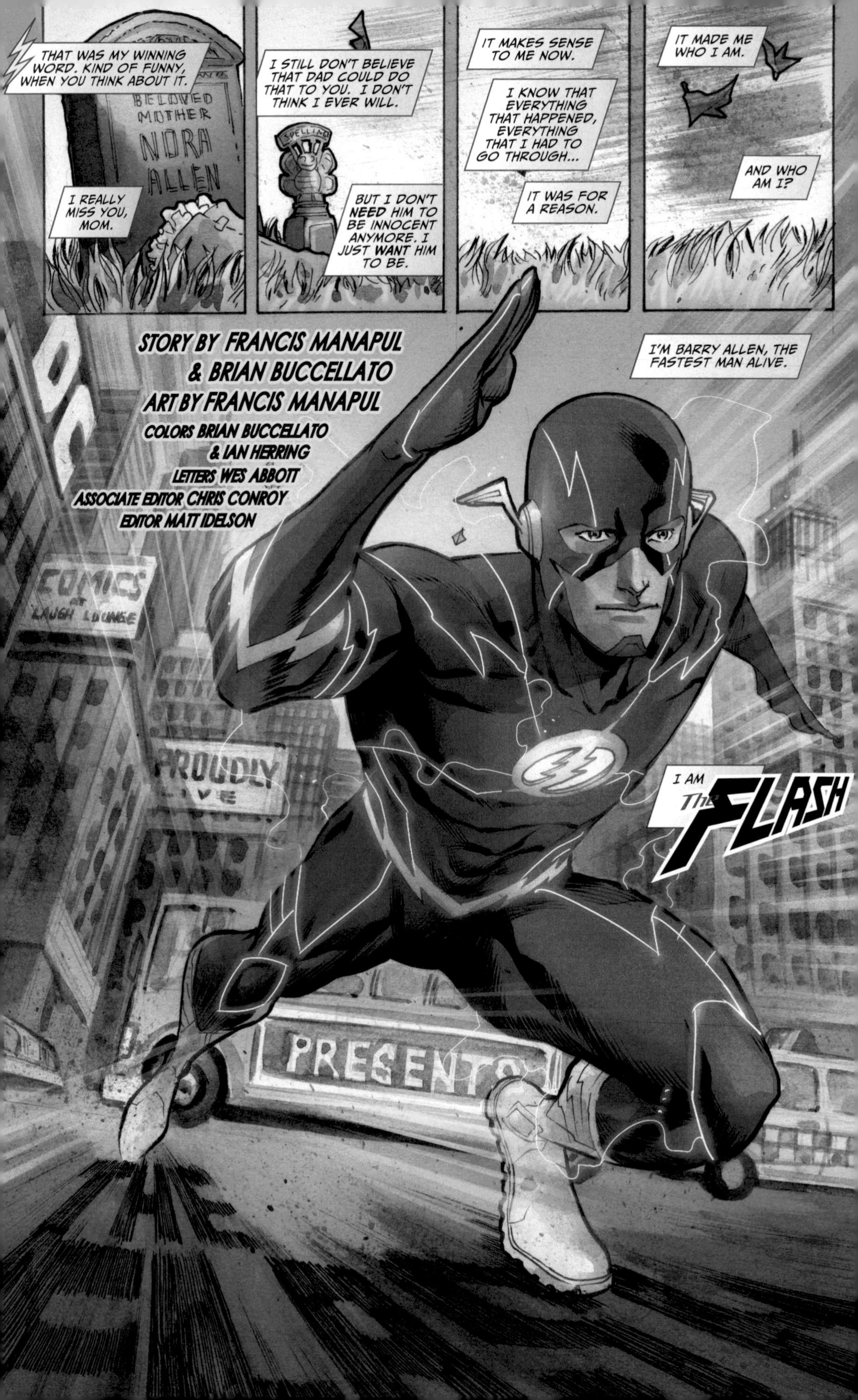
THAT WAS MY WINNING WORD. KIND OF FUNNY, WHEN YOU THINK ABOUT IT.
BELOVED MOTHER NORA ALLEN
I REALLY MISS YOU, MOM.
I STILL DON'T BELIEVE THAT DAD COULD DO THAT TO YOU. I DON'T THINK I EVER WILL.
BUT I DON'T NEED HIM TO BE INNOCENT ANYMORE. I JUST WANT HIM TO BE.
IT MAKES SENSE TO ME NOW.
I KNOW THAT EVERYTHING THAT HAPPENED, EVERYTHING THAT I HAD TO GO THROUGH...
IT WAS FOR A REASON.
IT MADE ME WHO I AM.
AND WHO AM I?
STORY BY FRANCIS MANAPUL & BRIAN BUCCELLATO
ART BY FRANCIS MANAPUL
COLORS BRIAN BUCCELLATO & IAN HERRING
LETTERS WES ABBOTT
ASSOCIATE EDITOR CHRIS CONROY
EDITOR MATT IDELSON
I'M BARRY ALLEN, THE FASTEST MAN ALIVE.
COMICS AT LAUGH LOUNGE
PROUDLY
PRESENTS
I AM The FLASH

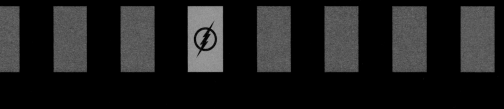

VARIANT COVER GALLERY

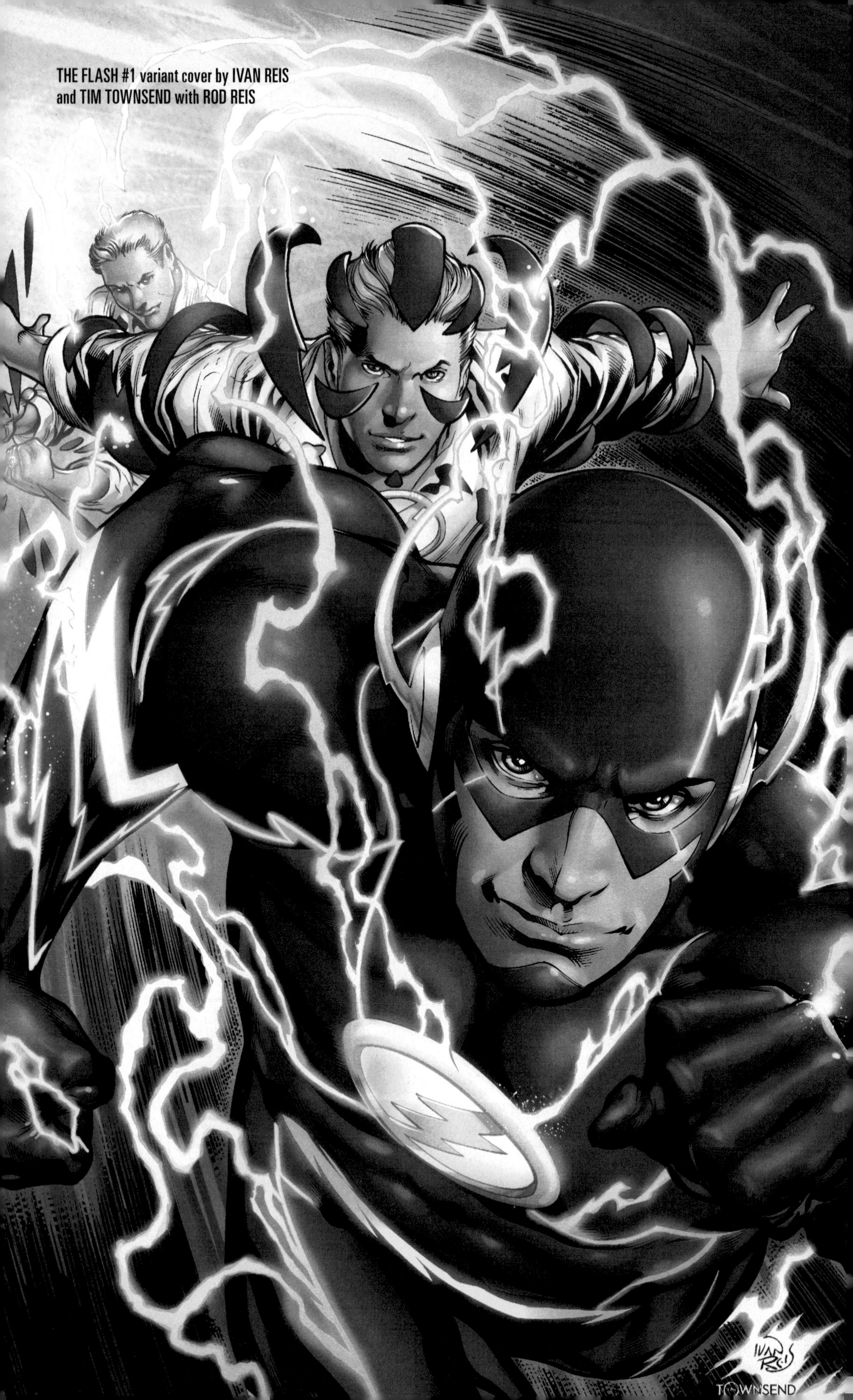
TOWNSEND

THE FLASH #1 variant cover by IVAN REIS
and TIM TOWNSEND with ROD REIS

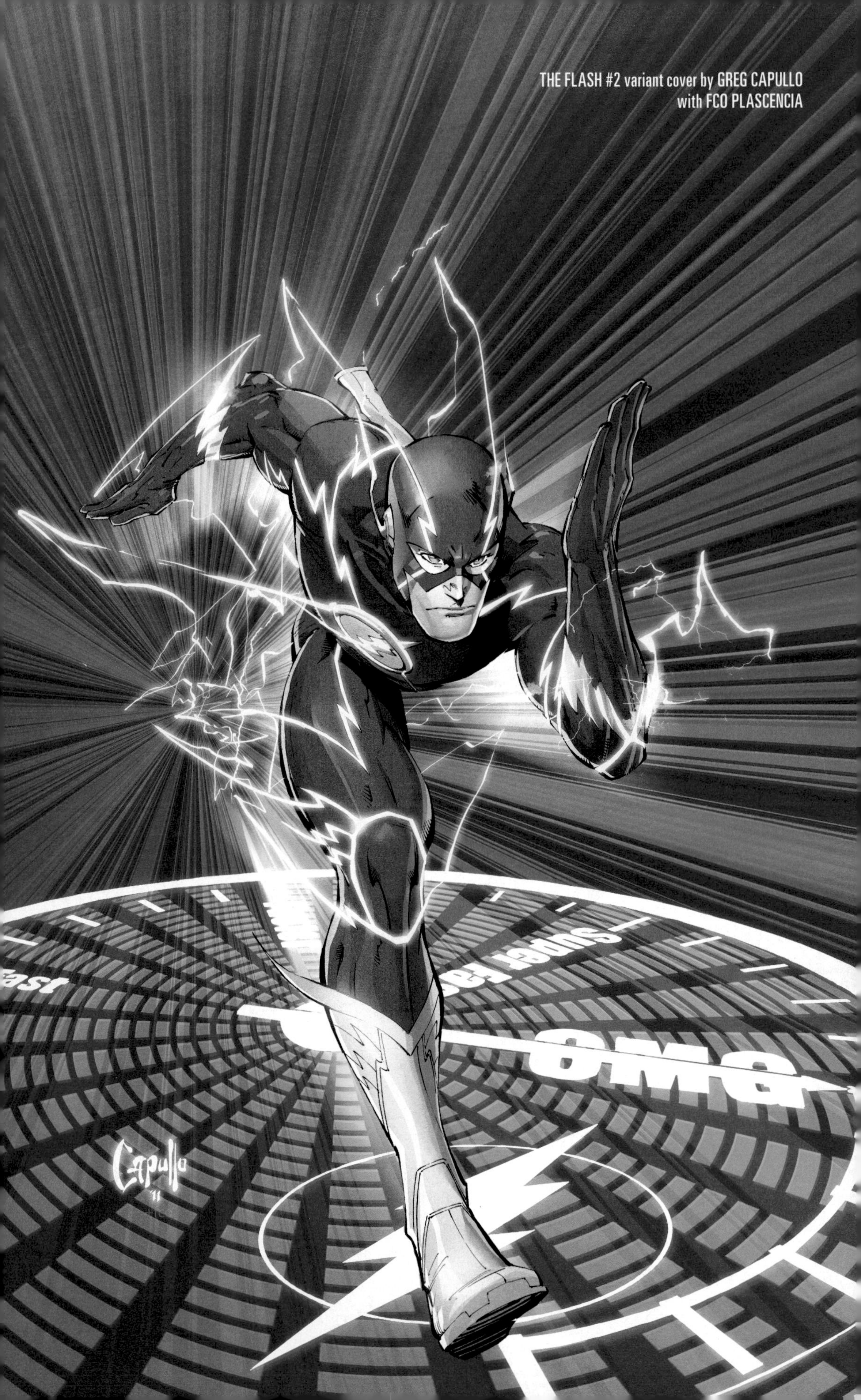
Capullo '11

THE FLASH #2 variant cover by GREG CAPULLO
with FCO PLASCENCIA

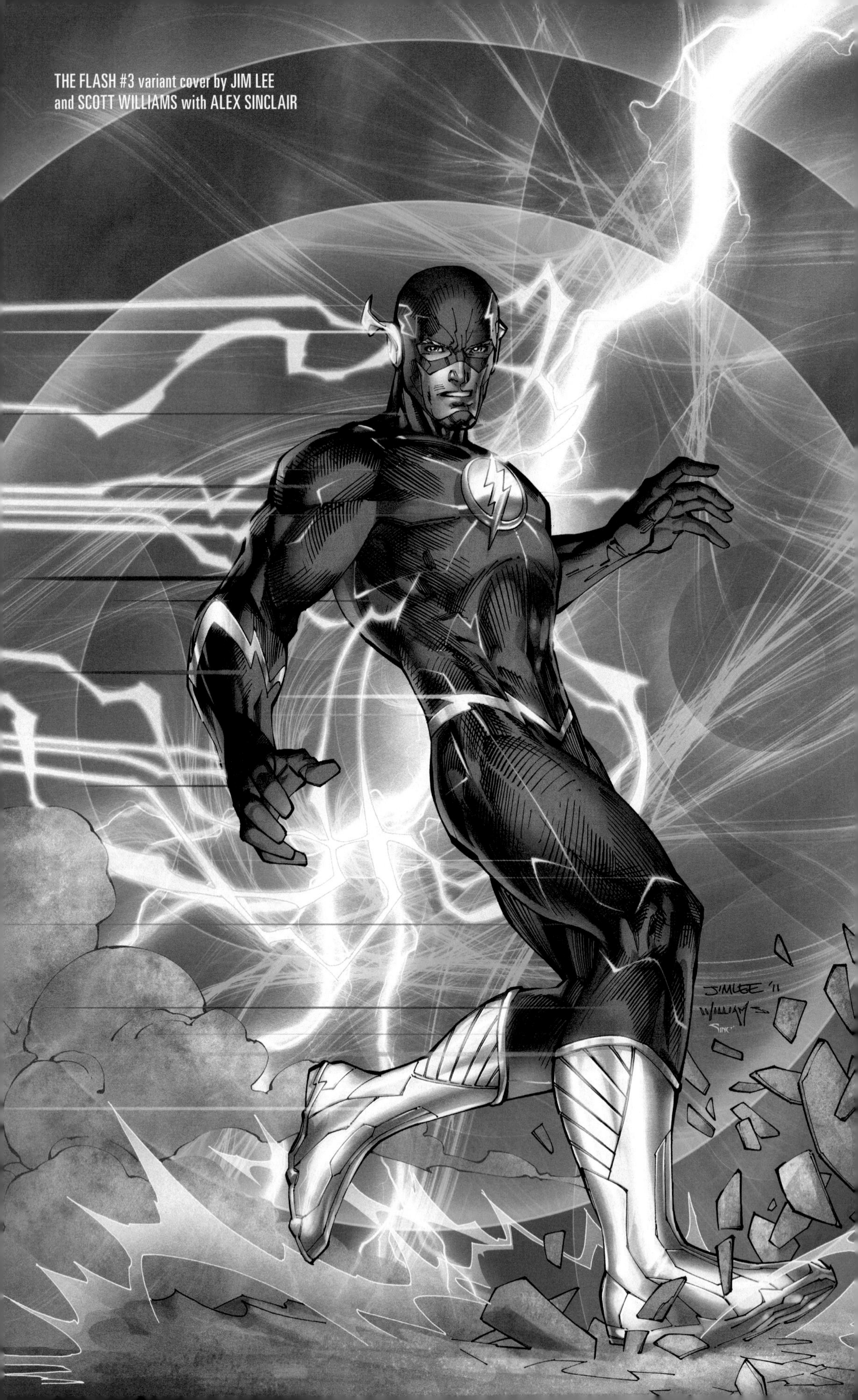

THE FLASH #3 variant cover by JIM LEE
and SCOTT WILLIAMS with ALEX SINCLAIR

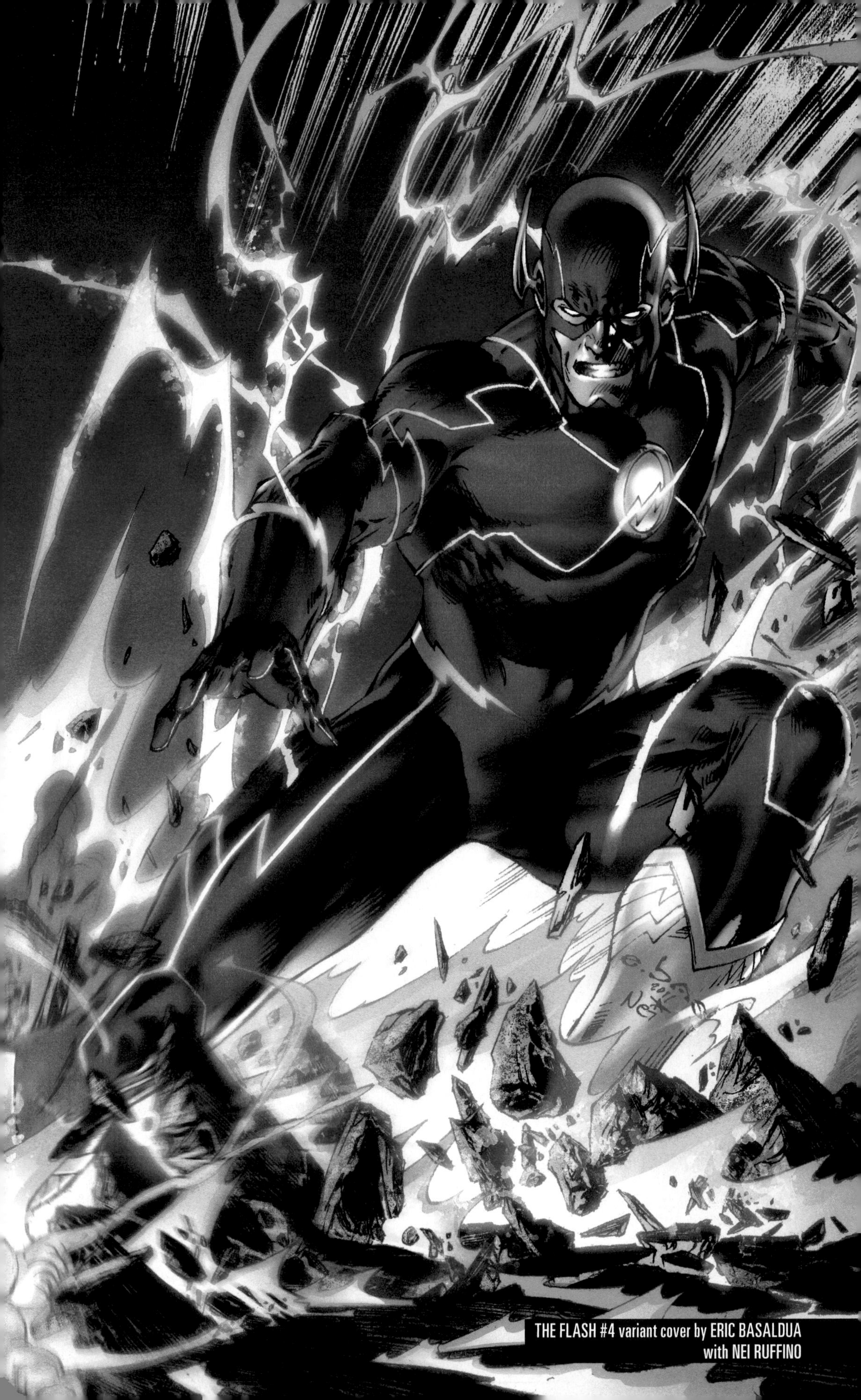

THE FLASH #4 variant cover by ERIC BASALDUA
with NEI RUFFINO

THE FLASH #5 variant cover by GARY FRANK
with BRAD ANDERSON

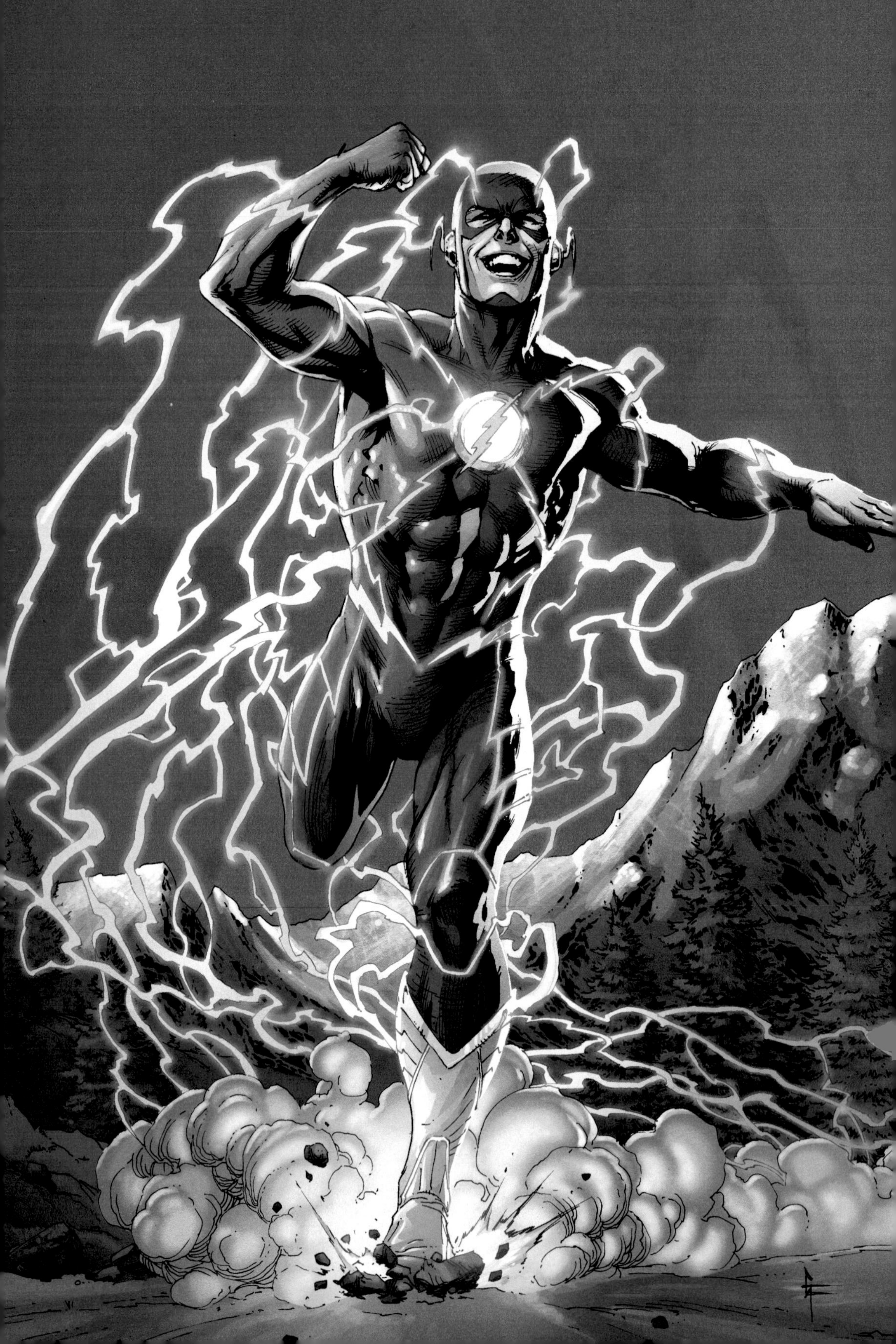

THE FLASH #6 variant cover by MIKE CHOI

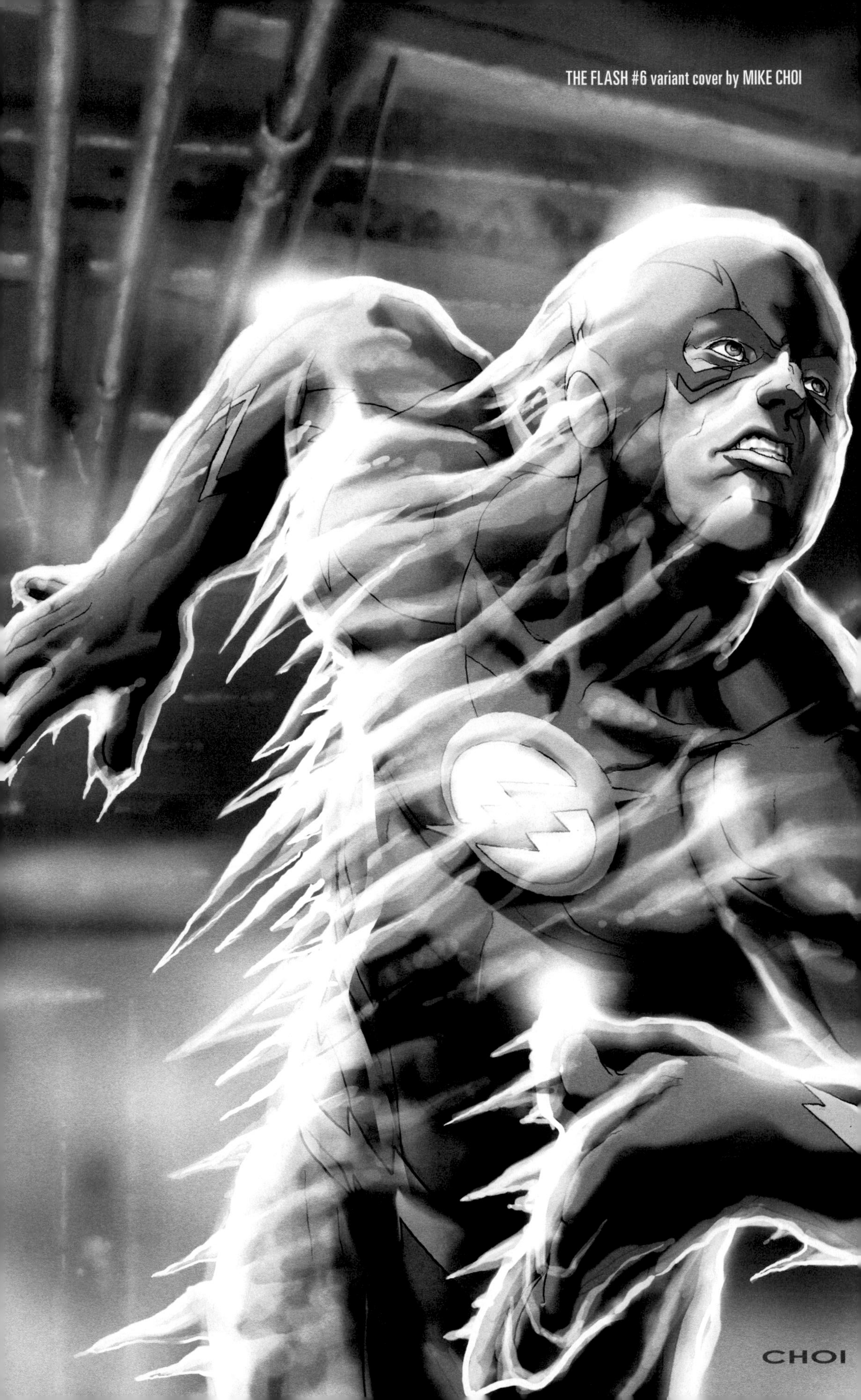
CHOI

THE FLASH #7 variant cover by DALE KEOWN

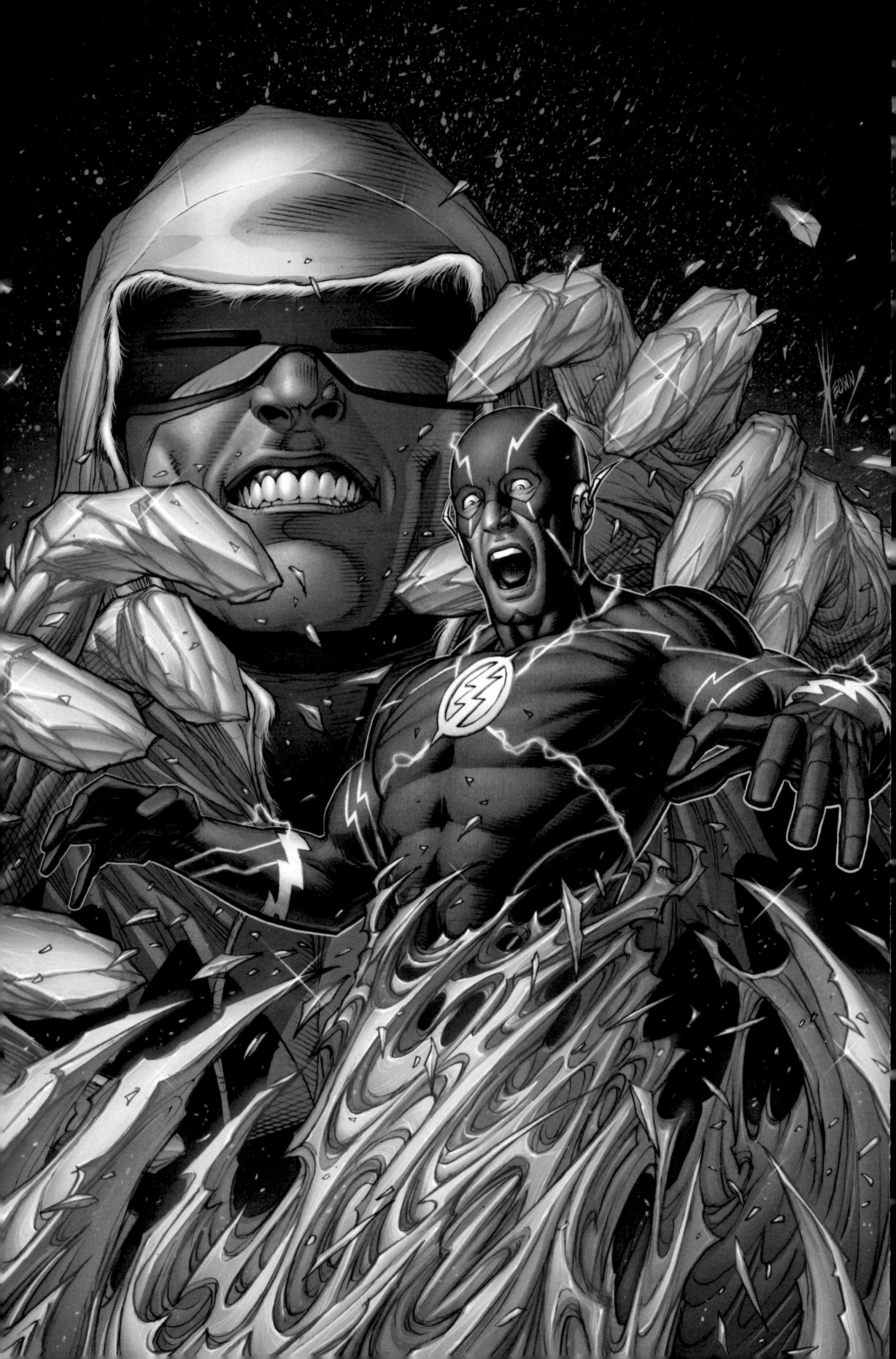

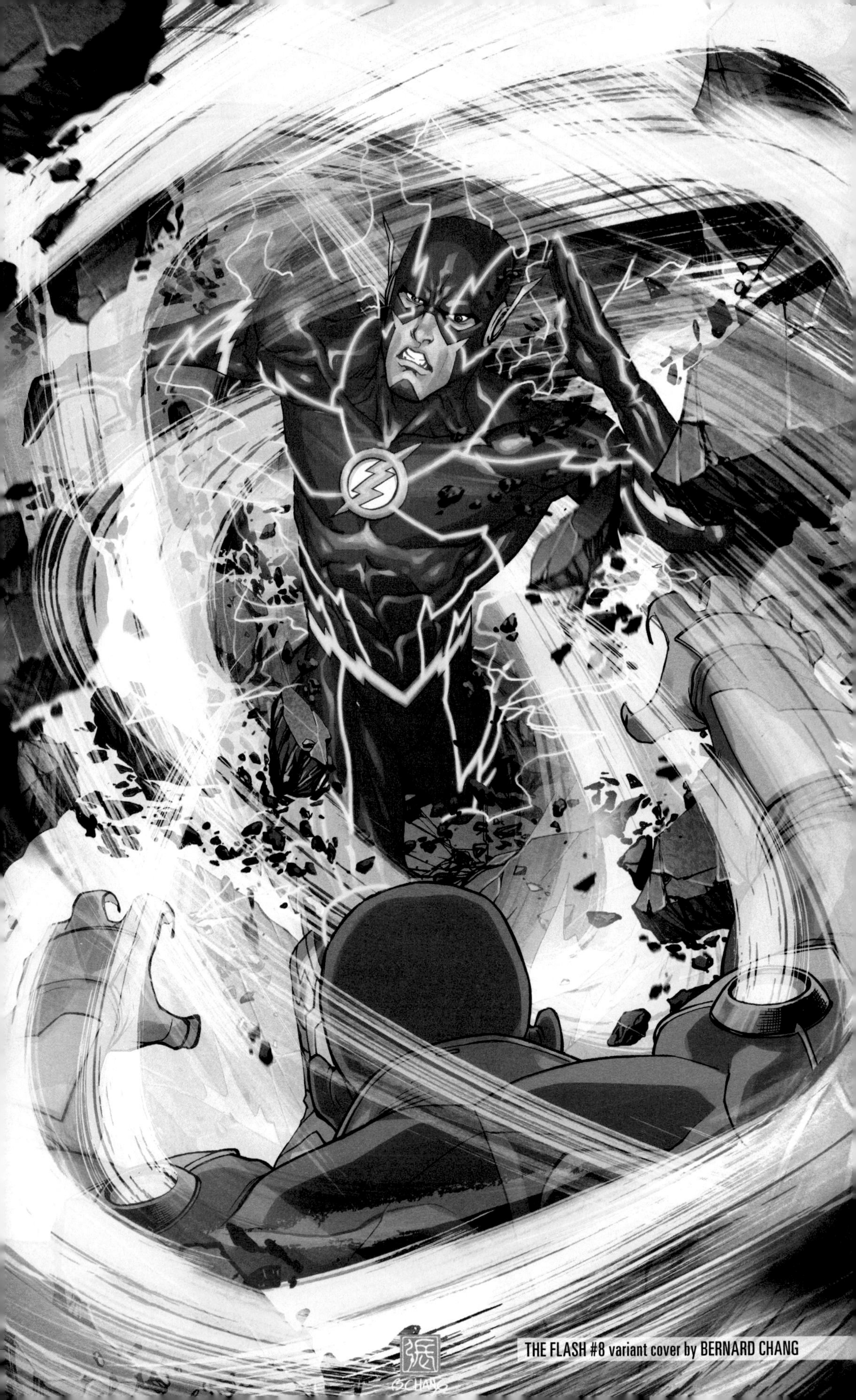

THE FLASH #8 variant cover by BERNARD CHANG

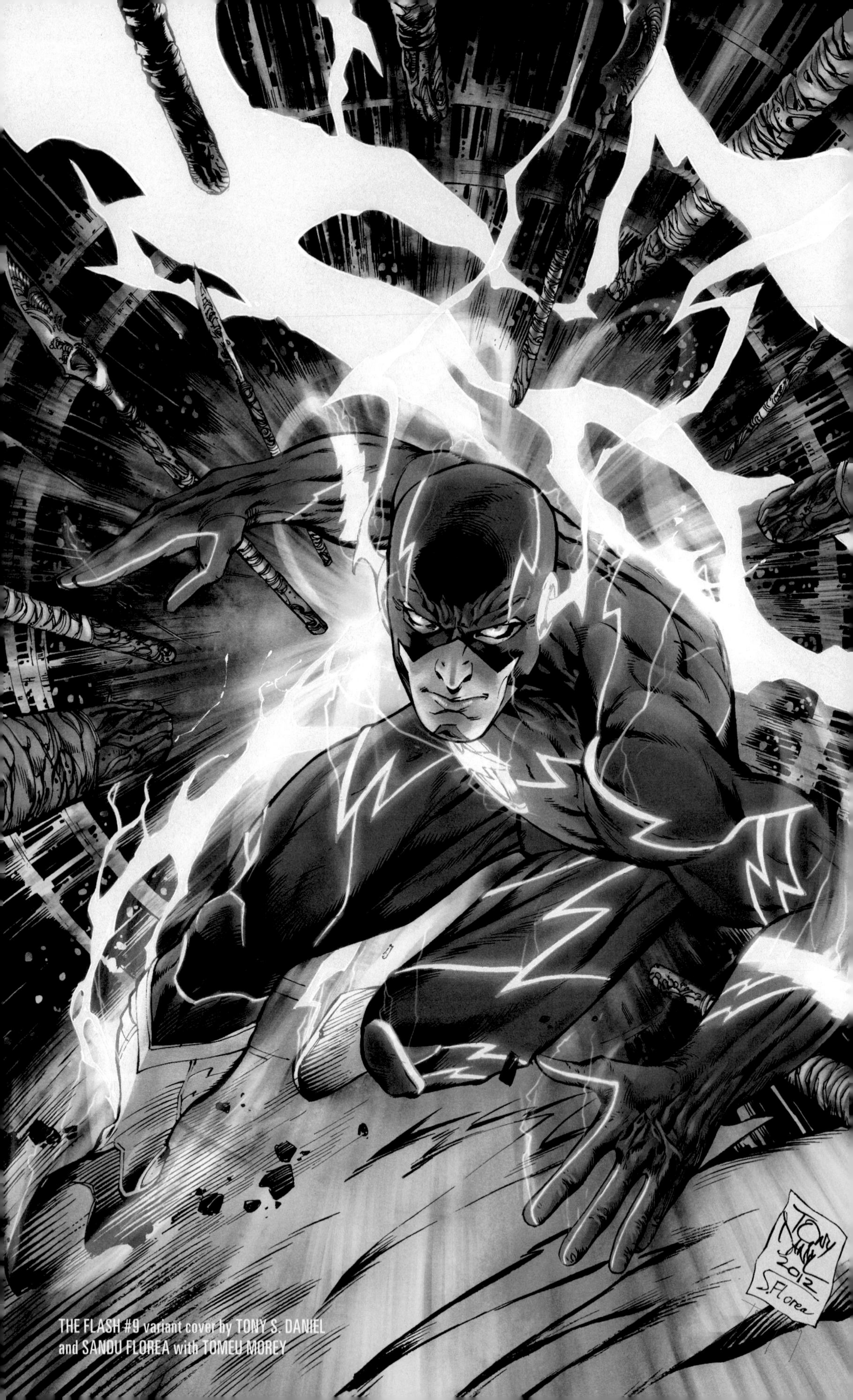

THE FLASH #9 variant cover by TONY S. DANIEL
and SANDU FLOREA with TOMEU MOREY

CHARACTER SKETCHES
BY FRANCIS MANAPUL

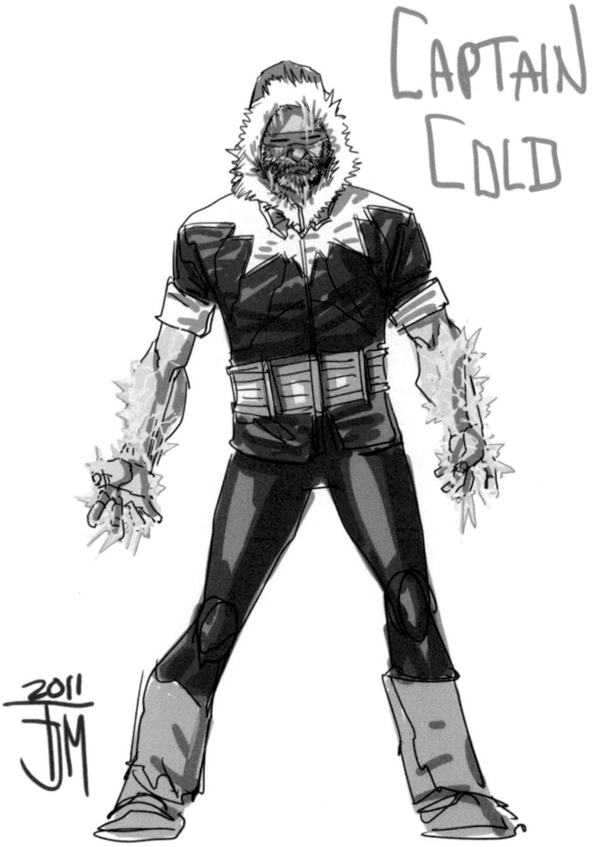
CAPTAIN COLD
2011

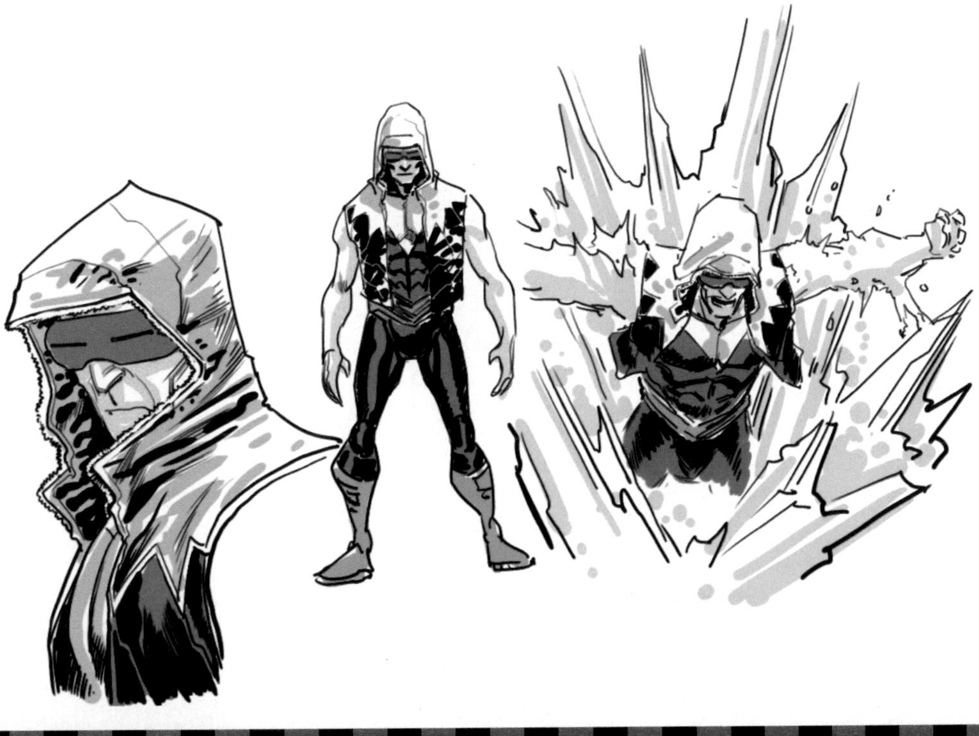

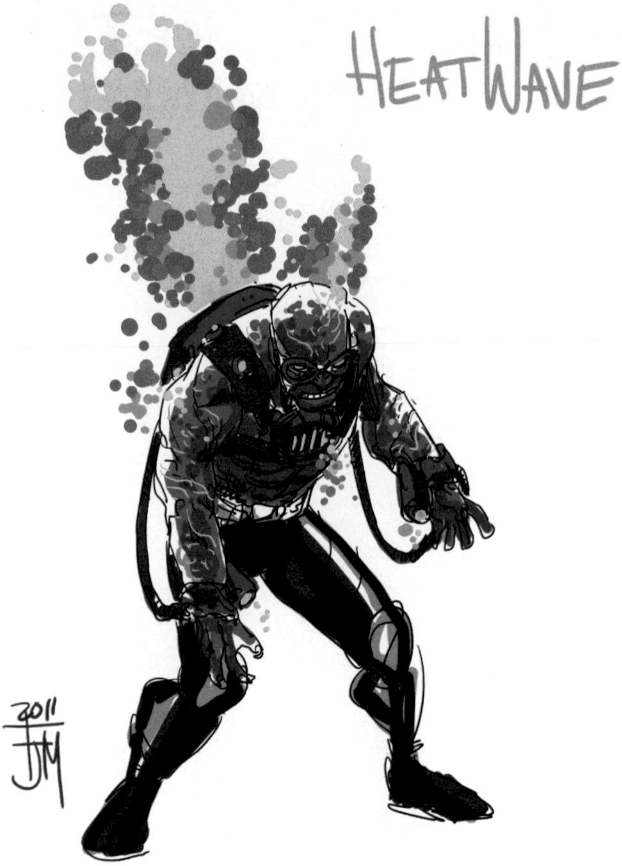
HEATWAVE
2011
JJM

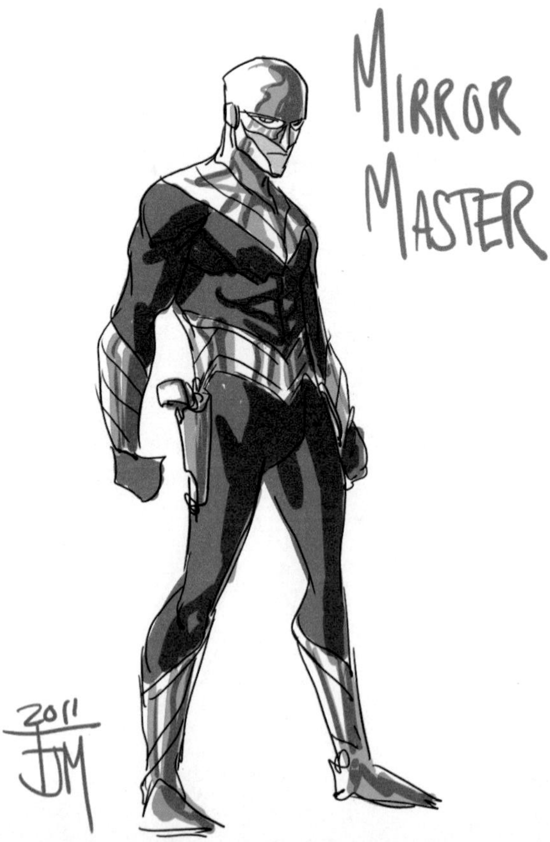
MIRROR
MASTER
2011
JJM

PIED
PIPER

2011 JM

THE
TRICKSTER

2011 JM

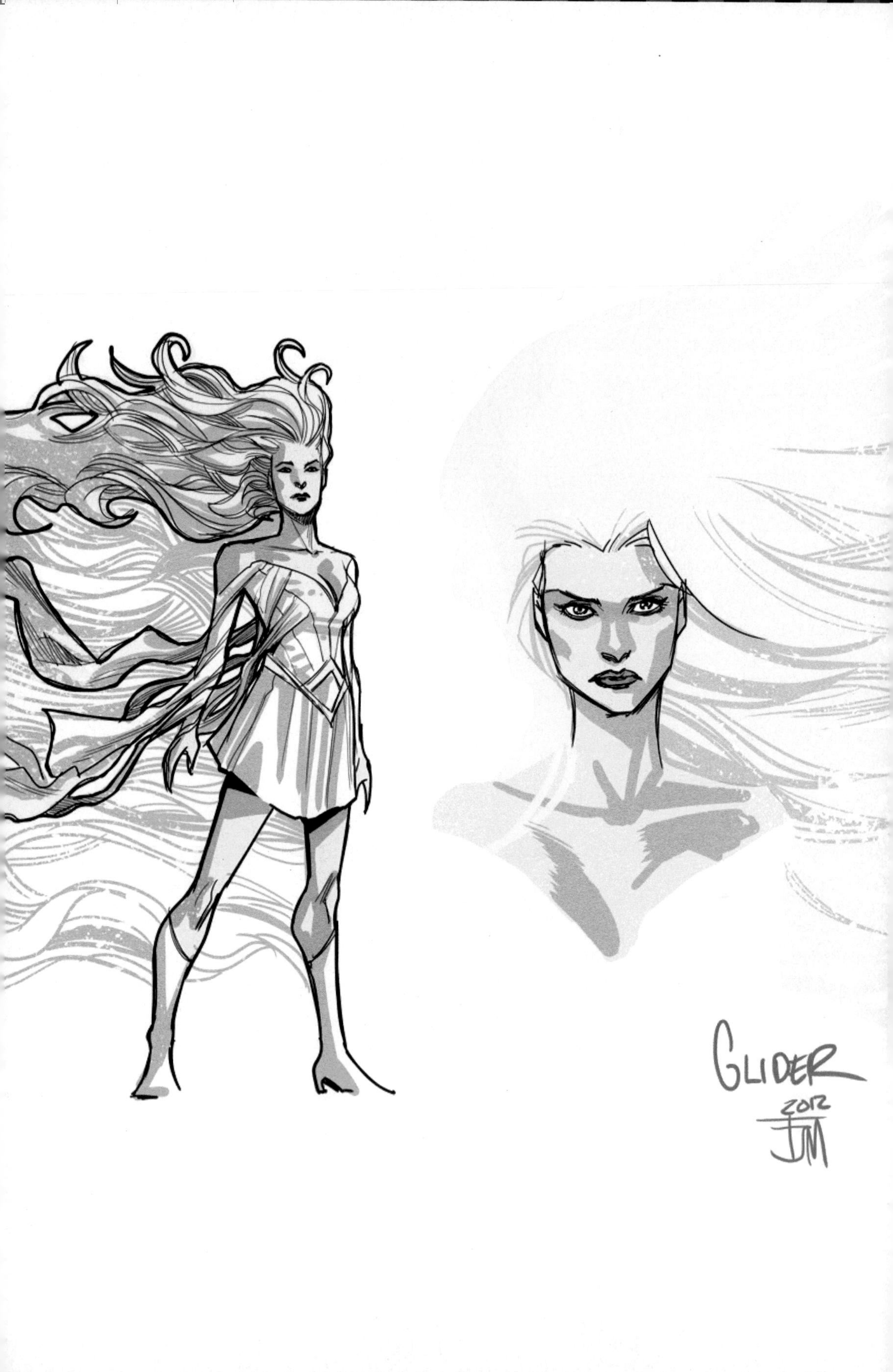
GLIDER
2012
JM